Law and Philosophy Library

Volume 111

Series editors
Francisco J. Laporta
Department of Law, Autonomous University of Madrid, Madrid, Spain

Frederick Schauer
School of Law, University of Virginia, Charlottesville, Virginia, U.S.A.

Torben Spaak
Department of Law, Stockholm University, Stockholm, Sweden

The Law and Philosophy Library, which has been in existence since 1985, aims to publish cutting edge works in the philosophy of law, and has a special history of publishing books that focus on legal reasoning and argumentation, including those that may involve somewhat formal methodologies. The series has published numerous important books on law and logic, law and artificial intelligence, law and language, and law and rhetoric. While continuing to stress these areas, the series has more recently expanded to include books on the intersection between law and the Continental philosophical tradition, consistent with the traditional openness of the series to books in the Continental jurisprudential tradition. The series is proud of the geographic diversity of its authors, and many have come from Latin America, Spain, Italy, the Netherlands, Germany, and Eastern Europe, as well, more obviously for an English-language series, from the United Kingdom, the United States, Australia, and Canada.

More information about this series at http://www.springer.com/series/6210

Michał Araszkiewicz • Paweł Banaś
Tomasz Gizbert-Studnicki • Krzysztof Płeszka
Editors

Problems of Normativity, Rules and Rule-Following

Springer

Editors
Michał Araszkiewicz
Department of Legal Theory
Jagiellonian University Faculty of Law
Kraków
Poland

Tomasz Gizbert-Studnicki
Department of Legal Theory
Jagiellonian University Faculty of Law
Kraków
Poland

Paweł Banaś
Department of Legal Theory
Jagiellonian University Faculty of Law
Kraków
Poland

Krzysztof Płeszka
Department of Legal Theory
Jagiellonian University Faculty of Law
Kraków
Poland

ISSN 1572-4395 ISSN 2215-0315 (electronic)
ISBN 978-3-319-09374-1 ISBN 978-3-319-09375-8 (eBook)
DOI 10.1007/978-3-319-09375-8
Springer Cham Heidelberg New York Dordrecht London

Library of Congress Control Number: 2014952461

Printed on acid-free paper

Springer is part of Springer Science+Business Media (www.springer.com)

Preface

The word "rule" is used in numerous disciplines in connection with various social practices. Jurists talk about legal rules, moral philosophers about moral rules, sociologists about various types of social rules, linguists about rules of language, logicians about rules of logic, and so on. For some of those disciplines (and in particular for jurisprudence, linguistics and moral theory) the problem of rules is a central issue. They cannot work without some concept of a rule. But does the word "rule" in all those contexts denote one and the same thing? Do rules have a common nature? Do legal rules, linguistic rules, moral rules and rules of logic have necessary features that make them into that what they are? Or is the concept of a rule a family concept, so that various types or instances of rules bear only family resemblances? Or is the word "rule" simply equivocal and denotes quite different things in each of the contexts listed above? Are rules (or at least rules of a certain type) reducible to mere regularities? Do all rules have the same function and structure? Does the differentiation of various types of rules extend across all social practices involving rules, or is it domain specific? What is the relationship between rules and values? What does it mean that a rule is conventional?

Other, but related puzzles arise in connection with the problem of normativity. Are all rules necessarily normative? What does it mean that a rule is normative? Can normativity be fully explained by recourse to the concept of reason for action? What is the role of rules in delivering reasons for actions? What type of reasons for actions should be distinguished? What is the link between a reason for action and motivation? Is the distinction between motivating reasons and justificatory reasons sound? In what sense should we talk about "objective" reasons? Can normativity of legal rules, moral rules, linguistic rules and so on be explained in the same terms? Or, rather, is the normativity in each of those domains specific? Can there be a general theory of normativity? How can the guiding and justificatory role of rules be explained? What is the role of cognitive science and neurosciences in explaining normativity? What does "authority" mean, and how is it related to rules and normativity? How can public reasons be separated from other reasons?

However, it was Ludwig Wittgenstein who asked probably the most fundamental question concerning rules and rule following. In the famous passage, Wittgenstein writes the following:

The paradox is how one can follow in accord with a role—the applications of which are potentially infinite—when the instances from which one learns the rule and the instances in which one displays that one has learned the rule are only finite? How can one be certain of rule following at all? (Philosophical Investigations, 201)

This was our paradox: no course of action could be determined by a rule, because every course of action can be made out to accord with the rule. The answer was: if everything can be made out to accord with the rule, then it can also be made out to conflict with it. And so there would be neither accord nor conflict. (Philosophical Investigations, 185)

Wittgenstein challenged powerfully the traditional picture, pursuant to which a rule is an abstract entity, transcending all of its particular applications. Knowing the rule involves understanding that abstract entity and thereby knowing which of its applications are correct and which incorrect.

Saul Kripke famously presented, in a broad philosophical context, his version of the Wittgensteinian paradox, which has invoked endless discussions. Hence, the problem of rule following has become one of the main topics in contemporary analytic philosophy.

It is not the ambition of the authors of this volume to propose answers to all questions listed above. Rather, the intention is to discuss those and other related questions from different perspectives and angles. The common feature of all papers contained in this volume is that they tackle the issues of rules, normativity and rule following, but they do it in various ways. Some of the papers discuss general problems, some specific ones. Some of them are written from the purely philosophical point of view, some from the perspective of general jurisprudence, logic or semantics. The editors of this volume believe that such an interdisciplinary approach is helpful because each of those disciplines may benefit from the insights the others provide. There is a certain lack of proportions among representations of particular disciplines in this volume. This was intended by the editors. The discipline that prevails is general jurisprudence (legal philosophy). The editors (as legal philosophers) have no doubts that the problem of rules and normativity is central for legal philosophy. Rules are a fundamental category for description and analysis of any legal system. A fundamental aim of legal philosophy is an explanation of the normative force of law. Any analysis of certain basic legal concepts such as duty, right or authority is probably bound to make recourse to the concept of a rule. The issue of rules is important for legal philosophy also in contexts of certain specific topics, such as legal reasoning and legal interpretation. Legal philosophy cannot ignore the problems of linguistic rules and rules of logic as law texts are written in natural languages and jurists are bound to perform certain logical operations on the sentences taken from those texts. Also, the development of modern legal knowledge systems in the domain of artificial intelligence (AI) and law requires a profound understanding of both contemporary logical calculi and logical features of legal rules.

Due to the reasons briefly sketched above, legal philosophy cannot develop in isolation from general analytic philosophy, linguistics and logic. Such a claim is a platitude for legal philosophers, at least since the date of publication of *The Concept of Law* by H. L. A. Hart. He has demonstrated in this magisterial work how much legal philosophy may benefit from analytic philosophy. Other thinkers have shown the same with respect to linguistics and logic.

But, as we believe, legal philosophy is not to take only from such cooperation. Legal philosophers are focusing on the problems of rules and normativity as their central issue. In other disciplines, such as analytic philosophy, linguistics and logic, this problem, however important, is just one of a multitude of important and interesting issues. Therefore, as we consider, philosophers, linguists and logicians may benefit from legal philosophy as well. A legal perspective may allow them to see certain problems in a new light.

The volume is divided into four parts. The first part "Philosophical Problems of Normativity and Rule Following" contains chapters relating to more general philosophical matters. It begins with the chapter written by Paul Boghossian. He presents a conceptual framework for talking about norms, rules and principles. The purpose of the author is to distinguish such matters which are purely verbal and matters which are substantive. Special focus in put on the crucial concept of rule-following, specifically in the cases, where there is no explicit intention. The author also asks important questions relating to normativity of rules. Are rules themselves normative? Is following a rule normative? Paul Boghossian argues that Kripke is endorsing an unqualified conception of rule following as normative. He concludes that rules and rule following facts are not normative in themselves. They derive what normativity they may on occasion have from the holding of some underlying moral truth.

Jaap Hage in his chapter questions the often accepted assumption concerning important (if not necessary) connections between rules and normativity. To justify his view that the connection between rules and normativity is much looser than it might seem, the author provides two main arguments. The first argument comprises a critique of a classical dichotomy involving regulative and constitutive rules. The author claims that regulative rules are in fact a subcategory of constitutive rules. Moreover, Hage advocates a concept of deontic facts that have the feature of being able to guide behaviour; in this connection, rules are not necessary as behaviour-guiding entities. The second argument is a novel account of (constitutive) rules as constraints on possible worlds. The constraining function is the most basic function of rules, and, as constraints, they cannot be regarded as behaviour-guiding entities. The chapter is concluded by Hage's views concerning the logic of rule application

William Knorpp discusses the issue of rule communalism, that is, the view according to which rule following is possible for communal individuals but not for solitary individuals. In this connection, the author refers to a famous Kripke-Wittgenstein view on this subject and assesses it as nihilism: according to Knorpp, the Kripke-Wittgenstein theory does not support the possession of rule-following capacity even for communal individuals. The author investigates the possibilities of defending genuine rule communalism in the context of nihilist arguments. The chapter's conclusion is negative: Knorpp states that communalism remains unproven and that it is almost certainly a false theory.

Krzysztof Posłajko deals in his chapter with Philip Goff's solution to the rule-following paradox as formulated from the point of view of certain interpretations of semantic phenomenology (its proponents suggest than one can literally hear meaning while listening to meaningful utterances—contrary to listening to expressions that one does not understand). For Goff, to perceive an utterance as meaningful is to perceive it as having specific meaning as well. Hence, phenomenal states can be seen as facts that make sentences about meaning true; however, existence of any such facts is denied by Kripkenstein's paradox. In his chapter, Posłajko argues that Goff's attempt is, however, unsuccessful because it goes against some basic intuition concerning the possibility of linguistic error.

The chapter by Leopold Hess analyses normativity of linguistic meaning and discusses the status of norms that determine whether language is used correctly. Rules can be perceived as either constitutive (a classical example is a game of chess where game rules determine not only whether a given move is a correct one but also whether it is a chess move in general) or prescriptive. A common view is that norms of meaning discourse are prescriptive; however, such a position must also face some difficulties (what does it mean that one ought to use a given word in a certain way?). Leopold Hess tries to show that one should understand linguistic norms as globally constitutive, having their normative force grounded in the notion of interpretability, which is connected with a more general linguistic practice rather than linguistic expressions only.

Przemysław Tacik, in his chapter, looks at Kripkenstein's paradox via a Kantian critique of Hume's scepticism. The author suggests a reinterpretation of Kant's arguments against Hume's ideas on causality and time's (dis)continuity. He describes analogies between Hume's and Kripkenstein's scepticisms so that the latter is reformulated in the following manner: How can one know that the rule that guides usage of a certain word at moment t_1 remains the same at moment t_2? Tacik claims that by appealing to the Kantian idea of "transcendental unity of apperception", one may contribute to solving Kripkenstein's paradox. The key for him is that linguistic normativity is based not on the community of language users but rather lies within our readiness to correct ourselves even before the community may perceive our language expressions as correct or incorrect.

Piotr Kozak, referring to the so-called "Pittsburgh school" of philosophy (W. Sellars), analyses the relationship between naturalism and normativism in connection with the rule-following problem. The author investigates a vicious regress threat and difficulties linked to any attempts to reduce rule following to merely regular actions. Then, a Third Way between regularism and intellectualism is proposed, and Sellar's idea of pattern-governed behaviour is critically discussed.

Joanna Klimczyk discusses in her chapter the relation between normativity and rationality. The problem she addresses is whether any normativity might be ascribed to the requirements of rationality. She argues that the so called *Double Binding View*, held by some philosophers who tend to agree on two general requirements of rationality: substantive and non-substantive, might be "far-fetched". Her claim is that at least the requirement of coherence (specific non-substantive requirement) might be already entailed by the substantive normative requirement. She concludes that the only normativity of rationality for which one might have (or should have) support is one connected with a "primitive" (as she calls it) desire of being comprehensible either to oneself or the other people.

Tomasz Pietrzykowski raises the important issue of the relationship between rules and rights. At the beginning, he compares two opposite versions of priority theses: The Priority of Rights and The Priority of Rules. The latter is based on a devastating criticism of the former. Despite this criticism, the idea of inherent natural human rights has been influenced by contemporary public discourse. For that reason, the aim of the author is to redefine the concept of rights. He considers "rights" as mental states, in which something is represented as "due" to someone. Such a mental representation was called "rights–feelings". The redefinition of the concept of "rights" makes it possible to defend a new formulation of The Priority of Rights Thesis, namely the hypothesis that rights–feelings may precede any developed internal point of view and, consequently, any full-fledged social rules. Such a reformulation of The Priority of Rights Thesis constitutes an attempt to present the relationship between rules and rights from the modern, naturalistic and cognitive perspectives.

The second part of the volume "Normativity of Law and Legal Norms" begins with the chapter written by Brian Bix. He discusses certain fundamental problems of legal philosophy—namely, the connections among law, rules and morality in the broad spectrum of contemporary theories of law. Law is a normative system, and any theory about its nature must focus on its normativity. The chapter starts with an overview of the relationship between law and rules, showing the issues that give rise to many of the debates in contemporary legal philosophy. Then, the author presents his interpretation of H. Kelsen's theory, according to which the Basic Norm is presupposed when a citizen chooses to read the actions of legal officials in a normative way. Kelsenian theory should be understood as an investigation into the logic of normative thought. Kelsen claims that all normative systems are structurally and logically similar, but each normative system is independent of every other system; thus, law is conceptually separate from morality. Then the author turns to H. L. A. Hart's theory, and in particular to the question of whether his approach views legal normativity as *sui generis*. This analysis allows the author to challenge the prevailing view in contemporary legal philosophy that law necessarily makes moral claims (L. Green, J. Raz and others). The author demonstrates that a less morally flavoured conception of the nature of law is tenable and may in fact work better than current morally focused understandings of law and its claims.

The chapter written by Stefano Bertea goes in the opposite direction. His topic is the concept of legal obligation. He starts with an analysis of the concept of obligation (such analysis is meant to mark the boundaries within which a theoretical debate on obligation is to take place) and on this basis develops his conception of obligation. This conception is built around the idea of obligation as having two essential aspects: one of these lies in the internal connection of obligation with moral practical reasons and is accordingly rational and moral; the other one instead lies in the conceptual link between obligation and mandatory force. In combination, these two aspects, which interlock to form what Bertea calls the "duality of obligation", frame obligation as a rational and morally justifiable categorical requirement. Thus, Bertea belongs to the camp of legal philosophers who believe that law necessarily makes moral claims.

Fundamental questions of legal theory are discussed in the chapter by Dietmar von der Pfordten. He asks the following question: What is the main form of expression in law? The classical conceptions maintained that such main forms are commands, orders and imperatives. For nonpositivistic theories, however, this question is of secondary importance because, for them, the aim of law is important, while the means of law are contingent. In the 20th century, Kelsen and Hart tried to identify one basic type of expression: norms (Kelsen) or rules (Hart). The author argues that there is no reason to indicate one and only one main form of expression in law, as law uses a multitude of conceptual means. The idea that there is any reason to reduce conceptually the choice of our means to realize the aim of law is false.

Dennis Patterson and Michael S. Pardo in their chapter develop the critique of the neuroscientific approach to fundamental problems of jurisprudence and *inter alia* to rule-following Their point of departure is the critical examination of the claims made by many authors that issues of mind are best explained as neurological events. Such an analysis shows that identifying the mind with the brain leads to a philosophical error. The authors discuss the nature of conceptual and empirical claims and their use in explanations of neuroscience. These considerations lead to the conclusion that psychological categories such as memory, knowledge, intention or belief are conceptual rather than empirical in nature. This allows the authors to deal with various conceptual issues: the distinction between criterial and inductive evidence, unconscious rule following, interpretation and knowledge.

Monika Zalewska reconsiders the classical Hartian problem of how law differs from a gunman situation. She asks the question regarding whether this problem arises as well with respect to Kelsen's theory of law. The principal problem of Kelsen's theory is that its answer to the question of the difference between law and the gunman situation puts this theory at risk of being trapped in *circulum vitiosum.* The solution proposed by the author is based on a combination of so-called relative categories *a priori*—a dynamic structure of law and primary and secondary norms.

Peng-Hsiang Wang and Linton Wang discuss a general problem concerning the relation between rules and normativity. They take Joseph Raz's challenge concerning normativity of rules by claiming that rules are not reasons, but reason-giving facts. The authors propose a theory referred to as a difference-making-based account of the reason-giving force of rules. According to the difference-making-based theory of reasons, reasons are difference-making facts. This theory may be instantiated in many ways because many types of objects may be considered as difference-making facts. The authors devote their attention to the possibility of constructing a theory of rules as reason-giving facts, and they focus on differences that are made in the world by actions conforming to rules or violating them. They define the difference that may be caused in the world by following or breaking legal rules as "the legality-based difference". Hence, the authors claim that the normativity of rules has the same structure of normativity of other types of reason-giving facts, with the qualification that difference-making facts obtained with regard to rules are different from those that are obtained due to the occurrence of other reason-giving facts. Consequently, they propose a theoretically grounded answer to Raz's questions concerning the normativity of rules.

Two chapters are directly related to the problem of autonomy of legal normativity vis-à-vis moral normativity. Aldo Schiavello deals with the "conventionalist turn" in legal positivism in relation to legal normativity. He argues that conventionalist legal positivism offers an explanation of legal normativity and preserves the autonomy of legal obligation, both vis-à-vis moral obligation and coercion. The position of the conventionalists has some defects, however. Two pathways should be distinguished. The first one (H.L.A. Hart in the Postscript) leads to a "weak" version of conventionalism, and, as such, it fails insofar as it does not preserve the autonomy of legal obligations from moral obligations. The second pathway (G. Postema) is able to develop a coherent theory of legal normativity but at the price of distorting reality.

A different conclusion relating to the distinction of legal and moral normativity in Hartian theory is developed in the chapter written by Adam Dyrda. Pursuant to H. L. A. Hart, the fundamental reasons for officials to apply the criteria of validity contained in the rule of recognition are of various provenience (moral, conventional, traditional and other). In order to be genuine, such reasons must be internal in the sense proposed by B. Williams (i.e., they must refer to agents' motivation). Therefore, the internal point of view should be defined in terms of internal reasons. It is argued that if fundamental legal reasons are to be normative (authoritative), they must be internal reasons of a moral nature. The conclusion is that Hart's original theory of internal point of view is too weak. If it is, however, supplemented by the concept of internal reasons, the autonomy of legal obligations cannot be sustained.

The third part of the volume "Rules in Legal Interpretation and Argumentation" deals with various problems of rules applied in interpretation and specifically with their normativity and validity.

The most general question is asked by Tomasz Gizbert-Studnicki: Are rules of interpretation applied in legal practice normative? The author distinguishes between two roles of such rules: they guide interpretation, and they justify interpretative decision by delivering justificatory reasons. In this sense, rules of interpretation are normative. Their normative force cannot be explained by recourse to the concept of convention. Rules of interpretation derive their normative force from values of political morality underlying a given legal system. They deliver justificatory reasons, which, however, are not exclusionary. Certain important differences in this respect between civil and common law legal cultures are described.

In his chapter, Paweł Banaś argues that legal interpretation should be perceived as a rule-guided process and as such cannot be reduced to following co called second order rules (e.g. *clara (non) sunt interpretanda*). There are different levels within a process of interpretation which are represented by different types of rules. The author draws an analogy between interpretation and some ideas present in contemporary philosophy of language concerning pragmatics and meaning. He argues that each level of legal interpretation process may be subject to Kripke's sceptical paradox which questions the very possibility of the existence of rules—a problem more fundamental than the one concerning their function in a legal discourse (either heuristic or justificatory).

Paolo Sandro investigates one of the most important problems in legal philosophy, that is, legal indeterminacy. The point of departure of his analysis is that according to a common view, notorious controversies in the theory of meaning lead to essential disagreement regarding the content of law understood as an interpretive practice. The author questions this view by pointing out that law is in the first place a vehicle of communication of patterns of certain behaviour that are prescribed by the lawmaker. Regarding this purpose, law is directed first and foremost to laymen. Sandro discusses important legal-philosophical views concerning the consequences of this thesis to conclude that a sound meta-theory of legal interpretation has to emphasize the central role of a linguistic criterion.

Ralf Poscher reconsiders Lon L. Fuller's argument that the positivist distinction between the law "as it is" and the law "as it ought to be" fails due to the need for creative interpretation even in easy cases. Poscher argues that Andrei Marmor's defence of positivism, based on Wittgenstein's remarks on rule following and the distinction between understanding and interpretation, is not successful. Positivism can be saved from Fuller's challenge, if we distinguish between two different elements of our practice of adjudication: the communicative interpretation of utterances and the application of a rule thus identified as the content of a communicative intention. We need to distinguish epistemic creativity and the creativity involved in amending the law via legal construction. Only the former is involved in communicative interpretation; only the latter concerns the distinction between the law "as it is" and the law "as it ought to be".

Brian Slocum revisits the matter of ordinary meaning of rules in the context of legal interpretation. The chapter contains a plea against the intentionalist position in the theory of legal interpretation. The question of what makes a certain meaning the ordinary one and the evidential question of how the determinants of ordinary meaning are identified are of crucial importance. Sometimes, the courts go beyond or reject the linguistic meaning, due to normatively based desires. The ordinary meaning principle is necessarily concerned with the linguistic meaning and not normative matters. Claims made by intentionalists are fundamentally inconsistent with how the ordinary meaning doctrine must be conceptualized.

Hanna Filipczyk raises a similar issue but refers to a distinct legal culture. Her topic is the *claritas* doctrine expressed by the maxim *clara non sunt interpretanda* and visible in the *acte clair* and *acte éclairé* doctrines of the Court of Justice of the European Union (ECJ). Referring to Wittgenstein's thoughts on rule following, the author develops a new understanding of this important doctrine.

An important issue directly related to legal interpretation is raised by Marcin Matczak. He criticizes the speech-act approach to rules, which is prevailing in legal philosophy. His main argument is that the speech-act theory provides an inadequate framework for the analysis of written discourse, including legal text. Such an approach is trapped into the fallacy of synchronicity and the fallacy of a discursivity. The former consists in treating legal rules as if they were uttered and received in the same context; the latter consists of treating legal rules as relatively short, isolated sentences. As a consequence, excessive focus is placed on semantic intentions of the lawmaker, and the discursive aspects of communication are neglected. The author proposes to look at the legal texts as complex text acts (as opposed to speech acts). Such an approach supports the idea of minimal legislative intent, developed by Joseph Raz.

The chapter by Andrzej Grabowski raises the problem of the validity of moral rules and principles. This issue becomes legally relevant frequently in cases when a judge is bound to take into account moral rules, principles or standards. Obviously, only valid moral rules, which the judge must identify, may be utilized by the judge. The author's aim is to clarify three basic questions: What does it mean when we say that a moral rule is valid? How do we identify valid moral rules and principles? How is the validity of moral rules and principles justified in the legal discourse? The author argues for a coherent juristic conception of the validity of moral rules and principles. He recommends the methodological approach based on the adoption of a morally detached and impartial point of view.

A problem relating to interpretation of law is addressed in the chapter authored by Izabela Skoczeń. She raises the problem of significance for legal theory of general-pragmatic theories, such as Grice's theory of conversational maxims and the competing "relevance theory" of Sperber and Wilson. Her main aim is to define the content of conversational maxims within the legal context. The author argues that none of the pragmatic theories delivers a satisfactory account of maxims in legal contexts, due to certain specific features of legal talk. Legislative speech is a collective speech act, while the tools developed by pragmatic theories apply rather to individual speech acts. Neither the content of maxims as defined by Grice, nor by Sperber and Wilson, provides an adequate account of what their content in legal contexts should be.

Michal Dudek in turn raises a very interesting (and rarely discussed) issue of traffic signs as a specific form of communicating legal rules. The author argues that traffic signs are not subsidiary instruments. To the contrary, they are in fact an integral part of rules and not just a way of communicating them. Traffic signs are a means of visual nonlinguistic communication with specific features that cannot be verbalized in an intelligible and concise manner. Due to that fact, in the context of traffic signs, a legal rule cannot be conceived of as a linguistic utterance. The concept of interpretation based on the vision of legal text as an aggregate of linguistic utterances proves to be inadequate. Certain legal norms cannot be adequately expressed in words.

Finally, the fourth part of the volume "Rules in Legal Logic and AI&Law" contains chapters devoted to logical analysis of rules.

Andrej Kristan contributes to the expressive conception of norms that was famously discussed in the 1980s by Carlos Alchourrón and Eugenio Bulygin. Kristan discusses important critical arguments that were raised against this conception in the literature. The author argues that expressivism is able to account for facultative states of affairs without obtaining a contradiction in the normative system. Additionally, he shows how this conception may account for describing the propositional content of rules of preference without semanticizing the force indicator of object-rules. Kristan also obtains a result according to which the expressive conception of norms accounts for the permissive closure and other types of conditional norms without admitting irreducible character of acts of permitting. This chapter shows the usefulness of the logical tools of hard analytical philosophy employed for the sake of legal-theoretical argument.

In his chapter, Jan Woleński discusses the problem of rule following, as formulated by Ludwig Wittgenstein and creatively interpreted by Saul Kripke, by appealing to some devices of contemporary deontic logic. The author develops a description of the rule-following paradox in logical terms. Finally, he sheds some light on the problem of rules in logic and analyses the specificity of following rules of logic.

The chapter by Giovanni Battista Ratti deals with an important logical problem concerning negation of rules and, more generally, with the role of negation in prescriptive discourse. The author discusses negation of both categorical rules and conditional rules and shows that using negation in the context of the latter leads to unclear and ambiguous consequences. These considerations lead also to problems concerning the proper accounting for contradiction between conditional rules. The chapter offers a systematization of different views concerning the application of negation to normative conditionals. The results brought by this contribution are mainly negative: the concept of negation in prescriptive discourse is unclear and problematic, which leads to serious problems concerning our understanding of the logical structure of rules themselves. Hence, according to Ratti, the development of a satisfying logical theory of negation of rules remains a powerful challenge.

The chapter by Michał Araszkiewicz deals with one of the most fundamental problems concerning logical characteristics of legal rules, namely, their defeasibility. The author distinguishes several different interpretations of this concept as discussed in the literature. Although non-classical defeasible logics are successfully employed in AI-based systems of legal knowledge, there is still an ongoing legal-theoretical debate concerning the adequacy of theories accounting for legal rules as defeasible ones. Araszkiewicz proposes a middle ground theoretical view that encompasses important intuitions present in the works of adherents of defeasibility on the one hand and of its critics on the other hand. He argues a concept of contextually complete legal rules, which encompasses the idea that defeasibility of rules depends on the context to which they are applied. This view is inspired by the very influential theory of epistemic contextualism.

The chapter by Marcello Ceci is a contribution to the understanding of rules in the domain of artificial intelligence and law research. The chapter should be seen as part of a broader ongoing work concerning bridging the gap between the layer of legal documents on the one hand and the layer of rule modelling on the other hand. Ceci rightly emphasizes that legal reasoning cannot be represented adequately in AI-based systems without taking the argumentation process into account. In this connection, Ceci refers to the theory of argumentation schemes advocated by T. Gordon and D. Walton. The author suggests an extension of the LegalRuleML standard in order to encompass the argumentative aspect of legal knowledge in Semantic Web technologies used for representation of legal reasoning.

Vytautas Čyras and Friedrich Lachmayer focus on the problem of visualization of legal rules. The authors offer a systematization of visualization of legal rules and patterns of legal inference using a criterion of the number of dimensions used in a given visualization. The illustrative materials chosen by Čyras and Lachmayer are diagrams and other pictorial representations that were presented during the JURIX 2012—the 25th International Conference on Legal Knowledge and Information Systems conference that took place in Amsterdam, Netherlands (December 17–19). The authors conclude that the creation of plausible visualizations of legal rules and reasoning is a difficult task due to its multidisciplinary character involving knowledge law, informatics, visual media and semiotics.

The idea for this volume came from the Rules 2013 conference held in Krakow, Poland in September 2013, organized by the Department of Legal Theory, Jagiellonian University. The conference, devoted to rules, rule-following and normativity, gathered a number of philosophers, legal philosophers, logicians, psychologists and specialists in AI & Law. This volume contains selected papers presented at the conference, however, expanded and revised for the purpose of the publication. We would like to thank all the participants, especially those who contributed to this volume, as well as members of the Program Committee.

Contents

Part II Normativity of Law and Legal Norms

Part III Rules in Legal Interpretation and Argumentation

Contributors

Michał Araszkiewicz Faculty of Law, Jagiellonian University, Kraków, Poland

Paweł Banaś Faculty of Law, Jagiellonian University, Kraków, Poland

Stefano Bertea Law School, University of Leicester, Leicester, UK

Brian H. Bix University of Minnesota, Minneapolis, USA

Paul Boghossian Department of Philosophy, New York University, New York, USA

Marcello Ceci AFIS GRCTC—University College Cork, Cork, Ireland

Vytautas Čyras Faculty of Mathematics and Informatics, Vilnius University, Vilnius, Lithuania

Michał Dudek Department of Sociology of Law, Faculty of Law and Administration, Jagiellonian University in Krakow, Kraków, Poland

Adam Dyrda Jagiellonian University, Krakow, Poland

Hanna Filipczyk Enodo Advisors Sp. z o.o., Warszawa, Poland

Tomasz Gizbert-Studnicki Faculty of Law, Jagiellonian University, Kraków, Poland

Andrzej Grabowski Jagiellonian University, Krakow, Poland

Jaap Hage Department Foundations and Methods of Law, University of Maastricht, Maastricht, Netherlands

Leopold Hess Uniwersytet Jagielloński, Kraków, Poland

Joanna Klimczyk Department of Philosophy and Sociology, Polish Academy of Sciences, Warszawa, Poland

Department of Philosophy, University of Szczecin, Warszawa, Poland

William Knorpp James Madison University, Harrisonburg, USA

Piotr Kozak Warsaw University, Warsaw, Poland

Andrej Kristan Tarello Institute for Legal Philosophy, University of Genoa, Genoa, Italy

Faculty of Law, University of Girona, Spain

Friedrich Lachmayer Faculty of Law, University of Innsbruck, Innsbruck, Austria

Marcin Matczak University of Warsaw, Warszawa, Poland

Michael S. Pardo University of Alabama School of Law, Tuscaloosa, USA

Dennis Patterson Law Department, European University Institute, Florence, Italy

Rutgers School of Law, Camden, USA

Swansea University, Swansea, UK

Tomasz Pietrzykowski University of Silesia, Katowice, Poland

Ralf Poscher Institute for Staatswissenschaft and Philosophy of Law, Albert-Ludwigs-Universität Freiburg, Freiburg im Breisgau, Germany

Krzysztof Posłajko Institute of Philosophy, Jagiellonian University, Kraków, Poland

Giovanni Battista Ratti Tarello Institute for Legal Philosophy, Department of Law, University of Genoa, Genoa, Italy

Paolo Sandro Liverpool Hope University, Department of Law, Liverpool, UK

Aldo Schiavello University of Palermo, Palermo, Italy

Izabela Skoczeń Department of Legal Theory, Jagiellonian University, Krakow, Poland

Brian G. Slocum University of the Pacific, McGeorge School of Law, Sacramento, USA

Przemysław Tacik Jagiellonian University of Cracow, Kraków, Poland

Dietmar von der Pfordten Georg-August-University, Goettingen, Germany

Linton Wang Department of Philosophy, National Chung Cheng University, Chia-yi County, Taiwan

Peng-Hsiang Wang Institutum Iurisprudentiae, Academia Sinica, Taipei City, Taiwan

Jan Woleński Jagiellonian University, Krakow, Poland

Monika Zalewska University of Łódź, Łódź, Poland

About the Authors

Michał Araszkiewicz is an adjunct lecturer in the Department of Legal Theory of Jagiellonian University (Kraków, Poland). His areas of research interest include theories of legal argumentation, application of AI tools to legal reasoning and general methodology of jurisprudence. He is a co-editor of several contributed volumes, including Coherence: Insights from Philosophy, Jurisprudence and Artificial Intelligence (with J. Šavelka), Law and Philosophy Library vol. 107, Springer 2013, as well as author of numerous papers published in monographs and journals.

Paweł Banaś is a PhD student at the Jagiellonian University. His studies focus on philosophy of law, philosophy of language and analytical metaphysics. His current research projects are "Non-factualism and the problems of law's normativity" and "Limits of Analytical Jurisprudence" under the supervision of Tomasz Gizbert-Studnicki.

Stefano Bertea is currently a Reader in Legal Philosophy at the School of Law of the University of Leicester. He worked as a Marie Curie Research Fellow at the University of Edinburgh in 2002–2004 and as an Alexander von Humboldt Research Fellow at the Christian Albrecht University of Kiel in 2005–2007. He has published widely in the fields of legal philosophy, jurisprudence, political theory and theory of legal reasoning.

Brian H. Bix is the Frederick W. Thomas Professor of Law and Philosophy at the University of Minnesota. He holds a D. Phil. (doctorate) from Balliol College, Oxford University and a J.D. (law degree) from Harvard University. He writes and teaches in the areas of Jurisprudence, Contract Law, Family Law, Philosophy of Language and Moral Philosophy. His publications in the area of Jurisprudence include A Dictionary of Legal Philosophy (Oxford, 2004), Jurisprudence: Theory and Context (6th ed., Sweet & Maxwell, 2012), and Law, Language, and Legal Determinacy (Oxford, 1993).

Paul Boghossian is Silver Professor of Philosophy at New York University and the Director of the New York Institute of Philosophy. His research interests are primarily in epistemology and the philosophy of mind, although he has written on a wide range of topics, including: color, rule-following, naturalism, self-knowledge, a priori knowledge, analytic truth, realism, relativism, the aesthetics of music and the concept of genocide. He is the author of Fear of Knowledge: Against Relativism and Constructivism (Oxford: 2006) and Content and Justification (Oxford: 2008).

Marcello Ceci holds Ph.D in Legal Informatics, CIRSFID—University of Bologna. Graduated in Law at the University of Pavia and at IUSS—Institute of Advanced Studies in 2008. His Ph.D research involved the semantic enhancement of judicial decisions through the technologies of the Semantic Web. His research won the "Best Paper Award" at the 2012 RuleML Doctoral Consortium, held within the ECAI conference in Montpellier. His fields of research include Legal Informatics (legal argumentation, legal ontologies, normative multi-agents systems), Philosophy of Law, Sociology of Law.

Vytautas Čyras is Associate Professor in computer science at Vilnius University, Lithuania. In 1979 he graduated from Vilnius University. In 1985 he obtained PhD degree (Candidate of Physico-mathematical Sciences) in computing from Lomonosov Moscow State University. In 2007 he obtained Master of Laws from Vilnius University. His research interests include computer science, law and legal informatics., Naugarduko 24, 03225 Vilnius, Lithuania

Michał Dudek holds PhD in Law, works at the Department of Sociology of Law, Faculty of Law and Administration, Jagiellonian University in Krakow, Poland. Among his main research interests are sociology of law, legal policy, axiology of law, communication of law and intercultural communication. In his monograph *Komunikowanie prawa w dobie pluralizmu kulturowego* [*Communication of Law in the Age of Cultural Pluralism*], he investigates the issue of how foreigners can acquire orientation about the law of the state in which territory they currently live.

Adam Dyrda is as an assistant professor in the Department of Legal Theory, Jagiellonian University, Cracow. He obtained PhD in Legal Theory in 2012. Author of the book "Convention as Foundation of Law. Controversies within Contemporary Legal Positivism" [in Polish: Konwencja u podstaw prawa. Kontrowersje współczesnego pozytywizmu prawniczego] (2013). He published articles on various topics connected with legal positivism and cultural theory. Presently he is working on pragmatist cultural theory and pragmatist theory of law.

Hanna Filipczyk holds degrees in law and in philosophy and a PhD in law from the Nicolaus Copernicus University in Toruń (2012). Her research interests focus on general theory of tax liabilities, tax procedure, legal interpretation, morality of taxation and tax avoidance. She is also a tax adviser specializing in tax litigation (Arthur Andersen, Ernst & Young, Accreo Taxand, Enodo Advisors), member of the International Fiscal Association.

Tomasz Gizbert-Studnicki is a Professor of Law, head of the Department of Legal Theory, Jagellonian University, Kraków. Former member of the Executive Committee of International Association for Legal and Social Philosophy. He has worked on the problems of language of law, legal interpretation and argumentation. Author of two books (in Polish) and numerous papers in Polish, English and

German. Currently he is a leader of a team working on a research project "Limits of Analytical Jurisprudence".

Andrzej Grabowski is an associate professor in the Department of Legal Theory at the Jagiellonian University in Krakow (Poland). His scientific interests include the theory of legal argumentation, the relationship of law and morality, the postpositivist theory of law and the problems of legal validity. He has published Judicial Argumentation and Pragmatics (Księgarnia Akademicka 1999) and Juristic Concept of the Validity of Statutory Law (Springer 2013).

Jaap Hage studied Law and Philosophy, and presently holds the Chair of Jurisprudence at Maastricht University. His research has focused on the nature of normativity, legal logic, basic legal concepts and methology of legal science. His books include: Reasoning with Rules (Kluwer 1997); Studies in Legal Logic (Springer 2005); Concepts in Law (co-edited with Dietmar von der Pfordten; Springer 2009); Introduction to Law (co-edited with Bram Akkermans; Springer forthcoming). More info can be found on his website: www.jaaphage.nl.

Leopold Hess is a PhD candidate in Philosophy at the Faculty of Philosophy, Jagiellonian University, Krakow. His main interests include Philosophy of Language, History of Early Modern Philosophy, issues of normativity and rationality.

Joanna Klimczyk is Assistant Professor of Philosophy at the Polish Academy of Sciences in the Section of Logic and Cognitive Sciences. Currently she also holds a post doc position at the University of Szczecin where she realizes the project 'Companions in Normativity: Normativity in Ethics and Language' funded by the National Science Centre within the FUGA Programme for years 2012–2015. Her main research interests revolve around the problem of normativity, broadly construed. Her recent research includes meta-theory of normativity and practical modals.

William Knorpp teaches philosophy at James Madison University in Harrisonburg, Virginia, USA. He received his Ph.D. from The University of North Carolina and has written on, among other things, relativism, logical psychologism, the private/solitary language arguments, methodological naturalism, and the relationship between logic and reasoning.

Piotr Kozak is a PhD student at Warsaw University. Interested in philosophy of mind and philosophy of law.

Andrej Kristan is a research fellow and doctoral candidate at the Tarello Institute for Legal Philosophy, University of Genoa (Italy). Lecturer at the University of Girona (Spain). With a dissertation on law's hypertextuality, his main work is on the crossroads of philosophy of law and philosophy of language, though he also serves as Program Coordinator of an international master in Global Rule of Law and Constitutional Democracy at the University of Genoa, and as Editor of Revus—Journal for Constitutional Theory and Philosophy of Law.

Friedrich Lachmayer born in Vienna in 1943. 1966 Doctor iuris (University of Vienna). 1967–70 Austrian Federal Law Office (Finanzprokuratur). 1971–2003 Austrian Federal Chancellery, Constitution Service. 1988 Habilitation at the University of Innsbruck (Legal Theory and Theory of Legislation). 1989–2003 Head of the Austrian Legal Information System (www.ris.bka.gv.at). Research interests include legal theory, legislation, legal informatics and legal semiotics.

Marcin Matczak is an associate professor at the University of Warsaw and a partner in DZP, one of the biggest Polish law firms. His academic interests cover legal theory and legal philosophy. His publications include articles and books on theories of legal interpretation, judicial reasoning and judicial formalism, with special focus on the application of philosophy of language in legal philosophy.

Michael S. Pardo is the Henry Upson Sims Professor of Law at the University of Alabama School of Law. His scholarship explores epistemological issues in the areas of evidence, criminal procedure, civil procedure, and jurisprudence, with a specific focus on legal proof. He is the author of Minds, Brains, and Law: The Conceptual Foundations of Law and Neuroscience (2013, with Patterson), Evidence: Text, Problems, and Cases (2011, with Allen, Kuhns, Swift, and Schwartz), and several academic articles.

Dennis Patterson is Professor of Law and Chair in Legal Philosophy and Legal Theory, European University Institute, Florence; Board of Governors Professor of Law and Philosophy, Rutgers University, New Jersey, USA; Professor of Law and Chair in International Trade and Legal Philosophy, Swansea University, Wales, UK. He is the author (with Ari Afilalo) of The new Global Trading Order (CUP, 2010) and Law and Truth (OUP, 1996).

Dietmar von der Pfordten is Professor for Philosophy of Law and Social Philosophy at the Georg-August-University Goettingen and there the Director of the Section for Philosophy of Law and Social Philosophy. He was visiting professor in Italy and the Netherlands. He is the author of several books, among it "Normative Ethik", Berlin 2010, "Suche nach Einsicht", Hamburg 2010, "Rechtsphilosophie. Eine Einführung", Munich 2013, and of various articles in the field of ethics, political philosophy and legal philosophy.

Tomasz Pietrzykowski is a lecturer at the Faculty of Law and Administration of the University of Silesia in Katowice, Poland. Author of several books and numerous articles on legal philosophy, including "Ethical problems of law" (2005), "Ethics in Public Administration" (2009), "Foundations of Intertemporal Law" (2011) and "Legal Intuition. Towards External Integration of Legal Theory" (2012). Practicing lawyer and former senior official in the governmental administration of the Silesian region.

Krzysztof Płeszka is Professor of Law in the Department of Legal Theory, Jagiellonian University, Kraków. His areas of research interest include problems of a legal system, theory of a legal interpretation and argumentation, and theory of legislation. His current research project is a part of a "Limits of Analytical

Jurisprudence" grant (funded by the Polish National Science Centre). He is an author of three books (in Polish) as well as of numerous papers in Polish, German and English published in monographs and journals.

Ralf Poscher is Professor of Public Law and Director of the Institute for Staatswissenschaft &Philosophy of Law, at the Albert-Ludwigs University Freiburg. Recent writings in English cover jurisprudential topics such as a critique of the principles theory, the Hart-Dworkin-debate, Concepts in Law, Ambiguity and Vagueness in Legal Interpretation and Legal Hermeneutics.

Krzysztof Posłajko is an assistant professor at the Institute of Philosophy, Jagiellonian University, Krakow. He works in the area of philosophy of language, metaphysics of mind and theories of truth.

Giovanni Battista Ratti is Lecturer in Legal Philosophy at the University of Genoa (Italy). Before his appointment with the University of Genoa, he has been Government of Canada Research Scholar (University of Toronto, 2004–05) and Government of Spain "Juan de la Cierva" Fellow in Law (University of Girona, 2008–2011). Amongst his most recent books are: Studi sulla logica del diritto e della scienza giuridica (Madrid, Marcial Pons, 2013), El gobierno de las normas (Madrid, Marcial Pons 2013), and The Logic of Legal Requirements (Oxford, OUP 2012, w/ Jordi Ferrer Beltrán).

Paolo Sandro teaches law at the University of Edinburgh. He holds a Ph.D. in Legal Theory (2014) from the University of Edinburgh and a Ph.D. in Public Law (2011) from the University of 'Roma Tre' (Rome). Paolo's main research interests lie in the juridical structure of constitutional democracies and in problems of applied legal theory, particularly in the context of transnational public law. His work has appeared on Res Publica (2011).

Aldo Schiavello is a full professor of Legal Philosophy at the University of Palermo. Co-director of Diritto & Questioni pubbliche; assistant editor of Ragion Pratica; advisory board member of Ethics & Politics. Coordinator of Ph.D Programme in "Human Rights: Evolution, Protection and Limits" (University of Palermo). His research is currently focused on legal positivism, legal reasoning and legal normativity, human rights.).

Izabela Skoczeń is a student at the Faculty of Law and Administration at the Jagiellonian University, Cracow. In 2013 she received a grant from the Polish Ministry of Higher Education for a research project entitled 'Pragmatics of the Legal Language' under the supervision of the Department of Legal Theory at the Jagiellonian University. Her research interests are: Jurisprudence, Linguistic Pragmatics and the Philosophical Legacy of Herbert Paul Grice as well as International Commercial Arbitration Law.

Brian G. Slocum is a Professor of Law at the University of the Pacific, McGeorge School of Law in Sacramento, California. Professor Slocum has expertise in the areas of administrative law, contracts, immigration law and statutory interpretation.

Professor Slocum's scholarship primarily focuses on the intersection of linguistics and legal interpretation. Professor Slocum has a juris doctorate from Harvard Law School and a Ph.D. in Linguistics from the University of California, Davis., Sacramento, USA

Przemysław Tacik holds a Ph.D. in philosophy. Graduated from Jagiellonian University (philosophy, sociology and law). Currently works on his Ph.D. dissertation in international law. Visiting scholar at Université de Nice oraz State University of New York w Buffalo. Judicial training trainee. Author of one published book (The Sociology of Zygmunt Bauman) and one in publishing process (Freedom of Lights. Edmond Jabès and the Jewish Philosophy of Modernity). His research fields include contemporary continental philosophy, philosophy of law, Jewish philosophy and international law.

Peng-Hsiang Wang is an assistant research fellow at Institutum Iurisprudentiae, Academia Sinica, Taiwan. He holds a Dr. iur. degree from the University of Kiel (Germany) in 2003. His research is focused on normativity of law and reasons and rationality in legal reasoning. His recent publications include Are Rules Exclusionary Reasons in Legal Reasoning (ARSP Beiheft 119), Principles as Ideal Ought. Semantic Considerations on the Logical Structure of Principles (ARSP Beiheft 124).

Linton Wang is an associate professor of philosophy at National Chung Cheng University, Taiwan. He holds a Ph.D. in philosophy from the University of Texas at Austin in 2005. His current research centers on three intertwined topics: (a) the epistemology of scientific methodology and reasoning, (b) the epistemological and logical characteristics of modality, and (c) the agent-based normativity. Several of his papers have been published in Erkenntnis, Synthese, and Philosophia., University Rd. Sec. 1 No. 168, 621 Chia-yi County, Taiwan

Jan Woleński is Professor Emeritus of Jagiellonian University, member of Polish Academy of Sciences, Polish Academy of Arts and Sciences, Academia Europea, International Institute of Philosophy. In 2013 he was awarded by the prize of the Foundation for Polish Science in humanities and social sciences, called the Polish Nobel. His research areas include philosophical logic, epistemology and legal philosophy. He published 30 books and 600 scholarly papers, many in foreign languages.

Monika Zalewska is an adjunct in Department of Theory and Philosophy of Law at Faculty of Law and Administration, University of Lodz (Poland). In 2012 Dr. Zalewska received PhD degree defending thesis about the problem of imputation in Hans Kelsen's theory. It was prevailed by a fellowship in Hans Kelsen's Institute in Vienna in 2009. In addition in 2012 Dr. Zalewska achieved master of philosophy degree at Faulty of Philosophy and History (University of Lodz).

Part I
Philosophical Problems of Normativity and Rule Following

Chapter 1
Rules, Norms and Principles: A Conceptual Framework

Paul Boghossian

Abstract This chapter develops a conceptual framework for talking about the notions of rules, norms and principles. It is hoped that this framework will allow us to properly distinguish between merely verbal and substantive issues concerning these notions. It is argued that the substantive debate about rules is not about whether a rule exists, or what a rule is, but about what it takes for a rule to be a norm on behavior. One result of this way of looking at things is a recasting of the problem about rule-following: what is it that constitutes correct following of a rule in a case where there is no explicit intention to conform one's behavior to a rule. Finally, some issues concerning the general problem of normativity of both rules and rule-following is discussed in the chapter.

Keywords Rules · Rule-following · Norms · Normative propositions · Principles · Kripke

1.1 Introduction

In looking at the literature on rules one is struck by two related observations: one is that different notions are often conflated; the other is that it is often hard to see when a dispute is merely *verbal* and when it is substantive. Part of the problem here is that ordinary language is not precise when it comes to the word 'rule'—one can legitimately talk in different ways and so there is a danger of people talking past one another.

In this paper, I will try to suggest a framework for talking about rules that will allow me to clearly pose the issues that interest me, and that will help us distinguish between merely verbal issues about rules and substantive ones.

This is the text of a talk that was given at the Conference on Rules that was held at the Jagiellonian University in Krakow in October of 2013, organized by Tomasz Gizbert-Studnicki. I have kept the informal and often highly schematic character of the presentation in preparing this version for publication. Large ideas are sketched rather than developed in any detail. I am grateful to the audience on that occasion, and to Jules Coleman, for helpful comments.

P. Boghossian (✉)
Department of Philosophy, New York University, New York, USA
e-mail: pb3@nyu.edu

M. Araszkiewicz et al. (eds.), *Problems of Normativity, Rules and Rule-Following*,
Law and Philosophy Library 111, DOI 10.1007/978-3-319-09375-8_1

1.2 What Is a Rule?

1.2.1 Rules as Abstract Objects

Let me start with the following basic question: *What is a rule?*

We should start with the fact that, whatever rules are, it must be possible for them to be the sorts of things that are *accepted*, either by a person or by a community. It must be *possible* for rules to be accepted, even if some are not. That suggests that rules themselves should be thought of as *contents*, as the possible objects of intentional states of acceptance. (An intentional state is a mental state that has an intentional object. This is not to be confused with the notion of an intention, although intentions are, of course, instances of intentional states).

Now, contents are best thought of as *abstract objects*. Exactly what an abstract object is, as we will presently see, is controversial. But the idea is that, on this conception, rules belong with such objects as numbers, properties and propositions, rather than with concreta like tables or (token) books. If we say that rules are abstract objects, what kinds of abstract objects should we take them to be?

I'll come back to this question below, but already we might be thought to face a puzzle: *How could rules be abstract objects?* Abstract objects, after all, are said to exist outside of time and space. That means that they can't come in and out of existence. But, surely, we do often want to say that *a rule came to exist* when it didn't exist before. For example, those who think that (legal) *laws* are rules will want to say that rules come to exist as a result of certain kinds of legislative activity and that those rules did not exist before. Another kind of example would be the rules of chess. Surely, an objector might insist, the rules of chess did not exist prior to the game's being invented.

However, on an abstract conception of rules, we seem committed to rules' existing atemporally and necessarily. How can we reconcile these two observations? One possible response to this problem might be to say that we *do* after all need to make sense of abstract objects coming in and out of existence. Some philosophers see the need to say this even in connection with abstracta that don't concern the topic of rules.

For example, a number of philosophers who hold that *concepts* are abstract objects have expressed sympathy for the idea that some of these concepts could not have existed since the dawn of time, but must have been brought into being by the creative activity of human beings. While knowing no good alternative to thinking of concepts as abstract objects, such philosophers find it odd to think that a distinctively *cultural* concept, such as that of a *piano,* for example, or a *high school prom*, could have been around before there were humans. One might feel a similar discomfort with the idea of a certain *type* of musical composition, for example, the symphony, pre-existing its invention by human beings.[1]

[1] For a recent endorsement of a temporal conception of abstract see Mark Sainsbury and Michael Tye (2012).

This sort of temporal thinking about abstract objects does not appeal to me. I lose my grip on the distinction between abstract and concrete objects if I think of abstracta as having temporal properties. Moreover, I believe that we can do justice to our intuitions about the role of conceptual and artistic creativity within a framework in which we talk not about *creating* abstracta, but about *selecting* them, or *discovering* them. But no matter, we will see below that our puzzle about rule existence can be solved on either the temporal or the atemporal view.

1.2.2 Imperatival vs. Normative Content

Let me turn next to the question: If rules are abstracta, what kinds of abstracta are they?

One kind of abstract object that one might naturally think a rule might be, is a certain sort of *normative proposition*—a proposition that specifies a permission or a requirement. These, for example, are among what we call the 'rules of chess':

a. White *must* move first.
b. If one's king and rook have not previously moved, and if the king is not currently in check, and if there are no pieces between the king and said rook, then, under those conditions and only under those conditions, one *may* castle.

Another kind of abstract object that is also often called a 'rule' is an *imperatival* content, or an *instruction*:

c. If C, write a 0, move to the next square and go into state S2!
d. If x is an email that calls for an answer and you have just received x, answer it immediately!

Both of these types of content have been called 'rules.' Yet they are quite different from one another. For example, normative propositions look to be truth-evaluable, whereas instructions or imperatives are not.

So, are rules abstract objects with normative contents, or imperatival contents? Which is it to be? I believe that it would be all right to say that a rule might be *either* an imperatival content *or* a normative proposition.[2] This may come as a shock to some in the philosophy of law, because in that literature it is very common to insist that there is an important three-fold distinction between imperatives, rules and normative propositions, and to claim that there is a big issue whether laws should be thought of as consisting in the one sort of thing or the other.

To put things very roughly, John Austin argued that laws are *imperatives* with a certain pedigree; H. L. A. Hart argued that laws are *rules* with a certain pedigree; and Ronald Dworkin argued that laws essentially involve certain sorts of normative propositions, *principles*, in addition to rules.[3]

---

[2] For some considerations that bear on this issue see Boghossian (2008).

[3] See Austin (1832), Hart (1961), and Dworkin (1977).

How could we make sense of this central debate in the philosophy of law if we adopt the framework I am suggesting?

The answer to both this puzzle and the one about existence lies in seeing that the substantive debate is not about *whether a rule exists* or *what a rule is*, but about *what it takes for a rule to be norm on behavior*. Assuming that a rule is an abstract object, under what conditions will such a rule come to be a *standard* that behavior must conform to on pain of being open to a certain kind of criticism.

On the view I am recommending, we can say that a rule exists before it becomes law. What the legislator does is to take an antecedently existing abstract object and turn it into a certain kind of *legal norm on behavior,* a standard on behavior violations of which open one to a certain sort of criticism. Analogously, what the inventor of chess does is take a certain number of antecedently existing rules and put them together in such a way that they become norms on the behavior of a person with the right sorts of *intention*—namely, the person intending to play a game of chess.

In terms of this framework, we can pose Dworkin's question whether there is more to law than imperatives and rules by seeing it as the question not whether law involves principles in addition to rules, but rather as the question:

> Are the rules that are involved in law norms on behavior *independently of whether they are accepted* or does the law involve *only* rules that have been somehow or other accepted (either directly or indirectly, via a rule of recognition)?

Dworkin's view, of course, was that certain normative propositions—namely, moral principles, could be norms on legal reasoning, even if they had not been explicitly accepted.

On the view I'm recommending, then, rules are just certain types of abstract content. Their essential feature is *generality.* Rules are about types of states of affairs, and types of action, not particular states of affairs and particular actions. The key question about them is whether some of them can be norms on behavior independently of acceptance, or whether acceptance is always a precondition on their being norms on behavior.

Intuitively, moral rules are norms on behavior independently of whether they are accepted—this amounts to saying that, intuitively, a relativistic view of morality is incorrect. Furthermore, rules of etiquette are not norms on behavior in a given community independently of whether they have been accepted by that community. In the way I am proposing we think about things, what Dworkin did is make a real issue out of the question whether legal laws always depend on explicit acceptance if they are to be regarded as normatively constraining one's behavior.

1.2.3 Rule-Following

What about the question what it is to *follow a rule* or to *obey a rule*? This is one of the most-talked about issues in connection with rules.

This notion has obvious application in the philosophy of law. Under what conditions is someone following the law? Let us ask first: what is the *intuitive* idea of someone's following a given rule R? Clearly, this is not just the idea of a rule's being *applicable* to one's behavior, being a norm on one's behavior. As we have just seen, a natural view about moral norms is that they can be applicable to one, even if one has not accepted them and so is not following them (see the ACER model of rule following below).

The idea of following rule R is also not just the idea of doing something and thereby *conforming* to R. Conformity to R is neither necessary nor sufficient for following R. It is not necessary because one could be following R but, for one reason or another, one fails to conform—for example, because of a performance error. And it is not sufficient because in conforming to R one simultaneously conforms to an infinite number of rules. So, what is it?

The intuitive account of rule-following is given by what we may call the ACER model: A, C, E, R (see Boghossian 2008):

(A) Acceptance: The agent must somehow or other accept the rule.
(C) Correctness: If an agent is following rule R, then there is a sense of correctness, according to which what he does is correct iff he conforms to R.
(E) Explanation: Acceptance of R explains what the agent does.
(R) Rationalization: Acceptance of R rationalizes or makes sense of what the agent does.

On this view, for an agent to be following R, she had to have accepted R. This marks a contrast with the notion of R's applying to her behavior as a standard, since R may apply to her even if she has not accepted it. A close approximation to the idea that an agent is following rule R is that, in following R, she is *trying* to conform to R. Now, as we all know, there is supposed to be a question, made famous by Wittgenstein (1953), about how rule following is so much as possible. Given the gloss I have just given, this raises another puzzle. How could there be any such problem? Isn't 'trying to conform to a rule' the most mundane of phenomena? For example, don't we all, typically, try to conform to the rule: *If the traffic light is red, stop!* How could there be a problem about this?

According to Saul Kripke's famous exposition, Wittgenstein is drawing our attention to the problem of explaining how there could be a determinate fact of the matter about *which* rule has been *accepted* by someone. Maybe the rule is: '*If the traffic light is red and it is before the year 3000, then stop! Otherwise, keep going!*'[4] After all, all the behavior we will ever observe will conform to that rule as much as to the normal one. But it looks as though there is a simple answer to Kripke: I am following the one rule and not the other because it is the one rule and not the other that I *intend* to conform to. Surely, there can be a fact of the matter about whether my intention involved anything about the year 3000 or not. Kripke thinks that this answer won't do because we need to explain how there could be a fact of the matter about what the determinate content of my intention is. But this threatens to look like just a generalized skepticism about determinate intentional content, and there are two things to be said about that.

[4] See Kripke (1982).

First, this has nothing specifically to do with rule-following. It's a very general skepticism about intentional content and, if it were to be accepted, we would be in trouble in a number of fundamental ways, and not just because we couldn't be said to follow determinate rules. Second, the very generality of the argument makes it vulnerable. At most, Kripke could hope to have shown that *naturalistic reductions* of intentional content don't work.

While I am inclined to agree that such naturalistic reductions don't work, I also think that he could not have refuted all possible anti-reductionist conceptions of intentional content. Surely, the conclusion that there is no meaning or content is bound to be less plausible than any premise leading up to that conclusion.

Given these considerations, it looks as though we may just think of rule-following as involving an intention to conform to a certain pattern, where that intention is non-reductively understood. And that state can then explain and rationalize my behavior. So is that all there is to the famous rule-following problem? Unfortunately, no.

1.2.4 The Problem of Rule-Following Recast

The further problem I have in mind is not about *vagueness*. Rules, like any contents, can be vague. They can have borderline cases. How should they be applied to borderline cases? What constitutes correct following of the rule in a borderline case? These issues are of great relevance to the study of law, but they are not my topic here. Once again, vagueness is a very *general* problem about contents and does not have to do with rules specifically.

The rule-specific problem I have in mind is that in addition to cases of rule-following where *there is an explicit intention*, there are cases of rule-following where there is *no* explicit intention. And the difficulty is to explain how we are to think about those cases. How do we know that there are such cases? We know this because we know that there are phenomena that cry out for saying that the agent is following a rule, but in which the agent *couldn't formulate the rule if asked*, without doing a great deal of empirical work. Why is the agent's ability to formulate the rule a good test for whether the rule is carried by explicit intention of his? Because with intentions, as we encounter them in ordinary action, we know their contents relatively effortlessly. If we didn't, they couldn't play the role in guiding our actions that they clearly play.

What are examples of phenomena in which rules are clearly involved but in which the agent could not formulate the rules without doing a lot of empirical work? Two central such phenomena involve the use of language and the fixation of belief in response to experience. In both of these central cases, our productive and general competence appears to require attributing to us the acceptance, or internalization, of rules that guide our behavior. Yet we would, of course, be hard pressed to give an account of what those rules are on a purely introspective basis.

So, there clearly look to be many cases of rule-following unaccompanied by explicit intention. Indeed, there is an argument, laid out in Boghossian (2008), to the effect that there *have* to be some such cases, that not all rule-following could be explicit.

The argument goes something like this. If all rule-following involved an explicit intention, rule-following would always involve inference from that intention. But inference itself is a form of rule-following. It can't be, though, that rule-following always involves inference and inference always involves rule-following (For details see Boghossian (2008). So, there has to be some rule-following that does not involve inference, and that in turn seems to imply that there must be rule-following that is not anchored in an explicit intention. But, in what sense could a rule be said to be *guiding* our behavior, if that does not amount to an intention's guiding our behavior?

One idea here that has appealed to many is that there is a representation of the rule guiding the behavior, but this representation is *sub-personal*, rather than being the sort of conscious mental state that an intention is. We can't know about this sub-personal state by introspection; but we can get at in various other more indirect ways—for example, by what we are inclined to say about possible scenarios (the method of cases), and by means of other analytic techniques.

One of the enduring difficulties with this line of thought is to say in what way such sub-personal regulation by rules can be properly said to rationally guide us in our use of language our in our reasoning. Many behaviors of ours, such as our digestion and breathing could be said to be regulated by homeostatic sub-personal systems, but we clearly don't think of them as rationally guiding those behaviors. Why would regulation by sub-personal systems be any different? I think we are still far from properly understanding these issues. I outline the matter here so we can properly distinguish those substantive issues that remain vexed, from those that we are relatively well understood.

1.2.5 The Normativity of Rules

Let me turn next to the question of the *normativity* of rules, a topic that has exercised quite a few scholars.

As we can see from the proposed framework, in asking about the normativity of rules one could be asking at least two rather different questions:

a. Are rules themselves normative?
b. Is following a rule normative?

Before we tackle these, let us briefly address a large question: what is it for something to be normative? Let us agree that something is normative when it provides *reasons* for doing something. This is, of course, very rough and terse, but it will do for now.

Question (a), then, is the question: are rules themselves normative? Do rules provide reasons? Well, rules are just abstract objects of a certain sort, we have agreed: among them we may find the following imperative: 'kill the first-born child of every family!' Or the normative proposition: 'you ought to kill the first-born child of every family.'

Clearly, this rule does not give anyone a reason to kill anyone. So, no rule, merely *qua* rule, gives one a reason to do anything. Some rules can be bad—and no one would have any reason for accepting them or following them. This ought not to be conflated with the fact that a *true* normative proposition gives ones a reason to do something. For example, among the normative propositions that exists is the following: 'one ought to educate girls and young women.' That true normative proposition gives one a reason to do something—namely, to see to it that girls and women are given an education along with boys and men. But it's trivial that a *true* normative proposition gives one a reason to do something.

What I have just said about normative propositions also applies to imperatival contents, perhaps more obviously so. No imperative, *qua* imperative, gives one a reason to do something. A *correct* imperative, on the other hand, namely one that corresponds to a true normative proposition, does do so—but again, that's trivial.

What about question (b)? Is there normativity that flows from the mere fact that one is following a given rule? Kripke famously claimed that there was. He said:

> (…)Suppose I [am following the rule for] addition by '+'. What is the relation of this supposition to the question how I will respond to the problem '68 + 57 ='? The dispositionalist gives a descriptive account of this relation: if '+' meant addition, then I will answer '125'. But this is not the proper account of the relation, which is *normative,* not descriptive. The point is not that, if I meant addition by '+' I *will* answer '125', but that, if I intend to accord with my past meaning of '+' I *should* answer '125'. Computational error, finiteness of my capacity, and other disturbing factors may lead me not to be *disposed* to respond as I *should,* but if so, I have not acted in accordance with my intentions. The relation of meaning and intention to future action is *normative,* not *descriptive.* (…).

Kripke uses this alleged fact to argue against naturalistic accounts of rule-following. But I think Kripke made a mistake here—not in being against naturalistic accounts of rule-following, but in endorsing an unqualified conception of rule-following as normative. Suppose I am following the invalid rule known as affirming the consequent.

From *q* and 'if *p*, then *q*', infer *p*!

Does it follow that I have *reason* to conclude *p* from *q* and 'if *p*, then *q*'? From a subjective point of view, it might *make sense* for me to draw that conclusion, given that I am following that rule. Drawing that conclusion is *rationalized.* But it would be odd to hold that it's *justified.* Similarly, if (like most people) I find plausible the fallacious probabilistic rule that says that if red has come up a number of times in a row in a game of roulette, it is much more likely than not that the ball will land on black the next time around, it might make sense for me to bet on black, but it wouldn't be justified. (The rule is fallacious if each spin of the ball is probabilistically independent of the other spins).

So, there is a *quasi*-normative notion that enters into the analysis of following a rule, but it is not a genuinely normative notion. That notion is *rationalization.* This is different from *justification.* It is one thing to say that a certain behavior makes sense from a subjective point of view. It is another thing to say that it is objectively justifiable. In general, nothing normative follows from the mere fact that one is following a rule. It all depends on the content of the rule. So, where does the normativity of obeying the law come from?

If what I've been saying is on the right track, it doesn't come from the mere fact that the law is a rule, nor does it come from the fact that the rule has been accepted. Where, then, could it come from? It looks as though it has to come from the truth of some underlying moral proposition roughly to the effect that:

When one is born into a society that has accepted certain norms and lives by them, and if one continues to live with and benefit from that society, then, other things being equal, one is obligated to live by the norms that are accepted in that society.

To formulate the moral proposition in question correctly would require a great deal of work. The main point right now is that it would be a mistake to look for a source of normativity either in the rule itself or in the mere fact that a rule has been accepted. If there is an obligation to obey a rule it cannot come from any source other than from the requirements of morality, which, as I previously emphasized, provide a norm on behavior independently of whether they have been accepted.

Conclusion

To sum up, then, these are the main elements of the framework that I am proposing for a talk about rules and norms.

Rules are themselves abstract objects: either normative propositions or instructions.

Their status as norms on behavior can be explained in some cases without anything—as in the case of true moral propositions—or, in other cases, via their acceptance, either directly or indirectly.

Following a rule is not in general a problem. What is a problem is explaining rule-following in cases where there is no explicit intention to conform one's behavior to a rule.

Finally, rules and rule following facts are not normative in themselves. They derive what normativity they may on occasion have from the holding of some underlying moral truth.

References

Austin, John. 1832. *The province of jurisprudence determined*. London: John Murray.
Boghossian, Paul. 2008. Epistemic rules. *Journal of Philosophy* 105 (9): 472–500.
Dworkin, Ronald. 1977. *Taking rights seriously*. Cambridge: Harvard University Press.
Hart, Herbert L. A. 1961. *The concept of law*. Oxford: Oxford University Press.
Kripke, Saul. 1982. *Wittgenstein on rules and private language*. Cambridge: Harvard University Press.
Sainsbury, Mark, and Michael Tye. 2012. *Seven puzzles of thought*. Oxford: Oxford University Press.
Wittgenstein, Ludwig. 1953. *Philosophical investigations*. New York: Macmillan.

Chapter 2
Separating Rules from Normativity

Jaap Hage

Abstract Often the notion of a rule is connected to the guidance of behaviour. The expression 'following a rule' nicely illustrates this. The aim of this paper is to show that this connection between rules and normativity is much looser than is often assumed, and that—although there are rules which aim to guide behaviour—the notion of a rule and the notion of normativity are not necessarily connected.

This aim is pursued by two arguments. The first argument tries to show that rules that guide behaviour, regulative rules, are at the same time constitutive rules and that therefore the opposition of regulative and constitutive rules is a bogus one. To this purpose, it is first shown that there are more constitutive rules than counts as-rules only. Secondly it is argued that there can be 'deontic facts', facts that specify what should be done, and which can therefore guide behaviour. These facts can fulfil the role of guiding behaviour, and therefore rules are not essential to fulfil this function. Thirdly it is shown that two main kinds of 'regulative' rules are in fact both kinds of constitutive rules, and more in particular duty imposing fact to fact-rules or obligation-creating dynamic rules. The existence of these obligations and duties are deontic facts. Fourthly it is argued, very briefly, that other kinds of regulative rules are, for similar reasons, also constitutive rules and that therefore regulative rules are a subcategory of constitutive rules.

The second argument tries to give an account of rules as constitutive rules by presenting rules as constraints on which facts can go together, or—to state the same in more technical jargon—as constraints on possible worlds. To this purpose the argument takes from model-theoretic semantics the ideas of a possible world and of constraints that define which worlds count as possible. The technical aspects of model-theoretic semantics are mostly ignored, however, since they are irrelevant

The argument in this paper elaborates some of the ideas that were mentioned in Hage (2013), and parts of this paper are adaptations of the texts of the Sects. 2.3 and 2.4 of that article. The argument in its present form has not only benefited from comments from the persons mentioned in the footnotes, but also from other participants in the Rules 2013 conference in Kraków, where an earlier version of the argument was presented, and in particular those of Michal Araszkiewicz, Andrzej Grabowski, and Marcin Matczak.

J. Hage (✉)
Department Foundations and Methods of Law, University of Maastricht,
Bouillonstraat 1-3, Maastricht, Netherlands
e-mail: jaap.hage@maastrichtuniversity.nl

M. Araszkiewicz et al. (eds.), *Problems of Normativity, Rules and Rule-Following,*
Law and Philosophy Library 111, DOI 10.1007/978-3-319-09375-8_2

for the purposes of this paper. The paper gives a mostly informal indication of the logic of constitutive rules by positing them as 'soft constraints' in between the constraints that define sets of possible worlds and declarative sentences which are contingently true or false.

Keywords Constitutive rules · Constraints on possible worlds · Deontic facts · Duties · Obligations · Regulative rules

2.1 Regulative and Constitutive Rules

The idea of a rule is traditionally associated with the guidance of behaviour. Rules prescribe behaviour, they can be followed, obeyed and disobeyed, and after the behaviour has taken place, rules can be used to evaluate behaviour as correct or incorrect. This association between rules and the guidance of behaviour is reflected in philosophical discussions about rule following[1], and in jurisprudential accounts of the nature of law. According to Aquinas, law is a rational ordering of things[2]; according to Kelsen[3], law consists of norms, where norms are defined in terms of 'ought', and according to Hart[4], primary rules are behaviour guiding rules. Moreover, recent discussions emphasise the behaviour guiding role of law.[5]

And yet some rules seem not to guide behaviour at all, or only in the marginal sense that they allow the evaluation of behaviour as correct (in agreement with the rule) or incorrect. Examples of rules which seem not to aim at guidance at all are the rules that confer competences, or define the institutions of, for example, the European Union. Examples of rules which do not strictly guide behaviour but which can nevertheless be used to evaluate behaviour as correct or incorrect are the rules of language and of mathematics, but also the definitions of terms used in legislation, and the rules that specify which procedure should be followed in order to reach a particular result.

Rules of games form an in between category in the sense that they only specify what should be done in order to play the game correctly. They do guide behaviour, but only for those who want to play the game. Some would see the 'rules' of morality[6] and legal rules[7] in a similar way: they only specify what somebody should do who wants to comply with morality or with the law.

---

[1] Wittgenstein (1953); Kripke (1982); Brożek (2013).

[2] Aquinas (S. Th.) I, II, qu. 90 Sect. 4; d'Entrèves (1970, p. 57).

[3] Kelsen (1960).

[4] Hart (2012, p. 94).

[5] Shapiro (2011, pp. 118–234); Bertea (2009); Bertea and Pavlakos (2011).

[6] Foot (1978).

[7] Raz (1977).

The phenomenon that not all rules can easily be said to guide behaviour has found philosophical recognition in the distinction between regulative and constitutive rules. This distinction has gained most of its popularity from the work of Searle.[8] According to Searle regulative rules regulate antecedently or independently existing forms of behaviour.[9] He mentions rules of etiquette as an example. Constitutive rules, on the contrary, would create or define new forms of behaviour. In a later work Searle discusses constitutive rules as a means to impose status.[10] An example would be the status of money which is imposed on pieces of paper. Constitutive rules are then assumed to have the form 'X counts as Y under circumstances C'; they are what will later be called 'counts as-rules'.

My aim in this paper goes far beyond Searle's however. I will argue that *all* rules are constitutive and that strictly speaking no rule guides behaviour. Norms may be defined as rules that prescribe or prohibit behaviour. My purpose is to separate these two aspects of norms into the rule-aspect of a norm and the normative aspect of a norm. The rule-aspect as such has no normative aspect, while the normative aspect can exist separate from the norm. It is this normative aspect, what I will call a deontic or normative fact, which guides behaviour and which can be followed or violated.

To this purpose I will argue that:

1. Searle's account of constitutive rules is too limited, and that there are more kinds of constitutive rules than only counts as-rules;
2. regulative rules can very well be interpreted as a kind of constitutive rules, and that therefore Searle's opposition between regulative rules and constitutive ones is a bogus one.
3. constitutive rules can be interpreted as a kind of constraints on what counts as possible.

The ultimate purpose of the argument is to disconnect the notion of a rule from that of normativity and to emphasise the role of rules as tools by means of which human beings impose ontological structure upon the world.[11] In my argument I will mostly use legal examples, but I do not think that this bias damages the strength of the overall argument.

[8] Searle (1969, 1979, 2010).

[9] Searle (1969, p. 33).

[10] Searle (1995, pp. 43–44).

[11] The exact opposite has been argued by Zelaniec (2013, p. 98), who states that constitutive rules cannot create anything unless they are followed. I became aware of this argument too late to discuss it extensively. My main objection would be that it is not the 'being followed' of constitutional rules that gives them their effect, but their existence. Moreover, it is not at all clear how, for instance, count as-rules can be followed.

2.2 Three Kinds of Constitutive Rules

The first step in my argument that regulative rules are constitutive is to distinguish between three different kinds of constitutive rules. It is not my intention to argue that these three kinds are the only constitutive rules, but their existence suffices to show that there is no need to assume the existence of regulative rules which are not at the same time constitutive rules. The three kinds of constitutive rules that will be distinguished are dynamic, fact-to-fact, and counts-as rules.

2.2.1 *Dynamic Rules*

Dynamic rules create new facts, or modify or take away existing facts, as the consequence of an event. Examples of events to which a dynamic rule attaches consequences are that:

- John promised Richard to give him € 100, which leads to an obligation for John to pay Richard € 100;
- Eloise was appointed as chair of the French Parliament, which has as consequence that Eloise has become chair of the French Parliament;
- a creditor informs his debtor that the latter will not have to repay the money before next year, which has as consequence that the debtor is not under an obligation to repay the money before next year;
- the legislator derogates a law, which has as consequence that the law does not exist anymore.

Dynamic rules may be conditional, in which case their consequences are only attached to the events under certain conditions. An example is the rule that if it is dark, the occurrence of a car accident obligates the drivers to place a light on the road next to the cars.

In law, some dynamic rules attach the presence of an obligation to the occurrence of a particular kind of event. The obvious examples are the rules of contract and tort law.

2.2.2 *Fact to Fact-Rules*

Fact to fact-rules attach a fact to the presence of some other fact. They make that facts of one type (almost[12]) always go together with facts of some other type. Fact to fact-rules are different from dynamic rules because the relation between the connected facts does not involve the lapse of time. An example is the rule that attaches

[12] This 'almost' has to do with the defeasible nature of rule application. To avoid complications which have nothing to do with the purpose of this paper, I will ignore defeasibility in the rest of this paper.

the fact that P is competent to alienate O to the fact that P owns O. For example, if Smith owns Blackacre, she is competent to transfer her property right in this real estate to Jones. This is a relation between two facts—being an owner and having the competence to transfer—which does not involve any change that occurs in time.

Fact to fact-rules may be conditional too. An example is the rule that the mayor of a city is competent to evoke the state of emergency in case of emergencies. This rule attaches the fact that some person has a competence to the fact that this person is the mayor under the condition that there is a state of emergency.

Fact to fact-rules often attach a duty to the presence of some status, such as being a house-owner, being the public prosecutor, or being the mayor of a city. Such rules are also duty-imposing rules.

2.2.3 *Counts as-Rules*

Counts as-rules have the following structure: Individuals of type 1 count as individuals of type 2. These 'individuals' may be human beings, as in the rule that the parents of a minor count as the minor's legal representatives. Often, however, the 'individuals' are events. For instance, under suitable circumstances, causing a car accident counts as committing a tort, or offering money to another person counts as attempting to bribe an official.

Usually counts-as rules are conditional, meaning that individuals of type 1 only count as individuals of type 2 if certain conditions are satisfied.[13] An example from Dutch law would be the rule that the delivery of a good counts as the transfer of that good if the person who made the delivery was competent to transfer and if there was a valid title for the transfer.[14]

2.2.4 *Constitutive Rules and the Direction of Fit*

All three kinds of constitutive rules, dynamic, fact to fact-, and counts as-rules, affect the facts in the world. A dynamic rules generates new facts, modifies existing ones, or takes existing facts away as the result of some event. Fact to fact-rules make that facts of particular kinds go together with other facts in a timeless fashion. This makes that the first-mentioned facts are attached by the fact to fact-rules to the last-mentioned facts. Counts as-rules, finally, make that some kinds of 'things', often events, are also 'things' of another kind.

Rules have a lot in common with descriptive sentences: they have a propositional content and they can in some sense 'correspond' with facts. For example, the rule that criminals are liable to be punished 'corresponds' to the fact that criminals are liable to be punished, just as the descriptive sentence 'Criminals are liable to be

[13] Searle (1995, pp. 43–45).

[14] Art. 3:84 of the Civil Code (*Burgerlijk Wetboek*).

punished' corresponds to this fact. However, in this correspondence lies also a major difference with descriptive sentences. Descriptive sentences are 'successful' in the sense of 'true' if they match the facts. They have the 'word-to-world direction of fit.[15] Constitutive rules are successful in the sense of 'valid', if the facts match the rule. With this match I do not mean that the rule is obeyed, but that the content of the rule is reflected in the world.[16] For instance, the rule that thieves are punishable is reflected in the world if (because of this rule) thieves are punishable. Valid constitutive rules—which I take to be the same as existing constitutive rules—impose themselves on the world. They have the world-to- word direction of fit because they constrain the world in the sense that not all combinations of facts are possible. As a consequence, these rules bring about facts, and in this sense they are constitutive.[17]

2.3 Regulative Rules

Having argued that there are more constitutive rules than counts as-rules only, the next argument step will lead to the conclusion that regulative rules can well be seen as a special kind of constitutive rules. To make this step, an intermediate conclusion is required, namely that there can be deontic facts.

2.3.1 Deontic Facts

Sentences that tell one what to do often take the form of declarations. For example, the sentence 'You ought to go to the supermarket' looks very much like the sentence 'You will go to the supermarket'. Is this similarity misleading, covering up a kind of order as a description? Or does the former sentence, if it is true, stand for a fact? Because the description contains a 'deontic operator', such as ought, should, must, is to … etc. the kind of fact at stake would then be a 'deontic fact'.[18] I will argue for the view that these sentences express deontic facts indeed.

---

[15] Searle (1979). See also Grabowski (1999).

[16] See also footnote 12.

[17] It might be asked—and I owe this question to Tomasz Gizbert-Studnicki—whether the use of the term 'constitutive rule' would not better be reserved for counts as-rules only. This would avoid confusion, given the restricted use of the term in prior work, in particular Searle's.

There is something to be said for that approach, but then we would still need a broader term that applies to counts as rules, fact to fact rules, and dynamic rules. Moreover, either one of the terms 'counts as-rule' or 'constitutive rule' would become superfluous, since the two categories to which the terms apply coincide. However, as we will see, the same objection applies to what I will propose, because then the category of constitutive rules will coincide with that of rules.

[18] The term 'deontic' is used, in particular in logic, for what should (not) be done, or be the case, and also for what is permitted. I would not mind giving up the term in favour of 'normative fact', if only this would not create confusion with norms in the sense of a kind of rules.

The following argument that there can be deontic facts is unavoidably too brief to convince readers who firmly believe in the gap between is and ought. It makes presuppositions about the role of the mind in structuring the world which I defended elsewhere.[19] Here my argument will essentially be limited to clearing away two possible misunderstandings.

One misunderstanding is that a sentence such as 'You ought to go to the supermarket' is 'really' a kind of order or exhortation, rather than the description of a fact, because it is, or can be, used to make somebody do something. Underlying this misunderstanding is the—often implicit—assumption that the world is inert and that (beliefs about) facts in the world cannot guide behaviour unless accompanied by a motivating factor such as a desire. This would be the reason why the fact that somebody ought to do something, or—probably better—that somebody is aware that he ought to do something, guides his behaviour.[20] Because facts by themselves, without accompanying desire, could not guide behaviour, it could not be a fact that somebody ought to do something.

This first misunderstanding has been attacked by Geach[21] and Searle[22] basically because the speech act which can be performed with a sentence does not determine the meaning of the sentence. The sentence 'You ought to do A' means the same when it stands on its own as when it is used the conditional sentence 'If you ought to do A, I will eat my hat'. So if the sentence expresses a fact in its second use, it also expresses a fact in its first use.

The other misunderstanding is that a 'real' fact cannot depend on what humans think, believe, project, accept or recognise. On the assumption that standards for goodness and for what should be done are mind-dependent, the misunderstanding becomes that 'real' facts cannot depend on standards. This misunderstanding is essentially that of applying an ontological realist stance to all domains, including those in which this is less suitable. One such domain is that of social reality, because social reality depends to a large extent on what people accept or recognise about it.[23] If there are some domains of facts (e.g. social reality) for which an ontological realist stance is not appropriate, there is no decisive reason why other domains could not be mind-dependent too. This opens up the possibility to recognise the existence facts that depend on standards, including facts that depend for their existence on rules. In law, the existence of such facts is assumed in a routinely fashion, for instance when it is said that (it is a fact that) somebody is the owner of a good. If facts can depend on rules, there is no good reason why there cannot be deontic facts.

Because normative judgments can very well, and often are, expressed by means of declarative sentences, apparently there are deontic facts which are expressed by these sentences. The two objections do not suffice to take the force of this appearance away.

---

[19] Hage 1987. See also Hage (2015), for an English rendering of one of the main arguments of my PhD-thesis.

[20] Cf. for instance, the account of 'internal reasons' in Williams (1980).

[21] Geach (1956).

[22] Searle (1969, pp. 136–140).

[23] Searle (2010, p. 8).

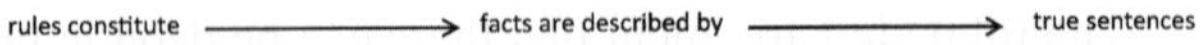

Fig. 2.1 Rules, facts and descriptions

2.3.2 Rules, Facts and Descriptions

A regulative rule is a rule that guides behaviour, either by prescribing or prohibiting particular kinds of behaviour or by indicating what should be done, or how something should be done, without imposing a duty or an obligation to do so.

Examples would be the rules:

- It is forbidden to torture sentient beings.
- Car drivers must drive on the right hand side of the road.
- If the king is in chess, the threat should immediately be removed.

However, these sentences can not only be interpreted as rule formulations, but also as descriptive sentences which, if they are true, express deontic facts. Moreover, if these sentences are true, the most likely explanation is that this is so because the rules with the same formulation brought about the facts which made the sentences true. In schema (Fig. 2.1):

Let us take a closer look at this mechanism according to which rules lead to facts which can be described by sentences that are identical to the rule formulations. To show that this has everything to do with the relation between constitutive rules and facts, and nothing in particular with regulative rules as such, I will start with a competence conferring rule. An example would be the fact to fact-rule that owners of real estate are competent to mortgage this real estate. Then, if Smith owns Blackacre, the rule makes that Smith is competent to mortgage it. The rule applies only to individual cases and makes that in all these cases the owners of real estate have the competence to mortgage it. Indirectly, via these individual cases, the rule also makes that (all) owners of real estate are competent to mortgage this real estate. And this general fact is truly described by the sentence ‘Owners of real estate are competent to mortgage this real estate’.

The same line of reasoning can—almost literally—be applied to rules that lead to deontic facts. An example would be the fact to fact-rule ‘Car drivers should drive on the right’. Let us assume that this is an existing (valid) rule. Then, if Schmidt drives a car, the rule makes that Schmidt should drive on the right. The rule is applicable to all persons who drive cars and imposes on all these persons the duty to drive on the right. The rule applies to all individual drivers and makes that they should drive on the right. As a result, car drivers should drive on the right, and this general fact is truly described by the sentence ‘Car drivers should drive on the right’.

A similar line or reasoning can be used in the case of dynamic obligation imposing rules. An example would be the dynamic rule that those who promise somebody else to do something are from then on under an obligation towards this other person to do what was promised. If this is a valid rule, then, if Smith promised Jones to pay her € 500, the rule makes that Smith is under an obligation towards Jones to pay her € 500. The rule is applicable to all individual persons who made a promise to do something and imposes on all these individuals the obligation to do what they promised. That all these individuals are under this obligation is truly described by the sentence 'Those who promise somebody else to do something are from then on under an obligation towards this other person to do what was promised'.

2.3.3 *Regulative Rules Are also Constitutive Rules*

I have discussed two examples of rules that constitute deontic facts, primarily duties or obligations for individual persons, but in a derived sense also for categories of persons. These two examples represent two kinds of regulative rules, namely fact to fact-rules which impose duties on categories of persons, and dynamic rules which impose obligations on persons as the result of events. There are still other categories of regulative rules, for instance the rule of etiquette, which do not really *prescribe* behaviour, but which still tell agents what to do.[24] Another example is the rule that if the king is in chess, the threat to the king should be removed immediately. These regulative rules are also constitutive in the sense that they make that agents *should* do something. Such should-facts exist in the same manner as duties and obligations, and if the latter two categories of facts are constituted by rules, so is the former. Therefore these non-mandatory regulative rules are no counter-examples against the general thesis that regulative rules are also constitutive rules. I submit here the thesis that all regulative rules are also constitutive rules, and that they only differ from other constitutive rules in that they constitute deontic facts, rather than other kinds of facts. This is not a sufficient reason to make a special category out of them.

2.4 Rules as Soft Constraints on Possible Worlds

If, as argued above, regulative rules are a subcategory of constitutive rules, one may wonder whether all rules are constitutive ones. A first reason to assume that this is indeed the case is that as yet no other kinds of rules than regulative and constitutive ones have been identified. If all these rules are constitutive, then at least it seems that all rules are constitutive. However, it is also possible to give a positive account of the nature of rules which leads to the conclusion that all rules are constitutive. According to this account, rules are a kind of 'constraints' on possible worlds, and more in particular a special kind of constraints, namely 'soft' ones.[25]

Possible worlds play an important role in model-theoretic semantics, an important part of modern logic. Therefore it is important to understand what these possible worlds are. The best technical approximation of logically possible worlds is the interpretation function that explains how truth values are assigned to compound

[24] This was pointed out to me by Paul Boghossian.

[25] The present account of rules as constraints on possible worlds is relatively non-technical. A technically more elaborate account can be found in Hage (2005).

sentences on the basis of the truth values of atomic sentences and to atomic sentences on the basis of individuals being elements of sets.[26] The nature of possible worlds is seldom discussed in an informal manner, however.[27] It may therefore be useful to say a little more about possible worlds, and to explain the role of constraints in defining which worlds count as possible ones.

2.4.1 States of Affairs, Possible Worlds and Constraints

For the purpose of this article, the terms 'possible world' and 'state of affairs' will be defined as follows:

A *state of affairs* is what is expressed by a declarative sentence. Notice that it is not necessary that the sentence is true. States of affairs are merely 'potential facts'. True sentences express *facts*, a subset of the states of affairs.

A *possible world* is a complete set of compatible states of affairs. Both completeness and compatibility are defined below.

Logic cannot determine which states of affairs are compatible, because logic presupposes the notion of (logical) compatibility rather than defining it. Which states of affairs are deemed compatible is not something that is 'objectively' given[28] but depends on the constraints that are imposed on the world. Constraints determine which states of affairs can go together in a possible word. It is possible that it rains and the sun is shining at the same time, but not that John is both a thief and not a thief.

Compatibility of states of affairs is by definition relative to a set of one or more constraints. The states of affairs that John is a thief and that he is not a thief are incompatible because of the constraints that a state of affairs cannot both exist and not. Another constraint is that the compound state of affairs that John is both a thief *and* a minor can only exist if *both* the states of affairs that John is a thief and that he is a minor exist. Such constraints are usually called *logical* constraints.

Besides logical constraints there are also other constraints. *Physical* constraints prevent a piece of metal being heated without expanding. *Conceptual* or *semantic* constraints make it impossible that something is both a square and a circle.

What is possible depends on the constraints that are taken into account. This brings us back to the notion of a possible world. A possible world is a set of states of affairs that are compatible relative to some set of constraints C, in the sense that the facts of that world satisfy the constraints in C. For instance, a logically possible world does not contain both the fact that the capital of Belgium is Brussels and the fact that the capital of Belgium is not Brussels.

[26] E.g. Kripke (1963).

[27] Cf. Lewis (1973); Chellas (1980, p. 4); Forbes (1995). But see Loux (1979) and Stalnaker (2011).

[28] Some may contest this with respect to physical necessities.

Since a set of constraints will usually not determine all the states of affairs in a possible world, every set of constraints defines a set of worlds that are possible relative to this set. For instance the set of logically possible worlds may contain one world in which Brussels is the capital of Belgium, and another possible world in which Belgium does not even exist. But, relative to a plausible set of constraints, there is no possible world that contains both facts.

If the traditional constraints of propositional logic are taken into account, a possible world cannot contain both states of affairs 'Snow is white' and 'Snow is not white'. If physical constraints are taken into account, no possible world will contain the states of affairs that a piece of metal is heated without expanding. But if only proposition-logical and physical constraints are taken into account, some possible world may contain a square which is at the same time a circle. To rule out that latter possibility, also some conceptual or semantic constraints need to be taken into account

Different sets of constraints may lead to different sets of possible worlds, and there is not one single set of possible worlds. So there is the set of worlds that are both logically and conceptually possible, and this set may include a world that is physically impossible. Another set includes the worlds that are physically and conceptually possible, but not necessarily logically possible. And so on …

There are not only constraints on the states of affairs that can exist together simultaneously. Many natural laws, for instance, operate in time and make that some things must happen after something else happened. These constraints confine which possible worlds can follow after a particular possible world in time.

Not any set of states of affairs that satisfies a set of constraints c is a possible world relative to c; the set must also be complete. Intuitively completeness means that a possible world determines for every sentence whether it is true or false.[29] This idea can be implemented by demanding that it is not possible to add any state of affairs to the possible world without violating a constraint on that world. For instance, if a possible world contains the states of affairs that John is a criminal and that the legal rule that criminals are punishable is valid, then it is possible (and—if the world is to be legally possible—even required) to add the state of affairs that John is punishable, but not to add the state of affairs that John is not punishable.

2.4.2 Contraints and Directions of Fit

The formulation of a constraint is very similar to a declarative sentence. For instance, one physical constraint might be that all pieces of metal that are heated expand, and a mathematical constraint would be that there is exactly one line parallel to some line L, which is through a point P which does not lie on L. However, there is a difference in the direction of fit between declarative sentences and constraints. Declarative sentences, even if they deal with what is possible, are true or false

[29] Forbes (1995).

depending on the states of affairs that exist in some particular possible world, or—if they aim to describe a regularity—in the set of all worlds that are possible relative to some set of constraints.[30]

Constraints, even though they can be formulated in language, are not linguistic utterances, let alone declarative sentences. The existence of 'hard' constraints, about which we are presently talking, does not depend on the facts in a possible world, or the facts in all possible worlds. It is rather the other way round: a world only counts as possible if it satisfies the constraint, if the facts in this world are as the constraint says they are. The constraint in that sense 'imposes itself' on the world.[31]

2.4.3 Constraints and Conditionals[32]

Because of their nature, constraints support conditional and even counterfactual sentences. An example of a conditional sentence would be: 'If John has committed theft, he is punishable'. This sentence tells us what is the case in the hypothetical situation that John has committed theft, without also informing us whether this hypothetical situation is actually the case. Metaphorically speaking, this sentence tells us what is the case in a possible world in which John has committed theft. Or rather, it tells us that John is punishable in all possible worlds in which John has committed theft, because it does not mention any other conditions for the punishability of John. The conditional sentence 'If John has committed theft, he is punishable' might be reformulated in possible world terminology as 'In all possible worlds in which John has committed theft, he is punishable'. These possible worlds may include the actual world, but the sentence does not inform us whether this the case.

A counterfactual sentence such as 'Even if Jane would have thrown a brick at the window, the window would still not have broken' is very much like a conditional sentence, informing us what is the case in all possible worlds in which Jane has thrown a brick at the window. But it also tells us that Jane did not throw a brick at the window in reality, that is in the actual world.

Constraints on possible worlds are the reason why conditional sentences, including counterfactuals, are true or false. If all possible worlds would be constrained in such a way that if they contained the state of affairs that Jane threw a brick to the window, they must also contain the state of affairs that the window did not break[33],

[30] For instance, the sentence 'Crows are black' deals with crows in general, and not only with the crows that presently exist in the actual world. This sentence is true if all crows are black in all possible worlds that satisfy some constraint which makes that only black birds can be crows.

[31] By the way, this still leaves the question open *how* constraints exist. My guess is that this is *in the end* a matter of how the brain functions and the way in which minds (as realised by brains) interact with a not yet conceptualised reality. This topic will not be discussed any further in the present article, but in his book *Rule-Following*, Brożek (2013) discusses relevant literature and formulates interesting hypotheses.

[32] The present account of conditional sentences was inspired by Stalnaker (1968).

[33] This is not a very likely constraint. Much more plausible would be the general constraint that if somebody had thrown a brick at the window, the window would not be broken. Moreover, the

then the counterfactual sentence 'Even if Jane would have thrown a brick at the window, the window would still not have broken' would for that reason be true. If all possible worlds would be constrained in such a way that if they contain the state of affairs that John has committed theft, they must also contain the state of affairs that John is punishable, then for this reason the conditional sentence 'If John has committed theft, he is punishable' is true.

Constraints also make that some facts are necessarily the case, or impossible. The constraint that if something is a square, it must have four straight angles makes that it is necessarily (in all possible worlds) the case that all squares have at least three straight angles.[34] The constraint that pieces of metal expand if heated makes it impossible that a heated piece of metal does not expand.[35] Analogously, a time constraint makes it impossible that a train arrives before it departed.

2.4.4 Rules as Soft Constraints

The reader may have noticed that the example about John who committed theft was based on a legal rule, and that this illustrates that rules can be seen as constraints. And, indeed, rules have a lot in common with more traditional constraints such as the logical and physical ones. They make that some things are necessarily the case (e.g. that thieves are punishable), and they support conditionals (If Jane bought this car, she owns it now) and counterfactuals (If the witness would not have lied, he would not have been punished for perjury).

However, many rules can be created or derogated, and in that sense they differ from the more traditional constraints which somehow seem outside the scope of human manipulation. As a consequence, there can be some logically and physically possible worlds in which a particular rule exists, and other similarly possible worlds in which the same rule does not exist.

In the world in which a rule exists, the rule functions as a constraint next to the other constraints to which this world is subjected. So if w1 is a world that is logically and physically possible and this world contains the rule that thieves are punishable, then in this world thieves are punishable, not merely as a contingent matter of fact (e.g. because all thieves happen to own a gun, which is punishable), but necessarily, because being a thief makes one punishable. Moreover, in this possible world the

counterfactual sentence strongly suggests that the window would not be broken either if nobody would have thrown a stone at it. This is not taken into account in the present analysis.

[34] The clause 'at least three' was used to show that a constraint can also have effects on possible worlds that are not described by a sentence with the same formulation as the constraint. It may be interesting to notice that the example only works if there is also a constraint that four is a bigger number than three. This also illustrates that necessities may be the result of the interaction of several constraints and not merely reformulations of constraints with the word 'necessarily' inserted.

[35] Arguably there are exceptions possible, but this only shows that constraints are amenable to exceptions. An intriguing hypothesis in this connection, which I only mention to stimulate research on it, would be that only constraints are amenable to exceptions. In Hage 2005, I treat rules as constraints on possible worlds and allow the possibility of exceptions to rules.

counterfactual state of affairs 'If John had been a thief, he would have been punishable' exists, and it exists because the rule is valid (exists). However, if the same rule does not exist in world w2, which is also logically and physically possible, thieves in w2 would not be necessarily punishable.

Apparently, rules are like other constraints, because they impose themselves upon the world and because they make that some facts necessarily obtain and that counterfactual states of affairs exist. But they differ from other constraints in that their existence is contingent. They can be created, and then the world is subjected to new constraints. They can be derogated, with as effect that existing constraints disappear again. For this reason, rules will be categorised as 'soft constraints', opposed to the hard constraints which do not depend for their existence on human decisions.

If rules are constraints on possible worlds, this explains their constitutive nature. The facts that are constituted by the application of a rule are the facts that must be present if the world is to count as a possible world. It also explains why all rules are constitutive, on the assumption that all rules function as constraints on possible worlds.

2.5 Logic for Rules

In this final section the focus will be on some logical implications of the idea that rules are soft constraints on possible worlds.

2.5.1 No Derivation of Rules

Rules have formulations which make them look like declarative sentences, but—amongst others—the fact that rules have the world-to-word direction of fit, while declarative sentences have the word-to-world direction of fit makes that rules are not declarative sentences. Moreover, there is much to be said for the view that rules are, from a logical point of view, individuals. Rules can be the topic of declarative sentences which are not part of a meta-language. Examples are statements that inform us how long a rule exists, when it was created and by whom, how popular it is, and—for logical purposes important (see the next subsection)—whether it exists (is valid).

Therefore rules cannot be the conclusions of arguments in the traditional sense, and it is not possible to derive rules from (declarative sentences and) other rules. Notice, by the way, that this has nothing to do with the supposedly 'normative' nature of rules, and not even with the fact that rules are constraints on possible worlds. However, the fact that rules are from a logical point of view individuals both makes it impossible to use rules as premises or conclusions in arguments, and makes it possible to treat them as *soft* constraints on possible worlds.

2.5.2 The Logic of Rule Application

Arguably a logic of rule application is possible. Take for instance the following rule applying argument:

Thieves ought to be punished
John is a thief
Therefore: John ought to be punished.

There is nothing wrong with this argument, if the first premise is interpreted as a declarative sentence about all thieves. But what if the first premise is interpreted as a rule? Then the argument is not deductively valid. Not only because rule-applying arguments tend to be defeasible (which they are), but first and foremost because rules are logical individuals and can for that reason not function as premises or conclusions of deductively valid arguments. (Only sentences with truth values can.)

The problem that rules are logical individuals and can therefore not occur in deductively valid arguments can to some extent be overcome by replacing the rule formulation as premise by the statement that the rule with this formulation exists (is valid). The argument then becomes:

Valid ([Thieves ought to be punished]).
John is a thief
Therefore: John ought to be punished.

This argument is not deductively valid either, but that problem can be worked around by a logic that has as an axiom (and allows as a well-formed sentence):

Valid ([Rule-formulation]) → □Rule-formulation.[36]

The use of this axiom is justified on the assumption that rules function as constraints on possible worlds. If a rule is such a constraint, the combination of states of affairs as presented by the conditions and the conclusion of the rule exists in all possible worlds. This means that the sentence that describes this combination is true in all possible worlds, or—to state it differently—necessarily true.

However, this sentence is not true in all possible worlds, because a rule in the actual world does not affect possible worlds in which the rule does not exist. Here the difference between hard and soft constraints plays a role, because hard constraints affect all worlds which are possible relative to these hard constraints (e.g. all worlds that are logically and physically possible).

The axiom 'Valid([Rule-formulation]) → □Rule-formulation' for a logic of rules can deal with this soft nature of the constraint if the □-operator is interpreted as expressing that in all possible worlds in which the rule [Rule-formulation] exists, the sentence 'Rule-formulation' is true.[37]

[36] The brackets should be interpreted as representing a function that maps sentences which can also be rule formulations on rules with those formulations.

[37] Technically, this might be accomplished by defining an accessibility relation over possible worlds such that precisely those worlds are accessible from a world w in which the same rules exist (are valid) that also exist in w. This would make the accessibility relation an equivalence relation.

On a more general level it should be noted that the above axiom nicely indicates the status of rules as soft constraints. The effects of hard constraints can be represented as sentences which are true in all worlds that are possible relative to these constraints, and in that sense necessarily true. The sentence that describes the effects of a rule is only necessarily true on the condition that the rule exists.

Conclusion

In this paper the thesis was argued that regulative rules are a subcategory of constitutive rules. In order to reach that conclusion, it was first shown that there are more constitutive rules than counts as-rules only. In particular fact to fact-rules and dynamic rules turned out to be important kinds of constitutive rules too. The second step was to argue that there can be 'deontic facts', facts that specify what should be done, and which can therefore take the behaviour guiding function that is often ascribed to rules. The third step was to show that mandatory and should-rules are both constitutive rules. On the assumption that all regulative rules are like mandatory rules or should-rules that conclusion leads to the further conclusion that regulative rules are a subcategory of constitutive rules.

If regulative rules are a kind of constitutive rules, this makes the latter category of rules even more important. Therefore the question needs to be addressed how constitutive rules relate to facts and to the sentences that describe these facts. That is the topic of the second part of paper, which discusses how constitutive rules can fruitfully be seen as 'soft' constraints on possible worlds. To this purpose the ideas of possible worlds and constraints on them were discussed. Building upon that discussion, constitutive rules are posited as 'soft constraints' in between the constraints that define sets of possible worlds and the declarative sentences that are contingently true. Moreover, from the result that rules are *soft* constraints on possible worlds and are therefore from a logical point of view individuals, the conclusion was drawn that rules themselves cannot occur as premises in deductively valid arguments because they are not sentences with truth values. A second conclusion was that statements about the validity of rules can function as a proxy, in particular if the axiom 'Valid ([Rule-formulation]) → □Rule-formulation' is added to the logic.

References

Aquinas, Th. *Summa theologica*, http://www.ccel.org/ccel/aquinas/summa/home.html. Accessed 20 Aug 2014.

Bertea, Stefano. 2009. *The normative claim of law*. Oxford: Hart Publishing.

Bertea, S., and Pavlakos G., eds. 2011. *The normativity of law*. Oxford: Hart.

Brożek, Bartosz. 2013. *Rule-Following*. Kraków: Copernicus Center.

Chellas, Brian F. 1980. *Modal logic: An introduction*. Cambridge: Cambridge University Press.

d'Entrèves, A. P. 1970. *Natural law, an introduction to legal philosophy.* 2nd ed. London: Hutchinson.
Foot, Philippa. 1978. Morality as a system of hypothetical imperative. In her *Virtues and vices,* 157–173. Oxford: Basil Blackwell.
Forbes, Graeme. 1995. Possible worlds. In *A companion to metaphysics,* ed. Jaegwon Kim and Ernest Sosa, 404–405. Oxford: Blackwell.
Geach, P. T. 1956. Good and evil. *Analysis* 17:33–42.
Grabowski, Andrzej. 1999. *Judicial argumentation and pragmatics*. Kraków: Księgarnia Akademicka.
Hage, Jaap C. 1987. *Feiten en betekenis* (Facts and meaning). PhD-thesis Leiden.
Hage, Jaap. 2005. Rule consistency. In his *Studies in legal logic*, 135–158. Dordrecht: Springer.
Hage, Jaap. 2013. The deontic furniture of the world. In *The many faces of normativity,* ed. J. Stelmach, B. Brożek, and M. Hohol, 73–114. Kraków: Copernicus Center.
Hage, Jaap. (2015). Facts and meaning. To appear in "The emergence of Normative orders", Krakow: Copernicus Center Press. Draft paper available on: http://www.jaaphage.nl/FactsAndMeaning.pdf.
Hart, H. L. A. 2012. *The concept of law.* 4th ed. Oxford: Oxford University Press.
Kelsen, Hans. 1960. *Reine rechtslehre*. 2nd ed. Vienna: Franz Deuticke.
Kripke, Saul A. 1963. Semantical considerations on modal logic. *Acta philosophica fennica* 16:83–94.
Kripke, Saul A. 1982. *Wittgenstein on rules and private language*. Oxford: Blackwell.
Lewis, David. 1973. *Counterfactuals.* Oxford: Blackwell.
Loux, Michael J., ed. 1979. *The possible and the actual: Readings in the metaphysics of modality.* Ithaca: Cornell University Press.
Raz, Joseph. 1977. Legal Validity. In his *The Authority of Law,* 146–159 Oxford: Clarendon Press 1979.
Searle, John R. 1969. *Speech acts.* Cambridge: Cambridge University Press.
Searle, John R. 1979. A taxonomy of illocutionary acts. In *Expression and meaning: Studies in the theory of speech acts*, 1–29. Cambridge: Cambridge University Press.
Searle, John R. 1995. *The construction of social reality*. New York: The Free.
Searle, John R. 2010. *Making the social world.* Oxford: Oxford University Press.
Shapiro, Scott J. 2011. *Legality*. Cambridge: The Belknap.
Stalnaker, Robert. 1968. A theory of conditionals. In *Studies in logical theory, American philosophical quarterly monograph series* 2:98–112. (Oxford: Blackwell)
Stalnaker, Robert. 2011. *Mere possibilities: Metaphysical foundations of modal semantics*. Princeton: Princeton University Press.
Williams, Bernard. 1980. Internal and external reasons. In his *Moral Luck,* 101–113. Cambridge: Cambridge University Press. (Originally in *Rational action* ed. Ross Harrison. Cambridge: Cambridge University Press).
Wittgenstein, Ludwig. 1953. *Philosophical investigations.* 2nd ed., trans. G.E.M. Anscombe. Oxford: Blackwell.
Zelaniec, Wojciech. 2013. *Create to rule. Studies on constitutive rules*. Milan: Edizioni Universitarie di Lettere Economia Diritto.

Chapter 3
Communalism, Correction and Nihilistic Solitary Rule-Following Arguments

William Knorpp

Abstract Rule communalism is the view that the rule *asymmetry claim* is true: rule-following (e.g. language-use) is possible for communal individuals but impossible for solitary individuals. The most notable argument of this general type is Kripke's Wittgenstein's argument in *Wittgenstein on Rules and Private Language*. Kripke's Wittgenstein's argument, however, is not a paradigmatic example of communalism because it does not attempt to show that genuine rule-following is possible in a community. Instead, Kripke's Wittgenstein is a full-blown rule nihilist; his view entails that there is no such thing as rule-following, even in communities. What he offers is an ersatz alternative to rule-following which purportedly useful in communities, but not in solitude. I examine the prospects for defending genuine rule communalism on the familiar grounds that interpersonal—but not intrapersonal—correction can make rule-following possible even in the face of nihilistic arguments. I conclude that such arguments are extremely unlikely to succeed.

Keywords Solitary language · Private language · Rules · Kripke · Wittgenstein

3.1 Introduction

On some interpretations—Kripke's, most notably—the private language argument is an argument for the conclusion that solitary individuals cannot follow rules nor use language, but communal individuals can (Kripke 1982). That is, it is an argument for the *Asymmetry Claim*:

> (AC) (i) It is logically impossible for a solitary individual to follow rules/use language; (ii) it is logically possible (in fact, not particularly difficult) for individuals in a community to follow rules/use language. (Knorpp 2003)

Such arguments can be called *solitary language arguments* (SLAs), and/or, more generally, *solitary rule-following arguments* (SRAs) and the position that accepts such arguments can be called *communalism*.

W. Knorpp (✉)
James Madison University, Harrisonburg, USA
e-mail: knorppwm@jmu.edu

M. Araszkiewicz et al. (eds.), *Problems of Normativity, Rules and Rule-Following*,
Law and Philosophy Library 111, DOI 10.1007/978-3-319-09375-8_3

There are many different versions of communalism and the SRA/SLA, and the literature is extensive. Obviously there is no way to examine all the relevant positions and arguments in one paper. In what follows, however, I hope to cast some additional light on the discussion of communalism by doing two things. First, I will examine several distinctions among types of communalism, and argue that the most important version of the view is the version I call *communalism simpliciter* (or unconditional communalism), the view that it is logically impossible for a solitary individual to follow rules (e.g. use language) no matter what s/he does. Second, I will examine the crucial role of interpersonal interaction in SRAs—efforts by one individual to condone, condemn, and/or correct the actions of another individual.

Communalism, of course, remains unproven—but it continues to tantalize philosophers who are inclined to believe that communities play not merely an important role, but an essential one, in thought, rule-following, and language-use. I will argue, however, that the prospects for communalism are dim, largely because there is reason to doubt that both conjuncts of the Asymmetry claim can be true. Once we fix the type of communalism that is under discussion, and limit our attention to the genuinely important version of the view, and once we reflect a bit on similarities between self-correction and correction by others, we can see that it is implausible that the conjuncts of AC can both be true in any given possible case.

3.2 Strategic and Dialectical Considerations

3.2.1 The Burden of Proof

There is at least one relevant issue in this vicinity that is easily settled, and that is the issue of the burden of proof—there is no doubt that communalism has it. Communalism is the view that makes the relevant positive claims, and claims that deviate significantly from common sense. It is the communalist who claims that something that seems prima facie logically possible (solitary rule-following … and, on some versions, *all* actual rule-following …) is logically impossible. One might, of course, question whether there is a burden of proof in philosophy (as Peirce does), or one might, I suppose, propose new criteria for establishing where the burden lies. However, in the absence of some non-standard theory of the matter, it seems that even communalists should agree that they are the ones with the case to prove. There is no reason to agonize over this point. However, since it is common for both communalists and anti-communalists to err with respect to this issue, it is, I believe, worth mentioning.

3.2.2 Anti-communalists' Common Strategic Errors

Anti-communalists often choose a strategy that is philosophically ambitious but strategically imprudent. Such critics typically also reject rule nihilism,[1] and are eager to defend more traditional conceptions of meaning and rule-following. In fact and unsurprisingly, they tend to be more concerned with rule nihilism that with communalism. Nihilism, after all, represents the more important challenge to our traditional understanding of rule-following and language-use. The overall situation here is a rather common one: skeptical/nihilistic arguments are directed against a traditional (realist or rationalist or objectivist) position. An ersatz or relativistic alternative is proposed. Defenders of the tradition as well as relativistic opponents of the tradition falsely assume—or, at least, act as if they assume—that defenders of the tradition must defeat the skeptical/nihilistic arguments in order to defeat the ersatz or relativistic alternative.

But this is not true, and, given that skeptical/nihilistic arguments tend to be particularly difficult to defeat, it is not a shrewd strategy. It is generally easier to attack positive views directly. People on both sides of the dispute apparently tend to forget that communalist positions, like relativistic ones, are *positive* positions. As such, *they cannot win the day on the strength of skeptical/nihilistic arguments*—and, in fact, such arguments pose the same threat to them as to more traditional positions. Since communalism itself is a perfectly legitimate topic/target, and since it should be the actual target of anti-communalist arguments, and since it is, furthermore, easier to defeat (in part because it can be defeated simply by showing that communalists fail to carry their burden of proof), the best and more prudent way to criticize communalism is, well, to criticize communalism. And that is what I will do here.

3.3 Sundry Considerations and Distinctions

3.3.1 The Asymmetry Claim

The essence of rule-communalism is the asymmetry claim—the claim that AC (i) and AC (ii) are both true, that rule-following is logically impossible for solitary individuals, but possible for communal ones. Rule communalism simply *is* the position that accepts AC, and SRAs are arguments that attempt to establish AC. The simplest, most direct route to refuting communalism is showing that communalist arguments fail to establish AC. A route that is, in some sense, more efficient or economical involves showing why AC is likely to be false, i.e. showing why arguments

[1] I favor the term 'nihilism' rather than the more standard 'skepticism' because, outside of its primary philosophical use to name an epistemological position, I am inclined to think that 'skepticism' still carries something of its non-philosophical suggestion of incredulity. 'Nihilism,' however, is less equivocal. The nihilist about x believes that there are no x's—that there is no such thing as x.

of a certain type for AC are not likely to succeed. That is the route I will take in Sect. 11.5.1, where I will explain why appeals to intersubjective correction are extremely unlikely to provide communalism with a route to the asymmetry claim.

Before we'll be in a position to see why this is so, we'll have to discuss several more preliminary considerations.

3.3.2 Possibility

It is not possible to make sense of the SRA unless we take the type of possibility referenced by AC to be logical possibility.[2] The SRA, like more orthodox versions of the PLA, does not seek to establish that there is some merely medical limitation of human beings that typically prevents them from following rules in isolation. *Everyone* believes that claim, communalists and non-communalists alike. *No one* thinks that a human being, isolated since birth, is *likely* to develop the ability to follow rules/use language. In order for communalism to be the astonishing philosophical discovery that it purports to be, it must be surprising. It must deny common sense and philosophical orthodoxy in some way. And it does—but only if it denies the *logical possibility* of solitary rule-following.

3.3.3 Conditional and Unconditional Communalism

Some versions of the SRA conclude that it is impossible for solitary, non-communal individuals to *learn* to follow rules; analogous versions of the SLA conclude that it is impossible for them to acquire/develop language. Such arguments are *acquisition arguments*. Other versions of the SRA/SLA conclude that it is *absolutely* impossible for isolates to follow rules/use language no matter what they do. A passably thorough discussion of this distinction alone might take up an entire paper, so, again, the discussion of this preliminary point will have to be somewhat abbreviated. But, to be more precise, the most important rough distinction in this vicinity is between the following two positions:

> Conditional/Acquisition communalism:
> It is not possible for a life-long isolate to learn to follow rules (e.g. use language); i.e. not possible for such a person to develop rules nor the ability to follow them (e.g. to develop a language/the ability to use it).
> Unconditional Communalism/Communalism simpliciter:
> It is not possible for a life-long isolate to follow rules (e.g. use language). (*Period.*) It is not possible for a life-long isolate to follow rules (e.g. use language) no matter what thoughts he has and no matter what actions he performs.

In these pure forms, the views are more accurately characterized when characterized more fully:

[2] Kusch (2002) suggests that it is metaphysical possibility which is at issue. That claim is plausible, too.

Conditional/Acquisition communalism elaborated:
It is not possible for a life-long isolate to develop rules nor the ability to follow them (e.g. develop a language/the ability to use it). In order to follow a rule, it is necessary and sufficient to have certain thoughts/perform certain actions. If it were possible for solitary individuals to think such thoughts/perform such actions, then they could follow rules. But it is not possible for life-long isolates to develop the ability to do these things.
Unconditional Communalism/Communalism simpliciter elaborated:
It is not possible for a life-long isolate to follow rules (e.g. use language) no matter what thoughts he has nor what actions he performs. This is not because there are thoughts/actions such that, could he only perform them, he would be following rules/using language. In principle, a solitary individual can have any thought/perform any action (narrowly construed) that a communal individual can have/perform. However, none of these things constitute rule-following (language-use) in the absence of (or: without reference to) other individuals.[3]

The ordinary, common-sense view of rule-following (e.g. language-use) goes roughly like so: ordinary humans like you and me follow rules (and use language). We do these things in virtue of some combination of (a) our thoughts and (b) our overt actions, verbal and otherwise—that is, some combination of what we do and what's in our minds. So, for example, when I follow syntactic rules of English, as I do as I type this sentence, I am having thoughts and doing things with my fingers. On the ordinary view, it is in virtue of these things that I follow the relevant rules. Let's say that people who follow a rule R have thoughts T and perform actions A, and it is in virtue of thinking/doing T/A (or as we can say: *being in state T/A*) that they follow R.[4] A straightforward acquisition argument concludes that solitary individuals that are not in T/A cannot switch into state T/A—and, therefore, they cannot follow R. If they could switch into/be in T/A, then they would *ipso facto* be following R, since following R simply *is* accomplishing T/A. That is: there is something—being in T/A—which constitutes following R. Since being in T/A constitutes following R, anyone who is in T/A follows R, regardless of whether they are in a community or not. In short, if a solitary individual could do the relevant things and have the relevant mental experiences, then s/he would follow rules. But s/he can't have/do them.[5]

Communalism simpliciter—unconditional communalism—is an extremely different view. According to this position, solitary individuals can, theoretically, have all the same mental experiences and perform all the same actions as communal individuals. I'm following rules as I write this; I'm having certain thoughts and

[3] It is, of course, possible for a communalist to accept both arguments. However, the arguments are so different that I think that would be reason to suspect that the conclusion is driving the reasoning rather than vice-versa.

[4] Communalists often raise an objection to such ways of speaking, objecting that thoughts themselves are infected by the same skeptical/nihilistic worries that afflict rules. The point seems to be that it is illegitimate to explain rule-following in terms of thoughts, since thinking is afflicted by the same problem that afflicts rule-following. Of course we can't track down and defeat every objection, but this objection seems easily deflected, since we can simply replace 'thought' with 'mental experience.'

[5] Such views rarely *explicitly admit* that solitary rule-following would be possible if solitary individuals could have the relevant thoughts and perform the appropriate actions. But that is what the pure version of the view is committed to.

performing certain actions. Communalism simpliciter is the view that: (a) it is logically possible for a solitary individual (say, my doppelganger) to have mental experiences and perform physical actions which are *indistinguishable* from the ones I currently have and perform; but (b) in the absence of an appropriate relation to a community, even an individual who had the appropriate experiences and performed the appropriate actions would not follow rules.

In this paper, I will be interested only in unconditional communalism/communalism simpliciter. Some of the arguments here are, in fact, applicable to conditional/acquisition communalism, and I discuss that view more extensively elsewhere—but considerations of space prevent me from considering the position here.[6]

The decision to focus on communalism simpliciter is not a purely practical one, however. Any acquisition argument will have the form: individual N can only acquire the ability to follow rules by interacting with another individual, N2. Only by interacting with N2 can N move into state T/A, which state constitutes following a rule. However, once we recognize that it is logical possibility that is at issue in the argument, it becomes extremely implausible that there is any such state—that is, a state that it is *logically impossible* for N to enter without interacting with N2. I acquired the ability to use language as a result of interacting with others, and, consequently, I am now in a mental/physical state that constitutes typing an English sentence. But it is logically possible for there to be a doppelganger of mine, solitary since birth/creation, who has never had any such interaction. There is no contradiction involved in the description of such an individual. Such a being is obviously imaginable—he could pop into existence randomly, or because of some weird cosmic occurrence, or God could make him.[7] Consequently, it seems that communalism's only hope is to argue that being in such a state does not constitute rule-following—that even an individual that is mentally and physically indistinguishable from me does not follow rules unless appropriately related to a community. And that view is unconditional communalism, communalism simpliciter.

To summarize the points of the previous section and this one: the SRA is not an anthropological nor psycholinguistic argument about what solitary *homo sapiens* are likely to accomplish. The SRA is a philosophical argument about what is possible, in the broadest sense of 'possible,' for any solitary being whatsoever. It is an argument about what language-use and rule-following *are*, about their logically necessary conditions, the conditions under which they are possible at all. If the SRA *were* an acquisition argument, it would rather obviously not come close to establishing its conclusion; in fact, it would be the merest philosophical speculation about a question that only biolinguists and other cognitive scientists have any hope of answering. Since the SLA is a serious argument, and a philosophical argument, only if it is about the in-principle possibility of a solitary language, that is how we should construe it.

---

[6] E.g. in Knorpp (2013).

[7] Some communalist have tried to argue that such a doppelganger is not conceivable, but such arguments are entirely unconvincing, often amounting to little more than simply denial that such things are conceivable. See e.g., (Lillegard 1998).

But let the fate of those arguments be as it may. It is communalism simpliciter that will be the focus of this paper.

3.3.4 Unconditional Communalism and the Primitive Bias

When we shift our attention away from acquisition arguments, we gain a certain advantage with respect to thought-experiments. Since acquisition communalism is not really the view that should be at issue in the disagreement about communalism and SRAs, arguments about an infant Super-Crusoe trying to *develop* rules and language on his own are not precisely to the point. In fact, simplistic pot-painting, bird-naming and rock-counting Crusoes are actually suboptimal and somewhat misleading. Among other things, the focus on very simple cases—e.g. sorting berries or making primitive marks—gives illicit advantages to the communalist by vaguely suggesting that we are concerned with primitive isolates *developing* primitive rules. And the more primitive the behavior, the more likely it seems that it might be automatic or instinctual and so non-rule-governed. And when such actions are compared to actual (communal) rule-following and language-use in all their current glory, communalism gains an illicit advantage with respect to plausiblity.

The unconditional SRA (that is, the argument for unconditional communalism), however, is an argument to the effect that even a solitary individual with complex behavior, even one who acts and thinks exactly like a communal rule-follower and language-user, cannot truly be said to follow rules, no matter what she does, and no matter what goes through her mind. The thoughts and actions of this individual need not be simplistic, and need not be of a type that a solitary *Homo sapiens* is likely to develop on her own. In fact—and this is an extremely important point—the individual in question need not be human, need not be mortal, need not have finite capacities, and can have a brain and behaviors that are orders of magnitude more complex than our own. (In fact, of course, the being in question need not be material, nor have a brain, at all.) If the SLA proves that solitary rule-following is impossible, then it proves that it is impossible not just for a solitary, primitive human, but also for an intelligent super-being who (apparently) understands (or even discovers) calculus and quantum physics—in fact, develops mathematics and physics far beyond anything we possess—builds starships, (apparently) understands and uses millions of languages much more complex than English, produces literary works incomparably more beautiful and profound than those of Shakespeare and Milton.… The unconditional SRA—the real SRA—entails that even such a solitary super-being cannot follow rules. Until, at least another individual—no matter how intellectually limited—arrives on the scene. In fact, the unconditional SRA entails that God, prior to the Creation, could neither follow rules nor speak a language. Since the SRA simpliciter is often conflated with various versions of the acquisition SRA, this point is almost invariably overlooked.

3.4 Kripke's Wittgenstein and Rule Nihilism

3.4.1 Nihilistic and Non-nihilistic Communalism

There is one more distinction we must address, the distinction between nihilistic (or skeptical) and non-nihilistic (or non-skeptical) versions of communalism and the SRA. Unfortunately, it is common for communalist arguments to be inexplicit about whether they are nihilistic or non-nihilistic. But the distinction is of crucial importance.

The most well-known nihilistic SRA is, of course, Kripke's Wittgenstein's.[8] A careful examination of the details of Kripke's Wittgenstein's complex and interesting account requires at least a paper unto itself; here, I can only provide a sketch of the conclusions and implications of the view, with a few details added where absolutely necessary.[9]

Kripke notoriously holds that "skeptical" considerations show that there are no facts about individuals in virtue of which they follow rules. Another way to say this is: take the sum total of all facts F1 … Fn about you up to and including time *t*; take any R-action (i.e., any attempt to follow rule R), RA1, subsequent to t; nothing about F1 … Fn determines whether RA1 is correct or incorrect as an application of R. Take any two possible actions that can be construed as attempts to follow some rule; no fact about your mind and no fact about your behavior can make either of those possible actions more correct than the other.

To put this in the way most favorable to communalism: when we consider only one person, isolated from a community, and consider any of his attempts to follow a rule, it is never true that any of these actions accord with his past intentions. Neither is it true that any of these actions contradict or violate his past intentions. Nor, in fact, do his attempts to follow the rule accord with nor violate any other fact about him, including his past behavior. Consequently, it is not possible for individuals to follow rules. For any individual and any attempt to follow a rule, that attempt is neither correct nor incorrect as an attempt to follow that rule. Rule-following is a fiction.

3.4.2 Kripkensteinian (Quasi-)Communalism

Kripke's Wittgenstein, however, thinks that there is some sense in which communal individuals are in a different position than solitary individuals. (Though, as we'll see, the difference turns out to be irrelevant …)

---

[8] Since the argument is, as Kripke is careful to note, neither really his, nor (probably) Wittgenstein's, I'll say that the argument is "Kripke's Wittgenstein's." I realize this is annoying, and I apologize, but this is better than attributing the argument to someone who did not/does not accept it.

[9] For my best go at a fairly complete account of Kripke's Wittgenstein's argument, see (Knorpp 2003).

According to Kripke's Wittgenstein's view, "practices" of making assertions are "legitimate" if and only if they meet two conditions:

a. There must be "specifiable" assertibility conditions for each type of assertion and
b. The "practice" of making such assertions must play a useful role in the lives of the practitioners.

The crucial—and widely-misunderstood—fact about this view, however, is this: according to it, *no individual, solitary or communal, ever actually follows any rule*. This position is firmly predicated on nihilism: no R-action ever actually accords or fails to accord with past behavior or intentions, rules do not, in fact, guide actions, no one, in fact ever applies a rule correctly or incorrectly. Again: rule-following is a fiction. However, according to Kripke's Wittgenstein, the "practice" of (falsely) *asserting* that some people are rule-followers—that, for example, they actually mean things by their words—plays a useful role in our lives. It is useful because it helps us identify people whose reactions we can predict and trust. If I frequently see you use, e.g., the word 'plus' in ways consistent with the ways that I am inclined to use the word, then I will assert things like "you mean addition by 'plus'," or "you mean what I mean by 'plus,'" or "We follow the same rule with respect to 'plus'." If your reactions differ more than incidentally from mine, I will say that you do not understand what 'plus' means; if they differ a lot, I may even say that you do not understand English, or do not follow rules at all. Thus, though no one ever *follows rules*, they sometimes "follow rules"—i.e., we are sometimes permitted to falsely assert that they follow rules because it is useful for us to do so.

It is absolutely crucial to realize that Kripke's Wittgenstein does not argue that the community is a stabilizing force that helps weed out our errors and assists us in genuinely following rules, nor anything of the sort. According to Kripke's Wittgenstein, the R reactions of the community, even when its members are in perfect consensus, are arbitrary, unjustified "leaps in the dark," just like the R-reactions of individuals. To ignore this point is to completely misunderstand the position.

Crucial to this account is Kripke's Wittgenstein's general conception of justification conditions for assertions:

> For any assertion, A, and any individual, N, N is permitted to assert A if and only if: (a) N is sincerely inclined to assert A, and (b) N is not corrected by other members of the community.

Kripke's view is famously asymmetrical as between solitary and communal individuals, however, because such a practice of "rule-following" allegedly cannot be legitimate and/or cannot be useful for a solitary individual. This is because the second condition, (b), is always trivially fulfilled. Without other individuals who might dispute a judgment/assertion, and given the first condition, a solitary individual would always be permitted to assert anything. In particular, he would always be permitted to assert of himself that he had correctly "followed" a "rule." Thus (allegedly) whatever a solitary individual thinks is right is right. Thus, for solitary individuals, there is (allegedly) no such thing as rightness. Thus solitary individuals cannot "follow rules."[10]

3.4.3 *The Failure of Kripke's Wittgenstein's Account*

Kripke's Wittgenstein's account fails in two very different ways.

First and most importantly: it simply does not constitute a defense of rule communalism. According to Kripke's Wittgenstein, AC (ii) is straightforwardly false. Communal individuals do not follow rules; they are merely warranted in asserting that they do because it is allegedly useful for them to do so.

Second and less importantly, the account fails even to prove that "rule-following" is impossible for solitary individuals. First, it begs the question; to make matters worse, does so in a way that violates the Wittgensteinian admonition to remain true to "our practice." "Our practice" clearly allows for self-correction; therefore to specify in (b) that correction must come, if at all, from other members of the community is to fail to capture crucial facts about our practice. To avoid these errors, the assertibility conditions must be altered at least like so:

> For any assertion, A, and any individual, N, N is permitted to assert A if and only if: (a) N is sincerely inclined to assert A, and (b) N is not corrected.

This leaves open the possibility of self-correction. This change does not entail that solitary "rule-following" is possible, however, because it does not entail that it is possible for solitary individuals to have a *useful* practice of "rule-following." And that is as it should be.

As it turns out, however, a solitary individual can, obviously, have such a practice. Any individual who corrects himself, and does so usefully, has a useful, legitimate practice of "rule-following." Of course on Kripke's Wittgenstein's view a self-correcting solitary individual is not actually *following rules*, since following rules is impossible. His acts of self-correction are not in accordance with his past intentions nor any such thing. But solitary and communal individuals are in the same boat in this respect: neither can follow rules. So on such an account, AC is false. And, since it is possible for both communal and solitary practices to be useful, solitary and communal individuals are in the same both with respect to "rule-following" as well.

3.5 Nihilism and Non-Kripkensteinian Communalism

Kripke's Wittgenstein's arguments fail to support the asymmetry claim, but one might plausibly argue that this is not a fair test of rule communalism. After all, Kripke's Wittgenstein does not even try to defend communalism about actual rule-

[10] This argument is full of problems, but an examination of them is rather beyond the scope of this paper.

following. Genuine communalists share Kripkenstein's hunch that it is correction (and other similar types of interpersonal interaction) that hold(s) the key to proving the asymmetry claim. But, unlike Kripke's Wittgenstein, they maintain the conviction that genuine rule-following can be made possible by such interaction. (Kusch 2006; Bloor 2011) In the final sections below, I explain why there is little hope that such a conviction is correct.

3.5.1 Correction, Community, and Non-Kripkensteinian Nihilism

Consider Smith, alone, facing a pile composed of red marbles and blue marbles, and trying to sort them into piles of uniform colors.[11] Rule nihilism entails that there is no such thing as following such a rule correctly as opposed to incorrectly—no such thing as acting correctly rather than incorrectly. Suppose that Smith has put a large number of red marbles into what we'll call pile A, and a large number of blue marbles into pile B, when suddenly, he notices that he has put a blue marble in pile A. Suppose he then judges that he has acted incorrectly. Imagine also that he does something obviously condemnatory and corrective of his previous action—switching the blue marble to pile B, laughing at himself, striking himself on the forehead … Imagine, if you like, that he even says 'incorrect!' This is the point at which communalists are inclined to assert that none of these things matter, because there is no one else around to correct Smith. There is no one there to condone, condemn nor correct his initial R-action, and no one there to condone, condemn, nor correct his correction of himself. Consequently, whatever Smith thinks is right—or, at least, whatever he thinks is right in his final or highest level judgment—is right. And so "here we cannot talk about right." Or, to be more precise: if Smith could follow rules, then whatever he thought was right would be right. But that is absurd. So, by reductio Smith does not follow rules.

Unfortunately for communalism, however, adding a second individual—or a third, or a thousandth, or a millionth—does nothing to change the situation in principle. If such considerations show that rule-following is logically impossible for a single person, then they show that it is logically impossible for any number of

[11] It might seem odd that I focus on a case of this kind given my complaints about "primitive case bias" in an earlier section. I do think that simple examples are often the best—and simple examples are fine here so long as we are not tempted by a certain common type of objection to the effect that "we can't really be sure" whether Smith is following rules, since his behavior is so primitive. As long as we recognize that this objection is utterly irrelevant here, there is no harm in focusing on simple cases. The complexity objection is irrelevant because Smith is not, in fact, following rules in any of these examples. Such an objection cannot, at any rate, help the communalist given that it would count against Smith's following rules even after Jones is added to the picture. Any reader bothered by such concerns, however, should replace these simple examples with examples that reference more complex behavior.

people, for individuals in any community, no matter how large. Let's consider what does happen if we add a second individual, Jones, to the situation.[12]

Note first that, assuming the truth of nihilism, Smith and Jones are in exactly the same situation with respect to the piles of marbles. There is no such thing as sorting them correctly rather than incorrectly. It is logically impossible for Jones to follow any rules with respect to the marbles just as it is logically impossible for Smith to do so. Every possible R-action of both Smith and Jones is necessarily an unjustified leap in the dark. Jones can no more follow marble-sorting rules than can Smith. So, thus far, nothing about adding Jones has changed the situation. And, of course, adding a third person, Brown, will not help, as she cannot follow rules, either—and so on.

Now, consider the kinds of interactions between Smith and Jones that communalism generally relies upon to allegedly make rule-following possible—acts in which Jones condones, condemns and/or corrects Smith's R-actions. Not only are Jones and Smith in the same position with respect to the marbles and the two (actually: the infinite number of) possible rules for sorting them, they are also in the same position with respect to the use of the words 'correct' and 'incorrect.' No use of 'correct' nor 'incorrect' can be guided by a rule. Each application of these words is an arbitrary, unjustified leap in the dark that can be neither right nor wrong. But, of course, this has nothing to do with the words 'correct' and 'incorrect.' Rather, the point holds with respect to *any* methods that might be thought to constitute (or be employed in) condoning, condemning, and/or correcting actions of any kind—patting on the head, swatting across the nose with a rolled-up newspaper, etc. It is logically impossible for Smith to follow rules with respect to sorting marbles because it is logically impossible for *anyone* to follow rules of *any* kind. And that entails that it is logically impossible for Jones to follow rules with respect to the use of any method of correction (including the use of 'correct' and 'incorrect'.) Jones's uses of 'correct' and 'incorrect' will simply be additional, unjustified, non-rule-governed actions that can do nothing to make Smith's actions rule-governed.

Furthermore, from Smith's perspective, the addition of Jones cannot alter his situation in principle, since Smith cannot follow rules with respect to Jones's attempts to condone, condemn, or correct his actions. Jones's utterances of 'correct' and 'incorrect' are simply additional features of Smith's environment, not in principle different than the piles of colored marbles. If nihilism is true, then there is no such thing as Smith reacting either correctly or incorrectly to Jones's utterance of 'incorrect.' Even if Smith alters his behavior in response to Jones's utterances,

---

[12] It is sometimes objected that it is illegitimate to focus on a case of only two individuals, since there are ways in which a community is not analogous to an individual (Kusch 2006b). These objections are indefensible. First, although individuals and communities are dissimilar in certain ways, they are similar in certain ways—and they are similar in the ways that matter here. Specifically, they can both be an external source of correction. Second, we are giving the communalist his best case by thinking about a second individual, since the reactions of another individual are analogous to the reactions of a community when there is complete consensus in the community. And when there is anything less than complete consensus in the community, this raises a whole new set of problems for the communalist.

shifting the red marble to the other pile, this new action will itself be arbitrary and unjustified, therefore no better (and no worse) than his original action. The situation becomes even worse when we realize that, if nihilism is true, there is not even any fact of the matter about whether or not Smith and Jones are agreeing or disagreeing in any of these cases.

So what we are faced with in this case is this: Smith has an arbitrary, non-rule-governed reaction to the distribution of marbles. Jones has an arbitrary, non-rule-governed reaction to the distribution of marbles. It is not possible for either of them to be right or wrong, and there is not even any fact of the matter about whether their judgments agree or disagree. Jones then, let us say, utters the word 'incorrect.' This new action is itself arbitrary and non-rule-governed, and it is impossible for it to be either correct or incorrect. Smith then reacts (or not) to Jones's utterance (or other action) in another arbitrary, non-rule governed way. Regardless of whether he alters his original action in response to Jones's utterance or fails to do so, either action is arbitrary and unjustified, and it is impossible for either response to be right or wrong.

Unless we are overlooking something here, there simply seems to be no hope whatsoever of grounding rule-governed behavior in this morass of random behavior. If we *start* with behavior that is necessarily non-rule-governed, and we can only *add* behavior that is necessarily non-rule-governed, there seems to be no hope of *producing* behavior that *is* rule-governed.

Communalists seem to recognize this point when they consider solitary individuals, but they seem to be blind to it when they consider groups of individuals. It seems clear to everyone, communalist and non-communalist alike, that in the case of a single individual, if one R-action, RA1, is necessarily non-rule-governed, and a second rule-action, RA2, is necessarily non-rule governed, then simply making RA1 the object of RA2 (that is, making RA2 a judgment about the correctness of RA1) is insufficient to make RA1 rule-governed. Communalists, however, seem be believe that this principle no longer holds if we simply move RA1 and RA2 into different individuals. That is to say: communalists seem to recognize that Smith's necessarily non-rule-governed attempts at self-correction cannot turn him into a genuine rule-follower; but for some reason they believe that Jones's necessarily non-rule-governed attempts to correct Smith can make Smith a genuine rule-follower. It is very difficult to see how such differential judgments can be sustained; communalism simply seems to be inconsistent on this point, applying more stringent standards to the solitary case than to the communal one.

3.5.2 *Wittgenstein's 257 Principle*

Communalists do sometimes attempt to defend such differential judgments by appealing to Philosophical Investigations 257:

> One would like to say: whatever is going to seem right to me is right. And that only means that here we can't talk about 'right' (Wittgenstein 1958).

The idea is, roughly, that in the case of a solitary individual, there is no court of appeal beyond his final or highest level judgment. If solitary Smith produces a distribution of marbles, D, and that is his final judgment, then that's that. If he then judges that he was wrong, and that is his final judgment, then *that's* that. He can continue to judge his previous judgments to be incorrect, but he will have to stop somewhere—and there is, in some sense, no further court of appeal.

There are many confusions in the paragraph above, but I want to focus only on the fact that—despite suggestions to the contrary (Summerfield 1990)—the situation does not change in any important way if we add another (or a million more) individual(s) to the picture. The argument of the previous paragraph (for one thing) depends on an unreasonably narrow interpretation of Wittgenstein's claim. Wittgenstein's thought in 257—at least to the extent that it is a plausible one—is that it cannot be true that *whatever is thought to be right is right*. And that thought is fully general, and indifferent with respect to the number of people involved. Moving the highest level, arbitrary judgment out of Smith and into Jones is legerdemain at best. It is an attempt to exploit the fact that Wittgenstein happened to express the thought at the end of 257 in the singular, rather in the plural.

And, of course, questions of Wittgenstein exegesis are largely irrelevant here. Even if Wittgenstein did mean to express the thought in the singular, limiting it in that way is indefensible. The reasonable thought, the defensible thought, is the general one: thinking that someone is right can't make them right, whether there are two people involved or just one.

3.6 Prospects for Non-nihilistic Communalism

Though any attempt to defend a non-nihilistic communalism on the basis of an appeal to asymmetries with respect to correction seems unpromising, that is not the final hope for communalism (even if it is the best hope). Another option is to try to defend a nihilistic communalism by appealing to phenomena other than correction to support the alleged asymmetry. Another option is to try to defend a communalism that is motivated by something other than nihilism about individual rule-following. (Rosenburg 1980) (Bar-On 1992)

In actual fact, however, most versions of communalism are not sufficiently explicit about their exact relationship to nihilism. This is what one might expect given that, in the absence of nihilistic arguments, there is little motivation for communalism—but once nihilism is accepted, communal rule-following seems doomed along with the solitary variety.

3.7 Some Perspective

One way to get some perspective on the communalist error to recognize that communities *do* matter with respect to rule-following and language-use. They matter a *lot* in practice, though they do not matter in principle. And they matter only on a fairly traditional view of rule-following. If there is a fact of the matter about what constitutes following rule R, then putting individuals together *does* typically help them follow R. They can check each other's R-actions, discuss controversial cases, and weed out obvious errors. If there is an objective fact of the matter about what constitutes following R, and if individuals have at least some tendency to get things right, then one individual can assist another individual in following R. But if rule nihilism is true, then there is no such thing as getting anything about rule-following right or wrong, and the addition of other individuals cannot change this. Given multiple judgments, where each has some tendency to be objectively correct, we can improve the accuracy of the judgments by aggregating them, testing them against each other, etc. But if there is no such thing as their being right or wrong, then aggregating them and testing them against each other is useless. Adding individuals and their judgments together only increases the probability that a rule will be followed if there is already a non-zero probability of individuals following it. But communalism is not the view that the probability of solitary individuals following rules is *low*; communalism is the view that the probability of solitary individuals following rules is necessarily zero. And so increasing the number of judgments—e.g. by increasing the number of people—does not help.

Conclusion

Communalism remains unproven, which is to say that the asymmetry claim remains unproven, which is to say that we do not yet know of a sound solitary rule-following argument (nor a sound solitary language argument). My own view is that communalism is almost certainly false, and that it survives largely because of the tendency to apply our doubts about rule-following more stringently to solitary cases than to communal cases. When we are scrupulous, however, about applying skepticism (in the sense of incredulity) to the solitary and communal cases in an even-handed way, the illusion of in-principle asymmetry evaporates. I have proven none of that here, however. All I hope to have done is to show that, once nihilism has been accepted at the individual level, we are unlikely to be able to salvage rule-following at the communal level merely by invoking alleged asymmetries having to do with correction. Such asymmetries apparently do not exist.

References

Bar-on, Dorit. 1992. On the possibility of a solitary language. *Nous* 26 (1): 27–45.

Bloor, David. 2011. Relativism and the sociology of scientific knowledge. In *A companion to relativism*, ed. Steven D. Hales, 433–455. Malden, MA: Wiley-Blackwell.

Knorpp, William Max. 2003. How to talk to yourself: Kripke's Wittgenstein's solitary language argument and why it fails. *Pacific Philosophical Quarterly* 84 (3): 215–248.

Knorpp, William Max. 2013. *Solitary language acquisition arguments* (unpublished).

Kripke, Saul. 1982. *Wittgenstein on rules and private language.* Cambridge: Harvard University Press.

Kusch, Martin. 2002. *Knowledge By Agreement.* Oxford: Clarendon.

Kusch, Martin. 2006. *A sceptical guide to meaning and rules.* Chesham: Acumen.

Lillegard, Norman. 1998. How private must an objectionable private language be? Paideia. http://www.bu.edu/wcp/Papers/Lang/LangLill.htm. Accessed May 2013.

Rosenburg, Jay. 1980. *Linguistic representation*. Dordrecht: D. Reidel.

Summerfield, D. 1990. Philosophical investigations 201: A Wittgensteinian reply to Kripke. *Journal of the History of Philosophy* 28:417–438.

Wittgenstein, Ludwig. 1958. *Philosophical investigations*, (ed. G. E. M. Anscombe). New York: MacMillan.

Chapter 4
Knowing Way Too Much: A Case Against Semantic Phenomenology

Krzysztof Posłajko

Abstract Proponents of so called "semantic phenomenology" claim that we are able to hear meanings when we hear meaningful utterances. Recently, Philip Goff has proposed his interpretation of semantic phenomenology that leads to the conclusion that the sceptical problem posed by Saul Kripke in his *Wittgenstein on rules and private language* must be solvable. My aim in this chapter is to question this view by showing that the way Goff conceives the epistemology of meanings is not compatible with the basic intuition about the possibility of linguistic error. Consequently, we cannot rightly say that our phenomenal experiences represent meanings. The conclusion is that the existence of the conscious phenomena described by semantic phenomenology is irrelevant to the ontological problem of existence of rules and meanings. At the end, I sketch an alternative picture of the role played by conscious experience in our use of language.

Keywords Meaning · Normativity · Rule-following · Self-knowledge · Semantic phenomenology

Proponents of semantic phenomenology claim that we are able to literally hear meanings while listening to meaningful utterances we understand (Goff 2012; Siegel 2006). The primary reason given for this claim is that there is a certain phenomenal difference between the situation when one hears an utterance and understands it and the situation when one hears words that one doesn't understand. The very idea of semantic phenomenology is subject to criticism (see e.g. O'Callaghan 2011). For the present purposes, I will however assume that we can speak of such a thing as experiencing a linguistic expression as meaningful. What will be contested, on the other hand, is what consequences can be drawn from that thesis.

Philip Goff has proposed his version of semantic phenomenology (Goff 2012), which leads to the conclusion which is at odds with scepticism about rule-following. My aim in this chapter is to show that even if we agree that semantic phenomenology exists, it doesn't lead to any definite conclusions about the solvability of Kripkenstein's sceptical problem.

K. Posłajko (✉)
Institute of Philosophy, Jagiellonian University, Kraków, Poland
e-mail: krzysztof.poslajko@uj.edu.pl

M. Araszkiewicz et al. (eds.), *Problems of Normativity, Rules and Rule-Following*,
Law and Philosophy Library 111, DOI 10.1007/978-3-319-09375-8_4

Let me briefly state the rule-following issue. As it's well known, Kripke introduces his sceptical problem using the following famous example (1982, p. 9): imagine that 56 is the biggest number you've ever used while performing addition (of course this is very improbable, but for any person an "upper limit" of his addition can be found). Now, you are asked to perform the operation of "57 + 68". Naturally, your answer is "125". But then you are confronted with the hypothesis that what you really mean by "+" is not a familiar addition function, but rather a *quaddition* function, which returns the same values as the original addition function for arguments that are both lower than 57 but 5 for all the other arguments. Kripke-Wittgenstein's sceptic is then to show that confronted with such a hypothesis we are unable to provide a satisfying answer to her challenge. There is nothing we can invoke in order to support our belief that we mean the "right" function.

The story is familiar enough so I won't elaborate it any further. It's important to keep two things in mind. First, the argument is meant to be strictly general—the sceptical conclusion applies to any meaningful use of language, not just arithmetics. Secondly, the negative conclusion is understood in ontological, not epistemological terms. It is not that we lack cognitive capacities to recognize some fact that makes it true that by "+" we mean addition, but that there is no such fact (Kripke 1982, p. 39). It is worth noting, however, that the negative epistemological thesis follows from the ontological one—if there is no fact of the matter regarding the meaning, then we are in no position to know it. Even an omniscient God would not be in a better position. Still, one should bear in mind that the ontological claim is more fundamental.

In my view, the way Goff conceives semantic phenomenology leads to the conclusion that the very fact of its existence is enough to show the solvability of the Kripknesteinian problem.

> When we consciously perceive someone using an assertoric sentence in a language we understand, our perceptual experience represents the speaker as making a certain claim; to return to the example, if I say to you 'God is a friend to all', your perceptual experience represents the utterance of that sentence as an act of literally claiming that God is a friend to all. This perceptual experience involves hearing the words in that sentence as meaningful, and this in turn is a matter of experience representing those words as contributing to the making of the claim in specific ways. Your experience represents the word 'God' as determining that God is the subject of the claim. Your experience represents the predicate 'is a friend to all' as determining that the utterance claims of the subject of the sentence that it is a friend to all (Goff 2012, p. 225).

The key thing about Goff's version of semantic phenomenology, as is clearly seen from the above quote, is that we perceive utterances not only as meaningful but also as having specific meanings. This is extremely important in the context of the sceptical debate. If we hear "+", not just as meaning something (as opposed to meaningless), but as meaning specifically addition, then, supposedly, we have a straightforward answer to the sceptic. We know that by "+" we mean addition just because we *perceive it*.

It is also instructive to look at the way Goff treats his version of the famous Mary example. His story runs as follows: Mary, a genial scientist is ask to determine what a person (called Cuthbert) means by a given expression. When Mary is given only physical information, regarding her subject dispositions etc., she is unable to determine whether Cuthbert is experiencing "plus" as plus or *quus*. But the task becomes simple when she is provided (by an evil daemon) with a glimpse of the subject's phenomenal states:

> instantly Mary knew everything there was to know about what it's like to be Cuthbert at *t*. She now had access to Cuthbert's semantic phenomenology at *t*; to what meaning Cuthbert's perceptual experience represented the word he was hearing at *t* as having. Mary had only to reflect for a moment before declaring, 'Cuthbert experiences 'plus' to mean plus' (Goff 2012, p. 231).

The primary aim of Goff's argument is to discredit physicalism, but this aspect will be left aside (Alex Miller and Ali Saboohi doubt whether Goff's paper poses a problem specific to physicalism (see: Miller and Saboohi forthcoming)). What will be the subject of interest is whether the answer to sceptical problem, which is more or less implicit in Goff's argument, is a successful one.

There might arise a more general worry that Goff's version of semantic phenomenology is not in the business of providing a direct answer to Kripke's sceptic. Nowhere does Goff suggest that the phenomenal states in question might serve as facts that make sentences about meaning true.

But let us remember that the negative ontological thesis about meaning-facts implies the negative epistemological thesis: if there are no facts about what we mean then there is no way we can know what we mean. By simple *modus tollens* we can infer that if there is a way to get to know what we mean (which is precisely what Goff claims) then there are indeed facts about what we mean. So, the very existence of semantic phenomenology disproves the sceptical conclusion, even if we are still in no position to give an account of meaning-facts.

Additionally, as the quotes above show, Goff often speaks of perceptual experiences as representing meanings, and if this talk about representation is to be understood in broadly realistic fashion, then the underlying assumption must be that semantic phenomenology provides us with knowledge that meaning-facts exist. So anyone who is even mildly sympathetic to the view that rule-following paradox shows that the realistic account of meaning and rules is mistaken must deny this interpretation of semantic phenomenology.

While I'm not inclined to claim that it is false that we might have conscious experiences in which we have the impression of perceiving meanings, I doubt whether it's right to say that such experiences provide us with knowledge of meanings (where knowledge is understood as realistically conceived representation). In order to show that, let us look more closely at the crucial notion of "knowing the meaning of a given statement". If we say "*X* knows what *P* means", it might be interpreted in at least two ways. First, it might mean that *X* knows that *P* means *p*, for example—Jones might know that "Snow is white" means snow is white. This phenomenon will be labeled, for the purposes of this chapter "disquotational knowledge of meaning". The basic test of possessing such knowledge is the ability to verbally exclude alternative interpretation of what one says. For example, when confronted with the sceptic, the subject would deny that she means quus by "plus" and insist that she means plus.

Two things might be said about this notion. First, possession of such knowledge is not enough to disprove Kripke's sceptic negative epistemological thesis. The fact that if someone asks me what I mean by "green" and I reply by saying that I just mean green doesn't get us any further in the context of rule-following dialectics. To quote John McDowell:

> When we say '"Diamonds are hard" is true if and only if diamonds are hard', we are just as much involved on the right-hand side as the reflections on rule-following tell us we are. There is a standing temptation to miss this obvious truth, and to suppose that the right-hand side somehow presents us with a possible fact, pictured as a unconceptualized configuration of things in themselves (McDowell 1984, p. 352).

The primary lesson from McDowell's observation is that if we hope to provide the sceptic with an answer we must do something more than just quote the expression which meaning is discussed, as the self-quotation is still liable to sceptical reintepretation.

Moreover, it seems that we don't need to invoke any phenomenology in order to account for disquotational self-knowledge. The fact that when asked "What do you mean by '2+2=4'?" I'm perfectly entitled to answer "I mean that 2+2=4" is easily explained in terms of there being rules of language which enable me to safely assume that while performing the semantic descent from meta-language to object language I do not, unbeknownst to me, change the language that I'm speaking (this point lies at the heart of Davidson's account of self-knowledge (see: Davidson 1984)). But this observation is licensed solely by the fact that the instances of T-schema seem to be nearly a priori truths in our language, and we don't need to engage in any phenomenological introspection in order to notice that.

Of course, the notion of "disquotational knowledge of meaning" should be much more elaborated, but this would get us too far from the central problem: does semantic phenomenology provides us with the kind of knowledge that is needed to deal with Kripke's problem?

In my opinion the kind of knowledge that should be discussed if we are about to answer this question is something along these lines: if we say that "*X* knows what *P* means" we mean that *X* knows the conditions of correct use of *P*. The notion of conditions of correct use is of uttermost importance in the debates on Kripkenstein's problem, especially in the discussions on normativity of meaning.

Many authors have strongly denied that meaning is normative in any philosophically interesting sense (see e.g. Hattiangadi 2006; Glüer and Pagin 1999; Wikforss 2001). However, what seems to be fairly uncontroversial is the fact that we frequently use normative vocabulary to describe how we speak the language. It is ubiquitous that we describe some uses as correct and some others as incorrect. What is debated is how we should interpret these assessments—most critics of normativity of meaning deny that the use of normative discourse indicates that we deal with "genuine" normativity here, and provide with an alternative account of this practice. Hattiangadi for example (2006, p. 228) suggests that in the semantic context we form merely hypothetical imperatives, which are not genuine normative statements.

Perhaps the only philosopher who denied the normativity of meaning in its entirety was Davidson who famously claimed "that there is no such thing as language" (2005, p. 107)—he asserted that the whole idea of there being rules with which one might (not) conform is an illusion.

It's not my aim here to provide a detailed critique of Davidson (see Whiting 2007 for such an endeavour) but it certainly seems that he is proposing a strongly revisionist account of a fragment of natural language—as if he suggested that ordinary users are wrong when they speak of correctness and incorrectness of linguistic behaviour. If we, however, take this commonplace practice in good faith, than we are committed to the claim that the essential feature of the concept of meaning is that there are certain uses which are, in some sense, incorrect.

An important ramification of this thesis was provided by Alan Millar, who distinguished between conditions of correct application and conditions of correct use (Millar 2002). The former might be summarised by a following schema: if an expression P refers to things which are Φ then it is only correct to use P to denote Φ-things—for example: it is only correct to call green things "green".

Conditions of correct use, however, allow for a greater liberty. It's just commonsense to observe that we can lie, make factual mistakes or be ironic while speaking and still conform to the semantic norms. If I, for example, want to deceive someone and say that my car is green when in fact it isn't, I do not stop to speak proper English; in fact the ability to lie or to be ironic might be considered a sign of the mastery of a language. So, lying etc. are cases of misapplication but still of correct use. Not every possible use of language, however, will count as correct—some utterances are so "off the hook" that they might only be classified as linguistic errors (notorious quotes by the former US president, George W. Bush, like "They misunderestimated me", are fine examples of this).

Patterns of correct use are fairly intricate. If asked about them, most competent users of language would be able to provide some (roughly correct) characterizations, but we shouldn't expect that these characterizations would capture all the details of how the given expressions should be used or that they would be immune to error. More importantly, even if we ignore for the moment the weird Kripkensteinian hypotheses, we should note that many competent speakers on different occasions might, and actually do, violate rules of correct use. People speak ungrammatically, mix their metaphors, use idioms in wrong contexts etc. What's crucial, however, is that such linguistic misdeeds don't stop them from speaking English. The speaker who makes such mistakes still means things we normally ascribe him to.

These observations, however, lead us to the conclusion, that, even if we ignore the sceptical challenge, it is simply implausible to ascribe any strong form of knowledge about the conditions of correct use to a normal language speaker. Someone might lack both know-that (in the sense that she might be unable to produce a list of statements that would give necessary and sufficient conditions of correct use) and a strong form of know-how (in the sense that she might make mistakes, even in a systematic way) in that respect, even if it would be completely plausible to ascribe meanings to her utterances in a standard way. This person, additionally, might be also in a possession of disquotational self-knowledge about the meanings of her expressions: for example when asked what she means by "plus" she might easily say that she means plus.

How are these observations relevant to question whether semantic phenomenology provides us with knowledge that is incompatible with scepticism about meaning? Giving any satisfactory answer to Kripke's sceptic must include some account of epistemology of what we mean. But, I would insist that we must be quite modest in such an endeavour. The adequate solution should render normal speakers competent about meanings of their expressions just to the extent they really are. This is important in the context of the dialectics, as the Kripkensteinian sceptic denies the speakers any knowledge of their meanings, and since his proposal seems clearly wrong, one might feel tempted to provide the users with too much knowledge in this respect. This is what, in my opinion, goes wrong in Goff's picture.

Goff's claim seems to be that knowledge of meaning should be accounted for exclusively along phenomenological lines. We know what we mean the same way we know what we actually experience. It is important to note here that, although Goff explicitly rejects the thesis that *qualia* are the only things that are present in the consciousness (Goff 2012, p. 226), he clearly thinks that raw feels and "conceptually saturated" phenomenal states are epistemologically on par.

The problem with this equation of epistemology of meaning and of *qualia* is that it is usually assumed that we know with a great deal of certainty what phenomenal experiences we have. The supposition seems to be that if we have a certain sensation and are attentive enough to it, then we are most likely to produce a correct report about what phenomenal experience we have. Frank Jackson went goes even as far as to claim that it is logically impossible to make a mistake in such case (Jackson 1973).

This is widely considered controversial, but the weaker thesis might be safely assumed. It's not necessary for our present purposes to subscribe to any theory which explains phenomenological self-knowledge. What is important is to see is that in case of knowledge of our qualitative mental states, we are in a better epistemic position than in the case in which we try to establish the conditions of correct use of the symbols we employ.

There is an important objection lurking here, though. It might be said that once we dispose of the notion of impossibility of error in the case of knowledge about *qualia* then the situation in both cases (of meaning and *qualia*) is fairly similar. In the context of "raw" phenomenal states as well as in the context of meaning we are in a position of a fairly good epistemic access, although we must concede that error is always possible. To what an extent, it might be asked, is our situation worse when it comes to knowing what we mean?

I think there is a crucial difference here. In the case of an attempt to gain knowledge about current qualitative mental states it might be said that everything we need to achieve them, is, in a sense, in front of us. Such states are—as long as we subscribe to the most standard view—fully present in the moment we experience them and "located" in the consciousness of the subject. There is nothing over and above to them, they have no "hidden dimensions" (of course, their physical basis might be thought of as such a hidden dimension, but this basis is not what interests us when we speak about phenomenal self-knowledge).

In contrast, I would conjure that whatever it is that we gain knowledge of when we get to know the meanings of the words we use (and since the Kripkenstein's ontological problem seems to remain unsolved, we do not know what it is) we gain knowledge about something in a broad sense *external* to our present conscious states. Such a thesis is fairly obvious to anyone willing to subscribe to any form of content externalism of the type advocated by Putnam (Putnam 1975) or Burge (Burge 1979). Of course it would be highly controversial to claim that some phenomenal states might be thought of as representations of external meaning facts, and Goff explicitly claims that:

> we can accommodate Twin Earth intuitions, together with a commitment to semantic phenomenology, by distinguishing narrow semantic content from broad semantic content, and claiming that only the former is representing in perceptual experience of language (Goff 2012, p. 227).

I would claim however, that even if we are committed to the internalist framework about meaning and content we should be willing to accept that any correct vision of epistemology of meanings should be fairly modest.

The important lesson from the normativity of meaning debate is that, even if we deny that meaning is normative in any strong sense, the uses of language are assessable as correct or incorrect. And this assessment is done in relation to certain standards or norms (see e.g. Hattiangadi 2007, p. 7). For the externalist such norms are (at least partly) constituted by something which is located "outside the head", like real essences of things or social conventions. The internalist, however, wishes to understand them only by means of what's going on "in the head"; most probably she will resort to the notion of meaning-intention. But it's extremely important to notice, that, in most cases, such meaning determining acts are something that happened in the past. The standard way of presenting the Kripkenstein problem as a worry which should be taken seriously by the internalist is to put some pressure on the notion of our present use being in accordance with our past intentions (Kripke 1982, p. 8). In the internalist framework we must take past intentions into account if we are to allow the possibility of using the same symbol more than just once (which seems much like a legitimate constraint).

What Kripkensteinian sceptic is questioning is, first, our epistemic access to our past intentions, and second, more importantly, whether there is something like a "conformity" relation between past intention and present use. Neither the past intention nor this alleged conformity relation is something that might be reasonably thought of as being "in front of us" in the sense that phenomenal mental states seem to be. So both on the externalist and internalist construals the things that we need to refer to in order to asses if our use is correct are more, as it were, epistemologically distant that the *qualia* we currently experience.

It might be said here that what is on par with "raw feels" are representations of meanings not meanings themselves, so there is no problem of equating *qualia* and meanings. Still, I would claim that if we say that phenomenal states represent meanings then we ascribe language speakers too much in terms of knowledge about their meanings. If conscious episodes provided us with representations of meanings it would be hard to explain how is mistake possible. Take a clear internalistic case: let's say that by a meaning-intention I decided to call certain colour "sepia" (to borrow an example from *Philosophical Investigations*).

The possible reply is that when I, at some later point, hear the word "sepia" I have a characteristic phenomenal state of experiencing the world as meaning *sepia*. But the problematic thing is: would such an experience provide me with an answer in case I were wondering whether this word, given its meaning, can be used in a certain situation? Let's imagine that I ponder if someone using the word "sepia" to describe a black chair is still using the word correctly (although lying) or is she simply showing that she doesn't understand the word (or understands it very differently from me).

If phenomenological experiences really gave us answers to such questions then the possibility of linguistic error would be hard to imagine. We would have to somehow counter what the experience is telling us or be not attentive enough in order to make a semantic mistake. This is, in my opinion, clearly implausible. Even attentive subjects with a honest intention to use language properly aren't immune to error. Consider Kripke's example of someone who is disposed to forget to "carry" numbers while performing addition (Kripke 1982, p. 29). It is quite believable that the person in question has the appropriate phenomenological experience of meaning plus, is attentive enough to it and acts in good faith. Still, this doesn't preclude her from making a mistake, and if phenomenology provided people with knowledge about conditions of correct use, such mistake would be hard to understand.

The worry might be that I greatly exaggerate the importance of linguistic mistakes, that are, leaving the sceptical problem aside, a minor phenomenon. It is true that there is something that Crispin Wright called "positive-presumptiveness" (Wright 2001, p. 202). It means that if we lack any evidence to the contrary we should take self-ascriptions of intentions as veridical. Still, rare as mistakes might be, their very possibility is central to the notion of meaning. Consequently, any epistemology of meanings which doesn't provide us with a clear account of error must be deemed inadequate. This, I reckon, is the semantic phenomenology case.

Where does this conclusion get us? Let us remind the basic structure of the paper's argument. Kripke's sceptic's negative ontological thesis implies that there is no way of knowing what we mean. In direct contrast to the later thesis, Goff claims that semantic phenomenology provides us with representations of meanings. So one must either reject sceptical conclusion or semantic phenomenology. My claim is that we should prefer the second option, as semantic phenomenology does provide us with too optimistic view on the nature of semantic knowledge and doesn't allow enough space for linguistic error. So, the sceptic might easily remain unmoved by phenomenological considerations.

At the beginning I suggested that even though semantic phenomenology doesn't solve the sceptical problem, we might nonetheless claim that such a thing exists. Is it not contradictory? I don't think so. We might claim that when we hear the word we know (at least in our mother-tongue), our perceptual experience present us this word as having specific meaning. But saying that is a far cry from claiming that our perceptual experience *represents* this specific meaning.

In order to make this distinction clear let me gesture at some rough vision of the alternative account of the role semantic phenomenology plays in our use of language. The conscious perception of meaning we get in such episodes is something that gives us *prima facie*, defeasible reason to use the symbol in the way that strikes us as correct. And as long as we don't get any countervailing information we might take ourselves as justified in doing as we do. But this is not to say that our perception gave us *knowledge* about what we mean.

The most important thing is that the vision I suggest is perfectly compatible with the view that there are no semantic facts which could be represented. The ontological sceptic might be quite ready to admit that our linguistic action might be more or less justified given certain reasons (like our internal states, evidence from the other users of language etc.) in a similar fashion to a meta-ethical expressivist, who might be open to the possibility that we base our moral judgments on reasons.

The rule-following problem is a substantial ontological issue. If one wants to prove that there are facts determining what we mean, one must provide an account of them. Phenomenological investigations, although they are valuable in their own right, are incapable of settling the debate. The possibility that there is nothing to be represented by meaning-discourse remains open.

Acknowledgments The author thanks Alex Miller and Jedrzej Grodniewicz for their helpful comments.

References

Burge, Tyler. 1979. Individualism and the mental. *Midwest Studies in Philosophy* 4:73–121.

Davidson, Donald. 1984. First person authority. *Dialectica* 38:101–113.

Davidson, Donald. 2005. Nice dearangment of epitaphs. In Donald Davidson Truth, language and history, 89–108. Oxford: Clarendon.

Glüer, Kathrin, and Peter Pagin. 1999. Rules of meaning and practical reasoning. *Synthese* 117:207–227.

Goff, Philip. 2012. Does Mary know I experience plus rather than quus? A new hard problem. *Philosophical Studies* 160:223–235.

Hattiangadi, Anandi. 2006. Is meaning normative? *Mind and Language* 21:220–240.

Hattiangadi, Anandi. 2007. *Oughts and thoughts*. Oxford: Clarendon.

Jackson, Frank. 1973. Is there a good argument against the incorrigibility thesis? *Australasian Journal of Philosophy* 51 (1):51–62.

Kripke, Saul. 1982. *Wittgenstein on rules and private language*. Cambirdge: Harvard University Press.

McDowell, John. 1984. Wittgenstein on following a rule. *Synthese* 58:326–363.

Millar, Alan. 2002. The normativity of meaning. In *Logic, thought and language*, ed. Anthony O'Hear, 57–74. Cambridge: Cambridge University Press.

Miller, Alex and Saboohi, Ali. forthcoming. Rule-Following and Consciousness: Old Problem or New? *Acta Analytica* 1–8.

O'Callaghan, Casey. 2011. Against hearing meanings. *The Philosophical Quarterly* 61:783–807.

Putnam, Hilary. 1975. The meaning of 'meaning'. *Minnesota Studies in the Philosophy of Science* 7:131–193.

Siegel, Susanna. 2006. Which properties are represented in perception? In *Perceptual experience*, ed. Tamar Szabo Gendler and John Hawthorne, 481–503. Oxford: Oxford University Press.

Whiting, Daniel. 2007. Meaning, norms, and use: Critical notice of Donald Davidson's truth language and history. *Philosophical Investigations* 30 (2):179–187.

Wikforss, Asa. 2001. Semantic normativity. *Philosophical Studies* 102:203–226.

Wright, Cripsin. 2001. Wittgenstein's Wittgenstein's rule-following considerations and the central project of theoretical linguistics. In Crispin Wright *Rails to infinity*, 170–214. Cambridge: Harvard University Press.

Chapter 5
The Meaning of Normativity of Meaning

Leopold Hess

Abstract In the three decades since the publication of Kripke's *Wittgenstein on Rules and Private Language* the claim that the meaning of linguistic expressions should be explained in normative terms has been one of the most debated issues in the analytic philosophy of language. A line of arguing against this claim that has gained prominence in the recent years starts off with the assumption that the norms that are involved in linguistic meanings must be either constitutive or prescriptive.

It is fairly obvious that linguistic norms cannot be understood as constitutive in the simple sense in which rules of chess are constitutive: a wrong use of a word is, in many cases, still a use of this word. However, if linguistic norms are understood as prescriptive norms, serious problems arise as well. For the relevant sense of "ought" is difficult to establish. What exactly ought I do to act in accordance with the norm? Ought I use the word "green" only in reference to things that are green? This is obviously not a genuine norm, as I might just as well be joking or lying. Ought I use the word "green" only when I mean green by it? This explains nothing.

I propose an analysis of the normativity of linguistic meaning that steers free of these problems. I will argue that we should understand linguistic norms as globally, but not locally, constitutive, and that the constitutiveness of linguistic norms is grounded in the structure of interpretability of linguistic practice.

Keywords Normativity of meaning · Linguistic practice · Constitutive norms · Radical interpretation · Normative pragmatics

5.1 Introduction

In the three decades since the publication of Kripke's *Wittgenstein on Rules and Private Language* the claim that the meaning of linguistic expressions should be explained in normative terms has been one of the most debated issues in the analytic philosophy of language. Some of the main controversies in this area have been focused on questions such as whether a normative dimension is essential for

L. Hess (✉)
Uniwersytet Jagielloński, Kraków, Poland
e-mail: leopoldhess@gmail.com

M. Araszkiewicz et al. (eds.), *Problems of Normativity, Rules and Rule-Following*,
Law and Philosophy Library 111, DOI 10.1007/978-3-319-09375-8_5

meaning and determines it, or whether it is only a consequence of its more properly semantic features; whether the normativity of meaning can be accommodated within a naturalistic account of semantics, and if not, whether it makes for a case against naturalism or against normativism; what is the role of intentional concepts such as "understanding" in an account of meaning, and what is the relation between normative aspects of meaning and dispositions and regularities that can be specified in a descriptive vocabulary. However, in the recent years, a variety of arguments against the claim of normativity has gained prominence that address a more fundamental issue of what in fact the normativity of meaning *means*, i.e. what kind of norms—or what is the nature of the norms that are involved, in one way or another, in linguistic meaning[1]. Although I will not discuss any specific arguments in detail, I want to focus on the basic question, which in a simplified form can be put as follows: are linguistic norms (the norms of meaning) constitutive or prescriptive?

The two terms of this alternative are related to two historically dominant models of thinking about normativity: rules of games and moral norms. (One should note that the idea of a specific kind of *semantic* or *linguistic normativity* is a fairly recent development in modern philosophy). Constitutive norms are understood on the model of rules of games such as chess: the norm constitutes its object, defining what is and what is not to be counted as realizing it. Prescriptive norms differ from constitutive ones most clearly in that it is possible to lapse from the norm while still being subject to it. The paradigm here is provided by moral norms: even if I do actually lie, I am still subject to the norm "one ought not lie", although I violate it. By contrast, if I move a piece on the chessboard in a way that is not in agreement with the constitutive rules of the game, I am not violating the relevant constitutive norm—I am not making a move in a game of chess at all (I might be violating a different norm, though, such as the norm obligating me to try and play chess if I agreed to do it).

There is some intuitive appeal to the idea that linguistic norms are constitutive in nature and somehow resemble rules of games, especially (but not exclusively) if one thinks of meaning in terms of proprieties of use, in a Wittgensteinian or Sellarsian manner. However, as opponents of this line of thinking point out, a construal of linguistic norms as constitutive makes it difficult to explain the possibility of error—and to distinguish between a properly semantic error and an empirical error. A wrong use of a word is, in many cases, still a use of this very word. If I say "this is green" pointing at a red apple in front of me, I am making a mistake, but the word "green" has its proper meaning.

[1] Cf. Gluer and Pagin (1999); Hattiangadi (2006); Gluer and Wikforss (2009). Gluer and Pagin consider a position of the kind that is advanced here: a claim that linguistic normativity is fundamentally a matter of a practice, and only derivatively a matter of particular words or speech acts. They reject it as a solution to the problem of "rules of meaning" because in their understanding such rules must be able to occupy a "motivational" position in a schema of practical reasoning which can give the correct explanation for a given speech act. The issue of the form of practical reasoning, however, is not relevant to understanding linguistic normativity in the way I suggest here.

On the other hand, if linguistic norms are understood as prescriptive norms, serious problems arise as well. For it is difficult to establish the relevant content of a norm governing, for instance, the use of the word "green". What exactly ought I do to act in accordance with the norm? Ought I use the word "green" only in reference to things that are green? This is obviously not a genuine norm, as I might just as well be joking or lying. Ought I use the word "green" only when I mean green by it? This, of course, explains nothing.

In the present paper, I want to suggest an analysis of the normativity of meaning that steers free of these problems. I will argue that linguistic norms should be understood as constitutive, but only in a *global*, rather than local sense. The consequence of this claim is that linguistic normativity is in the first place a matter of the pragmatic and practical dimension of language, rather than its strictly semantic aspect.

5.2 Local and Global Constitutiveness

We should begin by observing that the proper focus of an investigation into linguistic normativity is on use of words and sentences insofar as they are expressions or applications of *concepts*, and not merely physical events such as uttering a sequence of sounds or making some signs on a paper. The distinction is important, because it underlies the possibility of uttering sounds that correspond to a given word or sentence without actually applying the adequate concepts: either because the sounds do not express any meaning, or, more simply, because one uses the word with an incorrect meaning. I will come back to this shortly.

As I have mentioned, the main difficulty with construing linguistic norms as constitutive is what might be called the problem of error. Let me start with a basic and simple example of an individual concept, such as the concept expressed by the word "red". There is clearly a correct way of using this word (applying this concept)—to refer to things that are red[2]—and there are also incorrect ways of using it. The same concerns a simple judgment or sentence "This is red".

At a first glance, the norm governing the use of the concept "red" is not constitutive of its object: one can use the concept incorrectly and still be taken as using it. The norm is merely regulative in this sense and it leaves room for mistake. On the other hand, however, if we consider the use of a concept in a more general way, and not just a single application of it, we can see that incorrect applications are essentially dependent on correct ones. If someone never used the concept "red" in a proper way, there would be no sense in claiming that they are using this concept at all. It would be more reasonable to assume that they express a different concept with

[2] As remarked above, this is not quite as simple—one might use the word correctly in other ways, as a joke, for instance, or a metaphor, but let it suffice for now that there are correct and incorrect ways of using it, and among the former, referring to things that are red is one, while an earnest and literal application to a thing that is not red would count as an example of the latter. I will focus here on such basic cases.

the same word, if there was some discernible pattern of its use, or if there was none, that they are not really saying anything when uttering the sound “red”. A speaker can count as using a concept, whether correctly or incorrectly, only if he or she is *able* to use it correctly. In this sense, the norm governing the use of a concept is constitutive of its object.

To resolve this ambiguity, I propose to distinguish two senses of constitutiveness: local and global. Norms involved in games like chess are locally constitutive: nothing is subject to them, unless it is in accordance with them. Norms of concept-use are only globally constitutive: some performances can be both subject to a norm and incorrect according to it, *but it is impossible for all performances subject to a norm to be incorrect.* (Moral norms, on some views at least, are not constitutive even in this sense: something might be a moral obligation even if no one has ever done it and no one ever will).

The claim that linguistic norms are globally constitutive is based on the assumption that one could not be taken to be able to use a particular concept, if one never used it correctly. However, this is plausible only insofar as we consider examples involving merely one isolated concept. Things change when we consider the use of a concept in a broader context.

Imagine that we are dealing with someone who appears to be perfectly able of speaking a language, such as English, and correctly applying many of the concepts that this language enables her to express. She has no trouble with distinguishing apples from oranges and all sorts of fruit and correctly employing a rich color vocabulary. There is nonetheless one concept, “mauve”, that she never applies correctly (or even if she sometimes does—if she says of something that it is mauve and she is right—it is rarely enough for it to count as mere luck). Does the globally constitutive character of linguistic norms entail that she is not in fact using this concept at all?

There are of course numerous real-world examples of people consistently misusing some words and in the majority of such cases we are inclined to say that they are simply using the word incorrectly—and not that they are not using this particular word at all, but only making some sounds that resemble it. It might seem to follow from this observation that norms governing the use of concepts are not even globally constitutive.

In the case of our imaginary speaker, we would, in fact, probably agree that she is applying the same concept which other people apply when they say “mauve”, but she just uses it incorrectly. It is reasonable to assume, however, that we would only think so if she used it consistently as a color-adjective, for example to describe the particular shade that the pulp of unripe bananas has. It is easy to imagine circumstances in which we would hesitate to take her utterings of “mauve” as expressing the same concept, or any concept at all: she might use it to describe tastes (“this orange is very mauve, the other one was sweeter”), or apply it as an adverb (“I ate the apple so mauve, because I was hungry”); she could deny that being mauve implies being material (“but number three is mauve!”) or that it excludes being not-mauve (“my aunt is mauve and not mauve at the same time”); she could use it to express her personal feelings towards things (“I mauve the see at night”). Finally, there could be no meaningful pattern to be discerned in her uses of "mauve" at all ("I mauve number three, my aunt, and sea at night. Oh wait, James Bond is mauve, too. And mauves are so tasty."). In all such cases we would be more or less reluctant to take this speaker's utterings of "mauve" to express an incorrect application of the same concept we associate with this word, rather than some other concept, or maybe no concept at all.

Linguistic norms can, therefore, be treated as globally constitutive, but in an even less direct (less local, as it were) way than the isolated concept example at first suggested. What constitutes an application of a concept (what makes it an application of this particular concept) is not exhausted by an isolated rule that defines its correct and incorrect uses, such as the rule that says that the concept "mauve" is correctly applied only to things that are mauve. A speaker may be taken to use a determinate concept, even if she always applies it incorrectly, provided that her applications of it meet some other conditions. In the case of "mauve" the conditions (corresponding to the examples of misuse given in the preceding paragraph) include being used as a name of a color, being used as an adjective, describing material objects, obeying the law of non-contradiction, describing objective features of objects, being used according to some consistent grammatical pattern. (This list is not exhaustive and the conditions might differ for different kinds of concepts. More importantly, there are no absolute criteria or clear-cut distinctions here: what and how many conditions have to be met for an utterance to qualify as a use of a particular concept will always depend on the context, interlocutors, and practical or theoretical interests of the inquirer or interpreter.) The more of those conditions are violated, the more the interlocutors of the speaker will be reluctant to treat her as using this particular concept or any concept at all, when she utters the sound "mauve".

The most important conclusion from this analysis is that the norm governing the use of any particular concept is essentially related to norms governing the use of other concepts. For the globally constitutive function of linguistic norms has been revealed to have a *systemic* character: whether an utterance can be taken as an application of a concept does not depend solely on the isolated norm governing the use of this concept, but also on the proprieties of use of other concepts. Similarly, whether a speaker can be taken to be able to use a particular concept, depends also on whether or not she is able to use other concepts (thus, if our speaker was able to use a rich color vocabulary reliably we would be more inclined to treat her utterances of "mauve" as applications of the corresponding concept, even if incorrect ones). An example that is a reversed version of the one just discussed should help to illuminate this. Imagine now that our speaker's use of "mauve" is flawless: she has no trouble with picking out things that are mauve, and her utterances of "mauve" are reliably co-occurring with the presence of mauve things in her visual field. But she has no color vocabulary apart from this single word and she is unable to distinguish between things of different colors, if none of them are mauve. Her interlocutors would surely be reluctant to take her utterances of "mauve" as genuine applications of the concept.

One way of explaining their reluctance would be to say that the speaker does not seem able to *understand* what she is saying when she says "mauve"—she cannot really understand what "mauve" means, if she cannot discriminate other colors and employ concepts such as "red" and "green". The same point can be made without recourse to the mentalistic vocabulary of "understands" and "means". The speaker's differential responses to things that are mauve could in fact be triggered by a property of them other than being mauve; she might, for instance, call "mauve" things that she does not deem useful—and so it happens that of all the things in her environment, she finds no use for all and only those which are mauve; or maybe she just does not like mauve things (there are, of course, infinitely many properties that are co-extensive with being mauve for any finite set of objects). Her interlocutors have no way of telling which it is. In other words, even if they can take her to be correctly applying a concept, they cannot decide which concept it is—her utterances are correct according to a norm, but which norm?

This is an instance of a familiar type of problems that pop out wherever distinguishing between coextensive properties is necessary. Therefore I shall not go into the details of an equally familiar type of solutions that involve taking into account *counterfactual* situations. Let it suffice to say that with the use of counterfactuals it is in principle possible to single out the right property: our speaker can be taken to apply the proper concept "mauve", if she would respond appropriately to all mauve things in every possible world. Any solution of this sort, however, hinges in turn on the possibility of choosing the right counterfactuals (by definition, counterfactual situations are not directly accessible). This is where the systemic aspect of the global constitutiveness of linguistic norms comes into play: what makes the interlocutors of our speaker able to decide which concept she applies when uttering "mauve" is her use of other concepts. If she were able to apply other color-concepts (doing it at least sometimes correctly) and to classify things not only into those that are mauve and not mauve, but also into things red, green and so on, there would be no reason to doubt that she is in fact using the concept "mauve". If, on the other hand, she classified things into mauve, triangular, round and square, there would be good reason to take her to be applying some kind of a shape-concept when uttering "mauve".

5.3 Normativity of Linguistic Practice

So far I have distinguished two levels at which the use of concepts is determined by (globally constitutive) norms. At a basic, atomic level, where the use of a single concept is considered in isolation, I have argued that the possibility of incorrect applications of a concept is dependent on its correct applications (a speaker needs to be able to use a concept correctly in order to count as using it, even in the instances where the application is incorrect). At a systemic level, norms governing the use of concepts are interrelated in such a way that whether some utterance can count as an application of a concept (regardless of its correctness) depends on the ability of the speaker to use other concepts. In both cases the norms in question are globally, but not locally constitutive, because incorrect performances can still be subject to the norm in question, but they are essentially dependent on the capacity for correct performances (whether in application of the same concept or of other concepts). This line of argument can be pushed further to explore the limiting conditions of the constitutive function of linguistic norms.

At the atomic level the issue at stake was whether or not an utterance is subject to a conceptual norm (and thus constitutes an application of a concept), even if it is at odds with it. At the systemic level, the question was to which norm the utterance is subject, i.e. what concept is applied in it (considering that the individuation of the norm is underdetermined by circumstances of application). A more fundamental question can be asked now: what makes a piece of behavior, such as uttering some sounds, subject to any (linguistic) norm at all?

The answer to this question cannot rely on identifying any feature of an utterance taken in isolation by virtue of which it would count as an application of a particular concept. Because of the systemic character of linguistic normativity no such feature can be sufficient, not only to determine to which norm the utterance is (supposed to be) subject, but also if it is (supposed to be) subject to any norm at all. This might be difficult to see as long as we operate on examples involving utterances such as "mauve" or "red"—anyone who speaks English naturally assumes that they do express determinate concepts, even if we might sometimes wonder if it is the correct concept that is being applied. Imagine, however, a speaker of an alien tongue that no Westerner has ever encountered before, a native of the Amazon jungle, say, or a tall Venusian passing through—who can be observed to regularly react with a vocal response, sounding something like "gavagai", to the presence of a rabbit. Confronted with such behavior, not only we could not be sure, as Quine famously argued, if the word "gavagai" means "rabbit" or "momentary rabbit-stage" or something else entirely, but *we could not even tell if it means anything at all*. "Gavagai" could be just a meaningless expression of amusement or fear (like "wow" or "yikes") or even an involuntary response: it could turn out that our Venusian friend is allergic to rabbits and what seems to us like a word is in fact the alien counterpart of a sneeze. No amount of observational data could rule out all interpretations of a pattern of behavior as a non-linguistic one. The question whether some vocal response is to be taken as an expression of a concept is *empirically underdetermined.*

There is no answer to the question what makes a piece of vocal behavior count as an application of a concept on the atomic level, then. Moving to the systemic level of linguistic practice, we can easily see that there is no answer here, either. Even if we could establish a large set of correlations between the Venusian's response-types and stimuli-types, and even if those correlations seemed to be connected by a network of relations similar to the relations that connect the use of different word-types and parts of speech in human languages, we could never rule out the possibility that this intricate pattern of behavior has in fact nothing to do with language. After all, our friend could be allergic to many different Earth-things and react to them with various, although interrelated, symptoms. The question whether something is a language or not is itself empirically underdetermined.

A more realistic example of this is provided by the problems archaeologists often have with determining whether a pattern of marks—scratches, dots or whatnot—on a millennia-old shard of pottery or a piece of bone is to be interpreted as writing. No matter how regular the marks are, it is in principle always possible that they are a result of some random natural process. "In principle", because in a particular case such possibility may be highly improbable—if the marks clearly resemble signs of a known script, are arranged in some regular manner and, most importantly, if they make sense, that is, if assigning phonemic or morphemic values to them makes them interpretable as a meaningful linguistic expression, no one will doubt that they do in fact constitute a piece of writing.

The same is true in the case of our hypothetical contact with a Venusian. After having collected enough data on the patterns of our alien friend's behavior, we could reach a point at which it would just seem implausible that what we are observing is not a linguistic behavior. There is of course no clear-cut boundary here, but there is a guiding principle: an interpretation of some behavior as language-use is preferable, if treating this behavior as linguistic is the best way to make sense of it. Therefore, the answer to the question what makes a piece of behavior subject to any linguistic norm (that is, what makes it a linguistic expression, or an application of concepts) is the fact that this piece of behavior is an element of a pattern that is best interpreted as a linguistic one, where "best interpreted as a linguistic one" means that the best way to make sense of a piece or pattern of behavior, i.e. to explain it in a coherent way, is to ascribe linguistic values to particular response-types and to interpret relations between them on the model of syntactic, semantic and pragmatic relations obtaining between elements of known languages. (This is a Davidsonian thought, of course, and so are those that follow.[3])

One immediate, and fundamentally important, consequence of this is that being subject to a linguistic norm, being a linguistic expression, is a matter of being *interpretable* as such. Thus, there is no absolute criterion here, because interpretability is essentially relative to the interests, attitudes and capacities of an interpreter—and for two reasons. First, it is the interpreter that decides whether or not some pattern of behavior bears enough similarity to a linguistic pattern, and second, the interpreter also decides which of the countless possible ways of assigning linguistic values to the elements of this pattern is the "best" one. The criteria for both decisions are relative and empirically underdetermined. Language, we might say, is in the eye of the beholder.

Another consequence of this deserves closer attention in the present context, as it bears directly on the issue of the constitutive normativity of language. Any linguistic interpretation of a piece or pattern of behavior is based on the assumption of its

[3] I make no specific references to Davidson here, but my argument, and especially the notion of interpretability is in substantial—and easily recognisable—ways indebted to some of his canonical writings on radical interpretation. See esp. Davidson (1973). Nonetheless, my position is at the same time at odds with Davidson's famous claim that "there is no such thing as language", i.e. as a conventional, normative structure of the sort that philosophers of language and linguists are concerned with. There is no space here to discuss this issue in any detail, but what I believe is lacking in Davidson's conception—and this lack motivates his radical claim—is a workable notion of a (normatively structured) practice. In the present context I assume that such a notion is at our disposal.

essential interpretability. It is a normative assumption, as it serves as a guiding principle requiring (or at least enabling) the interpreter to choose the best interpretation, i.e. the one that makes the most sense of the observed behavior. In most situations, however, the assumption is implicit and comes to the fore only when the interpretation encounters serious obstacles or its adequacy and effectiveness become doubtful. This happens when there are too many elements or features of the pattern that cannot be accommodated within the chosen interpretation (when there are too many deviations from whatever regularities the interpretation picks out as significant): for instance, the person we were trying to talk to utters indistinct syllables that could be garbled words, but they could also just be inarticulate groans. There are, of course, always some irregularities, some deviations from linguistic norms: no one's speech is flawless (in terms of both grammatical and lexical correctness, and logical relations between statements), and even if it were, letters are not ideal geometrical figures and phones are not abstract phonemes—they are concrete material objects and no two of them are perfectly alike. What is revealed in situations of a breakdown of linguistic interpretation, when irregularities achieve a critical mass and the very fact that something is a language becomes doubtful, is that, by contrast, a successful interpretation is made possible by ignoring those deviations. *In this way the assumption of interpretability is a constitutive one*: it constitutes piece or pattern of behavior, which is necessarily irregular and devious, as candidate for interpretation as an application of a linguistic norm (or a set of norms).

The constitutiveness of interpretability is not global in the same sense as that of specific linguistic norms: the "standard" of interpretability is not in force, unless what is assessed against it is taken to be actually interpretable; non-linguistic behavior is obviously not subject to any linguistic norms. Interpretability is therefore locally constitutive, or constitutive *tout court*. But it provides a basis for the globally constitutive function of linguistic norms: something can be taken as subject to a norm, even though it is incorrect according to it, because it is an element of a pattern that is essentially interpretable as a linguistic one. On the other hand, interpretability is dependent on the constitutiveness of specific norms: what makes a pattern interpretable is that its elements are to a sufficient degree correct according to some set of linguistic norms. Therefore, it is the specific linguistic norms that give content to the formal notion of interpretability.

Put like this, the notion of interpretability might seem to lead to a vicious circle: something is interpretable, if it is "correct enough", that is, if it can be interpreted in accordance with some norms. However, we should note that interpretability is not a feature of linguistic expressions considered discretely, but of language as such, taken in its totality. Of course, particular expressions can be interpreted even when considered in complete isolation, but only because they belong to a broader linguistic *practice*. This is easily seen from the examples considered here. That the speaker who has difficulties with the word "mauve" can be taken to be applying the proper concept, although incorrectly, depends on the fact that the concept is correctly applied by uttering the same word by other people. The marks on a shard of pottery found in an ancient grave can be interpreted as writing only if they can be taken to express words of a language (whether the language is known to the researchers or not).[4] And likewise, we would have no reason to treat any piece of the behavior of a guest from Venus as linguistic expressions, until we had reason to think that our extraterrestrial friend is using a language at all. Only then we could start deciphering which of the Venusian's performances have a linguistic meaning and what their meaning is. It is primarily a *practice* that is interpretable as linguistic, and the interpretability of particular performances that belong to the practice is only derivative.

Conclusion

I have argued that linguistic norms should be construed as constitutive (rather than prescriptive), but only in a very specific and nuanced sense. They are only globally constitutive, insofar as the possibility of performances being incorrect with respect to a norm (but still subject to it) is essentially dependent on other performances being correct—whether with respect to the same norm (at the atomic level of language), or to other norms (at the systemic level). However, the most important conclusion of this argument is that linguistic normativity (on both levels) is not primitive, but it is derived from normative features of a linguistic practice as such. The most important feature of language that can be properly characterized as a normative one is, therefore, its interpretability as such.

References

Davidson, Donald. 1973. Radical interpretation. *Dialectica* 27:313–328.
Gluer, Katrin, and Peter Pagin. 1999. Rules of meaning and practical reasoning. *Synthese* 117:207–227.
Gluer, Katrin, and Asa Wikforss. 2009. Against content normativity. *Mind* 118:31–70.
Hattiangadi, Anandi. 2006. Is meaning normative? *Mind & Language* 21:220–240.

[4] This example reveals an important feature of the notion of interpretability that has to be kept in mind here: interpreting something as a linguistic behavior does not necessarily imply understanding it. Archaeologists and linguists can identify documents of the linear A script without being able to decipher them or knowing much about the so-called Eteocretan language in which they were supposedly written. Likewise, when new native communities are discovered in the Amazon, it is (quite naturally) presumed that they speak a language often long before the language itself is understood. Recognizing that something is a language, i.e. that it is a practice characterized by the right kind of normativity, is conceptually and at times chronologically prior to understanding it, i.e. understanding the particular norms that govern the practice.

Chapter 6
On the Kantian Answer to "Kripkenstein"'s Rule-following Paradox

Przemysław Tacik

Abstract This chapter aims to put Saul Kripke's formulation of Wittgensteinian rule-following paradox in the context of Kant's critical philosophy. I attempt to argue that a thorough re-examination of the Kantian critique can contribute to our better understanding of this paradox, because Kant himself strove to overcome a parallel form of scepticism—Hume's. Moreover, I seek to demonstrate that Kantian views on normativity may contribute to avoiding the consequences of "Kripkenstein"'s radicalism without a simultaneous refutation of its main premises. Taking the inter-linking between Hume's and Kripkenstein's thinking for a starting point, I attempt to reformulate Kantian arguments against Humean scepticism so that they could be applied to Kripkenstein's paradox. These reflections are organised around two main ideas of Kant's *Critique*: (1) arguments against the assumption of discontinuity of time; (2) the existence of two formal instances guaranteeing the coherence of experience: namely the "thing-in-itself" and the transcendental unity of apperception (TUA). Reassessment of the Kantian concept of the TUA gives an opportunity to propose a new perspective on normativity, whose core mechanism would lie in our readiness to correct ourselves. Finally, I juxtapose "Kripkenstein" and "Kant-stein"—the latter being Kripke's imaginary opponent, who accepts some premises of the rule-following paradox, yet puts them in a broader context which explains our effective usage of rules.

Keywords Wittgenstein · Kripke · Kant · Rule-following paradox · Normativity

6.1 Introduction

The famous book by Saul Kripke (1982) reassured Wittgenstein's position as one of the leading sceptics in twentieth century philosophy. "Kripkenstein"'s paradox poses a challenge to our previous understanding of rule-following and normativity in general, as much as Hume's scepticism posed a threat to pre-Kantian metaphysics. This comparison between both philosophers should not be taken for accidental:

P. Tacik (✉)
Jagiellonian University of Cracow, Kraków, Poland
e-mail: przemyslaw.tacik@gmail.com

M. Araszkiewicz et al. (eds.), *Problems of Normativity, Rules and Rule-Following*,
Law and Philosophy Library 111, DOI 10.1007/978-3-319-09375-8_6

not only both of them dealt a blow to their respective intellectual traditions, but—moreover—their sceptical paradoxes are marked by profound structural affinities. As I will attempt to demonstrate, Kripkenstein's paradox is much closer to Hume's scepticism than Kripke himself was willing to admit.

However, the mere comparison between Hume and Wittgenstein would not be particularly fruitful if a reference to Immanuel Kant were omitted. Kantian critique, born of the turmoil caused by Hume's scepticism, attempted to overcome obstacles posed by the legacy of the Scottish philosopher. It would be difficult nowadays to read Hume without making references to Kant. If Hume and Wittgenstein effectively share some basic intuitions, then interpreting the latter with no attention to Kantianism would be equally one-sided. Yet somehow we read Wittgenstein without Kant—and even Wittgenstein himself, although well-versed in Kantianism (at least in the period of *Tractatus*, when he read *The Critique of Pure Reason* extensively)—did not recognise how Kant's philosophy could be juxtaposed with his sceptical discoveries. If Hume's paradoxes met with a thorough reassessment by Kant—who generally accepted Humean premises but aimed to prove them incomplete—should not we expect that Kripkenstein's paradox could be solved with Kantian-like argumentation? Finally, some of Wittgensteinian remarks follow in Kant's footsteps, albeit implicitly and—in all probability—unintentionally. Therefore it seems reasonable to retrace the path from Hume to Kant in order to shed new light on the Kripkenstein's paradox.

Being convinced that the reconstruction of the Kantian background of this paradox can contribute to its re-examination, I will aim to apply Kant's thinking to Wittgensteinian terms and re-read Kripkenstein in a new context.[1] Firstly, I am going to outline some basic affinities between Hume's and Wittgenstein's scepticisms.

6.2 Relations Between Hume's and Wittgenstein's Scepticism

Let us begin by juxtaposing Hume and Wittgenstein in their respective formulations of sceptical paradoxes.

[1] My exposition—drawing chiefly upon Kant's *The Critique of Pure Reason*—converges in some regards with arguments developed by other commentators of Kripke. It should be of no surprise because the debate on "Kripkenstein" retraces old discussions on Hume and Kant. In some way I propose explicitly Kantian solution of the paradox, whereas manifold arguments in a Kantian spirit have been already formulated. P.G. Baker and P.M.S. Hacker reconsidered the scope of "blindness" of rule application and re-assessed the idea of grasping a rule in the logic of Kantianism (Baker and Hacker 1984, pp. 76–84). Colin McGinn (1984, p. 146 ff.), who suggested that rule-application might be viewed in terms of concepts—which changes the preservation of meaning of rules in time—makes an implicit reference to Kant. However, due to the limited length of this paper, I cannot refer to Baker's, Hacker's and McGinn's arguments. I will concentrate on applying Kant's reasoning to Kripkenstein's paradox.

6.2.1 Old and New Scepticism of Hume

The focal point of Hume's legacy is his critical reassessment of causality. It is well-known that he vigorously opposed causality construed as the necessary linkage between events (Hume 1992; Sect. VII).[2] In his opinion, what we perceive as relations between causes and effects boils down to our mere habit. Since we observe regularities in the functioning of nature, we tend to treat them—with no sufficient reason—as if they were necessary. Yet in truth there is no objective link between them and only our remembrance of past event sequences leads us to consider them intertwined. This argumentation, recited incessantly by new generations of philosophy students, is surprisingly more inspiring than its reverent status would suggest. Under close scrutiny it reveals its further consequences. According to Hume, the idea of causality stems from our memory: we remember past accidents and infer from them how causal links will work in the future (Hume 1739, pp. 40–93). If so, the only truly grounded empirical data must come from the present. As a consequence, even the most reliably observed and logged experience that already belongs to the past cannot be fully trusted.[3] Even the most inevitable experience that will happen in the future cannot be relied upon, since it does not happen here and now. In a nutshell, for Hume all the past is nothing but our recollection; all the future—nothing but our anticipation. Naturally, it does not mean that thinking of past and future events should be discarded altogether; yet they should be treated with scepticism grounded in the recognition of the primary role of the present.

The above formulated interpretation of Hume's sceptical paradox, based on a literal reading, is definitely bold, but it leads to a dead end: this scepticism must set aside its reservations and settle for practical everyday life, in which we act without persistent conscience of the groundlessness of our actions. Here we encounter the first affinity with Kripkenstein's paradox, whose practical consequences equally boil down to nothing. However, in order to explore further analogies between Hume and Kripkenstein, it is necessary to develop a more radical form of Humean scepticism. Let us then set aside references to Kripkenstein for a moment and try to change the perspective on Hume's paradox.

[2] As it is not the focal point of my argumentation, I will not discuss various interpretations of Humean theory of causality, which are abundant. Equally I set aside Hume's category of "relation of ideas", similar to analytical statements, which provide legitimate knowledge with no reference to empirical data.

[3] Hume comes to a conclusion that memory and imagination are effectively of the same nature and the only difference between them consists in liveliness of perceptions that memory presents (Hume 1739, pp. 49–50). "As an idea of the memory can by losing its force and liveliness degenerate so far that it is taken to be an idea of the imagination, so on the other hand an idea of the imagination can acquire such force and liveliness that it passes for an idea of the memory and has a counterfeit effect on belief and judgment." (Hume 1739, p. 50). Whereas there is no qualitative difference between memory and imagination, such a difference exists between memory and present impressions. As a consequence, present impressions constitute a privileged source of knowledge. If we do not experience hallucinations, imagination cannot produce impressions equally convincing as our senses.

This "new" Humean scepticism concerns the relation between time and validity of statements. If we attribute the privileged position to the present, as Hume did, time cannot be deemed continuous. There are myriads of moments which already happened, there are numerous moments which are yet to come, but there is always only one moment of the present. And only this one gives empirical support to our statements because even the best observed events from the past are now our recollection, which cannot be unconditionally trusted. But is it only this support that must necessarily pass, or *also the statement itself?* If I see a bird right now and I write down on a scrap of paper a statement: "I see a bird now", does this statement—formulated, let's say, at a moment t_1—belong to the past at a moment t_2? Does it pass? Or does it remain indefinitely valid? If the bird I referred to is still there at a moment t_2 and I say to myself: "I see a bird now" again, *is it the same statement? Or is it different?* Did the first statement pass with the moment in which it was formulated?

We are accustomed to perceive our judgements as independent from their concrete temporal pronouncements and believe in their abstract, atemporal validity. But if we reconsider Hume's paradox profoundly, we would have to conclude that there is nothing in language that would immunise it against the disastrous impact of time. Why would the empirical perceptions have to pass, whereas our statements—which do not exist without some empirical manifestation—would remain untouched and still valid? If only present perceptions are of any value in justifying our knowledge, as Hume assumed, then also past statements cannot be effectively reproduced in the present. If I read now my notes I jotted down an hour ago, I should not be misled that only the circumstances I referred to at that time are gone; on the contrary—*the very statement passed.* If so, what do I read now? Another statement, which I formulate currently, with only dim *recollection* of some past act of writing.

In this radicalisation of Humean scepticism, which challenges our approach to language, all statements belong to moments of their formulation and irrevocably pass with them. Statements are not only irretrievable, but there is no method of verifying their mutual conformity. I cannot say that some past sentences, for instance *p* and *q*, are identical, because by saying so I do not refer to them but to some *p'* and *q'* that I have just created. The moment I utter such a sentence, let's say *s*, it also belongs to the past and cannot be retrieved. It seems as if all my knowledge were reconstituted in the present, maybe in identical sentences (which I cannot ascertain), but definitely not the same. Yet this scepticism goes even further. If only currently formulated statements are fully legitimate and only those which relate to present impressions, then all our statements on past and future events are worthless. They might be pronounced or even believed, but nothing guarantees their reliability. Present statements are not valid for other moments of time, at least in terms of philosophical grounding.

What emerges from these questions could be described metaphorically as "the solipsism of the present". Only in the present and on the present could we formulate justified statements; speaking about the past or the future, although customary, would have no actual validity. Even though we tend to perceive time as a continuous sequence of equal units which we know from recollection or anticipation, only the shifting moment of the present would be the real moment of time.

6.2.2 Kripkenstein's Paradox in Humean Approach

After we have thus re-interpreted Hume, let us see whether a similar procedure might be applied to Wittgenstein *in Kripke's exposition* ("Kripkenstein").[4] Kripkenstein might formulate an analogous paradox, although applied not to affirmative statements, but to normative ones.

Kripkenstein's paradox, to recapitulate it very briefly, concerns the usage of a rule in two different moments (cf. Kripke 1982, pp. 7–54). Let us name them t_1 and t_2. How can I be sure, asks Kripke after Wittgenstein, that if I constructed my rule at the moment t_1, its meaning is preserved at the moment t_2, when I apply it to a new case? How can I pose a link between what I meant in the past—and the current usage of my rule? Apparently there is no "fact", as Kripke holds, that guarantees this meaning. Consequently, even though we project the use of a rule onto all future moments, nothing can guarantee the identity of a rule in its future applications. It is almost as if the time elapsing between two moments—of laying down a rule and its application—exerted a disastrous impact on the continuity of this rule in time[5]. At the moment of their formulation rules seem unproblematic, but as soon as this moment passes, their meaning starts to lack stability. Do they not resemble Humean statements in their link with the time of their creation?

Kripke acknowledges an evident analogy between Hume and Wittgenstein, yet for some reason he does not follow the path that this remark might open (Kripke 1982, pp. 62–64; cf. also McGinn 1984, p. 86). Let me then radicalise this analogy and suggest a conviction that both philosophers seem to share. Humean conception of causality and of the human self (which allegedly is nothing but a stream of changing impressions), as well as the Wittgensteinian rule-following paradox might be reasonably associated with both philosophers' views on relations between time and

[4] I set aside the question in which respects "Wittgenstein's paradox as it struck Kripke" corresponds to real Wittgenstein's views. My re-assessment of the paradox concerns the former. Moreover, I refrain from wider references to other commentators as they do not contribute substantially to the development of the Kantian answer to Kripkenstein.

[5] Naturally, to seek the core of Kripkenstein's paradox in the problem of continuity of rules in time remains a controversial and selective interpretative option. I am well aware that the paradox might be interpreted differently—for instance Crispin Wright attempted to demonstrate that it concerns not fixing meaning in time, but fixing it at all (Wright 1984). However, the temporal aspect of the paradox is clearly manifest in the original exposition by Kripke, who neatly separates the *current* application from the *past* formulation of a rule ("was there some past fact about me—what I 'meant' by plus—that mandates what I should do now?" asks Kripke (1982, p. 15). Other commentators—such as G.P. Baker, P.M.S. Hacker (1984, p. 27, 65) and Colin McGinn (1984, pp. 140–147)—also highlight the temporal aspect of the paradox in Kripke's formulation. I am convinced that "Kripkenstein's paradox" does not have one coherent formulation, but resembles a bundle of multiple inextricably intertwined paradoxes. It might be then justified to go in different ways and reduce the initial set of questions to various "subparadoxes". Wright's comments on McGinn, which aim at abstracting from the temporal aspect in favour of the general problem of meaning, is one of them. Nevertheless, it does not exclude other formulations. In this light I feel entitled to concentrate solely on the temporal aspect, bearing in mind that my reasoning is equivalent to constructing a new "subparadox".

language. *For both of them, time works against validity of statements and stability of meaning*. Interestingly, this effect of time does not manifest itself clearly: we speak about the past and the future, we read past writings, we lay down rules that will be followed in the future—with little concern about the justification of such actions. However, philosophical analysis reveals that no argument can support our expectation about future causal relations. Analogously, no fact guarantees that the rule currently applied remains identical with the one we established in the past.

To sum up these intuitions in one formula, one could say that for Hume and Kripkenstein there is no philosophical grounding that would assure preservation of validity of statements in time, either affirmative or normative ones. As long as the sceptical approach is adopted, continuous validity of statements (and rules) remains inexplicable. Yet in practice we assume that time is continuous and statements conserve their meanings. Both Hume and Kripkenstein are then tempted to accept a similar sceptical dualism between common practice and theoretical lack of justification. Both resort to acknowledging "blind action" that philosophy has to settle for. Nevertheless, we are unable to select one single "fact" that would accompany two separate moments and account for causality or stability of meaning.

6.3 Kant as a Critic of Kripkenstein

Once the link between Hume and Wittgenstein becomes apparent, we can return to Kant and ask how his anti-Humean critique could contribute to better understanding of Kripkenstein's paradox. I will select two main themes of Kantian critique and apply them to Kripkenstein's scepticism.

6.3.1 Continuity of Time and Rule-Following

Kant clearly identified the underlying presupposition of Humean sceptical paradox, namely the problem of continuity of time. As I suggested above, the ultimate consequence of Hume's critique of causality would be the following: only the present can be described in a justified manner, since only then do we perceive impressions which are substantially different from unreliable imagination or memory. Humean time lacks continuity, as the past and the future are only our recollections or anticipations in the present. Consequently, certainty concerns only present impressions and statements which are currently formulated on them.

In his "Transcendental Æsthetic", the opening part of *The Critique of Pure Reason*, Kant argues against selecting the present as the only legitimate form of time (cf. Kant 1855, pp. 28–35). In short, he points to the fact that time constitutes the ultimate "container" for all events—that is the only dimension in which all events can be compared (in terms of anteriority and posteriority). The following example will elucidate this argument. Contradictory statements, such as "It is raining" and "It is not raining" cannot be pronounced simultaneously with full assertion. We need to choose either of them, depending on the weather outside. Consequently, I cannot say "It is raining. It is not raining" and claim I speak the truth. However, once we differentiate moments of pronouncements of these statements, they might stand within the same narrative without contradiction (*p* can be true in t_1, whereas non-*p* in t_2). For instance, if I look from my window at noon, I might say "It is raining" and 1 h later I might say "It is not raining". Then the sentence "At noon I had said it had been raining and 1 h later I said it was not raining" is not contradictory. Thus differentiation in time allowed me to juxtapose in one narrative statements of apparent contradiction. Consequently, time provides the most basic framework organising our experience coherently.

Moreover, as Kant argues, time constitutes simultaneously the ultimate background onto which we can project all that happens—and it is the only one common frame of reference for all events. We might imagine events of which we would have no knowledge; there might be experiences that are inexplicable or indescribable, for which we would not be able to find any general term. We can imagine events so unique that they virtually transcend the scope of our experience. Yet even then there is one frame of reference that such events must belong to: time. *We cannot imagine an event that would not happen in time.* There are no impressions that could be experienced in some atemporal state. Naturally, we might lose consciousness of time (e.g. as a result of some accident or illness), but the event as such cannot be imagined as not linked with some period of time in which it happened.

Hence all human experience—however diverse it would be—can be organised within one temporal frame of reference. Furthermore, Kant argues that there is only one such a frame. Multiple "times" do not exist (I set aside the metaphorical use of this term), as they would have to be compared themselves within some "meta-time", encompassing them all—while this "meta-time" would be nothing but time as such. At any rate, it would be necessary to conceive time as one frame of reference. This argumentation might be divergent with the notion of time elaborated by post-Newtonian physics, but it describes the time we effectively experience. Our notion of temporality demands that there be one, all-encompassing sequence within which everything can be compared, at least in terms of anteriority and posteriority. This argument challenges Humean scepticism in both forms—original, against which it was propounded, and the above-mentioned. According to Kant, *the present is not the only moment of "real" time, because it can be perceived inasmuch as it is set against the whole temporal sequence. Once we acknowledge the present, we have already assumed all history of which the present is a part.* It is not that the past and the future are some flawed versions of the present and the present could be neatly separated from them. The past and the future equally belong to one temporal sequence, without which the present could not be experienced at all.

It is crucial to remember that Kant does not consider Humean paradox senseless, but he tries to challenge it by putting it in the context of our effective experience. Therefore he does not negate that from a purely abstract point of view there are no objective links between the past, the present and the future. He only claims that *we must perceive them as belonging to one temporal sequence, because if we did not, our experience would be nothing but a chaotical stream of always present impressions*. Bringing order into impressions means that they first need to be organised within the temporal frame of reference, which allows to compare them.

This concept was further explored in "Transcendental Analytic", the middle part of *The Critique*, which propounds more arguments against the discontinuity of time (Kant 1855, pp. 54–106). Let us start by remarking that Kant refutes Humean passivity of human senses. If our perception were only receptive, claims Kant, we would not recognise any objects, but chaotical impressions. This leads us to assuming that perception must actively form empirical data. How does it work? In a nutshell, time provides the most general framework for all impressions, which lose their absolute incomparability—that Hume assumed all too precipitately. Impressions experienced at different moments are not completely disparate because our perception assumes continuity of time. Thus basically reduced and sequentialised, impressions are subject to synthesis. Synthesis turns separate, but already comparable sensations into objects and allows us to name them. As a result, we do not perceive mere colourful stains and dispersed sounds, but recognise objects once these impressions reach our senses. Moreover, we can recognise them only when we assume that they do not change against the laws which form our knowledge. If gold, for example, changed its form in a radical and unpredictable manner, we would not be able to refer to gold as such.

The most significant consequence of this theory is that we can perceive present impressions only through a whole system of experience, which assumes continuity of time and stability of relations between names and objects. Kant does not presume that time is "truly" continuous. On the contrary, he underlines that experience is possible only when we approach impressions with such a set of presuppositions. No philosophical argument could support them, yet they turn out necessary for our knowledge, being generated retrospectively by the fact that our experience already works.

Let us now proceed to explain how Kant's argument could contribute to understanding of Kripkenstein's paradox. Kripkenstein—*in the above radicalisation*—follows in Hume's footsteps when he sets the current application of a rule as the only decisive moment. Past formulation of this rule remains relevant inasmuch as we apply it now. It is almost as if rules did not extend naturally their validity for all future applications, but were only *referred to* from a standpoint of the present. Current application virtually reconstitutes the rule, whose effective content becomes dependent on our present decision; "past content", if such a realistic term should be applied at all, remains inaccessible. In this vision the past is not binding as external to the present, but it is only a recollection entirely governed by laws of the present. As a consequence, *the present application would have no external point of reference and continuity of rules would be unverifiable.*

How could Kant oppose such a view? Firstly, he would point out that even when we apply a rule currently, we necessarily assume a continuous temporal sequence between the moment when the rule was laid down and the moment of its application. The mere distinction between the rule and its application entails this underlying presupposition: laying down a rule means that potentially it might be applied at least once, at a different moment. Hence the very concept of the rule is inextricably linked with the assumption of continuity between the moment of its formulation and the moment of its application. Consequently, the present is not privileged within the mechanism of rule-application. A given case never appears to us as "a case in itself", namely as a situation radically incomparable with past ones. On the contrary, it is always already perceived in the context of rules under which it might be subsumed. Continuous temporal sequence, in which past moments of rule-formulation and rule-applications are perceived as similar to the present moment of application, must be assumed if we are to have the very idea of a rule.

It is true, as Kripke argues that there is no fact which would guarantee the conformity of meanings of my rule in the past and now. There is no "objective" or "external" point of reference which would allow me to determine whether I apply my rule in the same way I did back then. Yet by applying a rule, I necessarily *assume* such external point: past applications. Even if this past application is just a dim recollection, or even worse—if it is an imagination—I have to consider it independent from my current will. Thus I create a minimal distance between past applications and the present one, a distance framed by the temporal sequence. *In this distance lies the binding instance of normativity*. As a result, I do not perceive the present as if it were the only real moment of time, over which my will would have absolute jurisdiction. The present—and my applying of a rule—becomes just a point of the continuous axis of time. All discrepancy between past and present applications disappears. Therefore, by applying a rule, I assume necessary continuity between the history of all (not only mine) applications of this particular rule and my present act.[6]

Finally, it would be misleading to challenge normativity—as Kripke did—by pointing to the fact that rules aspire to determining all future cases whereas they have been applied only a finite number of times (Kripke 1982, p. 18). On the contrary, once we establish a rule, it determines the whole context in which a given case is perceived. Hence rules cannot be opposed to a "finite number of cases", because *the very possibility of perceiving a finite number of cases assumes their continuity, which emerges only when a rule already works*. Rules establish a *potential* infinity of their applications. Therefore when a rule is applied, we should not compare the present case with a limited amount of past cases. The rule is not inferred from them, but it has always determined their position as cases. Kripke's stark nominalism in fact totally excludes the normative factor and leads to a perception of cases as completely independent from rules and not affected by them. It seems to preserve the idea of a rule, but rejects its consequences—hence the paradox.

Nonetheless it should be claimed that the application of a rule to a given case sets this case not against a limited range of singular and equal past cases, but against the whole potential infinity that the rule assumes. The rule does not emerge from a finite number of cases, just as the *possibility* of a temporal sequence does not emerge

[6] It is worth noting that in this Kantian approach we do not compare the present application and "real" past applications, which are inaccessible. We only juxtapose the present with its own record of past applications. Yet this record cannot be changed at will and continuity must be assumed.

from the units of this sequence. On the contrary, the assumption of a rule precedes its cases. Therefore it seems reasonable to claim that *the act by which a rule is laid down changes fundamentally the position of a case*. Clearly I draw here upon Kant's so-called Copernican revolution: just as the subject in the Kantian critique becomes a new starting point around which objects start to revolve, so does the rule change the role of its cases. Not accidentally, Kant's thought concerns epistemology as well as normativity and poses epistemological questions in normative terminology.

It should not be claimed, however, that Kant would accept any "objective" ground for rule application or a factor which would guarantee the stability of meaning. On the contrary, his critique seems to fully acknowledge Humean scepticism, yet it attempts to prove that Hume's presuppositions cannot be articulated in a justified manner. The same applies to the Kantian answer to Kripkenstein. *The mere fact that we formulate the rule-following paradox forces us to presume that time is continuous and that rules conserve their meanings*. Therefore, we must contradict ourselves. Kant would not claim that there is an objective fact which guarantees the stability of rules. However, he would point to the fact that we necessarily assume this stability, as it is inherent in the concept of rules. Therefore it is not possible to claim, as Kripke did, that due to the lack of an objective guarantee of meanings rules are followed blindly. We cannot speak about the lack of this stability, because we assume the contrary. *Thus we are unable to refer to our "blindness"*. It is not that practice works, however blindly, while theory cannot account for normativity and reveals its lack of justification. Even theory cannot point to this blindness, because it lies beyond our experience.

6.3.2 Transcendental Unity of Apperception as an Instance of Normativity

One of the most significant, though somewhat obscure parts of *The Critique of the Pure Reason* concerns the so-called "transcendental unity of apperception" (Kant 1855, pp. 81–96). It is a key factor in the synthesis of perceptions. We would perceive nothing but a blind play of representations—claims Kant—if it was not for this transcendental unity. However, I will argue that this concept might be very fruitful beyond the epistemological context—namely in explaining the functioning of normativity. I will also demonstrate how it can contribute to solving Kripkenstein's paradox.

Let us start by reconstructing the original role of the transcendental unity of apperception. Kant argues that experience requires a basic stable framework of reference, against which we recognise new phenomena. This framework does not come from objective "reality", but constitutes a key assumption making experience possible. We are inevitably forced to assume that phenomena are not disparate, but internally linked—and that there is some inner necessary element, let us call it "X", which accounts for this link. This "X", the famous "thing-in-itself", *is nothing but an empty remainder that our cognition puts into phenomena to make them coherent.* This element guarantees that different perceptions are attributed to one object. Yet Kant makes a step further and claims that this "X" does not come from consciousness. It corresponds to some deeper, inaccessible faculty—namely the transcendental unity of apperception[7]. Consciousness functions within a field already determined by the TUA and finds its "objects" divided into two categories: phenomena and "things-in-themselves". Just as "things-in-themselves" correspond to the activity of the TUA, so does consciousness correspond to phenomena. Therefore the split of object strictly matches the split of subject into consciousness and the TUA.

The TUA functions for consciousness just like the empty "X" for phenomena: it guarantees its unity. Both phenomena and consciousness are changeable and chaotical—but as soon as they are "projected" upon some unknown, purely formal and unchangeable element, they form a coherent whole. As a consequence, however, "pure data"—as well as our self—become inaccessible to perception. In Kant's view, "things-in-themselves" and the TUA—which split objects and the human self—are the inevitable price for the coherence of perception. Without them Hume's vision would come true, making experience chaotical, unpredictable and perpetually trapped in the present.

Let us now return to Kripkenstein's paradox. Kant's argumentation might be reconsidered as concerning not perception, but norms. In this version it may be applied to the rule-following paradox in three regards. Firstly, it might explain why Kripke felt compelled to seek some "fact" that would guarantee how the rule will be applied in the future (Kripke 1982, p. 108). Such searches are inconclusive as all potential candidates must be refuted; yet the paradox prompts us to seek them nonetheless. Kantian critique sheds some light on this mechanism. If some "X" is necessary to make impressions coherent, why could not we suppose that *a formal element must be assumed in order to link disparate cases and turn them into a set of applications of the same rule?* If for Kant the very possibility of recognising different phenomena as appearances of the same object necessitates the existence of some "X"—which transcends the phenomenal level and links its disparate points—is it not plausible that rules contain something more than the sum of their application? This "more" would be Kripkenstein's sought-after "fact". If so, Kripke would misinterpret the impossibility of its finding. We cannot pinpoint this normative "X", but such impossibility is not tantamount to reducing rules to their applications. *The irreducible gap that we hopelessly strive to bridge with some "fact" is exactly what separates rules from their applications.* In conclusion, Kripke followed the right path in search of his "fact", but he did not recognise that this very search—inevitably inconclusive—is already normativity itself at work.

Secondly, Kantian concept of the transcendental unity of apperception might account for a specific way of reasoning that Wittgenstein adopted. While remaining a staunch anti-introspectionist, he constantly investigated the status of mental states. It is almost as if he assumed their existence only to dismiss them in confrontation with linguistical practice. In his examples these mental states first appear

[7] In the following part of the text I will use the abbreviation TUA.

as real, subjective and incommunicable (in sentences like "You will never know whether I feel pain now"), but are later revealed to be dependent on an intersubjective communication ("pain" is meaningful only if it belongs to linguistical practice, e.g. if it is used in situations where somebody flinches or wriggles from pain and uses this word). However, if meaning can be so easily uncovered as equivalent to usage, why do we tend to imagine that some inner mental faculty provides a definitive criterion of correct applications of terms? Why do we think of meaning as linked to subjective mental states? The transcendental unity of apperception applied to normative statements might contribute to answering these questions. Perhaps the TUA, being a formal condition of stability and coherence of norms in their various applications, misleads us here. Symmetrically to the role of normative "X" (Kripke's "fact") for rules as such, the TUA would make us believe that *there is something in our minds that decides definitively on word usage*. The TUA would be here equivalent to an illusion of direct, self-contained and unquestionable perception (e.g. of pain), which is always possible and always present.[8] If such an illusion is accepted, all words referring to feelings and sensations are used accurately on the condition of their conformity with subjective certainty. Thus language would lose its intersubjective character, being only a "copy" of mental states.

Wittgenstein vigourously opposed such a vision of language, but effectively he could not do away with mental states completely. If we apply Kantian argumentation to this issue, we might conclude that the TUA, albeit unfathomable, cannot be removed. Perhaps its functioning accounts for the ineradicable tendency to find a condition of word usage in mental states, imagined as always present and directly perceptible.

Thirdly and most importantly, Kantian idea of the division of subject sheds light on the pivotal moment of Wittgenstein's thinking. The paragraph 202 of *Philosophical Investigations* reads:

> And hence also 'obeying a rule' is a practice. And to think one is obeying a rule is not to obey a rule. Hence it is not possible to obey a rule 'privately': otherwise thinking one was obeying a rule would be the same thing as obeying it (Wittgenstein 1974, §. 202).

Kripke draws upon this quote in his formulation of the argument against a private language (1982, p. 110). I am convinced, however, that Kantian critique allows of reworking this argument. According to Kripke no individual, *considered* in isolation, could be described as obeying a rule. Rule-application requires support of community—providing the assessment concerning correctness of application—in order to function. Thus Kripke transposes the difference between rules and private language onto the gap between community and individuals. Hence some tricky awkwardness of his reasoning: Kripke must explain why Robinson Crusoe could obey rules in seclusion. Being deprived of community assessment, Crusoe would never have true rules but some private pseudo-rules. In order to avoid this consequence, Kripke claims that a private language does not involve *physical isolation*

[8] Originally Kant described the TUA exactly in this way, claiming that it is some inner awareness of us thinking, present even when we are not conscious of it. Thus the TUA always refers impressions to us perceiving them.

but *considering* the act of rule application regardless of any community assessment. Crusoe might live on a desert island, but still—when we think about him—he is put in the context of community, which might verify his rule-following.[9]

The shift in the meaning of community that Kripke proposed makes this concept more dubious than ever. What is its status? Is it a real group of people? Does the rule have to be effectively followed in this community, or is it only abstract verification that matters? Maybe it is an imaginary group of men and women? Or is it just a mode in which rule-following is assessed, a *possibility* of putting someone's applications of a rule in the context of *potential* assessment, regardless of actual practice? Or, finally—extrapolating Colin McGinn's hints (1984, pp. 67, 189)[10]—is it some kind of community between applications of a rule, not between people?

Kantian critique might provide an answer here. Kant assumes that *the perceiving subject is split into consciousness and the transcendental unity of apperception*. The latter is this mysterious instance that provides stability of experience. In the logic of the previous reasoning, it might also be interpreted as the instance of normativity. If so, the subject would be divided into two faculties: conscious and normative. Before I try to develop this suggestion, I propose to identify Kripke's "community" with this normative faculty. It would no longer have to be associated with any kind of real community, but would be equivalent to the instance of normativity in the subject. *Therefore, as long as the subject remains internally split, it has its "community" within itself.*

The split of subject into two instances would mean that consciousness (and conscious application of rules) is not self-contained. It always refers to some inner, purely formal faculty which guarantees the continuity of rule-applications. As a consequence, even if I follow a rule in complete privacy, consciousness is not the same instance that both applies this rule and assesses its correctness.

This assumption sheds new light on Wittgenstein's intuitions concerning the private language. He seemed to suggest that thinking about obeying a rule and obeying a rule converge in privacy. Yet effectively, even in complete seclusion they might remain separate. *They would converge only if I lost my internal reference to the instance of normativity and were able to change at will the assessment it gives*. In this case I would arbitrarily change the content of my rule and would not be aware thereof. I would then claim that the meaning of the rule has always remained the

[9] Kripke writes: "*if* we think of Crusoe as following rules, we are taking him into our community and applying our criteria for rule following to him" (1982, p. 110).

[10] Baker and Hacker noted that community consent is not equivalent to the correctness of rule application (1984, p. 75). Kripke's community could not be then identified with a real group of people. McGinn pointed to the fact that even if my community—construed as a real group of people—produces a unanimous judgment on the correct application of a rule, nothing guarantees that this judgment would be in line with past applications (McGinn 1984, p. 189). The community itself cannot avoid Kripkenstein's scepticism. McGinn uses this argument to argue for a possibility of individual application of rules. However, it is not necessary to discard the idea of community. McGinn himself applied it to the description of Humean link ("community") between events (1984, p. 67). Kantian approach allows to dissociate the idea of community from any kind of society and transpose it to the abstract structure of experience.

same and that it converges with its most recent application. But if it came to such a situation, *I would de facto lose my history*, at least as far as this rule is concerned. Would I not lose then also the capability of distinguishing rules from their applications? My self would resemble Humean stream of disparate impressions.

However, if only the internal reference to the instance of normativity works, there is a distance between rule-application and its assessment; I distinguish the rule from its applications and remember its meaning. Kantian answer does not exclude that I might record it incorrectly, but I cannot simultaneously *remember past meaning of the rule and claim that a new application, which is discordant with this meaning, conforms to it*. Therefore, if language is to function properly and rules are to be obeyed, I can never identify current application of a rule with its general meaning. Even secluded, I must carry with me some inner instance severed from consciousness, which guarantees that *my* history of rule applications remains coherent.

Hence the core of normativity is not the existence of some community which assesses our application of a rule. The possibility of such community is nothing but a consequence of normativity that has already emerged in the split of subject. Where then can we spot the emergence of normativity? I would claim that *in our readiness to correct ourselves, not even before some imaginary community, but on our own.*[11] In this readiness manifests itself the aforementioned reference to the instance of normativity. As long as I am able to distinguish my application from general meaning of a rule and find my act incorrect,[12] normativity is at work. I am not stuck in the eternal present, in the stream of chaotical and radically disparate cases. Normativity would be thus linked to the elementary distance between the present and all history. Without normativity, I would perceive no continuity in time. To conclude, the readiness to correct myself is bound up with the split subject, which does not live in the Humean "solipsism of the present".

Finally, such readiness elucidates Kantian solution to Kripkenstein's paradox. As I already argued, we have to assume the continuity of rule application in time with no ground for it. It is true that now I might attribute a different meaning to a rule, but I cannot admit it. If I did, I would have to correct myself, claiming that *previously this meaning was incorrect*. This is a consequence of the necessity of the continuity presumption: no rule can be applied without assuming it has preserved its meaning. Therefore, I cannot claim that I interpreted this rule differently and still apply it now. Continuity demands that I give prevalence to one of these meanings

[11] Baker and Hacker note briefly that Robinson Crusoe might apply rules in isolation and correct himself (Baker and Hacker 1984, p. 39). In my exposition I put special accent on *the ability to correct oneself*, which in Kantian terms would prove that the instance of normativity is at work. An individual makes thus a distinction between herself applying a rule and the abstract order. Correcting oneself would not be just one of signs that an individual follows a rule, but a key feature of normativity.

[12] It does not matter here whether I recognise my mistake on my own or whether someone else points to it. As long as I am ready to acknowledge that my application might differ from what the rule entails, I am not using my private language, but true rules.

and correct the other one. The change of meaning, if it really happened, would have to remain elusive.

In the light of the above Kantian argumentation it might be claimed that Kripke confused two different issues: functioning of rules and possible changes of their meanings. Kant would not claim that meaning of rules is effectively preserved in time by some objective "fact". But contrary to Kripke's view, it does not undermine the theoretical possibility of accounting for normativity. Kant would point to the fact that normativity works even when "true" meaning of a rule changes—*if only we are still ready to correct ourselves when some evidence proves that our current application is based on a different meaning of a rule*. If there is no such evidence, the change of meaning is irrelevant. Kant would thus take a clearly anti-realistic stance.

If the above argumentation is correct, Kripke's community might be nothing more than the inner instance of the split subject—the instance equivalent to normativity.

6.4 "Kantstein"?

To sum up, Kantian views on Kripkenstein's paradox would be even more radical than Wittgenstein's or Kripke's. Kant would claim that at the moment of application of a rule, I have to assume a coherent and continuous version of my own previous history, including the moment I laid down the rule. However, no "real" fact could guarantee this continuity—but this is precisely what I cannot say. If I claimed that the rule I presume to follow changes in every case, my statement is meaningless because I have already assumed the opposite presupposition.

Consequently, it might be reasonably argued that "Kantstein"—a phantom philosopher, Kripkenstein's critic—acknowledges all results of his opponent's scepticism. Nevertheless, he attempts to demonstrate that this scepticism is necessarily incoherent. Due to this incoherence, Kripkenstein renounces theory and resorts to practice, claiming that rule-following is blind. Kantstein would not share this conclusion: theoretically speaking, rule-following cannot be described as blind. This "blindness" never appears to us directly. *It does not concern the mere application of the rule to a given case, but the whole system of experience within which we formulate and follow rules*. Thus "blindness" does not function within the scope of normativity, but describes it from the inaccessible outside.

Private language would be then impossible, not because we cannot imagine someone who lost the internal split and identified thinking of obeying the rule with its true obeying—but because without this split we cannot speak of language and rules at all. Such a person would live in the Humean stream of always present impressions, which could not be anyhow juxtaposed. However, as long as the instance of normativity is preserved, even totally isolated persons can use rules and language.

References

Baker, G. P., and P. M. S. Hacker. 1984. *Scepticism, rules and language*. Oxford: Basil Blackwell.

Hume, David. 1739. A treatise of human nature. http://www.earlymoderntexts.com/pdfs/hume-1739book1_3.pdf. Accessed: 20 Jan 2014.

Hume, David. 1992. *An enquiry concerning human understanding; my own life; an abstract of a Treatise of human nature*. La Salle: Open Court.

Kant, Immanuel. 1855. *The critique of pure reason*. London: Henry G. Bohn.

Kripke, Saul A. 1982. *Wittgenstein on rules and private language. An elementary exposition*. Cambridge: Harvard University Press.

McGinn, Colin. 1984. *Wittgenstein on meaning: an interpretation and evaluation*. Oxford: Basil Blackwell.

Wittgenstein, Ludwig. 1974. *Philosophical investigations*. Oxford: Basil Blackwell.

Wright, Crispin. 1984. Kripke's account of the argument against private language. *The Journal of Philosophy* LXXXI (12): 759–778.

Chapter 7
Rules as Patterns Between Normativism and Naturalism

Piotr Kozak

Abstract In the paper, basing predominantly on ideas of Sellars and so-called "Pittsburg school" of philosophy, I focus on the relation between naturalism and normativsim in rule following. In the first part I investigate a vicious regress threat in rule-following and problems that arise when one reduces rule-following to merely regular actions or extends rule-following to following representations of rules. In the second and third part as a Third Way between regularism and intellectualism I reintroduce and critically discuss Sellars idea of pattern-governed behavior that on the one hand helps to overcome sketched difficulties but on the other forces us to accept the irreal status of rules.

Keywords Rule-following · Sellars · Normativism · Naturalism · Pattern-governed behavior

7.1 Introduction

According to well established at least since Kant belief, the human practice, language and thought depend on an ability to follow rules. However, it is not clear what it means that we follow rules in practice, including using words and concepts. Commonsensical belief says that in order to follow a rule we need to be aware of the rule. However, if we agree on that, then we embark on a regress, for example, to be able to use rules, concepts and words we need another rules that would establish standards of correctness for the application of the first rules, the concepts and the words. To be able to apply the rules we require to follow further rules for the correct application of the rules. Therefore, following any rule would require following a further rule and so on. For instance, suppose the relevant rule for 'green' was formulated in the sentence: "Apply word 'green' when pointing at green objects". Then, the words in that rule such as 'object', 'apply' etc. would require other rules for their correct application. Wilfrid Sellars (1954 p. 204) sketches the regress as follows:

P. Kozak (✉)
Warsaw University, Warsaw, Poland
e-mail: piotr.kozak1@gmail.com

M. Araszkiewicz et al. (eds.), *Problems of Normativity, Rules and Rule-Following*, Law and Philosophy Library 111, DOI 10.1007/978-3-319-09375-8_7

> *Thesis*. Learning to use a language (L) is learning to obey the rules of L.
> *But*, a rule which enjoins the doing of an action (A) is a sentence in a language which contains an expression for A.
> *Hence*, a rule which enjoins the using of a linguistic expression (E) is a sentence in a language which contains an expression for E—in other words a sentence in a metalanguage.
> *Consequently*, learning to obey the rules for L presupposes the ability to use the metalanguage (ML) in which the rules for L are formulated.
> *So that* learning to use a language (L) presupposes having learned to use a language (ML). And by the same token, having learned to use ML presupposes having learned to use a meta-metalanguage (MML) and so on.
> *But* this is an impossible (a vicious) regress.
> *Therefore*, the thesis is absurd and must be rejected.

To put it roughly, using a language L is obeying rules of L; to obey rules of L we need metarules of ML for the correct application of the rules of L; the metarules for the correct application of the rules need further meta-metarules of MML and so on. The purport of Sellars's argument is the rejection of the thesis that learning to use language L is learning to obey the rules of L. One remark is necessary: the argument refers not only to language games but extends to the practice as such. Language games are an instance of practice in general.

The argument implies that, first, we can learn to participate in a rule-governed (language) practice without necessarily learn to obey rules of the (language) practice. Second, it suggests that we can partake in a in a rule-governed (language) practice without obeying the rules of the (language) practice. However, it does not mean that the (language) practice is not rule-governed. Just the opposite, if we want to speak sensibly about a practice, we have to speak about the practice in terms of rules of the practice. Without rules there is no practice at all. Therefore, it is not correct to say that a (language) practice does not establish what we must or must not or may or may not do. Partaking in a practice means that we have an operative knowledge what behavior counts as correct and incorrect behavior. If we do not know whether an application of the word 'green' when pointing at green objects is the correct application of the word 'green' or not, then we are not competent English speakers and we do not fully partake in the language practice. Nevertheless, if partaking in a rule-governed (language) practice does not depend on obeying rules of the practice, then it seems to follow that there is nothing we could recognize as a correct partaking in the practice.

In order to solve the difficulty and stop the regress it is tempting to distinguish, following Sellars, between learning to obey a rule and learning to conform to a rule. In *Some Reflections on Language Games* (1954 p. 205) Sellars writes:

> [T]here is a simple and straightforward way of preserving the essential claim of the thesis [that learning a language is learning to obey its rules] while freeing it from the refutation. It consists in substituting the phrase 'learning to conform to the rules… for 'learning to obey the rules…' where 'conforming to a rule enjoining the doing of A in circumstances C' is to be equated simply with 'doing A when the circumstances are C'—regardless of how one comes to do it.

The basic idea is that we can think about rule-following in terms of one's disposition or propensity to do what the rule R requires in the circumstances C. For example, small children can be said to follow the rule of the language grammar, so long as they have a disposition to speak in accordance with the grammar. However, conforming to a rule does not involve any conceptualizing of R and therefore it is contrasted with obedience to a rule that requires having the rule in mind and conscious intending to follow the rule. In short, rule-following is a matter of becoming conditioned to conform to a rule R but not yet to conscious obeying the rule R. As a consequence resulting behavior is *rule-governed* but it does not mean that it is *rule-obeying*.

The purport of the distinction is to include into rule-following considerations human activities for which there are rules and yet in which agents participate without being able to formulate the rules they conform to and consequently, where *obeying* the rules is not essential to participating in practice as such. The main advantage is that by the distinction between rule-conformity and rule-obedience we avoid the regress described above. If conforming to a rule is an instance of following a rule, then one can follow a rule without the necessity of having it in mind, where the rule-conformity means that one exhibits regularity in one's actions, i.e. a one has an inclination to do the right things in the right circumstances. Therefore, one conforms to a rule so long as one acts in accordance with what the rule says to do, even if one's intention is not to do so because of what the rule says.

However, after closer look this regress-stopping solution, at least at this stage, says too little. Conformity with a rule or a regularity of one's actions does not mean that one is following a rule. Our actions exhibit a variety of regularities we are not even aware of. One's action could be consistent with an infinite number of incompatible patterns. As a consequence, first, one is subject to infinite number of rules; second, if there is no single pattern that one's performance exhibits, then we cannot determine which rule one is following. If that is so, then we cannot determine what is and is not an error. Additionally, if that is true, then we cannot say that one is following a rule at all, because in order to say that one is following a rule we need a possibility of breaking the rule.

Similar point is made by Wittgenstein (2001). Let's take a sequence of numbers: 1, 2, 3. If we ask a student what number should follow the sequence, then the answer "4" is correct only if we apply a rule "add 1". However, a student could equally apply a rule "give a next prime number", and if that is so, then the correct answer is not "4" but "5". It could go on indefinitely, because one can find an adequate rule for every answer. Of course the issue concerns not only mathematical sequences. The same we can say about phenomenal properties. If the subject *s* possesses a mental image of a linden then this image is in accord with the representation of a linden as well as Berlin regardless what all past experiences of the subject *s*. Therefore one has no criterion to decide whether one actually possesses a representation of a linden or Berlin. As a consequence, the regularity of the sequence does not decide what rule one follows and what rule one ought to follow. At the end we are left, as McDowell (1998 p. 242) famously stressed it, between Scylla and Charybdis.

> [The] problem is to steer a course between Scylla and Charybdis. Scylla is the idea that understanding is always interpretation [...]. We can avoid Scylla by stressing that, say, calling something 'green' can be like crying 'Help!' when one is drowning—simply how one has learned to react to this situation. But then we risk steering onto Charybdis, the picture of a basic level at which there are no norms.

The problem, which is also called regularism-problem, is captured by Brandom (1994, p. 28). Regularism presupposes that exhibiting a regularity can count as following a rule, but without some kind of a supplement there is nothing that counts as an irregularity, hence nothing counts as an error. Nothing helps the reference to dispositions instead of one's past behaviors. Even if we constrain the infinite set of cases under consideration to finite set of one's dispositions, the problem remains. According to dispositionalist view, if one is disposed to add 1 to each predecessor, then one is following the rule to add 1 to each predecessor. On this basis one can exclude other incompatible rules by saying that one does not have a disposition to act in other way, and so following a rule is doing what one is disposed to do and breaking the rule is doing not what one is disposed to do.

The main problem with the dispositionalist view, what was most famously stressed by Kripke (1982), is that the dispositions as such do not say what one *ought to* do. Exhibiting a disposition does not say what is correct and incorrect. It is possible to imagine that one intends to do A in C, even if it is not correct to do A in C. The dispositions do not settle what should be done and what not, and so there is no necessary connection between what one is disposed to do and what is correct to do.

7.2 Pattern-Governed Behavior

At this point we can agree that to avoid the vicious regress in rule-following we must reject the intellectualist view that in order to follow a rule R we need another rule R', for R's correct application. Similarly we have to reject the view that rule-following is based on regularity of one's behavior. Yet, the question is how to reject the intellectualist view and avoid falling into regularism.

In order to solve the problem we need to make the next step and realize that the dichotomy between obeying a rule and conforming to a rule is a false dichotomy. If an appeal to obedience leads to the infinite regress, and an appeal to conformity leads to regularism, then we need to reject them and reconsider the issue. The alternative, introduced by Sellars, is to think about rule-following in terms of "pattern-governed behavior".

Still, what is pattern-governed behavior? The point of departure is that Sellars wants to save the possibility to act according to a rule, even if one is not aware of the rule, i.e., even if one does not intend to follow it. Let's consider an example. If I train my dog to act in accord with a rule R: "come when I say 'come'", then, after some time and training, the dog could develop a habit to act in accord with the rule R. What is important: we do not have to presuppose that my dog would have some kind of a rule in mind when it acts in accord with the rule, and intends to follow the rule, nor that its behavior would be somehow accidental. The behavior of my dog *could* be partly explained by the rule. My dog would act in accord with the rule *because I* have the rule in mind and I trained him to act in accord with it. That means that the dog's behavior is not accidental, nor merely conforms with the rule, nor is based on the discursive *obedience* to the rule. The dog's behavior is pattern-governed behavior, i.e., it exhibits a pattern not because it is brought about by the intention of exhibiting this pattern, but because the propensity to emit behavior of the pattern has been selectively reinforced (Sellars 1974a, p. 423). The same could be said about evolutionarily reinforced patterns. Sellars' favorite example is the "dance" of the bees, but we could say the very same about "logical inferences" in the case of animals or about our habitual behaviors. We can say that dogs have a use of reasoning modus ponens or disjunctive syllogism schema of inference even if we cannot ascribe them any discursive ability to infer. Another example, in daily life we habitually behave in accordance with many rules but we are very rarely aware of these rules. The basic idea in those cases is that pattern-governed behavior is performed because of the whole behaving system is achieving its goal, *resp.* it could be explained by reference to its goal. In a weak sense we could say, that there is a reason for those behavior—if by a reason in weak sense understand a function of a pattern in a system—and that distinguishes them from merely accidental and merely regular behavior.

It is easy to extend that idea to language use. We do not need to presuppose that in order to speak a language we need to have some rule in mind. In most cases we are not aware of rules of language and we use language habitually. Still, the rules of language could be an essential part of the explanation of one's language behavior. Therefore, we can say, that we are not merely conforming to the rule, because when we act in accord with a language rule we do so *because* we were trained to act in accord with the language rule. However, one doubt remains, i.e., how pattern-governed behavior could be correct or incorrect?

The important step, taken by Sellars in *Language as Thought and as Communication* (1969), is an introduction of the distinction between two kinds of rule. One, the 'ought-to-do' kind of rules, also called 'rules of action', which one can obey in the full sense. The basic form of the rule of action is conditional imperative: "If in circumstances C, do A!". The other kind of rules is 'ought to be' kind of rules, also called 'rules of criticism', which one can conform to. Ought-to-be rules specify what ought or ought not to be a case, that is, they endorse a state of affairs to be brought about. They may take a form: "Xs ought to be in state S, whenever such and such is the case". In such perspective one can say that my dog's behavior, our language behaviors or even regular events in the world are governed by rules of criticism. For example:

1. It ought to be the case that clock chimes strike on the quarter hour.

In the case of my dog:

2. It ought to be the case that my dog comes when I say so.

Something or someone could be governed by rules of criticism without intentionally obeying the rules, i.e., without having any concept of a rule in mind. Rules of criticism do not involve conceptualizing of the rules. In the case of my dog: we can say that the behavior of my dog is not an intentional *action*, at least in a traditional view of action, that is it does not need any concepts and goals. The behavior is rather, following another distinction made by Sellars, an *act*, i.e., it is not done on purpose but it is an actualization of a capacity or a capability in such and such circumstances. That means that the behavior of my dog is a response to such and such circumstances and it is an actualization of a capability to do so and so. The same in the case of the clock. The description of the event "clock chimes strike on the quarter hour" can be conducted in terms of causal responses or the actualization of a capability, and it obviously does not need to presuppose any intentional vocabulary.

What is important, with this distinction at hand we can say that pattern-governed behavior is subject to ought-to-be rules but not directly to ought-to-do rules. If that is so, then pattern-governed behavior is still rule-obeying behavior. It is normatively correct if it is in accordance with the ought-to-be rule in question, and it is otherwise incorrect. Thus the behavior of my dog is correct, if it comes when I say so, because the behavior fits the pattern that ought to be.

On the other hand, rules of criticism are opposed to rules of action. The latter specify what one ought or ought not to do. For instance:

3. I ought to train my dog to come when I say so.

In this case following rules of action requires that one possesses concepts to express the rule and the ability to guide one's actions in accordance with the rule, that is, one has to have a knowledge of the rule, a capacity to recognize the correct application-circumstances of the rule and a conative structure that motivates one to apply the rule and to act in accord with it.

More problematic is a relation between rules of action and rules of criticism. Sellars seems to say that each ought-to-be rule implies an ought-to-do rule, i.e., adoption of a rule of criticism by a conceptpossesing subject implies rules of action for that subject. For example, the statement (1) implies a relevant ought-to-do rule:

4. (If it is possible and other things being equal) one ought to bring it about that clock chimes strike on the quarter hour.

Analogously for the statement (2) one can formulate an adequate rule of action:

5. My dog ought to come when I say so, thus (if it is possible and other things being equal) I ought to train my dog to come when I say so.

The basic idea is that the recognition of a goal that Xs ought to be in state S if C by member(s) of a community commits the member(s) of the community to seeing to it that the goal is satisfied, and this may require teaching and requiring the member(s) of the community to be in state S if C. In such case we can say, that ought-to-be rules entail some kind of ought-to-do rules. We have also remember that it doesn't imply that rule-following is necessarily a social process. The community can have equally one member. Important is that this member can refer to him- or herself and guide his or her action following rule of action in accord with a recognized rule of criticism.

However, strictly speaking, this rough view lacks one important thing. When one says that it ought to be the case that one's dog comes when one calls, one has to presuppose a premise that it ought to be the case that dogs come when one calls. If not, then I could say that I *want* to be the case that so and so but there would be no reason that it *ought* to be the case that so and so. The relevant reasoning looks as follows:

It ought to be the case that dogs come when I call.
Therefore, it ought to be the case that my dog comes when I call.
My dog will come when called only if I train it to do so.
Therefore, I ought to train my dog to come when called.

On the other hand, for there to be rules of action there must be conformity with rules of criticism. In order to say that I ought to do so and so I need to presuppose that it ought to be the case that so and so. If not, analogously, I can say that I want to do so and so, but there would be no reason that I ought to do so and so.

At this stage three remarks are important. First, as long as subjects that do not possess concepts could be only the subjects of rules of criticism, the subject of the ought-to-be and the corresponding ought-to-do can be the same. Let's consider two statements:

6. One ought to feel sympathy for bereaved people.
7. One ought to bring it about that people feel sympathy for the bereaved.

Statement (6) expresses an ought-to-be rule since feeling sympathy is not an action. People in general ought to feel sympathy and ought also to bring it about that people in general feel sympathy for the bereaved. The respective rule-subjects coincide.

Second, with pattern-governed behavior and the distinction between rules of action and rules of criticism, we seem to avoid the infinite regress. If it is not true that our behavior, especially language behavior, could be reduced to rules of action, and if being engaged in pattern-governed practice we are abiding by rules of criticism, not rules of action, then danger of the regress disappears, since rules of criticism do not require conceiving or intending to follow these rules. The regress starts only if we assume that there are only rules of action.

Third, according to Sellars, ought-to-be rules could be realized in the world other ways that merely accidentally except insofar as there are agents who recognize them, infer relevant rules of action and undertake required actions. Unless there are agents that could follow rules of action, talk of any rules, including rules of criticism, turns out to be empty. It means that we are rule-governed creatures because we conceive of ourselves as rule-governed creatures. And as long as we conceive of ourselves as rule-governed and exercise and train ourselves to live in accord with rules, it is true that we are rule-governed creatures. The third remark will be crucial in the next point.

7.3 Ought-to-be's and the Division of Labor

However, there are some problems with Sellars' solution. On the one hand, it is not clear what kind of a relation "implication between rules" refers to. This relation cannot be a formal inference, since rules does not possess truth values. We could think about the relation in terms of material inference (at least Sellars does it) but, first, it is not clear what it is; second, even if it is so, then we face syntactical problems. The object of assessment of the relevant rule of criticism is different than the object of the relevant rule of action. Rule of criticism refers to a state of affairs; rule of action refers to actions. Thus, it is questionable whether we can easily combine these two.

The first doubt is connected with the second one. Sellars claims that in the case of pattern-governed behavior we do not need to be aware of the rule exhibited in the behavior. Prima facie it can seem as if pattern-governed behavior does not require having any understanding of the rule. Pattern-governed behavior can look merely as a way of being responsive to a rule that does not yet require being consciously aware of that rule. However, if it is so, then we seem to fall into a form of the famous (and introduced by Sellars) Myth of the Given.

Sellars' whole train of reasoning is based on a premise that one can conform to ought-to-be rules without having any conceptual understanding of them. On the other hand following ought-to-do rules presupposes having concepts and the ability to understand the rules. If it is so, then how to explain sudden conceptual leap from ought-to-be rules, to which we merely conform, to ought-to-do rules which we need to understand to follow? Nothing helps the reference to explicit formulation of rules, since then we fall into vicious regress. Prima facie reasonable would be to distinguish between grades of understanding a rule and, in turn, grades of following a rule. However, this alternative is questionable, for it implies that there is some degree of understanding shared by artifacts that are designed in accordance with specific rules held in mind by their designers, and which therefore conform to ought-to-be rules, which is implausible. A computer is designed to comply with various rules, but it does not understand what it is doing (if a computer is not a convincing example, consider a printer). Thus, we avoid Scylla and Charybdis of the regress and regularism but what we get instead are rocks of the Given.

Similar point is made by Marras. Marras (1973a, b, c) rises a doubt whether the solution given by Sellars satisfies the noncircularity requirement, i.e., whether the concept of intentional actions can be explicated in terms of states or acts that do not require any concepts, since the intentional actions presuppose the concept of rule as a standard of correctness for states and acts. According to Marras, Sellars must face the following dilemma. The main premise of the dilemma is based on an assumption that if we do not want to fall into regularism, then intentional actions could not be equated with merely behavioral items in some physicalistic sense. Exercised behavior is assumed to have such properties that enables us to speak about intentional actions in terms of correct or incorrect behaviors. Now, those properties are either ought-to-be rules at the level of pattern governed behavior or ought-to-do rules at the level of rule-obeying behavior. In the latter case we face the infinite regress, since every ought-to-do rule would require another ought-to-do rule for its correct application. The former alternative, Marras argues, leads to a vicious circle, since as soon as one accepts, as Sellars does, that ought-to-be rules imply a related ought-to-do rule and the ought-to-do rules depend on possessing concepts then, by means of hypothetical syllogism, ought-to-be rules depend on possessing concepts. If it so, then conceptual activities cannot be analyzed in terms of concept of rule in a non-circular fashion, since exercising concepts requires rules and rules require concepts.

The argument here says that when following a rule the agent must meet another criterion or standard, i.e., to follow a rule in a possibly wide sense that yet involves ought-to-do rules, which launches a regress. However, one can claim, that this charge can still be met by reference to pattern-governed behavior, which is rule-governed and meaningful by itself. The confusion may arise from the misunderstanding of pattern-governed behavior and the role of rules of criticism. Crucial here is to think about pattern-governed behavior in terms of meaningful *non-actions*.

First, we have to be more careful when we speak about correctness of actions. Most importantly, we have to distinguish the correctness of an intentional *action*, i.e., what is rational or morally appropriate thing for X to do, from the more basic correctness of sequences or events that are based on causal transition between volition/observation/thinking and (language) behavior. This transition is not an *action*, though it may be an essential part of such an action. Hence, the transition is something of which intentional actions are made, but the transition itself is not an intentional action. We can think about the transition in terms of unreflective, habitual behavior or basic acquired casual capacity that is necessary for the possibility of any action at all. Thus, what Sellars often underlines, it is a mistake to think about pattern-governed behavior in terms of action. Correctness and incorrectness of a pattern-governed behavior are not a correctness and incorrectness of an action but of an act. That is why we can speak about the correctness of feeling sorrow for someone who is bereaved. Feeling sorrow for the bereaved is a learned conceptual response and inference pattern but not an intentional action. Such responses and behavioral transitions can be thought for example, as it is commonly put, in terms of 'second nature'. Hence, I do not *intend* to take that such and such behavior is bereavement or not, nor I do not intend to take that such and such object is green or not, as if I might perform this recognition as an intentional action. Rather, this is how the behavior strikes me, given that I have learned how to recognize such and such behaviors and such and such green objects. The same in the case of animals. Parrots for example could be taught to recognize green objects and distinguish them from red objects but we do not have to presuppose here that parrots have some kind of concept of greenness. It is enough to say that a parrot recognizes such and such green object and that ability can be acquired causally. However, if pattern-governed behavior is reduced here to causal responses, then in which sense can we speak about the normative content of pattern-governed behavior?

Following Sellars (and late Wittgenstein), we can say that we can acquire such conceptual capacities in large part because we are *trained* as children to do so and so. However, we have to distinguish here two different *positions* in a process of learning, i.e., distinguish between position of *trainers* and *trainees*. Trainers follow rules of action that help shape the trainees' responses to be as they ought-to-be according to communally accepted standards. In the case of acquiring the capacity to feel sympathy for the bereaved, we can assume that very young trainees will at first lack the requisite conceptual capacities for recognizing cases of bereavement *as* cases of bereavement. However, through imitation as well as the trainers' encouragement of appropriate behavior and correction of inappropriate behavior, the developing sympathetic behavior (and feelings) of the trainee will gradually come to be of the right sort and to be channeled in the right direction. That is trainees' behavior will gradually come to be as it ought-to-be. Most importantly, the successful conforming of the trainee's behavior to the relevant ought-to-be rules does not require that the trainee herself initially possess the relevant conceptual understanding involved. Thanks to the trainers, the properly raised child will exhibit appropriate pattern-governed behavior before the stage at which we could say that the child has an understanding what situation of bereavement is. To characterize the trainee's behavior as pattern-governed rather than simply rule-obeying behavior is primarily to emphasize this point that while the trainee's behavior occurs because it fits pattern that ought-to-be, the trainee herself may as yet has no idea that her behavior conforms to that pattern.

Thus, the confusion arises only if we do not distinguish two positions we take in the division of labor, i.e., the position of the trainer and the trainee. That is why Sellars could say that we are rule-governed creatures *because* we conceive of ourselves as rule-governed creatures. There are no rules in the world except insofar as we conceive of ourselves as rule-governed and train ourselves to live in accord with rules. Rules are not *in* the world but in the way *how* we *perceive* the world and *how* we act.

References

Brandom, Robert. 1994. *Making it explicit: Reasoning, representing, and discursive commitment.* Cambridge: Harvard University Press.

deVries, Willes. 2005. *Wilfrid Sellars*. Montreal: McGill-Queen's University Press.

Kripke, Saul. 1982. *Wittgenstein on rules and private language*. Cambridge: Harvard University Press.

Maher, Chauncey. 2012. *The Pittsburgh School of Philosophy: Sellars, McDowell, Brandom*. New York: Routledge.

Marras, Ausonio. 1973a. Sellars on thought and language. *Nous* 7:152–163.

Marras, Ausonio. 1973b. On Sellars' linguistic theory of conceptual activity. *Canadian Journal of Philosophy* 2:471–483.

Marras, Ausonio. 1973c. Reply to Sellars. *Canadian Journal of Philosophy* 2:495–501.

McDowell, John. 1998. *Mind, value, and reality*. Cambridge: Harvard University Press.

O'Shea, John. 2007. *Wilfrid Sellars: Naturalism with a normative turn.* Cambridge: Polity.

Pagin, Peter. 1987. Ideas for a theory of rules. Doctoral Dissertation, University of Stockholm.

Peregrin, Jaroslav. 2010. The enigma of rules. *International Journal of Philosophical Studies* 18 (3):377–394.

Sellars, Wilfrid. 1949. Language, rules and behavior. In *John Dewey: Philosopher of science and freedom,* ed. Sydney Hook, 283–315. New York: Dial Press.

Sellars, Wilfrid. 1953. Inference and meaning. *Mind* 62:313–338.

Sellars, Wilfrid. 1954. Some reflections on language games. *Philosophy of Science* 24 (3):204–228.

Sellars, Wilfrid. 1969. Language as thought and as communication. *Philosophy and Phenomenological Research* 29 (4):506–527.

Sellars, Wilfrid. 1974a. Meaning as functional classification (a perspective on the relation of syntax to semantics). *Synthese* 27 (3/4):417–437.

Sellars, Wilfrid. 1974b. *Essays in philosophy and its history*. Dordrecht: D. Reidel.

Sellars, Wilfrid. 2007a. Some reflections on thoughts and things. In *In the space of reasons. Selected essays of Wilfrid Sellars,* eds. Kevin Scharp and Robert Brandom, 28–56. Cambridge: Harvard University Press.

Sellars, Wilfrid. 2007b. Some remarks on Kant's theory of experience. In *In the space of reasons. Selected essays of Wilfrid Sellars,* eds. Kevin Scharp and Robert Brandom, 437–453. Cambridge: Harvard University Press.

Tuomela, Raimo. 2001. *The philosophy of social practices*. Cambridge: Cambridge University Press.

Wittgenstein, Ludwig. 2001. *Philosophical investigations*. Oxford: Blackwell.

Chapter 8
Normativity and Rationality: Framing the Problem

Joanna Klimczyk

Abstract The paper is divided into four sections. The first one examines the hypothesis about whether the sharp distinction between two kinds of the normative requirements of rationality: the substantive and the non-substantive is a plausible view, given we can show that at least one particular non-substantive requirement of local attitudinal coherence is inscribed into the very idea of genuine normative requirement of whatever source. The second considers a particular version of a popular argument in favor of the substantive construal of the normativity of rationality that builds on the putative analogy between the normativity of rationality and the normativity of morality. The conclusion is that the argument remains unsuccesful because the analogy shows to be apparent. Section 8.3 explores the First-Personal Authority Account as an argument for the non-substantive normativity of rationality, and rejects it on the ground of its irrelevance. It is argued that the main problem with the the First-Personal Authority Account is that instead of establishing that attitudinal coherence is a normative claim of rationality, it provides support for the psychological interpretation of the normativity of rationality. Finally, granted that the arguments in the above sections are roughly correct, and the idea of the intrinsic normativity of rationality remains a muddle, a radical solution is advocated for. Instead of working hard on vindicating the normativity of rationality, we should rather rest content with the view that the only normativity of rationality for which we have support has external source in what we care about.

Keywords Local attitudinal coherence · Normativity · Rationality · Reasons · First-Personal Authority Account

---

J. Klimczyk (✉)
Department of Philosophy and Sociology, Polish Academy of Sciences,
Nowy Świat 72, Warszawa 00-330, Poland
e-mail: jklimczyk@ifispan.waw.pl

Department of Philosophy, University of Szczecin,
Nowy Świat 72, Warszawa 00-330, Poland

M. Araszkiewicz et al. (eds.), *Problems of Normativity, Rules and Rule-Following*,
Law and Philosophy Library 111, DOI 10.1007/978-3-319-09375-8_8

8.1 Introduction

Most participants in the debate over the normativity of rationality subscribe to three claims. The first says that you ought to reason correctly, where 'correctly' is a cover-term that includes various requirements of rational reasoning, such as *belief-consistency*: the requirement not to believe that *p* if you believe that not-*p*; *belief-closure*: the requirement to believe *q* if you believe that *p* and believe that if *p* then *q*; instrumental *rationality*: the requirement to intend to *B* if you intend to *A* and believe that your *B*ing requires that you *A*, just to mention the most noncontroversial from the list.

The second claim is that rationality requires you to respond correctly to reasons. 'Correctly' is a term of art here and there are hot debates about how to interpret correct responding to reasons. Interpretational query aside, the more important question concerns the issue whether rationality is to be appropriately thought of as consisting in responding to reasons at all (Broome 2007).

Finally, according to the third claim, what rationality requires of an agent is that she has to be in the relevant states of mind. If she fails to be in a certain state of mind at given circumstances, then she is not entirely as she *ought to be*. Behind that claim lurks the elusive thought that there is some normative truth about what states of mind an agent ought to be in, where that very truth is determined either by facts about how things are in the world, or by the contents of the agent's attitudes. Many philosophers who believe in the PLATITUDE also believe that the truth of the above claims can only be explained in terms of the normativity of rationality. To put the idea crudely, if we reject the view that rationality is normative, not only does the source of the PLATITUDE remain obscure, but also those who argue for the PLATITUDE are guilty of defective thinking. The accusation can take the following form: how can you truly believe in something if you lack satisfactory support for your claim? Or, how can you believe in something if you cannot vindicate the thesis you find to be true?

In the paper I shall try to make a preliminary contribution to the project of demystyfying the view that rationality is the source of normative claims on subjects. The view that I criticize consists of either one, or two of the following theses. The first says that the requirements of rationality form a distinct kind of requirements conferred on subjects, analogously to the requirements stemming from such sources as morality, or prudence. According to the second, conforming to the requirements of rationality, however one pleases to construe them, is a genuine normative issue. By the expression "genuine normative", I do not mean the issue of whether any individual requirements of rationality set out standards for correct reasoning either of theoretical, or of practical kind. Rather what I have in mind is something more substantive, regarding whether the requirements of rationality belong to the normative province of reasons. Normative reasons, I contend, are the only and appropriate extension of the term "normativity" that we are really interested in.

The paper takes as its point of departure the bundle of claims about what rationality requires that fall under the PLATITUDE, and then proceeds as follows:. I examine the first two claims of the PLATITUDE, and raise doubts whether it makes sense to think of two, independent, general requirements of rationality, which respectively I call the 'substantive' and the 'non-substantive' ones. Next, I put into question the suggestion that the PLATITUDE's credibility turns on the claim that rationality is normative. Finally, I sketch an alternative way of thinking of the requirements of rationality in terms of the requirements of comprehensibility. The main advantage of the comprehensibility approach, as far as I see it, is that this approach allows us to save what philosophers from the opposite sides want to save, that is, the idea of the first-personal authority of the requirements of rationality, yet dismiss the task with which we have fared so badly, namely the struggle to demonstrate that rationality *itself*, alike morality, is the source of intrinsically normative claims.

My suggestion, if plausible, obviously shares the fate common to bold philosophical theses: it has its own price. The price to be paid in this case is to come to terms with the possibility that normativity of rationality, if there is any, comes from somewhere else. This 'somewhere else', I have in mind, is what I call 'the desire of comprehensibility', which is a sort of a primitive desire of imperfect yet capable to rationality creatures such as we are. In short, I shall end with the conclusion that the apparent intrinsic normativity of rationality is confused with the straightforwardly non-normative requirements of comprehensibility.

8.2 Are There Really Two Kinds of the Requirements of Rationality?

Being in the grip of the requirements of one sort or another is something natural to social creatures of our kind. You can consider these various requirements that apply to human beings in terms of their *source* (Broome 2005, p. 324; 2008, pp. 96–97; Southwood 2008, pp. 17–18): moral, prudential, professional etc., or *object*. The requirements understood in terms of their object are the requirements that apply to the same object, yet stem from various sources. One example of requirements construed in terms of object are the requirements towards the poor. As a moral agent you have a certain set of obligations towards those who live in the poverty, and as a social worker you have another set of obligations that derive from your professional code. An alternative, simple way of thinking about requirements is to think of them in terms of *substance* and *coherence*. Requirements of substance are source-requirements, provided by morality, prudence or professional codes, whereas requirements of coherence seem to have no source in the sense that morality, or prudence are sources of various demands. The latter are usually construed of in terms of the general non-substantive requirement of rationality. What this general non-substantive requirement of rationality requires of you is not so much to conform to some particular norm of some particular source, or sources, but rather to think with certain pattern of correct thinking. Which pattern is the one you should think through depends on what sort of reasoning you are engaged in. If you intend to catch the 9 a.m. train to Cracow, and you know that this task will prove unfeasible unless you perform certain initial actions, including getting up at least two hours before the departure of the train on the day you plan to go to Cracow, then the norm or pattern of correct reasoning for your case is *instrumental rationality*. In this case the fact that you have intention to go to Cracow determines which other attitudes you ought to have, or ought not to have. For example, if it is true of you that you do intend to go to Cracow by train at 9 a.m. on the particular Monday, it must also be true of you that you do not have the intention not to go to Cracow by train at 9 a.m. on that very day. Or, it must be true that you do not have the intention to go there by plane and so on.

However, the sharp distinction between the requirements of substance and the requirements of coherence, as I label them, cannot be entirely correct. Recall what is the stipulated difference between the two kinds of requirements in question. Requirements of substance are the requirements whose normative force come from the relevant source, where what makes some source the province of normativity has to do with importance ascribed to the source in question. For example, morality is standardly thought of as a domain of value in one sense of the term "value" and prudence is thought of as a domain of value in another sense. On the other hand, the requirements of coherence amount to the general requirement of rationality that can be roughly characterized as the requirement to have attitudes that fit together in the coherent way. Call the source-normative requirements the *substantive normative requirements*, and the general requirement of rationality the *non-substantive normative requirement*.

Now, some philosophers are inclined to think that these two general requirements make for the requirements of rationality, though in a somewhat different sense. The rationale behind that view, which I label the *Double Binding View*, as I understand it, is that, if it is true that morality, prudence or any other source of substantive normative claims require of you something, conforming to that particular source-requirement is what is rational for you to do in one sense of the term "rational", in which rationality is construed of in terms of appropriate responding to reasons. According to that line of thinking on rationality, if it is true that you ought to comply with a particular moral norm, or a particular norm of prudence, or a particular norm of ettiquette, you "gain", so to speak, the relevant normative reasons to conform to them, and because it is true that you ought, or have normative reasons to conform to the substantive requirement in question, complying with this requirement is also the correct way of responding to the normative reasons you have. Consequently, if responding to correct normative reasons is one of the hallmarks of rationality, then responding to the source-normative requirements is one way of manifesting one's rationality.

In what follows, I shall not discuss the issue whether the substantive connection between rationality and reasons is a tenable view, and specifically whether rationality consists in responding correctly to reasons, though I am sceptical about that. Rather, what I am interested in, and what will be the focal point of this section, is the problem that, as it seems to me, has not been given due attention in the ongoing debate over the normativity of rationality. The problem I have in mind concerns whether assuming the existence of two distinct kinds of the normative requirements of rationality along the lines of the PLATITUDE: the substantive one and the non-substantive one is not a bit far-fetched. The hypothesis I find worth testing is whether at least certain requirement of rationality in the non-substantive sense that is certain specific requirement of coherence among one's attitudes is not already included, or entailed by the substantive normative requirement itself. To put the same idea in less complicated words: what I want to inquire about is, whether, if it is true that you ought, or have normative reason to conform to a particular requirement in the source sense of normative requirement, then it is also true that the content of that very requirement forces upon your attitudes certain requirement of attitudinal consistency of the local character.

Let us, provisionally, take the tentative thesis to say:

Inter-normative Transmission Rule of Rationality (ITRR) Necessarily, if it is true that you ought to X or have normative reason to X, where X is what is required of you in the substantive, source sense of normativity, then it is also true that there is a certain pattern of local attitudinal coherence, such that you are required to satisfy if you are to satisfy a substantive requirement of normativity.

Spelt out more carefully, the *Inter-normative Transmission Rule (ITRR)* says that being under some normative requirement of substantive kind (in the source-sense of the normative requirement) entails being also under the particular non-substantive requirement of rationality of not having the combination of attitudes that in principle are irreconciable with the content of the particular requirement in the substantive sense of rationality that applies to you.

To see how the IRRR works, consider moral requirements, for example. Moral requirements require you to do, or not to do certain things, but they also require you to have coherent attitudes as determined by the content of some particular substantive moral requirement that applies to you at some particular time. Thus, if it is true that morality requires you not to cheat on other people, thus requires you not to behave in a certain way, it also requires you to *believe* that cheating on others is morally wrong, or generally morally reprehensible. Moreover, most people find what I here coin the *requirement of content-fitting attitudes*, a necessary condition on being moral at all. By 'content-fitting attitudes' I understand the attitudes that the subject is required to have when s/he remains under some particular source-normative requirement(s). Morality is an obvious case of such source-normative requirements that entail the relevant requirements of content-fitting attitudes. That this is so is what Kant has taught us when he claimed that acting on a moral principle is not yet the evidence of moral action. Such acting can merely be the evidence of acting in accordance with a moral principle. Moral action, if it is to deserve the name 'moral', must also spring from moral motivation, and moral motivation is nothing other than having the very attitudes that morality in the source sense of normativity requires you to have. What about prudence? Prudence is also unanimously taken to consist of a set of normative requirements in the source sense of normativity. *Prudence requires you to do this or that.* Suppose prudence requires you not to jump from the fourth floor of your apartment in order to attract the attention of by-passers on the street in which you live. Does the requirement of prudence, in the source sense of normativity, imply any particular requirement of content-fitting attitudes, for example one which says that if it is against the requirement of prudence to jump from the fourth floor of your apartment for no good reason, it is also against the requirement of prudence to *believe* that jumping from the fourth floor is something imprudent or stupid? It seems to me that it does. Generally and necessarily, normative requirements in the source sense of normativity go together with the relevant source-derivative requirements of content-fitting attitudes, being the part of the same package of what amounts to the requirements of rationality.

The tentative view defended here says that genuinely normative requirements, in the source sense of normativity, entail the requirements of local coherence among your attitudes, where the requirements in question are determined by some particular requirement you should in some particular context satisfy. If that is so, as I think it is, then the idea of introducing two distinct kinds of normative requirements: the substantive and those that concern coherence among one's attitudes is, in an important sense, mistaken. Instead of bringing us closer to understanding the nature of the requirements of rationality, the idea in question makes us plunge into more confusion. That is so because we are told that there is a normative reason to have coherent attitudes or that we ought to have coherent attitudes, as if the required coherence among one's attitudes formed a separate requirement that would be added to the one provided by some specific source-normative requirement. As if it were truly possible to satisfy the second (the substantive one) without satisfying the first (the coherential one). As if, for example, the *moral* requirement that forbids you cheating on other people could be genuinely satisfied without your having the relevant belief (if you are a moral cognitivist), or having some non-cognitivist attitude, say the attitude of being committed to the norm in question (if you are a non-cognitivist) that is determined by the very moral norm in question.

To put the idea I try to make plausible in the form of a slogan: the *substance* of the normative source-requirement *implies* the requirement of *local* attitudinal *coherence* as framed by the very content of a particular source-requirement. Hence, on the proposed view, if it is true that morality, prudence, professional codes, etiquette etc. require from you something in the substantive sense, it is also true that this substantive requirement entails the relevant requirement regarding what attitudes you ought to have/ought not to have if you remain under some normative requirement in the source sense of normativity. What this non-detachable and non-substantive requirement amounts to is that you ought to have the very attitudes that render it possible for you to genuinely satisfy the requirement in the source sense of normativity. In other words, you are required to have the very attitudes that are the necessary conditions of your truly satisfying some substantive requirement that on some particular occasion applies to you. And if I am not mistaken about this claim then what it also implies is that at least some structural rationality seems to be inscribed into the very concept of substantive normative requirement. In other words, it turns out that if being under some substantive normative requirement entails being under the relevant normative content-fitting requirement, then given what the ITRR states, introducing a separate normative requirement of rationality cashed out in terms of some requirement of coherence is spurious.

8.3 Is the Inter-normative Transmission Rule of Rationality Mistargeted?

Some may object to what I have argued, and say: "You are right but in a somewhat trivial sense. Nobody denies that you cannot be moral if you do not have moral beliefs, or the relevant non-cognitive commitments, as you cannot be truly prudent if you lack correct beliefs on what prudence is, or if assuming you are a non-cognitivist about normativity, you lack the relevant attitude of norm-acceptance. But how does what you say here touch upon the problem we discuss? When we hold that rationality requires you to have coherent attitudes, what we mean is that rationality, in the sense we are after, requires you to follow the rules of logic when engaged in reasoning. Thus, what we want to capture is the logical structure of reasoning that forces upon the reasoner, either in theoretical or practical contexts, certain requirements s/he ought to satisfy".

If that is your—my possible opponent—line of defence, then my reply goes as follows: It is not the case that we can innocuously say "There are requirements of rationality in the source, substantive sense, and other requirements in the non-substantive sense that concern relations among attitudes. And both of them make up for the normative requirements of rationality so that rationality requires you to be rational in the substantive sense of acting on the correct/best reason (or however you specify the requirement of rationality in the substantive, general sense), and additionally, to have coherent attitudes". That this *Double Binding View* cannot be true is explained by your claim's being in some sense redundant. Note that what you suggest is that rationality in the source sense requires one to do[1] *A*, when doing *A* cannot be fulfilled without doing *B*, where *B* means having the relevant attitudes needed to satisfy *A*. Shortly, if it is true that rationality requires you to respond to reasons (given that this is the correct, rough formulation of what rationality requires of you in the source sense of normativity), then it also requires you to have the relevant attitudes towards the proposition that is the object of the particular normative source-requirement that applies to you. Specifically, it requires you to have attitudes that do not conflict with the content of what you are required in the particular situation you are in.

Therefore, if it is generally true that rationality requires you to respond to reasons, it also requires you not to believe that rationality does not require you to respond to reasons. This is because if you do not believe that rationality requires you to respond to reasons, then the idea that rationality requires you to respond to reasons is not a part of your standpoint. And being no part of your standpoint, it has no authority over you, in the sense that you cannot rationally act on the substantive requirement of rationality (the requirement to respond to reasons) without believing that rationality requires you not to believe that rationality does not require you to respond to reasons. Note that the connection between the source sense of the normative requirement of rationality, the requirement to respond to reasons, and the non-substantive sense of the normative requirement of rationality, that is, the

[1] I count forming attitudes as a form of acting.

requirement of having coherent attitudes within the framework of what rationality requires of you in the source-sense of normativity is not a psychological connection. It is not the case that if it is true that rationality requires you to respond to reasons (source-sense), and you believe that this is what rationality requires of you, you can (in the sense of its being a true option) have a belief that stands in conflict with what you believe rationality requires of you, and end up with the belief that rationality does not require you to respond to reasons. Consequently, you cannot violate the non-substantive requirement of having coherent attitudes if you truly satisfy some substantive requirement in the source sense of normativity.

8.4 One Bad Result for the Double Binding View

If it was plausible to assume that there are two senses in which rationality imposes on an agent normative requirements, the substantive sense and the non-substantive one, then we would have to accept the unwelcome consequence that sometimes rationality is the source of conflicting normative requirements. It requires of you, in the first sense of normative requirement, something that you ought not to do if you are to satisfy what rationality requires of you in the second sense of normative requirement. To illustrate that problem suppose that among the normative requirements of rationality in the non-substantive sense is the *principle of belief-intention*, which says that if you believe you ought to *phi*, then you ought to intend to *phi*. Now, imagine that your satisfying the requirement in question will have a disastrous effect on the planet: if you satisfy the *belief-intention* requirement of rationality, some evil demon will cause a cosmic incident that will bring life on the Earth to an end. If the demon's threat were a real scenario, then rationality would require you not to think along the belief-intention requirement that rationality in some other sense requires you to follow. Therefore, rationality would require from you two different things you cannot satisfy at once. But that would be an odd result.

In order to avoid the paradox of conflicting claims that rationality requires you to satisfy, perhaps you would be tempted to modify the PLATITUDE in a way that would fit the highly untypical circumstances of the sort mentioned above, and propose a disjunctive general requirement of rationality of the following form: *either* rationality requires you to do something in the substantive sense of normativity, *or* it requires you to have coherent attitudes (call this requirement the *Rationality in Emergency (RE)*). To render the new requirement more plausible, you could express the new disjunctive requirement in the following words:

Rationality in Emergency (RE) when satisfying a certain non-substantive requirement of rationality is supposed to bring about an effect that is destructive to what is of genuine value, then non-conformance to the relevant non-substantive requirement of rationality is what rationality in the substantive sense requires of you.

Despite being attractive on the surface, the *Rationality in Emergency* is seriously flawed. It invites an obvious complaint, which is that it is simply not true that in the case at hand rationality gives you a choice of being rational either in one way or another. In a sense, the requirement of having coherent attitudes, as I have tried to argue in this section, is only an apparent normative requirement since coherence among one's attitudes is not something that the subject whose cognitive system functions properly can decide to satisfy or not to satisfy. To illustrate briefly my point, suppose that you recognize that having a belief is holding some proposition as true. Moreover, you take it to be noncontroversial that if there is a tight conceptual connection between having a belief and its object's being true, then if you are about to have any belief, you ought to believe what is true. Suppose next that you believe that snow is white because snow is white. However, unluckily to you, some evil demon demands of you, on the threat of causing a cosmic incident that will destroy all life on the Earth, that you stop believing that snow is white. How are you to think about the requirements you are under?

It seems to me that it is plausible to assume that your thinking goes as follows: you are convinced that if there is anything that rationality truly, in the substantive sense, requires of you, it requires you to prevent this cosmic catastrophe. However, it also seems to me that you would find it hard, if not impossible, to do what you think you have most normative reason to do, namely to suddenly stop believing that snow is white if it is white. My explanation of why it is impossible for you to conform to the demon's wish is that ceasing to have a certain attitude is something different from realizing how disastrous effect maintaining this very attitude might bring about. If having attitudes is in no sense similar to the activity of choosing clothes from one's wardrobe, having or not having them cannot be properly thought of as an object of some independent normative requirement. If I am correct in this respect, then such extraordinary examples as the one with the evil demon that are supposed to demonstrate possible conflicts between different requirements of rationality, miss the target. Requirements that lack success conditions are no requirements at all.

What I have attempted to show in this section is that, if the normativity of rationality is conceived of in the source sense, analogously to the source-normativity of prudence and the source-normativity of professional codes, then a particular normative requirement in the source sense (for example, the one that says that you ought to respond correctly to reasons), if it is truly normative, precludes the possibility of the local incoherence among one's attitudes by forcing the subject to adjust her attitudes to the substantive normative requirement that applies to her. If that view is not mistaken, then strong incoherence among one's attitudes is not an option, and consequently the general requirement of coherence cannot be an independent normative requirement of rationality.

8.5 Why 'Why be Rational?' Is a Good Question?

If rationality indeed can be conceived of in terms of source-normative requirements, as many philosophers propose, and against what I have argued in the preceding section, then it should (in the non-normative sense of "should") also share the fate of other source-normative requirements, and allow us to ask "Why ought I to do what the source-requirement of rationality requires me to do?". A proper answer to the question of that format is to be supplied in terms of reasons.

However, that this very question is essentially mistaken remains the view held by a great number of the participants to the debate, who argue in one way or another that the question 'Is rationality normative?', when understood as the question pressing you to give reasons why be rational, rests on a fatal mistake (Southwood 2008, p. 17).[2] The mistake in question, as Nicholas Southwood diagnoses it, consists in "looking for a justification for rational compliance *outside* of rationality" (Southwood 2008, p. 18; my emphasis), whereas it seems plausible to Southwood and many others to assume that, if rationality is normative, it is normative in the very or at least similar sense to the normativity of morality. Or, as Broome suggests, it is normative in its own right, in some special way (Broome 2007, p. 350; 2008, p. 97).

This section is devoted to provide a brief explanation of why I think that Southwood's suggestion is unconvincing, which in turn will form a part of my negative assessment of Broome's suggestion, according to which rationality is "the independent source of normative requirements" (Broome 2007, p. 350).

To support his conviction that they key to understand the normativity of rationality lies in the appropriate understanding of the normativity of morality, Southwood invites us to recall Prichard's seminal paper, in which Pritchard argues that there is something gravely wrong with attempting to answer moral sceptic by seeking some independent justification for compliance with moral claims. The lesson to be derived from Prichard's elucidation, in Southwood's view, is to learn that the normativity of morality is *inside,* not *outside* morality. In other words, the only sensible answer to the question why be moral can be given by some *moral* reason. Likewise, the only sensible answer to the question why be rational can be given by reason(s) of rationality. Given that this is true, we can still sensibly ask whether the normativity of morality is in all relevant aspects alike the putative normativity of rationality. My conjecture is that it is not since we can effortlessly understand what it means when it is said that morality gives us normative reason, which is not so easy decipherable when it comes to understanding the claim that rationality provides us with normative reason.

The feature to which Southwood draws special attention in pursuing the analogy in normativity between the moral and the rational domain is that the source of normativity in both cases resides within these domains themselves. Put another

---

[2] If they are right, then they invite us to have two incoherent attitudes. First, they want us to believe that rationality is normative in the source-sense, similarly to morality and prudence, where such source-normative requirements admit of the question about reasons to comply with them. And second, they also want us to believe that rationality is similarly normative to morality, in the sense that both make no room for the question 'Why be moral/rational?', which intuitively seems to be a good question to ask in the context of any source-normative requirement. What we are left with is a fuzzy picture of the putative similarities in normativity between morality and rationality, which does not help us much to understand the normativity of either of these two sources. That is because it turns out that though both morality and rationality are source-normative, the source-normativity of one is so special in comparison to the source-normativity of the other that we lack grounds to derive any substantive conclusion about the character of the normativity that morality and rationally seem to share.

way, when we say that the normativity of moral claims is internal, we mean that the reasons for being moral are of moral kind. To say that they are of moral kind is another way of saying that they have source in moral values. If I ask you, why it is morally wrong to cheat on others, one quick answer that springs to your mind is that there is something wrong in cheating on others. Properly speaking then, moral reasons are normative in virtue of moral values they embody, which in turn indicate that they are, normative in themselves. However, if we explore the suggestion that what makes demands of morality normative is that they concern intrinsic values, standardly accrued to the objects of moral claims, then the analogy between the normativity of rationality and the normativity of morality shows superficial. A bulk of apt questions arises to be dealt with. Are there any values essentially connected with rationality? Is there any intrinsic value in being rational? Or, to approach the problem from the other angle, if there is something intrinsically good about being rational *tout court*, then where lies the intrinsic badness of being irrational? What values are neglected when one is irrational? These questions make perfect sense for me. And unless I am proposed a satisfactory answer to them, the claim that rationality is normative out of itself remains attractive, though a bit far-fetched slogan.

Notice that what I ask for when I ask for a vindication of the claim that rationality is normative in the sense analogous to the way that morality is normative is not a sophisticated answer, but quite a simple one. I want you to explain me in what exactly consists the badness of being irrational, or what wrongness I commit when I am irrational? I think that you cannot give me a satisfactory reply because the only reply to the question so articulated that comes to one's mind is that, if you are not rational, you are not as you ought to be. But the latter statement is as obscure and begs explanation as the question initially raised.

I have no problem with understanding the claim that causing others to suffer is morally wrong, because I understand the wrongness of suffering. However, when you tell me that there is something similarly deeply wrong with being irrational, I am puzzled and perplexed. What I find hard to comprehend is the alleged intrinsic badness of being irrational. Where exactly does it reside?

One available answer is that it resides in not conforming to the norms of rationality, which in themselves constitute normative reasons. But granted that, I can raise another question concerning why I ought to think that norms of rationality are the source of the normative commitments for me? Any available on the philosophical market answer to that question strikes me as unsatisfactory. Teleological, or constitutivist accounts, according to which being rational is, so to speak, a part of one's nature or constitution, collapse since if rationality somehow frames my way of thinking and acting, no serious violation of rationality seems possible. If my cognitive capacities have been designed to recognize, and then to observe to the claims of rationality, my true intentional departure from rationality cannot be effectuated.

The distinctive object approach of the Broomean kind also fails unless we explain the distinctive character of the normative claims of rationality. However such a line seems to me an unpromising one because it is very difficult to make plausible the assumption that there is some source of the normative requirements, which is so unlike to any other source we encounter in everyday life. So-called 'familiar' normativities speak to us through reasons we can recognize, so we can further either comply with them or not comply. They are able, at least in principle, to be a part of our motivation. I can understand that inflicting pain is something I ought not to do to others, or have normative reason not to do to others because pain is something what animals (including me) try to avoid. But if you tell me that there is something *normatively* wrong in being inconsistent, I am afraid; I cannot truly grasp your point. The bare idea of intrinsic normativity as something simply instilled into certain kind of requirements, in our case in the requirements of rationality, seems to me hard to swallow unless I am clearly explained what exactly renders the requirements of rationality in either of the two stipulated senses normative *in themselves*. And more importantly, what if anything, makes it the case that I should be truly concerned about being rational.

8.6 What Is Wrong with the First-Person Authority Account?

Many answers have been offered in the recent literature on how to meet the "Why Be Rational?" question, which Southwood labelled Broome's Challenge, the challenge to demonstrate that the thesis that rationality is normative is true (Southwood 2008, p. 12). In the view of many one promising way of dealing with that task is to allude to the first-personal authority account. In this section I shall focus on the critical assessment of a particular version of the defence of that account as put forward by Nicolas Southwood (2008, p. 25). According to his proposal, as I understand it, that the subject is under certain normative requirement becomes transparent to her once she thinks of her attitudes, and the attitudes she ought to have, given the ones she has now. In a sense, such a picture seems familiar and correct. Suppose I have the belief that snow is white, of which I remain unconscious because it is so obviously true to me that I have never bothered to give it any thought. Suppose next, that surprisingly to me I meet people who doubt in this proposition being true. Their lack of conviction that snow is white makes me realize that I indeed believe that snow is white. Next, given that I am now aware of my having the belief that snow is white, Southwood's suggestion goes, that very fact stops me from adopting a conflicting attitude, say, of believing that snow is not white. So far so good. I agree with him that, if the subject believes that snow is white, the fact of having the particular belief is *taken* by her as normative reason not to believe in the proposition that snow is not white. That I ought not to have contradictory beliefs about the colour of snow is due to the fact that I *think* I cannot at the very same time have confidence in self-contradictory propositions.

The disagreement between us lies in the nature of explanation of why I ought not to have incoherent attitudes. According to Southwood, there seems to be something normative involved in the explanation of why I should not believe that snow is not white if I hold the belief in the opposite proposition. Moreover, this essential normative 'something' has to do with the fact that this is me who has the belief in question.

Here come my two worries. First, I do not quite see what is this normative element that it is essentially attached to the first-personal point of view on Southwood's account. Instead, what I can see is some psychological element inscribed in how we think about having attitudes. I take my belief that snow is white as 'forbidding' me to have the opposite belief not because there is something normative in having this particular belief but because the concept of belief imposes on me certain constraints. The concept of belief tells you that in order to have belief; you ought to hold some proposition being true if it is true. So, if you formed a belief, it is plausible to assume that you formed it on the basis of evidence. And the same piece of evidence could not give support to the conflicting claims. Therefore, if you do believe that snow is white, yet also do not believe that snow is white, you are incomprehensible to yourself. Unless you treat your attitudes as putting constraints on what attitudes you are allowed to have, it does not make much sense to talk about your having any attitudes at all. Therefore, if it is true that you ought not to have contradictory beliefs, the 'ought' at stake is not a "mighty" ought since it does not confer any proper normative requirement on you, it only signals that if you happened to have contradictory beliefs, something had gone wrong, where 'wrong' is to be read as suggesting some cognitive rather than volitional defect.

Nevertheless, what seems to me a plausible suggestion in Southwood's account is the idea that there is some sort of connection between the requirements of rationality and the first-person perspective, though what I find dubious is his assumption that the connection in question is of the *normative* nature. Southwood thinks that normativity in question is obvious because of the authority of the first-personal standpoint period. But then enters my second worry. Why does he link the first-personal standpoint with the normative authority? Why, to put the same idea in different words, *my* being the subject of deliberative thinking entails, or produces straightforward *normative* consequences? Notice that to say that there are requirements of rationality, which have the first-personal authority over your attitudes, is another way of saying that from your own perspective the requirements of rationality seem to be normative. But that judgment, if it is true, perfectly fits with the view that Southwood rejects out of hand, namely that so-called normative authority of the first-personal requirements of normativity is of *psychological* kind. That I ought to respect the logical relations between concepts in my thinking is something that makes my thinking possible, but from that nothing yet follows to the effect that thinking along the patterns of correct thinking is what I ought to do, or have normative reason to do. It is one thing to say that thinking correctly is essential to rationality and quite another to identify the rules of correct reasoning with first-personal *normative* requirements of rationality.

In fact, it seems to me that, if it was true that demands of rationality were genuinely normative, their normativity would not have to do with the standpoint one adopts, but rather would be a matter of certain normative fact being true, precisely that you ought to be coherent. However, in such a case the standpoint from which the reasoning runs would be devoid of any substantive importance.

It also seems to me that, if there are any true normative demands they have less to do with the first-personal authority, and more with the content of the very requirements under consideration. People may let their attitudes be authoritative in the normative sense and yet behave in a way they have normative reason not to behave. Southwood's proposal does not prevent such a result. What it says is only that given, for example, my views about the moral significance of poverty, I am subject to certain standpoint-relative demands concerning how to share my income (cf. Southwood 2008, p. 27). Therefore, if I had different, for instance, crazy views on what morality requires me to do, these views would commit me normatively to conform to them. And that would be so not because I find the content of the moral requirements to be of normative significance, but only because having attitudes is, generally, commitive.

My main objection towards Southwood's proposal of how to account for the normativity of rationality concerns grounding normativity in the first-personal authority before one argues successfully that authority of the first-personal standpoint is to be properly conceived of in terms of *normative* demands. In other words, *that* I *think* that certain attitude *necessarily* commits me to another, or prevents me from adopting another, is the result of my first-personal recognition of the normative truth about the particular requirement of rationality.

Southwood seems to be aware of the difficulties in understanding the nature of these standpoint-relative requirements *qua* normative requirements, and in order to show that they are unmotivated, he introduces the example, in which the requirements of friendship are assumed to be normative similarly to the way the requirements of rationality are normative. If the analogy works, it is supposed to bring us closer to the answer to the question in what the normativity of standpoint-relative demands consists in.

One preliminary methodological remark will be in place here. Note that the argument from analogy is supposed to work given two conditions are satisfied. First, Southwood manages to show that the normativity of standpoint-relative requirements of rationality is of the same kind as the normativity of the requirements of friendship. Otherwise no instructive lesson could be derived from comparing them. Second, that these requirements, which serve as the illustration of the normativity that Southwood is after will successfully reveal the essence of normativity.

My complaint is that Southwood's analogy fails at the outset because the delivered example with friendship does not pass the above-mentioned methodological test. Neither it succeeds in capturing the essence of normativity, nor does it give us a correct explanation of what normativity consists in.

Consider the following features of the demands of friendship that he takes to be illuminating in the context of the debate over the normativity of rationality:

1. Demands of friendship are *genuine* demands, rather than merely believed, or perceived demands.
2. These demands are *essentially* agent-relative demands, which is to say that they are relative to some particular friendship in question.
3. These demands also partially *constitute* friendship (Southwood 2008, p. 27; my emphasis).

Now think of the demands of optimism. Optimism, as I roughly characterize it, is a general attitude that requires of you to have positive attitude towards future events, irrespectively of whether these events will involve you personally or not. If one wants to be more precise, she may characterize Optimism in terms of the general requirement of coherence that requires of optimist not to have any attitude, which in principle is irreconcilable with the optimist credo. Hence, no matter what kind of attitude is at stake, whether you hope that something is to happen, believe that something has happened, or expect something to happen, if you really are an optimist, your attitudes should be guided by the thought that "everything's gonna be alright". Having suggested what being optimist consists in, let us see whether Optimism passes the test of normativity that Southwood offers. If Optimism is construed in terms of the requirements, these requirements satisfy all three conditions that friendship does. It satisfies (1) because what Optimism requires of you is not a matter of your beliefs but rather the definition of what such an attitude to life, broadly construed, consists in. It also satisfies (2) because if you are not an optimist, the requirements of optimism do not apply to you. If you are not an optimist, requirements of optimism are not relative to your standpoint, and if that is the case, the requirements of optimism also have no authority over you. Finally and not surprisingly, the demands of Optimism also satisfy (3) if certain demands constitute such an attitude as Optimism, as I suggested at the beginning by stipulating what being an optimist consists in, then obviously they also partially constitute Optimism. Since if some requirements make for certain attitude or relation, then they also make for this attitude or relation partially. Therefore Optimism turns out to be in all relevant respects such as friendship. And being in the relevant aspects like friendship renders it also similar to rationality by the light of Southwood's argument. But such a view strikes me as obviously false! Optimism is not normative in the sense, in which rationality is supposed to be normative. If you are not an optimist, there is nothing wrong with you that render you vulnerable to the sort of criticism that you can expect, if you violate some requirement of rationality. Moreover, being optimist or not is your choice whereas being rational seems not to be something entirely in your hands. Even if you do not care about coherent thinking, it is far from obvious whether you are truly capable of not being coherent, at least to a certain degree. That is to say, it is not clear whether having incoherent attitudes is a true option for you, given you know what having some particular attitude consists in, and how your mind operates. Moreover, the comment that explains why Optimism is not normative, though survives the normative test designed for friendship, also applies to friendship as portrayed by Southwood.

If that is the case, then what important lesson about the nature of normative requirements we are supposed to learn from contrasting the requirements of optimism, the requirements of friendship and the requirements of rationality? It seems to me that the lesson is that the features Southwood finds to be crucial in order to understand the nature of the normative requirement do not capture the essence of normativity since after the analysis of his example we are still justified in asking why we would care about friendship, as we are justified in asking why we would care about being optimist. That we feel even more awkward to ask why we would care about rationality has nothing to do with Southwood's explanation of normativity, but rather with the fact that we barely have any idea what exactly amounts to the normative requirements of rationality that we should respect. Lack of a compelling story speaking in favor of the normativity of rationality, as my diagnosis goes, finds explanation in our fundamental inability to think of the very grounds that would be needed to guarantee the success of the argument that rationality is normative.

If these sketchy considerations are on the right track, then we have sufficient ground to conclude that the first-personal authority account fails as a vindication of the normativity of rationality. There are three crucial flaws about the considered proposal. First of all, this position gets off the ground due to the assumption that rationality is normative without explaining first why we would think so. Analogy with morality collapses since moral requirements have grounds in objective values, which is not so obvious in the case of the stipulated value of being coherent. Second, it attempts to account for the normativity in terms of vague notions such as "first-personal authority" that are not necessarily encumbered with the alleged normative flavor, and equally well allow for a psychological interpretation.Finally, given that it is true that rational commitments are standpoint-relative, as it seems to be true, some requirement being standpoint-relative does not yet make it being normative.

Being an optimist is a standpoint-relative requirement (precisely a set of particular requirements), though such that you need not satisfy, if you are not, or do not want to become an optimist. Note that even if I am deeply wrong and Southwood succeeded in providing us with some vindication of the normativity of rationality, in the sense that he has convincingly argued that the essence of the normative requirements resides in the very conditions he highlighted by means of his example with the normative requirements of friendship, then his vindication is still seriously flawed.

The flaw that remains is that on Southwood's account the normativity of rationality turns out to be a conceptual truth. That conceptual truth generates normative consequences is however no part of the normative truth itself and needs to be demonstrated.

8.7 Requirements of Comprehensibility

I shall end up this paper with my brief suggestion of how to think about the requirements of rationality in the situation, where we have no convincing vindicatory story about their normative nature at hand. My proposal tries to do justice to the two opinions that seem to be captured by the PLATITUDE. The first says that, if you have incoherent attitudes, there is something wrong with you, in the sense that you are not entirely as you ought to be. For example, if you believe that snow is white and you simultaneously believe that it is not white, you are irrational. According to the second, when your glass contains petrol instead of gin, it is irrational of you to drink the liquid from the glass. In the first case, irrationality comes from having the attitude, whose content is in sharp conflict with your initial attitude. This sort of irrationality appears when your cognitive system suffers from some defect, as when you mistakenly think that having the belief in *p* poses no constraint on whether you can also have the belief that not *p*. The second case is mistakenly interpreted as an example of genuine irrationality since if you have no way of finding out that the glass you keep in your hand contains petrol, by drinking petrol you did what you had had most reason to do. And that is perfectly what rationality requires of you: acting on the reasons that you have best evidence to treat as the correct ones.

Nevertheless, it also seems to be true that by drinking petrol you did something that you ought not to have done in some objective sense of the term "ought". However, what you ought to do in the light of all relevant and true information is not what human rationality is all about. Human rationality is about reasoning correctly, and manifests in responding correctly to the available normative reasons. It is in the broad sense standpoint-relative. Consequently, on my view, if you have strong evidence in favor of doing something and no evidence against not doing that thing, your doing something that you objectively ought not to do, if you possessed all relevant and true information, is not a violation of some requirement of rationality you ought to conform to. In contrast, when you have contradictory beliefs, you are irrational and not as you ought to be. However the crucial question is whether by being not as you ought to be you violate any genuinely *normative* requirement. My answer is in the negative.

I have attempted to show that rational requirements and normativity are worlds apart. First of all, this is so because we cannot truly think of them along the model provided by morality, or prudence, in which case we are at least able to understand the reasons underlying the normative claims they put on us. Second, we are confused as to in what their alleged normativity consists, and how it retains connection to motivation. Unclarity as to the the latter point seems to me a serious obstacle since if you tell me that something is normative, yet I cannot perceive, or comprehend the normativity you are talking about, how can the alleged normativity have a grip on me? How can something be a true source of *normative* constraints on the subject, if the reason-giving force of the requirements in question remains inaccesible to her?

Of course, there is still an option that there is some normativity that cannot be adequately grasped through reasons. But in such a case the burden of demonstrating that that is the case with the requirements of rationality is on the part of those who advocate for the specific normativity of rationality. Until they offer us a plausible suggestion to that very effect, our suspiciousness seems to me well supported.

Having said that the requirements of rationality are not properly speaking normative, or normative in themselves does not necessarily entail skepticism about the existence of such requirements. They may be real, but being real is not sufficient to generate or imply normative consequences. By saying that the requirements of rationality that amount to the general claim of having coherent attitudes are real, I mean that they do form a part of rational thinking. Not satisfying them is a genuine signal that there is something wrong with us. But again, it is one thing to say that certain set of requirements describe a correct way of operating, and quite another to infer from that claim certain normative consequences of practical valence. Normative requirements, on my view, do guide our thinking but not independently and not in terms of reasons, but from within and through particular attitudes we form when we respond to the individual normative requirements in the substantive sense of normativity.

To sum up: the view I have tried to make attractive is that, if there is any normativity to be ascribed to the requirements of rationality, and consequently there is some truth in the claim that you ought to be rational, the 'ought' in question has to do with a primitive desire most of the typical representatives of our species share. The desire in question is the desire of being comprehensible, either to oneself, or to other people. This desire of being comprehensible, as I further contend, governs our deliberation in a specific way by navigating our reasoning to keep with the norms of correct reasoning. So on my view, that we usually take care of not commitng fatal errors in reasoning, and tend to take seriously the threat of incoherence finds explanation not in the mysterious normativity of rationality, but in the plain interest in being intelligible to ourselves and others.

References

Broome, John. 2005. Does rationality give us reasons? *Philosophical Issues* 15 (1):321–337.
Broome, John. 2007. Does rationality consist in responding correctly to reasons? *Journal of Moral Philosophy* 4 (3): 349–374.
Broome, John. 2008. Reply to Southwood, Kearns and Star, and Cullity. *Ethics* 119 (1):96–108.
Southwood, Nicholas. 2008. Vindicating the normativity of rationality. *Ethics* 119 (1):9–30.

Chapter 9
Rules and Rights

Tomasz Pietrzykowski

Abstract The relation between rights and rules has always been one of the basic conceptual problems of legal and moral philosophy. Since Bentham's "nonsense upon stilts" the traditional idea of "natural" rights has been an object of devastating critique. In particular, all positivist accounts of law regard rights to necessarily derive from rules. This paper defends a redefined priority of rights. I assume that when rights are conceived as a content of specific mental states in which something is represented as due to someone, they may precede any fully fledged social rules effectuating them. Moreover, in many cases, such right-feelings cause the development of instrumental rules created to protect and enforce such rights. In this sense, the priority of rights thesis is fully reconcilable with the contemporary approaches to naturalizing explanations of legal phenomena. Since my argument claims that the development of rules may depend on more primitive mental representations of rights or proto-rights rather than seeks any objective justification of any "natural" or "inherent" rights, it has very little (if anything) in common with the natural law tradition.

Keywords Law · Right · Rule · Naturalism · Human

9.1 Introduction

One of the most interesting and controversial aspect of rules is their relationship with subjective rights. Rules can be treated as the only conceivable source of rights, but also as just a means to protect some independently existing rights. Various versions of both these positions have been endorsed in philosophical and legal thought. My aim is to reexamine this relationship in view of the contemporary science contributing to our understanding of the phenomenon of normativity, as well as the naturalistic approach to moral and legal rules.

T. Pietrzykowski (✉)
University of Silesia, Katowice, Poland
e-mail: tomasz.pietrzykowski@us.edu.pl

M. Araszkiewicz et al. (eds.), *Problems of Normativity, Rules and Rule-Following*,
Law and Philosophy Library 111, DOI 10.1007/978-3-319-09375-8_9

9.2 The Priority of Rights Thesis

According to the popular idea, there are at least some rights that are held by human beings just "by virtue" of their being human. Thus, they are not derived from any rules, but rather precede any rules declaring or enforcing them. The conceptual and ontological distinction between subjective rights and objective rules has deep, even if unclear, historical and philosophical roots. The beginnings of an idea of subjective right distinguished from an objectively "right" behaviour (justified by a rule) can be traced back to the famous medieval argument advanced by William of Ockham in defense of the Franciscan order against Papal accusations of heresy. Yet, even in the much later writings of Thomas Hobbes, Jean Bodin, Hugo Grotius, or Samuel Pufendorf it remained ambiguous whether right meant subjective entitlement or conduct justified by objectively binding rules.

The modern idea of rights as inherent "endowments" of human beings was born in the Age of Enlightenment [1] As Thomas Paine put it, "natural rights are those which appertain to man in right of his very existence," originating ultimately in the divine creation of man and providing foundation for all civil rights.[2] Since that time, as J. Griffin has pointed out, the "extension" of the concept of inherent human rights has evolved considerably, but its "intension" has remained practically unchanged.[3] Thus, contemporary ideology of human rights remains fully subscribed to an idea of an inborn rights held by human beings just by virtue of their membership in the human species.

Moral and legal rules should reflect such inherent rights of human beings instead of pretending to create or justify their existence.[4] An illuminating example of this idea can be found in Article 30 of the Polish Constitution, which affirms that "an inherent and inalienable dignity of the person is the source of all rights and freedoms of persons and citizens. The respect and protection thereof is the duty of all public authorities." Interestingly enough, the political success of the idea of inherent human rights has coincided with a noticeable decline of the idea of natural law as a system of universally binding, objective rules. I will call the claim that some rights may exist without any prior rules "the Priority of Rights Thesis."

9.3 The Priority of Rules Thesis

When only the Priority of Rights Thesis had been openly formulated, it attracted the severe criticism of many moral and legal philosophers. One of the earliest and probably most famous rebuttals came from Jeremy Bentham. According to the leader of

---

[1] See, e.g. Hunt (2007).

[2] Paine (1791).

[3] Griffin (2009).

[4] See, e.g. Ishay (2008), Morsink (2009), Osiatyński (2010).

the group of "philosophical radicals," each right may be nothing else than a "child of law." The notion of a right without a previously assumed rule is like an offspring without parents. The very idea of such a right amounts to "simple nonsense." There might be good reasons to wish that there were rules instituting and protecting some rights, but this does not entail that such desired rights can "exist" in any sense even if there are no rules establishing them. As Bentham puts it clearly: "wants are not means, hunger is not bread."[5] From this perspective, the fallacy of the Priority of Rights Thesis relates to a well-known gap between "ought" and "is." The belief in rights prior to rules conflates a wish that some rights "ought" to exist (through the adoption of postulated rules) with rights that actually do exist. Moreover, as Bentham claimed, the idea that one's desired, imagined rights constrain all present and future rule-making authorities amounts to "self-conceit exalted into insanity" and commits its advocates to an extremely dangerous "anarchical fallacy."

An extensive argument against the Priority of Rights Thesis was developed by Bentham's famous follower, John Austin.[6] Later on, in the twentieth century, similarly penetrating critique of the concept of independently existing subjective rights was provided by another champion of positivistic legal thought, Hans Kelsen.[7] According to his "pure" theory of law, subjective right is nothing more than the very legal norm (rule) taken in its relation to a certain subject (its beneficiary). Any subjective right, as well as the corresponding obligation of another agent, has to be established by a norm. Subjective right is just the content of a rule described from the perspective of its beneficiary.[8] Hence, any dualism of subjective rights and objective rules is illusory. They are the same thing conceived from two different perspectives. Further analytical critiques of the Priority of the Rights Thesis, together with the concept of right itself, were offered by leading Scandinavian realists such as Karl Olivecrona and Alf Ross.[9] I will consequently call the views according to which all rights necessarily derive from rules the "Priority of Rules Thesis."

9.4 Conceptual Confusions and the Noble Dreams

Despite devastating critiques of the Priority of Rights Thesis, contemporary legal, political, and public discourses have been dominated by an idea of inherent natural human rights. This "rights-talk" seems to flourish despite its weak philosophical foundations, mainly due to the nobleness of an ideological dream of a world in which each human being is duly respected, independently of the caprices of any

[5] Bentham (2011 [1795]).

[6] Austin (1832).

[7] Kelsen (2000 [1960]).

[8] Kelsen (2000 [1960]) also distinguished the "narrower" meaning of a legal right, in which it is a more technical legal term referring to a situation in which the rule in question grants the beneficiary of another's obligation the additional power to demand fulfillment of that obligation.

[9] Olivecrona (1971), Ross (1958).

rule-making authorities. Even if the Priority of Rights is based on an incoherent idea of rights not awarded by any rules, there can by hardly any doubt that the world would be much better if the Priority of Rights Thesis were actually true. Therefore, attitudes toward the modern ideology of human rights (as a version of the Priority of Rights Thesis) seem rather ambivalent. On the one hand, it may exert beneficial effects on the respective political communities only as long as it is widely shared by their members and their authorities. Effectively undermining its philosophical foundations may bring dangerous and unwanted outcomes. On the other hand, beliefs in the existence of some inherent human rights lack sound foundations. They either rely on an act of pure faith, involving an incoherent idea of rights existing independently of any rules, or remain committed to a kind of naturalistic fallacy where the potential moral consequences are held to make related statements concerning the existence of rights descriptively true. It seems that this kind of ambivalence permeates most legal and philosophical accounts of the versions of the Priority of Rights Thesis that remain popular today.

I would like to argue, however, that the widespread skepticism concerning the Priority of Rights Thesis can be challenged by changing paradigms of legal analysis that gradually become more naturalistic and empirically oriented. In particular, some developments in science involving the examination of biological roots and the psychological underpinnings of all normative phenomena may make the case against the Priority of Rights Thesis less persuasive than it seemed in the purely conceptual and logical analysis that used to dominate philosophical inquiry. From this perspective, conceptual critique along Benthamian-Kelsenian lines may turn out to be rather superficial and largely missing the point (even if undoubtedly clarifying some obvious confusions and obscurities).[10] In my opinion, there can be at least some plausible interpretations of the Priority of Rights Thesis that seem compatible with the emerging naturalistic account of mental, cultural, and legal phenomena. If this is correct, the unqualified Priority of Rules Thesis resulting from simple refutation of any possibility of rights existing independently of rules may amount to throwing the baby out with the bathwater.

9.5 Rights as Mental Representations

In order to discuss the Priority of Rights Thesis, it is necessary to have a sufficiently clear idea of what rights are. It is also obvious that in any version of a defensible Priority of Rights Thesis, a "right" cannot be identified with a normative situation of an agent in relation to rules granting some entitlements or imposing duties on others. Such a conception of rights would by definition exclude their existence without previous rules. On the other hand, it is hardly possible today to understand rights as any kind of mysterious entities belonging to some Platonic heaven or metaphysical

[10] For some doubts concerning the value and validity of conceptual arguments see Pietrzykowski (2012).

endowments possessed by humans solely by virtue of their very "nature" or the will of their Creator.

Given these considerations, I would like to attempt to redefine rights as content of particular kind of mental representations held by individuals. Rights so conceived would ultimately be (similar to as rules) "thought-objects."[11] As famously proposed by Herbert L. A. Hart, for a social rule to exist there has to be some concordant practice determined by "internal point of view" on the side of at least some of its users.[12] Following a rule involves an internal attitude of some normative content (in which some pattern of behaviour is represented as an "ought" of a given agent). Only due to such a normative mental state may a pattern of conduct constitute a subjectively relevant reason for action. Hence, I would consider "rights" as mental states of this basically normative kind, in which something is represented as "due" to someone (including the cases when it is represented as due to the holder of this mental state herself). I will call this kind of mental representation "rights-feelings." Such rights-feelings underlie social actions of claiming, asserting, recognizing, accepting, or fulfilling what is perceived as "due" to someone (including oneself). Arguably, not only intentional rule-governed behaviour (based on an internal point of view), but also actions determined by more primitive rights-feelings seem to depend on internal representations of a pattern of conduct that "ought" to be effectuated.[13]

The contents of rights-feelings, like all kinds of mental states, are shaped by interaction between internal and external factors. They emerge, develop, and evolve under the predominant pressures of an agent's socio-cultural environment, interacting with internal needs, goals, affections, processes of thought and associations. This makes all sorts of "greedy" psychological reductionisms unable to adequately and completely explain normative phenomena.[14] On the other hand, any such phenomena may exist only as expression in the behaviour and speech of some internal representation belonging to specific mental states of a normative content (in which something is perceived as someone's "ought"). Thus, all collective actions and attitudes that constitute reality of a normative order are rooted in individuals' internal, psychological states. Thus, no empirically credible explanation of normative phenomena that would ignore the centrality of mental states in triggering the actions and reactions of agents is conceivable. In this sense, any theory of normative order, including law, has to be at least partially a psychological one.

[11] I borrow the notion of norms as "thought-objects" from Weinberger (1986).

[12] Very similar points were previously developed by Alf Ross (1958), who pointed to the patterns of behaviour grounded in normative ideology shared by participants of a given community.

[13] The ideas developed here rely on a monistic ontology in which there is no separate domain of "ought" (Stelmach 2011).

[14] In many cases, such psychologism exists rather as a straw man for critiques than an actually held position. A classic example may be the "psychologism" of Leon Petrazycki's theory of law and morality and its critique by such anti-psychologists as Czeslaw Znamierowski.

9.6 The Defense of the Redefined Priority of Rights Thesis

The version of the Priority of Rights Thesis I would like to defend here is a hypothesis that rights-feelings—regarded as some kind of primitive mental representations of something as due to someone—may precede any developed internal point of view, and consequently any fully fledged social rules.[15] Such rudimentary rights- or proto-rights feelings (without even being conceptualized as "rights") consist of representing some conduct as someone's benefit that "should" be effectuated by someone or at least allowed to be effectuated because of the needs or wants of its beneficiary.[16] The argument in favor of this hypothesis refers to the evolutionary origin of the human mind and the nature of mental phenomena. Animal and human minds have evolved as mechanisms facilitating pursuit of strategies that have proven adaptively successful. In order to achieve that the human mind developed as a structure capable of generating complex combinations of cognitive, affective, and motivational processes allowing it to perceive the world in a meaningful way and flexibly react to changing circumstances. The driving force of such reactions are needs and affections including fear, anger, empathy, love, shame, gratitude, envy, joy, hope, and the like. Such motivations, along with associated patterns of conduct, incline humans toward such strategies as kin and reciprocal altruism, seeking retaliations, tribal and egocentric biases, conformity, collecting means of comfort and safe living, avoiding filth, and so on. Primitive, proto-normative passions of this kind may also occur in some non-human species of animals—for example, empathy or fairness has been demonstrated in famous experiments conducted on monkeys.[17] Probably only humans, however, have developed sufficiently advanced cognitive skills to conceptualize such recurrent combinations as an "ought" and thus convert them into conscious normative expectations. Nevertheless, the main building blocks of normative mental states, including primitive rights (or proto-rights) feelings, seem to consist simply in combined affective and cognitive processes that make one perceive some pattern of conduct as necessary to satisfy one's needs or wants that deserve to be met.

---

[15] The primitive right-like representations are responsible for cooperative dispositions that Wojciech Załuski (2009) considers the natural underpinnings of law.

[16] I do not attach to much value to the precise definitional difference between the notions "rights-feelings" and "proto-rights feelings." Roughly, by proto-rights feelings, I mean a mental state representing something (behavior, object, benefit, harm) as due to someone without any conceptualization of such desert as right. By "rights-feelings," I mean a similar state that is more developed toward a representation of a rule effectuating a right that should be recognized by others (although the existence of a right is not derived from the awareness that is granted by already socially recognized rules). Primitive rights (or proto-rights) feelings may to some extent correspond to the idea of "rudimentary rules" as proposed by Bartosz Brozek (2012) or proto-norms of conduct developed by Stanislaw Ehrlich (1997), but I will not analyze the relationships and differences between those accounts here.

[17] DeWaal (2008).

Primitive rights or proto-rights feelings should be distinguished from more complex forms of mental representations of rights that are dependent on awareness of the content of recognized rules of conduct. This kind of mental representation is therefore derivative and secondary to rules. The Priority of Rights Thesis I defend here does not deny the obvious fact that rights (including their underlying mental representation) can be based on awareness of some already existing rules. It claims only that there can exist simple, primitive rights or proto-rights feelings which may emerge without any reference to socially established rules effectuating them. Furthermore, this kind of rudimentary rights-feelings may actually causally underlie the later development of respective rules that are proposed, formulated and accepted to address sufficiently strong or widespread representations of what is (ought to be) due to whom.

My conjecture is that primitive rights-feelings precede the emergence of social rules and create a link between pure wants or desires and normative rules implicating a fully developed internal point of view. They may play a crucial role in the phylogenesis of social normative orders. Paving the way for the development of fundamental rules of such orders, later on they are to a large extent overshadowed by complex representations of rights based on the internalized content of rules actually functioning in the social milieu of an agent. Nevertheless, in many situations, the discrepancy between rights-feelings and the content of externally existing rules may inspire individuals to object to rules or demand their adoption. The hypothesis of the priority of rights and their partial independence from adopted rules would also help to elucidate the famous "anarchical" potential of rights-feelings motivating individuals to demand establishment of rules aiming to effectuate postulated rights. It would also explain the persistence of an idea of inherent rights of human beings despite its obvious conceptual weakness, which has been clear at least from Bentham's time.

Two important comments should be made, however, in relation to such a version of the Priority of Rights Thesis. First, there is no reason to believe that the complex mental processes underlying primitive rights or proto-rights feelings will constitute a fully unified, harmonized order of normative representations. The variety of incentives triggering many parallel, interwoven processes that influence the course and content of our mental life suggests rather a multiplicity of such attributions and suggest that they coincide and conflict with one another. This implicates notorious intra-personal dilemmas and inter-personal controversies concerning what is due to whom as well as whose and what kind of actions should address this. Only to some extent may such representations be made homogenous by similarity of basic needs, cognitive mechanisms, and social environment of particular individuals.

Second, basic rights-feelings may give rise to whole chains of instrumental rules. Most rules constituting such chains are only indirectly related to the original attribution of something as due to someone. Arguably, modern normative orders—not only law but also customary rules of behaviour (such as rules of etiquette, good-manners, or fashion)—include plenty of rules that are direct or indirect means developed to satisfy some ultimate rights-feelings. Typical examples of such instrumental rules could include legal rules of procedure or extra-legal rules of polite behaviour aimed ultimately to avoid harming or embarrassing others. Such instrumental rules in turn stimulate the emergence of secondary rights derived solely from recognition of the content of such instrumental rules. Nevertheless, the rules in question would be pointless unless there were some ultimate rights-feelings underlying the development of the whole chain of instrumentally related rules of conduct.

Conclusion

The Priority of Rights Thesis is an attempt to capture the relation between rules and rights from a modern naturalistic perspective. This kind of naturalism is related only to an assumption that normative phenomena can ultimately be explained only in terms of biological, psychological, and sociological processes of causes and effects. It attempts to elucidate the emergence of rules and the normative orders they compose as a further cultural development of primitive rights or proto-fights feelings (as well as primitive duty-feelings) experienced because of the contingent shape of human mind and its environment. Thus, this naturalistic approach to normativity has nothing in common with the natural law tradition aiming to find justification for rather than the elucidation of rules. From a naturalistic perspective, normativity as such is fully explainable in terms of causal relations between psychological, sociological, biological, and historical facts. Methodological naturalism by no means, however, regards rights as some objectively valid normative entities that morally or legally bind all rule-makers. It rather helps to understand the basis on which widespread beliefs in the existence of mysterious "natural rights" could flourish.[18] To this extent, the naturalistic account of the Priority of Rights Thesis defended here undermines rather than endorsing the traditional idea of absolute natural rights.[19]

[18] I leave open the question of whether it is reconcilable with some radically subjectivist and empirical reinterpretation of some accounts of natural law, such as those by John Finnis or Michael Moore. At any rate, this would require a reading that was in clear opposition to the philosophical attitudes and intentions of these authors.

[19] My account is based on the assumption that there is no special puzzle of "normativity" that needs to be solved. The domain of normativity is reducible to the mental states and behavioural patterns they trigger. There is much to be explained regarding how such mental states develop and control behaviour.

References

Austin, John. 1832. The province of jurisprudence determined. http://archive.org/details/provincejurispr04austgoog. Accessed 22 Aug 2014.

Bentham, Jeremy. 2011 [1795]. Anarchical fallacies. In *The selected works of Jeremy Bentham,* ed. E. Stephen. New Haven: Yale University Press.

Brożek, Bartosz. 2012. *Normatywność prawa*. Kraków: Copernicus.

DeWaal, Frans. 2008. *Primates and philosophers. How morality evolved.* New Jersey: Princeton University Press.

Ehrlich, Stanisław. 1997. *Norma, Grupa, Organizacja.* Warszawa: Państwowe Wydawnictwo Naukowe.

Griffin, James. 2009. *On human rights*. Oxford: Oxford University Press.

Hunt, Lynn. 2007. *Inventing human hights: A history*. New York: W. W. Norton.

Ishay, Micheline R. 2008. *The history of human rights. From ancient times to the globalisation era*. Berkeley: University of California Press.

Kelsen, Hans. 2000 [1960]. *Reine Rechtslehre. Nachdruck.* 2nd ed. Wien: Verlag Österreich.

Morsink, Johannes. 2009. *Inherent human rights. Philosophical roots of the universal declaration.* Philadelphia: University of Pennsylvania Press.

Olivecrona, Karl.1971. *Law as fact*. 2nd ed. London: Stevens and Sons.

Osiatynski, Wiktor. 2010. *Prawa człowieka i ich granice*. Kraków: Znak.

Paine, Thomas. 1791. Rights of man. http://ebooks.adelaide.edu.au/p/paine/thomas/p147r/. Accessed 22 Aug 2014.

Pietrzykowski, Tomasz. 2012. The nature and limits of conceptual truths. In: *Jurispridence and Political Philosophy of the 21st Century*, ed. M. Jovanovic, B. Spaic, P. Lang and Frankfurt A. M. Bern-Bruxelles New York: Oxford-Wien.

Ross, Alf. 1958. *On law and justice*. London: Stevens and Sons.

Stelmach, Jerzy. 2011. And if there is no "ought". In *Studies in the philosophy of law, Normativity of law,* 6 vol, ed. Bartosz Brożek and Jerzy Stelmach. Kraków: Copernicus.

Weinberger, Ota. 1986. The norm as thought and as reality. In: The institutional theory of law, ed. W. Ota and M. Neil. *New approaches to legal positivism*. Dordrecht: Reidel Publishing Company.

Załuski, Wojciech. 2009. *Ewolucyjna filozofia prawa*. Warszawa: Wolters Kluwer.

Part II
Normativity of Law and Legal Norms

Chapter 10
Rules and Normativity in Law

Brian H. Bix

Abstract Two of the persistent questions in the philosophy of law concern the relationship between law and rules and the relationship between law and morality. Both topics are most sharply raised through the topic of "legal normativity." Many contemporary legal theorists purport to "explain legal normativity," but often fail to articulate what it means to say that law is normative or in what way that property requires explanation. As a way of resolving some problems of legal normativity, this article offers a reading of Hans Kelsen's legal theory as a limited claim about the logic of normative claims: that when one reads the actions of legal officials normatively, this assumes or presupposes the validity of the foundational norm of that legal system, a Kelsenian "Basic Norm." This article also looks at a different aspect of legal normativity through a focus on the work of H. L. A. Hart. Legal norms frequently prescribe what one ought to do or ought not to do. However, the rush of legal theorists to describe law as thus making moral claims seems ungrounded and unnecessary.

Keywords Normativity · Rules · Kelsen · Hart · Law and morality

10.1 Introduction

The connection between law, rules, and morality, remains a central topic of modern legal theory. In this article, I will revisit these debates, and suggest some corrections and some challenges. Central to the work of many important legal theorists is the idea that law is a normative system, and that any theory about the nature of law must focus on its normativity. There are familiar questions connected with explaining legal normativity: e.g., What is the connection between legal normativity and other normative systems, in particular, morality? And there are methodological questions: when theorists claim that we need to (and that they will) "explain the normativity of law," what is it that is being explained? In the course of looking at issues relating to the normativity of law, many of the major figures of modern legal theory (primarily English-language legal theory, to be sure) will be revisited and perhaps

B. H. Bix (✉)
University of Minnesota, Minneapolis, USA
e-mail: bix@umn.edu

M. Araszkiewicz et al. (eds.), *Problems of Normativity, Rules and Rule-Following*,
Law and Philosophy Library 111, DOI 10.1007/978-3-319-09375-8_10

reconsidered, including Hans Kelsen, H. L. A. Hart, John Finnis, and Joseph Raz. Part I gives a necessarily brief overview of the relationship between law and rules, showing the tensions and connections that give rise to many of the debates in contemporary legal philosophy. Part II offers a view regarding the nature of law and legal normativity that I believe could reasonably be read off of some of Kelsen's work. It is a slightly unconventional reading of Kelsen, but one that is grounded clearly in some of Kelsen's work and has the support of some Kelsenian scholars. And while I recognize that a more careful analysis of Kelsen's texts[1] and their historical context might undermine the proposed reading on exegetical grounds as the best overall understanding of Kelsen's views, I will argue that my reading has the benefit of being more defensible than alternative readings—I will defend it as right on the merits, even if I am willing to defer to others on whether it is the best understanding historically of that theorist's perspective. That is, my discussion of the view will be offered on its merits as a legal theory, whatever its merits as an exegesis of Kelsen. In summary, the basic argument will be that the Basic Norm[2] is presupposed when a citizen chooses to read the actions of legal officials in a normative way. Kelsen's analysis should be understood as an investigation into the logic of normative thought, in particular legal normative thought. In this Kelsenian approach, all normative systems are structurally and logically similar, but each normative system is independent of every other system—thus, law is, in this sense, conceptually separate from morality. Part III will turn to H. L. A. Hart's theory, analyzing the extent to which his approach views legal normativity as *sui generis*. This investigation will offer an opportunity to raise questions regarding what has become a consensus view in contemporary jurisprudence: that law makes moral claims. I will show how a more deflationary (and less morally-flavored) understanding of the nature of law is tenable, and may in fact work better than current conventional (morally-focused) understandings of law and its claims.

10.2 Law and Rules

Is a legal system primarily a matter of rules? For H. L. A. Hart, what was distinctive of a legal system (in its most developed form) was that it was a combination of primary and secondary rules, and that the system contained a rule of recognition, by which the officials determined which rules were and were not part of that legal system(see Hart 1958, 2012).

Lon Fuller equated law with rules, at one point defining law as "the enterprise of subjecting human conduct to the governance of rules" (Fuller 1969, p. 96; see also Fuller 1958). The strength of Fuller's "internal morality of law" was that it

[1] As Michael Hartney notes, in "[Robert] Walter's definitive bibliography of Kelsen' works, there are 387 titles, 96 of which are on legal theory." Hartney, General theory of norms, pp. ix–lx, 1991, x.

[2] In this article, I will use "Basic Norm" and "*Grundnorm*" interchangeably.

presented principles ("the principles of legality") that were simultaneously rules of thumb for the effective guidance of behavior through rules while maintaining the moral tone of one form of justice—procedural justice. More recently, John Gardner has modified the Fullerian view as being that law is not a particular functional kind, but rather a particular modal kind: that it is a certain kind of means—governance through general rules (Gardner 2012, pp. 206–207).

In recent decades, various legal theorists have challenged the equation of law with rules. Both Ronald Dworkin (see Dworkin 1977, pp. 22–45, 71–80) and Robert Alexy (see Alexy 2002b, pp. 44–110) famously argued that, along with rules, legal systems contain "principles."[3] In Dworkin's version, legal principles contrast with rules by giving general weight towards one outcome in a dispute rather than another, rather than being conclusive (as rules are). In most difficult legal cases, there will be principles both on the plaintiff's side and on the defendant's side. The weight a given principle has may vary from one area of law to another (*e.g.*, the way the importance of certainty and predictability is stronger in commercial law and property law than it is in disputes dealing with civil liberties) and from case to case.

John Gardner has reflected that Dworkin's idea of legal principles may be an unnecessary entity created to solve a problem that does not really exist. The problem Dworkin raised is that either judges are applying pre-existing legal norms (beyond legal rules) or they are legislating contrary to important rule of law principles when they decide cases in ways that go beyond the clear application of legal rules. Gardner's response is that there is a kind of legal reasoning, a reasoning "according to law," that works with existing legal rules in a way that creates new legal norms, but does not require the recognition of "legal principles" as a separate sort of entity (Gardner 2012, pp. 37–42).

Robert Alexy's distinction between rules and principles is perhaps less sharp than Dworkin's, and also differs on some matters of detail. For Alexy, principles are more general, more the justifications for rules rather than the specific rules themselves, and perhaps best thought of as goals to be optimized to the extent possible (Alexy 2002b, pp. 45–50; see also Jakab 2010, pp. 145–147).

A number of theorists have argued that a distinction between legal rules and principles will not hold up: that in the end purported legal principles, upon closer analysis, will be seen to be either a kind of rule or a kind of (moral or policy) argument for changing legal rules or interpreting or applying them in a particular way (see *e.g.*, Alexander 2013; Gardner 2012, pp. 37–42; Jakab 2010; Raz 1983).

The American legal realists raised a number of hard challenges for the role of rules within law: sometimes regarding the way that general rules might fail to determine the outcome of particular cases (without being supplemented by moral or policy judgments), and sometimes regarding the way that the existence of legal rules can mislead us into believing either (a) that citizens always follow what the legal rules prescribe; or (b) that judges always cite legal rules when those rules are relevant to the cases they decide; or (c) that when judges appropriately cite legal

[3] There are other important theories relating to legal principles that, unfortunately, I do not have time to consider in this piece, *e.g.* Ávila (2007).

rules it always means that those rules have in fact guided the judges' reasoning. That is, there is almost always a gap with rules between text and behavior, whether considering the behavior of judges or of citizens; this gap (especially as it pertains to judges) Karl Llewellyn (following an idea of Roscoe Pound) called the problem of "paper rules" as against "real rules" (see Llewellyn 1930, pp. 444–457; Pound 1910).

This gap is pervasive to rule-based guidance, though it is not clear what we should take from that observation in constructing our ideas about the nature of law. Perhaps like the pervasiveness of coercion in law, the slippage between legal rules on paper and the rules "in action" is an important element to understanding law, even if it is not an "essential" or "necessary" attribute of law[4].

The gap between "real rules" and "paper rules" might remind us of another gap important to understanding rules and how they operate—including *legal* rules, but not exclusive to them. This is the gap between the reasons that justify the rule and the rule itself, such that rules, as written, and certainly as applied, are always both over-inclusive and under-inclusive relative to the reasons that justify them (see Alexander 1991; see generally Schauer 1991). This gap leads to the idea of the equitable exception to rules (suggested as long ago as Aristotle, and exemplified in the English tradition of separate Courts of Equity and (now, in many countries) separate equitable rules and equitable defenses to the strict application of legal rules) and the idea of interpreting legal texts purposively and in ways that avoid absurd outcomes (relative to the purpose of the statute or the mischief it was meant to prevent).

This gap between rules and justifying reasons is also evident to those who are directly affected by legal rules. When people are governed by rules (to paraphrase Fuller's definition of law), there will always be circumstances where even good citizens and officials, acting in good faith, must face the question of whether to obey the rule (as written) or not, where there are good reasons to act contrary to the rule—and these reasons often include the reasons that originally justified the rule in the first place.[5] Both citizens and judges morally should try to do the right thing, but sometimes that may point in the direction of acting contrary to the rule rather than consistently with it. At the same time, there are good second-order reasons for citizens to do what the law says, and for officials to apply the law "as written," just because the law says so; that is, there are good practical and institutional reasons for being governed by rules, and not just by reasons. We understand why there are long-term prudential reasons for why citizens and officials should not second-guess the legal rules, and substitute their judgments for those of the legislature. This is a big subject that we do not have time to explore fully here; suffice it to say that any discussion of the role of rules within law and within legal practice must pay due consideration to this problem of the gap between reasons and rules.

---

[4] *Cf.* Schauer (2014) (on coercion as an important but not essential aspect of law).

[5] A comparable analysis led David Lyons to argue that rule utilitarianism inevitably collapses into act utilitarianism, for the best rule to follow is one that would allow one to violate the rule when the benefits were great enough (Lyons 1965).

10.3 Kelsen and Normativity

10.3.1 Normativity

Hans Kelsen's jurisprudential work, through most of his long scholarly career,[6] centered on the normative nature of law—that law is essentially made up of norms, and that this requires an approach to understanding law distinctively different from descriptive, empirical approaches (e.g. Kelsen 2013, p. 217). Kelsen's approach assumes or is grounded on the view (often attributed first to David Hume, though questions remain as the best understanding of Hume's text[7]) that there is a sharp division between "is" and "ought" statements, in particular, that no conclusion about what one ought to do can be derived from statements regarding what is the case. Whatever its origins, this view about not deriving "ought" conclusions from "is" statements (sometimes called "the fact-value distinction") is generally accepted in modern philosophy[8].

The importance of the Humean division between "is" and "ought" statements is the implication that for every normative conclusion (*e.g.* about what one ought to do), there must be at least one normative premise (*e.g.* about what one ought to do or what one ought to value). In the context of a normative system like law (or morality or religion), every statement of what one ought to do (or ought *not* to do) requires justification from a more general or more basic ought statement, leading through the normative hierarchy[9] until one reaches a foundational normative premise[10]. Thus,

[6] Over the course of Kelsen's many decades of writings there were some radical changes of views – particularly if one contrasts his very earliest works and his very last works with most of what came in between (Paulson 1992a, 1998, 1999). My focus throughout this article will be in the better known work of Kelsen's middle periods. I would also note that my knowledge of Kelsen comes from those works of his currently available in English.

[7] Hume wrote: "In every system of morality, which I have hitherto met with, I have always remark'd, that the author proceeds for some time in the ordinary way of reasoning, and establishes the being of a God, or makes observations concerning human affairs; when of a sudden I am surpriz'd to find, that instead of the usual copulations of propositions, *is*, and *is not*, I meet with no proposition that is not connected with an *ought*, or an *ought not*. This change is imperceptible; but is, however, of the last consequence. For as this *ought*, or *ought not*, expresses some new relation or affirmation, 'tis necessary that it shou'd be observ'd and explain'd; and at the same time that a reason should be given, for what seems altogether inconceivable, how this new relation can be a deduction from others, which are entirely different from it…[I] am persuaded, that a small attention [to this point] wou'd subvert all the vulgar systems of morality, and let us see, that the distinction of vice and virtue is not founded merely on the relations of objects, nor is perceiv'd by reason" (Hume 1978, Section 3.1.1, pp. 469–470).

[8] Though there remain prominent dissenters (*e.g.* MacIntyre 1959; Searle 1964). One might also, in the present context, mention the recurrent questions legal theorist Lon Fuller raised to any sharp division of "is" and "ought" (Winston 1988).

[9] This is the *Stufenbaulehre* that Kelsen adopted from Adolf Julius Merkl (see Kelsen 1992, pp. 28, 57; Jakab 2007). One can find a similar hierarchy of normative analysis from Hart, with his concept of a "rule of recognition" playing a similar role to Kelsen's "Basic Norm" (Hart 2012, p. 107).

[10] One alternative to this line of analysis would be to justify normative conclusions as part of a holistic or coherentist argument. (I am grateful to Ralf Poscher for this point.) I have my doubts

the rules in a religious system that one ought not pray to idols will be grounded ultimately in the norm, "do whatever the creator God tells you to do"; one's secular ethical rule of thumb not to lie unless there is a very good reason may be grounded ultimately on either the Kantian norm, "so act that the maxim of your will can be a universal law," or the Utilitarian norm, "maximize the greatest good of the greatest number"; and the legal norm not to drive more than 65 miles per hour on a specified highway may be grounded ultimately on the norm, "act according to what has been authorized by the historically first constitution." This foundational norm for legal normative systems Kelsen called "the Basic Norm" ("*Grundnorm*")[11].

This view regarding the separation of "is" and "ought" statements, and the hierarchical structure of normative systems, leading to ultimate norms, could lead to somewhat skeptical conclusions regarding morality (and religion and law). The reason is that under this approach every normative system is shown to be necessarily grounded on a foundational norm that is itself subject to no (direct) proof. One simply accepts (or not) the ultimate norm, whether it be "do what the Creator God commands" or "maximize the greatest good of the greatest number" or "act in accordance with the historically first constitution." And the fact that the important normative systems of one's life, like morality, religion, and law, may be grounded on an ultimate norm that cannot be proven, and can be accepted or rejected with seemingly equal legitimacy, seems to invite skeptical or relativistic implications. However, these implications must be left to others to discuss, or for other occasions[12].

In Kelsen's understanding of "the science" of norms[13], every "ought" claim—whether legal, moral, religious, or of any other kind—implies the (presupposition

---

that this is, in the end, a viable alternative, but I do not have the time here to get into a full critique of coherentist approaches to (normative) truth, and the even greater difficulties such approaches would likely have for law. On those topics, see Young (2013); Olsson (2012); Raz (1994, pp. 261–309).

[11] There is a common confusion in understanding both Kelsen's "Basic Norm" and H. L. A. Hart's analogous concept, the "rule of recognition" (Hart 2012, pp. 94–95, 100–110). While there is an understandable temptation to equate these fundamental norms with foundational texts of a legal system (like the United States Constitution), this equation is at best imprecise. First, as Kelsen points out, the current foundational text may have been created under the authority of a prior foundational text of the same legal system, so the Basic Norm should refer to the historically first foundational text. Second, there remain questions of how to interpret the provisions of the foundational text, and to determine what priority it has in that legal system in relation to other national and international legal norms. Third, at least with the case of Kelsen's Basic Norm, the norm is an instruction to act in accordance with a particular legal text, a prescription that is in principle separate from the legal text itself.

[12] There are, of course, numerous responses in the philosophical and jurisprudential literature to this potential skeptical challenge. Brief but thoughtful responses from one well-known legal theorist can be found in Finnis (Finnis 2011a, pp. 29–48, 441–442; Finnis 2011c, pp. 201–204).

[13] Kelsen refers more commonly to "the science of law" (or "legal science") – "*Rechtswissenschaft*." As Paulson notes in the Supplementary Notes to his translation of one of Kelsen's works (Paulson 1992c, pp. 127–129), the reference to "science" in Kelsen's work, and in German generally, means objective academic enquiry, without necessarily implying all the extra baggage that the term "science" carries in English (such that one might comfortably refer to literary theory in German as a "science," while it would be an unlikely, and certainly controversial, description in English).

of the) foundational norm of that normative system. And the corollary is that every normative system is self-contained and logically independent of every other normative system. The normative system that is law, with its foundational norm, is necessarily separate from the normative system of a particular religion or a particular moral system. However, it is important to note: this would not exclude lawmakers from in fact being influenced by the content of another normative system—*e.g.* morality or religion. One must distinguish the logical structure of (all) normative systems from the empirical/historical/causal claims regarding why certain lawmakers promulgated the legal norms they did.

10.3.2 Presupposing the Basic Norm

In Kelsen's works, one can find language to the effect that the presupposition of the Basic Norm is required to make "possible the interpretation of the subjective sense of [certain material facts] as their objective sense, that is, as objectively valid norms ...."[14] At the same time, Kelsen makes it clear, in a number of places, that one need not presuppose the Basic Norm.[15] In particular, Kelsen notes that anarchists need not, and would not, perceive the actions of legal officials as anything other than "naked power" (Kelsen 1992, § 16, 36), with the legal system being for them nothing more than the "gunman situation writ large."[16]

Similarly, Kelsen writes: "For the Pure Theory strongly emphasises that the statement that the subjective meaning of the law-creating act is also its objective meaning—the statement, that is, that law has objective validity—is only a possible interpretation of that act, not a necessary one" (Kelsen 2013, pp. 218–219).[17] Kelsen adds: "The Pure Theory aims simply to raise to the level of consciousness what all jurists are doing (for the most part unwittingly) when, in conceptualizing their object of enquiry, they ... understand the positive law as a valid system, that is, as a norm, and not merely as factual contingencies of motivation"[18].

[14] Kelsen (1960a, p. 34(d)), quoted in translation in Paulson (2013, p. 50).

[15] I recognize that there may be other passages in Kelsen's text that support a different reading. For a good overview of the different tenable readings of Kelsen's writings on the Basic Norm, see Paulson (2012).

[16] This last phrase is, of course, not from Kelsen, but from Hart (1958, p. 603). However, Kelsen writes in similar terms: "The problem that leads to the theory of the basic norm...is how to distinguish a legal command which is considered to be objectively valid, such as the command of a revenue officer to pay a certain sum of money, from a command which has the same subjective meaning but is not considered to be objectively valid, such as the command of a gangster". (Kelsen 1965, p. 1144).

[17] Later in the same passage, Kelsen adds, helpfully: "The concept of normative validity is, rather, an interpretation; it is an interpretation made possible only by the presupposition of a basic norm," and that such an interpretation is well-grounded "*if* one presupposes the...basic norm." Kelsen (2013, p. 219) (emphasis in original).

[18] Kelsen (1992, pp. 29, 58). (The omitted text states "[they] reject natural law as the basis of validity of positive law..."). And once more: "This presupposition [of the Basic Norm] is possible but not necessary... Thus the Pure Theory of Law, by ascertaining the basic norm as the logical

Thus, Kelsen speaks about those who perceive legal actions as norms, in some places noting, in other places simply implying, that one can also choose *not* to perceive such actions in a normative way. Here, by perceiving actions as normative, what is meant is that one perceives those actions as giving reasons for action. In H. L. A. Hart's terms, it is the difference between an "internal" and "external" view of normative systems, or the difference between "accepting" or not "accepting" the system (Hart 2012, pp. 87–91; see also Morawetz 1999). At that same time, I can understand that a legal institution *purports* to create reasons of actions (for me and for other citizens), even if I do not accept the system, and thus do not perceive it as ("actually") normative.

This point can be generalized across normative systems. Some look at events in our (natural, empirical world) and perceive norms: obligations (reasons) to act according to the requirements of etiquette, the dictates of a religious system, or the norms of a legal system. Other equally competent and intelligent adults can look at the same world and perceive *nothing* normative: etiquette systems may seem like the trivial rules of a pointless game; religious norms may seem like the superstitions of the ignorant and the self-deluded; and legal rules may seem like just one more way by which the powerful control and oppress the less powerful. And, of course, some people may perceive in a normative way in some of these areas but not in others. One could just as easily say that some people *accept* certain normative systems that other people do not "accept"; these, I think, come to the same thing.

One idea that may help clarify the distinction between systems that purport to be normative (reason-giving) but one does not *perceive* as normative, and those one perceives as normative (reason-giving), is Joseph Raz's idea of "detached normative statements". Raz's basic idea is that one can speak of what a normative rule or system requires, without necessarily endorsing or accepting that rule or system (Raz 1990, pp. 170–177). Thus, someone who is not a vegetarian can say to a vegetarian friend, "you should not eat that (because it has meat in its ingredients)," and a nonbeliever can say to an Orthodox Jewish friend, "you should not accept that speaking engagement (because it would require you to work on your Sabbath)." Analogously, the radical lawyer or anarchist scholar can make claims about what one ought to do if one accepted the legal system (viewed the actions of legal officials in a normative way), even if that lawyer or scholar saw the actions of legal officials only in a non-normative way, as mere acts of power.

(When one says that one can *choose* to view the (legal) actions of officials normatively or not, it is important to note that this does not mean that this "choice" is always or necessarily a *conscious* choice. The reference to "choice" indicates primarily that there is an option; one could do (or think) otherwise.)

Yet another way to get at the general point is John Gardner's observation that law is voluntary in a way that morality is not. Gardner argues that morality's claim upon

condition under which a coercive order may be interpreted as valid positive law, furnishes only a conditional, not a categorical, foundation of the validity of positive law" (Kelsen 1960b, p. 276).

all of us, as human beings, is "inescapable" (Gardner 2012, p. 150)[19]. According to Gardner, one cannot reasonably ask whether one should follow the dictates of morality[20]. But one *can* reasonably ask that question of law (Gardner 2012, pp. 160–176)[21].

However, it may be that the reference to "inescapability" is too vague to be useful here. One might argue that the sanctions pervasively and importantly present in all (or almost all) legal systems (past and present)[22] make law, in a sense, "inescapable"[23]. One might choose not to perceive the actions of legal officials as creating valid norms, but law (at least in systems that are generally efficacious) is not something that a practically reasonable person could ignore, the way that she could ignore (say) fashion, etiquette, or chess. Still, while one may be unable to "escape" or ignore the coercive power of the State, one *can* choose not to think of the State's actions in a normative way.

Also, I am not sure that the Kelsenian approach (as I am interpreting it) would go even as far as declaring morality to be "inescapable," for morality (or one's moral system) would be, under this analysis, just one more normative system that one could choose or not choose, internalize or not internalize, assert or not assert. Certainly, we perceive around us a wide variety of (secular and religion-based) moral systems being advocated or assumed—with, for example, a broad range of variations on consequentialism, deontological ethics, and virtue ethics (and mix-and-match combinations of the three), just among the secular approaches to morality, even without noting the approaches to morality that are more theologically based.

The general view of normativity underlying the present analysis is often explained in analogy to games. For example, one might say to people playing chess that they ought not (*e.g.*) to move the bishop a certain way. However, those same people could decide never to play chess, in which case prescriptions about how one ought to move the bishop would have no application.[24] (Of course, one might make an all-things-considered judgment as to whether it is right to play chess on a particular occasion, or whether it is wise to devote significant time to chess as a

---

[19] Foot also refers to morality's purported "inescapability" in the course of her discussion questioning the view of morality as a categorical imperative (as opposed to hypothetical imperative) (Foot 1978, pp. 160–164) Cf. Raz (1999, pp. 94–105), on whether reasons are optional.

[20] To be clear: this is Gardner's view, and Gardner here reflects the conventional position, though, of course, radical thinkers like Friedrich Nietzsche appear to raise exactly the question Gardner's quotation implies cannot or should not be raised: whether one should follow the dictates of morality (though one can also read Nietzsche less radically, as simply arguing for a rejection of conventional morality in favor of the moral system he espouses). See also Foot (1978, pp. 157–173 (on whether morality is merely a "hypothetical imperative"), 181–188 (questioning whether moral considerations are "overriding")).

[21] Robert Alexy points out similarly that "[o]ne can of course refuse…to participate in the (utterly real) game of law" (Alexy 2002a, p. 109).

[22] Cf. Schauer (2010).

[23] I am indebted to Frederick Schauer for this suggestion.

[24] For one good analysis on the similarities and differences between the normativity of a system of law and the normativity of the game of chess, see Marmor (2007, pp. 153–181).

hobby, but these are very different inquiries, and, in any event, few would argue that everyone has an unconditional (moral?) obligation either to play chess or to avoid playing chess.)

However, the game analogy does not entirely work. If after we gave people advice regarding the rules and restrictions of chess, those people responded that they were not playing chess, we would accept that the chess rules and reasons did not apply to them. With etiquette, though, we would (or could) insist that the rules and reasons applied even if our listeners stated that they did not "accept" or "participate" in etiquette. (Foot 1978, p. 160)

The voluntariness of affiliation with religions is somewhat more complicated. On one hand, in many societies today the normative rules of a particular religion are not thought to be binding on those who are not members of that religious group. Of course, the way we think about religion today is far different from the way people thought about it in the past. As Jacques Barzun points out, "in earlier times people rarely thought of themselves as 'having' or 'belonging to' a religion.…Everybody 'had' a soul, but did not 'have a God,' for God and all that pertained to Him was simply *what is*, just as today nobody has 'a physics'; there is only one and it is automatically taken to be the transcript of reality" (Barzun 2000, p. 24). And similarly, true believers even today (especially in countries in which fundamentalist views have greater social and political influence) perceive the dictates of their religion not as something chosen, but as "the Truth," binding on all.

Back to law: if one views legal rules and official actions as things that people may or may not view in a normative way, this understandably affects how one views Kelsen's Basic Norm—the role it plays and how it is justified. As Stanley Paulson and others have pointed out (*e.g.*, Paulson 1992b, 2000, 2012, 2013), it is common now to view Kelsen's argument for the Basic Norm as a neo-Kantian version of the Kantian transcendental deduction. A transcendental argument (to simplify) goes from a conclusion of what must be true, lest the conclusion be false, or, at any rate, unsupported. Kant's transcendental deduction (again, to simplify) went from the unity of our experience to the conclusion that certain categories of thought (e.g., time, space, substance, and causation) are projected by us onto sense data[25].

For Kelsen, the relevant transcendental deduction is something along the following lines: since law is (experienced as) normative, the Basic Norm must be presupposed. The difficulty, as Paulson has pointed out (*e.g.* Paulson 2012, 2013), is that Transcendental Arguments depend on there being *only one* available explanation for the matter being examined (in Kant's case, the unity of experience; in Kelsen's case, the normativity of law), and that Kelsen did not come close to proving that his approach was the only available explanation[26].

The approach discussed in this article does not require the full machinery of a Kantian Transcendental Deduction: it needs only belief in the basic and gener-

[25] This particular way of phrasing the matter (e.g., the reference to "sense data") is likely *not* a way most Kantians would choose, but it should suffice for the rough summary needed here.

[26] Paulson argued, correctly in my opinion, that Kelsen's analysis was far too quick to dismiss natural law approaches and was not convincing in its effort to show that there was no possible explanations beyond the limited number of alternatives he considered.

ally accepted Humean division of "is" and "ought," combined with a comparably conventional idea that law is a normative *system*. Where one asserts the validity of any lower-level norm in a legal system[27], one implicitly asserts or presupposes the validity of the foundational norm of the system.

10.3.3 Concerns

In an earlier work (Paulson 2012), Paulson expressed concerns about the sort of reading of Kelsen's work I am offering here[28]. His primary worry is that this reading leaves the Basic Norm in particular, and Kelsen's Pure Theory of Law in general, doing little work, and not the important task that Kelsen seemed to set for himself. Kelsen's offers the Basic Norm (and its presupposition) as the key to explaining the objective meaning of norms generally, not just for those who happen to choose to interpret official actions in a normative way.

I disagree that my proposed reading of Kelsen leaves Kelsen's theory unimportant, and the reading has the distinct benefit of being more defensible than more ambitious readings of Kelsen's aims[29]. Kelsen's Pure Theory, as I read it, is offering important insights about the logic of norms, about what follows from the fact that someone perceives the actions of officials normativity, and it offers related insights regarding the connections (or lack thereof) between law and morality, and regarding whether (or not) one has an obligation to accept or presuppose the Basic Norm of one's legal system.

10.4 H. L. A. Hart and the Relationship of Law and Morality

10.4.1 Hart and the Internal Point of View

H. L. A. Hart, like Kelsen, emphasized the normativity of law in his criticism of earlier legal theorists (particularly John Austin), and in the development of his own, more hermeneutic theory of law. Hart argued that Austin's command theory did not sufficiently distinguish a community acting out of fear, the "gunman situation writ

[27] A comparable point could be made, as earlier mentioned, for a moral or theological normative system, or any other kind of normative system.

[28] In private e-mail communication, Paulson reasserted his objection to this reading of Kelsen – while he noted that the reading was supported by some of Kelsen's texts, he characterized the reading as "trivial" and question-begging. For the "question-begging" criticism, Paulson refers to Robert Alexy's analysis, where Alexy makes that charge against Kelsen (Paulson 2012, pp. 68–70). However, Alexy's accusation is based on a "justified normativity" reading of Kelsen's Basic Norm, a reading I do not share. I believe that the problem of begging the question disappears when one reads Kelsen's theory in a less ambitious way.

[29] As Paulson shows, indirectly, by his critique of other readings (Paulson 2012).

large" (Hart 1958, p. 603), from a community where the officials and at least some portion of the citizens treated the law as giving them reasons for action—what Hart called "the internal point of view."

As part of the legal positivist separation of law and morality that he advocated, Hart is careful (a) not to claim that citizens *must* accept the law as giving them reasons for action (he does not even discuss the circumstances under which citizens *should* do so); and (b) he offers a broad and open-ended set of reasons for why citizens *might* accept the law as giving them reasons for action. Hart writes that a citizen "may obey it [the law] for a variety of different reasons and among them may often, though not always, be the knowledge that it will be best for him to do so" (Hart 2012, p. 114). And later: "[A]dherence to law may not be motived by it [moral obligation], but by calculations of long-term interest, or by the wish to continue a tradition or by disinterested concern for others" (Hart 2012, p. 232).

10.4.2 Hart's Legal Normativity

The question still remains for Hart: what is the nature of this normativity of or in law? The law prescribes behavior—to act in certain ways, and to avoid acting in other ways—and also empowers citizens to use legal institutions and processes for their own purposes (through wills, contracts, incorporation, and the like). If under a Hartian analysis someone accepts the legal system as giving reasons for action, *what kind of reasons* are those? Is there any alternative to understanding these reasons as *moral* reasons?

One alternative that comes to mind is that people often obey the law for purely prudential reasons: to avoid the financial penalties, potential loss of liberty, or public humiliation that can come from being adjudicated as a law-breaker. However, Hart builds his theory of law from a critique of Austin's command theory of law, and a key part of Hart's critique is that for many people law is more than (that phrase again) the "gunman situation writ large"—that a perception of (legal) obligation can frequently be something different from merely feeling obliged (coerced) (Hart 2012, pp. 82–91). Hart clearly intends an understanding of legal normativity where legal reasons are something distinct from (mere) prudential reasons.

Hart could be read as treating law as a *sui generis* form of normativity, a form of normativity distinct from all others, and there is support for this position in a number of his writings (see, *e.g.* Hart 1982, pp. 262–268; cf. Finnis 2011b, pp. 248–256; Himma 2013). As mentioned, Hart, as legal positivist, does not explore whether there are good *moral* reasons for accepting a particular legal system (or *all* legal systems) as giving reasons for action. Analogously, Hart does not explore in any length *what kind of reasons* people might think that the law gives them. It is sufficient for Hart that some people treat the law as giving reasons for action; this is a fact for which the descriptive or conceptual theorist should attempt to account. As Hart sees it, it is not for the theorist of law to be too concerned about what sort of reasons these might be, and whether they are well grounded. Elsewhere (as part of his debate with Lon Fuller), Hart emphasizes that one should not confuse "ought" with morality—that there were many forms of "ought," many sorts of reasons for action (Hart 1958, pp. 612–614).

Along the same lines, one could read Hart as saying that for the person who accepts the law, the sort of reason the law gives is a *legal* reason, just as those who make other choices might consider themselves as subject to *chess* reasons (while playing that game—*e.g.*, reasons within the game for moving the bishop diagonally rather than otherwise, and to this square rather than another one), *etiquette* reasons, or *fashion* reasons. There is, to be sure, something a little strange about this line of analysis—one can understand the force of the objection that "*legal* reasons" should reduce either to prudential reasons, on one hand, or moral reasons, on the other. However, it is not clear that Hart, or a modern follower of his approach, needs to concede this point. Why should one assume that one has a moral obligation to do as the law says, simply because the law says so? While it may once have been the accepted view that just legal systems create such general moral obligations to obey their enactments, many theorists today have offered strong arguments against such a general obligation (*e.g.*, Smith 1973; Raz 1994, pp. 325–338; Edmundson 2004; Higgins 2004). The alternative view is that law *sometimes* creates moral obligations, and that this is a case-by-case analysis, relative to the individual citizen, the particular legal rule, and the coordination problems or expertise claims that may be involved (Raz 1994, pp. 325–338; Enoch 2011). There are good reasons to avoid constructing one's theory of the nature of law around the view that law generally does create, should create, or even *claims* to create moral obligations (Schauer 1998).

Even John Finnis, the foremost theorist working today within the Natural Law tradition, rejects the idea that law makes moral claims, and accepts the view that law creates only indefeasible *legal* obligations (Finnis 2013, pp. 553–556), which are then slotted into

> a flow of general practical reasoning—by good citizens in terms of the common good … by careerists in the law in terms of what must be done or omitted to promote their own advancement towards wealth or office, and by disaffected or criminally opportunistic citizens in terms of what they themselves need in order to get by without undesired consequences (punishment and the like) (Finnis 2013, p. 555).

Similarly, for those who accept the law as giving them reasons for action, why should we assume that these reasons are *moral* reasons? For example, with etiquette or chess, we understand how a practice can give reasons that are not moral reasons. Perhaps law similarly gives reasons that are not moral reasons, but are merely *legal* reasons.

As Kenneth Einar Himma points out, Hart grounded his theory of law on a social practice theory of rules: that rules exist when individuals accept a rule as giving them reasons for action (and grounds for criticizing deviations from the rule) (Himma 2013)[30]. However, Hart held that a legal system exists when *officials* accept the foundational rules of the system, and he said little about citizens' obligations. Himma argues that theories of legal obligation should track the usual understand-

[30] The discussion of Himma here is adapted from an analysis first published in Bix (2013a).

ings and practices of legal officials and citizens, or face a strong burden of justifying deviation from those usual understandings and practices. Himma is concerned in particular with the conventional understanding that the law creates (legal) obligations *for all citizens*—regardless of whether those citizens accept the law or not. Himma's reading of Hart is that a legal system creates legal obligations for its citizens when the citizens acquiesce to the system of norms, a passive acceptance of the norms combined with a willingness to conform generally to those norms, and this, in turn, is combined with coercive enforcement of the norms. The difficulty is that under Himma's analysis, it is not clear that anything follows from claiming that citizens have a legal obligation, other than the fact that they are in a functioning legal system. Determining the existence conditions of legal systems is of independent philosophical significance, as is distinguishing legal *obligations* from other normatively significant legal actions (*e.g.*, permissions, authorizations, and powers). However, one still might be concerned that "having a legal *reason* to do X" seems to mean more than that there is a norm prescribing X in a functioning legal system[31].

The next section returns to the question of the connection between law and morality.

10.4.3 Law and Morality

A great deal of attention in analytical legal philosophy, going back decades, if not centuries, has been focused on claimed connections, or claimed absence of connections (and various permutations of "possible," "contingent," or "necessary" connections) between law and morality.

It has become common for legal theorists to claim a close connection between law and morality (Raz 1994, pp. 325–338; Green 2003, pp. 14–17; Alexy 2002a)[32]. And in this category I include not only the traditional natural law theorists, some of whom offer a moral test for what counts as valid law, but also modern critics of legal positivism like Robert Alexy who argues that all legal systems claim (moral) "correctness" (see, *e.g.* Alexy 2002a, pp. 34–39)[33], and legal positivists, like Joseph Raz who argues that law, by its nature, claims moral authority (though Raz is also quick to note that he thinks that legal systems' claims to moral authority are usually mistaken)(see Raz 1994, pp. 199–204).

This purported connection between law and morality is often presented in contrast to older theories that emphasized power and sanction: for John Austin, law is essentially the command of a sovereign, where "command" means that the sover-

[31] Himma asserts or assumes that there are "no other kinds of basic reason other than prudential, moral and possibly aesthetic reasons" (Himma 2013, p. 181); however, as discussed that is likely a too-quick conclusion to a difficult foundational question.

[32] There are, to be sure, notable dissenters, at least from the view that such claims are essential to law. *E.g.*, Dworkin (1996, pp. 198–211); Kramer (1999, pp. 100–101); Himma (2002, pp. 155–157); Ehrenberg (2013); Schauer (2014).

[33] For a critique of Alexy's theory of correctness, see Bix (2013b, pp. 38–39).

eign is willing and able to impose a sanction if the directive is not followed. (Such theories, especially Austin's, were also distinctive for reducing law to or equating law with factual descriptions (like a habit of obedience, and an ability and willingness to impose a sanction) (see Austin 1995). Most theorists view the effort to reduce law to the factual rather than the normative as doomed to failure, but that is a debate for another day).

For some commentators, the existence of a sanction is essential to law, even if a sovereign is not. Robert Cover argued that "[l]egal interpretation is either played out on the field of pain and death or it is something less (or more) than law"(Cover 1986, pp. 1606–1607). Similarly, Frederick Schauer has maintained that even if coercion is not "essential" or "necessary" to law—in the sense that one can imagine a system that was "legal" that lacked coercion—in the real world, legal systems are *always* associated with coercion, and this is important for understanding law and legal systems (*e.g.* Schauer 2014).

None of this is to deny the important point made by many natural law theorists (and some legal positivists), that one important aspect of legal rules and legal reasoning is the way they operate in a form of practical reasoning, the reasoning towards what both citizens and legal officials should *do*.

To return to the main topic: Why should one assume that law makes moral claims (let alone that law *by its nature always* makes such claims)? As with all claims regarding the relationship of law and morality, the difficulty is that both terms in the equation—"law" and "morality"—are hard to define, and all likely definitions will be controversial.

As already mentioned, Hart pointed out a similar objection when responding to Lon Fuller in their famous debate published in the *Harvard Law Review*. Fuller had argued that legal interpretation often displays no sharp separation between "is" and "ought," with statutes (and other legal texts, like contracts and wills) often being interpreted not only according to the clear meaning of the text, but also in line with the lawmaker's or drafter's purpose (Fuller 1958, pp. 661–669). Hart responded that there were many kinds of "ought," and many of these forms of normative reasoning had little to do with morality (Hart 1958. pp. 612–614). Nazi Germany had its own demonic objectives, which judges could further by interpreting statutes one way rather than another; this is an "ought," but not one we would likely call truly "moral." At a more mundane level, one could well imagine statutes that either sought to promote corporate profit-making or treated corporate avarice as an evil to be fought; in both cases, a judge could apply the statute in ways that furthered those (contrary) purposes (one's moral or political beliefs will determine which one of those views one considers moral, and which one not). Hart's own example was of the failed poisoner who states with regret that he should have used a second dose, reminding us again that normative language is appropriate whenever one speaks of a purpose, however immoral or amoral the objective.

The advantage of the approach discussed in this article—that the normativity of law is a matter that individuals assume (presuppose) or not, but it carries no direct connection with moral normativity—is that it accounts for the normative nature of law, at least in a thin way, without the requirement of substantial metaphysical assumptions or controversial moral claims. This approach agrees with the modern view that denies that the law always creates moral obligations—or even that is *almost always* does so, or that it does so presumptively, or that it does so as long as the legal system is otherwise "generally just".

To take a naïve position for just a moment: we all know the difference between law and morality. We do not confuse the two. Law is made up of the rules the government promulgates—many of them guiding behavior directly through imposing sanctions on actions the government wishes to discourage, and other rules affecting behavior in more subtle ways by imposing selective tax benefits or payments due, or by offering legal enforcement to certain contracts, trusts, wills, and so on. Morality, by contrast, involves the rules and principles for how one should live one's life. For those for whom morality is a secular matter, morality is not tied to any institution, and the only sanctions are those that come from the reproach of one's peers or from self-reproach. For those who have a more religious approach to moral matters, law and morality may come to seem similar: there may be institutions which clarify what that religion's morality requires, moral rules may be thought to be the directives of a law-giver, in this case a divine law-giver, and the believer may think that there are punishments for transgression, in this world or in a world to come. At the same time, sharp differences remain: religious morality purports to show us time-less truths, while legal rules are always relative to a particular system that is tied to a time and a place, and legal rules are changed by the fallible choices of fallible law-makers.

Consider the same comparison from a different, more analytical direction: when a legal system says "do X" or "don't do Y," the basic meaning is that certain things are to be done or not done, because authorized officials so declared. By contrast, when the same prescriptions ("do X," "don't do Y") are *moral*, the understanding is that individuals have reasons to do or not do certain things, and that those reasons having no necessary connection to any (non-divine) speaker or official[34].

One standard argument for the view that law makes moral claims points to the overlap of terminology between law and morality: both law and morality speak in terms of "right," "duty" "permission," "authority," and so on. One response to this argument is that these are not terms limited to morality and morality-like claims. These are the terms of any normative (rule-governed) activity. One can find most if not all of these terms in discussions of etiquette, fashion, bridge, and chess. Yet I would think it very strange to say that chess makes moral claims upon us, and only slightly less strange to offer that characterization of fashion or etiquette (etiquette is, I think, a genuinely hard case, in that many of the rules of etiquette are meant to be rules for how one goes about expressing appropriate respect and deference, and thus *are*, in a sense, aspects of morality).

As part of Leslie Green's analysis that "[n]ecessarily, law makes moral claims on its subjects" (part of his list of ways in which he states that there *are* necessary connections between law and morality, contrary to some understandings of legal positivism's "separability thesis" (Green 2003, pp. 14–17)), Green explains that

[34] This paragraph tracks a similar argument offered by Marmor (2014, Chap. 3).

law "make[s] categorical demands" upon citizens, and that these demands require citizens "to act without regard to our individual self-interest but in the interests of other individuals," and that these criteria together constitute "moral demands" (Green 2003, p. 16)[35]. I do not find this definition of morality (or this characterization of law's demands) persuasive. Even putting aside, for the moment, Hart's essential point that law does not merely command, it also empowers (Hart 2012, pp. 27–33, 1958, pp. 604–606), legal rules do not make the same sort of (implied or express) claims as do moral rules: they do not, as moral rules do, (purport to) reflect universal and unchanging moral truths, nor do they purport to be integral aspects of the Good, as moral rules are.[36]

Joseph Raz offers a somewhat different explanation of why he believes that law's claim to authority is a moral claim: "it is a claim which includes the assertion of a right to grant rights and impose duties in matters affecting basic aspects of people's life and their interactions with one another" (Raz 2009, pp. 315–316). I am not sure that this will go much further towards persuading those not already persuaded that law's claims are moral claims. Many normative systems, including those of etiquette and even fashion, seem to involve claims of "rights to grant rights and impose duties." And while it is true that law, like morality, covers "basic aspects of people's life and their interactions with one another", this does not seem sufficient to turn claims on behalf of law into moral claims.

I do not mean this to be a dispute about the proper way to define morality; in any event, such disputes are unlikely to get far beyond one person's "that seems right to me" evoking "but it does not seem right to me" by another. I think it is sufficient to the perspective I am trying to elaborate that few of us confuse morality and law. We may be inclined to overestimate the moral merits of the law, but we still do not confuse the two. Who besides a strong believer in a Sharia legal system thinks that law is essentially an instantiation of morality, grounded in divine command or otherwise? It is true that the early Common Law judges in England (and commentators on the Common Law from that period) sometimes cited "Reason" with a capital "R" as the justification for why the Common Law rules were the way they were (those same judges also frequently characterized their actions as declaring existing law, while modern observers would describe their decisions as making new law or modifying existing law), but even legal figures from that period did not conflate or confuse law with morality.[37] For example, in English (and later American) Common Law, there was no legal obligation to rescue another, however easy and low-risk the

[35] His precise language: "But to make categorical demands that people should act in the interests of others is to make moral demands upon them" Green (2003, p. 16). A similar argument is offered by Shapiro (2011, pp. 113–115).

[36] According to some, there is a connection between morality and divine command (*e.g.* Quinn 1990), while law (at least outside Sharia systems) does not claim any direct connection with divine command.

[37] The proper understanding of the Common Law, and of what the Common Law judges thought that they were doing, is a large topic on its own. Simpson (1973) emphasized the connection between the Common Law and customary practices and ideas, while Berman (1994) argued forcefully that the Common Law judges and commentators should be understood as precursors of the Historical Jurisprudence School, emphasizing the historical developments of both law and society.

rescue might be (*e.g.*, Weinrib 1980, p. 247), and there was no legal obligation to keep one's promises (only those promises that were supported by "consideration"—that is, that were part of a bargain)[38]. In these, and many other cases, the Common Law judges distinguished what individuals had a moral obligation to do and what their (Common Law) legal obligation was.

Perhaps I speak too quickly in saying that people do not conflate law and morality. Some very able theorists seem to be advocating just such a merger. For example, Mark Greenberg argues that "when the law operates as it is supposed to, the content of the law consists of a certain general and enduring part of the moral profile" (Greenberg 2011, p. 57; see also Greenberg 2013). Heidi Hurd, in an earlier article, offered a comparable view: that law should be seen as a theoretical authority regarding our moral obligations (Hurd 1991). However, such equations of law and morality seem sufficiently distant from how most people perceive law to be non-starters as theories about the nature of law.

An approach put forward by David Enoch explains a way of understanding the connection between law and morality that does not require us to think of the law as making a moral claim or as being some sort of subset of morality. Enoch's argument is the legal enactments and other actions by legal officials can act as "triggering reasons," giving us reasons to act under the moral reasons for action that we already had (Enoch 2011). This parallels a more common observation that law may make more articulate or determinate our general obligations: for example, where our obligation to drive safely means driving on one particular side of the road and below a specified speed because the law makes that choice, and supporting the basic needs of society and helping the poor means paying a set percentage of one's income to a government fund as taxes again because of the choices of legal officials. Legal rules sometimes—not all legal rules, and not all the time—work effectively as salient solutions to coordination problems, and to make more determinate otherwise vague moral obligations.

What may remain mysterious is why many legal theorists, including prominent legal positivists, have taken a more ambitious starting point about law's claims and law's role. For example, Jules Coleman and Brian Leiter, in their otherwise excellent overview of legal positivism, asserted that it was part of the task of a legal theorist to explain the "normativity" or "authority" of law, by which they meant "our sense that 'legal' norms provide agents with special reasons for acting, reasons they would not have if the norm were not a 'legal' one" (Coleman and Leiter 2010, pp. 228–229; see generally Bix 1996, 2006). One might reasonably question whether we (whoever "we" might be in this case) do in fact believe that legal norms "provide [us] with special reasons for acting," separate from the prudential reasons associated with legal sanctions, or the general moral reasons that *some* legal norms might *sometimes* trigger. Additionally, even if a significant number of people believe that law *qua* law gives them reasons for action, this may be a matter calling more for a psychological or sociological explanation (see *e.g.* Tyler 1990) rather than a philosophical one.

[38] *E.g.*, *Mills v. Wyman*, 20 Mass. (3 Pick.) 207 (1825).

10.4.4 Stefano Bertea's Argument

In a number of important recent works (*e.g.* Bertea 2009, 2011), Stefano Bertea has offered an important and intricate analysis regarding the normativity of law. Bertea argues that "the law (not only its individual provisions but also the system as a whole) claims to guide conduct by providing its addressees with reasons for acting as directed" (Bertea 2009, p. 62).[39] I do not have time here to give Bertea's sophisticated analysis—which ties together law, practical reasoning, human agency, and Immanuel Kant—the attention it deserves, but I did want to make one brief observation.

What I find problematic about Bertea's approach is similar to what I find problematic about the approach of Coleman and Leiter, and many others: that he assumes that theorists should attempt to explain "the source of the obligatory force of law, that is, an elucidation of the source of what enables law to apply to us and hold us bound to do anything, and hence why legal statements should be taken to be binding" (Bertea 2011, p. 200). I think that this is a starting point that needs to be established by further analysis[40]; of course, theorists can choose their own starting point for their own purposes, but can then have no objection if those who do not accept their starting point do not then accept their analysis.

Conclusion

In this article, I have presented in necessarily abbreviated form some of the basic issues regarding two of the persistent questions in the philosophy of law: the relationship between law and rules, and the relationship between law and morality. Both topics are most sharply raised through the topic of "legal normativity."

Many contemporary legal theorists purport to "explain legal normativity," but often fail to articulate what it means to say that law is normative or in what way that property requires explanation. This article has offered a reading of Hans Kelsen's approach as a limited claim about the logic of normative claims: that when one reads the actions of legal officials normatively, this assumes or presupposes the validity of the foundational norm of that legal system, a Kelsenian "Basic Norm." This article also looked at a different aspect of legal normativity, through a focus on the work of H. L. A. Hart. Legal norms frequently prescribe what one ought to do or ought not to do. However, the rush of legal theorists to describe law as thus making *moral* claims seems ungrounded and unnecessary.

Acknowledgement I am grateful for the comments and suggestions of Sean Coyle, William A. Edmundson, John Finnis, Andrew Halpin, Stanley L. Paulson, Ralf Poscher, and Frederick Schauer. An earlier version of portions of this article will be published as Bix (2014), and a version of the article was presented at Hebrew University; I am grateful for the comments and suggestions of those who attended the Hebrew University talk and the Krakow Conference.

[39] Bertea labels this approach "the minimally normative claim".

[40] For a similar response to Bertea, and a generally very thoughtful analysis, see Hage (2011).

References

Alexander, Larry. 1991. The gap. *Harvard Journal of Law & Public Policy* 14:695–701.

Alexander, Larry. 2013. What are principles, and do they exist? http://papers.ssrn.com/sol3/papers.cfm?abstract_id=2277787. Accessed 26 Jan 2014.

Alexy, Robert. 2002a. *The Argument from injustice* (Trans. Bonnie Litschewski Paulson and Stanley L. Paulson). Oxford: Oxford University Press.

Alexy, Robert. 2002b. *A Theory of constitutional rights*. Oxford: Oxford University Press.

Austin, John. 1995. *The Province of jurisprudence determined*, (ed. Wilfrid E. Rumble). Cambridge: Cambridge University Press.

Ávila, Humberto. 2007. *Theory of legal principles*. Dordrecht: Springer.

Barzun, Jacques. 2000. *From dawn to decadence: 500 Years of western cultural life, 1500 to the present*. New York: HarperCollins.

Berman, Harold J. 1994. The origins of historical jurisprudence: Coke, Selden, Hale. *Yale Law Journal* 103:1651–1738.

Bertea, Stefano. 2009. *The normative claim of law*. Oxford: Hart Publishing.

Bertea, Stefano. 2011. Law and obligation: Outlines of a kantian argument. In *New essays on the normativity of law*, ed. Stefano Bertea and George Pavlakos, 199–218. Oxford: Hart Publishing.

Bix, Brian. 1996. Jules Coleman, legal positivism, and legal authority. *Quinnipiac Law Review* 16:241–254.

Bix, Brian. 2006. Legal positivism and 'explaining' normativity and authority. *American Philosophical Association Newsletter* 05 (2): 5–9.

Bix, Brian. 2013a. Book review (reviewing *Philosophical Foundations of the Nature of Law* ed. Wil Waluchow and Stefan Sciaraffa), http://ndpr.nd.edu/news/44711-philosophical-foundations-of-the-nature-of-law/, *Notre Dame philosophical reviews*, Dec 3, 2013, Accessed 26 Jan 2014.

Bix, Brian. 2013b. Ideals, practices, and concepts in legal theory. In *Neutrality and theory of law*, ed. Jordi Ferre Beltràn, José Juan Moreso and Diego M. Papayannis, 33–47. Dordrecht: Springer.

Bix, Brian. 2014. Kelsen and normativity revisited. In *Festschrift for Stanley L. Paulson*, ed. Carlos Bernal Pulido and Marcelo Porciuncula. Madrid: Marcial Pons, Forthcoming.

Coleman, Jules L., and Leiter, Brian. 2010. Legal positivism. In *A Companion to philosophy of law and legal theory.* 2nd ed., ed. Dennis Patterson, 228–248. Malden: Wiley-Blackwell.

Cover, Robert M. 1986. Violence and the word. *Yale Law Journal* 95:1601–1629.

Dworkin, Ronald. 1977. *Taking rights seriously*. Cambridge: Harvard University Press.

Dworkin, Ronald. 1996. *Justice in robes*. Cambridge: Harvard University Press.

Edmundson, William A. 2004. State of the art: The Duty to obey the law. *Legal Theory* 10:215–259.

Ehrenberg, Kenneth M. 2013. Law's authority is not a claim to preemption. In *Philosophical foundations of the nature of law*, ed. Wil Waluchow and Stefan Sciaraffa, 51–74. Oxford: Oxford University Press.

Enoch, David. 2011. Reason-giving and the law. In *Oxford studies in philosophy of law,* vol. I, ed. Leslie Green and Brian Leiter, 1–38. Oxford: Oxford University Press.

Finnis, John. 2011a. *Natural law & natural rights*. 2nd ed. Oxford: Oxford University Press.

Finnis, John. 2011b. *Philosophy of law: Collected essays volume IV*. Oxford: Oxford University Press.

Finnis, John. 2011c. *Reason in action: Collected essays volume I*. Oxford: Oxford University Press.

Finnis, John. 2013. Reflections and Responses. In *Reason, morality, and law: The philosophy of John Finnis*, ed. John Keown and Robert P. George, 459–584. Oxford: Oxford University Press.

Foot, Philippa. 1978. *Virtues and vices*. Oxford: Basil Blackwell.

Fuller, Lon L. 1958. Positivism and fidelity to law – A Reply to Professor Hart. *Harvard Law Review* 71:630–672.
Fuller, Lon L. 1969. *The Morality of law*, rev. ed. New Haven: Yale University Press.
Gardner, John. 2012. *Law as a leap of faith*. Oxford: Oxford University Press.
Green, Leslie. 2003. Legal positivism. In *Stanford encyclopedia of philosophy*, ed. Edward N. Zalta, plato.stanford.edu/entries/legal-positivism. Accessed 26 Jan 2014.
Greenberg, Mark. 2011. The Standard picture and its discontents. In *Oxford studies in philosophy of law*, vol. 1, ed. Leslie Green and Brian Leiter, 39–106. Oxford: Oxford University Press.
Greenberg, Mark. 2013. The Moral impact theory of law. http://papers.ssrn.com/sol3/papers.cfm?abstract_id=2309689. Accessed 26 Jan 2014.
Hage, Jaap. 2011. Elusive normativity. Review article on Stefano Bertea: The normative claim of law. *Rechtsfilosofie en Rechtstheorie* 40:146–168.
Hart, H. L. A. 1958. Positivism and the separation of law and morals. *Harvard Law Review* 71:593–629.
Hart, H. L. A. 1982. *Essays on Bentham: Jurisprudence and political theory*. Oxford: Clarendon Press.
Hart, H. L. A. 2012. *The Concept of law*. 3rd ed. Oxford: Oxford University Press.
Hartney, Michael. 1991. Introduction: The Final form of the pure theory of law. In Hans Kelsen, *General theory of norms* (Trans. Michael Hartney), ix–lx. Oxford: Oxford University Press.
Higgins, Ruth C. A. 2004. *The Moral limits of law: Obedience, respect, and legitimacy*. Oxford: Oxford University Press.
Himma, Kenneth Einar. 2002. Inclusive legal positivism. In *The oxford handbook of jurisprudence and philosophy of law*, ed. Jules Coleman and Scott Shapiro, 125–165. Oxford: Oxford University Press.
Himma, Kenneth Einar. 2013. A comprehensive hartian theory of legal obligation: Social pressure, coercive enforcement, and the legal obligations of citizens. In *Philosophical foundations of the nature of law*, ed. Wil Waluchow and Stefan Sciaraffa, 152–182. Oxford: Oxford University Press.
Hume, David. 1978. *A Treatise of human nature* (analytical index by L. A. Selby-Bigge; 2nd ed., with text revised and notes by P. H. Nidditch). Oxford: Clarendon.
Hurd, Heidi M. 1991. Challenging authority. *Yale Law Journal* 100:1611–1677.
Jakab, András. 2007. Problems of the *Stufenbaulehre*: Kelsen's failure to derive the validity of a norm from another norm. *Canadian Journal of Law and Jurisprudence* 20 (1): 35–67.
Jakab, András. 2010. Re-defining principles as 'important rules': A Critique of Robert Alexy. In *On the nature of legal principles*, ed. Martin Borowski, 145–159. Stuttgart: Franz Steiner Verlag.
Kelsen, Hans. 1960a. *Reine rechtslehre.* 2nd ed. Vienna: Deuticke.
Kelsen, Hans. 1960b. What is the pure theory of law? *Tulane Law Review* 34:269–276.
Kelsen, Hans. 1965. Professor Stone and the pure theory of law. *Stanford Law Review* 17:1128–1157.
Kelsen, Hans. 1992. *Introduction to the problems of legal theory*. Trans. Bonnie Litschewski Paulson and Stanley L. Paulson. Oxford: Clarendon Press.
Kelsen, Hans. 2013. A 'Realistic' theory of law and the pure theory of law: Remarks on Alf Ross's on law and justice. In *Kelsen revisited: New essays on the pure theory of law*, ed. Luís Duarte d'Almeida, John Gardner and Leslie Green, 195–221. Oxford: Hart Publishing.
Kramer, Matthew. 1999. *In Defense of legal positivism: Law without trimmings*. Oxford: Oxford University Press.
Llewellyn, Karl N. 1930. A Realistic jurisprudence—The Next step. *Columbia Law Review* 30:431–465.
Lyons, David. 1965. *Forms and limits of utilitarianism*. Oxford: Oxford University Press.
MacIntyre, A. C. 1959. Hume on 'is' and 'ought'. *The Philosophical Review* 68:451–468.
Marmor, Andrei. 2007. *Law in the age of pluralism*. Oxford: Oxford University Press.
Marmor, Andrei. 2014. *The language of law*. Oxford: Oxford University Press.
Morawetz, Thomas. 1999. Law as experience: Theory and the internal aspect of law. *SMU Law Review* 52:27–66.

Olsson, Erik. 2012. Coherentist theories of epistemic justification. In *The Stanford encyclopedia of philosophy*, ed. Edward N. Zalta, http://plato.stanford.edu/entries/justep-coherence/. Accessed 26 Jan 2014.
Paulson, Stanley L. 1992a. Kelsen's legal theory: The Final round. *Oxford Journal of Legal Studies* 12:265–274.
Paulson, Stanley L. 1992b. The Neo-Kantian dimension of Kelsen's pure theory of law. *Oxford Journal of Legal Studies* 12:311–332.
Paulson, Stanley L. 1992c. Supplementary notes. In *Introduction to the problems of legal theory*. ed. Hans Kelsen (Trans. Bonnie Litschewski Paulson and Stanley L. Paulson), 127–137. Oxford: Clarendon Press.
Paulson, Stanley L. 1998. Four phases in Hans Kelsen's legal theory? Reflections on a periodization. *Oxford Journal of Legal Studies* 18:153–166.
Paulson, Stanley L. 1999. Arriving at a defensible periodization of Hans Kelsen's legal theory. *Oxford Journal of Legal Studies* 19:351–364.
Paulson, Stanley L. 2000. On transcendental arguments, their recasting in terms of belief, and the ensuing transformation of Kelsen's pure theory of law. *Notre Dame Law Review* 75:1775–1795.
Paulson, Stanley L. 2012. A 'Justified normativity' thesis in Hans Kelsen's pure theory of law? Rejoinders to Robert Alexy and Joseph Raz. In *Institutionalized reason: The Jurisprudence of Robert Alexy*, ed. Matthias Klatt, 61–111. Oxford: Oxford University Press.
Paulson, Stanley L. 2013. A Great puzzle: Kelsen's basic norm. In *Kelsen revisited: New essays on the pure theory of law*, ed. Luís Duarte d'Almeida, John Gardner and Leslie Green, 43–61. Oxford: Hart Publishing.
Pound, Roscoe. 1910. Law in books and law in action. *American Law Review* 44:12–36.
Quinn, Philip L. 1990. The Recent revival of divine command ethics. *Philosophy and Phenomenological Research* 50 (Suppl):345–365.
Raz, Joseph. 1983. Legal principles and the limits of law. In *Ronald Dworkin and contemporary Jurisprudence*, ed. Marshall Cohen, 73–87. Totowa: Rowman & Allanheld.
Raz, Joseph. 1990. *Practical reason and norms*. Princeton: Princeton University Press.
Raz, Joseph. 1994. *Ethics in the public domain*. Oxford: Clarendon Press.
Raz, Joseph. 1999. *Engaging reason: On the theory of value and action*. Oxford: Oxford University Press.
Raz, Joseph. 2009. *The Authority of law*. 2nd ed. Oxford: Oxford University Press.
Schauer, Frederick. 1991. *Playing by the rules*. Oxford: Oxford University Press.
Schauer, Frederick. 1998. Positivism through thick and thin. In *Analyzing law: New essays in legal theory*, ed. Brian Bix, 65–78. Oxford: Clarendon Press.
Schauer, Frederick. 2010. Was Austin right after all?: On the role of sanctions in a theory of law. *Ratio Juris* 23:1–21.
Schauer, Frederick. 2014. *The force of law*. Cambridge: Harvard University Press (forthcoming).
Searle, John. 1964. How to derive 'ought' from 'is'. *Philosophical Review* 73:43–58.
Shapiro, Scott J. 2011. *Legality*. Cambridge: Harvard University Press.
Simpson, A. W. B. 1973. The Common law and legal theory. In *Oxford essays in jurisprudence (second series)*, ed. A. W. B. Simpson, 77–99. Oxford: Clarendon Press.
Smith, M. B. E. 1973. Is there a prima facie obligation to obey the law? *Yale Law Journal* 82:950–976.
Tyler, Tom R. 1990. *Why people obey the law*. New Haven: Yale University Press.
Weinrib, Ernest J. 1980. The Case for a duty to rescue. *Yale Law Journal* 80:247–293.
Winston, Kenneth I. 1988. Is/Ought redux: The Pragmatist context of Lon Fuller's conception of law. *Oxford Journal of Legal Studies* 8:329–349.
Young, James O. 2013. Coherence theories of truth. In *The Stanford encyclopedia of philosophy*, ed. Edward N. Zalta, http://plato.stanford.edu/entries/truth-coherence/. Accessed 26 Jan 2014.

Chapter 11
Obligation: A Legal-Theoretical Perspective

Stefano Bertea

Abstract In this study, I intend to contribute to a better understanding of what kind of thing an obligation is and what its defining features are. Central to the conception I will put forward is the idea of obligation as having two essential aspects: one of these lies in the internal connection of obligation with moral practical reasons and is accordingly rational and moral; the other one instead lies in the conceptual link between obligation and requiredness, or mandatory force. In combination these two aspects, which interlock to form what I would call the duality of obligation, frame obligation as a rational and morally justifiable categorical requirement.

Keywords Obligation · Reasons · Command · Rationality · Wrongness · Rules

11.1 Introduction

In this contribution I intend to discuss a specific component of rules: the obligatory component incorporated in some rules and rule-like standards. I thus scrutinise the notion of obligation, which I consider a central element to both ruleness and the practice of rule following. And I will do so from a distinctive perspective, that of a legal theorist.

From the vantage point of legal theory one can appreciate that law, rules, and obligation are intimately connected and ultimately inseparable. This is not to say that any legal system consists either exclusively or primarily of rules or that all legal directives are obligatory. In fact, there is broad recognition in contemporary jurisprudence that law both consists of different kinds of standards—some of which arguably do not have the structure of a rule (think of principles and policies, for instance)—and at least occasionally fails to generate obligations.[1] Yet the claim

---

[1] The dominant view, legal positivism, in some of its most influential contemporary versions, holds that while the law provides reasons for action, it only *purports* to impose obligations, and in fact may well fail to do so (See Coleman 2002, p. 2). Even these variants of legal positivism, however, grant the existence of some form of connection between law and obligation, even if only at the level of mere claims, or of what is *purportedly* the case.

S. Bertea (✉)
Law School, University of Leicester, Leicester, UK
e-mail: stefano.bertea@leicester.ac.uk

M. Araszkiewicz et al. (eds.), *Problems of Normativity, Rules and Rule-Following*,
Law and Philosophy Library 111, DOI 10.1007/978-3-319-09375-8_11

that law, rules, and obligations stand in a close relationship is hardly deniable, this for a number of reasons. First, law is generally understood to be deeply shaped by regulative norms: an important part of the legal domain has to do with statements prescribing courses of conduct and instructing individuals on how they ought to behave. The recognition of the prescriptive structure of law provides strong support for the thesis that key legal statuses can be expressed only through the use of such notions as those of obligation and duty, along with their correlate, the notion of a right[2]. Secondly, paradigmatic legal materials—such as statutes, judicial decisions, and legal commentaries—make reference to obligations either directly, by specifying what one is obligated to do, or indirectly, by attributing rights, powers, and privileges to some of us, which positions are intrinsically connected to the obligations of other individuals. Likewise, practitioners in legal proceedings (judges, prosecutors, lawyers, and juries) as well as citizens in their ordinary lives, frequently make claims about which obligations arising out of law certain individuals have in specific circumstances. This means that the deontic language, including the language that explicitly refers to obligation, is pervasive in discourse within and about law. This widespread attitude is deeply rooted in our practices and experience. For, on the one hand, phrases such "being under an obligation" and "being required" are typically used in connection with law and legal requirements; on the other hand, the vocabulary associated with obligation has entered the philosophical debate with the "law conception" of ethics, which over the centuries has progressively replaced virtue ethics as the dominant ethical approach in the Western tradition.[3] Finally, law, rules, and obligation are regarded as going hand in hand, because a legal system is commonly understood to be an authoritative institution. Now, an essential component of what is ordinarily meant by having or claiming authority in practical matters consists in having or claiming the legitimate power to influence or even control the normative standings of others. And one of the paradigmatic ways (though certainly not the only way) in which the normative standings of others can be affected consists in creating rule-based obligations binding on them.

This extensive use of rule- and obligation-related notions and language contributes to entrenching the widespread belief that legal systems use their rules (and other prescriptive standards) in an effort to impose obligations, and that they actually succeed (at least sometimes) in determining the duties of those subject to the same systems. This being the case, law, rules, and obligation are regarded as conceptually connected even by those legal theorists who, quite understandably, object to reducing law to a merely obligation-imposing system of rules, and who instead opt for a conception under which the normative dimension of law encompasses more than

---

[2] In this article I will treat *obligation* and *duty* as synonyms. In the existing literature some theorists prefer to differentiate between a duty, which is a requirement someone has by virtue of occupying a given position within an institution and so is independent of that person's acceptance, and an obligation, which by contrast is grounded in a previously performed voluntary transaction between two parties, who accordingly stand in a mutual relation and so have correlative claims each other. For such a distinction see Brandt (1964), among others. There is hardly an established or set practice in this regard, though.

[3] These points are argued at some length in Anscombe (1981, pp. 26–42).

just rules and obligations. These theorists accordingly conceptualise a legal system as an order framed by different kinds of normative standards, and as having the capacity not simply to bring obligations into being but also to confer powers, grant permissions, and attribute immunities, just to name a few of the normative statuses that can be kept distinct from obligation. On these grounds, a significant number of legal theorists, especially within mainstream jurisprudence, agree that an account of the obligatory dimension of legal rules must be central to the philosophical study of the concept of law and other fundamental legal concepts. Related, they recognise that the distinctive way in which law governs human conduct can hardly be made intelligible without bringing in the idea of obligation.

In consideration of the fact that obligation is regarded as a notion that figures centrally in the experience and practice of law, I will focus here on the idea of obligation to determine what kind of thing an obligation is and what its defining features are. In pursuing this aim I will work toward a theoretical account of obligation by reflecting on the fundamental characteristics of obligation understood as a concept with its own distinctive defining features.

The basic assumption underlying the discussion is that obligation singles out a general idea used in different realms and is accordingly given different meanings in different contexts. This differentiation is attested, for instance, by the fact that we ordinarily speak not only of obligation, period—obligation *simpliciter*—but also of moral obligations, social obligations, legal obligations, associative obligations, positional obligation, and natural obligations, just to name a few. Despite this range, obligations of different varieties are regarded not as referring to altogether disparate notions but as pointing to the existence of a general overarching idea—obligation *simpliciter*—to which specific kinds of obligation can be traced and from which they derive. For this reason in this contribution I will argue for an account of obligation in general, addressing such questions as What is an obligation? and How can obligation be distinctively characterised? The account of obligation so provided can then be used as the fundamental benchmark against which to critically assess the models of legal obligation currently defended, and as the essential tool making it possible to move beyond the current debate in legal theory, putting forward an account of legal obligation irreducible to the ones presently discussed and superior to them, or so I think.

11.2 The Essential Traits of Obligation

The chief aim of this section is to single out the general traits, or set of properties, which in the existing literature are commonly associated with the notion of obligation. This should give us a general meaning of what an obligation is, that is, a *concept* of obligation as distinct from a *conception*, or theoretical *account*, of obligation. A *concept* of obligation is meant to mark the boundaries within which a theoretical debate on obligation is to take place: it thus identifies the ground common to otherwise conflicting, or at least alternative, theoretical views. By contrast, a *conception* of obligation will identify a far more controversial view of obligation, a view closely aligned with the specific philosophical preferences underlying one's approach to obligation as well as with the specific contents, criteria, and conditions of existence that different theorists associate with obligation.[4] The perspective I will take in this section will thus be theoretically lightweight: rather than embarking on a potentially controversial and partisan analysis of obligation, I will extract from the literature the current views of what an obligation is so as to reduce them to a common core encapsulating a broad understanding of obligation, or a general framework within which to think about obligation.

Since in this section I will be discussing the traits that define obligation as a (distinctive) concept, the resulting characterisation—to be interpreted as providing us with a general meaning of obligation—should be expected to be "thin" and tolerant. In this sense, the concept should be able to accommodate a vast range of specific accounts, or conceptions, of obligation reflecting the distinct philosophical perspectives endorsed by those who have defended those accounts. At the same time, this general meaning of obligation is neither pointless nor irrelevant. While it does not give a comprehensive answer to the basic questions about obligation, as these questions are debated among those who study obligation, it at least makes sense of them. Accordingly, the general meaning of obligation that will be introduced in this section will be framed in terms sufficiently clear and precise to render intelligible such questions as What is the nature of obligation? How are obligation and "ought" related? What is the distinctive force of an obligation? Is the existence of an obligation independent of the specific perspective, goals, interests, and desires of those who are subject to that obligation, or is it rather ultimately tied to those persons' attitudes? How is obligation related to other paradigmatic normative notions like justification, reasons, responsibility, and wrongness? What is the kind of justification, if any, that should be associated with the existence of obligation? Is obligation essentially tied with sanction and coercion, or at least with the possibility of sanctioning and coercing deviant conduct? and What kinds of entities—persons, institutions, states of affairs—can have or lack the property of obligating?

11.2.1 Obligation as a Normative and Practical Notion

Among the traits most commonly associated with obligation are practicality and normativity.[5] Obligation is a concept at once practical and normative, since it can

---

[4] This distinction between concepts and conceptions has been made popular by Rawls (1971, p. 5).

[5] These two traits are recognised as essential to obligation in Prichard (1949, pp. 87–163), for instance, where the mistake is criticised of resolving obligation into different categories of thought, such the category we use to state what ought to *exist*, on the one hand, and the one we use to state what ought to be *done*, on the other. The idea of obligation as being both practical and normative also finds a clear statement in Himma (2013, p. 20), arguing that obligations are associated with "claims about what someone (or some class of persons) ought to do in some state of affairs." Similarly, Hage (2011, pp. 178–83) distinguishes the "ought" into two kinds—which he calls the

be so described: (a) on the practical side, it serves as a means by which to guide our conduct (and so is action-related) and (b) on the normative side, it does so by providing a basis for *judging* conduct as good or bad, or right or wrong, worthwhile or worthless, and the like. Obligation thus sets itself up as a *practical ought*:[6] it indicates that which an agent *ought to do*, and can accordingly be broken down analytically into an "*ought*" component (the normative part) and a "*do*" component (the practical part).

This breakdown helps us to distinguish obligation, on the one hand, from that which is practical but *descriptive* (indicating not what agents *ought to* do but what they *in fact* do or can be expected to do) and, on the other hand, from that which is normative but *theoretical*, by virtue of its depicting an account of the world as it ought to *be* (not necessarily implying any agency or action on our part but mere contemplation), in turn distinguished from the world such as it *is*, which places us in a sphere conceptually separable from that of obligation, a sphere at once theoretical and descriptive, that of the "*is*".[7]

11.2.2 Obligation as a Non-trivial Requirement

An obligation is widely understood as a requirement. Our having an obligation means that we are *bound*, or required, to act in accordance with what the obligation prescribes. Thus, there is in obligation the idea of a *binding* ought, or requiredness: an obligation does not make something desirable and good; it makes conduct exactable and compulsory.[8] More to the point, an obligation encapsulates a demand that, if recognised as valid, has the quality of a pronouncement urging one to engage in some course of conduct. This means that obligation is conceptually connected to an imperative, making any alternative course of conduct normatively ineligible and unviable: when an obligation exists, there is just one course of action that, normatively speaking, is available to the agent. Obligation, in sum, is a kind of necessitation issuing from a binding directive whose nature is imperative.

In addition, the kind of requirement associated with the existence of an obligation is widely understood to be more than just trivial. Obligation is associated with a

---

"ought-to-do" and the "ought-to-be"—and then goes on to argue that obligations are instances of the former kind, in that they determine what ought to be *done*, and so are constraints on behaviour. See also Baier (1966, p. 210) and, more recently, Owens (2008, p. 406).

[6] The connection between normativity and ought is widely accepted today. For an exemplary statements of this connection see Dancy (2000a, p. vii).

[7] The breakdown thus works by way of two oppositions (normative vs. descriptive and practical vs. theoretical) yielding four kinds of concepts, which may be (i) theoretical and descriptive (the world such as it is); (ii) theoretical and normative (the world as it ought to be); (iii) practical and descriptive (what agents do); or (iv) practical and normative (what agents ought to do). Only in this fourth class we find obligation.

[8] On the idea of obligation as a requirement, see Brandt (1964, p. 374), Pink (2004, pp. 159–61), Owens (2008, p. 403), and Darwall (2009, pp. 31–36).

stringent compelling force.[9] To further elaborate on this point, the form of demandingness accompanying an obligation is peculiar in a twofold sense. On the one hand, we cannot be said to have an obligation if we can easily dispose of it or effortlessly free ourselves of it. An obligation is a serious constraint. As such it is non-optional: it puts genuine pressure on us by significantly limiting our practical freedom. In that sense, obligation comes with a built-in resistance, since it is stringency that distinguishes obligation from other forms of ought. This also means that those under an obligation are not in the position to legitimately remove that obligation or distance themselves from it. In the words of David Owens (2008, p. 404), an obligation is

> something that takes the matter out of your hands: it is no longer up to you to judge whether doing the required thing would be best, all things considered.[10]

On the other hand, the pressure you have when you are under an obligation is not inexorable. The necessity of obligation (its demanding that you do something) is *normative*, not metaphysical or logical: it is not a conceptual kind of necessity. Precisely for this reason obligations can as a matter of practical possibility be ignored and violated. Likewise, we can even act against the requirements set by the obligations we have. In so doing, we challenge, and so disobey, a real constraint imposed on us: a decision to so act will not come without consequences, to be sure; but the act is neither naturalistically nor metaphysically impossible.

11.2.3 Obligation and Responsibility

Finally, obligation is widely thought to be inextricably connected to responsibility: if we are under an obligation, we are responsible for complying with the corresponding requirement. In this context, *responsibility* means both "answerability to others" and "liability for one's own failure." For, on the one hand, those subject to obligations are regarded as responsible in the sense that they can be called to account for their action and can be made to respond to charges (let us call this "responsibility as answerability"). If we are under an obligation, then, we are accountable or can be held accountable for our conduct. On the other hand, if we fail to honour an obligation, we will be responsible in the specific sense of being liable to some negative reaction from others (call this "responsibility as liability"). This additional sense of responsibility stems from the fact that (a) violating an obligation is *prima facie* an act of wrongdoing, and (b) we are presumptively entitled to regard those acting in breach of their obligations as wrongdoers, that is, as persons who in some way can justifiably be rebuked. Obligation, accountability, and liability should thus be treated as interdefinable notions.

---

[9] The stringency of obligation is emphasised in Baier (1966, p. 211), Gewirth (1970, pp. 55–56), Forrester (1975, p. 219), and Cupit (1994, pp. 439–41).

[10] This idea is aptly rendered by Margaret Gilbert (1992, p. 34), who claims that because "obligations are recalcitrant to one's will," "people may feel trapped by them": obligations cannot be changed by "a simple change of mind".

11.3 A Theoretical Account of Obligation

Thus far I have argued for a view of obligation as a practically normative requirement that makes a nontrivial claim on us, who in turn are both bound to comply with it and responsible for our compliance or disobedience. I take this to be the general meaning, or concept, of obligation, a meaning that any competent user of the term "obligation" would acknowledge as the core idea of obligation.

In this section I will be building on this general concept to develop a *conception* of obligation. To this end, I start out from the body of material about obligation that I have just introduced and then I critically synthesise this material so as to make the idea of obligation fully intelligible. This will give us a theoretical account of obligation, namely, a framework in which the general traits widely associated with the existence of obligation find meaning by virtue of the broader and more comprehensive picture they are part of. This means that we will be leaving the relatively uncontroversial territory of the ordinary understanding of obligation and moving into a partly uncharted territory where theoretical considerations informed by potentially controversial assumptions and presuppositions need to be introduced and defended.

11.3.1 Obligation, Justifications, and Reasons

In the reconstruction offered in Sect. 11.2, it was claimed that obligation is widely regarded as a practical and normative notion. Describing obligation as a normative notion, thus locating it within that broader domain, implies that it will not suffice to frame obligation as something that guides conduct; by contrast, it has to do so in a certain way, by providing *reasons* for us to so behave.

This intuitive idea can be worked into a more specific thesis, which I will be calling the "reasons thesis"[11]. The reason thesis states that reasons are essential to normativity in a constitutive sense, in that they *define* what it means for something to be normative. Accordingly, normative discourse essentially consists in reasons offered in support of this or that course of conduct. This is to say that the reasons thesis posits reasons as the fundamental normative concept, the concept to which any other notion inhering in the normative dimension of human experience must be traced, and in terms of which any other normative notion can ultimately be captured.

The statement of the reason thesis carries direct implications for the study of obligation. If we accept that obligation is a practical normative concept and that, as such, it belongs in the realm of practical normativity—a realm where nothing becomes normative except through the use of practical reasons (this is the reasons

[11] This is in accordance with an established tradition in contemporary philosophy, and specifically with what Broome (2004, p. 28) calls the "turn to reasons," which has characterised the philosophy of action and normativity since the 1970s. The turn to reasons has been summarised in Raz's (1999, p. 67) statement that "the normative of all that is normative consists in the way it is, or provides, or is otherwise related to reasons". For a critical approach to the turn to reasons, see Broome (1999, 2004).

thesis, or rather, its practical instantiation)—then we should be able to conclude that obligation itself is essentially defined by the use of practical reasons. A conceptually necessary link, therefore, obtains between obligation and practical reasons, to the effect that something can be regarded as obligatory only by virtue of its being supported by reasons for action. In turn, obligation rests in an essential way on the use of reasons. That is, obligation cannot be fully understood unless its indispensable and essential reliance on practical reasons is made apparent.[12] Hence the central position a discussion of the meaning of a practical reason occupies within a theory of obligation shaped by the reasons thesis.

Contemporary philosophy offers a range of different, often conflicting views of what a practical reason is. These views differ by their underlying metaphysical, epistemological, and semantic premises. Here I will not offer a complete overview of this panoply of conceptions, because that would take me too far from the immediate task of elucidating the idea of obligation. So instead of taking in the full landscape, I will explain the meaning of practical reasons by looking at the role such reasons play in our normative discourse. My treatment can accordingly be described, in more technical language, as a study into the semantics of a practical reason. It is therefore a circumscribed study, not a full conception of a practical reason[13].

By a practical reason, in the current debate, is generally meant any consideration offered in support of some course of action. Such a supporting consideration can in turn be understood in any of three ways, namely, as something that attempts to (a) *justify* some act, that is, rationalise it or show why it is a good action or the right or proper thing to do; or (b) say what *motivates*, or drives, someone to do something; or (c) *explain* why somebody did, or would do, something, with more of a descriptive or a predictive interest. Practical reasons, then, have traditionally been grouped into three classes, depending on whether they are meant to serve as justifications, as motivations, or as explanations.

Now, which of the classes of a practical reason can specifically be used to define obligation? Stated otherwise, which of those classes singles out that specific segment of the normative dimension inhabited by obligations? The question is relevant, since not all the three classes of practical reasons come to bear in this connection. In order to appreciate that, one only need further elaborate on the stringency requirement, as it is associated with the existence of an obligation. The generic idea of stringency, as it applies to an obligation, can be more specifically spelled out in terms of the categorical, or non-hypothetical, character of a requirement. It is only insofar as a class of practically normative stringent requirements can be characterised as categorical and so enjoys some form of independence of an individual agent's subjective states and personal goals, or projects, that those requirements can be considered obligatory. In turn, a requirement can be qualified as categorical if it

[12] This point is clearly stated in Gilbert (1992, pp. 27–30).

[13] This can be appreciated by considering that different conceptions of a practical reason may well agree on a certain meaning of a practical reason—on its semantics—while diverging in significant, even irreconcilable, ways on its metaphysics and epistemology.

binds us regardless of whether we have a personal stake in it and therefore applies to us unconditionally.[14]

To further elaborate on this point, categoricity is such that a practical requirement qualifies as an obligation if the reason why we should act accordingly is not essentially connected with what we happen to personally like, or what we might be naturally inclined to do (for instance, as a matter of habit or disposition or by virtue of our psychological makeup or subjective states), or what we might have a personal interest in doing.[15] Accordingly, a categorical requirement is impermeable to, and independent of, the inner states of the specific individuals subject to the requirement. An obligation should be regarded as categorical in quality, since the moment we are under an obligation we are required to comply with it, whether or not doing so comports with or advances our plans, objectives, and projects.[16] This means that we have before us a practical requirement we cannot opt out of for reasons that only apply to us specifically.

This idea can be reformulated by saying that our complying with an obligation is a question of objective necessity and has little to do with what we like or dislike doing: an obligatory act is one we are normatively expected to do, period, no matter what we wish or are inclined to do or are actually committed to doing: the specific perspective one has as an individual agent does not exhaust the framework within which obligation finds its proper place.[17]

Once we see obligation in this way—namely, as an ought enjoying some degree of independence from the one's personal preferences, wishes, and plans—it is possible to further specify which class of practical reasons defines obligation. For, what it means for a reason-based requirement to be obligatory depends on the degree of independence from individual states as it is that the reason supporting that requirement has. Hence, it is only insofar as a class of practical reason can be characterised in terms of its independence—as a class comprising of, and inhabited by, standards that can have categorical character that one can use a practical reason to define

[14] Categoricity, so conceived as a form of non-hypotheticalness, is a notion I am borrowing from Railton (2003, pp. 120–23). It can be described as a humanised variant of the Kantian idea of categorical imperatives.

[15] On this point, see Gilbert (1992, pp. 30–31).

[16] On this aspect of obligation, see Baier (1966, p. 216) and Gardner and MacKlem (2002, pp. 464–70).

[17] The preceding remarks should not be taken to mean that an obligation, with the categorical claim it makes on us, must be acted on, since that would take us to the level of what is *conclusively* binding. What it means for a requirement to be categorical is not that it must be acted on, regardless of any consideration, but that we cannot "undo" our obligation for reasons of personal preference, or interest. The categorical bindingness of an obligation may well be presumptive, not final, to be sure. Therefore, an important caveat in thinking about the categoricity of an obligation is that this idea should not be confused with the idea of what is conclusively binding all things considered. A practical ought is non-hypothetical if we cannot opt out of it for personal reasons; it is conclusive if it is backed by reasons that on balance trump all other reasons—or can be shown to do so in the course of practical reasoning among moral agents—and we are therefore expected to comply no matter what. An obligation can apply to us categorically and still be inconclusive: what makes it categorical is a criterion different from that which makes it conclusive.

obligation (which, to reiterate, stands not just for any requirement but for a categorical demand).

Now, not all kinds of practical reasons stand on the same ground or exert the same force. There are classes of reasons that are established by, or are directly related to, subjective states, contingent personal ends, and undertakings of the relevant agent. This means that not all (classes of) practical reasons partake of the categorical quality.

In fact, there is a strong presumption that motivating reasons, as personal as well as psychological reasons, do not have what it takes to make a practical reason non-hypothetical and, hence, unconditionally binding. To see this, we have to critically engage with Dancy's (2000b, pp. 14–15) contrary claim that at least some motivating reasons are not psychological states. This is relevant because the moment we unhinge motivating reasons from psychological states, we have thereby opened the possibility of making these reasons non-hypothetical, by so making them an essential part of what is obligatory. That is, if we identify a motivating reason with something other than a psychological state—for instance, with a fact or a state of affairs—we are in position to establish a conceptual link between obligation and the class of motivating reason. By contrast, if a motivating reason is identified with a psychological state it is then impossible to characterise a motivating reason as a reason with categorical force. For, in this case, we will not be able to show that such a class can provide support on a non-contingent basis. Accordingly, one can define obligation in terms of motivating reasons only as long these reasons are predicated not on an agent's psychology (which is contingent) but on certain facts, or states of affairs, having inherent normative and thus motivating force.

The argument showing how a motivating reason can be anything other than a psychological state looks unconvincing, because there is simply no such thing as a fact, or state of affairs—a non-psychological condition existing out there in the world—that can be pointed out as a motivating reason for action, however obvious or self-evident it may be as such a reason. The point is that this fact, or state of affairs, however straightforward it may be as a motivating reason for action, does not become such a reason until we complete the thought by showing how we are to take that fact, or state of affairs, namely, until we spell out the kinds of beliefs and desires needed to act on that fact, or state of affairs, and the frame of mind through which to relate to it. It is therefore fair to conclude that an agent's beliefs, psychological features, attitude, interests, and frame of mind play an unavoidable mediating role in establishing what ultimately counts as a motivating reason for action. This mediating role rules out the possibility that a motivating reason can hold categorically. From which it follows that motivating reasons—as reasons whose point would be defeated if they were decoupled from the psychology of action and whose basis lies in a personal view of what is valuable in life—cannot bear any *essential*, or constitutive, relation to obligation, at least not when obligation is acknowledged to be a non-hypothetical requirement.

This conclusion leaves us with only two candidates for the role of a defining element of obligation: justificatory reasons and explanatory reasons. Explanatory reasons can be ruled out straightaway as a defining element of obligation, since these reasons are concerned with the *causes* of action—with why an action *is* performed, and not with why a course of conduct *ought to* be engaged in. And the discourse concerned to explain why agents behave the way they behave has little to do with obligation, since that kind of discourse is not normative. Accordingly, it is as far removed from the "ought" of action, which instead is constitutive of what is obligatory, as one can imagine when contemplating action. This is to say that it is justificatory reasons that we find at the core of obligation qua practical and normative notion. Only justificatory reasons (a) can make something distinctly normative and (b) can do so in such a way as to make it categorically binding. Motivating reasons may in some sense succeed in that first role (a), by prompting agents to act in one way or another when faced with a practical decision. But they definitely fail in the second role (b), because that decision cannot be divorced from an agent's psychological makeup and unique system of beliefs and so is contingent, even when felicitously congruent with what turns out to be the normatively validated course of action.

To restate this point, since motivating reasons are reasons which reveal an agent's psychology, personal character, and individual inclinations, they are not specifically designed to bind us regardless of how well we may be disposed toward it or how we may feel in contemplating it. Explanatory reasons, for their part, fail on both counts, for they neither (a) say how we ought to act nor do they (b) concern themselves with determining whether someone's actions were non-hypothetically right, good, commendable, appropriate, reasonable, or what have you. Only justificatory reasons fill both of those seats, which are central to the definition of obligation understood as a practical and normative requirement. For, justificatory reasons are the reasons that make an agent's performance acceptable when measured up against certain standards of practical correctness: they are conceptually connected to notions—justification, evaluation and grounded criticism—that are constitutively normative. In addition, on the one hand, justificatory reasons grant the possibility that specific instances of practical normativity bind non-hypothetically, since justificatory reasons do not make psychology-related features essential to determining what they support as, instead, motivating reasons do; on the other hand, justificatory reasons engage with what one ought to do, vis-à-vis with what one does, and so they secure the distinctiveness of the normative realm when compared to the cause-shaped descriptive domain marked out by explanatory reasons. Accordingly, the reference to justificatory reasons has the potential to account for two central aspects of what is obligatory: its distinctiveness from what is factual and descriptive and its categorical quality.

This argument ultimately grounds the conclusion that obligation need be conceptualised in terms of a specific class of reasons—justificatory reasons. Obligation, in other terms, is essentially defined by the use of *justificatory* reasons, not motivating or explanatory ones. Namely, the obligatory quality of certain demands depends on the existence of justificatory reasons—the reasons which (at least occasionally succeed to) make it the case that someone non-hypothetically ought to perform certain actions and refrain from doing something else. This is also how it will be in the rest of the discussion, where the unqualified term "reason" will designate neither motivating nor explanatory reasons but justificatory ones[18]. This is because, as I hope to have clearly illustrated, only justificatory reasons can have any categorical normative force in discourse involving that which ought to be done (that is, in any practical discourse).

In summary, the argument offered in this section has shown that obligation should be understood as inextricably bound up with justification, in that it fundamentally revolves around the use of *justificatory* reasons (as against motivating or explanatory reasons). A conceptual link can thus be said to exist between obligation and justification, a link by virtue of which these two notions ought to be regarded as intimately connected. When viewed as a notion pertaining to the sphere of practical normativity, obligation is essentially defined by the use of practical reasons. Since in this context practical reasons are to be understood as *justificatory* reasons, not as motivating or explanatory ones, obligation is essentially and primarily a matter of justification. Because obligation as a practical notion would make no sense but for the reason-giving practice through which it comes into being—the practice of offering *justificatory* reasons for action—the proper domain of obligation is going to find its main focus in the ideas of answerability, or standard-relatedness, and legitimate criticism. The foregoing argument therefore takes us to the conclusion that obligation is best conceived and understood by locating it in the domain of justification, where it is shaped through the activity of giving reasons, an activity by virtue of which the action identified as the object of an obligation can be rationally justifiable. This means that a necessary link obtains between obligation, practical reasons, and justification.[19]

11.3.2 The Moral Nature of Obligation

Obligation, I have just argued, is shaped by justificatory reasons. A theoretical account of obligation will therefore need to further specify what kinds of justificatory reasons define an obligation. To this end we will have to draw a rough map of the practical sphere within which to locate justificatory reasons.

The starting point of this exercise is provided by a distinction that is widely acknowledged to be fundamental in ethics, a distinction between two basic modes of thinking about the practical ought, as well as two ways of supporting a course, or plan, of action: the distinction between moral reasons and prudential reasons. Both prudential reasons and moral reasons provide support to certain undertakings to be sure; namely, they both justify the performance of a given conduct while, at the same time, grounding criticism of acts that conflict, or are incompatible with, the supported one.[20] Nevertheless, prudential reasons and moral reasons justify action in different ways.

---

[18] For remarks supporting the terminological stipulation just made, see Greenspan (2005) and Wallace (2006, pp. 63–70).

[19] Support for this conclusion can also found in Prichard (1949, pp. 142–52) and Hacker (1973, pp. 142–8).

[20] This quality of (all) practical reasons derives from the very definition of a practical reason.

On the one hand, with *prudential* reasons, we are presented with the argument that we ought to do, or avoid doing, something because that would lead to good or bad consequences, as the case might be. The consequences are measured by a criterion of comparative advantage of the agent: the agent would be better off or worse off than she is now as a result of pursuing or not pursuing the course of action at issue. An example of this kind of practical reasoning would be as follows. We should stay on a healthy diet because otherwise we will be at risk for a variety of medical conditions. This can be described as prudential practical thinking. It is practical because it involves reasoning about what to do; it is prudential, and so nonmoral, because its essence lies in hypothetical means-end reasoning where the ends need only be consistent with the value inherent in the idea of that which is in our best interest, however construed. On the other hand we have *moral* reasons, which, by contrast, point something out as being good, regardless of whether realising the good in question gives us an "edge" or an advantage (paradigmatically construed in terms of self-interest). Thus, going back to the diet example, we may eat vegetarian because we believe it to be healthier than an omnivorous diet, in which case we would be said to act prudentially; but it may be that we choose to so act because we feel that it is wrong to kill animals, and in that case we can be said to act out of properly moral reasons.

This construction means that prudential reasons secure practical justification by making appeal to the interests of the agent who performs the relevant piece of conduct; moral reasons, instead, grant practical support by showing that the course of conduct one is justified to undertake matches with interests that go beyond the concerns of the person who act. To elaborate further on this point, prudential reasons appeal to the personal interests of the agent and so disregard other subjects and their needs. As a result, they rely on considerations that are exclusively concerned with private gain and one's own advantage. By doing so, prudential reasons are entirely self-regarding in so that they neglect the concerns of others and exclusively cater to the needs of the acting self: when one acts on prudential reasons, she guides her action by the measure of personal advantage and, hence, she simply adduces her own preferences, aspirations, ends and desires in justifying the undertaking she carries on. By contrast, moral reasons take into account not just the interests of the agent but the interests of other individuals who are affected or may be affected by the action as well[21]. From the point of view shaped by moral reasons, then, everyone's concerns count equally. This means that one uses moral reasons to account for the needs of each individual impartially, give full weight to each need, and make each count in practical deliberation.

This is a crucial distinction to bear in mind as we work our way toward an account of obligation because it brings into focus the distinctive kind of force that

[21] This statement follows from the thesis that the moral point of view factors in the needs of others as well as the first-person needs of the self-interested subject, so that self-regarding reasons, too, play a role in moral reasoning, alongside other-regarding reasons. For a defence of this all-encompassing view of morality see Stroud (1998, pp. 179–181).

justificatory reasons have in giving rise to obligations[22]. There is the force of advice (of that which is recommended or held up as good in giving practical guidance); and there is the force of requirement (of that which is mandatory or demanded in pointing out what is right). The latter is the proper domain of obligation, since only in this latter domain we can frame obligation in the categorical sense we are pursuing. So, in summary, the practically normative sphere can be roughly divided into two broad camps for the purpose of locating obligation. On the one hand we have the whole range of practical considerations we formulate from a first-person framing perspective in pointing out a prudential reason for action: anything contrary to such a proposition will be amenable to criticism as either inadvisable, or, insensible, or unwise, or ineligible, or even foolish, *qua* not in accordance with the agent self-interest. This means that prudential reasons come with a specific force attached to them: recommendatory force. Recommendatory force is attractive. A course of conduct is justified in the recommendatory sense as long as it is found appealing, to the effect that departing from it is unreasonable, *qua* ill-advised. On the other hand we have the more circumscribed camp of moral reasons we formulate from a broader and more inclusive perspective in pointing out what we argue to be mandatory or demandable (an obligation proper): anything contrary to such a proposition will be amenable to criticism as being wrong and categorically forbidden. Accordingly, departing from what is justified by moral reasons will not be considered merely inadvisable or foolish—a course of conduct that is less than sensible and hence one has a personal interest in avoiding it. It will rather be considered wrong—an instance of wrong-doing. In other terms, the form of criticism that is appropriate when one departs from moral considerations—the considerations that define what an obligation is—is qualitatively different from the form of criticism attached to an act performed against a prudential practical reason. Deviance from what is morally due is qualified as, and is criticised for being, wrong when compared to a set of reason-based standards. That is, the departure from moral reasons legitimises the accusation of wrongness, which, when contrasted with, say, the accusation of inadvisability, or lack of wisdom, is a distinct reason-based criticism.

This element associated with the existence of a moral reason—peculiarity of criticism—means that moral reasons possess a distinctive kind of justificatory strength, a kind of justificatory strength that cannot be found in association with prudential reasons. More to the point, the justificatory force of moral reasons has mandatory quality. Mandatory force is binding and compulsive, as opposed to attractive. An action is supported in the mandatory sense as long as it is demanded and exactable, namely, the agent is not simply advised to perform it, but rather she is bound, or required, to do so.[23] Therefore, action supported by practical reasons with mandatory force is justified in the strong sense of being demanded, required

[22] I would like to thank Aldo Schiavello for discussing this point with me and providing valuable insights into the relation between prudential reasons and recommendatory force, on the one hand, and moral reasons and mandatory force, on the other. If there is any error or failing in this discussion, however, I am entirely responsible for it.

[23] In sum, thus, for all their diversities and nuances the variable kinds of the strength with which practical reasons justify a course of action can be reduced to two basic broad types: the force of

or necessitated. And therein lies the distinctive force of obligation. It is a force we can appreciate by looking at justification in comparison with all the other forms of practical discourse so far considered, and by bearing in mind the close conceptual connection that justification has been argued to bear to obligation and the categorical ought grounded in the moral perspective.

In this context, it cannot be overemphasised that it is because a course of conduct supported by moral reasons can be not merely advisable and recommended, but indeed mandatory and required, that deviating from it is not just a hardly commendable choice, but it can be criticised as a wrong decision. Hence, a relation of mutual interdependence can be established between moral quality of a practical reason, its mandatory force and the practical criticism expressed in term of wrongness. This makes the link between moral reasons, mandatory force and wrongness definitional, or constitutive: an act is supported by moral reasons insofar as it is backed by practical reasons that have mandatory force and justify the criticism of the deviant conduct as wrongful.

This conclusion is key in the context of a study of obligation. For, obligation has the force of a demand and a directive, namely, the force of a mandatory requirement, as opposed to the force of a recommendation. In addition, action performed in breach of an obligation is at least presumptively not just inadvisable but wrong. This means that obligation is conceptually and distinctively associated with moral reasons, as opposed to prudential reasons. One has an obligation to act so and so by virtue of the fact that the relevant course of conduct is supported by moral reasons, since only when practical reasons come with mandatory force—the force which is distinctive of moral reasons—and single out a wrongdoing—as moral reasons characteristically do—an obligation arises. That is, having an obligation can hardly be equated to having a practical reason recommending one to act in a certain way, as it is the case when prudential reasons apply. Unless the reason supporting a certain conduct possesses the force of a requirement no obligation can be said to arise. And this is why obligation links up conceptually with a specific subset of practical reasons—moral reasons—by so singling out a narrow division within that which is rationally justified and secured from criticism.

To put it otherwise, not everything that is supported by practical reasons in their justificatory mode is made obligatory: not practical reasons whatsoever but rather practical reasons the nature of which is moral give rise to obligations. Obligation, therefore, refers to a situation where practical reasons are present that are endowed with some enhanced strength, to the effect that the supported action is compellingly due from the moral point of view.[24]

From this it also follows that there is no conceptual space for anything like a "prudential obligation". Prudential reasons and considerations cannot by themselves support any obligation to carry out given actions: they can do so only if associated with *moral* reasons and considerations. This is to say that we cannot be

---

advice and the force of requirement. This reduction is argued for in Pink (2007, pp. 416–23). See also Pink (2004).

[24] Similar remarks can be found in Darwall (2009, pp. 31–6).

said to be under an obligation unless moral reasons apply to us; conversely, prudential reasons may induce or even compel someone to act, but the force of compulsion based on prudence cannot be qualified as obligatory. Related, self-interest cannot take us into the realm of obligation[25]: obligations are grounded not in prudence but in morality. Similarly, although an obligation can originate out of different kinds of considerations and situations—and so, genealogically speaking, can be religious, social, institutional, natural, and so on—its quality is distinctively and intrinsically moral[26].

11.4 Tacking Stock: The Duality of Obligation

Central to the conception of obligation I have put forward in this contribution is the idea of obligation as having two essential aspects: one of these lies in the internal connection of obligation with moral practical reasons, and is accordingly rational and moral; the other one instead lies in the conceptual link I have argued to exist between obligation and requiredness, or mandatory force. These two aspects interlock to form what I would call the duality of obligation. Namely, by virtue of the dual conceptual link which ties obligation to moral reasons, on the one hand, and to mandatoriness, on the other, obligation at once acquires moral justificatory force and sets itself up as a categorical requirement. In combination, the two aspects frame obligation as a morally justifiable and rational categorical requirement.

In the theoretical framework worked out in this contribution, therefore, obligation can be defined in terms of two claims: (a) the claim that obligation is shaped by moral practical reasons, such that no obligation can arise unless the conduct it prescribes is morally and rationally justifiable—hence the moral and justificatory element in the definition—coupled with (b) the claim that obligation carries a distinctively mandatory force—hence the non-hypothetically imperative element of the definition. It is only the interplay of moral and rational justification with categorical imperativeness that gives us a full picture of obligation.

The two axes around which the concept of obligation can so be organised makes the proposed account of obligation as irreducible to any alternative conception equating obligation to either a rational component (where reason-relatedness is taken to be the sole fundamental constituent of obligation) or a constraining component (where requiredness, or imperativeness, is understood as summarising by itself alone the core of obligation). On this basis, one should concluded that if we leave either one of these two elements out of the picture—as by defining obligation exclusively in terms of moral and rational justification or exclusively in terms of categorical requirements—we will therefore have a *partial* account, one that chooses to bring out some features of obligation without duly acknowledging other features.

[25] In Prichard's (1949, p. 97) words, "conduciveness to our advantage is simply irrelevant to the question whether it is a duty to do some action."

[26] See Baier (1966, pp. 211–3) for an argument supporting this conclusion.

Acknowledgement I wish to express my indebtedness to the participants in the workshop *Rules 2013* (27–29 September 2013, Jagiellonian University in Krakow) for their insighful comments on the paper from which this essay originates. Also, the argument has benefited from the valuable feedback received at one seminar organized by the Philosophy of Law Research Group at the Law Department of the Pompeu Fabra University of Barcelona (10 June 2013).

References

Anscombe, Elizabeth. 1981. *Ethics, religion and politics. The Collected Philosophical Papers of G.E.M. Anscombe, vol. 3*. Oxford: Blackwell.
Baier, Kuert. 1966. Moral obligation. *American Philosophical Quarterly* 3:210–226.
Brandt, Richard. 1964. The concepts of obligation and duty. *Mind* 73:374–393.
Broome, John. 1999. Normative requirements. *Ratio* 12:398–419.
Broome, John. 2004. Reasons. In *Reason and value*, ed. Jay Wallace, et al. 28–55. Oxford: Clarendon.
Coleman, Jules. 2002. Conventionality and normativity. In *Legal and political philosophy*, ed. E. Villanueva, 157–175. Amsterdam: Rodopi.
Cupit, Geoffrey. 1994. How requests (and promises) create obligations. *Philosophical Quarterly* 44:439–455.
Dancy, Jonathan. 2000a. Editor's Introduction. In *Normativity*, ed. Jonathan, Dancy, vii–xv. London: Blackwell.
Dancy, Jonathan. 2000b. *Practical reality*. Oxford: Oxford University Press.
Darwall, Stephen. 2009. Moral obligation: Form and substance. *Proceedings of the Aristotelian society, supplementary volume* 110:31–46.
Forrester, Mary. 1975. Some remarks on obligation, permission, and supererogation. *Ethics* 85:219–226.
Gardner, John and Timothy MacKlem. 2002. Reasons. In *The Oxford handbook of jurisprudence and philosophy of law*, eds. Jules Coleman and Scott Shapiro. Oxford: Oxford University Press.
Gewirth, Alan. 1970. Obligation: Political, legal, moral. In *Political and legal obligation*, ed. R. Pennock and J. Chapman, 55–88. New York: Atherton.
Greenspan, Patricia. 2005. Asymmetrical practical reasons. In *Experience and analysis, proceedings of the 27th international Wittgenstein symposium*, eds. M.E. Reicher and J.C. Marek, 8–14 Aug 2004, Kirchberg Am Wechsel (Austria), 387–94. Vienna: ÖBV & HPT.
Gilbert, Margaret. 1992. *On social facts*. Princeton: Princeton University Press.
Hacker, Peter. 1973. Sanction theories of duty. In *Oxford essays in Jurisprudence*, ed. A.W.B. Simpson, 131–170. Oxford: Oxford University Press.
Hage, J. 2011. Legal transactions and the legal ought. In *Studies in the philosophy of law*, eds. J. Stelmach and B. Brozek, 167–190. Krakow: Copernicus.
Himma, Kenneth. 2013. The ties that bind: An analysis of the concept of obligation. *Ratio Juris* 26:16–46.
Owens, David. 2008. Rationalism about obligation. *European Journal of Philosophy* 16:403–431.
Pink, Thomas. 2004. Moral Obligation. In *Modern moral philosophy*, ed. A. O'Hear, 159–85. Cambridge: Cambridge University Press.
Pink, Thomas. 2007. Normativity and reason. *Journal of Moral Philosophy* 4:406–31.
Prichard, Harold. 1949. *Moral obligation*. Oxford: Clarendon.
Railton, Peter. 2003. *Facts, values and norms*. Cambridge: Cambridge University Press.
Rawls, John. 1971. *A theory of justice*. Cambridge: Harvard University Press.
Raz, Joseph. 1999. *Engaging Reason*. Oxford: Oxford University Press.
Stroud, Sarah. 1998. Moral overridingness and moral theory. *Pacific Philosophical Quarterly* 79:170–189.
Wallace, Jay. 2006. *Normativity and the Will*. Oxford: Clarendon.

Chapter 12
On Obligations, Norms and Rules

Dietmar von der Pfordten

Abstract What is the main form of expression in law? The classical philosophers of law like Grotius, Hobbes, Pufendorf, Achenwall, Kant, Hegel and Austin thought that commands/orders/imperatives/prescriptions are these main forms. However, non-positivistic philosophers did not pay much attention to this question because for them the aim of law was important, while the means of law, like forms of linguistic expression, were a secondary concern. The linguistic means are contingent and will be chosen freely to attain this aim. In the twentieth century positivists like Kelsen or Hart tried to identify one main type of expression to characterize the law: norms (Kelsen) or rules (Hart). In this essay I will argue that neither norms nor rules can be assumed as the main form of expression of law. Furthermore, there is no reason why we could or should identify one and only one main form of expression in law. In contrast, law can use a multitude of linguistic means. There does not even exist a limited number of expressions in law but a whole plethora: commands/orders/imperatives/prescriptions, evaluations, permissions, derogations, authorizations, rules, norms, but also descriptive speech acts like statements, definitions. We have to liberate ourselves from the false and dangerous idea that there is any reason to reduce conceptually or a priori the choice of our linguistic means to realize the aim of law. The same holds for means, which are part of our thinking like concepts, institutes, obligations, duties, propositions, values etc. Like in any other human endeavour means can be selected freely to attain the chosen aim, provided these means are effective, proportional and not forbidden because of other reasons.

Keywords Rules · Norms · Commands · Imperatives · Orders · Aims · Means · Philosophy of Law

D. von der Pfordten (✉)
Georg-August-University, Goettingen, Germany
e-mail: rechtsph@gwdg.de

M. Araszkiewicz et al. (eds.), *Problems of Normativity, Rules and Rule-Following*,
Law and Philosophy Library 111, DOI 10.1007/978-3-319-09375-8_12

12.1 Introduction[1]

What is the main form of expression in law? Or put it in another way: What is the main semantic mean that law uses to attain its aims? Concerning this main form of expression in law, that is its main semantic mean, the theoretical assumptions have changed fundamentally. This change took place in two main respects.

Firstly classical philosophers of law like Grotius, Hobbes, Pufendorf, Achenwall, Kant and Hegel from the seventeenth up to the nineteenth century believed that *commands/orders/imperatives/prescriptions* (all these words have for our question no decisive difference in meaning[2]) are the prevalent form of expression in law that is the main means used in and by the law.[3] Later authors like Kelsen and Hart argued instead that the main form of expression in law does not consist in commands/orders/imperatives/prescriptions, but in *norms* (Kelsen) or *rules* (Hart).

Secondly while many of the classical philosophers of law like Grotius, Pufendorf, Kant and Hegel but also Radbruch in the twentieth century didn't put much effort on identifying *one and only one of these means*, authors of the positivist tradition began to lay great emphasis on the fixation of *one decisive form of expression*, that is *one decisive mean* of law: E. g. already Hobbes started his discussion of the law with the thesis that law is *command* not counsel (Hobbes 1991, Chap. 26, p. 183). And John Austin stated similarly to Hobbes: "Every law or rule (…) is a command" (Austin 1995, p. 21). But some pages later Austin admits that the term "laws" is also applied to objects, which have nothing of an imperative character and which are therefore not commands but declaratory laws, laws to repeal laws or imperfect laws (Austin 1995, p. 33). According to Austin the frequent habit of calling these objects "laws" shall be an improper application of the term. Nevertheless, he concedes that these improper signified laws shall be properly included into the province of jurisprudence (Austin 1995, p. 33). Therefore, he must concede that they are part of "the law" even if they are—as he thinks—not "laws". All in all, that attempt to reform the language and to identify one and only form of laws is quite confusing and not very convincing. Nevertheless, it set the stage for all the following positivistic attempts to identify one and only one of the means of law as decisive.

What might be the reason for this fixation of positivist authors on one and only one decisive form that is specific as linguistic mean of the law? The reason is surely this: Because the positivist authors did not acknowledge some aim like the good,

---

[1] I would like to thank Tomasz Gizbert-Studnicki for many very helpful comments, which have improved this article considerably.

[2] There are some slight differences in meaning. But the core meaning is identical as we will see in what follows. The core meaning is this: They all make an action necessary via a meaningful act.

[3] Hugo Grotius, De Jure Belli ac Pacis (1625), I, 1, X, p. 6: "dictatum"; XIV, p. 10: "praecepta"; XVII, p. 14: "obligatio"; Thomas Hobbes, Leviathan (1991, Chap. 26, p. 183): "command"; Samuel Pufendorf, De Officio Hominis et Civis Juxta Legem Naturalem, Libri Duo (1673, Chap. 2, § 2); Gottfried Achenwall/Stephan Pütter, Elementa Iuris Naturae, (1995, II, S. 38): "obligatio"; Immanuel Kant, Die Metaphysik der Sitten, (1907, p. 347); Georg Wilhelm Friedrich Hegel, Grundlinien der Philosophie des Rechts oder Naturrecht und Staatswissenschaft im Grundrisse (1986, § 212, p. 364).

justice or freedom as specific aim of the law, which can be used to distinguish law from other social facts, they were forced to concentrate on specific means, especially specific semantic means like commands, norms and rules. They couldn't accept any more the reality of means in the law, a unlimited plethora of various means: commands/orders/imperatives/prescriptions, evaluations, permissions, derogations, authorizations, rules, norms, but also declarative speech acts like statements, definitions, and finally means which are not or not purely linguistic but part of our thinking like: concepts, institutes, obligations, duties, propositions, values etc.

We will here look only at the first aspect of this fundamental change:[4] At the end of the nineteenth and the beginning of the twentieth century the picture became—as was already said—radically different. In the positivist tradition Kelsen did not only hold that one form of expression is decisive for law, he also changed that characteristic mean of the law: He held that *norms* are the main form of expression in the law (Kelsen 1960, 3 ff.; 1979, 1 ff.). And Hart assumed—very heavily influenced by the late Wittgenstein and taking up his most important concept (Wittgenstein 1977, §§ 53, 54, 81 ff., 142 ff.)—that the concept of *rules* is the best way to describe the main tool of the law (Hart 1994, 12 ff.).[5] Dworkin then added a new type of expressions of law, that is *principles*, but didn't question Hart's basic assumption that rules are prevalent in law (Dworkin 1977). So his critique of Hart, which is in the secondary literature often assumed to be very radical, was in reality only an addition within the new paradigm of a linguistic-means-centered and even more narrowly rule-centered understanding of the law.

This change from *commands/orders/imperatives/prescriptions* to *norms* and *rules* is not a mere accident but carries with it some very fundamental assumptions about the law. In my article I will try to identify some of these assumptions and discuss in the light of this result, whether the change in legal theory from a plethora of legal expressions to norms and rules as an assumed main form of expression in law is justified.

12.2 The Meaning of Commands/Orders/Imperatives/Prescriptions

Commands/orders/imperatives/prescriptions have a common core meaning. They refer respectively create obligations/duties.[6] One can assume that these obligations/duties are characterized at least by the following three elements[7]:

[4] For the second one, see: von der Pfordten (2011).

[5] By the way already Austin (1995), spoke initially of "law or rule" before introducing "commands".

[6] As it is not necessary for my argument, I will not discuss here to what extend commands refer or rather create obligations.

[7] Jaap Hage (2005, 166 ff, p. 201) distinguishes orders, which are mere directives from commands which require as constitutives a setting, in which the commanding person has some authority over

1. a necessity
2. of an action
3. which is transferred by some meaningful act.

These three elements are necessary conditions of the concepts of an obligation/duty and will be explained after the following note concerning Kant's definition of a *duty*:

In the "Groundwork to the Metapysics of Morals", Kant (1911 p. 400) says: "duty is the necessity of an action out of respect for the law". "Law" does not mean a positive juridical act that is a positivist law here, but morals and ethics ("Sittengesetz"). We can see that the first two elements of the definition are similar to those conditions of the concept of obligation etc. stated above, whereas the third element is completely different.

12.2.1 Necessity

Let us now turn to the first element, necessity. The necessity implied by an obligation/duty is neither a logical/mathematical/conceptual necessity, that is an a priori necessity nor an empirical necessity, that is an a posteriori necessity, brought about by causal effects. It is a sort of mental necessity, created by the person who obliges another person or herself (if one believes like Kant in duties to oneself) in an individual and social realm of meaning. It is worth keeping in mind that this necessity does not have to be realized. In the context of the concept of obligation, necessity is a mode in which all factual orders like morals, law, religion, medicine, technics, conventions etc. *can* be realized. Henceforth, it is assumed, that there are no logical or empirical obstacles to realize the necessity. This is stated by the well known principle "ought implies can."

12.2.2 Action

The second element, action, is also to be taken in the widest possible sense. For example, only the intentional change of a state of affairs is required for an action, while nothing is decided about the means and the way of achieving this change. These findings of both means and methods are left to the agent.[8] "Action" is moreover not restricted to outer action, but also comprises inner actions, e.g. the willful change of our emotions, attitudes, opinions, evaluations, wishes, aims and so on.

the person that is commanded, and obligations which are the outcome of commands. But neither ordinary language nor the technical languages of law or philosophy distinguishes the concepts in this way. So Hage's distinction is an ideal language proposal which is based on the—in my view even in military command structures not realistic—thesis that the prescriptive force of a command is totally created by the constitutive rule. Hage mixes up authorization, which is dependent on special authoritative rules with the prescriptive force of speech acts, which is dependent on many factors.

[8] See for such a wide understanding also v. Wright (1963, p. 13 ff.).

12.2.3 Transfer by Some Meaningful Act

Taking only the first two conditions, not only external physical forces, but also purely internal, necessary causes of actions would constitute a form of obligation, for example the free and contingent intention of the actor to walk to the university. Therefore, we need the additional element of the transfer by some meaningful act. This meaningful act will be very often communication by others. And in the case of the law it even must be always communication by others. But conceptually required is only some sort of meaningful act. So it might be also a meaningful act within the obliged himself, e.g. if we realize that we are morally obliged by duties to oneself (if these exist).

If we go back to Kant's definition and his third condition of acting out of the respect for the law we notice that Kant's third prerequisite is quite narrow, as it states that the action has to find its reason in the respect for the law, it is specific for a morality that is concerned with the categorical imperative as a moral law. Yet in other normative orders, like in law, the reason to act according to the obligation does not have to be a reason coming from the norm/law itself. We are allowed to pay our taxes for whatever reasons, e.g. avoid sanctions or remain a responsible citizen. Therefore, Kant's third requirement for the definition of "duty" cannot be assumed to be a standard requirement of the concept of obligation in general. It can at best hold for some moral duties, but not for the duties of the law. Therefore, we have to stick to the definition of obligation etc. given above. It has to be remarked that the concept of obligation/duty is very fundamental because we find it also in all versions of the standard systems of deontic logic and legal logic (Joerden 2005; Weinberger 1989, 232 ff.).

Commands/orders/imperatives/prescriptions and their meaning, that is obligations/duties, can be general or singular. E.g. a statute is a general order and creates a general obligation, while a judicial judgment is normally a singular order and creates normally a singular obligation.

H. L. A. Hart has (mis-)understood Austin's use of the concept of command only in the sense of a singular order when he constructed his gunman-example and argued on the ground of this example against Austin (Hart 1994, p. 19). But Austin himself hasn't reduced the meaning of "command" to singular obligations, neither has Hobbes.[9] And also the normal meaning of the word "command" is not reduced to singular obligations. It is not understandable how Hart came to this misunderstanding of Austin, because Austin stated explicitly at several points in the text that commands are general and create general obligations.

---

[9] Austin (1995, p. 25): "Commands are of two species. Some are laws or rules. The others have not acquired an appropriate name, nor does language afford an expression which will mark them briefly and precisely. I must therefore, note them as well as I can by the ambiguous and inexpressive name of 'occasional or particular commands'."; Hobbes (1991, Chap. XXVI, p. 183): "Civil Law, Is to every Subject, those Rules, which the Common-wealth hath Commanded him, by…."

12.3 The Difference Between Commands/Orders/Imperatives/Prescriptions and Norms

What does the switch from commands/orders/imperatives/prescriptions to norms and then rules imply? Or formulated in another way: Why did positivist authors propose this change from commands etc. to norms and then to rules as main semantic means of the law?

One main semantic and conceptual difference between commands and norms lays in the fact that the concept of a norm is wider in two main respects:

Firstly norms are not only commands/orders/imperatives/prescriptions but also *evaluations*. That is, they are not necessary prescriptive like commands, but can also be *evaluative*. So they create not only obligations but also values.[10]

Secondly norms grant or create besides obligations also *permissions*, *derogations*, *authorizations* and perhaps other similar forms of expressions, which are not clearly descriptive like statements or definitions (Kelsen 1979, 76 ff.).[11]

A second main difference concerns the reality to which the expressions refer. Commands/orders/imperatives/prescriptions require—at least in law—a source. If they are human orders of the positive law, they are therefore necessary speech acts. Instead, norms can refer only to mere regularities. These regularities constitute a fact of normality. So if somebody has developed the habit to drink a cup of coffee every morning he follows the norm and therefore normality to do this. But there exists no command and henceforth no obligation to drink a cup of coffee every morning. Nobody has uttered the speech act that one is obliged to drink a cup of coffee every morning and there is no internal moral law to do this. If he feels one morning, that today this habit of coffee-drinking will make him too nervous, he can switch to tea or orange juice without any restriction or necessity placed on his action. As a symptom of this lack of prescriptive force, there is no remorse or shame or any other sanction, which comes along with deciding to not follow in this case or change the habit for all future cases. I do not think that one could hold that this additional meaning of normality of the term "norm" is just an ambiguity or synonymy. For this, the wording of the expressions "norm" and "normality" is too close.

Why then does Kelsen replace commands/orders/imperatives/prescriptions with norms? I think, for him the first of these reasons is decisive. Because his legal theory knows no necessary aim of the law like the good, justice or freedom any more he needs to center on one and only one specific type of legal expression which not only refers to obligations but also permissions, derogations and authorizations. The last function of authorization is especially crucial for Kelsen and his central requirement to create "validity" (Geltung), because for him norms are initially only factual speech acts and can receive their necessary validity only by the authorization by higher norms. According to Kelsen, we need higher norms as a scheme of

---

[10] See von der Pfordten (1993). This might be debatable because the term "norm" is rather artificial and not as "command" or "order" a term of everyday use. Hans Kelsen (1960, p. 4), has reduced "norms" to their prescriptive meaning of "soll".

[11] "Definitions" are meant here in the sense of "real definitions", not only nominal or stipulative definitions, which can be certainly conveyed by norms.

interpretation (Deutungsschema) to transfer a subjective fact (Sein) into an objective obligation (Sollen) and create the objective validity, which he holds to be necessary in law (Kelsen 1960, 3 ff.).

Norms can, according to Kelsen, be *general*, but they might also be *singular*. E.g. a court decision or an administrative act is for him a singular norm (Kelsen 1960, pp. 20, 74, 85).

12.4 The Difference Between Commands, Norms and Rules

What is now the implication of considering the main legal expression, that is the main semantic mean in *rules* by Hart?

Rules imply the same semantic enlargement in respect to commands/orders/imperatives/prescriptions as norms. They embrace also evaluations as well as permissions, derogations and authorizations.

But in one decisive respect the meaning of the term "rule" is narrower than that of the term "norms". Even more, it is surprisingly narrower than that of commands/orders/imperatives/prescriptions: *Rules are always general. They cannot be singular*. So a singular juridical judgment or an administrative act can semantically and conceptually not be a rule. Singular juridical judgments can become instances of rules by a second order principle of generalization like the rule of precedents in the anglo-saxon case law or an explicit order of a statute which declares them to be general like specific decisions of the German Bundesverfassungsgericht according to § 31 II Bundesverfassungsgerichtsgesetz. But even in this last case the singular juridical judgments are not rules but only singular instances of rules and externally declared to create the same general obligations as rules—which is a fundamental ontological difference.

But singular juridical judgments and administrative acts are *undoubtedly parts of the law*. Even more: They are *important* and—in the case of juridical judgments—even *crucial* parts of the law. And there are not only juridical judgments but also singular administrative acts and singular contracts which are important parts of the law. These singular acts are much more numerous than rules in law. But if this is so, it makes no sense to characterize the main or decisive expression or means of the law as rules. So Hart's change from commands or norms to rules as main expression of the law is not justified.

This result has to be distinguished carefully from an assessment of Hart's theory of secondary rules as constitutive elements of law, that is, rules of adjudication, rules of change and rules of recognition. This theory of secondary rules is in no way affected by the outcome reached above, because it is perfectly consistent to assume that second order rules refer to singular first order commands or norms. So Hart's theory of recognition and therefore authorization of primary norms is not rebutted by this finding.[12]

[12] But see for a critique of this theory of second order rules: von der Pfordten (2011, 161 f).

12.5 What About Norms?

If the concept of rules is not adequate to describe the main expressions, that is, the semantic decisive means of the law, might then not the concept of norms be the best choice? Should we therefore replace the classical proposal of commands/orders/imperatives/prescriptions as main but not exclusive expressions by norms as e.g. Kelsen suggested? As we saw, norms do not have the disadvantage to be necessary general and therefore too restricted. So singular juridical judgments and administrative acts can be understood as norms. And the concept of norms has—as was the result—the advantage to be quite encompassing. But it is still not encompassing enough, because in the law we find in principle all forms of speech acts, not only norms but also statements and definitions.[13] Therefore, every attempt to look for an all-embracing notion which can include all legal expressions and henceforth, linguistic means is in vain. And there is no reason why we should need such an all-embracing notion.

Such an attempt is the unfortunate consequence of the positivistic rejection of a more specific aim of the law. If we acknowledge a more specific aim of the law, we do not need to identify a main semantic expression or linguistic mean of the law to distinguish it from other social facts. Instead, we can assume that many or even most expressions of the law are commands/orders/imperatives. Some other expressions are evaluations, permissions, derogations and authorizations, that is, norms. Additionally we find statements, definitions and perhaps other sorts of expressions.

Consequently, law encompasses not only obligations but also propositions, concepts and institutes. So we are free to hold a liberal and open view about the expressions of the law and their meanings. This freedom corresponds with the freedom of the lawmaker. In addition, the lawmaker is not restricted to use only one type of speech act or a limited number of speech acts. He uses what he needs to attain the aim he wants to attain by issuing law. This liberality and openness concerning the expressions and semantic means of the law is possible, because we have to recognize some more specific aim and more specific non-linguistic means, which are not recognized by Kelsen and Hart and which will be identified in the last chapter.

12.6 Necessary Aims and Means of the Law

My proposal is this: Law has, as its conceptually necessary aim (and, thus, necessary feature of its concept) the mediation between possibly contrary, conflicting concerns[14].

For instance, statutes mediate between various general concerns of people, judges' holdings mediate between interests in particular conflicts, administrative acts

[13] See footnote 11.

[14] See von der Pfordten (2011, 151 ff).

mediate between the specific wishes of individual citizens and/or the interests of the general public.

So we have four elements of the necessary aim of law: (1) at least two concerns or interests, (2) which are contrary, (3) the possibility that these concerns may conflict, and (4) a form of mediation. These elements need careful explanation:

1. *Concerns/Interests*: Concerns or interests (for present purposes, these concepts are used synonymously) are not reducible to an economic or egoistic will. An important concern or interest, for example, is that one's children be able to attend a good school. The concept "concern" is derived from more concrete properties. I think four properties have to be taken into consideration: *strivings*, *needs*, *wishes* and the *aims* of individuals who can be thought to be bearers of interests. These four properties form a sort of continuum between purely bodily and purely mental properties.[15] Some strivings of our bodies like the immune system are purely bodily. Needs such as the need for food, drink, warmth and shelter are bodily but can be wilfully controlled. Wishes often have bodily origins but are primarily mental and can be suppressed, like the wish to read a book. Aims are purely mental, like the aim to set up a valuable theory of law. For lack of a real body, collective and theoretical entities like juridical persons cannot develop strivings, needs or wishes. Only aims, set forth by the real persons who function as their representatives, can be attributed to them.
   In order for the mediation of concerns to be legally relevant, the concerns in question must be sufficiently weighty. This is presumably one of the reasons why—in spite of their obvious mediating function—we do not generally consider rules of games as law. In a way, games are self-sufficient, that is, they have no necessary external aims. Their respective internal aims only refer to the game in question itself. Hence, also the corresponding aims and desires of the participants only pertain to the game; they fail to gain the inherent weightiness of those concerns that are susceptible to legal mediation. If someone takes a game too seriously, he misses its peculiar character as a game. For this reason, the referee in a game does not engage in adjudication—even if his mediating function resembles that of the judge. By contrast, in arbitration outside games agreements can generate law perfectly well.
2. *Contrariness*: The concerns must in some way be contrary in a wide sense, that is at least incompatible to some extent. If they are perfectly parallel there is no need for law to solve the conflict between them. Again, the contrariness need not be actual. Its possibility suffices, whether it is the possible contrariness between the concerns of living persons or between the concerns of living persons and that of future generations.
3. *Possibility of Conflict*: Even if two concerns are contrary to each other, a resolution of the conflict between them—or, more precisely: about them—may be

[15] The relationship between bodily and mental properties is of course controversial in philosophy. While some hold like Descartes a dualism others prefer a reductionism of mental properties to bodily properties (materialism, Hume,) or vice versa (idealism, Plato, Hegel). A compromise is the suggestion that mental properties supervene on bodily.

impossible or unnecessary. In that case, there is either no possibility or at least no reason for mediation. Consider the following example: A farmer wants rain, the tourist sunshine. For as long as local weather cannot be influenced, there can be no resolution of the conflict between their contrary concerns. Mediation by law is not possible and therefore not necessary.

4. *Mediation*: There must be a weighing or considered decision resolving the conflict between these possible contrary concerns. That does not mean that law must be good or just in a perfectionist sense. The necessary condition is only that the entities which are of concern have to be taken into consideration in some way. If persons are murdered or their being murdered is ordered—that is, they are killed without a criminal inquiry or fair trial—this cannot be law, because it does not mediate between actual or possible contrary concerns at all.

The conceptual features of law proposed here are relatively abstract and weak. Law does not have the fulfilment of all or even the main demands of morality or ethics as its necessary aim. But it does have a conceptually necessary aim, without which it is impossible to identify a social fact as law. We may call this aim "justice" in some weak sense. This is to be taken, however, not as a normative, ethical standard, but as a conceptually necessary ingredient of the concept of law.

By reference to this aim of mediation between possibly contrary, conflicting concerns, we can distinguish law from many social facts. But some social facts have the same, or at least a similar, aim. This holds in particular for morals, politics, religion, and non-moral conventions. Law can be distinguished from these social facts which have the same or a similar aim only by reference to its necessary means.

By comparison with other social facts, the following distinctive means of law can be identified:

(1) *Conventions*: Conventions have the concrete agreement or concrete lack of disagreement of the obliged as a necessary condition. Law comprises not only such weak-obligatory, that is voluntary norms, e.g. in most of the contract law, but also at least some categorical obligations, that is, obligations, which do not have the concrete agreement or concrete lack of disagreement of those obliged as a necessary condition (which does not mean that all norms of the law are categorical). So it is—like morals—distinguished from pure conventions by its partially *categorical character*.[16] Their categorical character distinguishes judgements also from mere mediation.

(2) *Morals*: Law has, in all its various manifestations, only external sources and means (judging, agreeing, issuing, ordering, voting) but no purely internal sources, such as human conscience, which is one necessary source of morals.[17] So the distinctive feature of law, in comparison to morals, is its *externality* in all singular instantiations.

(3) *Politics*: Law, in all its manifestations, is marked by a certain formality in its making, promulgation, or application, which simple political acts, for example,

[16] Note that the categorical character has to be distinguished carefully from coercion.

[17] This was already stated by Immanuel Kant, Metaphysics of Morals, Metaphysical Foundations of the Theory of Law, Introduction.

a decision in foreign politics, even in the form of a rule like the Monroe Doctrine or the Breschnew Doctrine, do not have.[18] So the distinctive feature of law in comparison to politics is its *formality* in all its singular instantiations. This formality lends support to legal certainty. In its final realisation, the requirement of formality also holds for common law that has to find its form in parliamentary, judicial, or administrative proceedings.

(4) *Religion*: Even as 'divine' or 'natural' law, law refers to immanent states of affairs within human life and agency. By contrast, religion, as the practice of a faith, also refers to a transcendental goal—the goal, say, of beatitude, reincarnation, or eternal peace of the soul. Accordingly, the distinctive feature of law in comparison to religion is its *immanence* in all its singular instantiations. This holds at least under the condition that law and religion are separated in reality and are not more or less interwoven, as in Jewish or Islamic law.

Conclusion

If we accept a more specific aim and more specific non-semantic means of the law, we come in our understanding much closer to the very liberal and open reality of the use of semantic means in law. There does not exist one and only one decisive form of expression in law like norms or rules. There does not even exist a limited number of expressions in law but a whole plethora: commands/orders/imperatives/prescriptions, other norms like evaluations, permissions, derogations, authorizations, rules, but also descriptive speech acts like statements, definitions, and finally means, which are not purely linguistic like: concepts, institutes etc. In order to achieve its aim to mediate between possibly contrary, conflicting concerns, law will normally use in a higher degree commands and other prescriptive expressions. But this statistic statement is the only thing we can say about the relative frequency of the means of the law. We have to liberate ourselves from the false and dangerous idea that there is any conceptual or a priori reason to reduce the choice of our means to realize the aim of law to one or several expressions or one or several other means.

References

Achenwall, Gottfried, and Stephan Pütter. 1995. *Elementa Iuris Naturae/Anfangsgründe des Naturrechts*. Frankfurt a. M.

Austin, John. 1995. *The province of jurisprudence determined*. Cambridge.

Dworkin, Ronald. 1977. *Taking rights reriously*. Harvard.

Grotius, Hugo. 1625. *De Jure Belli ac Pacis*. Paris.

Hage, Jaap. 2005. *Studies in legal logic*. Dordrecht.

[18] See for a comprehensive study of the formality of law: Summers (2006). Summers's concept of formality is in many respects wider than would be necessary in order to distinguish law from politics.

Hart, H. L. A. 1994. *The concept of law*. Oxford.
Hegel, Georg Wilhelm Friedrich. 1986. *Grundlinien der Philosophie des Rechts oder Naturrecht und Staatswissenschaft im Grundrisse*, Werke 7. Frankfurt a. M.
Hobbes, Thomas. 1991. *Leviathan*. Cambridge.
Joerden, Jan C. 2005. *Logik im Recht, Grundlagen und Anwendungsbeispiele*. Berlin.
Kant, Immanuel. 1907. *Die Metaphysik der Sitten,* ed. Prussian Academy, vol. VI. Berlin.
Kant, Immanuel. 1911. *Grundlegung zur Metaphysik der Sitten*, ed. Prussian Academy, vol. IV. Berlin.
Kelsen, Hans. 1960. *Reine Rechtslehre*. Wien.
Kelsen, Hans. 1979. *Allgemeine Theorie der Normen*. Wien.
Pufendorf, Samuel. 1673. *De Officio Hominis et Civis Juxta Legem Naturalem, Libri Duo*. Heidelberg.
Summers, Robert. 2006. *Form and function in a legal system*. Cambridge.
von der Pfordten, Dietmar. 1993. *Deskription, Evaluation, Präskription*. Berlin.
von der Pfordten, Dietmar. 2009. About concepts in law. In *Concepts in the law*, ed. Jaap Hage and Dietmar von der Pfordten, 17–33. Heidelberg.
von der Pfordten, Dietmar. 2011. What is law? Aims and means. *Archiv für Rechts- und Sozialphilosophie* 97:151–168.
von Wright, Georg Henrik. 1963. *Norm and action. A logical inquiry*. London.
Weinberger, Ota. 1989. *Rechtslogik*. Berlin.
Wittgenstein, Ludwig. 1977. *Philosophische Untersuchungen*. Frankfurt a. M.

Chapter 13
Philosophy, Neuroscience and Law: The Conceptual and Empirical, Rule-Following, Interpretation and Knowledge

Dennis Patterson and Michael S. Pardo

Abstract The intersection between law and neuroscience is one of the most-discussed subfields in legal scholarship. In this article, we consider fundamental issues in the field. These include: the distinction between the conceptual and the empirical, rule-following, and the nature of knowledge. We maintain that the conceptual issues are fundamental to all aspects of this enterprise.

Keywords Neuroscience · Rule-following · Conceptual · Empirical · Analytic · Philosophy

13.1 Introduction

A staple of any good argument, be it a philosophical argument, a public policy position, or even a debate about the relative merits of daily exercise, is clarity. What clarity accomplishes is both good and bad for arguments. A clear argument draws its power, in part, from the compelling nature of the connections made in the course of the argument. Likewise, clarity can reveal the flaws in an argument, leaving the proponent of the position to either concede defeat or reformulate the argument in better terms.

One of the principal virtues of philosophy (as method) is the relentless search for flaws—clear or hidden—in argument. As every college student knows, there are multiple fallacies. Fallacies such as the fallacy of composition, appeal to authority, and begging the question are quotidian features of daily newspapers and faculty

D. Patterson (✉)
Law Department, European University Institute, Florence, Italy
e-mail: Dennis.Patterson@EUI.eu

Rutgers School of Law, Camden, USA

Swansea University, Swansea, UK

M. S. Pardo
University of Alabama School of Law, Tuscaloosa, USA

M. Araszkiewicz et al. (eds.), *Problems of Normativity, Rules and Rule-Following*,
Law and Philosophy Library 111, DOI 10.1007/978-3-319-09375-8_13

lounges. In addition to these relatively well-known, common forms of fallacious argument, there are more sophisticated and more difficult argumentative errors. It is with these latter forms of argument that we focus in this chapter. The fallacies we focus on are logical or philosophical in nature.

One might rightly ask what is a "philosophical fallacy"? There are errors in computation, mistakes in reasoning, but what is a "philosophical error"? Throughout this paper, we answer this question by carefully scrutinizing the claims made by a broad spectrum of authors who take the view that matters of mind are best understood or explained as neurological events. The mantra for this group is "your mind is your brain." Adopting this view leads to the philosophical errors we highlight. These errors are logical or philosophical in the sense that the claims made take language beyond "the bounds of sense". Claims transgress the bounds of sense when they apply terms expressing concepts to contexts in which they do not apply—without stipulating or presupposing a new meaning for the term. So, for example, we take issue with the idea that a rule or norm can be followed "unconsciously." The very idea of "following" a rule means that one is cognizant of it and ready to invoke it in any context that implicates the rule. Through example and exegesis, we show why the idea of "unconscious rule following" makes no sense.

Before advancing our arguments, we wish to dispel a potential confusion at the outset. Our discussion of problematic conceptions of mind and other mental attributes may suggest to some readers that we are setting up a classic dualist versus materialist discussion, with the neuroscience proponents falling on the materialist side. This is not so. Indeed, as we will discuss, the putative dichotomy is a principal source of the problems we survey. Cartesian dualism—with its picture of mind as an immaterial substance, independent of but in causal relation with the body—is typically set up as the foil in many neuroscience discussions. For example, in introducing the journal *Neuroethics*, Neil Levy writes that "Cartesian (substance) dualism is no longer taken seriously; the relation between the brain and the mind is too intimate for it to be at all plausible… [N]euroscientific discoveries promise… to reveal the structure and functioning of our minds and, therefore, of our souls." (Levy 2008, p. 2) Likewise, in discussing the implications of neuroscience for jurisprudence, Oliver Goodenough writes that the "Cartesian model… supposes a separation of mind from the brain", whereas models of mind for "a nondualist like myself" are "what the brain does for a living." (Goodenough 2000–2001, pp. 431–432) The dichotomy between dualism and mind-as-brain is a false one. Moreover, materialists like Goodenough are *too* Cartesian—he, like many neuroscientists and neurolaw scholars keep the problematic Cartesian structure in place by simply replacing the Cartesian soul with the brain.

Rather than arguing about where the mind is located (e.g. in the brain or elsewhere) we need to step back and contemplate whether this is the right question to ask. First, notice that the question of the mind's location presupposes that the mind is a kind of "thing" or "substance" that is located "somewhere" (e.g. in the body). Why must this be so? Our answer is that it need not be, and is not. An alternative conception of mind—the one that we contend is more plausible—is as an array of powers, capacities, and abilities possessed by a human being. These abilities implicate a wide range of psychological categories including sensations, perceptions, cognition (i.e. knowledge, memory), cogitation (i.e. beliefs, thought, imagination, mental imagery), emotions and other affective states (i.e. moods and appetites), and volition (i.e. intentions, voluntary action).

To be clear, we do not deny that a properly working brain is required for a person to exercise the diverse array of powers, capacities, and abilities the exercise of which we collectively identify as mental life. Although neural activity is required for a human being to exercise these powers, capacities, and abilities, neural activity alone is not sufficient. The criteria for their successful exercise are not a matter of what is or is not in the brain. These criteria—which are normative in nature—are the basis for our attribution of mental attributes. To outline briefly one of the examples that we will explore below, consider what it means to "have knowledge". We believe that "knowing" is not (just) having a brain in a particular physical state. Rather, it is having the ability to do certain things (e.g., to answer questions, correct mistakes, act correctly on the basis of information, and so on). Thus, if behavior of various sorts, and not brain states, constitutes the criteria for "knowing," then it will make no sense to say that knowledge is "located" in the brain. The same is true for other psychological predicates—and for the mind itself. So, to the question, "what is the mind: an immaterial substance (Descartes) or the brain?" we answer "neither". To the question, "where is the mind located: in the brain or in a non-spatially extended realm (Descartes)?" we answer "neither." Human beings have minds, but minds are not substances located somewhere within their bodies.

We recognize that our claims may initially strike those operating within the dualist versus mind-as-brain dichotomy as unorthodox. Thus, to undermine what we see as entrenched but problematic presuppositions underlying many neurolaw claims, we proceed deliberately and carefully. We begin our argument by introducing an important methodological distinction between conceptual and empirical questions. In the context of neuroscience research, empirical claims are those that are amenable to confirmation or falsification on the basis of experiments or data. By contrast, conceptual questions concern the logical relations between concepts. We explain why the questions of what the mind is and what the various psychological categories under discussion are (e.g. knowledge, memory, belief, intention, decision making), are conceptual rather than empirical questions.

Given that these are conceptual issues, we next discuss the distinction between criterial and inductive evidence. This issue concerns the inferences that may be drawn from a body of evidence (neuroscience research) regarding various capacities and their exercise. We then turn our attention to philosophical problems that arise with claims regarding norms. Again, the critique we offer is philosophical in nature. The topics of unconscious rule following and interpretation are staples of the philosophical literature. We show why the approaches of several neurolegalists to these issues engender conceptual confusions.

We then take up the question of knowledge. Knowledge is a central concept in law, having a wide range of applications from tort law to criminal law and beyond. We make the case that knowing something to be so is best understood as an array of abilities or capacities and not as a particular state of mind or brain.

13.2 The Conceptual and the Empirical

The important issue of the relationship between conceptual and empirical claims has, unfortunately, received little direct attention in the current debate over the present and future role of neuroscience in law. Empirical neuroscientific claims, and the inferences and implications for law drawn from them, depend on conceptual presuppositions regarding the mind. As we see it, many of the proponents of an increased role for neuroscience in law rest their case on a controversial and ultimately untenable account of the nature of mind. Although we recognize the need for greater emphasis on and interrogation of the empirical claims regarding neuroscience applications in law, we believe that the fundamental conceptual issues regarding the mind are of equal, if not greater, importance.

Devoted as they are to understanding the physiology of the brain, neuroscientists are principally interested in physical processes. Of greatest interest to neuroscientists are questions regarding neural structures, the functioning of the brain, and the physiological bases for a wide range of mental attributes, including consciousness, memory, vision, and emotion. Scientific explanations, including those of neuroscience, are framed in a language of explanation most readily identified as "empirical". Grounded in theories and hypotheses, scientific claims are tested by means of experiment. Experimental confirmation or disconfirmation of hypotheses forms the basis of the scientific method.

Empirical and conceptual questions are distinct. We would go so far as to say that they are logically distinct. In addition to their distinct characters, the conceptual relates to the empirical in a certain way: the very success of empirical inquiry depends upon conceptual clarity and coherence. An experiment grounded in confused or dubious conceptual claims can prove nothing.

Conceptual questions concern the logical relations between concepts. Concepts like mind, consciousness, knowledge, and memory are exemplary instances of the sorts of concepts implicated in neuroscience discussions. To be well-founded, and thus to ground successful empirical claims, conceptual claims must make sense. But what does it mean to say that conceptual claims must make "sense"? The concept of sense is bound up with the forms of expression for the use of words in a language. Therefore, to say that a particular claim lacks sense (literally, is nonsense) is not to say that the claim is frivolous or stupid (although the claim may be). It is to say that the claim fails to express something meaningful and as such cannot be evaluated for its truth or falsity. Often mistakes or ambiguities in use can generate "nonsensical" claims—for example, what is meant by one's claim that a Dworkinian legal principle "weighs" more than an elephant? We suppose no one would endorse the truth of this claim, but we also suppose no one would endorse that it is false either. Or consider a judge's claim that, having heard the arguments from both sides, she will decide the case "in her brain"? It is neither clear what this means (other than that she will decide) nor what evidence would confirm or falsify it. Sometimes mistakes in usage can take the form of simple grammatical errors—compare "he has almost finished his breakfast" with "he has not already finished his breakfast."

More importantly, however, they sometimes ramify in more problematic and significant ways.

One such mistake occurs when we think that the mind must be a substance. This error underlies the fundamental reductionist move in many positive arguments for neuroscience in law. The "reduction" is the reduction of the mind to the brain, and it typically takes one of two forms: an identity form (the mind *is* the brain) or an explanatory form (mental attributes can be explained fully in terms of information about the brain). By making this move, many proponents of an increased role for neuroscience set the stage for their enterprise, which is the explanation of human behavior in causal, mechanical, and non-volitional terms. As we will show, the reductive impulse is driven by a conceptually problematic account of the relationship between mind and brain. Once this account is undermined, many of the aspirations of the neurolegalists diminish significantly. We expose the problematic foundations of these accounts by focusing on a variety of conceptual issues: the distinction between criterial and inductive evidence, unconscious rule following, interpretation, and knowledge.

13.3 Criterial and Inductive Evidence

Suppose we were asked to look for evidence of various kinds of psychological faculties or attributes such as perception and belief. Some evidence would provide criterial support—that is, it would provide constitutive evidence for the faculty or attribute (Wittgenstein 1958, pp. 24–25). Another class of evidence would provide inductive support—that is, although not constitutive of the faculty or attribute, it might be empirically correlated with the faculty or attribute so that we could say with some degree of confidence that the presence of this evidence increases (or decreases) the likelihood of the phenomena with which it is correlated.

Criterial evidence for the ascription of psychological predicates, such as "to perceive" or "to believe," consists in various types of behavior. Behaving in certain ways is logically good evidence and, thus, partly constitutive of these concepts. For visual perception, this includes, for example, that one's eyes track the phenomena one perceives, that one's reports match what one observed, and so on. For belief, this includes, for example, that one asserts or endorses what one believes, that one acts in ways consistent with one's beliefs, that one does not believe directly contradictory propositions, and so on. This behavior is not only a way to determine whether someone perceives or believes something in particular. The behavior also helps to determine (indeed, it partly constitutes) what it means to engage in these activities. In other words, it helps to provide the measure for whether someone is in fact engaged in this activity (not just a measurement in a particular instance). If these forms of behavior were not in principle possible for a creature, then it would not make sense to ascribe the predicate to it truly or falsely. Note, however, that this criterial evidence is defeasible; people can assert propositions they do not believe, or say they perceived things they did not, and people can perceive or believe without ever describing what they perceived or asserting or acting on what they believe. The primary point is that the behavior not only provides evidence of whether someone on a given occasion is perceiving something or has a belief, but it also partially determines what it means to perceive or believe.

By contrast, some evidence provides only inductive support for whether one is perceiving or believing. This would be the case if there were, as an empirical matter, a correlation between some evidence and perceiving or believing. For example, there may be a relatively strong inductive correlation between wearing glasses and perception, but the behavior of wearing glasses does not constitute (or partly constitute) what it means to perceive. Neural activity, as demonstrated by neuroscience research, may fill this role; searching for these correlations is precisely the goal of much current research. But note that this inductive correlation only works once we know what to correlate the neural activity with. Physical states of the brain are not criterial evidence for—because they are not partly constitutive of—psychological faculties and attributes such as perception or belief. To refer back to the metaphor in the above paragraph, neural activity may help to provide a measurement—but not the measure—of whether one has perceived or believes something on a particular occasion.

To know whether a brain state is correlated with a particular psychological faculty or attribute, we must first have criteria for identifying the faculty or attribute. Physical states of the brain cannot fulfill this role. To illustrate this, consider a claim that a certain brain state, or pattern of neural activity, constitutes perceiving X or thinking that P is true, but that a person whose brain was in either of these states engaged in none of the behavior that we associate with thinking or perceiving. Suppose we ask the person and she sincerely denies that she had perceived or thought anything. In this example, the claim that the particular brain states constitute thinking or perceiving would be false, based in part on the constitutive evidence to the contrary (her experiences and her sincere denial). Any purported inductive correlation between the particular brain states and thinking or perceiving would have to be reexamined.

13.4 Unconscious Rule Following

One of the most basic questions of ethics and law concerns norms and conformity with them (or lack thereof). Interest in this question stems from the desire to learn more about the nature of moral cognition; how it is that we decide what norms there are and what is required by those norms. This is the issue of norm application or, in the language of some philosophers, what it means to follow a rule.

Many scholars take the view that moral knowledge is "encoded" or "embedded" in the brain. (Mikhail 2009, 2011) This view of the nature of moral knowledge assumes that the capacity for moral judgment is "hard wired" in the brain. In other words, moral knowledge is "innate." To explain moral knowledge is to explain how the brain exercises choice in making moral judgments. Under this explanation, making a moral judgment is a matter of actuating "the machinery to deliver moral verdicts based on unconscious and inaccessible principles." (Hauser 2006, p. 42) These principles, so the argument goes, are brought to bear on an ethical problem in a manner described as "unconscious". The idea of unconscious rule following, grounded in the notion that moral knowledge is "encoded" or "embedded" in the brain, is a fundamental feature of the neurological explanation of human ethical and legal judgment. As a form of explanation for human judgment, this approach is conceptually problematic. To be clear, we are not contesting the empirical correctness of the view; we are saying that the view makes no sense, as such, as an explanation. Why does the idea of unconscious rule following make no sense? There are two reasons.

First, the idea of "tacit knowledge" has to be separated from that of "correct performance." It is not enough to say that one's brain "possesses" tacit knowledge because one performs correctly (i.e. in accordance with an ethical standard). Invoking tacit knowledge to explain behavior requires something more than the mere invocation to show exactly how tacit knowledge is doing the work claimed for it. If tacit knowledge is to be more than a question-begging explanation, there must be independent criteria for it. Lacking such criteria, the explanation is empty.

Second, we question the intelligibility of the very idea of "unconscious" rule following. What does it mean to say that a person or a brain "follows rules unconsciously"? Of course, a person can follow a rule without being "conscious" of it (in the sense of having it in mind or reflecting on it) while acting, but one must still be cognizant of the rule (i.e., be informed of it and its requirements) in order to follow it. A person cannot follow a rule if he is unconscious (accordingly, unconscious bodily movements are not considered acts for purposes of criminal law doctrine). Brains are neither conscious nor unconscious and so cannot follow rules consciously or unconsciously. Rules are not causal mechanisms in the sense that they do not "act at a distance." Rule following is something human beings do, not alone with their brains, but in concert with others.

This last point can be detailed further. Consider that in many contexts in daily life where rules come into play, the following things seem to be implicated. We may (1) justify our behavior by reference to a rule; (2) consult a rule in deciding on a course of conduct; (3) correct our behavior and that of others by reference to a rule; and (4) interpret a rule when we fail to understand what it requires. Rule following occurs in a wide variety of contexts, each of which has its own unique features. These contexts are not "in the brain" but in the world. They are referred to in the course of any explanation of what a subject thinks is required by a norm and what, on the subject's view, that norm requires. When disputes break out about what norms require, appeal to what is in one's head is irrelevant, for the very presence of a different point of view on what a norm requires signals that such appeals would be question-begging. Reason giving in defense of a challenge about what a norm requires cannot be done "unconsciously".

Moreover, there is a fundamental difference between following a rule and acting in accordance with a rule. Consider a simple example. In the entrance to a club in central London, the following sign appears on the wall: "Gentlemen are required to wear a jacket in the dining room". Mr. Smith is a dapper man, who happens to be the guest of a club member. If Mr. Smith has his jacket on as he enters the dining room, we can safely say that he is "acting in conformity with the rule". But is he "following" the rule? For that, more is required.

To actually "follow" the rule, Smith would have to be cognizant of it. If Smith had no knowledge of the rule prior to his entrance into the club, it is difficult to say how he was "following" the rule. How would he have conformed his conduct to the rule through a course of behavior (e.g., being told the dress code by his friend, the club member)? If Smith had his jacket on his arm and did not see the rule posted on the wall, he would not be acting in accordance with the rule and would, presumably, conform his conduct to the rule once he was apprised of it.

The point here is that there is an epistemic component to rule following: one has to be cognizant of the relevant rules. Making one's conduct conform to rules is an essential feature of "rule following". Without this epistemic component, one is merely acting in accordance with what a rule requires. This is not rule following in any meaningful sense.

13.5 Interpretation

In the view of many neuroscientists and their enthusiasts, the brain does all manner of things. It describes, understands, computes, interprets, and makes decisions. In this section, we will focus our attention on one of these claims, to wit, that the brain achieves knowledge through a process of "interpretation". While they are not alone in this regard, many scholars writing about neuroscience are enthusiastic in their belief that the brain grasps norms through an internal process of "interpretation". Here is Oliver Goodenough singing the praises of Michael Gazzaniga's "interpreter module" in the legal context:

> [Gazzaniga] has postulated the existence of an interpreter module, whose workings are also in the word-based arena. A similar word-based reasoner could work with the word-based rules of law. In experiments on split-brain patients, whose central corpus callosum had been cut as a cure for severe epileptic problems, the interpreter supplied completely erroneous explanations for behavior originating in some nonword-based thinking module (Goodenough 2000–2001, p. 436).

Our problem with this account of mental life is that it fails to appreciate the fact that interpretation is a "parasitic activity," one that is secondary in moral and legal practices. While we agree that interpretation is certainly an important element of both ethics and law, it is an activity that depends upon existing and widespread agreement in judgment. In short, interpretation cannot "get off the ground" without widespread agreement in judgment already being in place.

As Wittgenstein pointed out, practice and settled regularity are the grounds of normativity and the distinction between understanding and interpretation ("Im Anfang war die Tat"). The point of Wittgenstein's example of the signpost (Wittgenstein 1953, section 85) is that only practice and settled regularity can provide the ground for correct and incorrect judgment. Without a practice of following it—a way of acting—the signpost by itself provides us no clue as to its proper use. In theory, there are as many potential ways of "following" the signpost as there are possible conventions for determining how it is to be used and what counts as following it. But once a convention for following signposts takes hold, a background of understanding evolves. It is against this background that the need for interpretation arises. Interpretation is a reflective practice we engage in when understanding breaks down. Understanding is exhibited in action. For example, we show that we understand the request "Please shut the door" by closing the door. The need for interpretation arises from a firmament of praxis.

As an account of correct and incorrect action in a practice (whether in ethics, law, arithmetic, or measurement), interpretation is a non-starter because interpretation draws our attention away from the techniques that make understanding possible. Correct and incorrect forms of action are immanent in practices. Correct forms of action cannot be imposed on a practice, by interpretation or otherwise. It is only when we master the techniques employed by participants in a practice that we can grasp the distinction between correct and incorrect action (e.g. in ethics or law). Claims about what morality and law require are adjudicated through employment of intersubjectively shared standards of appraisal. As Wittgenstein says, "It is not the interpretation which builds the bridge between the sign and what is signified// meant//. Only the practice does that" (cited in Baker and Hacker 1985, p. 136).

13.6 Knowledge

In the previous sections, we examined two issues that relate to particular kinds of knowledge: namely, what it means for a person to know how to follow a rule, and what it means for a person to know (and to interpret) what is required by a norm. In this section, we turn to the concept of knowledge more generally. We first articulate a general conception of knowledge as a kind of ability, and we then apply this conception to legal examples that scholars have claimed neuroscience may inform.

The concept of knowledge has been a topic of intense philosophical interest for thousands of years, and understanding its contours is the main agenda for many epistemologists. Aside from theoretical issues in epistemology, knowledge also relates to important ethical and practical issues. Ethical and legal judgments about whether to ascribe moral blame and/or criminal responsibility to someone's actions often depend on what that person did or did not know when they acted, as well as what they were capable of knowing. Similarly, someone's knowledge of where they were and what they were doing on a particular occasion will virtually always be highly probative evidence of, for example, whether they are the perpetrator of a crime and ought to be held criminally liable. The promise that neuroscience might help us to determine conclusively what someone knows, or what he is or was capable of knowing, is a seductive one.

We outline a number of conceptual points regarding knowledge as a general matter. As with rule following and interpretation, our fundamental methodological point is this: in order to assess the role that neuroscience may play in contributing to these issues, we must be clear about what knowledge is and what would count as someone having knowledge. More specifically, before we can determine whether someone knows something on a particular occasion, or is capable of knowing something more generally, we need some sense of the appropriate criteria for ascriptions of knowledge.

Ascriptions of knowledge generally take one of two forms: that someone knows how to do something (e.g., ride a bicycle, juggle, find one's way home, or recite the State capitals while juggling and riding a bicycle home) and that someone knows that things are so (e.g., "that Springfield is the capital of Illinois," "that he lives on Sherwood Drive"). There is considerable overlap between these two types of knowledge ascriptions. Both knowing-how and knowing-that, in other words, manifest themselves in the ability to display the relevant knowledge. These manifestations—that is, expressions of knowledge—may take a variety of forms depending on the particular circumstances. You may manifest your knowledge of how to do something, for example, by doing it or by saying how it is to be done. You may manifest your knowledge that something is so, for example, by asserting that things are so, by answering questions about it correctly, by correcting others who are mistaken about it, or by acting appropriately based on that knowledge. It is also possible that you may do nothing at all with your knowledge (how or that). The primary point is that knowledge is a kind of cognitive achievement or success—it consists in a kind of power, ability, or potentiality possessed by a knowing agent.

To be sure, this is not to suggest that knowledge just is the relevant behavior. On the one hand, it is possible to have knowledge without expressing it. On the other, it is possible to engage in the relevant behavior without having knowledge. A lucky guess, for example, that something is true or how to do something is not knowledge.

Although knowledge is typically (but not always) manifested in behavior, one might object that certain types of syndromes or injuries pose a fundamental challenge to the conception of knowledge as an ability. Consider the tragic case of "locked-in syndrome," in which victims, due to injury to their brain stems, remain fully conscious—with their memories and knowledge intact—but are unable to move or talk (Bauby 1998). Plainly, they have knowledge—but they lack the ability to manifest their knowledge in the typical ways. Does this mean that knowledge is not, in fact, an ability, but rather is something else (a brain state)? We think not. First, those with locked-in syndrome can, quite remarkably, learn to communicate their knowledge through a series of complex eye movements. These communications do manifest knowledge consistent with an ability conception of knowledge. And before a locked-in sufferer learns to communicate in this way—or in cases of "total locked-in syndrome" in which no movements of the eye or any other body parts are possible—he is still able to reflect on his knowledge, to reason from what he knows to be so, and to feel emotions grounded in what he knows. These, too, are abilities or capacities and, indeed, these are reasons why we ascribe knowledge to patients in this situation. If such patients were not conscious of their knowledge in any way, and could not manifest it in any way, on what basis would we ascribe knowledge to them? We would not. Thus rather than posing a challenge to the claim that the criteria for knowledge ascriptions includes an ability or capacity to manifest that knowledge, this example is consistent and reinforces that conception.

A second potentially challenging example is someone in a vegetative state. This example raises several issues. Does someone in a vegetative state possess knowledge? It depends. If he is in a vegetative state, then there may be no reason to suppose that he knows anything at all. If he recovers, then we would say that he retained whatever knowledge he continues to possess post-recovery.

Moreover, patients in persistent vegetative states are reported to sometimes engage in behaviors that, under other circumstances, might be consistent with manifestations of knowledge. For example, although patients in this condition are thought to be unconscious, they are reported to "respond to sounds, to sit up and move their eyes, to shout out, to grimace, to laugh, smile, or cry." (Noë 2010, p. 17) When this occurs, does the patient have knowledge? If they do not, but they have an ability to manifest responses to their environment, does this mean that knowledge is not an ability (to manifest such responses)? We think not. First, as noted above, one may engage in behavior that is consistent with knowing (how to do something or that something is so) without in fact possessing that knowledge (e.g. someone who answers a question correctly by guessing). The behavior, in other words, is not sufficient for knowledge. Second, while knowledge implies an ability to do something, the reverse is not true: being able to do something does not imply knowledge. The ability to do something may apply to many circumstances in which an ascription of knowledge is inappropriate. The ability of a metal to conduct electricity, for example, does not mean the metal knows how to conduct electricity. The ability of a thermometer to display the correct temperature does not mean the thermometer knows, for example, that it is currently 70 °. Knowledge involves a kind of "two-way ability": agents may typically choose to or refrain from exercising it at will. With knowledge, as with rule following, it makes sense to say that an agent knows how to do something correctly, as well as what it means to do it incorrectly, to make a mistake, or to do it wrongly. [1]

References

Baker, G. P., and P. M. S. Hacker. 1985. *Wittgenstein: Rules, grammar and necessity 136* (Volume 2 of An analytical commentary on the philosophical investigations). Oxford: Blackwell.

Bauby, Jean-Dominique. 1998. *The diving bell and the butterfly: A memoir of life in death*. New York: Knopf Doubleday

Goodenough, Oliver R. 2000–2001. Mapping cortical areas associated with legal reasoning and moral intuition. *Jurimetrics* 41 (2): 430–466.

Hauser, Marc D. 2006. *Moral minds: How nature designed a universal sense of right and wrong*. Massachusetts: Ecco.

[1] This article is drawn from our book *Minds, Brains, and Law* (OUP 2013).

Levy, Neil. 2008. Introducing neuroethics. *Neuroethics* 1:1–13.
Mikhail, John. 2009. Moral grammar and intuitive jurisprudence: A formal model of unconscious moral and legal knowledge. *Psychology of Learning and Motivation* 5:28–41.
Mikhail, John. 2011. *Elements of moral cognition: Rawls' linguistic analogy and the cognitive science of moral and legal judgment*. New York: Cambridge.
Noë, Alva. 2010. *Out of our heads*. New York: Basic Books.
Wittgenstein, Ludwig. 1953. *Philosophical investigations. Trans. Anscombe G. E. M.* New York: Macmillan.
Wittgenstein, Ludwig. 1958. *The blue and brown books*. Oxford: Blackwell.

Chapter 14
Gunman Situation Vicious Circle and Pure Theory of Law

Monika Zalewska

Abstract As H.L.A Hart's gunman case serves as an illustration of the weakness of Austin's theory of command, we could ask if this also true for Hans Kelsen's Pure Theory of Law. One possible answer could be that the gunman situation doesn't apply to his theory, as, *inter alia*, Kelsen's theory is strictly bound with the concept of primary and secondary norm. When he speaks about legal norms, he distinguishes primary and secondary norms, the most important of which for law is the primary norm, which consists of two elements: the condition which is needed for an execution of a sanction, and the obligation to impose the sanction. Why does the gunman situation not apply here? Let's imagine a gunman who says: 'give me the money, or I'll shoot'. Such a statement seems to be very similar to the construction of a secondary norm, for example: 'register a car, or receive fine. However, what distinguishes them is the fact that legal norms, especially secondary norms, must refer to a competent authority who represents the state. But this claim seems to be source of another problem. If we agree on such an interpretation, we risk being trapped in a vicious circle defining law: if law is a set of norms which come from the state, and the state is just a legal order, we return to the starting point. In this paper, I will examine whether a more favorable explanation can be found for this dilemma, or if such a vicious circle really exists in Kelsen's legal theory. I will then demonstrate that the solution is based on a combination of so-called relative categories *a priori*, dynamic structure of law and primary and secondary norms.

Keywords Hans Kelsen · Pure theory of law · Relative categories a priori · Definition of law · Gunman situation

14.1 Introduction

When a gunman enters a bank, points a gun and issues the command *give me the money,* then he will probably get what he wants: if not, he will shoot. Such a situation sounds very similar to the description of law provided by John Austin, which

---

M. Zalewska (✉)
University of Łódź, Łódź, Poland
e-mail: mzalewska@wpia.uni.lodz.pl

M. Araszkiewicz et al. (eds.), *Problems of Normativity, Rules and Rule-Following,* Law and Philosophy Library 111, DOI 10.1007/978-3-319-09375-8_14

consists of such elements as *command* and *threat of force*, both of which can be found in the armed robbery described above. However, taking such an approach makes it difficult to identify a difference between law and the coercive factors involved in the situation given above (Dworkin 1978, p. 19). It also might lead to the conclusion that it is unclear whether more sophisticated legal theories based on positivistic paradigms such as Hans Kelsen's pure theory of law are valid in this context. On the other hand, Herbert L. A. Hart, successfully tries to determine how law can be distinguished from the kind of command delivered by the gunman (Hart 1961, pp. 18–20). Does his solution apply to Kelsen's pure theory of law? Or does it really fail in the example of the gunman given above?

In Sect. 14.1 of this paper, I will outline this problem. In Sect. 14.2, I will describe another problem with Kelsen's theory: how to distinguish law from other types of rule. I have chosen two examples, a multinational corporation and the mafia, and I will argue that in kelsenian terms, they represent the two most common normative orders apart from law, and resemble law to some extent. In Sect. 14.3, I will firstly present the most obvious solution, that Kelsen binds all elements of his legal theory with the state, and then I will demonstrate that this solution leads to a further problem: namely, that Kelsen's legal theory might fall into a vicious circle. However, in Sect. 14.4, I will argue that no such vicious circle exists in Kelsen's theory, thanks to the presence of such elements as category of ought, basic norm and imputation, and I will suggest other possible solutions. In the final section, I will try to demonstrate that Kelsen's theory does not fall into a vicious circle and is able to distinguish law from other sophisticated normative orders on the bases of basic norm, imputation and the concept of primary and secondary norm.

14.2 Gunman Situation and Pure Theory of Law

Hart provides a very simple and satisfactory answer for the gunman problem. He notes that the interaction implied by the gunman situation differs from law in several aspects. First of all, law has a general character, while the command provided by the gunman is individual. Secondly, the gunman's command has a temporal character, valid only in the presence of the gunman in the bank, while law is more eternal. Thirdly, in law, there is no need for a direct relationship between the sovereign and the subject of command as in the bank: the two subjects doesn't have be at the same place and time (Hart 1961, pp. 21–25).

Let's examine whether Kelsen's theory conforms with this description of law. He cannot consider the second and third conditions, since they belong to the sphere of facts. At first glance, Kelsen's theory is about general norms, however, he considers also those individual ones. Does it mean that Kelsen's theory is unable to distinguish law from the bandit's command? This question is crucial for Pure Theory of Law since as Zirk-Sadowski notes Kelsen's main objective was to build an autonomous science of law, and to achieve this purpose, a definition of law needs to be constructed which would distinguish law from other normative orders, especially sophisticated ones. If he fails to do so, it would mean that the construction of an autonomous science of law in normativistic terms is impossible, since normativity is the preserve of legal science rather law itself (Zirk-Sadowski 2000, p. 49), law is, according to a neokantian paradigm, alogical material. Assuming that the "method of cognition constitutes the subject of cognition", law itself is not normative, but it gains normativity through a normative method which is valid for the science of law. This argument can be demonstrated in three simple steps:

If:

1. Law itself is alogical material and:
2. Method of cognition constitutes the subject of cognition then:
3. Normative method constitutes normativity of law.

Hence, if this method fails to distinguish law from other normative orders, especially sophisticated ones, it would imply that the Pure Theory of Law fails in two crucial dimensions: first of all, in building a legitimate science of law, since it is impossible to build a science of something which the applied methodology fails to distinguish from other similar objects, and secondly, it fails as a description of law based on the is-ought dichotomy. Kelsen cannot afford that conclusion.

Fortunately for Kelsen, he proposed a dynamic structure for law (*Stufenbau*) which can distinguish law from such a command. Kelsen chose to adapt an innovative idea first proposed by Adolf Merkl (1931) for his theory, which is arguably one of its most successful elements. According to this concept, law has a specific structure with a dynamic character, which stands in contrast to the static nature of the moral order. The hierarchical relations between norms in the sphere of morality are determined by their content. It is possible to infer the content of a lower norm from the content of a higher one. For example, from the norm *love your neighbor as yourself*, it can be presumed that it such norms as *you shall not kill*, *you shall not steal*, *help your neighbor* are valid within this moral system. In contrast, law has no such relations. The legal system is characterized by formal links between norms and is based on the rule of delegation. This is to say that an authority higher in the hierarchy passes an act with the competence for a lower authority to pass another act of a lower degree. This chain of competences ends with an individual norm (Kelsen 1934, p. 93): a structure which is rather hard to visualize in the simple gunman example given above.

14.3 Vicious Circle and Pure Theory of Law

Even if we provide a plausible answer to the gunman situation (and any other type of simple orders), there is also another related problem: how to distinguish, in Kelsenian terms, law from a set of rules associated with other formal or informal groups such as the mafia or a multinational corporation? I have chosen this two examples, as they represent the two most common types of complex normative systems which are not law. The reason for choosing the mafia structure as an example was that as such an organization is illegal, and against the legal order, the argument that this structure is in fact incorporated into the legal order and could be considered part of it must be invalid. Such organizations also have their own structure, members of higher and lower ranks and people with more and less power, which makes them hard to distinguish from a legal order.

A possible difference between the two is that a system like that employed by the mafia is based more on temporary commands than eternal norms, and lacks the regularities and predictability of the law. However, there are at least two possible answers to this argument. First of all, is it really impossible to imagine a mafia organization with a very sophisticated structure, a very sophisticated code, that has the same, dynamic character of law? Even if it is less likely, such a possibility can't be excluded. What is more, a more sophisticated normative structure with a high level of formality can certainly be found in multinational corporations. Also even law itself doesn't fit so perfectly into the schema of dynamical structure and it is possible to imagine a legal system incorporating both norms and commands of a similar character to those which exist in the mafia. To solve this puzzle, firstly I will look closer at these two types of structure: the mafia and a multinational corporation.

A mafia structure, which I will define as a type A normative order, is based on the existence of a highest authority bearing absolute power. It is easy to imagine the highest norm of such a structure: *you shall listen to the godfather.* Such a normative system assumes the highest authority which everyone should obey. Religious organizations could be described as having a similar character, where God is the highest authority.

The other type of normative order, henceforth defined as type B, illustrated by the organisation of a multinational corporation, is a normative order with a very strict structures based on delegation of competences. I have chosen the example of a multinational corporation because of its complex structure, which is difficult to ascribe to one particular legal order. They are powerful enough to choose the most suitable legal order for them, lowering costs of production and taxation. In such organization there is a hierarchy, and there are empowerments.

While the type A structure is very often bound with some kind of ideology, from which we can reconstruct the content of the highest norm, ideology doesn't seem to be a necessary component of type B. Although profit could be regarded as such an ideology in the case of a multinational corporation, firstly it is unclear whether profit can be regarded as the ideology or the goal of a company, and secondly, non-profit NGOs could also arguably be included in this type. Of course type A structures are mostly based on some kind of ideology, or rather they set specific goals, but it is not necessary to include ideology as a necessary factor for this group.

In type B, even if some kind of ideological rule is breached, a sanction doesn't have to be necessarily automatically imposed, according to a normative system. For example, if member of environmental NGO owns a car and uses it instead of a bicycle he doesn't have to be necessary punished, although his transportation policy is not environmentally friendly. Obviously, it is possible, but it is not a necessary rule for such organization. On the contrary, in a type A structure such as the mafia or church, breaching a mafia code or a commandment is bound with some kind of sanction, such as execution or atonement, which is necessary in such a normative order. In mafia, disloyalty is to be punished as soon as it is discovered, while in the church, committing a sin is always bound with a punishment, even if later it is forgiven by God.

To sum up, the first normative system, the type A system, is characterized by some sort of ideology which determines the content of the highest norm in the hierarchy and also determines some set of material norms. The second type, type B, can also be bound with some kind of ideology, but not necessarily. It can be one of many options which are possible in this type. I believe that most normative systems belong to either type A or type B, and law can be distinguished from both of them in Kelsenian terms. This division is crucial for the next part of my argumentation and as I will demonstrate later is not arbitrary, but is grounded in Kelsenian legal theory. Specifically its elements which allowed me to make such a division, such as hierarchical structure of law, basic norm and imputation.

The final conclusion of this part is that as both type A and B could possess dynamic structure, we should look further afield to find the *differentia specifica* of legal norms. At first glance, it appears that both problems can be solved quite easily. It should be sufficient to add one component to the Kelsenian definition: the state. The state distinguishes the formal from the informal. However, in this case, we fall into the even more serious problem of the vicious circle of the pure theory of law. As Lande noticed (Lande 1959, p. 271) if we accept the Kelsenian definition of the law as a set of norms, and to distinguish them from morality we claim that these norms have institutionalized sanction, and to distinguish the norms from mafia rules we argue that they need to come from a state, we fall into a vicious circle, because Kelsen claims that state and the law are equal. They are two sides of the same coin (Kelsen 1926, p. 1411). Let's examine this problem more carefully. The schema presented above is very simplified, and doesn't concern many elements of the Pure Theory of Law, elements which add further sophistication to this theory: My next step will be to prove that Kelsen's theory doesn't fall into a vicious circle.

A vicious circle is something which every scientist would prefer to avoid. As Hans Albert points out, if a scientist wishes to build a well-grounded theory, at some point he will face the so-called Münchhausen-Trillema: his theory will either fall into a vicious circle, *regressus ad infinitum* or a break of searching will have to occur at some point. (Albert 1968, p. 15) Nevertheless, as these two options are not acceptable for the scientist, I will try to examine whether Kelsen's theory can be solved in a third way, which assumes that fundamental elements of a theory do not demand any further justification.

Three elements which do not require justification are *ought* category, imputation and basic norm. The ought category is included in this list as its meaning can be understood only through the context in which it appears. Kelsen doesn't define ought, a fact that is made particularly clear when Kelsen discusses the separation of *is* and *ought* or, from the neokantian perspective, when he claims that it is a relative category *a priori* (Kelsen 1934, p. 33) then defining a norm, Kelsen argues that a norm is a hypothetical judgment: that something should happen or someone ought to behave in certain way (Kelsen 1960, p. 4). *Ought* is also contrasted with *is*: while *is* implies necessity, *ought* only possibility. These are key principles which refer to ought, but it is hard to regard any of them as a 'definition'.

The question is whether *ought* is capable of breaking this vicious circle, whether it brings something new to Kelsen's theory or whether it too is accommodated within the circle. As there is no definition of ought the context in which it appears demands further examination. In neokantian terms, Kelsen perceives *ought* as a second degree category (Alexy 2002, p. 193) which enables the recognition of norms, as all norms exist in the *ought* world. However, as it is not enough to distinguish legal norms from other norms, we need to find the *differentia specifica* of legal norms (Alexy 2002, pp. 181–202). The conclusion is that pure *ought,* without any further interpretation, doesn't suffice as a criterion for the law because it cannot distinguish the law from other normative systems.

Hence, there needs to be a much more specific element which distinguishes the law from other normative orders. Kelsen combines *sollen* with the doctrine of imputation as a relative *a priori* (Kelsen 1934, pp. 33–35): Imputation is equivalent to causality in the world of *ought*. Causality can be seen in the structure (Kelsen 1934, pp. 34–35):

If A then B.

Imputation is to be found in a statement which has another structure:

If A then should be B.

Kelsen defines imputation as the link between legal fact and legal consequence (Kelsen 1934, p. 34), indicating that imputation binds two elements: a condition to imply sanction, i.e. the violation of a secondary norm by the subject, where the secondary norm imposes legal obligations on the subject, and a statement that the legal authority ought to impose a sanction. According to Kelsen, legal norms are the only ones which consist of such an imputation. No other normative system contains binding links for norm infringement and duty of legal authority. What is more, if we look closer at the definition of imputation, it can be seen that this definition doesn't capture the essence of the term: It is rather vague and fails to address the nature of imputation, because, as Paulson notes Kelsen considered imputation as a category in his neokantian scheme of cognition of norms (Paulson 2004). So this would be a second break of searching for his theory.

Kelsen also considers a third category, the basic norm (Kelsen 1960, p. 205). If we ask why a particular norm is binding, the answer seems simple: because it was passed on behalf of a higher authority. However, we can then ask why this higher act is binding, and the answer will be because there is a constitution. This way, we will be forced to ask a question about the nature of the first constitution: a question which has two common answers. Firstly, we could recall natural law, that the first constitution is binding because it conforms with natural law. Or secondly, we could explain that the first constitution was binding because, historically, people gathered and the first constitution was passed. As Paulson notes, for Kelsen, who denied that the law could be explained through facts, and who stood for separability of the law and morality, neither solution was acceptable (Paulson 1992, p. 313). As a normativist, he was restricted to the world of *ought*. So he provided the only answer that a normativist could give: he used transcendental argument to prove that a hypothetical assumption, the basic norm, is a necessary assumption which every lawyer has to make. He did this in three steps: Firstly he stated that the law is valid. Then he assumed that the law is valid only when there is an assumption of a basic norm. Finally, Kelsen argued that as the first premise is true, the basic norm must also be assumed to be true. In other words, Kelsen claimed that if we want to (as Stanley Paulson named it) play the game called law (Paulson 2004, p. 112) and if we assume that the law is in force, we need to assume that a basic norm exists at the top of every normative legal system. This argumentation indicates that a basic norm might also be understood as a point of break in searching. It has a formal character but no content.

Hence, there are at least three elements which are able to break the vicious circle, the categories of *ought*, imputation and basic norms, while only one is sufficient. But at this stage, this answer is insufficient to address the problems created by type A or type B normative systems. It only demonstrates that Kelsen's legal theory doesn't fall into a vicious circle, as implied by the simple schema. Hence, there is still a need to either show that at least one of those categories differentiates law from another set of rules, or determine the role of the state in Kelsen's theory.

14.4 Can Pure Theory of Law be Distinguished from Other Sophisticated Normative Orders?

First let's examine whether these categories are really specific only for the legal system, and consider these main elements of law:

1. *Ought* distinguishes legal statements from factual statements.
2. Imputation binds primary and secondary norms: While the primary norm imposes a sanction, the secondary norm provides the conditions under which the sanction can be imposed.
3. Basic norm empowers the whole normative system.

Arguably, none of these conditions is specific for law but if they are combined, and the vertical aspect that is the dynamic structure of law is added, maybe this could be the hidden combination? A basic norm in the form described by Kelsen is specific only for the normative system created by a human being. Its character also distinguishes law from mafia structure, insofar that the mafia's supreme norm is reminiscent of a natural law rule, filled with content (e.g. '*you shall be loyal to the Godfather*'). At this point, one could question the difference between a basic norm characteristic of a legal order and a supreme norm characteristic of a type A normative system: the basic norm is specific because it doesn't have any determined content. While *any* content could be incorporated to make a legal order valid, the list of the content of supreme norm for mafia structure seems much more limited, and is determined by the specific character of such organization, making it rather similar to religion and its supreme norm (*you shall listen to God*). Conversely, the supreme norm of the legal system, for example *you shall obey the first constitution*, would make no sense in the context of either a type A or B structure. Furthermore, imputation offers a guarantee that the system in which it exists is characterized by highly institutionalized sanction. Finally, a dynamic structure guarantees the complexity of the system. Without a doubt, if all these conditions are gathered, the reward will be laws with a perfectly adequate character. However, still it is possible to imagine an institutionalized organization with a similar structure, especially type B.

It seems that there are two ways to deal with this problem. The first way leads through positivistic paradigm, where again the presence of the state is a very important component in the differentiation of law from other normative orders. This begs the question of how Kelsen's theory defines the state. Kelsen asserts that the state is the component which unifies law. Although it is also the endpoint of imputation, Kelsen employs a different kind of imputation: central imputation as opposed to the peripheral imputation described above. This central imputation concerns the hierarchical structure of law, in that it links a certain type of behavior with an authority. As all single imputations meet at one final point, a state which is called the endpoint of imputation (Kelsen 1926, p. 1408), we could say that the concept of central imputation creates a detailed picture of the dynamic structure of norms. As noted above, in itself, such a structure doesn't distinguish law from other normative orders; when sufficiently sophisticated, it could also be described in terms of dynamic structure and points of imputation. But is it possible to imagine the endpoint of imputation in any such structure? Of course it is. It is possible to conceive of a sophisticated normative structure such as type B, which will have all the components characteristic of law described in the same way as Kelsen's. In this case, the endpoint of imputation wouldn't be a state but rather the multinational corporation itself. Of course, according to Kelsen, the state is an essential component which unifies legal norms and which is the 'endpoint of imputation' (Kelsen 1926, p. 1408). However, Kelsen also points out that the state is just a metaphor and a personification of the legal order (Kelsen 1960, p. 294). From this statement, the conclusion can be drawn that Kelsen needed the concept of the state to make his argumentation clearer. The state could be eliminated from his theory but this would be at the expense of this clarity. Even if the line of argumentation ended at this point, something could still be gained. For example, we could ask whether the state is equal with law, which would imply that maybe his theory is much better adjusted to today's multicentric world and stateless law than it first seemed? Such an approach might beg the question about the usefulness of Pure Theory of Law, one recent criticism of which is that it does not accommodate present legal circumstances, which are strongly influenced by multicentric relations and stateless law (Golecki et al. 2009, p. 8) But maybe if Kelsen doesn't need the state in his theory, then in fact, Pure Theory of Law does concern, to some extent, stateless law? If this is the case, a new interpretation of what Kelsen has written in his books and a broad analysis of both Pure Theory of Law and todays legal relations would be needed. This question will have to remain open, firstly as it is rather off topic, and secondly another solution is even more favorable for Kelsen.

14.5 The Final Solution

In conclusion, the most obvious answer to the question 'how to differentiate law from other sophisticated normative orders' does not provide a satisfactory explanation. However, there is another way to solve the problem. It is a problem of primary and secondary norms. As it was mentioned above, imputation binds two elements: a condition to imply sanction as a result of the violation of a secondary norm, where the secondary norm imposes legal obligations on the subject, and a statement that the legal authority ought to impose a sanction. The presence of a secondary norm, despite being unable to distinguish law from morality (*you shall not kill* is both a moral norm and can be a secondary legal norm), can make it possible to distinguish law from type B normative orders. This structure resembles that of law, but only in the vertical, or procedural, aspect. Fewer secondary norms, and fewer norms with sanctions, exist in corporations and even if they do, they tend to come from outside, from the legal order. Hence, our solution to the present dilemma is through imputation, which binds a primary norm, distinguishing law from morality, with a secondary norm, distinguishing law from such sophisticated normative structures as corporations.

There is, however, one interesting case which could contradict this argumentation. One could ask, what about the Holy See? It is organized as a state, and while it is subject to international law and can maintain diplomatic relationships, it is also obviously a religious structure and fails to fulfill the criteria of statehood established by international law. However, as it consists of all the required components given by Pure Theory of Law and the criteria mentioned above, the Holy See would have to be considered a state, this does not necessarily mean that Kelsen's theory fails. According to international law doctrine, the most important criterion of statehood which is not fulfilled by Holy See is that it is a non-territorial institution. But, first of all, this criterion belongs to the sphere of facts, which is irrelevant for the Kelsenian definition of law, and secondly, Kelsen regards the state as having rather a supportive meaning in a metaphorical sense than being an autonomous component which defines the essence of law. Again it seems that Kelsen's theory could support, to some extent, the concept of stateless law. On the other hand, the fact that Holy See is strictly bound with religion rather supports the thesis that a basic norm can have content, even content which incorporates the whole of a normative system of another type into law.

Conclusions

To sum up, this paper argues that firstly, although Kelsen's theory doesn't fit the gunman situation described earlier, because of the concept of the dynamic structure of law, it encounters the much more serious problems of the vicious circle and the distinction of law from other sophisticated normative structures. The vicious circle problem can be solved by demonstrating that there is a break of searching in Kelsen's theory manifested by the category of *ought*, imputation and basic norm. While imputation and the concept of primary and secondary norms are able to distinguish law from such sophisticated normative structures as multinational corporations (the type B normative system), the presence of basic norms distinguishes the legal system from the mafia's normative order (a type A normative system). Therefore, according to Pure Theory of Law, as law has its own unique components, Kelsen was able to fulfill the first condition on the way to his primary goal, which was to build an autonomous science of Law, and he provides a very complex and sophisticated concept of law, distinguished from other normative systems.

References

Albert, Hans. 1968. *Traktat über kritische Vernunft*. Tübingen: Mohr Siebeck (1991).

Alexy, Robert. 2002. Hans Kelsens Begriff des relativen Apriori. In *Neukantianismus und Rechtsphilosophie,* eds. Robert Alexy, Lukas H. Meyer, Stanley. L. Paulson, and Gerhard Sprenger, 179–202. Baden Baden: Nomos Verlagsgesellschaft.

Dworkin, Ronald. 1978. *Taking rights seriously*. Cambridge: Harvard University Press.

Golecki, Mariusz, Bartosz Wojciechowski, and Marek Zirk-Sadowski. 2009. Editorial; introduction. In *Multicentrism as an emerging paradigm in legal theory,* eds. Mariusz Golecki, Bartosz Wojciechowski, and Marek Zirk-Sadowski, 7–14. Frankfurt a. M.: Peter Lang.

Hart, Herbert L. A. 1961. *The concept of law*. Oxford: Clarendon (1994).

Kelsen, Hans.1926. Das Wesen des Staates. In *Die Wiener rechtstheoretische Schule,* eds. H. R. Klecatsky, Rene Marcic, and Herbert Schambeck, 1403–1416. Stuttgart: Franz Steiner Verlag (2010).

Kelsen, Hans. 1934. *Reine Rechtslehre*. Tübingen: Mohr Siebeck (2008).

Kelsen, Hans. 1960. *Reine Rechtslehre*. Wien: Verlag Franz Deuticke.

Lande, Jerzy. 1959. *Studia z filozofii prawa* [Studies on legal philosophy]. Warszwa: PWN.

Merkl, Adolf. 1931. Prolegomena einer Theorie der Rechtlichen Stufenbaues. In *Die wiener rechtstheoretische Schule,* eds. H. R. Klecatsky, Rene Marcic, and Herbert Schambeck, 1071–1112. Stuttgart: Franz Steiner Verlag (2010).

Paulson, Stanley L. 2004. Die Zurechnung als apriorische Kategorie in der Rechtslehre Hans Kelsens. In *Zurechnung als Operationaliesierung von Verantwortung,* eds. Matthias Kaufmann, and Joachim Renzikowski, 93–122. Frankfurt a. M.: Peter Lang.

Paulson, Stanley L. 1992. *The Neokantian Dimension of Kelsen's Pure Theory of Law*. Oxford Legal Studies, vol. 12, no. 3, 311–332. Oxford: Oxford University Press.

Zirk-Sadowski, Marek. 2000. *Wprowadzenie do filozofii prawa* [Introduction to legal philosophy]. Kraków: Zakamycze.

Chapter 15
Rules as Reason-Giving Facts: A Difference-Making-Based Account of the Normativity of Rules

Peng-Hsiang Wang and Linton Wang

Abstract In his "Reasoning with Rules," Joseph Raz raises a puzzling question about the normativity of rules: "How can it be that rules are reasons when they do not point to a good in the action for which they are reasons?" In this paper, we put forward a difference-making-based theory of reasons to resolve Raz's puzzle. This theory distinguishes between reasons and reason-giving facts, and we argue that rules are not reasons but rather reason-giving facts. Based on this distinction, we recast and criticize some of Raz's theses about the nature of rules, such as their opaqueness, the normative gap, and the breakdown of transitivity in the content-independent justification of rules. Finally, we propose a difference-making-based account of the reason-giving force of rules.

Keywords Difference-making · Normativity of rules · Raz · Reasons · Reason-giving facts

15.1 Introduction: Raz's Puzzle About the Normativity of Rules

The aim of this paper is to give an account of the normativity of rules in terms of reasons. A representative view of this approach is that of Joseph Raz, who writes:

> The normativity of all that is normative consists in the way it is, or provides, or is otherwise related to reasons. The normativity of rules … consists in the fact that rules are reasons of a special kind …. (Raz 1999a, p. 67)

P.-H. Wang (✉)
Institutum Iurisprudentiae, Academia Sinica,
Academia Rd. Sec. 2 No. 128, 11529 Taipei City, Taiwan
e-mail: philaw@sinica.edu.tw

L. Wang
Department of Philosophy, National Chung Cheng University,
University Rd. Sec. 1 No. 168, 621 Chia-yi County, Taiwan
e-mail: lintonwang@ccu.edu.tw

M. Araszkiewicz et al. (eds.), *Problems of Normativity, Rules and Rule-Following*,
Law and Philosophy Library 111, DOI 10.1007/978-3-319-09375-8_15

The claim that rules are reasons for action seems at odds with the value-based theory of reasons advocated by Raz, when he says that "reasons for action are facts that establish that the action has some value" (Raz 2011, p. 70). As Raz observes,

> Yet rules are unlike most other reasons. Most reasons are facts which show what is good in an action, which render it eligible: it will give pleasure. It will protect one's health, or earn one money, or improve one's understanding. It will relieve poverty in one's country, or bring peace of mind to a troubled friend, and so on. What is the good in conforming to a rule? (Raz 2009, p. 205)

Raz thus raises a puzzling question about the normativity of rules: "How can it be that rules are reasons when they do not point to a good in the action for which they are reasons?" (Raz 2009, p. 205). He calls this puzzle *the opaqueness of rules*. For example, the fact that smoking in a public place damages others' health is a reason not to do it, because this fact shows the good in refraining from smoking in a public place: it will protect others' health. By contrast, suppose that the fact that there is a legal rule prohibiting smoking in a public place constitutes another reason not to do it. This fact tells us that it is legally required to refrain from smoking in a public place, but it does not indicate that there is some good or value in the action required by this rule.

Of course, one can circumvent Raz's question by denying that reasons depend on values, but we will not adopt this strategy here. Rather, we will draw on a difference-making-based theory of reasons, of which the value-based theory is just a special case, to resolve his puzzle. Although we think Raz is right when he says that the normativity of rules is to be explained in terms of reasons, we will argue, based on this difference-making account, that rules are not reasons but reason-giving facts.[1] In terms of rules as reason-giving facts, we shall reformulate Raz's puzzle about the opaqueness of rules and then provide an alternative way to account for the normativity of rules.

15.2 Reasons and Reason-Giving Facts

The main idea of the difference-making-based theory of reasons is that reasons are *difference-making facts*. Consider the fact that smoking in a public place damages others' health. This fact is a reason not to smoke in a public place. When one asks whether there will be any difference if one does not smoke in a public place, the answer is positive: the health of other people will not be damaged. Therefore, this fact is a difference-making fact in that smoking in a public place makes a difference

[1] A reviewer of the Rules 2013 conference reminds us that whether rules can be facts is a controversial matter. Strictly speaking, it is not rules but their existence which are facts. A statement about the existence of a rule, such as "there is a rule prohibiting smoking in a public place," can be true or false. If such a statement is true, as Raz (1979, p. 147) points out, then it is a fact that there is such a rule. For the sake of brevity, however, we will adopt the shorthand of referring to rules as reason-giving facts.

to whether or not others' health will be damaged. To take another example, driving to work will lead to an increase in your gasoline expenses, as opposed to if you take the metro. This is a difference-making fact because it shows that driving to work makes a difference to your gasoline expenses. It is therefore a reason for you not to drive to work.

This idea can be made more precise as follows:

> **(Reasons)** R is a reason for A to φ if and only if R is a fact that A's φ-ing makes a difference to X.

There can be varied versions of the difference-making-based theory of reasons, each corresponding to a different way to characterize X in **Reasons**. For example, if X is characterized as the fulfillment of A's desires, then we get a desire-based theory of reasons. A value-based version of the difference-making-based theory can be formulated as follows:

> **(Value-Based Reasons)** R is a reason for A to φ if and only if R is a fact that A's φ-ing makes a difference to whether a good or valuable outcome occurs, in other words, A's φ-ing leads to some good or valuable consequence.

Such a difference, characterized in **Value-Based Reasons**, might be called "*evaluative difference.*" In this regard, Raz's value-based theory of reasons can be viewed as a special case of the difference-making-based theory of reasons.

The motivation to define reasons as difference-making facts is to capture the idea that normative reasons can be, and must be, *practically deliberationally useful*. By "being practically deliberationally useful," following DeRose (2010, p. 25), we mean that an agent can make use of a difference-making fact to deliberate over whether or not to perform a certain act as a way of producing (or preventing) some consequence. For instance, you can deploy the fact that driving to work leads to a rise in your gasoline expenses to consider whether to take the metro as a way of saving money. Likewise, the fact that smoking in a public place damages others' health can be used to deliberate over whether to extinguish a cigarette before entering a public place in order to prevent damage to others' health.

The deliberational usefulness also takes the explanatory dimension of normative reasons into account. A normative reason for A to φ, as Broome (2004) defines it, is a fact that explains why A ought to φ. By means of pointing out what difference an act makes, difference-making facts provide *quasi-teleological* explanations of ought facts. For example, an explanation of why you ought not to drive to work is that your gasoline expenses will increase if you drive to work. For the sake of reducing your gasoline expenses, you ought not to drive to work. In the same way, the fact that one ought not to smoke in a public place is explained by the fact that this act causes damage to others' health; in order to avoid this undesirable consequence, one ought to refrain from smoking in a public place.

An explanation provided by a difference-making fact differs from one that a difference-maker provides. That the health of other people will be damaged may be explained by the fact that someone smokes in a public place, given that the damage to others' health is a difference "made" (or "caused") by smoking in a public place.

In this sort of explanation, which may be called the *canonical* explanation, the explanans is a difference-maker, that is, an action (or a fact) that makes a difference to whether or not some consequence (the explanandum) occurs.[2] By contrast, the explanans in an explanation of why one ought to φ is not a difference-maker but rather a difference-making fact that one's φ-ing makes a difference to whether or not some consequence occurs. In such an explanation, which may be called the *inverted* explanation, the explanandum is a fact that a certain action, which plays the role of the difference-maker in a difference-making fact, ought to be done. Reasons as inverted explanations are useful for practical deliberation in that they can be so deployed in order for agents to deliberate the consequences of actions for which they are reasons, thereby providing the intellectual base for normative considerations concerning whether one should perform a certain action for some reason.

In light of practically deliberational usefulness and inverted explanations, reasons are to be distinguished from reason-giving facts. A reason-giving fact is not a difference-making fact, but rather a fact in virtue of which a difference-making fact obtains. For example, suppose the price of gasoline goes up. This fact does not point to what difference that an action, such as driving to work, makes, but it provides the background condition for the difference-making fact that driving to work leads to an increase in your gasoline expenses: Were the price of gasoline not to be raised, driving to work would not make a difference to your gasoline expenses. Therefore, the fact that the price of gasoline goes up, though it is not a reason, gives you a reason not to drive to work. Likewise, while the fact that smoking in a public place damages others' health is a difference-making fact, the fact that tobacco contains toxic chemicals is not. It is, however, the fact in virtue of which smoking in a public place causes damage to others' health. The fact that tobacco contains toxic chemicals is therefore a reason-giving fact.

Reason-giving facts can be defined as follows:

> **(Reason-Giving Facts)** The fact P gives A a reason to φ if and only if, in virtue of P, A's φ-ing makes a difference to X.

Since a reason-giving fact does not point to any difference an action makes, it is not practically deliberationally useful, nor can it provide an inverted explanation in its own right. Consider the following statement: "Because the price of gasoline goes up, you ought not to drive to work." This is merely an enthymematic explanation. To deliberate over whether to perform a certain action, such as driving or not driving to work, you cannot rely only on the fact that the price of gasoline goes up, because it does not show what consequences will be produced (or prevented) by driving to work. Without resort to the difference-making fact that driving to work causes an increase in your gasoline expenses, it is unintelligible why you ought not to drive to work just because the price of gasoline goes up, and we do not know what reasons you really have not to drive to work, either. In other words, in order to provide an inverted explanation of why you ought not to drive to work, we still have

[2] For a detailed discussion of difference-making in the causal explanation, see, among others, Strevens (2004).

to appeal to a difference-making fact that obtains in virtue of a rise in the price of gasoline, and this fact accounts for the reason-giving force of the fact that the price of gasoline goes up.

15.3 The Opaqueness of Rules

Let us return to the opaqueness of rules. If rules are reasons, then the fact that an action is required by a rule has to be a difference-making fact. Rules automatically make a "difference" in one sense: they distinguish between what is correct and incorrect, or what is legal and illegal. An action is correct if it complies with a rule and is incorrect if it does not. However, the difference in this sense only reveals a feature of an action, that is, being correct (or incorrect), and is not deliberationally useful because it does not point to the consequence to which performing a correct (or incorrect) action will lead. In other words, the fact that an action is required by a rule is not the one that an agent can employ to deliberate over whether to perform it as a way of producing or preventing a certain consequence.

For example, smoking in a public place is illegal because it is banned by a legal rule, but the fact that it is illegal to smoke in a public place does not show a difference this act makes, let alone any valuable outcome of refraining from it. Alternatively, consider Raz's example: a chess club's rule that members are entitled to bring no more than three guests to the club's social functions. According to this rule, it is correct to bring three or fewer guests and incorrect to bring a fourth guest. However, from this rule, we cannot see any practically significant difference between bringing three and bringing four or more guests, nor can we discern that bringing fewer than three guests will lead to any desirable consequence.

In terms of the difference-making-based theory, Raz's puzzle about the opaqueness of rules can be generalized in the following question: How can rules be reasons if they do not show what difference the actions they require make? In fact, since reason-giving facts are not difference-making facts, they are all opaque in this sense. For example, one might ask: "How can the fact that the price of gasoline goes up be a reason for you to not drive to work, even though it does not point to any difference this action makes?" or "The fact that tobacco contains toxic chemicals does not show what difference smoking in a public place makes, how can it be a reason not to smoke in a public place?" Although these facts are not reasons (that is, difference-making facts), they can still be reason-giving facts inasmuch as there are some difference-making facts which obtain in virtue of them. By the same token, if reasons are difference-making facts but rules are not, the straightforward answer to the question above is that rules are not reasons. Even though rules are not reasons, this should not preclude rules from being reason-giving facts.

With regard to the normativity of rules, instead of questioning whether rules are reasons, perhaps it is more sensible to ask how rules can be reason-giving facts. In other words, the problem about the normativity of rules will shift from "How can it be that rules are reasons?" to "How can rules give reasons?" Applying **Reason-Giving Facts**, we get the following condition for the reason-giving force of rules:

> **(Reason-Giving Force of Rules: First Attempt)** The fact that a rule requires A to φ gives A a reason to φ if and only if, in virtue of this fact, A's φ-ing makes a difference to X.

If we endorse the value-based theory of reasons, the right-hand side of this condition can be formulated as "in virtue of this fact, A's φ-ing leads to some valuable consequence."

According to this condition, if rules are reason-giving facts, there must be some difference-making fact R that obtains in virtue of the existence of rules, and R is a reason to do what they require. On this matter, rules are not different from other reason-giving facts. In order to account for why a fact is a reason-giving one, we have to point to a difference an action makes in virtue of this fact. However, whereas it is relatively clear what difference-making facts obtain by virtue of ordinary reason-giving facts, it is not straightforward to find out what (evaluative) difference an action makes in virtue of its being required by a rule.

For instance, because of the fact that the price of gasoline goes up, driving to work makes a difference to whether or not your gasoline expenses increase; the fact that tobacco contains toxic chemicals makes smoking in a public place dangerous to others' health. But what difference does bringing no more than three guests make in virtue of the fact that it is required by the rule? What is the difference-making fact that obtains by virtue of the legal rule prohibiting smoking in a public place? Now we face a puzzle similar to Raz's. This puzzle can be presented in the following way:

> **(The Opaqueness of Rules as Reason-Giving Facts)** How can we account for the reason-giving force of rules if we cannot show that an action makes a difference in virtue of the fact that it is required by a rule?

At issue here is how to explain the normativity of rules, that is, their reason-giving force, given that they are opaque in the above sense. To answer this question, we have to look into Raz's view on the nature of rules in more detail.

15.4 Content-Independent Justification and Normative Gaps

According to Raz,

> When we ask 'what makes rules bind?' the answer will revert to evaluative considerations. The rules of the Mastergame chess club may be binding because it is *better* for the affairs of the club to be governed by its committee than to be organized some other way, or be left in chaos.... *Normativity is ultimately based on evaluative considerations*, but in a way which leaves room for a normative gap. (Raz 2009, p. 209)

If the binding force of rules is understood as their reason-giving force, Raz's idea might be put another way: In order to explain the reason-giving force of rules, we still have to appeal to certain evaluative difference-making facts that obtain in virtue of the existence of rules. With respect to this difference-making-based account of the normativity of rules, there are two related problems: First, what kind of difference-making facts are those that can explain the reason-giving force of rules? Second, are they concerned with the evaluative difference made by the actions required by rules?

Let us start with the latter problem. Raz's answer to this question is negative. In his view, the evaluative considerations on which the normativity of rules is based do not turn on the value of the actions for which they give reasons. Take the chess club rule as an example. The considerations which explain its normative force, as Raz claims,"do not turn on the desirability of members having a small number of guests, nor on the desirability of members having the option to bring guests, but on the desirability of the affairs of the club being organized by the committee which laid down the rule" (Raz 2009, p. 210).

Raz calls such an explanation of the normativity of rules *content-independent justification:*

> It is content-independent in that it does not bear primarily on the desirability of the acts for which the rule is a reason. Here we see clearly how rules differ from other reasons. The insightfulness and subtlety of a novel are reasons for reading it because they show why reading it is good. But the considerations which show why the rule is binding, ie why it is a reason for not bringing more than three guests, do not show that it is good not to bring more than three guests. They show that it is good to have power given to a committee, and therefore good to abide by decisions of that committee. (Raz 2009, p. 210)

Since the justification of rules is content-independent, that is, it does not depend on the value of the actions they require, Raz claims that "[r]ules … allow for a potential gap, a gap between the evaluative and the normative, that is between their value and their normative force" (Raz 2009, p. 208). Displaying a *normative gap* is a unique feature of rules:

> Contrast this with 'ordinary' reasons. That a novel is insightful and subtle is a reason to read it. We cannot here drive a wedge between the evaluative and the normative, between the two questions 'is it good?' and 'is it binding or valid?' If being insightful and subtle are good characteristics of novels then they are reasons. There is no gap between being valid reasons and being good or of value, between the normative and the evaluative, as there is in the case of rules …. (Raz 2009, p. 208)

Let us make a clarification. According to the distinction between reasons and reason-giving facts, it is somewhat misleading when Raz says, "That a novel is insightful and subtle is a reason to read it." The fact that a novel is insightful and subtle does not show the difference to which reading this novel will lead. It is not a difference-making fact but rather provides the background condition for an evaluative difference-making fact, such as the fact that reading this novel will bring you enjoyment. This difference-making fact is an explanation of why you ought to read it, thereby being a reason for you to read it. Therefore, the fact that a novel is insightful and subtle is not a reason but a reason-giving fact.

Nevertheless, the content-independent justification and the idea of normative gaps help us see a difference between rules and other reason-giving facts. If the fact that a novel is insightful and subtle gives you a reason to read it, that is because, in virtue of this fact, reading this novel will lead to some valuable consequence. The reason-giving force of "ordinary" reason-giving facts derives from the evaluative difference made by the actions for which they give reasons; thus they do not display a normative gap.

By contrast, in Raz's view, rules display a normative gap in that their normative force does not turn on the value of the actions they require. To put it another way, the normative gap consists in the fact that the reason-giving force of rules does not derive from the evaluative difference made by the actions for which they give reasons. For example, if the club rule gives its members a reason to bring no more than three guests, it is not because this act leads to some valuable consequence, such as reducing the cost of social functions. Likewise, the reason-giving force of the fact that smoking in a public place is illegal is not grounded in the fact that refraining from doing it will prevent damage to others' health.

Yet we think that Raz's view about the normative gap of rules is inaccurate in some respect. Just as the reason-giving force of the fact that a novel is insightful and subtle derives from the evaluative difference-making fact that obtains by virtue of the insightfulness and subtleness of the novel in question, so, if rules give reasons, their reason-giving force must be established on the difference-making facts that obtain in virtue of the existence of rules. But the evaluative difference-making facts mentioned above—that is, "Bringing no more than three guests will reduce the cost of social functions" or "Refraining from smoking in a public place will prevent damage to others' health"—are not those facts that obtain in virtue of the existence of rules. Smoking in a public place will damage others' health no matter whether it is forbidden by the law. Even if the club committee did not issue the three-guests-rule, bringing no more than three guests could still reduce the cost of social functions.

Since such difference-making facts, though they are concerned with the value of the actions required by the rules, are independent of the existence of rules, by definition, they cannot figure as the considerations that account for the reason-giving force of rules. Let us draw an analogy to illustrate this point: We cannot deploy the difference-making fact that not driving to work will reduce air pollution to explain why the fact that the price of gasoline goes up gives you a reason not to drive to work, because this difference-making fact is not a reason given by a rise in the price of gasoline. Whether the price of gasoline goes up or not, not driving to work will reduce air pollution.

Hence, the crucial issue in explaining the reason-giving force of rules is whether an action can make a distinctive difference in virtue of its being required by a rule. In Sect. 15.6 below, we will argue that it is possible to give an affirmative answer to this question. If so, rules will not differ so much from ordinary reason-giving facts. However, Raz seems to ignore this possibility and pursues another question: How can justification be content-independent? He says, "For a content-independent justification to be possible there must be reasons for an agent to behave in a certain way other than the value of the behavior in question" (Raz 2009, p. 212). In terms of the difference-making-based theory, this point can be put as follows: In order to explain the normativity, that is, the reason-giving force, of rules, we still have to appeal to some difference-making fact that obtains in virtue of rules, but this difference-making fact is not concerned with the evaluative difference made by the actions for which rules give reasons (the so-called "content-independence"). So we are back with the first question above: What kind of difference-making fact would it be?

Consider the content-independent justification for the club rule: the goodness of governing club affairs by rules issued by the committee. To see that it is good to regulate club affairs by rules, let us imagine a counterfactual situation: What would be different if the affairs of the club were not governed by rules? The social functions would be in chaos if it were left to each member to decide how many guests she/he were entitled to bring, or it would be controversial and inefficient if members had to coordinate the policy on the number of guests by means of bargaining with each other. Hence, in our view, what the content-independent justification of rules appeals to is nothing more than a difference-making fact that governing club affairs by rules will lead to some valuable consequence. Such a difference-making fact, which can be called an "*institution-involving difference-making fact*," is distinguished from "ordinary" ones in that its difference-maker is an institution (i.e., governing club affairs by rules) rather than an action.

15.5 The Breakdown of Transitivity in the Justification of Rules

Given that the content-independent justification appeals to the value of institution (the evaluative difference made by institution) rather than to the value of action, Raz claims that the most important feature of rules is the lack of transitivity in justification:

> As a rule, normative justification, and justification in general, are transitive. If A justifies B and B justifies C then A justifies C. So if there is reason to read the novel because it is a good novel, and if it is a good novel because it is insightful and subtle, then that it is insightful and subtle is reason to read it. … The opacity and content-independence of rules mean that transitivity does not hold. That it is good to uphold the authority of the committee is a reason for the validity of its rules, including the rule that one may not bring more than three guests to social functions of the club. But the desirability of upholding the authority of the committee is not a reason for not bringing more than three guest (not, that is, under this description). (Raz 2009, pp. 213–214)

The point of intransitivity in the justification of rules can be recast in the following claim: What accounts for the reason-giving force of the club's rules is not an action-involving difference-making fact but rather an institution-involving one; in other words, it does not point to the (evaluative) difference made by the actions required by the rules; therefore, it cannot directly be a reason to perform these actions.

If intransitivity indeed holds in the justification of rules, the formulation of the condition for the reason-giving force of rules in our first attempt appears not entirely correct. Before making a slight revision to our first formulation, however, we will examine the structure of Raz's "normative justification" in more detail.

Once again, we have to stress that Raz's characterization of normative justification will be more enlightening if reason-giving facts are distinguished from reasons. As argued above, a reason to read a novel is a difference-making fact, such as the fact that reading it will promote some value, which obtains in virtue of its insightfulness and subtlety. Therefore, in Raz's case, the fact that a novel is insightful and subtle is not a reason but gives one a reason to read it. The distinction between reasons and reason-giving facts is not a verbal one. Rather, it is significant for a more precise analysis of the structure of normative justification.

In fact, if the justifying relation in Raz's normative justification is interpreted as the explaining relation between reason-giving facts, difference-making facts, and ought facts, the breakdown of transitivity is not unique to rules but common to all reason-giving facts. As argued in Sect. 15.2, a reason-giving fact, since it is not a difference-making fact, cannot provide an inverted explanation of an ought fact. For example, the fact that tobacco contains toxic chemicals explains why smoking in a public place damages others' health, and the difference-making fact that smoking in a public place damages others' health provides an inverted explanation of why one ought not to smoke in a public place, but the fact that tobacco contains toxic chemicals on its own cannot explain this ought fact. In Raz's case, by the same token, the fact that a novel is insightful and subtle, because it does not show the difference that reading this novel will make, cannot directly explain why you ought to read it. The explaining relation between reason-giving facts, difference-making facts (reasons), and ought facts is thus intransitive: Even if a reason-giving fact P explains why a difference-making fact R obtains and R explains why A ought to φ, P by itself does not explain why A ought to φ.[3]

Perhaps the structure of Raz's normative justification is not intended to characterize the explaining relation, but rather to provide a general structure to account for the reason-giving force of a fact. But this general structure can also be viewed in terms of the explaining relation. As mentioned above, a reason-giving fact P alone cannot intelligibly explain why A ought to φ. There is an explanatory "jump" from P to the fact that A ought to φ. In order to eliminate this "jump," we have to add a difference-making fact R (A's φ-ing makes a difference to X), which obtains in virtue of P and provides an inverted explanation of why A ought to φ. Without this difference-making fact, which is a reason for A to φ, we cannot answer the question why P gives A a reason to φ. P explains why R obtains, and R is a normative reason for A to φ; therefore P gives A a reason to φ.

The general structure of normative justification can thus be formulated as follows:

[3] Raz seems to agree with the claim that the explaining relation is intransitive. He says (2011, p. 30), "[I]t is plausible to think that 'being an explanation of' is not a transitive relation. Sometimes even if C explains B and B explains A, C does not explain A."

> **(Normative Justification)** In virtue of the fact P, an *action-involving* difference-making fact R obtains, and R is a reason to φ, therefore P gives a reason to φ.

Let us take Raz's example to illustrate it. Because of its insightfulness and subtleness, reading a certain novel will lead to some valuable consequence. This evaluative difference-making fact is a reason for you to read it, therefore the fact that this novel is insightful and subtle gives you a reason to read it. Without the action-involving difference-making fact in question, we cannot explain why you have a reason to read this novel just because it is insightful and subtle.

It should be noted that Raz's characterization of intransitivity in the justification of rules has a structural problem. If the general structure of normative justification is formulated in the above way, a rule of which the reason-giving force is to be explained should play the role of the former term P in this structure, and the middle term R should be an action-involving difference-making fact that obtains in virtue of this rule. In Raz's characterization, however, the former term is an institution-involving difference-making fact, that is, it is good to uphold the authority of the committee, the middle term is that certain rules are valid (have binding force), and the consequence seems to be the fact that one has reason to do what these rules require.

But let us put aside this structural problem for a moment. As stated above, the insight of Raz's claim about intransitivity in the justification of rules is that the difference-making fact accounting for the reason-giving force of rules is an institution-involving one, which is not concerned with the evaluative difference made by the actions for which they give reasons and therefore cannot be a reason to perform these actions. If so, how can we deploy the general structure of normative justification to explain the reason-giving force of rules? This brings us back to the opaqueness of rules as reason-giving facts: How can we explain the reason-giving force of rules if we cannot show that an action makes a distinctive difference in virtue of its being required by a rule? In the following section, we will propose a solution to this problem.

15.6 A Difference-Based Account of the Reason-Giving Force of Rules

In our view, Raz might have exaggerated the significance of intransitivity. It is possible to transform an institution-involving difference-making fact into an action-involving one. In fact, Raz has suggested the possibility of this transformation, when he says that "all *prima facie* justifications are description-sensitive" (Raz 2009, pp. 210 fn. 12, 213 fn. 16). Precisely speaking, Raz's claim about content-independent justification is meant to indicate that the justification of a rule does not bear on the desirability of the action under the description in this rule, but he does admit that "the justification of rules bears on the desirability of actions required by the rules when they are described as 'actions required by the rule,' etc." (Raz 2009, p. 211 fn. 15).

The key point here is that the same action, as Davidson (1980, pp. 4–5) argues, can be described in various ways. For example, bringing no more than three guests can also be described as an action conforming to the club rule; smoking in a public place can also be described as an illegal act. Since the existence of rules makes it possible to describe the actions that fall under the rules as actions conforming to (or violating) the rules, the institution-involving difference-making fact that figures in a content-independent justification can be transformed into an action-involving one which has a rule-conforming action as its difference-maker. This action-involving difference-making fact constitutes a distinctive reason to perform a certain action if this action can be described as a rule-conforming one. Accordingly, an action *qua* rule-conforming action can make a difference that is distinct from other differences it makes.

For example, suppose the desirability of governing club affairs by rules consists in the fact that the club will run smoothly if its rules are followed. On this account, the institution-involving difference-making fact that figures in the content-independent justification of the club's rules can be transformed into an action-involving one, as follows:

(R*) Performing an action conforming to the club's rules makes a difference to the smooth operation of the club.

R* is obviously a reason for members to do any action required by the club's rules. It would not be a reason for a certain action if this action could not be described as one that conforms to the club's rules; therefore, it is a reason given by the club's rules.

There are two things to be noted, however. First, R* can account for the reason-giving force of various rules in a system, such as the rules of the chess club. As long as an action is required by some rule in this system and, accordingly, can be described as a rule-conforming action, R* constitutes a reason for this action, thereby explaining why this rule gives a reason to do it. To borrow Raz's phrase, the very same considerations can justify a variety of rules; they are in this sense content-independent (Raz 2009, p. 210). Furthermore, R* is concerned with the evaluative difference made by an action *qua* rule-conforming action instead of other differences made by this action under the description in the rule; therefore, R* constitutes a distinctive reason to do what the rules require.

Second, and more importantly, R* is a difference-making fact *in abstracto*. It cannot directly figure as a reason to bring no more than three guests, unless bringing no more than three guests can be described as an act conforming to the rule. At this point, Raz is correct when he says that "the lack of transitivity is that the reasons for the validity of the rule (in our phrase, the considerations that account for the reason-giving force of rules) are not in themselves reasons for performing the act required by the rule, as described in the rule" (Raz 2009, p. 210 fn. 12).

But this should not be a very serious obstacle. Whether R* can be a reason to perform a certain action depends on whether this action can be described as a rule-conforming one. Hence, for R* to be a reason to bring no more than three guests, it must be possible to describe "bringing no more than three guests" as a rule-conforming action. Such a description can be given precisely because there is a rule forbidding members to bring a fourth guest. In virtue of the existence of this rule, the act of bringing no more than three guests turns into the difference-maker in R*, and accordingly, a difference-making fact *in concreto* obtains:

(R) Bringing no more than three guests, as an act conforming to the club's rules, makes a difference to the smooth operation of the club.

R can be viewed as an instantiation of R*. R is a reason to bring no more than three guests and would not obtain if the three-guests-rule did not exist because, but for this rule, the act of bringing no more than three guests could not be described as a rule-conforming action and thereby would not make the difference that can be activated only by rule-conforming actions. Therefore, R is an action-involving difference-making fact that obtains in virtue of the existence of the three-guests-rule; in other words, it is a reason given by this rule.

On this construction, the account of the reason-giving force of rules still fits into the general structure of normative justification: Because there is a rule forbidding members to bring a fourth guest, the difference-making fact R obtains. R is a reason to bring no more than three guests; therefore, this rule gives members a reason to bring no more than three guests.

Now the condition for the reason-giving force of rules can be reformulated as follows:

(Reason-Giving Force of Rules: Second Attempt) The fact that a rule requires A to φ gives A a reason to φ if and only if, in virtue of this fact, A's φ-ing *qua an action conforming to the rule* makes a difference to X.

The second attempt differs from the first only in the qualifying phrase "*qua an action conforming to the rule.*" This qualification indicates that the difference made by A's φ-ing as a rule-conforming action is a distinctive one: A's φ-ing would not make such difference if it were not required by the rule; in other words, this difference is distinct from others that A's φ-ing could still make even if the rule did not exist. Hence, the difference-making fact in this formulation is a rule-given reason and can explain why the rule gives A a reason to φ.

Finally, the difference-making-based account of the normativity of rules invites us to reconsider Raz's *autonomy thesis*, which says: "[R]ules, at least man-made rules, make a difference to practical reasoning. … If valid, they constitute reasons which one would not have but for them" (Raz 2009, p. 214). In terms of rules as reason-giving facts, the autonomy thesis can be put the following way: No matter what reasons we have to do a certain action, the fact that it is required by a rule gives us another reason to do it, and this reason is distinguished from other reasons that we have for the same action.

In light of the difference-making-based account, it is quite clear why rules can affect the reasons one has in this way, because a difference-making fact that obtains in virtue of the existence of a rule—that is, a reason given by the rule—is not the same as other difference-making facts that obtain independently of the rule, even if both are reasons to do the action required by the rule.

Consider the smoking example: The fact that smoking in a public place damages others' health is a reason not to do it. If smoking in a public place is forbidden by the law, its being an illegal act will make another difference. The difference-making fact that performing a legal or illegal action will lead to a distinctive kind of difference, which might be termed "the legality-based difference,"[4] is another reason not to smoke in a public place. If there were no legal rules forbidding smoking in a public place, this act would not make the legality-based difference. In this case, we still have other reasons not to smoke in a public place because this action is able to make other differences, such as causing harm to others' health, but there would no longer be a law-given reason not to do it.

In this view, rules are "autonomous" in the following sense: The difference an action *qua* a rule-conforming action makes is distinguished from other differences it makes. Hence, a rule-given reason is distinct from other reasons that one has independently of rules. But we have to point out that the autonomy thesis in this sense can be generalized to apply to all reason-giving fact: Any reason-giving fact gives a distinctive reason that one would not have but for it.

To illustrate this, let us consider another example: Whether or not the price of gasoline goes up, driving to work will produce air pollution. This difference-making fact is also a reason not to drive to work, but it is given by the fact that cars emit exhaust, not by the fact that the price of gasoline goes up. If the price of gasoline goes up, you will have another reason not to drive to work, but this reason is different from the former one, because the fact that driving to work produces air pollution and the fact that driving to work leads to an increase in your gasoline expenses are two distinct difference-making facts; in other words, they are two different reasons. If the price of gasoline does not go up, driving to work will not make a difference to your gasoline expenses, but it still makes a difference to air pollution. In this case, although you have the former reason, which is given by the fact that cars emit exhaust, you do not have the latter reason not to drive to work. Therefore, the reason given by the fact that the price of gasoline goes up is distinguished from reasons given by other facts, and the same is true for the reason given by the fact that cars emit exhaust.

To sum up, if the normativity of rules is understood as their reason-giving force, an account of the normativity of rules has the same structure as that of the reason-giving force of ordinary facts. Rules differ from other reason-giving facts only in that the difference-making facts which obtain in virtue of rules are distinct from those that obtain in virtue of other reason-giving facts.[5]

---

[4] Note that the legality-based difference can be interpreted in different ways, such as avoiding a sanction, promoting the common good, or fulfilling the law's moral aim, but we will not pursue this issue here.

[5] One might think that rules still differ from other reason-giving facts in that what a rule gives is an *exclusionary reason*, i.e., a reason not to act for some conflicting reasons. See Raz (1999b, pp. 39–48, 73–80; 2009, p. 216). But the exclusionary character of rules concerns the relation among competing reasons and has less to do with the question of whether and how rules give reasons, so we will not deal with this issue here.

15.7 Conclusion

In this paper, we put forward a difference-making-based theory of reasons to argue that rules are not reasons but reason-giving facts. What distinguishes rules from other reason-giving facts is not their opaqueness, normative gaps, or the breakdown in transitivity, but rather the distinctive kind of difference an action makes in virtue of its being required by a rule. Instead of questioning whether rules are reasons, perhaps there are more interesting issues to be explored about the nature of difference-making facts that account for the normativity of rules.

Acknowledgments The authors would like to thank Richard Hou, Sermin Shei, and two anonymous reviewers of the Rules 2013 conference for helpful suggestions and comments. Funding for this study was supported by research grants of Taiwan National Science Council (NSC-100-2410-H-001-003-MY3, NSC-99–2420-H-194–137-MY3, NSC-100-2410-H-194-085-MY3).

References

Broome, John. 2004. Reasons. In *Reason and value. Themes from the moral philosophy of Joseph Raz*, ed. R. J. Wallace, P. Pettit, S. Scheffler, and M. Smith, 28–55. Oxford: Oxford University Press.
Davidson, Donald. 1980. *Essays on actions and events*. Oxford: Oxford University Press.
DeRose, Keith. 2010. The conditionals of deliberation. *Mind* 119:1–42.
Raz, Joseph. 1979. *The authority of law*. Oxford: Oxford University Press.
Raz, Joseph. 1999a. *Engaging reason*. Oxford: Oxford University Press.
Raz, Joseph. 1999b. *Practical reason and norms*. 3rd ed. Oxford: Oxford University Press.
Raz, Joseph. 2009. *Between authority and interpretation*. Oxford: Oxford University Press.
Raz, Joseph. 2011. *From normativity to responsibility*. Oxford: Oxford University Press.
Strevens, Michael. 2004. The causal and unification approaches to explanation unified—causally. *NOÛS* 38:154–176.

Chapter 16
Rules, Conventionalism and Normativity: Some Remarks Starting from Hart

Aldo Schiavello

Abstract The paper deals with the "conventionalist turn" in legal positivism in relation to the matter of the duty to obey the law and legal normativity. In this respect, conventionalist legal positivism is worth considering (a) because it offers an explanation of legal normativity partly different vis-à-vis previous ones and (b) because it tries to preserve the autonomy of legal obligation from moral obligation and coercion, respectively. Here I will only focus on legal conventionalism as sketched out by Hart in the *Postscript*. Indeed, Hart's conventionalism comes up against problems which to some extent also affect other distinguished versions of legal conventionalism like, for example, those worked out by Jules Coleman, Andrei Marmor and Scott Shapiro. Other "stronger" versions of legal conventionalism like, for example, those advanced by Chaim Gans and Gerald Postema, succeed in avoiding some of the traps into which the previous ones fall but, paraphrasing Hart, the outcome is distortion as the price of internal coherence. To sum up, legal conventionalism follows two pathways, both of them in the end unsatisfactory. The first pathway—opened up by Hart—leads to a "weak" version of conventionalism. This approach fails insofar as it does not succeed in preserving the autonomy of legal obligation from moral. The second pathway—followed in different ways by Gans and Postema—does not soften conventionalism and so it achieves the outcome of designing a coherent conventionalist model of legal normativity but at the price of distorting reality.

Keywords Legal positivism · Legal conventionalism · Normativity · Justificatory reasons · Law and morals

16.1 Introduction

This paper deals with the "conventionalist turn" in legal positivism (Green 1999, pp. 35–52) in relation to the matter of the duty to obey the law and legal normativity.

In this respect, conventionalist legal positivism is worth considering (a) because it offers an explanation of legal normativity that is partly different vis-à-vis previous

A. Schiavello (✉)
University of Palermo, Palermo, Italy
e-mail: aldo.schiavello@unipa.it

M. Araszkiewicz et al. (eds.), *Problems of Normativity, Rules and Rule-Following*, Law and Philosophy Library 111, DOI 10.1007/978-3-319-09375-8_16

ones and (b) because it tries to preserve the autonomy of legal obligation from moral obligation and coercion, respectively. Here I will mainly focus on legal conventionalism as sketched out by Hart in the *Postscript*. Indeed, Hart's conventionalism comes up against problems that to some extent also affect many versions of legal conventionalism like, for example, those championed by Jules Coleman (2001), Andrei Marmor (1996, pp. 349–371, 2001a, b, pp. 193–217, 2009) and Scott Shapiro (2011).

Other "stronger" versions of legal conventionalism like, for example, those defended by Chaim Gans (1981) and Gerald Postema (1982), succeed in avoiding some of the traps into which the previous ones fall but, paraphrasing Hart, the outcome is distortion as the price of internal coherence.

To sum up, legal conventionalism follows two pathways, both of them are in the end unsatisfactory. The first pathway—opened up by Hart—leads to a "weak" version of conventionalism. This approach fails insofar as it does not succeed in preserving the autonomy of legal obligation from moral. The second pathway—followed in different ways by Gans and Postema—does not soften conventionalism and so it achieves the outcome of designing a coherent conventionalist model of legal normativity but at the price of distorting reality.

16.2 Three Models of Legal Normativity

The debate on legal normativity deals with law's capability to provide reasons justifying action (Raz 1990; Raz 2009, pp. 186–189; Nino 1984, pp. 489–490). The term 'reason' is an ambiguous one: it means either 'explanation' or 'justification'. To clearly distinguish these two meanings is a hard task and I will not go further into this point here. Suffice it to observe that a clear link exists between the couples *explanation/justification* and *external/internal point of view* (Hart 1994, pp. 56–57, 79–91). A reason is a justification for those who accept it as a good reason or a valid one to believe or do something (Scanlon 1998, p. 17). Therefore, a reason justifies beliefs and behaviors for those who adopt an internal perspective towards it. Conversely, the very same reason is just an explanation of other beliefs and behaviors for those who adopt an external perspective towards it. Be it as it may, the debate on legal normativity revolves around the following question: is the law a reason justifying action?

All the (affirmative) answers to this question focus on the relationship between law and coercion on one side and law and morals on the other. In this regard, there are three possible options: (a) the normativity of law depends on coercion (John Austin's gunman model); (b) the normativity of law depends on moral reasons (natural law doctrine, but also some legal positivists like Joseph Raz and Carlos Nino); (c) the normativity of law is autonomous from both coercion and moral reasons and must be linked to "legal reasons." "Conventionalist" legal positivism corresponds to the latter option.

On the basis of the first model, law would be a prudential reason affecting the hierarchical order of the preferences of individuals through the threat of the use of force. With rare exceptions, human beings prefer to keep their money for themselves rather than hand it over to others. The robber's gun pointed at an individual's head changes the latter's preferences: he will prefer to forego his money in order to save his life. Law, for those who adopt this model, works in a similar way: nobody would pay taxes if there were not severe penalties for tax evasion.

The remaining two models have in common the fact that they share the refusal of the gunman model. The main limit of the latter is failing to perceive a crucial difference between legal norms and the gunman's orders. The gunman, through threats, induces particular behavior but does not make that behavior obligatory in a strict sense. It is correct to say that a bank cashier that undergoes a robbery "has been forced" or even "obliged" to hand over the money, but not that he "had the obligation" to hand over the money. Law, by contrast, seems to be able to produce genuine obligations. This is also proved by the fact that, in relation to the prescriptions laid down by legal norms, expressions like "has the obligation to …" or "must …" from a semantic point of view are perfectly adequate. According to the supporters of the last two models this means that the normativity of law cannot be based upon prudential reasons but must be linked to moral reasons or, alternatively, to legal reasons.

Here I will only deal with the conventionalist conception of legal normativity.[1]

In the next section I will highlight the main reasons which caused the conventionalist turn of (part of) contemporary legal positivism; then, I will look more deeply into the main features of Hart's conventionalist conception of legal normativity in the *Postscript*; with this done, I will deal with the flaws of this conception. Finally, in the conclusive section I will present a summary critical analysis of the versions of "hard" conventionalism respectively proposed by Gans and Postema.

16.3 Hart's Conception of Legal Normativity Before the Conventionalist Turn: An Outline

In *The Concept of Law*, Hart supports a theory of social rules whose aim is to distinguish social rules from mere habits. One of the sharper criticisms that Hart makes of John Austin's imperativism is precisely not having taken into account the relevance of this distinction and, as a consequence, having overlooked the concept of norm. "The root cause of [Austin's] failure", Hart observes, "is that the elements out of which the theory was constructed, viz. the ideas of orders, obedience, habits, and threats, do not include, and cannot by their combination yield the idea of a rule, without which we cannot hope to elucidate even the most elementary forms of law" (Hart 1994, p. 97).

[1] For a detailed analysis of all these three options see Schiavello (2010, pp. 39–89).

Social rules, unlike habits, in addition to regularity of convergent behaviors, also present an internal aspect: "what is necessary is a critical reflective attitude to certain patterns of behavior as a common standard, and that this should display itself in criticism (including self-criticism), demands for conformity and in acknowledgements that such criticism and demands are justified, all of which find their characteristic expression in the normative terminology of 'ought', 'must', and 'should', 'right' and 'wrong'" (Hart 1994, p. 57).

For Hart, the rule of recognition, the "rule of rules" identifying the validity criterion of other legal norms, is a social rule. The acceptance of a rule of recognition does not necessarily imply moral acceptance, but only a reflective critical attitude that is empirically verifiable by analysing the linguistic expressions that go with legal obligations and by observing that officials, in particular judges, act in accordance with the rule.

According to Hart, the rule of recognition is, at one and the same time, the norm closing the system and the basis of legal obligation. Hence the definitive answer to the question: "why do we have to do what the law prescribes?" will be "because a social rule exists that obliges us to do what the law prescribes". The practice theory of norms tells us that a rule of recognition exists when it is accepted (at least) by officials and by judges in particular. This ontological claim on law—that is to say, the claim that the rule of recognition and, more in general, the law of a community is determined by the attitudes and convergent behaviors of the participants, and of judges in particular—has some implications at a methodological or meta-theoretical level: law is a fact that can be described in a non-evaluative way looking at the attitudes and convergent behaviors of the participants (neutrality thesis). Hart (1994, p. 244) also confirms this conviction in the *Postscript*: "Description may still be description, even if what is described is an evaluation."

Starting from the theory of social rules, Hart also works out his general theory of legal obligation. According to Hart, the existence of a social rule is a necessary condition and yet not a sufficient condition for a determined behavior to be configured in terms of obligation: if a person has an obligation to do something, then it will always be possible to trace a social rule at the basis of this obligation; nevertheless, not every social rule is a mark of the existence of an obligation. Hart highlights three conditions that, together with the existence of a social rule, make it possible to reconstruct a certain behavior in terms of obligation (see also Hacker 1977, pp. 12–18; Lagerspetz 1995, pp. 141–146; Schiavello 2013, pp. 69–73).

The first is that there should be an "insistent general demand for conformity" to the model of conduct prescribed by the rules and a "great social pressure" on those people whose behavior configures a deviation from this model.

The second condition is that "the rules supported by this serious pressure are thought important because they are believed to be necessary to the maintenance of social life or some highly prized feature of it" (Hart 1994, p. 87). As Neil MacCormick observes, "obligations depend, at least in part, on degrees of importance of rules" (MacCormick 1986, p. 133).

The third and last condition is that the behavior that shapes the fulfilment of an obligation should imply a sacrifice or a renouncement and, accordingly, there is a "standing possibility of conflict" between the obligation on one side and personal interest on the other (Mackie 1977, pp. 105–107).

To sum up, according to Hart, the ultimate foundation of legal obligation is the rule of recognition, which is a social rule. The existence of a social rule depends on its acceptance by a group of individuals as a criterion of behavior. Acceptance of a social rule as a criterion of behavior implies (a) that this rule is generally obeyed, (b) that its application is prescribed and (c) that behaviors different from what is prescribed are criticized.

According to Hart, legal obligation is grounded on the social rule that arrests the infinite regress of the chain of validity of law. The definitive answer to the question "why do we have to do what law prescribes?" will therefore be "because a social rule exists forcing us to do what the law prescribes." As María Cristina Redondo puts it:

> the fact that the majority of the norms of a system must be applied because this is imposed by other norms presupposes the fact that the latter norms, which prescribe the application of other norms, must be applied in virtue of a practice. *In other words, from this positivist perspective, a distinctive trait of every existing legal system is constituted by the fact that the norms that form it must only be applied because, in the last resort, they are founded on social rules*. (Redondo 1999, p. 209 italics added; see also Hart 1982, pp. 153–161; Bayón 2000, pp. 326–327 and Bulygin 2007, pp. 173–186)

The idea underlying this claim is that the acceptance of a norm is a mental or interior act and, as such, is not relevant to the justification of a given behavior. As Hart (1994, p. 57) puts it, "…feelings are neither necessary nor sufficient for the existence of 'binding' rules". Elsewhere Hart (1994, p. 203, italics added) is even clearer:

> Not only may vast numbers be coerced by laws which they do not regard as morally binding, but it is not even true that those who do accept the system voluntarily, must conceive of themselves as morally bound to do so, though the system will be most stable when they do so. *In fact, their allegiance to the system may be based on many different considerations: calculation of long-term interest; disinterested interest in others; an unreflecting inherited or traditional attitude; or the mere wish to do as others do*.

So, a legal norm can be accepted for prudential or moral reasons, just as a moral norm can be accepted for moral reasons, for prudential reasons or for reasons of simple conformism. What counts, in order to justify an action, is the nature of the norm that is adopted as a model of conduct: if it is a legal norm, then we find ourselves facing a legal obligation; if instead it is a moral norm, then we find ourselves facing a moral obligation. This implies that in justifying an action it is not possible to go beyond the norm that is adopted as a model of conduct. It is appropriate to specify that setting a social rule, and hence a social practice, at the basis of the legal obligation does not necessarily involve a violation of Hume's law. In relation to a social fact like the existence of a social rule two different attitudes can be imagined. One is the theoretical and descriptive attitude of the observer. The other is instead the normative attitude of the person who takes the internal point of view and derives normative judgments not from a social fact but from his or her own "practical engagement with descriptive facts" (Shapiro 2011, pp. 99–101).

16.4 What Is Wrong with Hart's Theory of Legal Normativity

For Hart, the existence of a legal obligation implies the possibility of identifying a social rule at the bottom of this obligation. Starting from this insight, on the one hand, Hart criticizes Austin who, by reducing the law to orders backed up by threats, fails to distinguish instances in which there is an obligation to do something from instances in which one is forced or compelled to do something; on the other hand, Hart claims that it is possible to distinguish legal obligation from moral obligation in that the source of an obligation of the first type is a legal rule, while the source of a moral obligation is a moral rule.

The main criticisms of this claim challenge precisely the possibility of distinguishing legal obligation from moral obligation starting from the idea of social rule (Dworkin 1978, pp. 46–80 and Dworkin 2006, pp. 223–240).

Hart's fundamental mistake would then be that of believing that an obligation necessarily presupposes the existence of a social rule. A vegetarian could affirm that a duty exists not to eat any living being even in the lack of a social rule that effectively prescribes a model of conduct of this kind.

What this example is meant to show is that the sources of obligations are not social rules but moral rules, rules of individual critical morality, that is rules which are not necessarily *also* social rules. If this is true, it follows that the only genuine obligations are moral obligations and therefore, in spite of what Hart affirms, that it is not possible to distinguish legal obligations from moral obligations.

Against this objection one could concede that in some cases, like the case of the vegetarian, the practice theory of norms, which sets up a conceptual link between the existence of an obligation and the existence of a social rule, is not appropriate, and nevertheless continue to state it in connection with those cases in which the generalized agreement on the existence of a certain obligation is somehow connected to the existence of a problem of coordination: to solve a problem of coordination presupposes an agreement, in a broad sense, between those people that find themselves involved in this problem and, consequently, the agreement (which can consist in acceptance of a social rule) becomes at least a necessary condition for the existence of an obligation.

In relation to these cases, it seems reasonable to believe that a social rule can justify certain behaviors. For instance, a social rule that prescribes driving on the right (or, alternatively, on the left) is what is needed for coordinating the traffic. In connection with cases of this kind, the practice theory seems to maintain a certain plausibility: after all, what "obliges us" to drive on the right side except the existence of a social rule that gives the necessary salience to this practice?

The hallmark of these cases is what I call, following Bruno Celano, "dependence condition" (Celano 1995, pp. 35–87, 2003, pp. 347–360). As I will clarify in the next section, it is crucial to specify that the dependence condition can be seen in a strong sense or a weak sense. If it is maintained that the only reason that an individual has for considering a social rule as a model of conduct is that the other members of the group also consider it as such, then the dependence condition is seen in a strong sense (like in the case of a pure coordination problem); if instead it is maintained that general conformity of the members of the group is only one reason for the acceptance of a rule, then the dependence condition is seen in a weak sense.

At this point, Hart's next step is to show that the rule of recognition is a conventional rule. He attempts to do this in the "Postscript" to the second edition of *The Concept of Law*.

16.5 The Origin the "Conventionalist Turn" in Legal Positivism

In the "Postscript", though conceding to Dworkin that the practice theory is not acceptable as a general theory of obligation, Hart maintains that it continues to be correct in relation to conventional rules and that the rule of recognition is a conventional rule.

Hart, influenced by the argumentative route dictated by Dworkin (Dickson 2007, pp. 382–386), affirms that the rule of recognition is a conventional rule, in the sense that its compulsoriness for each judge is also necessarily linked to the fact that it is considered mandatory by the judicial class as a whole.

The passages in the *Postscript* that are relevant for characterizing Hart's conception of legal obligation as conventionalist are in the third section, entitled "The Nature of Rules", and in the fourth section, entitled "Principles and the Rule of Recognition."

In the third section, after conceding to Dworkin that the scope of his theory of obligation must be restricted, Hart nevertheless maintains that it applies to conventional rules, and adds that the rule of recognition is a conventional rule. He offers the following definition of conventional rule:

> Rules are conventional social practices if the general conformity of a group to them is *part* of the reasons which its individual members have for acceptance…. (Hart 1994, pp. 255, italics added)

In what sense is the rule of recognition a conventional rule? Hart gives the following answer to this question in the fourth section:

> Certainly the rule of recognition is treated in my book as resting on a conventional form of judicial consensus. That it does so rest seems quite clear in English and American law for surely an English judge's reason for treating Parliament's legislation (or an American judge's reason for treating the Constitution) as a source of law having supremacy over sources *includes* the fact that his judicial colleagues concur in this as they predecessors have done. (Hart 1994, pp. 266–267, italics added)

The fact that Hart considers "general conformity" to a conventional rule only "part of the" reasons for accepting it shows that he accepts the dependence condition in a weak sense; this means that his theory of obligation cannot be considered an alternative to the model of the gunman and the model of morality. At this point it is already possible to understand Hart's worry, which is reported by Nicola Lacey's

(2004, p. 335) biography, that any change he made to the original version of the theory of obligation would force him to forego the autonomy of legal obligation.

This worry induces Hart to reemphasize in the *Postscript* the claim originally defended. In brief, according to Hart, it is not correct to attribute hierarchical superiority to any of the reasons for accepting a conventional rule with respect to acceptance by the other participants:

> Plainly a society may have rules accepted by its members which are morally iniquitous, such as rules prohibiting persons of certain colour from using public facilities such as parks or bathing beaches. Indeed, even the weaker condition that for the existence of a social rule it must only be the case that participants must *believe* that there are good moral grounds for conforming to it is far too strong as a general condition for the existence of social rules. [...] Of course a conventional rule may both be and be believed to be morally sound and justified. But when the question arises as to why those who have accepted conventional rules as a guide to their behavior or as standards of criticism have done so I see no reason for selecting from the many answers to be given [...] a belief in the moral justification of rules as the sole possible or adequate answer. (Hart 1994, p. 257, italics in the original)

Hence for Hart the reasons that can induce acceptance of a social rule are manifold, in many respects are unfathomable and are all on the same plane. In this respect, the only significant difference between the original edition and the "Postscript" is that in this posthumous work Hart further clarifies the idea that, in the case of social rules, acceptance by the other members of the group is a necessary reason for the existence of an obligation.

As already mentioned, similar limits afflict other versions of weak conventionalism. Shapiro's *Legality* is perhaps the most ambitious attempt to propose a reconstruction of law in a conventionalist key. In brief, Shapiro proposes a theory of law founded on the notion of "plan" worked out by Michael Bratman (1999). To use Shapiro's words, "the main idea behind the Planning Theory of Law is that the exercise of legal authority, which I will refer to as 'legal activity', is an activity of social planning. Legal institutions plan for the communities over whom they claim authority, both by telling their members what they may or may not do and by authorizing some of these members to plan for others" (Shapiro 2011, p. 195; see Schiavello 2013, pp. 80–86).

A legal system is therefore a highly sophisticated planning organization and is composed by a master plan shared by a group of planners and by the norms (subplans, mainly) that this group adopts and applies. There are five characteristics, according to Shapiro, that make it possible to distinguish law from other planning activities: "a group of individuals are engaged in legal activity whenever their activity of social planning is shared, official, institutional, compulsory, self-certifying, and has a moral aim" (Shapiro 2011, p. 225). In relationship to the normativity of law, the last characteristic is important.

The law is a planning activity the main aim of which is that of solving the moral problems that arise inside society in the most appropriate way possible. We do not only expect the law to coordinate actions in one way or another, but alsoto choose the morally correct solution. This characteristic makes it possible to distinguish law from phenomena that are in many respects similar like organized crime. The point is not that legal activity is connoted by being morally correct while that of an organization like the mafia is not; the difference consists, rather, in the fact that the law has the necessary purpose of morally organizing a society correctly, while this is not the purpose of a criminal association (see also Alexy 1989, pp. 167–183).

However, if this is true, the rational constraints that force us not to break away from a plan once it has been adopted do not authorize us to put in brackets the moral reasons that have led to that plan being adopted. In conclusion, Shapiro simply presents a sophisticated version of the dependence condition in a weak sense. Hence in this case too the desire to distinguish justifying the obligation to obey the law on the basis of non-moral reasons is only very partially satisfied.

16.6 The "Conventionalist Turn" Taken Seriously (and its Limits)

There are two salient characteristics of a genuinely conventionalist conception of legal obligation.

The first is identification of the peculiar function of law in the resolution of coordination problems, mainly seen in a narrow sense. A typical coordination problem is a case of strategic interaction in which (a) it pays all the individuals involved to cooperate rather than not to cooperate; (b) the preference granted by an agent to one action rather than to another depends on the fact that the other agents too prefer the same action (we should not overlook the connection between this characteristic and the dependence condition), (c) there exist at least two possible combinations of actions that the agents substantially set on the same plane as a solution to the coordination problem.

The second characteristic is the necessary link between legal obligation and the capacity of law to resolve coordination problems. This characteristic implies acceptance of the dependence condition seen in a strong sense: the only reason to consider a legal norm as a model of conduct is the fact that the other individuals too consider it such. In other words, what counts is solving the problem, not how it is solved. In relation to law, this implies that the importance of the content of the norms is reduced while there is emphasis on the importance of the formal mechanisms (of the criteria that revolve around the *pedigree*, Dworkin would say) making it possible to identify in a certain and easy way what the legal norms are and what they prescribe.

These are demanding characteristics and indeed in the literature, there are very few conceptions of legal obligation able to satisfy them. Here I will limit myself to presenting a brief critical analysis of the two most interesting versions, worked out respectively by Chaim Gans and Gerald Postema. The conceptions of legal obligation put forward by these two authors, though they share the same basic assumptions, are very different from one another.

Gans holds out a conception of legal obligation founded on the notion of coordinative authority. He makes a very broad analysis, which also applies to law insofar as law is a coordinative authority. Gans identifies two recurrent characteristics making it possible to maintain that all legal systems are coordinative authorities.

The first characteristic is that when we wonder, for practical purposes, whether a legal obligation exists and what its sphere of application is, we necessarily have in mind a legal system in force. In other words, discourses with practical aims on legal obligation imply an effective legal system in the background. This does not hold, for instance, for moral obligation. When it is maintained that a behavior or an action is morally obligatory, this is done in the abstract, that is to say aside from the fact that the moral norm and/or the moral system as a whole from which the moral obligation in question springs are indeed in force, are shared, in a given spatio-temporal sphere.

The second characteristic is the "completeness" of legal systems: law regulates all aspects of social life and claims to be superordinate to all other norms or systems of norms.

These two characteristics, common to all legal systems, make law the normative system that is most able to produce coordination of actions and, accordingly, "it is therefore most reasonable that a system of concordant expectations will evolve round this system, producing co-ordination" (Gans 1981, p. 342). The central thesis upheld by Gans (1981, p. 335) is that "… Co-ordination […] comes to obligate acts specified in legal rules in defiance of at least some sorts of reasons for action."

A weak point of the conception of legal obligation put forward by Gans is the distinction between external aims and values on one side and instrumental aims on the other. He clarifies this distinction through an example. Knives have the instrumental purpose of cutting; this constitutive characteristic of knives then makes it possible to pursue external purposes like cutting bread, meat or people's throats. Equally, coordination is the instrumental objective of law, through which it is possible to pursue external values like social justice and internal safety, but also the extermination of other nations or internal minorities. Just as the capacity of knives to cut takes on a positive or negative connotation according to the external goal for which they are used, so the ability of law to coordinate actions takes on practical importance, is a reason for action, only for those people who share the external aims that it pursues. This conclusion weakens the genuinely conventionalist nature of legal obligation and the autonomy of the latter in relation to moral obligation.

The model of legal obligation delineated by Postema springs more directly from the debate on the *practice theory of norms* discussed in the previous sections and it is an attempt to shelter legal conventionalism from Dworkin's criticisms. "The crucial insight of [Hart's rule of recognition]", Postema observes (1982, p. 166), "is that law rests, at its foundations, on a special and complex custom or convention." "This notion of convention", he adds (Postema 1982, italics in the original), "when properly understood, successfully bridges the gap between social fact and genuine obligation […], because a convention is both to social fact and a framework of reasons for action."

According to Postema, in law, coordination problems appear at three different levels. The first level identifies those coordination problems whose existence is independent of law and that law has the task of resolving in an authoritative way; the other two levels identify coordination problems that arise in the context of the interpretation/application of law and concern, respectively, officials and citizens (second level) or only officials (third level).

Postema expressly maintains that his conventionalist conception of legal obligation exclusively applies to officials and, in particular, to judges. This, by itself, it is a serious limit to this conception of legal obligation, even if one considers it plausible for the rest. A conventionalist conception of legal obligation limited to officials is *not* a conventionalist conception of legal obligation, precisely because it says nothing about the reasons for citizens to obey the law. In brief, insofar as Postema links citizens' obligation principally to the moral correctness of legal norms, then his conception of obligation is a version of the moral model. If instead he broadens the role of the sanction, then his conception of obligation veers toward the gunman model.

Despite the differences, both the conceptions of legal obligation presented here are affected by serious defects that lead one to reject once and for all an explanation of legal obligation in a genuinely conventionalist key.

The reductionistic operation on the basis of which law is given the exclusive (or at least greatly prominent) task of resolving coordination problems is already suspicious at first sight.

Ultimately, an analysis of the proposal of reducing law to machinery that solves coordination problems, carried out starting from the versions of legal obligation proposed respectively by Gans and Postema, supports the initial suspicion. Without considering anything else, the obvious difficulty that both authors come up against by isolating legal evaluations (referable to law's function of solving coordination problems) from moral evaluations (concerning the justice or correctness of the content of norms) is a crucial sign of the implausibility of this reductionistic operation.

Gans also emphasizes that coordinative authority is chosen, and has to be chosen, because of its characteristics of excellence; as Raz puts it, an authority is legitimate if it is legitimate to presume that one is more likely to do the correct thing by following its directives rather than by acting according to one's own mind. Nevertheless, if things are so, the solutions to the problem that authority is called on to settle are not equivalent and, in conclusion, the problem is not a coordination problem in a strict sense. To give an example, we are not indifferent to whether law allows women to abort or not; we are not satisfied with law giving us a clear directive, but also want it to give us the directive that is just, i.e. that we deem to be just.

As we have seen, Postema maintains that law is a reason for action by citizens insofar as it incorporates and defends moral principles and values accepted by them. Hence it is Postema himself that recognizes that, in the case of citizens, legal obligation is not independent of moral obligation. Regarding the obligation of officials to respect the interpretative conventions of the second and third levels, on one hand, Postema claims that, beginning from a given conception of the political responsibility of judges, this obligation is independent of the content of the existing conventions and therefore proves to be independent of a moral obligation that could consist, for instance, in adopting the interpretation of law considered just on the basis of given moral parameters. On the other hand, he is forced to concede scope to morality, granting that evaluations of a moral type can influence *ex ante*, that is to say before an interpretative convention is consolidated, orienting the choice towards one of the possible interpretations of a disposition and, *ex post*, to the extent that it is the interpretative convention itself that grants exercise of discretion to the interpreter. The rather large scope that Postema assigns to moral evaluations in the legal sphere clearly clashes with the thesis that the principal function of law is to solve coordination problems in a strict sense. Then the fact that Postema (1987, p. 311 ff.; 1989, pp. 50–56; 2004, pp. 203–226; 2008, pp. 41–55) over the years has weakened this thesis is a sign, together with others, of its limited plausibility.

To conclude, the conventional nature of the rule of recognition is not strong enough to warrant the autonomy of legal obligation with respect to moral obligation. The only way conventionalism can preserve the autonomy of legal obligation is to treat the rule of recognition as a convention in the manner of Lewis, making it possible to solve coordination problems seen in a narrow sense. In relation to a typical coordination problem it is indifferent what solution is selected; the important thing is that all converge towards the same solution. In other words, in order to be effective, the conventionalist turn should adopt the dependence condition in the strongest version. In this way, it would effectively be possible to distinguish legal obligation from moral obligation: the normativity of law would not depend on its capacity to ensure a morally appreciable social order, but on its capacity to solve coordination problems.

However, this version of conventionalism does not appear very plausible. The fact is that it is not enough for us that the law should coordinate social action in one way or another, since we desire that it should do so in the correct way. As Shapiro, among others, notices, a constitution is not generally considered an arbitrary solution that can be replaced by another text at any moment; on the contrary, many believe that "the text of the Constitution is sacred and that they had a moral obligation to heed it, regardless of what everyone else did" (Shapiro 2011, p. 109). Strong conventionalism could then guarantee the autonomy of legal obligation but only at the price of a serious distortion of reality.

Acknowledgment The Author is grateful to the anonymous referees for their comments to a previous version of this paper. He also warmly thanks the participants in the conference "Rules 2013"—Jagiellonian University, Krakow, 27–29 September 2013, for their observations and comments. Last but not least, he is particularly grateful to Stefano Bertea for his comments and observations to a previous version of this paper.

References

Alexy, Robert. 1989. On necessary relations between law and morality. *Ratio Juris* 2 (2): 167–183.

Bayón, Juan Carlos. 2000. Deber jurídico. In *El derecho y la justicia,* ed. Valdés. Ernesto Garzón and Francisco J. Laporta, 313–331. Madrid: Editorial Trotta.

Bratman, Michael E. 1999. *Intention, plans and practical reason.* Stanford: Center for the Study of Language and Information.

Bulygin, Eugenio. 2007. *Il positivismo giuridico* (It. trans. P. Chiassoni, R. Guastini, G. B. Ratti). Milano: Giuffrè.

Celano, Bruno. 1995. Consuetudini, convenzioni. In *Analisi e diritto 1995. Ricerche di giurisprudenza analitica,* ed. Paolo Comanducci and Riccardo Guastini, 35–87. Torino: Giappichelli.

Celano Bruno. 2003. La regola di riconoscimento è una convenzione? *Ragion Pratica* 21:347–360.

Coleman, Jules Leslie. 2001. *The practice of principle. In defense of a pragmatist approach to legal theory*. Oxford: Oxford University Press.

Dickson, Julie. 2007. Is the rule of recognition really a conventional rule? *Oxford Journal of Legal Studies* 27 (3): 373–402.

Dworkin, Ronald. 1978. *Taking rights seriously*. Cambridge: Harvard University Press.

Dworkin, Ronald. 2006. *Justice in robes*. Cambridge: The Belknap Press of Harvard University Press.

Gans, Chaim. 1981. The normativity of law and its co-ordinative function. *Israel Law Review* 16 (3): 333–349.

Green, Leslie. 1999. Positivism and conventionalism. *Canadian Journal of Law and Jurisprudence* 12 (1): 35–52.

Hacker, Peter M. S. 1977. Hart's philosophy of law. In *Law, morality, and society. Essays in honour of H. L. A. Hart,* ed. Peter M. S. Hacker and Joseph Raz, 1–25. Oxford: Clarendon.

Hart, Herbert L. A. 1982. Legal duty and obligation. In Id., *Essays on Bentham. studies in jurisprudence and political theory*, 127–161. Oxford: Oxford University Press.

Hart, Herbert L. A. 1994. *The concept of law*. 2nd ed. with Postscript, eds. Penelope A. Bulloch and Joseph Raz. Oxford: Clarendon (1st. ed. 1961).

Lacey, Nicola. 2004. *A life of H. L. A. hart*. The Nightmare and the Noble Dream. Oxford: Oxford University Press.

Lagerspetz, Eerik. 1995. *The opposite mirrors. An essay on the conventionalist theory of institutions*. Dordrecht: Kluwer.

MacCormick, Neil. 1986. Law, morality and positivism. In *An institutional theory of law. New approaches to legal positivism,* ed. Neil MacCormick and Ota Weinberger, 127–144. Dordrecht: Reidel.

Mackie, John L. 1977. *Ethics. Inventing Rights and Wrong*. Harmondsworth: Penguin Books.

Marmor, Andrei. 1996. On convention. *Synthese* 107:349–371.

Marmor, Andrei. 2001a. *Positive law and objective values*. Oxford: Clarendon.

Marmor, Andrei. 2001b. Legal conventionalism. In *Hart's postscript. Essays on the postscript to the concept of law,* ed. Jules L. Coleman, 193–217. Oxford: Oxford University Press.

Marmor, Andrei. 2009. *Social conventions: from language to law*. Princeton Monographs in Philosophy Series, Princeton: Princeton University Press.

Nino, Carlos Santiago. 1984. Legal norms and reasons for action. *Rechtstheorie* 15:489–502.

Postema, Gerald J. 1982. Coordination and convention at the foundations of law. *Journal of Legal Studies* 11:165–203.

Postema, Gerald J. 1987. "Protestant" interpretation and social practices. *Law and Philosophy* 6 (3): 283–319.

Postema, Gerald J. 1989. Bentham on the public character of law. *Utilitas* 1:41–61.

Postema, Gerald J. 2004. Melody and law's mindfulness of time. *Ratio Juris* 17 (2): 203–226.

Postema, Gerald J. 2008. Salience reasoning. *Topoi* 27: 41–55.

Raz, Joseph. 1990. *Practical reason and norms (with a new postscript)*. 1st edn. Oxford: Oxford University Press (1975).

Raz, Joseph. 2009. Reasons: Explanatory and normative. In *New essays in the explanation of action,* ed. Constantine Sandis, 184–202. Basingstoke: Palgrave Macmillan.

Redondo, María Cristina. 1999. Sulla rilevanza pratica del diritto. *Ragion Pratica* 13:203–218.

Scanlon, Thomas. 1998. *What we owe to each other*. Cambridge: The Belknap Press of Harvard University Press.

Schiavello, Aldo. 2010. *Perchè obbedire al diritto? La risposta convenzionalista ed i suoi limiti*. Pisa: ETS.

Schiavello, Aldo. 2013. Rule of recognition, convention and obligation. What shapiro can still learn from hart's mistakes. In *The planning theory of law. A critical reading,* ed. Damiano Canale and Giovanni Tuzet, 65–87. Dordrecht: Springer.

Shapiro, Scott J. 2011. *Legality*. Cambridge: The Belknap Press of Harvard University Press.

Chapter 17
Are Fundamental Legal Reasons Internal? A Few Remarks on the Hartian Idea of the Internal Point of View

Adam Dyrda

Abstract The fundamental reasons for officials to apply the criteria of validity available within the system's rule of recognition, according to a basic reading of *The Concept of Law*, could be of various provenience (moral, conventional, traditional, other). However, to think of these criteria as genuine reasons it must be supposed that they are internal reasons that refer to agents' motivational set. In this paper, the idea of the internal point of view is juxtaposed with the notion of "internal reason" as introduced by B. Williams. It is argued that if fundamental legal reasons are to be normative (authoritative)—at least in a conceptual sense—they must be internal reasons, which are moral in character. It is just another way to build an argument that Hart simply presented an "over-weak" theory of the internal point of view.

Keywords Internal reasons · External reasons · B. Williams · Internal point of view · H.L.A. Hart · Legal positivism

17.1 Introduction

There is an old philosophical claim (i.a. ascribed by S. Kierkegaard to G. W. F. Hegel) according to which what is "inner" turns out to be "outer," and vice versa (Kierkegaard 2011). This claim cannot, however, be interpreted independently of the discussion on the role of dialectics in metaphysical investigations and cannot be considered as a premise in an argument against the potential usefulness of this distinction in other fields of philosophy. It seems that the strict, analytical distinction between these two categories—the inner (the internal) and the outer (the external)—could be very useful, especially in such fields as the investigation of human motivation, knowledge, truth and practical reasoning. Actually, the field of practical, normative reasoning is the one I'd like to focus on initially. Indeed, we should first briefly consider the nature of practical, normative reasons, especially the difference between internal and external reasons, before we turn to legal theorizing.

A. Dyrda (✉)
Jagiellonian University, Krakow, Poland
e-mail: adam.dyrda@uj.edu.pl

M. Araszkiewicz et al. (eds.), *Problems of Normativity, Rules and Rule-Following*, Law and Philosophy Library 111, DOI 10.1007/978-3-319-09375-8_17

17.2 Internal and External Reasons

The difference between internal and external reasons appears to be sound, as far as reasons of the first type are somehow connected with the agents' motivation for taking a certain kind of action, and therefore can be equated with normative reasons (and not explanatory or theoretical ones). On the contrary, external reasons are reasons that cannot be considered to involve any *interesting* dependence on the facts about the subjects' motivation (Finlay and Schroeder 2012). The most popular version of such an approach is probably Humean[1] internalism: an agent has no reason to do *A* if she has no desire that could motivate her to do *A*. However, for the sake of brevity and simplicity, I introduce a broad understanding of motivation here and leave the question of whether it is fundamentally dependent on desires or some other type of inner feelings open (and even whether the famous discrimination[2] of B. Pascal in this matter can be considered true). The "internal" explanation of the normativity of reasons is rejected by externalism. In fact, it is sometimes suggested that external reasons, which are not dependent upon the subject's motivational states, are themselves normative. Such a claim is characteristic of some versions of moral absolutism, according to which some actions are morally wrong for any agent, no matter what motivations and desires the agent has (Finlay and Schroeder 2012). Externalism tries to justify the normativity of practical reasons without reference to the subjects' motivation. It is usually construed by reference to certain presuppositions about the possibility of human moral cognition, but it is enough to say that if the external reasons are not desires, they are simply beliefs (about what ought to be done)—and mere beliefs by themselves cannot motivate someone to act. External reasons are like hypothetical imperatives that are made categorical by substantial, cognitivist moral theories. In contrast, internalism can be connected with a variety of views about the nature of morality, e.g., G. Harman's relativism, or the error theory of J. Mackie. It can also be complementary with some versions of moral non-cognitivism. The only thing that is presupposed here is that the normativity of reasons is dependent on their relation to the agents' actual motivations.

I take for granted the (revised) reading[3] of internalism proposed by B. Williams in his famous article "Internal and External Reasons" (Williams 1981). In this paper, Williams claims that practical reasons have an "explanatory dimension," which contributes to the "meaning of our thoughts and claims about practical reasons, where the possibility of an error and ignorance about them is simply excluded" (i.e., the agent's actual reasons are the explanation of the agent's behavior only if our agent is not somehow mistaken)[4]. In brief, the core of Williams' argument is

[1] I write "Humean" because it is controversial whether Hume actually had such a view himself.

[2] "The heart has its order, the mind has its own, which uses principles and demonstrations. The heart has a different one. We do not prove that we ought to be loved by setting out in order the causes of love; that would be absurd" (Pascal 2013, thought 283).

[3] See Finlay and Schroeder 2012.

[4] Such interpretation is in Finlay and Schroeder 2012. They write that according to Williams, "[t]o think that a fact is a reason for an agent to act is not to think it is an explanation of an action that

that practical reasons must be able to explain actions, and one cannot explain actions without reference to one's motivations. Explanations that adduce to the set of subjects' motivations are internal. I think this is plausible[5]. Moreover, I suppose that many leading legal theorists build their theory of law's normativity by implicitly referring to basic intuition as developed by Williams in the context of the analysis of moral reasons. According to Williams there are no external reasons, but for the purpose of this paper I will interpret his statement as claiming that external reasons are just not genuine, normative reasons, and cannot play any explanatory role in explaining normativity (both in morality and law).

17.3 Law as Practical Reason

Having said this, we can move into the area of legal theory. There are theorists who claim that law is a social phenomenon that aspires to be normative in the most fundamental sense. What they have in mind is that the idea of legal obligation is strictly connected with the role legal rules are supposed to play in agents' practical reasoning. Law purports to govern conduct as practical authority. As J. Coleman notices, "the distinctive feature of law's governance on this view is that it purports to govern by *creating reasons for action*" (Coleman 2001, p. 71). J. Raz asserts that "the law claims that the existence of legal rules is a reason for conforming behavior" (Raz 1979, p. 30). The group of "legal rationalists" (philosophers who are convinced that "the law's normativity is to be explained in terms of the law's effect on the reasons of its subjects," Essert 2013, p. 2) includes A. Marmor, S. Shapiro and many others. All of them are to some extent continuators (or constructive critics) of the refined version of legal positivism presented by H. L. A. Hart in *The Concept of Law*. We might say that their main concern is to construe a "full-fledged theory of law," which not only gives an adequate picture of legal practice as a social fact, but also aims at convincingly explaining the very nature of the characteristic normativity of law (sc. its reason-giving character). However, it is quite controversial whether Hart's own original theory had such character. There are some interpreters of Hart who claim that it was not Hart's main aim to present any theory of legal obligation and, what's more, any detailed account of law's normative force. Rather, they say, Hart's project was profoundly descriptivist ("descriptive sociology")[6] and any concerns about whether we should treat legal provisions as actually justified

she actually performs, but rather it is to think it an explanation of an action that she would have performed (or would have been somewhat motivated towards performing) if not for her error or ignorance."

[5] In particular, I agree with the main supposition that underlies the argument about external reasons, namely, the claim that our ethical life is too untidy to be captured by any systematic theory (the view that Williams connects with utilitarianism especially, but which I think can be connected with any kind of anti-substantialism and non-cognitivism or anti-formalism in ethics).

[6] Actually, in my opinion, descriptive sociology in the sense presented by Hart is not sociology at all.

and reason-giving, binding norms, are a matter of normative, political philosophy justifying legal order, as opposed to descriptive legal theory. In this interpretation, Hart is supposed only to propose a general sketch of the relationships between the central legal concepts (obligation, sanction, legal practice, rules, etc.) as a "reflection of the composite character of a legal system" (Hart 2013, p. 117). With such an interpretation, to say that the criteria of legality are conventional, as Hart does, is simply to say that there is a widely shared agreement among officials who apply the same criteria to identifying law (i.e., the same rule of recognition)—and nothing more. Interpreted this way, Hart himself cut off political and normative deliberation in the context of law by simply evoking the concept of the internal point of view connected with the notion of "serious social pressure," which does not need any further explanation.

I do not share this interpretation of Hart's theory. In my opinion, if we want to perceive his theory as a full-fledged theory of law, the most important problem is to present such a general interpretation of his theory that would both save its descriptive value and present a coherent and plausible understanding of the internal point of view (on which almost the whole burden of law's normativity rests) towards certain social rules (esp. the ultimate rule of recognition). I would like to stress that I do not make any historical claim about what Hart actually had in mind. My objective is different; namely, I would like to propose an interpretation of his theory that answers the normativity question also. Such a task would reveal some internal contradictions in Hart's own theory, which would be the main reasons for further amendments. To clarify, my basic assumption is that post-Hartian positivism is not worth much if it does not aspire to be a "full-fledged theory of law." Legal rationalists are trying to build such a theory by making serious amendments to Hart's original project—by providing a better theoretical scaffolding for our understanding of the role legal reasons (norms) play in the practical deliberation of subjects and by analyzing the reasons for rule acceptance more carefully. The starting point is the assumption that the idea of the general acceptance of the foundational rule of recognition (which is a social rule that defines the ultimate criteria of legal validity) makes it a duty-imposing rule[7]. To allow this there must be a special sphere of the subjects' own reasons for acceptance of the ultimate rule and, moreover, a "mechanism" constituting motivations for acceptance that should be dependable and not selective.

I think that Hart was generally inclined to be a legal rationalist, who, however, thought that one can combine both non-cognitivism in relation to moral reasons and values with the appreciation of the role of the agents' personal motivations, which can only be used as an "explanation" for the acceptance of a rule. Simultaneously, Hart feverishly argued for the claim known as the "separability thesis" (the claim that roughly speaking, the meaning of legal "ought" need not be reduced to the meaning of moral "ought," and vice versa. However, as I will briefly argue below,

[7] The so-called "conventionality thesis," according to S. Shapiro, is as follows: "Every legal system contains a conventional rule that imposes a duty on courts to evaluate conduct in light of rules that bear certain characteristics" (Shapiro 2000, p. 128).

the latter claim is at odds with the former. Moreover, to think of Hart as a legal rationalist, we must interpret his work holistically, in the context of his other writings[8]. A basic reading of *The Concept of Law* can give an impression that Hart himself wasn't a legal rationalist, and (while putting aside the problem of the plausibility and proper meaning of Hart's critique of Austin and the realists[9]) may lead to the conclusion that the notion of the "general acceptance of the rule," as strictly connected with the idea of the "internal point of view," refers to nothing but a simple attitude of endorsement (Perry 2006). And the reasons observed within such an endorsement are at least external reasons that explain only the hypothetical, not the genuine, normativity of law. So, in this case, Hart would be viewed as not interested in providing a theory of why legal reasons are authoritative, but just in giving a description of law as an effectively endorsed social institution.

17.4 Is the Internal Point of View Internal Enough?

If we treat the idea of law's normativity seriously, and want to develop it upon Hart's original writing, we should consider the following. The internal point of view should explain why a statement like "It is the law of Poland that everyone has an obligation to do *X*" is a normative statement at all. So, the key to explaining the law's normative force together with the concept of legal obligation is to present the notion of having an internal point of view towards the social rule in detail, such that the notion breaks the vicious regress in tracing the very foundations of legality (cf. Lagerspetz 2011; Perry 2006) and supplies the Polish people, both officials and laymen, with practical reasons to do *X*. According to S. Perry:

> The internal point of view, properly understood, is the perspective both of the authorities who make this claim and of the subjects of law who accept it. To accept the legitimacy of the law's claim to authority is to *believe* that the law has such authority, and not simply to adopt an attitude of endorsement towards the law's requirements (Perry 2006, p. 1174).

I think the main reason why internal reasons could play an explanatory role is valid for such a notion of the internal point of view that refers to the set of reasons that underlie agents' action[10]. In this case, these reasons have to be only formally characterized without reference to any substantial, and, I would say "over-cognitivist"

[8] See Hart 1982, pp. 243–268, where he discusses the relevance of "content independent and preemptory reasons."

[9] Hart famously argued against Austin's sanction-based theory of law in part on the grounds that it could not account for the fact that, at least sometimes, people take their legal obligations as reasons for performance (see Hart 2013, p. 84).

[10] It is worth noticing that the title-term "fundamental legal reasons" refers to the reasons that agents have to submit themselves to legal authority (which consists in an internal attitude or a belief of acceptance). However, these reasons have to be distinguished from legal reasons par excellence, i.e. the reasons that law purports to give itself. In this article I am primarily concerned with the former. Nevertheless, it seems obvious to me that, at least in an explanatory scheme, the plausible understanding of the former is a necessary condition of the proper understanding of the latter.

(or even absolutist), and therefore "external," claims about morality. Rather, the term "morality" is used here "personally" and "critically" to refer to the scope of the agent's reasons for action, which are based on the agent's preferences, desires, or motivations. Putting it this way, Hart took the right way, but unfortunately, wasn't inquisitive enough. In order to save his basic distinction between legal and moral obligation, he was bound to formulate a proper *criterium divisionis*. After R. Dworkin's famous critique, he argued that at least as far as legal obligation is concerned, the criteria of validity are partly conventional, whereas morality can be either conventional (as based on social rules) or critical (private). He then didn't want to discuss moral obligation at all (due to his meta-ethical non-cognitivism) and focused on a different kind of obligation: legal obligation. This can be clearly read as a reason why Hart rejects the assimilation of an internal point of view, which he introduces to explain the basic, normative characteristics of law, with a moral point of view. S. Perry calls it "the non-cognitivist understanding" of the internal point of view. The non-cognitivist understanding of the internal point of view means that the acceptance of law can come about for different reasons that are all on the same level[11], none of which seems to be a necessary reason[12]. What's more interesting is that simple, non-cognitivist understanding seems to be at odds with the idea that the explanation of the agent's practical action has to refer to her desires, preferences and motivations (the characteristics of the internal reasons) and not only to sets of beliefs, present in certain social groups, about what ought to be done. Non-cognitivist understanding focuses on the idea that for a social rule to be accepted there is, *inter alia*, a need for the belief of "serious social (punitive) pressure" in the case of breaking the rule. Nevertheless, non-cognitivism grants the idea that such a belief

---

[11] Cf. Schiavello 2012. Hart himself writes: "[…] Of course, a conventional rule may both be and be believed to be morally sound and justified. But when the question arises as to why those who have accepted conventional rules as a guide to their behaviour or as standards of criticism have done so I see no reason for selecting from the many answers to be given […] a belief in the moral justification of rules as the sole possible or adequate answer" (Hart 2013, p. 257). This claim can be understood as a claim that reasons for the acceptance of a social rule can be manifold. However, as A. Schiavello notices, in his posthumously published writing Hart changes his mind to a certain extent and further clarifies the idea that, in the case of social rules, acceptance by the other members of the group is a necessary reason for the existence of obligation (Schiavello 2012). In this he could have been influenced by the writings of G. Postema and J. Coleman who, from the beginning of the 80 s, tried to defend Hartian positivism against Dworkin's critique by developing the idea that the rule of recognition is a coordination convention in the Lewisian sense.

[12] The unnecessary character of reasons for accepting the rule of recognition, characteristic of the non-cognitivist understanding of the internal point of view can be called, after B. Celano, "a weak-dependence condition" of the rule's normativity. On the other hand, the cognitivist understanding of the internal point of view, according to which some of the reasons (of a certain type: e.g., conformist/bad man's/conventional/moral) are considered to be necessary, can be called "a strong dependence condition". As A. Schiavello writes: "The dependence condition can be seen in a strong sense or a weak sense. If it is maintained that the only reason that an individual has for considering a social rule as a model of conduct is that the other members of the group also considered it as such, then the dependence condition is seen in a strong sense; if instead it is maintained that general conformity of the members of the group is only one reason for acceptance of a rule, then the dependence condition is seen in a weak sense" (Schiavello 2012).

is one thing, and the real (genuine) reasons for conformity is another. Therefore, it is not only the case that all reasons for conformity are equal, but, moreover, these, as being actual, practical motivations of agents, cannot be mere external reasons (simple beliefs). This has much to do with what N. MacCormick calls the "over-weak characterization" of the internal point of view. Non-cognitivist interpretation asserts that from the whole scope of reasons for the acceptance of the rule of recognition by officials, including bad man's reasons, conformist reasons, moral reasons and conventionalist reasons, there is no type of reasons that can grant law's peculiar normativity per se: the reasons for conformity are manifold, and we cannot reduce law's normativity to reasons of any particular kind. Especially, we cannot equate legal reasons with moral reasons, because in such a case, as Hart would think himself, the crucial distinction between "the legal" and "the moral" would be lost.

Many of the reasons that Hart thinks can validate the internal point of view in a non-cognitivist interpretation are simply external reasons. It is most obviously visible in the case of conventional reasons, where the crucial part of the reasons for accepting a rule is the fact that others accept it as well, and in the case of conformist reasons, where the attitude of the endorsement of a rule is based simply on the fact that it has been endorsed so far (whatever it is, and for whatever reasons). The main argument against "non-cognitivism" is that such an interpretation is too weak and lacks explanatory power. To explain why law has normative force, one must refer to the special types of reasons that can exclude other reasons from deliberation (especially reasons to go against the law). When people rationalize their decisions concerning their actions, they balance different types of reasons, many of which could be equal, and in these cases, the decision could be made only by reference to some kinds of reasons that could outweigh others (second order and preemptory reasons)[13]. I suppose that external reasons are basically reasons of the same type, from the same level—there is nothing special in them that allows an agent to develop a conviction that what they account for would be a proper thing to do (what the agent ought to do). According to Williams, such a normative function can only be fulfilled by internal reasons that refer strictly to the agents' motivations. We should remember that Williams is concerned with what the agent comes to believe when he comes to believe that some consideration *R* is a reason for him to do *X*. Granted the conceptual premise, an "internal reasons statement" is a claim that some consideration is an explanation of why *by virtue of the contents of the agent's actual "motivational set"* he would be motivated to do *X* under the conditions of sound deliberation, while an "external reasons statement" is a claim that some consideration is an explanation of why *independently of the contents of the agent's actual motivational set* he would be motivated to do *A* under those conditions (Williams 1981).

If we propose a non-cognitivist interpretation of the internal point of view towards certain social rules (esp. the rule of recognition), we circumscribe only the general set of reasons for conformity. The question remains open whether these reasons are really normative, unless agents are truly motivated to act upon them. Was Hart really thinking of these reasons as internal, normative ones, or only as general

[13] Cf. Raz 1979; Raz 1990; Green 1988.

reasons that agents can refer to when describing (or even justifying by reference to certain beliefs) the fact that the rule is generally obeyed (simple endorsement)? I think Hart does not give a clear answer. On the one hand, Hart seems to be a Humean, and to believe that each of these reasons should be conceived theoretically as internal reasons, including conventional reasons, bad man's reasons and reasons for simple conformism. Moreover, his argument is built in such a way that it allows the agent to act for whatever reasons, as well as to act for no reason at all. Hart thinks that the internal point of view is the point of view of someone who is just simply motivated[14] to do *X* (what the rule requires). On the other hand, Hart is supposed to think of external reasons only, as far as he tries to defend the strict, rigid gulf between legal and moral normativity. As he says: "To feel obliged and to have an obligation are different though frequently concomitant things" (Hart 2013, p. 88)[15]. However, the problem is that in terms of the distinction between internal and external reasons, such a distinction cannot be made, simply because this differentiation applies only to the discussion about the nature of morality. Internal reasons are *par excellence* moral reasons. They are normative because of the motivation that the agent has for acting upon them. External reasons are not normative, because they are only general statements about what one ought to do. External reasons may have many sources: tradition, convention, social morality. This inevitably leads to the conclusion that if we do not want to argue for some kind of "essentialist objectivism" about reasons, we should try to explain why people conform to the rules by introducing the idea of moral, internal reason. Hart tries to refer to agents' motivations or desires in conforming to *X*, but he simply forgets that the reasons (if only such behavior can be evaluated as reasonable) for doing it must be moral and internal in character.

I think basically the same intuition may be ascribed to many critics of Hart (J. Raz, S. Perry, N. MacCormick, A. Schiavello and many others), who point out that the normative reasons for acting along law's requirements must be genuine moral reasons. However, this "cognitivist" interpretation of the internal point of view can still secure the relative independence of the concept of law and the concept of morality. It is true that the concept of morality, esp. the concept of internal reason, is

[14] I'd like to differentiate between my own use of the word "motivation," which I've borrowed from Williams and which equates with the base of the Hartian reasons for "acceptance," and Hart's use of the word "motive," which he appears to use in the case of describing the situation of someone simply being obliged (for example, due to the fear of punishment, where there is no "acceptance" in Hartian terms). See the citation in the next footnote.

[15] Further, Hart indicates two conditions for a legal system to exist. First is the general obedience of the law; second, the internal point of view of officials towards the criteria within the rule of recognition. He then writes: "The first condition is the only one which private citizens need satisfy: they may obey each 'for his part only' and from any motive whatever [...]. The second condition must also be satisfied by the officials of the system. They must regard these as common standards of official behaviour and appraise critically their own and each other's deviations as lapses. [...] The assertion that a legal system exists is therefore a Janusfaced statement looking both towards obedience by ordinary citizens and to the acceptance by officials of secondary rules as critical common standards of official behavior" (Hart 2013, pp. 116–117). Here, I'm trying to explain the notion of acceptance in terms of underlying, internal reasons.

necessary to explain normativity of any kind. That's why it is conceptually possible for law to be normative only if it can at least imitate morality—by using the same concepts, and—what is most important—by trying to play the same role in practical reasoning as morality does. That's why many authors say that "law's claim to authority is actually a moral claim." I think that idea has been developed in the right way by contemporary legal rationalists who took the basic idea from Hart, but have deepened it enough to make the theory plausible.

17.5 Some Possible Ways of Improvement—Final Remarks

There are many interesting ways of improving the Hartian account of the rule of recognition as a "social duty-imposing rule." There is a strong temptation to put greater focus on the matter of how this kind of social phenomenon or fact (social rule, convention) is construed. Such an approach tends to ignore what I've tried to show above: that the reasons for action that are considered to be within the attitude of acceptance (internal point of view), if there are any, are to be understood as reasons of critical morality that are based in the agent's motivational set. In such circumstances, where focus is put on the social mechanism necessary for legal institutions to exist, at least two ways of improvement can be proposed. One way to improve Hart's account is to abandon the non-cognitivist understanding of the reasons for rule conformity and reduce these reasons, at least conceptually, to conventional, coordinative reasons, which would surely save the crucial positivist distinction between legal and moral obligation. I think that such a reduction accepts the individualistic picture of acting agents, but in the end fails due to Hume's Guillotine. Therefore, it cannot explain legal reasons as internal reasons at all. (Moreover, I think that the argument of Hume's Guillotine is strictly connected with the inability of external reasons to create normative judgments, but this thesis would require a deeper inquiry.) An attempt to build law's normativity on conventional reasons (understood as coordinative reasons, by use of the concept of convention introduced by Lewis 1969) must fail as far as the reasons for conformity are not in themselves understood as internal reasons. Conventionalist theory provides only a hypothetical or, more precisely, conditional explanation of law's normativity (cf. Green 1988, 1999). We may say that law is conventional because it is arbitrary, but it still doesn't necessarily lead to a claim that the normative reasons agents have for taking part in the legal game are conventional at all (conventional reasons are neither sufficient nor necessary for legal authority to exist).

The other way is to explain the normativity of a social rule (e.g., the rule of recognition) that falls under the general label of "conventionalist" theories (built upon certain criticism of a standard, Lewisian account) by making special reference to the role that such conventional beliefs play in our thinking about our duties. In this case we can either claim that due to being a part of a social community, each and every "command" or "imperative" that comes from the group-conscious acts (group *fiat*) is actually a kind of self-imposed norm. This theory has been developed by M. Gilbert (Gilbert 1999). However, I'm not sure whether such an account helps to explain the law's peculiar normativity, or if it only postpones an answer. It seems to me that this theory simply presupposes that due to some ontological commitments (in the context of an idea of group membership), there is always an internal obligation (internal reason) to act along the rules created by the group. I think this is against Hart's conception, which is rather individualistic and not holistic. The other alternative, which saves us from such an individualist picture, is A. Marmor's idea that apart from coordinative conventions, there are more fundamental, constitutive conventions that underdetermine basic social institutions (Marmor 2009). This picture is a bit more complicated than the Hartian one. It preserves the distinction between law and morality by incorporating Razian's service concept of authority. In this case, the sole idea of law's peculiar normativity rests on a conceptual premise that law claims to have a legitimate authority and the whole set of conventional norms that aspire to be authoritative builds a system that is normative, but only internally (law's internal normativity). The internal normativity of the law is only hypothetical. However, in order to give a genuine explanation of law's normativity we must refer to the idea of external normativity, i.e., genuine reasons that are external to the rules of the "legal game." Such reasons are genuine reasons of morality, which may be well considered as internal reasons. By the way, we should differentiate between the object-criterion, by reference to which the relationship between the internal and external normativity of the law is considered, and the subject-criterion, which allows us to consider the relationship between internal (genuine, moral) and external reasons (hypothetical beliefs about "oughts"). It allows us to say that Marmor's amendment to Hartian's positivism, in my view, explains the genuine normativity of law by suggesting that it must be described by reference to internal, moral reasons (subject-perspective), which are actually external to the scope of reasons that are provided by the law itself (object-perspective). The only important thing to remember is that law, conceptually, is a kind of social institution that always claims to be normative in the most internal, genuine and moral sense. It makes no difference for the theory whether such an immanent aspiration of the law is actually considered true. I find such a "rationalist" improvement of Hartian's account quite promising.

Acknowledgments The Author thanks to the Participants of the Rules 2013 Conference for comments to the presented version of the paper. In addition, special thanks go to T. Gizbert-Studnicki who provided incisive and helpful written comments on a draft of this article.

References

Coleman, Jules. 2001. *The practice of principle.* Oxford: Oxford University Press.

Essert, Chris. 2013. Legal obligation and reasons. *Legal Theory* 19:1–26.

Finlay, Stephen and Mark, Schroeder. 2012. Reasons for action: Internal vs. external. Stanford Encyclopedia of Philosophy. http://plato.stanford.edu/entries/reasons-internal-external. Accessed 20 April 2013.

Gilbert, Margaret. 1999. Social rules: Some problems for Hart's account, and an alternative proposal. *Law & Philosophy* 18 (1999): 141–171.
Green, Leslie. 1988. *The authority of the state.* Oxford: Oxford University Press.
Green, Leslie. 1999. Positivism and conventionalism. *Canadian Journal of Law and Jurisprudence* 12 (1999): 35–52.
Hart, Herbert. 1982. *Commands and authoritative legal reasons in Herbert Hart. Essays on Bentham.* Oxford: Oxford University Press.
Hart, Herbert. 2013. *The concept of law.* 3rd ed. Oxford: Oxford University Press.
Kierkegaard, Soren. 2011. *Albo-albo* [Either-or]. Polish translation: Jaroslaw Iwaszkiewicz. Warszawa: Wydawnictwo Naukowe PWN.
Lagerspetz, Eerik. 2011. *The opposite mirrors: An essay on the conventionalist theory of institutions.* Dordrecht: Springer.
Lewis, David. 1969. *Convention: A philosophical study.* Cambridge: Harvard University Press.
Marmor, Andrei. 2009. *Social conventions.* Princeton: Princeton University Press.
Pascal, Blaise. 2013. *Thoughts.* Bartelby.com. http://www.bartleby.com/48/1/4.html. Accessed 21 April 2013.
Perry, Stephen. 2006. Hart on social rules and the foundations of law: Liberating the internal point of view. *Fordham Law Review* 75:1179–1207.
Raz, Joseph. 1979. *The authority of law. Essays on law and morality.* Oxford: Oxford University Press.
Raz, Joseph. 1990. *Practical reason and norms.* Oxford: Oxford University Press.
Schiavello, Aldo. 2012. Rule of recognition, convention and obligation. What Shapiro can still learn from Hart's mistakes. In *The planning theory of law. A critical reading,* ed. Damiano Canale and Giovanni Tuzet, 65–87. Dordrecht: Springer.
Shapiro, Scott. 2000. Law morality and the guidance of conduct. *Legal Theory* 6:127–170.
Williams, Bernard. 1981. Internal and external reasons. In *Moral luck,* ed. B. Williams, 101–113. Cambridge: Cambridge University Press.

Part III
Rules in Legal Interpretation and Argumentation

Chapter 18
The Normativity of Rules of Interpretation

Tomasz Gizbert-Studnicki

Abstract Rules of interpretation of law have both heuristic and justificatory functions. They are normative in the sense that they deliver justificatory reasons for interpretative decisions. The normativity of these rules cannot be explained by recourse to the concept of convention. Rules of interpretation are based on various (and sometimes conflicting) values of political morality. Rules of interpretation reduce the complexity of the judicial decision-making process by delivering second order reasons for interpretative decisions—the first order reasons being values of political morality that underlie those rules. The reasons supplied by rules of interpretation are not exclusionary, as their application does not exclude the need for recourse to the first order reasons. Such recourse is necessary if particular rules of interpretation remain in conflict with respect to the case to be solved. The question of justifying rules of interpretation is not a semantic question. These rules are not supported by any definite semantic theory, but by political philosophy, justifying the adoption of a certain set of values pertaining to political morality. In this respect, certain differences pertaining to the mode of resolution of conflicts between various rules may be observed between common law and civil law legal cultures.

Keywords Interpretation · Legal culture · Normativity · Reasons · Rules of interpretation

18.1 Is the Interpretation of Law Rule-Guided?

It is a common occurrence that judges present their interpretative decisions as based on rules, canons, maxims or methods of interpretation. For the sake of brevity, I will refer below exclusively to "rules" as a general term covering all designations listed above. In this broad sense of the term, rules of interpretation may have various forms. Some of them are strict rules, providing for a definite outcome (for example: *if the same word occurs more than once in the statute, the same meaning should be ascribed to each of those occurrences*), but some are rather prudential maxims, the

T. Gizbert-Studnicki (✉)
Faculty of Law, Jagiellonian University, Kraków, Poland
e-mail: t.gizbert-studnicki@uj.edu.pl

M. Araszkiewicz et al. (eds.), *Problems of Normativity, Rules and Rule-Following*, Law and Philosophy Library 111, DOI 10.1007/978-3-319-09375-8_18

application of which must be based on a judgment (for example: *adopted interpretation should not be in conflict with fundamental constitutional values*). Others just indicate which factors should be taken into account by the interpreter (for example: *take into account the legislative history of the statute*). In the discussion that follows, I will not discriminate between these different types of rules. Further, I will deal exclusively with statutory interpretation, leaving aside the interpretation of other legal materials.

The question of whether the interpretation of law is a rule-guided enterprise may pertain to two distinct issues. The first issue is whether the interpreters, while considering the matter of the proper meaning of the text of a statute, actually engage rules of interpretation as a device to help them solve the problem that they face. Thus, the first issue is the role of rules of interpretation in the heuristics of the interpretation of law (in the context of deliberation). The second issue is the role of rules of interpretation in the process of justifying the interpretative decision, or in other words, the question: "What is the role of rules in the process of presenting the reasons for the adopted interpretative decision (in the context of justification)?"

As far as the first issue is concerned, the answer can only be based on empirical research. In the absence of such research, it is impossible to say whether rules of interpretation are actually applied by interpreters for the purpose of finding the right solution to interpretative problems that they face, or whether, as maintained by legal realists, such a solution is selected by intuition, "hunch" or moral beliefs, and the exclusive role of the rules is to justify the solution so identified. It is possible that no uniform answer to this question can be given—some interpreters take rules of interpretation seriously, as devices to help them find the right solution, and others rely on their own intuition and make use of the rules only for the purpose of rationalizing the outcome of their morally-driven or intuitive interpretation. Alternatively, it may be argued that the distinction between the context of deliberation and the context of justification is not sound with respect to legal interpretation, or at least not clear-cut, and therefore, the solutions of both issues should run congruently.

For the purpose of this paper, I assume that rules of interpretation have both a guiding and a justificatory role, but I will be interested exclusively in the latter role. An obvious feature of the judicial decision-making process is that a judge must present his or her decision based on, and driven by, the law. If the text of a statute is ambiguous or if there is a basis for departing from the plain meaning of the statute, the judge is bound to give reasons for his or her interpretative decision. But even if the language of a statute is clear and does not give rise to any doubts, the tacit reason for the decision based on such plain meaning is provided by the rule prescribing that the judge is bound by the wording of the statute. The question of whether such reasons reflect the actual psychological motives behind the judge's decision is impossible to answer, due to the fact that there is no practical means to check what the actual motives are. While discussing the interpretation adopted by the judge (for instance, in the context of an appeal against his or her decision), we only have access to the reasons which have been explicitly revealed by the judge (or we may attempt to reconstruct reasons implicitly assumed), as we are not able to gain access to his or her actual psychological motives. On the other hand, we have no basis to assume that the actual motives always, or even usually, dramatically depart from the reasons given for justification. Thus, rules of interpretation probably play a certain role as devices that provide motivating reasons[1].

I assume, therefore, that the principal function of rules of interpretation in legal practice is to give justificatory reasons supporting interpretative decisions. Below, I will discuss this role exclusively. Rules of interpretation are normative in the sense that they supply such reasons.

18.2 Rules of Interpretation Supply Justificatory Reasons

In order to be able to supply a justificatory reason, a rule must jointly satisfy three requirements (Brożek 2012, p. 10):

(i) it must be objective,
(ii) it must be applied in a conscious way (at least potentially), and
(iii) any departure from the pattern established by such a rule must be (at least potentially) subject to critique.

Let us check whether those requirements are satisfied by rules of statutory interpretation. As far as the requirement of objectivity is concerned, it is plausible to argue that objectivity as mind-independence is what is meant here. Let me borrow from M. Kramer the distinction between strong and weak mind-independence (Kramer 2007). Strong mind-independence is the mind-independence *tout-court*. It means that the existence of the thing in question does not depend on anyone's thoughts or beliefs. The Earth's moon is mind-independent in this sense, as it would exist even if nobody were aware of its existence. Obviously, rules of interpretation are not mind-independent in the strong sense, as they would not exist in absence of the thoughts and beliefs of the members of a particular legal culture. Weak mind-independence means that the existence of the thing in question does not depend on the thoughts, beliefs or attitudes of any particular individual, but depends on collective attitudes or beliefs which individuals share in their interactions. Rules of interpretation are mind-independent in the weak sense, since their existence depends upon collective beliefs shared by a community of judges, lawyers and other state officers in a given legal culture. This does not mean that all rules of interpretation must be uncontroversial within a legal culture. To the contrary, certain rules and/or the mode of their application are a matter of dispute (I will revert to this problem below). This means only that rules of interpretation, in order to perform their justificatory function, cannot be private rules invented by a particular interpreter. They must be

[1] As it follows from the above, I adopt an externalist position based on the distinction between justificatory reasons and motivating reasons. I follow D. Enoch (2011) in proposing that these kinds of reasons can be distinguished at least conceptually, and therefore, I do not need to engage in the discussion of the connection between motivating reasons and justificatory reasons (Williams 1981; Smith 1994).

generally shared by the community of interpreters (or at least by a substantial part of such a community), which does not mean that each individual interpreter must accept (or even be aware of) each of these rules. An interpretative decision would not be deemed sufficiently justified if it were solely based on private rules adopted by a given interpreter. Such private rules would not be considered as giving justificatory reasons since they lack objectivity (weak mind-independence).

It also appears that the second requirement is satisfied as well. Rules of interpretation are applied in a conscious way. This does not mean that they are always explicitly worded, since usually, in easy cases, they are only tacitly assumed. It is, however, a fact of legal interpretation practice that interpreters, when asked for justification of their interpretative decision, are usually prepared to refer to the rules that they have consciously applied or at least tacitly assumed. If they fail to indicate such rules, their interpretative decisions are deemed to be unjustified. The same applies to the third requirement. In legal disputes relating to interpretation or application of the law, rules of interpretation are frequently evoked as the basis of a critique of the interpretation adopted by an opponent. An interpretative decision is claimed to be wrong if it has been made in breach of certain rules of interpretation, unless other rules sufficiently support such a decision. Departure from a generally accepted rule requires justification.

Therefore, rules of interpretation are normative in the sense that they supply justificatory reasons for actions (interpretative decisions). My claim that rules of interpretation supply justificatory reasons for actions (interpretative decisions) is a descriptive, and not a normative, claim. I do not want to say that rules of interpretation always give good or sufficient reasons for interpretative decisions. My only claim is that rules of interpretation are utilized in the practice of interpretation to provide justificatory reasons. The question of whether any particular reasons are good or sufficient is to be answered by a normative theory of interpretation. For the purpose of this paper, I do not assume any normative theory of statutory interpretation.

Further, for the purpose of this paper, it is not necessary to answer the question of whether rules of interpretation are normative in a weak or strong sense. This may depend upon specific features of a given legal culture and on specific features of particular rules. In some legal cultures, certain rules of interpretation may be normative in a strong sense (for example, when the rules of interpretation are explicitly formulated in a statute[2]). In other cultures, most of the rules of interpretation are just prudential rules, canons or maxims with a weak normative force, which may be overweighed by an opposite rule. Another interesting question is what kinds of reasons are delivered by rules of interpretation, and in particular, whether they deliver epistemic, triggering or robust reasons (Enoch 2011). For the sake of brevity, I will leave this question unanswered.

One more thing needs to be explained to avoid misunderstanding. Rules of interpretation as such do not constitute justificatory reasons, but only define what facts or circumstances count as justificatory reasons. To give a simple example: if an interpreter adopts the rule that the actual intention of the lawgiver should be taken

[2] For specific problems with the application of such rules, see Tutt (2013).

into account in the interpretation of a statute, the reason for a definite interpretative decision is the fact that the lawgiver has had a certain intention. In order to justify the decision, it is not sufficient to refer to that rule, but the actual intention (as a certain fact) must be demonstrated. Such a fact, however, constitutes a justificatory reason only due to the existence of the rule. In the absence of the respective rule, the actual intention of the lawgiver would not constitute a justificatory reason.

18.3 Are Rules of Interpretation Conventional?

Where does the normative force of rules of interpretation come from and how can it be justified? This question appears to be important, as justification is a necessary component of normativity (Bertea 2009, p. 25).

The first hypothesis is that the normativity of rules of interpretation is a consequence of their conventional nature. The reasons delivered by rules of interpretation have a justificatory force due to human conventions, which ascribe such a force to them. This hypothesis is supported by the trivial observation that knowledge of the rules and the ability to apply them are acquired in the course of legal education, which is a sort of socialization process. Lawyers learn and master the rules of interpretation in much the same way as everyone acquires various conventional rules of social life (for example, rules of language or rules of etiquette), although the process of the acquisition of rules of interpretation is more institutionalized, conscious and explicit in the course of legal education. Legal practice is sometimes perceived as a sort of a conventional game or discourse, governed *inter alia* by the rules of interpretation, which exclude certain moves in such a game as wrong and endorse other moves as right.

I do not think, however, that the picture of legal practice as a conventional game is adequate. Legal practice is not a sort of chess game, as it involves human values and not just conventional moves. The hypothesis that the normativity of rules of interpretation is a consequence of their conventional nature, fails for the reasons described below.

Obviously, the notion of convention is subject to numerous philosophical controversies. For the sake of brevity, I will refer only to the theory of convention developed by D. Lewis (1969), though I believe that my conclusions also remain valid if another account of convention is adopted[3]. For Lewis, a convention is a solution to a coordination problem (which arises in non-zero sum coordination games in which there are two or more proper coordination equilibria). The rule commanding people to drive on the right side of the road may be used as an example. The same coordination problem would be solved (and in some countries is actually solved) by the opposite rule, commanding people to drive on the left side. It is clear that the

[3] The rationale for my belief is that each conception of convention (even a non-coordinative one) must assume that every convention is arbitrary, at least in the weak sense that it is not necessary (in the sense that another convention could have been adopted as well). See Dyrda (2013, p. 233).

adoption of any of these opposite rules is a matter of arbitrary decision. One of the opposite rules acquires the status of a convention if further requirements are met. Those requirements refer *inter alia* to the overwhelming conformity of behaviour to a rule within a certain community, and the existence of a mutual expectation that other people will follow the rule too.

There are several arguments against the thesis that rules of interpretation are of a conventional nature. The most important arguments are as follows:

First, it seems implausible that the main function of rules of interpretation is to solve a coordination problem. Such coordination problems may be identified only at a very high and general level (Dyrda 2013), equivalent to the question of how to ensure that interpretation of the law is uniform in the framework of the whole legal culture. A solution to such a global coordination problem would not require the adoption of any specific rules of interpretation. Arbitrary adoption of any rules would be sufficient, provided that they are accepted and applied by all, or almost all, interpreters (similarly, the coordination problem in road traffic can be solved by the adoption of any of the opposite rules: either by the right side rule or the left side rule).

Second, rules of interpretation are not perceived as arbitrary in the same sense as traffic rules are. Such rules are justified by appeal to other reasons and are usually not perceived as the solution to a coordination problem, although they probably also play a coordinative role in legal practice. In particular, rules of interpretation are justified by appeal to certain fundamental values of political morality underlying legal orders (such as formal justice, legal certainty and fairness) and to the assumption of the rationality of the lawgiver. Therefore, the decision to adopt certain rules of interpretation is not value-neutral, and in this sense is not arbitrary. Rules of interpretation may be accepted or criticized as right or wrong, justified or non-justified in the light of adopted values. An effective solution to a coordination problem is not a sufficient reason to adopt a certain set of rules of interpretation[4].

Third, a convention requires the fundamental convergence of behaviour of all (or nearly all) persons engaged in a given social practice. This requirement is not satisfied with respect to rules of interpretation for two reasons. The first reason is that the application of a given rule of interpretation to a certain case sometimes leads to different or even contrary results to the application of another rule (although *in abstracto* those rules are not conflicting). The second reason is that, as indicated above, certain rules are controversial within a given legal culture. For example, it is controversial whether the actual intention of the lawgiver should be taken into

[4] Certain purely "technical" rules of statutory interpretation may be, however, conventional in the sense that the adoption of an opposite rule would be consistent with the values underlying the legal system. For example, the gender and number rule of U.K. Interpretation Act of 1978, providing that *In any Act, unless the contrary intention appears, (a) words importing the masculine gender include the feminine; (b) words importing the feminine gender include the masculine; and (c) words in the singular include the plural and words in the plural include the singular* is arbitrary in the sense that the opposite rule could have been adopted as well, without damage to the value of legal certainty. Adoption of such an opposite rule would, however, make the drafting of statutes more complicated.

account. Although a convention does not require absolute convergence of behaviour, such fundamental divergences relating to certain rules of interpretation do not allow a conventional nature to be ascribed to them. Further, if an interpreter is asked the question, "What are the reasons for your decision?" an answer referring only to the applied rules of interpretation is not always sufficient, as the interpreter may still be asked for reasons to justify the adoption and/or the mode of application of such rules. This would be puzzling if rules of interpretation were conventional, since convention (provided that it effectively solves the coordination problem) does not usually require any further justification. Paraphrasing Bix (2012), it can be said that: it does matter which rules of interpretation one chooses (unlike which side of the road one drives). Certain differences, in this respect, between various legal cultures will be described below.

18.4 Rules of Interpretation Supply Second Order Reasons and Reduce the Complexity of Judicial Decision-Making

Thus, the normative force of rules of interpretation as devices that provide reasons for interpretative decisions cannot be explained in terms of their conventional nature. Apparently, such normative force is based primarily on the values underlying those rules. The interpreters accept and apply certain rules of interpretation because they accept (at least tacitly) the values of political morality supporting such rules. The rules, as such, constitute second order reasons for interpretative decisions, with first order reasons being the respective values of political morality. If an interpreter applies the rule giving priority to the plain or ordinary meaning of words contained in the statute, such a rule is a second order reason for his or her decision, while the value of legal certainty and transparency of law constitutes the first order (or "deep") reason for such a decision. If an interpreter departs from the plain meaning in order to find a fair or just solution to the case on the basis of the "golden rule", the first order reason for his or her decision is the value of justice or fairness (Stawecki 2010). Thus, rules of interpretation derive their normative force from underlying values. Different values may justify different rules. Conflicting values may justify conflicting rules. This explains (at least partially) the disputes relating to certain rules of interpretation within one and the same legal culture, such as, for example, the dispute between textualism and purposivism in the USA (Tutt 2014). Such disputes mirror the fact that particular values of political morality and/or their hierarchy are controversial within legal culture.

The fact that rules of interpretation are supported by values of political morality does not mean that each instance of the application of such rules requires a careful consideration of various values constituting first order reasons. If such a consideration were necessary, rules of interpretation would be redundant, as interpretative decisions would be guided and justified directly by reference to values. As it is, rules of interpretation play an important role in legal practice, reducing the complexity of the judicial decision-making process and providing justification of interpretative decisions. An average judge is not Hercules. Rather, he or she is subject to the usual limitations of time in which his or her decision must be made, the limitations of mental capacity, the limited knowledge of the external world and the inability to foresee all the consequences of his or her decision and all the ramifications of the case under consideration. In particular, a judge is usually unable to critically examine all axiological aspects of the case and of the law to be applied. A judge may, at least *prima facie*, rely on the rules of interpretation prevailing in the legal culture he or she belongs to, without needing to consider and critically examine the values underlying those rules. Application of "ready-made" rules of interpretation allows for a reduction of the level of complexity of the matters a judge must deal with. A judge does not have to directly consider the axiological matters if the application of a rule gives him or her a clear answer. A justification of an interpretative decision by recourse solely to such rules is, at least *prima facie*, sufficient and does not require making explicit recourse to the underlying values. The burden of argumentation rests not on the interpreters who follow generally accepted rules, but on their opponents (Gizbert-Studnicki 1990). This explains why the practice of interpretation is, at least in easy cases and to a certain extent, conventionalized (in the sense that it relies directly on rules and not on the underlying values), even though rules of interpretation are not based on conventions. In the absence of rules of interpretation, each judge would have to consider, *ab ovo*, all axiological problems connected with the application of law.

I think, therefore, that the primary function of rules of interpretation is the reduction of complexity within the judicial decision-making process by releasing the judge from the burden of considering all the values of political morality underlying the legal order and, in particular, the values on which the adopted rules of interpretation are based. Rules of interpretation deliver only second order reasons for an interpretative decision, and in most cases, such second order reasons are sufficient. Only in more complicated cases, where two or more rules collide, does the need arise to make reference to the values constituting the first order reasons for the purpose of solving the collision.

This does not mean, however, that the recourse to "ready-made" rules of interpretation (also in the absence of a collision) is always perceived as sufficient. The reasons delivered by the rules are not "exclusionary" or "pre-emptive" in the Razean sense (Raz 1994). They neither forbid recourse to the first order reasons nor exclude the need of such recourse, if the relevance of the second order reason is challenged. In the practice of interpretation, rules of interpretation are perceived as delivering only *prima facie* justification of an interpretative decision.

This conclusion does not apply to those rules of interpretation which are explicitly formulated in the binding statutes. Such rules have the same binding force as the rules of substantive law and deliver conclusive exclusionary reasons, excluding any need to refer to underlying values (unless they have the form of principles in the Dworkinean sense).

18.5 How the Conflicts Among Rules of Interpretation Are Resolved—The Diversity of Legal Cultures

As far as the use of rules of interpretation as second order reasons is concerned, there exists a substantial difference between continental and Anglo-Saxon legal cultures. This is an empirical hypothesis which would require a deeper comparative study of legal practice in various legal orders. I am not able to offer sufficient empirical evidence to fully support this hypothesis. I am only able to support this hypothesis by certain selected examples, and namely by the comparison of certain features of Polish legal culture (in which I participate) with features of US legal culture, the knowledge of which I acquire only from legal literature. I believe, however, that the difference I intend to describe is not accidental, but is somehow linked to the general features of continental and Anglo-Saxon legal cultures.

In Polish theory of legal interpretation, two levels of rules of interpretation have been distinguished (Wróblewski 1992). At the first level, a distinction is made between linguistic, systematic and functional (or teleological) rules. Most of the particular rules of each of these sorts, considered *in abstracto*, are usually uncontroversial, in the sense that all or almost all interpreters recognize their existence as a part of the legal culture and agree that such rules may be utilized as second order reasons for an interpretative decision. For example, nobody denies the rule that the meaning of a word prescribed by a legal definition should be followed or that if the same word or phrase occurs more than one time in the same text of law, the same meaning should be ascribed to each such occurrence. Similarly, nobody challenges the rule that the structure of the law text should be taken into account in the process of interpretation or that the statute should be interpreted in accordance with its purpose. The number of these generally accepted rules is quite substantial, though some other rules remain controversial. Therefore, at least in Polish legal culture, the set of generally accepted rules of interpretation of the first level is relatively well determined (Zielinski (2010). Taken *in abstracto*, none of these rules is inconsistent with any other.

The problem, however, arises if the application of a certain rule of the first level leads to the ascription of different meanings to the same statute than the application of another rule. In such a situation, the first level rules remain in conflict. The existence of such a conflict cannot be identified *in abstracto*. For example, there is no logical inconsistency between the first level rules of linguistic and teleological interpretation. They just indicate different facts or circumstances as justificatory reasons for an interpretative decision, but such reasons taken *in abstracto* do not remain in conflict. Such conflict may only arise *in concreto,* e.g. with respect to the application of various first level rules to a specific question of interpretation. Obviously, the application of a generally accepted rule of linguistic interpretation, that the plain meaning of the law text should be followed, may *in concreto* (but does not have to) be in conflict with the application of the rule of teleological interpretation, requiring that the interpretation should accomplish the purpose of the statute or that the interpretation should lead to a fair or just result, or with the rule of systematic interpretation—that the interpretation should not lead to inconsistency or a contradiction of legal norms. The theoretical models of legal interpretation developed in Polish legal theory maintain that if such a conflict arises, it should be resolved by the application of rules of interpretation of the second level (Gizbert-Studnicki 2010). Those rules determine:

(i) the sequence in which the first level rules are to be applied and
(ii) the priority relation between them in case of a conflict.

A conflict between the results of linguistic and teleological interpretations can obviously be resolved in two ways: either by giving priority to the former or to the latter. The problem with second level rules is twofold. First, there are no unconditionally and generally accepted second level rules. Second, even individual judges do not apply any second level rules in a consistent manner (one and the same judge, for example, will sometimes give priority to the rules of teleological interpretation and sometimes to the plain meaning rule). Usually, the justification of such a decision does not simply refer to any particular "ready-made" second level rule. Such a reference is usually not deemed to be a sufficient reason for an interpretative decision, due to the highly controversial nature of second level rules. A proper justification requires direct reference to the values underlying the conflicting first level rules and resolution of the conflict between those values. Such an axiological justification, however, is presented only if a conflict between the first level rules arises.

To sum up in Polish legal culture there exist quite a large number of first level rules of interpretation which are generally accepted and applied. Those rules have different provenance (linguistic, systematic or teleological). As long as their application does not lead to a conflict, they remain uncontroversial. Nobody is questioning, for example, the legitimacy of teleological rules of interpretation, or of a rule requiring that the actual intention of the lawgiver should be taken into account. The application of first level rules does not usually invoke any axiological considerations. The theoretical models of legal interpretation maintain that conflicts between those rules are resolved by making recourse to second level rules. In legal practice, however, such conflicts are resolved not by making reference to any "ready-made" rules of interpretation, but usually by direct recourse to the underlying values (legal certainty, justice, fairness, flexibility of law, etc.). The conflict between competing interpretations is resolved by the resolution of the conflict of values underlying the applied rules of the first level. Therefore, in legal practice, the second level rules, as a matter of fact, do not function as devices delivering justificatory reasons for interpretative decisions. This role is played directly by values underlying the first level rules. This means that the second level rules are rather a theoretical construction of legal theory, and not a practical device of legal practice. An important feature of legal practice is that axiological justification of an interpretative decision by direct reference to underlying values is usually invoked only if a conflict between reasons delivered by the first level rules arises.

My impression, based on American legal theoretical literature, is that the approach characteristic of US legal culture is different[5]. The main difference is that the legitimacy of particular sorts of first level rules of interpretation (commonly called "canons of construction") is frequently challenged *in abstracto,* which is not the case in Polish legal culture. I'll give a few selected examples. Textualists and formalists challenge the legitimacy of rules of purposive interpretation (Schauer 1988), originalists (adopting "original public meaning" position) challenge the legitimacy of rules based on the actual or construed intentions of the framers of the Constitution (Scalia 1997) and supporters of living constitutionalism challenge the legitimacy of the rules based on the plain language of the Constitution (Strauss 2010). Most discussions between the supporters of conflicting views are of the axiological nature. These discussions relate directly to the legitimacy of the first level rules and not to ways of resolving conflicts between various first level rules[6]. At stake is the existence or absence of the proper axiological justification of various first level rules. It is recommended that those rules which are considered (*in abstracto*) as lacking axiological justification are abandoned and not applied to any problem of interpretation. The consequence of such an approach is that within one and the same position in the theory of interpretation, no conflict between various rules may arise. For example, purposive rules are rejected *in abstracto* by adherents of formalism and any rules referring to the intention of the lawgiver are rejected by the "original public meaning" originalists. The proponents of the respective positions maintain that due to the lack of axiological justification, certain rules should simply not be applied in any case, and therefore, for a formalist or an originalist, no conflict of the purposive rule with the plain meaning rule may arise. If this is the case, there is no need to introduce the theoretical construction of rules of interpretation of the second level.

In both legal cultures, the theorists of legal interpretation frequently refer to various semantic theories which they present to support their recommendations of the rules of interpretation that should be adopted and/or the modes of resolution of conflicts between particular rules. I am sceptical whether this is the right approach (Patterson 1995). In my opinion, controversies as to the proper interpretation of law cannot be solved solely by any semantic theory, since matters of interpretation are, in the last instance, matters of axiology, and therefore, the matters of political philosophy, not semantic matters. As J. Raz (1996, p. 23) said, "The choice of methods of interpretation is part of the constitution of every state". Therefore, no semantic theory can deliver definite, valid justification for the adoption of any definite rules of legal interpretation, although semantic theories may help in developing and justifying such rules (Brink 2001).

[5] American literature on statutory interpretation is enormous. I can refer here to only a few selected positions.

[6] Important discrepancies exist as to the proper rules of interpretation within one and the same position, for example, within textualism (Tutt 2014).

References

Bertea, Stefano. 2009. *The normative claim of law*. Oxford: Hart Publishing.

Bix, Brian. 2012. The nature of law and reasons for action. *Problema. Anuario de Filosofia y Teoria de Derecho* 5:400–415.

Brink, David O. 2001. Legal interpretation, objectivity, and morality. In *Objectivity in law and morals*, ed. Brian Leiter, 12–65. Cambridge: Cambridge University Press.

Brożek, Bartosz. 2012. *Normatywność prawa (Normativity of Law)*. Warszawa: Kluwer.

Dyrda, Adam. 2013. *Konwencja u podstaw prawa. Kontrowersje pozytywizmu prawniczego (Convention as foundation of law. Controversies of legal positivism)*, Warszawa: Kluwer.

Enoch, David. 2011. Reason-giving and the law. In *Oxford studies in the philosophy of law 1,* ed. Leslie Greed and Brian Leiter 1–38. Oxford: Oxford University Press.

Gizbert-Studnicki, Tomasz. 1990. The burden of argumentation in legal disputes. *Ratio Iuris* 3 (1): 118–129.

Gizbert-Studnicki, Tomasz. 2010. Dyrektywy wykładni drugiego stopnia (Rules of Interpretation of the Second Level). In *W poszukiwaiu dobra wspólnego (In search for common good),* ed. Agnieszka Choduń and Stanisław Czepita, 49–68. Szczecin: University of Szczecin Press.

Kramer, Mathew. 2007. *Objectivity and the rule of law*. Cambridge: Cambridge University Press.

Lewis, David. 1969. *Convention: A philosophical study*. Cambridge: Harvard University Press.

Patterson, Dennis. 1995. Against a theory of meaning, 73. *Washington University Law Quarterly* 1153:1153–1157.

Raz, Joseph. 1994. *Ethics in the public domain*. Oxford, Oxford University Press.

Raz, Joseph. 1996. On the nature of law. *Archiv fuer Rechts- und Sozialphilosophie* 82:1–25.

Scalia, Antonin. 1997. *A matter of interpretation: Federal courts and the law*. Princeton:Princeton University Press.

Schauer, Frederic. 1988. Formalism. *Yale Law Journal* 97:509–548.

Smith, Michael. 1994. *The moral problem*. Oxford: Blackwell.

Stawecki, Tomasz. 2010. Złota reguła wykladni (The Golden Rule of Interpretation), In *W poszukiwaniu dobra wspólnego (In search of common good)*, ed. Agnieszka Chodun and Stanisław Czepita, 113–128. Szczecin: University of Szczecin Press.

Strauss, David A. 2010. *The living constitution*. Oxford: Oxford University Press.

Tutt, Andrew. 2013. Interpretation step zero: A limit on methodology as "Law". *The Yale Law Journal* 122:2055–2067.

Tutt, Andrew. 2014. Fifty shades of textualism. *Journal of Law and Politics* XXIX:309–351.

Williams, Bernard. 1981. *Moral luck*. Cambridge: Cambridge University Press.

Wróblewski, Jerzy. 1992. *The judicial application of law*. Dortrecht: Kluwer.

Zielinski, Maciej. 2010. *Wykładnia prawa. Zasady, reguły, wskazówki (Interpretation of law. Principles, rules and recommendations)*. 5th ed. Warszawa: LexisNexis.

Chapter 19
Legal Interpretation as a Rule-Guided Phenomenon

Paweł Banaś

Abstract The content of law is derived from legal texts in a process of interpretation that is not random but is rather supposed to follow some rules. There are different types of rules of interpretation, and they govern different levels of every interpretation process. In describing this process, an analogy can be drawn between some notions present in the contemporary philosophy of language and legal interpretation. Rules of interpretation constitute legal content; i.e. they provide it with truth conditions. Rules of interpretation are given by a political theory adopted together with semantic theory grounded in social practice. Ontologically, the most problematic issue is the question of what makes an application of rules of interpretation correct or incorrect. It is part of a certain view of law to suggest that indeed there are always facts of some kind (either social practice or moral values) that guide the application of given rules of interpretation. This common picture of law is built on some presuppositions, among them normativity (guidance and justification), objectivity and classical realism. Within this view, it is also presupposed that there are right answers to questions about the content of law. It is argued that Kripkenstein's sceptical paradox poses a threat to this view, as it questions the existence of any facts that could guide any types of rules of interpretation. Such an ontological threat does not necessarily weaken the justificatory function of legal interpretation.

Keywords Interpretation · Meaning theory · Content of law · Rule guidance · Rule scepticism

19.1 Introduction

Law can be seen as a system that contains a certain set of rules and relations between them. In legal practice, these rules are derived from legal texts in a process of interpretation. Interpreters look for the proper meaning of what is written so they can say that what is meant by a text is in fact a legal rule. Hence, the aim of legal interpretation is to provide the meaning of a given text of law (i.e. the content of

P. Banaś (✉)
Faculty of Law, Jagiellonian University, Kraków, Poland
e-mail: pawel.banas@uj.edu.pl

M. Araszkiewicz et al. (eds.), *Problems of Normativity, Rules and Rule-Following*,
Law and Philosophy Library 111, DOI 10.1007/978-3-319-09375-8_19

law). The 'proper meaning' of a legal text can be arrived at only if some rules of interpretation are followed. This is a platitude about law stating that the process of interpretation should never be random; instead, there are a number of so-called second-order rules, such as e.g. *clara (non) sunt interpretanda* (if the text is clear on how the first-order rule should be understood, one should (not) engage in a 'deep' interpretation process), that should guide it.

Interpretation serves legal discourse in many ways: its function can be seen as explanatory or heuristic, i.e. providing adequate descriptions of judges' practices; it can also be seen as justificatory, i.e. providing reasons for judges' decisions (see Studnicki, Chap. 18). However, the most fundamental aspect of legal interpretation is that it constitutes the content of law. For a judge to say that a certain rule is a valid legal rule, there must exist a rule of interpretation (a second-order rule) that, when applied, points to this first-order rule as what is meant by a legal text. However, to say that law is constituted by the interpretation of a legal text does not automatically entail an interpretivist theory of law in the Dworkinian style.[1]

The interpretation of law is a multi-layer phenomenon; on the deepest level, however, it must at least provide some theory of linguistic meaning. The starting point of every interpreter of law is always a piece of language that requires some further processing. In the sense in which the output of such processing is constituted by the latter, interpretation must be seen at least minimally constitutive of the content of law. In this chapter, an analogy will be drawn between the interpretation of legal texts and some notions from the contemporary philosophy of language to develop this issue further.

In this chapter, I also aim to show that legal interpretation is a rule-guided process that operates on different types of rules, some of which can be perceived as grounded in some semantic theory and others in a kind of social practice, moral values or political theory. Finally, I would suggest that all levels of interpretation are subject to some version of Kripkenstein's sceptical problem that questions the intuitively realist picture of law where there exists an answer to the question of law arrived at via correct interpretation.

19.2 Legal Interpretation as a Multi-Level Process

As previously stressed, legal interpretation aims at providing the (correct) meaning of a given legal text. The journey starting with a legal text, a linguistic entity, requires some theory of linguistic meaning in the beginning. Legal discourse is quite different from meaning discourse, and every analogy drawn between them must be well justified. However, I assume (and strongly believe) that this difference is not qualitative and the latter is simply more general than the former (at least in terms of linguistic properties). Legal discourse includes discourse about the meaning of legal texts. What makes a discourse about the meaning of legal texts a part of a legal

[1] As e.g. Stavropoulos (2003) describes it.

discourse is that truth-evaluable sentences within the former require truth-makers provided (or suggested) by some legal theory.

If my assumption is acceptable (and it does not seem very controversial), then I may draw some analogies between certain notions present in the contemporary philosophy of language and legal interpretation.

Philosophers of language tend to distinguish different levels of interpretation. Borg (2004, p. 38)[2] points to three such levels:

1) Linguistic decoding, which results in a logical form [according to e.g. Carston (1988), unlike in Borg (2004)—an incomplete one]. This is a purely formal stage, guided by syntactic rules of language. It is debatable whether it provides in the end anything truth-evaluable, any propositional content so that minimal formal semantic theory can be of any use here (as Borg suggests). Nonetheless, interpretation (whether legal or not) requires some semantic theory, part of which describes formal syntactic rules that at some very basic level guide any use of meaningful expressions in any language.
2) Primary pragmatic inference, the result of which is an explicature ('what is said'[3]). According to e.g. Carston (1988) or proponents of dual pragmatics in general, unlike Borg (2004), this is a level that provides us with propositional content to which truth value can be assigned. For Carston (1988), explicature is built on a linguistically determined content as well as anything pragmatically inferred[4] that seems necessary to obtain whatever is really said (still, however, not implied). At this level, different types of development of the logical form obtained as a result of level-one processes are allowed: reference assignment, disambiguation, specification of vague terms, the supply of empty grammatical categories with conceptual content, the building of certain relations between events and states, free enrichment, completion, saturation, etc. It must be noted that pragmatic inferences at this level are local. They operate on subparts of a logical form [in an example by Carston and Hall (2011), free enrichment e.g. replaces an encoded concept with an inferred concept or adds material to change the interpretation of some encoded element]. However, all the pragmatic inferences are somehow context-dependent; alas, rules that guide interpretation at this level are very different from those at level one.
3) Secondary pragmatic inference, which results in an implicature ('what is implied'), a fully pragmatically enhanced item (Borg 2004, p. 38). It is either 'the act of meaning, implying, or suggesting one thing by saying something else' or 'the object of that act' (Davis 2013). For Grice, an implicature is arrived at by following the cooperative principle and maxims of quality ('Say what you believe is true'), quantity ('Be informative'), relation ('Be relevant')

[2] In her book, Borg talks about utterances rather than written text. I think, however, that as far as this chapter goes, it does not make much difference.

[3] However, it was Sperber and Wilson (1986, pp. 182–183) who introduced the term 'explicature', not Grice, and it was probably Carston (1988) who identified the Gricean 'what is said' with an explicature as described in relevance theory.

[4] For Griceans, disambiguation and reference assignment only.

and manner ('Be perspicuous') (Grice 1975; for more about the issues, see I. Skoczeń's Chap. 26). Alternatively, Sperber and Wilson (1986) and Carston and Hall (2011), as proponents of relevance theory, in contrast to Grice, claim that implicatures are globally derived speaker-meant contextual implications. They are global because they do not encode a logical form provided by level one but operate on fully propositional content. An example (taken from Carston and Hall 2011, p. 21) is as follows:

X: Does John like cats?
Y: He doesn't like any animals.

1. Cats are animals.
2. John doesn't like cats.
   a) Dogs are animals.
   b) John doesn't like dogs.

Sentences 2 and b (so-called 'implicated conclusions') are not said but rather communicated by the speaker, and they are not in any way developed from an initial logical form; hence, they must be implicatures (according to relevance theory). Again, different rules of interpretation must be applied at this level to arrive at 'what is communicated.'

I do not intend to advocate any particular framework (either the Gricean or that of relevance theory), as there are strong arguments that neither of them is adequate to accommodate discourse about the meaning of a legal text fully (see Skoczeń, Chap. 26). However, the general idea that the process of legal interpretation can be divided into at least three stages governed by different types of rules (all of which can be labeled 'rules of interpretation') seems a natural implication of my previous assumption that a discourse about the meaning of a legal text is just less general but qualitatively the same as a meaning discourse in general.

First, within any process of legal interpretation, a judge is supposed to follow formal syntactic rules that provide him with logical form-like structures of what is written in a text of law. For that, he needs some syntactic theory or even a minimal formal semantic theory [as Borg (2004) or Cappelen and Lepore (2005) would like to suggest]. This is not actually a problem of philosophy of law to decide whether linguistic decoding results in a type-like (compared to a token-like) truth-evaluable propositional form. Whether literal meaning can be formally derived or requires some contextual input does not change the fact that any theory of interpretation must deal with the problem of the literal meaning of a text of law anyway. Literal meaning can be (and in the case of a legal language, it is perhaps even more apparent that it is) a product of free enrichment and saturation processes (governed by interpretation rules such as '*every use of the same word in a given statute ought to be given the same meaning*'). However, the theory of linguistic meaning must operate on this explicature-like input even if rules applied at the implicature-like level aim to allow in the end that what is meant ('communicated' or 'implied') by a legal text is much different from what is literally stated in it. This is because the output of the subsequent level of interpretation is constituted by its input (even if this constitutiveness is to some extent mutual).

Finally, rules that guide the implicature-like level must be taken into consideration. These are global, heavily context-dependent rules. Since discourse about the meaning of a legal text is a highly specialized discourse, one should expect that it will employ principles that may not always (or, more probably, cannot) be applied to any other discourses and are far too specific to be discussed within the general meaning discourse. These are principles that may appeal to some systematic aspects of law e.g. they may '*be in accord with constitutional values*'.

To sum up, any judge should, in the process of interpretation, follow (not necessarily consciously) formal rules of syntax and semantic rules that locally govern literal meaning—both type-like and token-like as well as higher-order global rules. These rules guide different levels of the processing of any legal text. Each level results in an output that becomes an input of the subsequent level and constitutes this level's eventual output, etc.

19.3 Metaphysics of Interpretation

What do I mean by saying that any judge should follow certain rules in the process of interpretation? Well, certainly I do not mean that every judge should be familiar with different levels of interpretation and types of rules that guide processing at each particular level. Being aware that legal interpretation is a multi-level phenomenon is of little (if any) use for legal practice. This is mostly due to the fact that the aforementioned theory of meaning (including legal meaning) is hoped to be a descriptive (explanatory) rather than a normative one.

As far as the justificatory function of legal interpretation is concerned, one should probably note that higher-order rules (appealing to moral or political values of some kind) must always operate on a material that is a result of some kind of linguistic processing. Hence, any political theory that defines the content of higher-order rules is required to adopt or at least silently agree on some kind of semantic theory that will deliver input for the secondary pragmatic processes.

In the remaining part of this chapter, however, I do not intend to deal with the justificatory function of legal interpretation, as I find this a problem of legal epistemology. My concern here is more fundamental, namely ontological. So far, I have claimed that a logical form-like structure is constituted by some formal syntactic rules and, together with local rules that guide the development of the logical form, constitute the explicature-like 'what is stated' propositional content of law. This explicature-like structure, together with higher-order rules, constitutes the implicature-like content of law. However, what exactly do I mean by claiming that rules of interpretation (operating on logical form-like and explicature-like structures) constitute the content of law? Within philosophy, including the philosophy of law, the notion of constitutive rules has been discussed in many different contexts and as such may entail some strong associations. Hence, to clarify this claim of constitutiveness, I would rather discourage any quick analogies between it and potentially similar notions present in debates concerning either constitutive vs. prescriptive (see Hess, Chap. 13)[5] or constitutive vs. regulative[6] (see Hindriks 2009) nature of rules. As far as this chapter is concerned, to constitute something is to provide truth conditions for sentences about it. Any sentence such as, 'The explicature-like structure E is so and so' is a true sentence only if it is a result of the correct application of semantic rules that govern literal meaning while operating on a logical form-like structure.

The claim of constitutiveness, therefore, is the claim that the assignment of truth value to any sentence about the meaning of a legal text (and hence any sentence about the content of law) is admissible only if this sentence about the content of law is a result of the proper application of appropriate rules at every level of the whole process of legal interpretation.

Whether a given rule is an appropriate one is a matter of a political theory adopted[7] (a part of which is a certain semantic theory) and grounded in our social practice. From an ontological point of view, an important question is, however, what makes the application of a given rule (assuming that it an appropriate rule) correct. I will focus on this question in the remaining part of this chapter.

19.4 Common Picture of Law

It actually seems rather intuitive to assume that there is always a fact of some kind that makes the application of a given rule of interpretation correct. Such a fact (or set of facts) would serve as a truth-maker for sentences about the content of law. Hence, the character of this fact (or set of facts) lies at the very center of legal theory; e.g. Scott Shapiro (2007) describes the core of the Hart-Dworkin debate as follows:

> Dworkin's basic strategy throughout the course of the debate has been to argue that, in one form or another, legality is ultimately determined not by social facts alone, but by moral facts as well. In other words, the existence and content of positive law is, in the final analysis, governed by the existence and content of the moral law. This contention, therefore, directly challenges and threatens to undermine the positivist picture about the nature of law, in which legality is never determined by morality but rather by social practice.

It seems that positivists as well as non-positivists generally assume[8] that the content of law is grounded in either social practice (the former ones) or some moral or

[5] In this case, the constitutive nature of rules would mean that they are chess-like rules. Anyone who is not following the rules of the game of chess is not playing chess at all. On the other hand, rules of grammar that govern the use of language are rather prescriptive in nature. To speak correctly, one ought to follow them, but failing to do so does not necessarily mean that she does not speak the language at all.

[6] As introduced by Searle (1969).

[7] For a discussion see Gizbert-Studnicki 2014.

[8] This, of course, is an oversimplification (for discussion of some factual as well as nonfactual theories, see Grabowski, 2013). It seems a controversial claim to suggest that Dworkin was some kind of factualist. However, for the purpose of this chapter, some generalization seems acceptable.

political values (the other ones). I think that such an assumption is a part of a larger picture of how legal discourse is commonly perceived. Let me call this picture 'a common picture of law.' A picture can hardly be seen as a theory (or some meta-theory) of law; instead, it is some general set of views concerning legal discourse.[9]

An important element of the common picture of law is the normativity of the rules of interpretation. This normativity consists of at least two aspects: guidance and justification. Other elements are objectivity and classical realism. Hence, this picture can be described as follows: there is something (let us call it a fact of some kind) that guides a judge on how to apply a rule of interpretation and at the same time can be referred to for this application to be justified. This guidance, however, does not determine how the rule of interpretation will be applied (as there would be no place left for normativity at all) but rather how it ought to be applied. Objectivity in this picture is built on two assumptions: first that no rule of interpretation may be of a private (a judge cannot justify her decision by appealing to a rule unavailable to anyone else) or a mind-dependent character and second that any guiding fact itself cannot be private or mind-dependent. Classical realism requires that whether or not a rule of interpretation is correctly applied is somehow mirrored in a sentence where the aforementioned guiding fact serves as a truth maker.

Guidance, justification, objectivity and classical realism are not the only elements of the picture set above. However, they point together to the most fundamental principle it employs, namely that there is always an answer to the question about the content of law that is independent of any individual and her thoughts, attitudes or conceptual vocabulary and that, nonetheless, human beings are somehow cognitively capable of conceiving it [Crispin Wright (1992) calls the former a 'modest' and the latter a 'presumptuous' thought of realism]. This picture is not only intuitive but certainly appealing as well. If there is an answer to any question about the content of law that is at least potentially accessible to anyone ready to make the minimum effort, then my confidence in a judge's decision rises (or should rise).

However, no matter how intuitive the common picture of law seems to be, it requires well-established candidates for guiding facts that serve as truth makers for any sentences about legal content (meaning of legal texts). The answer, after all, is constituted by the correct application of appropriate rules of interpretation, and this 'correctness of application' depends on a fact (or set of facts of some kind).

To develop the problem further, the previously provided description of legal interpretation as a multi-level phenomenon is required. Indeed, there are different types of rules of interpretation: formal rules of syntax and semantic rules that locally govern literal meaning—both type-like and token-like as well as higher-order global rules. Different types of rules may require different candidates for the

[9] Here I follow Martin Kusch's idea (2006) to read Kripke's *Wittgenstein on Rules and Private Language* (1982) as a 'critical study of philosophical analyses of meaning attributions' to a word or sign. Kusch points out that these analyses are based on a certain picture of language, which he calls 'meaning determinism'—a picture Kripke attacks and rejects on the merit of his reading of Wittgenstein's sceptical argument. I think that there is an analogy between the picture offered by the meaning determinism and the common picture of law, which, I assume, is strongly connected with how the process of the interpretation of law is usually perceived.

truth-makers. For a sentence about legal content to be true, it must (probably) be grounded in a non-reducible set of facts about at least language and our social practice. What kinds of facts make good candidates? Among potential social facts, consensus (either real or theoretical), a majority vote, experts' opinion or some kind of convention have been or still are postulated as fine truth-makers.

Social facts and facts about language (either social or not) do not necessarily exhaust the list of all potential facts guiding legal interpretation. Much attention has also been given to values, either political or moral, external or even internal to law and at the same time independent of law practices and 'genuine value facts' (Greenberg 2004). Nonetheless, whether of social or moral pedigree, every candidate fact to be considered a proper truth-maker must first face the greatest single threat to the 'common picture of law'—Kripkenstein's sceptical argument.

19.5 Kripkenstein's Sceptical Argument

In his famous book *Wittgenstein on Rules and Private Language*, Kripke proposes an interpretation of Ludwig Wittgenstein's *Philosophical Investigations* (passages 138–242; 'the private language argument'), where two different but strongly connected ideas are present (Boghossian 1989). I am going to sketch them here briefly. First, any meaning offers an infinite number of truths about how the meaningful term should be applied. Second, as Kripke points out, this infinite number of truths to be formulated with a meaningful expression is normative in nature. These truths are truths about how a given expression ought to be applied, not how it will be applied. These two assumptions are elements of the 'meaning determinism' picture of language (Kusch 2006).

In this picture, a linguistic term's meaning can be seen as a rule that 'tells' its user how the term ought to be applied if it is to be applied correctly, and this covers an infinite number of possible applications of the term. The problem, termed Kripke's sceptical paradox, is, however, that there is actually nothing that serves as a criterion that allows a language user to differentiate between the correct and incorrect applications of a semantic rule. In other words, there are no truth conditions for any sentences about meaning.[10] To illustrate this problem, Kripke provides his famous example: if I add 68 and 57, the obvious result is 125. When I say, hence, that '68 plus 57 is 125,' I think that I use the term 'plus' correctly, while if anyone said that e.g. '68 plus 57 is 5,' I would think that she uses the term 'incorrectly.' However, Kripke claims, there is no fact about this world that constitutes either correctness or incorrectness in both these cases. E.g. from the previous applications of the rule, I cannot tell whether it is something like 'x plus $y=x+y$' rather than 'x plus $y=x+y$ when $x, y<57$ and $x+y=5$ when $x, y>57$'. If the previous applications of the rule are not enough to determine the correctness of the new use, then maybe it is the case that we, in fact, do not follow an abstract rule when deciding on the application

[10] Kripke dismisses some potential candidates for such truth-making facts, e.g. Platonic entities, past uses and dispositions. However, these are of less importance for legal discourse.

of meaning in question. A language user could e.g. already know all the potential applications or at least have dispositions for every possible use of the term in question. If my use of the term is the same as the disposition, then it is correct. Kripke, however, points out that there is an infinite number of potential applications and that it is impossible for a finite mind such as ours to possess an infinite number of dispositions.

What follows from Kripke's sceptical paradox is that our semantic discourse is non-factual; in other words, whenever one utters a declarative sentence about the meaning of a linguistic term, there is nothing that makes such a sentence true or false (and hence makes a given use of a meaning predicate correct or incorrect).

If the semantic aspect of any language is to be seen as a certain set of meanings, conceived of as semantic rules for applying linguistic terms, then Kripke's argument claims that we cannot say which rule application is right and which is wrong, as there are no criteria that make it possible to say when one acts correctly, i.e. according to the semantic rule. This leads to the counterintuitive conclusion that meaning cannot be normative, which is the essence of the paradox.

Kripkenstein's paradox is not, however, limited to general meaning discourse. It threatens every meaning discourse, including our discourse about the meaning of a legal text (legal interpretation discourse). Moreover, it actually can be easily applied to every rule-governed discourse. To arrive at some truth-evaluable content, a legal interpreter must provide some facts (either social or moral) that could serve as truth-makers for a corresponding proposition. She must also bear in mind that legal interpretation is a multi-level phenomenon and that the rules of every level of processing require their own truth-makers.

Conclusions

This chapter aimed at introducing legal interpretation as a multi-level rule-guided phenomenon. I began by showing that there are different types of rules that guide the whole process, i.e. formal rules of syntax and semantic rules that locally govern literal meaning—both type-like and token-like as well as higher-order global rules. All these rules are supposed to constitute the legal content, which means that the correct application of appropriate rules should provide sentences about the meaning of a text of law with truth conditions. I further claimed that his idea, together with some others, was an element of the common picture of law that adopted a realist view of legal discourse. However, I finished this chapter by introducing Kripke's argument against such a view with an indirect suggestion that it may pose a serious threat to the very existence of truth-makers for sentences in a discourse about legal content. The result of this would be a strong claim that no statement about the meaning of a legal text is true or false. Such a non-factual conclusion seems a very strong one as well as counter-intuitive. However, Kripkenstein's sceptical paradox is a strong enough argument seriously to consider alternatives to the common view of law—this, however, is not the aim of this chapter. It should probably be noted that the claims of non-factualism are strictly ontological. Epistemic functions of legal interpretation, the justificatory one in particular, should retain their force—even if a sentence is not truth-evaluable, it still may be at least better or worse justified, and it is the justificatory[11] force of legal interpretation that affects legal practice in the first place.

Acknowledgments This paper is a part of a project funded by National Science Centre of Poland (UMO-2012/07/N/HS5/00999).

References

Boghossian, Paul. 1989. The rule-following considerations. *Mind* 98:507–549.

Borg, Emma. 2004. *Minimal semantics*. Oxford: Clarendon.

Cappelen, Herman, and Lepore, Ernie. 2005. *Insensitive semantics: A defense of semantic minimalism and speech act pluralism*. Oxford: Blackwell.

Carston, Robyn. 1988. Implicature, explicature and truth-theoretic semantics. In *Mental representations: the interface between language and reality*, ed. R. Kempson, 155–181. Cambridge: Cambridge University Press.

Carston, Robyn, and Hall, Alison. 2011. Implicature and explicature. In *Cognitive pragmatics, vol.4 of handbooks in pragmatics*, ed. Hans-Jörg Schmid. Hawthorne: Mouton de Gruyters.

Davis, Wayne. 2013. Implicature. *The stanford encyclopedia of philosophy* (Spring 2013 edition) ed. Edward N. Zalta. http://plato.stanford.edu/archives/spr2013/entries/implicature/. Accessed 25 Aug 2014.

Gizbert-Studnicki, Tomasz. 2014. The normativity of rules of interpretation. In *Problems of normativity, rules and rule-following*, ed. Michał Araszkiewicz, Paweł Banaś, Tomasz Gizbert-Studnicki, and Krzysztof Pleszka. Heidelberg: Springer, [pp].

Grabowski, Andrzej. 2013. *Juristic concept of the validity of statutory law. A critique of contemporary legal nonpositivism*. Heidelberg: Springer.

Greenberg, Mark. 2004. How facts make law. *Legal theory* 10:157–198. Los Angeles: University of California.

Grice, Paul. 1975. Logic and conversation. In *The logic of grammar*, eds. D. Davidson and G. Harman. Encino: Dickenson.

Hindriks, Frank. 2009. Constitutive rules, language, and ontology. *Erkenntnis* 71 (2): 253–275.

Kripke, Saul.1982. *Wittgenstein on rules and private language*. Cambridge: Harvard University Press.

Kusch, Martin. 2006. *A sceptical guide to meaning and rules: Defending Kripke's Wittgenstein*. Canada: Acumen & McGill-Queen's.

Searle, John. 1969. *Speech acts: An essay in the philosophy of language*. Cambridge: Cambridge University Press.

Shapiro, Scott. 2007. The "Hart-Dworkin" debate: A Short guide for the perplexed. U of Michigan Public Law Working Paper No. 77. SSRN: http://ssrn.com/abstract=968657 or http://dx.doi.org/10.2139/ssrn.968657. Accessed 25 Aug 2014.

Sperber, Dan, and Wilson, Deirdre. 1986. *Relevance: Communication and cognition*. Oxford: Blackwell.

Stavropoulos, Nicos. 2008. Interpretivist theories of law. *The Stanford encyclopedia of philosophy* (Fall 2008 Edition), ed. Edward N. Zalta. http://plato.stanford.edu/archives/fall2008/entries/law-interpretivist/. Accessed 25 Aug 2014.

Wright, Crispin. 1992. *Truth and objectivity*. Cambridge: Harvard University Press.

[11] See the previous chapter for more discussion about the justificatory function of law.

Chapter 20
To Whom Does the Law Speak? Canvassing a Neglected Picture of Law's Interpretive Field

Paolo Sandro

Abstract Among the most common strategies underlying the so-called indeterminacy thesis is the following two-step argument: (1) that law is an interpretive practice, and that evidently legal actors more generally hold different (and competing) theories of meaning, which lead to disagreements as to what the law *says* (that is, as to what the law *is*); (2) and that, as there is no way to establish the prevalence of one particular theory of meaning over the other, indeterminacy is pervasive in law. In this paper I offer some reflections to resist this trend. In particular I claim that a proper understanding of law as an authoritative communicative enterprise sheds new light on the relation between the functioning of the law and our theories of interpretation, leading to what can be considered a neglected conclusion: the centrality of the linguistic criterion of meaning in our juridical interpretive practices. In the first part of the chapter I discuss speech-act theory in the study of law, assessing its relevance between alternative options. Then I tackle the 'to whom does the law speak?' question, highlighting the centrality of lay-people for our juridical practices. Lastly, I examine the consequences of this neglected fact for our interpretive theories.

Keywords Indeterminacy thesis · Law as communication · Legal interpretation · Norm-addressees · Speech-act theory

20.1 Introduction

A growing bulk of legal scholarship, conceiving of law as a communicative phenomenon (e.g. Van Hoecke 2002),[1] revolves around the question 'what does the law say?' On a first approximation, to ask this question is tantamount to ask 'what is the law?', in general or as to a specific case. This is indeed a common way in which a layperson would seek legal advice from her solicitor: 'What does the law *say* on

[1] This trend is particularly evident in criminal law and criminal justice (see for an overview Stark 2013).

P. Sandro (✉)
Liverpool Hope University, Department of Law, FML Building,
Hope Park, Liverpool, L16 9JD, UK
e-mail: p.sandro@leeds.ac.uk

M. Araszkiewicz et al. (eds.), *Problems of Normativity, Rules and Rule-Following*,
Law and Philosophy Library 111, DOI 10.1007/978-3-319-09375-8_20

buying land estate without a written contract?' The solicitor would then go on and explain the *content* of the law, that is, she would tell her client what the law *is* (at least from the best of her knowledge) on real estate. But on a more careful consideration, what the law *says*—i.e. the text of legal sources such as statutes and judicial decisions—does not always correspond with what the law *is*, viz with the norms (rules, standards, principles, etc.) that govern a certain activity or situation.[2] Such variance depends on the role one assigns to pragmatics (and context in particular) in the determination of the content of legal utterances, and this point represents one of the most debated issues in jurisprudence nowadays (e.g. Marmor 2008; Marmor and Soames 2011), straddling the philosophies of law and language.

In this chapter I shall focus on a different, albeit clearly related, question. Operating within the same understanding of law as communication I ask, 'to whom does the law speak?' Such a question might sound naïve, at best, or pointless, at worse. For if we skim through law books and manuals, it seems that the law *speaks* only to judges, officials, lawyers and (sometimes) jurists,[3] as it is only their interpretive practices which are analysed. In other words, the law addresses only those agents whose interpretation bears some authoritativeness, directly (judges, officials) or indirectly (lawyers, jurists). Hence our theories of legal interpretation are (and must be) modelled around their operations, taking into account the specificity of the resulting interpretive field and considering legal interpretation as a highly specialised practice. Now, is this picture of law's interpretive field apt? I seriously question this contention. Of course, to deny the high degree of complexity of legal interpretation as carried out by judges and other institutional agents would be readily counterintuitive as a descriptive claim. Rather, in this chapter I plan to suggest that this picture of law's epistemic field is, at best, incomplete, and that a different, more comprehensive, picture of it must be canvassed. But why is this operation worth pursuing? If the arguments I put forward are sound, important consequences for our theories of legal interpretation arise, and in particular as to the so-called 'indeterminacy problem'.

In this regard underpinning our liberal institutional paradigms is the belief that legal 'facts' are in some sense, and at least partially, objective and determinate Coleman and Leiter 1995). On the interpretive side, this position is usually defined as 'mixed' theory (see e.g. Hart 1994; Marmor 2005; Moreso 1998) precisely because it acknowledges an area of objectivity and determinacy in our adjudicative practices. And yet we see judges, lawyers and academics constantly disagreeing about what the law is, both in general and in particular cases: for legal actors interpret the (text of the) law in different ways, and thus they obtain different answers as to what the law is. Viz, they seem to disagree about the *meaning* of legal utterances, because they hold different theories of meaning: so that, descriptively, no one among them can be considered to be prevalent (Guastini 2011, pp. 153–154). But if this is so, legal utterances cannot be truth-apt—they do not have '*one* definitive objective

[2] This variance presupposes the distinction, still slightly underdeveloped especially in Anglo-American jurisprudence, between norm-sentences and norms *tout court* (e.g. Guastini 2011).

[3] cf Hart 1994, pp. 35–41, criticising Kelsen on the point.

meaning' (Guastini 2011, p. 152, italics original). As such, the indeterminacy of law would follow from its interpretive nature and two seem the main strategies available to us:[4] either we resort to the Dworkinian approach that might allows us to reach always a right answer (thus preserving the legitimacy of adjudication), but at the cost of embracing the idea of law *as integrity* all the way down (Dworkin 1986, 2011); or we are faced with the necessity to acknowledge the pervasiveness of indeterminacy in law, and to draw the ensuing implications in terms of the legitimacy of our liberal institutional practices.

My contention is that the considerations offered in what follows as to law's interpretive field help assessing, and rebutting, the indeterminacy thesis as we have just outlined it. As such they are not sufficient to establishing the case for objectivity and determinacy in law, but they offer corroborating reasons to uphold a mixed theory of interpretation against critical and radical indeterminacy positions. The chapter breaks down like this. In Sect. 20.2 I discuss the use of speech-act theory in the analysis of law, briefly assessing the suitability of the former vis-à-vis the communicative nature of the latter. To this end, Sect. 20.3 examines the peculiar relationship between sender and receiver of legal utterances, and statutes in particular. This leads to the question of 'who are law's addressees?', which I take up in Sect. 20.4. I argue that there are sound meta-theoretical reasons to consider laypeople as the first and foremost addressees of legal communication. Finally in Sect. 20.5 I deal with the consequences of this latter claim for our theories of interpretation, the most important being the need to recognise the prevalence of the linguistic criterion of interpretation amongst the ones available. This is necessary, I argue, for the existence of a legal system as such.

20.2 Preliminaries on Speech-Act Theory and The Study of Law

The use of speech-act theory to analyse law represents one of the principal waves that have swept legal philosophy over the last few decades. Beginning with the collaboration between J.L. Austin and H.L.A. Hart in Oxford, legal rules have been understood in their quality of performatives—in their being not just *words* (like when we describe the motion of planets), but actual *actions* through *words* ('I hereby declare you man and wife'). Since then speech-act theory has progressively gained relevance in legal-philosophical discourse, providing it with a 'general orientation and framework for analysis and research' of 'legal utterances with which it is confronted.' (Amselek 1988, p. 199) Through speech-act theory several interpretative issues have been tackled and (purportedly) resolved (e.g. Marmor and Soames 2011).

[4] Granted, there might be even more theoretical options available to us (see e.g. Stoljar 2003); but for the sake of this chapter I group all 'moderate' or 'mixed' views about determinacy and interpretation together, hence leaving as alternatives only holistic views à-la-Dworkin and radical indeterminacy theses (as those held by most legal realists and critical legal scholars).

Among these, the relationship between semantics and pragmatics in legal utterances (and particularly legislative texts) has been clarified, showing the (potential) degree of difference between the communicative and the legal content of legislative utterances (e.g. Marmor and Soames 2011). But parallel to the far-reaching, mainstream popularity that speech-act theory has gained in legal discourse, a mounting sense of uneasiness with it has come to the fore in the work of several authors. This is precisely the subject of the contribution of Marcin Matczak in this volume.[5] Following a certain, minority orientation in philosophy of language, he argues that speech-act theory cannot be fruitfully applied to legal utterances because it cannot explain in the first place written text. That is, the development of speech-act theory—in the seminal works of J.L. Austin, J.R. Searle, H.P. Grice, P.F. Strawson, and many others—has revolved only upon face-to-face oral interaction, and in this regard speech-act theory is plagued vis-à-vis legal utterances by what he calls (i) the fallacy of a-discursivity and (ii) the fallacy of synchronicity. That is, it is not true that legal rules can be analysed as (i) single oral utterances, to be analysed in isolation from other statements and (ii) utterances which are performed between a hearer and a speaker who share a *conversational* context (i.e., one in which contextual factors are *directly* accessible to both interlocutors, and as such can be presupposed by both parties). We shall come back to this latter fallacy shortly. For now I want to jump to Matczak's conclusions as to the role of speech-act theory in legal scholarship. As I just said, the problem is that speech-act theory has focussed almost exclusively on the oral, *face-to-face* mode(l) of communication thus neglecting written—or anyway, 'non-conversational'—ones (see e.g. Stubbs 1983).[6] Hence applying the traditional model of speech-acts to the legal situation—statutes in particular, but also judicial decisions—yields ill-formed results. I have reached the same conclusion within my own line of research (Sandro 2014); and as if this was not enough, Brian Slocum's contribution in this volume too points to the fundamental distinction between oral conversations and texts that requires a rethink of the relationship between speech-act theory and legal analysis.[7] Here though it is not entirely clear to me whether Matczak argues for abandoning speech-act theory in legal philosophy altogether (as it seems from the title of his contribution, and from having read previous drafts

[5] This is, I believe, precisely one of the distinctive features of collected volumes, originating from conferences' proceedings, such as this one: namely that of allowing different authors to cross-interact directly on one or more topics, enhancing not only debate but also mutual cognitive enrichment.

[6] Indeed, two parties could be communicating by means of written text and yet be in a conversational situation, that is in a situation in which contextual resources can be accessed by both independently of the communication itself, and such epistemic resources be presupposed by both parties. Hence the problem is not with written communication as such—but with communicative instances in which context is, or better the contexts are, epistemically inaccessible to one or both parties.

[7] The concurrence between Matczak, Slocum and myself on this central claim, considering that we reach it starting from different backgrounds and through autonomous theoretical routes, is quite exceptional: as such this volume could constitute the beginning of a larger 'movement' or 'doctrine' that purports to reconceive of the relationship between philosophy of language and the study of law.

of it), embracing alternative theoretical frameworks ('complex text-acts'), or rather for amending speech-act theory in light of the peculiarity of legal utterances (as one could think from some passages in the text).[8] Surely, most applications of speech-act theory to legal discourse have been plagued by these fallacies: but there are also a few relevant exceptions (Kurzon 1986; Duarte 2011) that Matczak overlooks and on which the next section builds upon. That is why, between abandoning speech-act theory in the study of law or amending it to such purpose, I opt for this latter possibility: for one can use the legal example to address speech-act theory general shortcomings and to begin to address satisfactorily the differences between conversational and non-conversational communicative instances. This last endeavour of course goes far beyond the scope of this chapter;[9] here I am only going to focus on the relationship between sender and receiver of legal utterances.

20.3 Sender and Receivers in Law: A Peculiar Relation

In our ordinary conversations we usually have a speaker and a hearer who interact being in the same place and at the same time. They can be said to share a *situational* context.[10] This latter often enriches the semantic content of the utterance, so that in philosophy of language, following the seminal work of Grice, we have come to distinguish consistently between sentence and speaker meaning (Korta and Perry 2012). Imagine the following situation: my friend John screams '*We* won!' in front of the television just after the football match. The situational context of his utterance consists of, among other things, the fact that John's favourite football team won the finals and that we just watched the match together (so that I know that he knows that, and vice versa) and thus I am able to make sense of his exclamation, i.e. I am able to understand what he means by uttering '*We* won!'[11] Traditional speech-act theory builds upon these 'ordinary conversation' situations (Matczak, Chap. 24).

Things seem different when we consider legal utterances, and in particular those as contained in statutory instruments, whose sender is the normative authority and

[8] Matczak clarifies to me, in a private conversation, that it is indeed the second case: he wants to amend the theory to make it more suitable for the analysis of written utterances, that in this sense must be conceived of as 'text-acts' and not as 'speech-acts'.

[9] But the reader might be interested to know that this is a route I have already begun to explore (Sandro 2014).

[10] This is the context surrounding the utterance, viz the state of the world (consisting of material and immaterial things, such as beliefs) as it exists at the time$_X$ and space$_X$ of the utterance$_X$. This type of context must be contrasted with what, following Habermas, I call 'lifeworld' context, which is instead the set of cultural and linguistic conventions somehow shared between subjects of any (minimally) successful communication (Sandro 2014; cf Habermas 1989, pp. 122–123).

[11] In this case, I successfully understand that the indexical 'we' does not refer to us, me and John, as it would do literally, but to John's football team, to which he feels some sense of belonging or membership—so that the meaning of his utterance is really 'My football team just won the game!'

whose receivers are the agents within an institutional system.[12] I limit my focus to statutory texts—statutes, directives, etc—and more generally to all those official normative texts which are addressed to the public in general and which contain norms that purport to regulate people's behaviour. Such a restriction is arbitrary—legal communication is constituted by a variety of speech-acts which are different from each other, judicial decisions being a paradigmatic example of them—but justified: if law is the enterprise of 'subjecting human conduct to the guidance of rules' (Fuller 1969; cf Rawls 1999, pp. 208–212),[13] statutory communication represents the only viable means, at least so far, to do so when to be regulated is a large society like modern ones (Hart 1994). As such, it constitutes the core of legal communication. This seems confirmed by the fact that law is, in the first place, only conceivable as such within a 'common sense' discourse that originates from the social practice of the society—that is the general public at large—itself (Jori 2010).[14]

There is a first important difference between ordinary speech-acts and legal ones, for it seems clear that legal utterances are 'closed unilateral speech acts' (Duarte 2011, p. 116), in the sense that they normally do not require an answer by their recipients. Rather, they require a 'human behaviour'—which by the way is not even 'oriented towards the normative authority' (ibid). This is a very important qualification, as their aim as speech-acts then is not the successful *exchange* of information, but the successful *reception* of information that *can*, together with non-linguistic factors (Pattaro 2005), lead the receiver to act in a certain way (Marmor 2008).[15] This consideration has to be taken into account when interpreting a legal utterance, for it puts already a relevant constraint not only on the illocutionary value(s) of the act itself,[16] but also to the potential enrichment brought to the utterance's meaning by the implied content, which is in this sense limited by both the strategic nature of the act performed and the ultimate aim of the communicative endeavour (Marmor 2008, p. 428).

Another significant sense in which legal utterances are different from speech acts taking place in ordinary conversation has to do with the inevitable lack of direct *relation*, in terms of time and space, between 'who' performs the speech act and who

[12] cf the analysis in this section with the (mostly) concurring one in Slocum (Chap. 22).

[13] This is particularly true, again, in criminal law (see e.g. Stark 2013, p. 163). This should not surprise, being criminal law the context in which our most basic freedoms are usually at stake and thus in which the requirements of the principle of legality should be applied strictly (see Ferrajoli 1990).

[14] Jori purports to amend—or to reallocate—Hart's rule of recognition and his insistence on the role of officials in determining it: in the sense that even the rule of recognition of a legal system cannot but exist on the ground of a 'common sense' social practice that identifies both 'law' (the concept of law, in general) and 'the law' (the law in force in a given jurisdiction, e.g. Italian law or English law).

[15] To be clear: successful reception of information on the part of the agent is not tantamount to compliance, nor implicates it as a matter of *necessity*—for compliance is always, and merely, a possibility. My point is rather the opposite: if there is no successful reception of information, how can the agent be thought of complying with, that is, of *following* the rule?

[16] Thus diminishing the relevance of context in determining the illocutionary values of legal speech-acts; cf Bianchi (2013); contra Matczak (2014).

is (supposed to be) its recipient. This roughly corresponds to Matczak (Chap. 24) 'fallacy of synchronicity'. Here though I am not referring only to the lack of a 'situational context', that is to the fact that sender and receiver of legal utterances are not in the same place at the same time; rather, the point is that 'norm sentences are a kind of speech act where the connection speaker→hearer (reader) is played out on both sides by indeterminate actors', [so that] '[e]ven though it is possible to connect a norm sentence with the person or group of persons that at a certain time act as the normative authority, from the speaker's point of view, the fact is that the speaker is, precisely, the normative authority and not that person or group of persons' (Duarte 2011, p. 117).[17]

The importance of this remark should not be underestimated. While Matczak (Chap. 24) deploys it to highlight the role of multi-contextuality in determining the lawmaker's intention, and thus in order to justify the need to distinguish between the locutionary and the illocutionary intentions of lawmakers,[18] I want to stress how this 'a-synchronicity' of legal utterances, far from being accidental, constitutes instead a distinctive and necessary feature of law as an institutional normative system (MacCormick 2007). For otherwise nothing like the rule of law, as opposed to the rule of men, can (ever) exist. That is, one of the differences between the two lies precisely in the fact that the *power to rule* ceases to be held by one or more individuals in their quality as such, and it is instead conferred upon an institution or *officium*—the 'legislator'—that pushes into irrelevance the people temporarily exercising it. At the same time, the fact that legal utterances contained in statutory texts are not addressed to individual subjects, but to categories (types) of them, ensures the formal rationality ('like cases should be treated alike') of law and thus equality (of treatment and consideration) among its subjects.

The overall peculiarity of the relationship between sender and receiver of legal utterances vis-à-vis ordinary conversational situations leads us to ask: 'Who are the addressees of legal utterances?' At first glance, this question might seem just foolish.[19] Especially if we are heavy consumers of jurisprudence books and articles, we might get the impression that legal utterances' addressees are judges, lawyers and more generally legal officials, i.e. the agents within the system that are institutionally called to interpret (and apply) those very legal utterances (Cao 2007, p. 76). Only these agents' interpretations 'count'—after all, isn't this idea that both Hart's rule of recognition and Kelsen theory of norms presuppose, and only to name perhaps the two most prominent theorists of last century?[20] And isn't this the perspective from which radical sceptics and legal realists start off in order to criticise the traditional

[17] cf Hart (1994, pp. 21–22).

[18] Whereas Duarte (2011) shows how multi-contextuality reduces the pragmatic impact of context in determining the semantic value of the utterance.

[19] Perhaps not so much in the criminal law context: cf Duff (2007, Chap. 2) (thanks to Findlay Stark for the pointer).

[20] Hart's rule of recognition seems to be predominantly official-oriented despite the fact that he criticises Kelsen's idea that (primary) norms are addressed only to officials (Hart 1994, pp. 35–42). I owe this point to Alex Latham.

picture of legal interpretation (Guastini 2011)? The convergence among different authors on this point seems difficult to set aside.

And yet, isn't something missing from this picture? Namely, where are *we, the people*? Aren't we statutes' addressees, first and foremost? This especially in light of the consideration that adjudication, as Green (2009, p. 21) reminds us, is always 'law's Plan B'. Law's 'Plan A', as often left unspoken, is that of a successful communication, on part of the law-maker, and application, on part of the public, of legal rules that does not lead at all to adjudication; for the guidance offered by rules is effective in offering reasons for action and thus constraining behaviour.[21] As such, isn't the way in which laypeople interpret and apply the law at least as worthy of theoretical consideration as that of legal officials? And if this so, why seem theories of law and legal reasoning to be overlooking this (rather apparent) fact so often?

20.4 Laypeople as the First (and Foremost) Addressees of Legal Communication

I cannot speculate on this last question. But I readily argue that there is something wrong with our mainstream theories of interpretation when they simply remove laypeople from law's interpretive field. I contend that this is an unwarranted move, one that yields non-negligible effects on the way in which we understand law. Before stating what are these consequences, let me make the case for the claim that laypeople are the first—and at least in one sense, the foremost—addressees of legal communication.

First, as we have briefly touched on it already, there is a flaw in all those theories that narrow down law's interpretive field to that of institutional agents and judges in particular. For they seem to forget that adjudication is always an only merely *potential* 'moment' in juridical phenomenology (Fuller 1969, p. 55; Levenbook 2006, p. 74; Miers 1986). That is, a legal system could be said to be in place even without a system of courts or in any case without an 'adjudicative moment',[22] provided that the (primary) communication of normative standards is successful amongst its subjects, in the sense that they comply with what the law requires.[23] The fact that such scenario perhaps never historically occurred does not make the remark any less

[21] As I said already, to this end non-linguistic factors are necessary—I assume them for granted for the purposes of this chapter.

[22] Raz (1979, p. 105) and Waldron (2008, pp. 20–24) strongly resist such claim. Perhaps there is a way to explain such a stark opposition, which seems to leave no space for a middle position: it has to do with the dual nature of law, as an institutional and as a normative system. Hence, while it seems impossible (as Raz and Waldron hold) to conceive of law as an institutional system without a hierarchy of courts, it is instead possible to do so when law is understood in its normative sense, that is as a system of norms that purport to guide behaviour.

[23] Of course, this presupposes non-contradiction and completeness on part of the legal system, and this is all but self-evident—yet being only an argumentative strategy the reader can assume both conditions.

theoretically relevant.[24] But the opposite does not hold, i.e. a normative system with a fully functional hierarchy of courts[25] but where there is little or no compliance of primary norms (for whatever reason) is no legal system at all.[26] Hence on what grounds do mainstream theories establish the exclusive relevance of institutional agents' interpretive practices, and of courts in particular, if a (hypothetical) legal system could do without the *moment* in which this latter kind of interpretation takes place?

Granted, this is no objection to the claim that the first and foremost recipients of legal utterances are indeed lawyers and not laymen. This neglected fact would come to the fore by adopting the (disputed) distinction between the official, the implied and the instantial author of a given text, mirrored by that between the official, the implied and the instantial reader: Kurzon (1986, pp. 26–29) argues that notwithstanding which one of the three simultaneous relations we entertain, in the case of statutory communication authors and readers are always, substantially, lawyers and not laypeople. Now, although this description might have been empirically sound until some time ago, it is questionable that it is still the case nowadays.[27] For the role of lawyers as *medium* both in the process of coding and decoding deontic content seems shrunk. This is due to a variety of factors, among which one can think of the developments of information technology as applied to communication, the always higher level of literacy and higher education amongst citizens in developed countries, the specialisation of entire market-sectors and the always expanding regulative sphere of the law that has embraced fields progressively more and more directly connected to every day's life. The result is that laypeople are constantly, in their daily business, confronted directly by the text of the law, either on newspapers, on the internet, in their professional environments and so on—and are called upon to act *applying* the law. Hence they seem to be after all the first (and foremost) addressees of statutory communication, at least in non-specialised cases,[28] and this fact wins them back centre-stage within law's interpretive field. As Surden (2011, p. 66) puts it,

---

[24] Cf Priel 2013, pp. 8–10.

[25] Notwithstanding the fact that, for a hierarchy to be there, there must be some successful communication and application (at least) of primary rules.

[26] Cf Hart's claim that '[I]f it were not possible to communicate general standards of conduct, which multitudes of individuals could understand, without further direction, as requiring from them certain conduct when the occasion arose, nothing that we now recognize as law could exist' (Hart 1994, p. 124).

[27] Stark (2013, p. 163) convincingly argues that '[i]n planning their lives, citizens must be able to understand properly the nature of what the law declares to be a criminal offence, and it is obvious that this will usually be conducted without the benefit of legal advice.'

[28] That is, clearly I do not mean to claim that a particular statute regulating a specific, technical area (medical, engineering, and so forth) is addressed first and foremost to laypeople, as this would appear unsound on the descriptive level but also on the theoretical one: for likely the addressees of such norms are highly-specialised individuals who possess the skills not only to understand, but also to comply with the requirements of the law. What I do claim though is that these 'specialised' statutes can but only constitute a subsidiary part of statutory communication, one that necessarily presupposes the successful outcome of the non-specialised one.

in law generally, it is probably true that the vast majority of legal analysis and assessment of legal outcomes is conducted, not by officials like judges or by trained lawyers, but by lay (non legally-trained) individuals.

This latter claim seems confirmed from yet another perspective, namely from considering the systemic relationship that establishes between law as an 'administered' language (Pattaro 2005) and the natural language Y in which legal utterances are encoded. In this sense, if we agree that there is a formal reception by the legal system X of the given natural language Y (Duarte 2011), then the [rules of the] interpretive practice of speakers of Y *must* be taken into account by any theory of interpretation of X. For that interpretive practice (of the community of speakers of the given natural language as a whole) becomes constitutive of the meaningfulness of the law as much as the law-specific interpretive practices established by institutional actors like courts (cf Velluzzi 2008, pp. 502–503; Stark 2013, pp. 164–166). Clearly the *transformative* power of the two interpretive practices will be different, as natural language processes usually extend over a considerable timespan whereas the law can be changed (in theory) day by day; what is relevant is that *we* use today the expression 'personal device' in quite a different way than we did just 20 years ago, so that a norm containing 'personal device' will not apply to the same situations as 20 years before. This seems also to offer some grounds to the thesis—on which I cannot dwell upon in the context of this chapter—that the normativity of law is premised to some extent upon that of language (Sandro 2014); so that transformative processes in the latter will directly produce effects in the former too.[29]

20.5 So What?

The prominence of laypeople as the first addressees of statutory communication is usually used to support the so-called 'plain language' movement in law-making, whose aim is to ensure that public agencies use 'clear Government communication that the public can understand and use.'[30] I want instead to shift the focus on the potential consequences that can follow from this move as to our theories of interpretation.

I believe that two very different pictures of law's interpretive field stem from whether we assume that both laymen and legal officials are recipients of legal communication or not. In the latter case, which seems to be the traditional starting point for mainstream theories of legal interpretation, the fact that we consider only legal officials as addressees of legal utterances requires us to hold complex theories of

[29] The take-home point is the overall interaction between the two systems, language Y and law X, and the fact that the rules governing meaning in Y must be considered governing the same practice in X—this without denying the possibility for X to 'atomistically' re-define words and concepts from the set Y (Duarte 2011, p. 115).

[30] US Plain Writing Act of 2010 (HR 946, Pub L 111–274).

interpretations, for our theories *must* account for the (pragmatic) characteristics of this community of legal interpreters. These pragmatic characteristics are, roughly:

1) the *authoritativeness*, and in some case the *finality*, of their decisions;
2) the high-level of specialisation, in terms of practical reasoning, of interpreters;
3) their self-reflexive understanding as being *part* of the normative institutional system, in particular as exclusive addressees of Hart's 'secondary rules' (Hart 1994);
4) their (superior) epistemic abilities as to both questions of law and questions of fact as opposed to lay-men;
5) the vast array of interpretive methods developed (Leiter and Coleman 1995, p. 213);
6) so-called juristic theories or 'legal dogmatics' (Guastini 2011, p. 148).

As a matter of course, a theory of interpretation that has to take into account (likely) even more than these listed features cannot but possess a highly degree of complexity. For several different theories of interpretation can be, and have been, put forward (linguistic, constructivist, consequentialist, originalist, coherentist, moral, etc.), each stressing different aspects of the practice of law. The result is the highest theoretical and pragmatic disputability of the (universal) adoption of *any* theory of legal interpretation; but more importantly a compelling ground—*rebus sic stantibus*—for the (radical) indeterminacy thesis of law.[31] Different theories of interpretation may lead to different (interpretive) results in a given case, and as there is no superior meta-principle that enable us to pick one of them as the right or correct one, we must do so, as realists say, by resorting to extra-legal, normative, considerations (moral, political, etc.),[32] as such acknowledging the *pervasive* indeterminacy of law.

What if then we adopt the former possibility, viz the idea that laypeople are addressees of legal communication (at least) as much as legal officials? Is there any difference, in particular as to the indeterminacy thesis? Well it seems to me that in this case the possibility of pragmatic enrichment of our interpretive working field changes altogether, and the fact that we consider laymen as the *first* recipients of deontic communication (Cao 2007, p. 76) yields relevant constraints upon our theory-elaboration process. In this regard, our theory of interpretation must now take into account, among other things:

1a) the relative non-specialisation of the *great majority* of norm-interpreters;
2a) the difference of the non-institutionalised pragmatic meta-context in which the deontic communication takes place (Duarte 2011);
3a) the different epistemic abilities of members of the public compared to those of high-skilled legal officials;
4a) the relative absence of second-order theories (juristic theories) which constrain interpretation;

---

[31] Here, I think, determinacy stands also for objectivity, notwithstanding the fact that Coleman and Leiter warn specifically against conflating the two concepts (Coleman and Leiter 1995, p. 600).

[32] Cf Guastini (2011, p. 148).

5a) the coordinating and action-guiding function of law (Fuller 1969, Kramer 2007) and legal reasoning (Spaak 2007).

As we have seen, amongst the most prominent legal realist theses is that there is no way (and perhaps no meta-theoretical reason) to establish the predominance of *one* criterion of interpretation—and of the linguistic one in particular –[33] over the others in the interpretive practices of legal officials (Guastini 2011, pp. 153–158; Leiter 1995). But does this still hold if, as I argue, we broaden our field and consider as the relevant community of interpreters the sum of the two groups, laypeople and legal officials? In this case things seem quite different. If law is the enterprise of 'subjecting human conduct to the guidance of rules' (Fuller 1969), and if laypeople are the first and foremost addressees of legal utterances, it follows the prevalence, already at the descriptive level, of the linguistic interpretive criterion over the other available –[34] so that these latter become only residual or supplementary (Velluzzi 2008, pp. 501–502). We must in other words acknowledge that in the great majority of cases laymen can be understood as *applying* the law[35] in their everyday lives by relying on the linguistic meaning of legal utterances.[36] For the linguistic criterion is the only one that squares with laymen's original epistemic abilities and that as such is shared with (specialised) legal officials.[37] This 'horizon of common meaning' between law's different types of addressees also ensure—in the sense of *making possible*—law's *certainty*, particularly in the negative sense of excluding whatever

[33] By 'linguistic' criterion of interpretation I roughly mean what Asgeirsson (2012) calls 'textualist thesis of legal content', according to which 'the legal content of a statute is the linguistic content that *a reasonable member of the relevant audience* would, knowing the context and conversational background, associate with the enactment' (italics added). I want to stress how in such definition identifying the 'relevant audience' is preliminary to assessing the meaning of a given utterance—which is precisely the overall point I am trying to make in this chapter. cf also with Slocum's (Chap. 22) very compelling defence of an objective approach to interpretation and with his concept of 'ordinary meaning'.

[34] The prevalence of the linguistic criterion is positively established in some civil codes, see for instance art 12 of the Italian Civil Code.

[35] Cf Hart (1994, p. 39). This is what sociology of law does for instance when measuring the effectiveness or lack thereof of the law. Obviously this is but a theoretical reconstruction: many people are actually partially or completely ignorant of the text of the law.

[36] This is a descriptive claim that is paired, on the normative level, by claims that the law *ought* to be interpreted linguistically, first and foremost—see e.g. the 'presumption of common natural language' in Wróblewski (1992). This convergence between descriptive and normative claims, in turn, strengthens the meta-theoretical point I am defending here.

[37] Hence the only one that can be required by the law on their part. Two qualifications are in place here. First, this contention has to do with the epistemic, and not moral, problem of *agency* in a deontic system (cf Fuller 1969, pp. 162–167; Duff 2007, Chap. 2). In this regard, ascription of responsibility is premised upon so-called 'reason-responsiveness', that is, 'a responsible agent is one who is *capable* of recognising and responding to the reasons that bear on his situation' (Duff 2007, p. 39, italics added). But being able to recognise reasons implies, it seems to me, being able to understand the medium in which those reasons are communicated—hence, being able to understand language. As such, linguistic capacity is a necessary but not sufficient element for the ascription of any type of responsibility in our legal systems. Second, I am not claiming that laypeople are always incapable of interpreting the law according to criteria other than the linguistic one, but all these different types of interpretation (e.g. teleological) presuppose the linguistic one, viz are parasitical on it.

is outside the range of possible linguistic meanings of a legal utterance from its legal meanings (ibid), thus constraining interpretative operations. This allows legal rules to constitute *intelligible* reasons for action for their addresses (Sandro 2014) and as such to give rise to *genuine* rule-following practices (Wittgenstein 2009).[38] What are the consequences for our meta-theory of interpretation then?

I can think only of two alternatives here. Either we still maintain, notwithstanding this move, some sort of fundamental difference between the two types of addressees, so that we are forced to predicate two different theories of legal interpretation in our domain; or we must say that the linguistic criterion is the most relevant one, to be ranked descriptively above the others. The former option is indeed found in existing scholarship (Dan-Cohen 1984; Marmor 2008). It is based upon the well-known distinction between 'conduct' and 'decision' rules,[39] conceived of though as two *independent* sets of rules addressed to two *independent* sets of receivers, lay-men and courts (Dan-Cohen 1984, pp. 626–630). Dan-Cohen has purported to show, using a theoretical model of 'acoustic separation', on the one hand the beneficial effects—in terms of the realisation of both sets of norms' underlying policies—if one communicative deontic 'channel' is more or less concealed from the other set of receivers, so that lay-men are more or less unaware of (some) decision rules that must be applied by courts in their jurisdictional function; on the other, to highlight that the law indeed makes use to a greater or lesser extent of 'strategies of selective transmission' to 'segregate its normative messages' in some cases, e.g. in criminal law (Dan-Cohen 1984, p. 636). This has brought Marmor to talk of a 'legislative double-talk' that must be understood as implying almost a 'conflicting implicature' on part of legislators (Marmor 2008, pp. 437–438).

Now, Dan-Cohen's thesis that conduct and decision rules are *logically* independent has been already convincingly criticised (Duarte d'Almeida 2009). But even if we were to accept his thesis, the argument that decision rules *should* be to a greater or lesser extent concealed from the public seems unsound also on the normative one. In particular, I refer to his claim that 'by definition, conduct rules are all one needs to know in order to obey the law. Decision rules, as such, cannot be obeyed (or disobeyed) by citizens; therefore, knowing them is not necessary (indeed, it is irrelevant) to one's ability to obey the law.' (Dan-Cohen 1984, p. 673) It seems to me that Dan-Cohen fails to realize that the distinction between conduct and decision rules is, if any, a *relative* one—given that those same decision rules might become 'conduct' ones if infringed upon by a judge (Ferrajoli 2007, p. 681). So, how would it be possible for a citizen to file a lawsuit and report the violation of one of those rules (e.g. a procedural rule), if those very rules are to be concealed from her?[40] Hence those normative arguments that question whether these strategies of selective

[38] Cf Stark (2013, p. 166) for the convergent claim that law must respect citizens as 'planning agents' (in the context of criminal law at least).

[39] For the origins of the distinction (tracing back to Bentham and lately Kelsen and Hart) see Dan-Cohen (1984, pp. 626–630).

[40] Indeed, Dan-Cohen (1984, p. 632, ft 14) explicitly supposes that decision-makers would not give reasons for their decision, thus in this way preserving the acoustic separation between themselves and the public. I hope the unacceptableness of the claim is so crystal clear that I do not need to linger at all on it.

transmission can be deemed compatible with the rule of law in the first place seem reinforced (cf Duff 2007, p. 43).[41] For 'far-reaching incongruities between the law as it is articulated and the law as it is administered will be fatal to the existence of a legal system' (Kramer 2007, p. 138), and the legislature talking with 'two voices' would not but lead to increase such gap.

Conclusions

If what has been argued above is persuasive, one ought to recognise the prevalence of the linguistic criterion as it ensues from a sound elaboration of law's interpretive epistemic field—and more generally from correctly conceiving of law as an authoritative communicative enterprise. This entails that our meta-theory of interpretation must acknowledge this point and elaborate models of interpretation that display the interaction between the linguistic criterion of meaning and the other available (Velluzzi 2008, p. 502). Without acknowledging the necessary centrality of the linguistic criterion of meaning, it is not clear how a theory of law can account for the great bulk of legal phenomenology that allows more complex interpretive practices—like those of judges and lawyers, or those in specialised sectors of society—to take place. According to Kramer (2007, pp. 139–140)

'[t]wo constraints are met by any genuine legal system. First, a key aim of the officials is to interpret and apply the formulations of the norms of their legal system in accordance with what would be expected by a dispassionate observer who knows those formulations and who also knows the interpretive canons that prevail within the system. Second, naturally, those canons themselves—which consist of technical conventions for dealing with specialized legal terminology and concepts, but which also draw upon all or most of the ordinary conventions of the language in which the formulations of the legal norms are written—are such as to satisfy rather than dash the expectations of a dispassionate observer who is familiar only with the formulations and with the language (such as English) in which they are written. This second constraint is a crucial supplement to the first, since it rules out interpretive canons that would license and indeed require significant aberrations from the terms of the law on the books.'

In other words, that the content of legal utterances which guides people's behaviour must be interpreted (first and foremost) according to the linguistic criterion of meaning used by the norms' addressees themselves [42] seems a very important requirement for the existence of a *genuine* legal system.[43]

[41] *Contra* Dan-Cohen (1984, pp. 667–677).

[42] Cf Raz (1979, p. 217): 'it is obvious that it is futile to guide one's action on the basis of the law if when the matter comes to adjudication the courts will not apply the law and will act for some other reasons'; see also Slocum (Chap. 22).

[43] The argument proposed in this chapter can be understood as taking the cue from, and thus in some sense as supporting (but from a different angle, that of philosophy of language), the early legal positivist project that purported to vindicate law's autonomy from morality through its scientific and technical method. This political project, which can be retrieved more clearly in the

Acknowledgments My warm thanks go to Felipe Oliveira de Sousa, Martin Kelly, Alex Latham, Euan MacDonald, Marcin Matczak, Haris Psarras, Francisco Saffie, Luiz Fernando C. Silveira and Findlay Stark for valuable comments on previous drafts of this chapter, which forced me to improve it substantially; and also to the participants in the 'Rules 2013' conference, held at the Jagiellonian University, Krakow, 27–29 September 2013, for their observations. I remain the only person responsible for every error or omission in this piece.

References

Amselek, Paul. 1988. Philosophy of law and the theory of speech acts. *Ratio Juris* 1:187–223.

Asgeirsson, Hrafn. 2012. Textualism, pragmatic enrichment, and objective communicative content. Monash University Faculty of Law Legal Studies Research Paper No. 2012/21. http://papers.ssrn.com/sol3/papers.cfm?abstract_id=2142266. Accessed June 2013.

Bianchi, Claudia. 2013. How to do things with (recorded) words. Philosophical Studies. http://link.springer.com/article/10.1007%2Fs11098-013-0111-0. Accessed June 2013.

Cao, Deborah. 2007. Legal speech act as intersubjective communicative action. In *Interpretation, law and the construction of meaning,* eds. Anne Wagner, Wouter Werner, and Deborah Cao, 65–82. Berlin: Springer.

Coleman, Jules L., and Brian, Leiter. 1995. Determinacy, objectivity, and authority. In *Law and interpretation: Essays in legal philosophy,* ed. Andrei Marmor, 203–278. Oxford: Clarendon.

Dan-Cohen, Meir. 1984. Decision rules and conduct rules: On acoustic separation in criminal law. *Harvard Law Review* 97:625–677.

Duarte, David. 2011. Linguistic objectivity in norm sentences: Alternatives in literal meaning. *Ratio Juris* 24:112–139.

Duarte d'Almeida, Luis. 2009. Separation, but not of rules. In *Criminal law conversations,* eds. Paul H. Robinson, Stephen Garvey, and Kimberly Kessler Ferzan, 17–18. Oxford: Oxford University Press.

Duff, Anthony R. 2007. *Answering for crime.* Oxford: Hart.

Dworkin, Ronald. 1986. *Law's empire.* Cambridge: Harvard University Press.

Dworkin, Ronald. 2011. *Justice for hedgehogs.* Cambridge: Harvard University Press.

Ferrajoli, Luigi. 2007. *Principia Iuris. Teoria del Diritto e della Democrazia. Vol. 1. Teoria del Diritto.* Roma-Bari: Laterza.

Ferrajoli, Luigi. 1990. *Diritto e Ragione. Teoria del Garantismo Penale.* Roma-Bari: Laterza.

Fuller, Lon L. 1969. *The morality of law.* New Haven: Yale University Press.

Green, Leslie. 2009. Law and the causes of judicial decisions. Oxford Legal Studies Research Paper No. 14/2009. http://papers.ssrn.com/sol3/papers.cfm?abstract_id=1374608. Accessed June 2013.

Guastini, Riccardo. 2011. Rule-scepticism restated. In *Oxford studies in philosophy of law,* Vol. 1, eds. Leslie Green and Brian Leiter, 138–161. Oxford: Oxford University Press.

Habermas Jürgen. 1989. *The theory of communicative action. Vol. 2. Lifeworld and system. A critique of functionalistic reason.* Cambridge: Polity

Hart, Herbert L. A. 1994. *The concept of law.* 2nd ed. with Postscript. eds. Penelope A. Bulloch and Joseph Raz. Oxford: Clarendon.

Jori, Mario. 2010. *Del Diritto Inesistente. Saggio di Metagiurisprudenza Descrittiva.* Pisa: Edizioni ETS.

Korta, Kepa, and John, Perry. 2012. Pragmatics. The Stanford encyclopedia of philosophy (Winter 2012 Edition). http://plato.stanford.edu/archives/win2012/entries/pragmatics/. Accessed April 2013.

---

works of Friedrich Carl von Savigny, Jeremy Bentham and Gaetano Filangieri, highlighted the dangers, among other things, of interpretation when this latter carries the law too far away from the posited text of the legislation. I owe this point to Francisco Saffie.

Kramer, Matthew H. 2007. *Objectivity and the rule of law*. Cambridge: Cambridge University Press.

Kurzon, Dennis. 1986. *It is hereby performed...: Explorations in legal speech acts*. Amsterdam: John Benjamins.

Leiter, Brian. 1995. Legal indeterminacy. *Legal Theory* 1:481–492.

Levenbook, Barbara. 2006. How a statute applies. *Legal Theory* 12:71–112.

Marmor, Andrei. 2005. *Interpretation and legal theory*. Revised 2nd ed. Oxford: Hart

Marmor, Andrei. 2008. The pragmatics of legal language. *Ratio Juris* 21:423–452.

Marmor, Andrei, and Scott Soames (eds.). 2011. *Philosophical foundations of language in law*. Oxford: Oxford University Press.

MacCormick, Neil. 2007. *Institutions of law. An essay in legal theory*. Oxford: Oxford University Press.

Miers, David. 1986. Chap. 7: Legal theory and the interpretation of statutes. In *Legal theory and common law,* ed. William Twining. Oxford: Blackwell.

Moreso, José J. 1998. *Legal indeterminacy and constitutional interpretation*. Dordrecht: Kluwer.

Pattaro, Enrico. 2005. The law and the right: A reappraisal of the reality that ought to be. In *A treatise of legal philosophy and general jurisprudence,* Vol. I, ed. Enrico Pattaro. Dordrecht: Springer.

Priel, Dan. 2013. Fuller's argument against legal positivism. *Canadian Journal of Law and Jurisprudence* 26:399.

Raz, Joseph. 1979. *The authority of law: Essays on law and morality*. Oxford: Clarendon.

Rawls, John. 1999. *A theory of justice: Revised Edition*. Cambridge: Belknap.

Sandro, Paolo. 2014. Creation and application of law: A neglected distinction. Ph. D. Thesis. Edinburgh: University of Edinburgh.

Spaak, Torben. 2007. *Guidance and constraint: The action-guiding capacity of theories of legal reasoning*. Uppsala: Iustus förlag.

Stark, Findlay. 2013. It's only words: On meaning and mens rea. *Cambridge Law Journal* 72:155–177.

Stoljar, Natalie. 2003. Survey article: Interpretation, indeterminacy and authority: Some recent controversies in the philosophy of law. *Journal of Political Philosophy* 11:470–498.

Stubbs, Michael. 1983. Can i have that in writing? Some neglected topics in speech act theory. *Journal of Pragmatics* 41:393–400.

Surden, Harry. 2011. The variable determinacy thesis. *Columbia Science & Technology Law Review* 12:1–100.

Van Hoecke, Mark. 2002. *Law as communication*. Oxford: Hart.

Velluzzi, Vito. 2008. Interpretazione degli enunciati normativi, linguaggio giuridico, certezza del diritto. *Criminalia. Annuario di scienze penalistiche* 3:493–510.

von Wright, H. Georg. 1963. *Norm and action*. London: Routledge and Kegan Paul.

Waldron, Jeremy. 2008 The concept and the rule of law. *Georgia Law Review* 43:1–61.

Wittgenstein, Ludwig. 2009. *Philosophical investigations*. 4th ed, eds. Peter MS Hacker and Joachim Schulte. Oxford: Wiley-Blackwell.

Wróblewski, Jerzy. 1992. *The judicial application of law,* eds. Zenon Bańkowski and Neil MacCormick. Dordrecht: Kluwer.

Chapter 21
Inerpretation and Rule Following in Law. The Complexity of Easy Cases

Ralf Poscher

Abstract Lon L. Fuller challenged the positivist distinction between the law "as it is" and the law "as it ought to be" by insisting on the need for interpretation even in easy cases of adjudication. Fuller argued that interpretation is always creative in the light of the purpose of the rule to be applied and thus always draws on the law "as it ought to be". Andrei Marmor tried to defend positivism against this challenge by advancing the thesis that there is no need for interpretation in easy cases. He drew on Ludwig Wittgenstein's remarks on rule following to suggest that in easy cases the law is just in need of understanding not of interpretation. Although I also think that positivism can be saved from Fuller's challenge, I do not think that it can be done with the help of Wittgenstein's distinction between interpretation and understanding. Fuller's challenge and Wittgenstein's remarks on the relation between a rule and its application address different aspects of the process of adjudication in easy cases, which build upon, but which cannot be played out against each other. We have to distinguish between two different elements of our practice of adjudication in easy cases: On the one side the communicative interpretation of utterances—in the case of the law legal texts—in the sense Paul Grice was concerned with; on the other side the application of a rule thus identified as the content of a communicative intention and its application that Wittgenstein's remarks on rule following are concerned with. Fuller can be understood to have insisted rightly on the ubiquity of the former, which cannot be refuted by any account of the latter. The upshot, though, is not that Fuller's challenge is successful. Its flaw, however, does not lie in the insistence on the ubiquity of communicative interpretation, but in its exploitation of an ambiguity of the creative element in interpretation, which can designate epistemic and the creativity involved in amending the law via legal construction. In principle only the former is involved in communicative interpretation; only the latter concerns the distinction between the law "as it is" and the law "as it ought to be".

Keywords Easy cases · Rule following · Legal interpretation · Understanding · Legal positivism · Legal construction · Hart · Fuller

R. Poscher (✉)
Institute for Staatswissenschaft and Philosophy of Law, Albert-Ludwigs-Universität Freiburg, Freiburg im Breisgau, Germany
e-mail: rechtsphilosophie@jura.uni-freiburg.de

M. Araszkiewicz et al. (eds.), *Problems of Normativity, Rules and Rule-Following*, Law and Philosophy Library 111, DOI 10.1007/978-3-319-09375-8_21

21.1 Introduction

Lawyers and legal theorists alike are fascinated by hard cases. They are central to law as a professional practice; they are the cases dealt with in appellate and supreme courts; they are preserved for posterity in the law reports; and they are the cases doctrinal legal scholars spend their intellectual energy on. In legal theory, the most central debates of the twentieth century on the relation of law and morals, on one-right-answer-theories and on legal realism have centered on or taken their starting point from hard cases.

Deep in the shadow of these wide-ranging debates on hard cases there has been a far quieter debate on their counterparts: easy cases. At first sight it might seem that easy cases could hardly be of interest. What could be interesting about the legal question of whether someone who jumped a red light or exceeded the speed limit by 30 mph violated the law. In legal practice they might be of some pecuniary interest for lawyers, but do not demand their professional expertise. In legal theory there might be some self-centered theoretical interest in belaboring the obvious, but easy cases seem to have no strong theoretical import.

21.2 Lon Fullers's Easy Case Challenge to Positivism

There is, however, an argument which links easy cases to the mother of all Anglo-Saxon legal theory debates—the debate on legal positivism. The link is not only interesting for the import of easy cases on the debate about positivism, but also because the arguments exchanged in this segment of the debate can help to shed light on the relation between the interpretation and the application of rules—besides legal construction two of the most basic operations in the process of adjudication. The link was made by Lon Fuller in his interpretation of H.L.A. Hart's distinction between the core and the penumbra of legal concepts. Hart famously held:

> If we are to communicate with each other at all and if, as in the most elementary form of law, we are to express our intentions that a certain type of behavior be regulated by rules, then the general words we use—like 'vehicle' [...]—must have some standard instance in which no doubts are felt about its application. There must be a core of settled meaning, but there will be, as well, a penumbra of debatable cases in which words are neither obviously applicable nor obviously ruled out. (Hart 1958, p. 607)

For Fuller, Hart's distinction was connected to the central claim of legal positivism, namely that there is a conceptual separation between the law "as it is" and the law "as it ought to be". Fuller stressed that—in Hart's account—when "applying the word to its 'standard instance', no creative role is taken by the judge. He is supposed to simply apply the law 'as it is'" (Fuller 1958, p. 662). At their core, in standard instances of their application, legal rules thus seem to vindicate the claim that the law can be applied "as it is", without recourse to how it "ought to be", which Fuller attributes to positivism.

Things look different, though, in the penumbra.

> When the object in question … falls within this penumbral area, the judge is forced to assume a more creative role. He must now undertake, for the first time, an interpretation of the rule in the light of its purpose or aim. … When questions of this sort are decided there is at least an 'intersection' of 'is' and 'ought,' since the judge, in deciding what the rule 'is,' does so in the light of his notions of what 'it ought to be' in order to carry out its purpose. (Fuller 1958, p. 662)

In Fuller's reconstruction of Hart's argument, the need for interpretation of a legal rule threatens the core positivist distinction between the law "as it is" and the law "as it ought to be". If positivism is to live up to its central claim, there have to be—according to Fuller—core cases of application, where "no doubts are felt", where the law can be applied without interpretation. Penumbral cases are contaminated by interpretation, which is creative and dependent on ideas about the law "as it ought to be".

Fuller, though, rejects Hart's core and penumbra distinction and the idea of cases in which a legal rule could be applied without recourse to its purpose and thus without interpretation. "If in some cases we seem to be able to apply the rule without asking what its purpose is, this is not because we can treat a directive arrangement as if it had no purpose. It is rather because, for example, whether the rule be intended to preserve quiet in the park, or to save carefree strollers from injury, we know, 'without thinking', that a noisy automobile must be excluded" (Fuller 1958, p. 663).[1] Fuller does not reject the idea that there are easy cases, but he rejects the idea that there can be easy cases which do not need purposive interpretation, even if we know the purpose and right interpretation "without thinking".

21.3 Taking the Bait

There are a number of ways supporters of the positivist core separation thesis can react to Fuller's challenge. The direct one is to dismiss the whole idea that the creativity involved in the application of the law—be it in easy or hard cases—does in any way affect the separation of law and morality that is central to legal positivism. At its core positivism merely holds that the *validity* of the law does not necessarily depend on its conformity with the right moral standards. Positivism is not concerned with the reasons out of which a specific legal rule is set into force—be it by the legislator or a court. Just as the separation thesis is not challenged by the fact that the legislator can turn to certain moral standards to design its legislation—e.g. "thou shalt not steal."—, it is not challenged by the fact that courts in their function of doctrinally developing the law can turn to—*inter alia*—moral considerations. Positivism does not deny that the creation of law—be it by a legislator or a court—can be influenced by moral considerations. Positivism just denies that the validity of the law created by a legislator or a judge depends necessarily on its conformity with

[1] Cf. the similar account of easy cases by Dworkin (1986, p. 353 f).

some moral standard. This claim is not challenged by the fact that courts are sometimes motivated *inter alia* by moral standards when they create law in the process of adjudication. That courts might rely on moral standards in the creation of law, does not entail that the validity of the law created by courts depends on its morality. Just as legislators, judges can rely on moral standards and just as legislators they can rely on immoral ones. Positivism only holds that the validity of the law created out of whatever reason does not rely on its conformity to morality. Fuller's attack on positivism is a red herring. The separation thesis cannot be challenged by hinting at the creative function of adjudication—be it in hard or easy cases.

Some positivists, however, took the bait. They granted Fuller the premise that a throughout creative role of adjudication would challenge central positivist tenets. Andrei Marmor accepts Fuller's premise that "positivism cannot accept the view that law is always subject to interpretation" (Marmor 2005, p. 124). He also accepts it for the same reason—namely that "interpretation adds something new, previously unrecognized, to that which is being interpreted" (Marmor 2005, p. 125). Accordingly, there have to be easy cases that do not require interpretation if positivism is to be upheld. For Marmor, too, "the distinction between easy and hard cases is entailed, or rather required, by the distinction between the law as it is and the law as it ought to be" (Marmor 2005, p. 125). Easy cases thus take center stage. If Fuller's premise is accepted, the whole positivist agenda seems to hinge on easy cases not requiring interpretation. Only if it can be proven that there are easy cases that allow for the application of the law without interpretation, positivism seems to be saved from Fuller's challenge.

To defend the thesis that easy cases do not require interpretation Marmor makes recourse to an idea developed by Ludwig Wittgenstein in the context of his considerations on rule following. Wittgenstein was concerned with the gap between a rule and its application.

> 'But how can a rule show me what I have to do at this point? Whatever I do is, on some interpretation, in accord with the rule.' This is not what we ought to say, but rather: any interpretation still hangs in the air along with what it interprets, and cannot give it any support. Interpretations by themselves do not determine meaning. (Wittgenstein 1953, § 198)

Wittgenstein had in mind rules like "add 2" which can be interpreted to accommodate whatever series of numbers is given. For any series of numbers like 1000, 1004, 1008, 1012 there is a mathematical function that can be associated with "add 2" (Cf. Wittgenstein 1953, § 185). Saul Kripke later turned Wittgenstein's observation into a skeptical argument against rule following (Kripke 1982). For Wittgenstein, however, his thoughts on rules and their interpretation were not meant to support skepticism, but to suggest that there must be something wrong in how we understand interpreting and applying a rule. "This was our paradox: no course of action could be determined by a rule, because every course of action can be made out to accord with the rule. … It can be seen that there is a misunderstanding here" (Wittgenstein 1953, § 201). For Wittgenstein the possibility of bringing any course of action into agreement with some interpretation of a rule testifies to the fact that there must be another explanation as to how we judge whether an application is in accord with a rule. Wittgenstein continues: "What this shows is that here is a way of grasping a rule which is *not an interpretation*, but which is exhibited in what we call 'obeying the rule' and 'going against it' in actual cases" (Wittgenstein 1953, § 201).

That there is a way of grasping a rule which is not an interpretation is the idea that Marmor picks up to support his claim that in easy cases there is no need for interpretation, but only for understanding (Marmor 2005, p. 149).[2] In accord with a Wittgenstein interpretation along the lines of Baker and Hacker, Marmor regards the understanding of a rule as a practical ability to exhibit behavior that is in accord with the rule. What counts as "obeying a rule" is not vindicated by an interpretation, but by our ability to judge which acts are in accord with it and which would run against it (Marmor 2005, pp. 347–355). So it seems that there is a way of applying a rule that is not dependent on interpretation. Wittgenstein's rule-following seems to show that there must be a way of applying the law in easy cases that does not require interpretation. Legal positivism seems to be saved from Fuller's challenge.

21.4 The Necessity of Communicative Interpretation in Easy Cases

For the reason mentioned above already the premise of Fuller's and Marmor's arguments—namely that creative adjudication threatens the positivist separation thesis—should be rejected. But if it is accepted for the sake of the argument, it can be shown that both rely on a flawed account of easy cases and of the role that interpretation and understanding play in the process of adjudication. Fuller's argument for the creative element in applying the law even in easy cases cannot be unhinged with the help of Wittgenstein's distinction between interpretation and understanding. Fuller's challenge and Wittgenstein's remarks on the relation between a rule and its application address different aspects of the process of adjudication, which build upon, but which cannot be played out against each other. We have to distinguish between two different elements of our practice of adjudication in easy cases: On the one hand the communicative interpretation of utterances—in the case of the law legal texts—in the sense Paul Grice was concerned with; on the other hand the application of a rule thus identified as the content of a communicative intention and its application that Wittgenstein's remarks on rule following address. Fuller can be understood to have insisted rightly on the ubiquity of the former, which cannot be refuted by any account of the latter. The upshot, though, is not that Fuller's challenge is successful. However, its flaw does not lie in the insistence on the ubiquity of communicative interpretation, but in its exploitation of an ambiguity of the creative element in interpretation, which can refer to epistemic or substantial creativity. In principle only the former is involved in communicative interpretation;

[2] Cf. already Patterson (1996, pp. 86–88), also pitting understanding against interpretation in the constructive sense of Dworkin's account of easy cases without discussing the role of communicative interpretation.

only the latter would—accepting Fuller's premise—challenge the positivists' distinction between the law "as it is" and the law "as it ought to be".

A Gricean perspective on language, communication and meaning stresses the fact that meaning is an intentional phenomenon (Grice 1989). Meaning is tied to intentions. There is no meaning without at least the presupposition of intentions. The famous letters drawn in the sand by the waves (Knapp and Benn Michaels 1982, pp. 727 f.)[3] or in the sky by cloud formations have no meaning and cannot be interpreted as such. We can assign meaning to them, only by presupposing some kind of intentional subject. When waves formed the signs "I love you", we could only assign meaning to the signs, if we presuppose some normal context like a couple on a romantic walk and one of them stating her or his affection.

Since meaning is tied to intentions our first task when confronted with an utterance is to decipher the communicative intentions that a speaker connected with them. We have to interpret the utterance with respect to the meaning intentions the speaker connected with them to discover its "speakers meaning" as Grice called it or its pragmatic meaning as it is often called in contemporary semantics. The most important clue for inferring speakers meaning from an utterance is what Grice called sentence meaning or what linguists refer to as semantic meaning of the terms employed in the utterance. Semantic meaning refers to some kind of standard or average or core type of intentions expressed with an utterance type. Semantic meaning is usually the stepping-stone for our inferences about the intentions of a speaker, because in a first instance we infer that she connected the intentions standardly connected with an utterance type with her utterance token. Grice and linguistic pragmatics have taught us, however, that semantic meaning is only a first approach and usually in need of other contextual factors to determine speakers or pragmatic meaning. This is most obvious for all openly indexical terms like pronouns, indexical descriptions of time or location, but also holds for many other aspects of an utterance like ambiguities, granularity and the like. Some of the most important contextual factors are all those that allow us to make inferences as to the purpose of the utterance.[4] "We meet at the bank." is ambiguous as to whether we meet at the river- or savings-bank. However, if we know that the purpose of the meeting is to renegotiate our mortgage, we are able to infer the right communicative intention of the speaker.

In law there are some constructive hurdles and normative implications of reconstructing the pragmatic or speakers meaning of the legislator. The constructive hurdles are due to the theoretical difficulties of making sense of the collective intentions we can assign to our complex legislative institutions. The normative implications concern the relation between pragmatic and semantic meaning in the light of rule of law values like the publicity and predictability of the law, which can set limits to what kind of legislative intentions can still be considered as authoritative for legislative acts. But leaving aside these constructive and normative intricacies,

[3] The argument has been picked up for the law by Alexander and Prakash (2004); see also Fish (2008).

[4] Cf. the critique of Marmor by Goldsworthy (1995, pp. 457, 462); also Fish (2008, p. 1138).

we need to work with some kind of intention—however construed—in the law, too, to give meaning to otherwise meaningless signs.

This entails that communicative interpretation must always take place when we are confronted with a legal utterance and that the purposes of the legislator are of import in inferring the pragmatic content of the law. This was the point that Fuller was trying to drive home and which later Hart accepted (Hart 1983, p. 106; Cf. also Schauer 1993, pp. 207 f.). When confronted with a legal text, we have to engage in communicative interpretation in this sense even in easy cases. For inferences in the process of communicative interpretation, however, the purposes of the utterance can always play a role—even if we make our interpretative inferences "without thinking", i.e. if we draw our inferences unconsciously. We do not have to engage in conscious inferences to determine which kind of bank is meant in the above remark, and we do not have to engage in much conscious reasoning to infer that a legal rule that imposes a tax on the ownership of a "bank", relates to river-banks if stated in an environmental regulation of river ownership and to savings and investment banks if stated in some financial oversight code—but we have to infer nevertheless. This also holds for easy cases. The ownership of a bank on the Mississippi is as much an easy case of a river-bank as the ownership of the Bank of America is an easy case of a savings-bank. First, however, we have to infer, the ownership of which kind of bank the tax-code that just speaks of "banks" is intended to tax.

The fact that easy cases rely on the interpretation of utterances, too, cannot be challenged by associating them solely with semantic meaning. An argument in this direction could be made by associating semantic meaning with semantic rules. The application of the law would then come down to a two-leveled pure rule following procedure: At the first level the linguistic—semantic and syntactic—rules of the language used in the legal rule formulation would be followed to establish the legal rule as the content of the utterance; at the second level the thus by mere linguistic rule following established rule would be followed in its application. Leaving aside the intricate question of whether language is guided by rules in any normative sense (Glüer 2009)—a position at least Wittgenstein seems to have given up in his later writings—, (Glüer and Wikforss 2010) even if there is rule following involved in semantic meaning, there are a series of shortcomings with a reduction of easy cases to linguistic rule following. First, even die-hard defenders of the importance of semantic meaning (Cf. Salmon 2005, p. 324) admit that semantic meaning is parasitic on pragmatic meaning. Semantic meaning relies on the intentions that speakers usually, on average, or in the core instances of the utterance type connect with it. To get to the semantic meaning of a term we infer the intentions connected with an utterance token from the usual, average or core type of intentions connected to the utterance type. Second, for the reasons already mentioned "pure" semantic meaning will hardly ever suffice to connect sensible meaning intentions with an utterance. The meaning intentions an addressee connects with an utterance on the basis of the semantics of the terms employed have to be specified with regard to the context of the utterance as is most obvious for any kind of indexical. Even if legislative intentions were discarded for the interpretation of legal texts as some scholars advocate (e.g. Hurd 1989, p. 983; Waldron 2001), the intentions that an average addressee would be licensed to connect with it would have to be assigned to it by an inferential process drawing on standard usage and context. Third, in an easy case pragmatic and semantic meaning have to be aligned. If they were not, the case would not be an easy one. Cases in which the intentions of the legislator differ from the semantic meaning of the text the legislator uttered are never easy. They involve difficult normative considerations about whether and under which circumstances which kind of meaning can prevail. Easy cases require the inference of legislative intentions, because without such an inference we could never know if the case is an easy one. If we were to know in the above tax code case that the legislator did not want to tax financial banks, but only insurances, the Bank of America case would not be an easy one. For the Bank of America to be an easy case the legislator must have intended to tax banks in the semantic sense of the word. That—in easy cases—these inferences about the legislative intentions are made "without thinking" does not render them superfluous. Easy cases require interpretation of utterances in a Gricean sense.

It also goes without saying that the inferences of legislative intentions can be erroneous, which entails that we can err on whether a case is an easy one. When applying the law in easy cases there will usually be no further information to base our inferences on than the semantic meaning of the legislative text and some knowledge about the standard context to which the law is supposed to be applied. In easy cases we will usually infer that the intentions of the legislator are in line with the contextually enriched semantic meaning of the law. This inference, however, might prove to be wrong as in the fictitious case of a legislator that wanted to refer to insurances with the word "bank". Since we lack any knowledge about the non-standard intentions the legislator connected with the word "bank", we will be led to erroneously consider the Bank of America an easy case.

21.5 Interpretation and Rule-Following

In his remarks on rule-following Wittgenstein is not concerned with the inferential process of figuring out what is meant by a speaker by way of an utterance and its context. He is not concerned with issues like establishing whether a legal rule that imposes a tax on the owners of "banks" is directed at river- or financial-banks or at savings- or investment-banks. His topic is not the inference of meaning from an utterance, but the application of a rule after it is established as the meaning of an utterance. Wittgenstein does not reflect on the relation between an utterance and its meaning but on the relation between a rule and its application. When he talks about interpretation in this context, he does not refer to communicative interpretation in the Gricean sense but in the sense of "the substitution of one expression of the rule for another" (Wittgenstein 1953, § 201). He highlights that interpretation in this paraphrasing sense will ultimately not close the gap between the rule and its application. The substitution of the expression the speaker uttered to express her intention by another expression might help to better understand her intention. If in the above examples the utterance "bank" is substituted by "savings-bank", it is easier to understand at which kind of bank the speaker wanted to meet or which kind of bank the legislator wanted to tax. However, no substitution of one rule formulation by another can close the gap between the rule and its application. The effort to close the gap between the rule and its application by another interpretation will just lead to an end- and fruitless series of interpretations.

The reason is not, however, that the gap cannot be closed, that we have to subscribe to rule-skepticism, but that the ability to paraphrase a rule is just one aspect of what it means to understand a rule. In terms of our ontogenetic cognitive development it seems even a rather late addition to our practice of rule following. Children are able to follow rules long before there is any evidence that they are able to form any conceptual representation of the rule that they are following (Zelazo 2014). But even when we have acquired the ability to conceptualize rules, we find ourselves in multiple rule following practices without the possession of a conceptual representation of the rule—the rules of grammar of our mother tongue being an obvious example. And worse still—in some cases we are not able to come up with a rule conceptualization even though we have firm intuitions on the cases that we are not able to integrate in a conceptualization of a rule: the definition of knowledge and the Gettier-problems would be a case in point.[5] Understanding a rule is a complex ability that inter alia consists in being able to paraphrase expressions of the rule. But understanding a rule includes above all the ability to apply it in standard cases in various intertwined practices, which include judging others according to rules, as in the case of a court judging the behavior of defendants and parties according to the law. It might be possible to come up with an interpretation of "add 2" that creates a bizarre pattern—as in Wittgenstein's famous examples—, but following through with such bizarre interpretations in our practice when we calculate our taxes, our rent and the statics of our houses and bridges would be a very different story. Our understanding of a rule is not vindicated by interpretations of rule formulations—let alone bizarre ones , but by applying it in the various practices that constitute our form of life. Since the ability to paraphrase a rule is just one and not even the most important aspect of understanding a rule, it cannot account for the complex practice as a whole. So one might speak of a gap between a rule and its application, but there is no gap between understanding a rule and knowing how to apply it in standard cases, because being able to apply it to standard cases is just what understanding in Wittgenstein's sense most importantly includes. The rule that is established via communicative interpretation as the content of an utterance demands the use of the ability to follow it, just as giving a series of examples would. In applying the rule to a given case the ability to follow the rule is exercised. Just like other abilities are exercised in given circumstances: as a swimmer exercises the capacity to swim on various occasions—in a lake on a hot summer day, in a pool for a work out etc.—, or as a jockey exercises the capacity to horse-ride on different horses in different races.

In contemporary pragmatism the relation between a rule and its application is reversed in an even more radical way. Rules are regarded just as the attempt to make our practice in standard cases explicit. Applications do not follow from rules, but

[5] For an excellent explanation of our conceptual problems Keil (2013).

rules supervene on applications (Brandom 1994, Chap. 1; Brandom 2002, pp. 230–234). This would also explain why we do sometimes not succeed in coming up with a rule that covers all of our practice in individual cases as the Gettier-problems seem to illustrate. We just cannot oversee all the possible cases of application. Just as Wittgenstein remarked: "A main source of our failure to understand is that we do not command a clear view of the use of our words.—Our grammar is lacking in this sort of perspicuity" (Wittgenstein 1953, § 122).[6]

But in whatever way the relation between understanding a rule and its application is conceptualized—be it as a grammatical relation in Wittgenstein's sense or as an attempt to make our practice in standard cases explicit in the sense of Robert Brandom—, the relation between a rule and its application addresses a different issue than the relation between an utterance and the content of the intentions associated with it. While the meaning of an utterance is extracted by inferences to the communicative intentions connected with it, the applications of the rule are not extracted from the rule via interpretation or any other inferential means. The rule that is the content of the communicative intention does not "contain" its applications just as the ability to swim does not "contain" the swim in a specific lake. Communicative interpretation and following a rule that is the contingent content of an utterance are very different operations. For the latter Wittgenstein insisted that there must be other ways of understanding a rule than providing "the substitution of one expression of the rule for another"; this, however, has no implication for the need to interpret an utterance in the former sense, i.e. to infer the—rule-establishing—intentions connected with it by a speaker.

The two activities involved in the process of adjudication also account for two ways in which easy cases can become difficult or even hard. First, problems can arise in establishing the communicative intentions connected with a legal utterance. In these cases there exists a legislative intention for the case at hand, but it is difficult to establish. The legislator might have used a common term in a non-standard sense or a technical term the interpreter is not familiar with, or it might not have expressed its intentions clearly for some other semantic or contextual reason. These cases produce not only difficulties in establishing the legislative intent, but also normative rule of law questions regarding the relation between legislative intent and the publicly accessible semantic meaning.

Second, a different kind of problem arises in cases in which our ability to follow the rule that the legislator communicated runs out. We might be well aware of the rule that the legislator communicated, but our ability to apply it to a specific case might run out. Just as our ability to swim might run out with respect to some particularly troubled waters in river rapids, our ability to apply the rule that the legislator communicated might run out. We are perfectly aware of the rule the legislator communicated and we can easily apply it to standard cases, but there are cases for which we do not know how to apply. We have no trouble understanding that the legislator wanted to limit the surface of windows allowed in facades and we can apply his 20 % rule with ease to standard windows, but we do not know how

[6] On the importance of this insight for the Gettier cases Keil (2013, p. 135 f).

to apply it to glass bricks. The inability to apply a rule can have multiple reasons: it might stem from semantic or pragmatic vagueness or ambiguity; it might stem form horizontal systematic considerations within the specific regulation; it might stem from vertical or norm hierarchical considerations if e.g. the application in the particular case would violate fundamental rights guaranteed in the constitution.

In both cases the application of the law becomes difficult, but for different reasons which pertain to the different kind of activities involved in the application of the law in easy cases: interpretation and understanding. Adjudication is a complex process even in easy cases. It involves a series of capacities and operations. First, legal texts, like any text, have to be interpreted in the sense that the relevant communicative intentions connected with them have to be inferred from the utterance and its context. Legal rules are only a contingent content of communicative intentions. Utterances can have any kind of communicative intentions connected with them: assertions, questions, demands, requests etc. Rules, let alone legal rules, are just one possible content of communicative intentions. Their application is not at stake in the communicative interpretation of an utterance that first aims at reconstructing a specific legal rule as the contingent content of a specific utterance. Second, only after it has been established that a specific legal rule is the content of the relevant communicative intention, the legal rule inferred as the communicative intention connected to a legal utterance has to be applied to the cases at hand. Communicative interpretation and rule application are thus ordered chronologically in the process of adjudicating easy cases: communicative interpretation being prior to legal rule application. Gricean communicative interpretation addresses the former, Wittgenstein in his rule following considerations the latter.

21.6 Two Types of Creativity

This does, however, not entail that Fuller's argument succeeds even if one were to grant its premise that the creation of law by judges in accordance to moral standards would threaten the positivist separation thesis. Fuller implied that the creative element of every interpretation does threaten the positivist separation of the law "as it is" and "as it ought to be", because—as Marmor put it—interpretation always "adds something new, previously unrecognized, to that which is being interpreted" (Marmor 2005, p. 125). Even if the premise were granted that adding something to the law in the process of its application threatens the positivist separation thesis, this, however, could only hold if what is added by interpretation would change or amend the law pre-existing to the interpretation in the process of adjudication. Interpretation in the Gricean sense of inferring the intentions connected to an utterance from the utterance, its semantic meaning and its context adds something "previously unrecognized" to the utterance, but what it adds does not change or amend the law. The creativity that can be involved in communicative interpretation is merely epistemic (Cf. Moore 1995, p. 4). We might need epistemic creativity to infer the intentions of the speaker from the utterance and its context. But interpretation of an utterance in a Grecian sense aims at the preexisting communicative intentions of the subject of the utterance. By inferential means it adds the preexisting communicative intentions of the speaker to our knowledge—initially limited to the utterance and its context. In law it aims at the pre-existing communicative intentions of the legislator—in whatever way these are construed. But in easy cases nothing has to be added to these intentions to be able to apply the rule identified in this inferential way to a given case. Fuller's argument exploits the ambiguity of "creativity" in the process of adjudication. It can relate to the epistemic creativity which might be involved in interpretation in the Gricean sense. Then it leaves the content of the pre-existing law untouched. The creativity can, however, also relate to the creativity required in hard cases, in which the law has to be amended through the doctrinal development of the law. The latter is yet another type of hermeneutic activity often also referred to as "interpretation", but traditionally—and more properly—addressed as "legal construction". The traditional term "legal construction" marks well the difference between legal interpretation in a Grecian sense and the creative doctrinal development of the law. In easy cases, though, only the former type of interpretation is involved. Legal construction, which creatively amends the law, plays no role in easy cases. The epistemic creativity that might sometimes be involved in communicative interpretation, which is necessary in easy case fits just fine with the distinction between the law "as it is" and the law "as it ought to be" even if the Fuller-Marmor-thesis on the incompatibility of positivism and substantive creativity in adjudication were correct—which it is not.

Acknowledgment Next to the discussants of the Krakow workshop I thank Dennis Patterson, Giorgio Pino and the members of the Legal Theory Workshop at the European University Institute in Florence (EUI) for their comments.

References

Alexander, Larry, and Saikrishna Prakash. 2004. Is that english you're speaking? Why intention free interpretation is an impossibility. *San Diego Law Review* 41:967–995.

Brandom, Robert. 1994. *Making it explicit: Reasoning representing and discursive commitment.* Cambridge: Harvard University Press.

Brandom, Robert. 2002. *Tales of the mighty dead: Historical essays in the metaphysics of intentionality.* Cambridge: Harvard University Press.

Dworkin, Ronald. 1986. *Law's empire.* Oxford: Hart Publishing.

Fish, Stanley. 2008. Intention is all there is. A critical analysis of Aharon Barak's purposive interpretation in law. *Cardozo Law Review* 29:1109–1146.

Fuller, Lon. 1958. Positivism and fidelity to law—a reply to professor Hart. *Harvard Law Review* 71:630–672.

Glüer, Kathrin. 2009. The normativity of meaning. In *The Stanford encyclopedia of philosophy*, ed. Edward Zalta.

Glüer, Kathrin, and Åsa Wikforss. 2010. Es braucht die Regel nicht: Wittgenstein on rules and meaning. In *The later Wittgenstein on language,* ed. Daniel Whiting, 148–166. Basingstoke: Palgrave Macmillan.

Goldsworthy, Jeffrey. 1995. Marmor on meaning, interpretation, and legislative intention. *Legal Theory* 1:439–464.

Grice, Paul. 1989. *Studies in the way of words*. Cambridge: Harvard University Press.
Hart, H. L. A. 1958. Positivism and the separation of law and morals. *Harvard Law Review* 71:593–629.
Hart, H. L. A. 1983. Problems of the philosophy of law. In *Essays in jurisprudence and philosophy,* ed. H. L. A. Hart, 89–119. Oxford: Oxford University Press, Clarendon.
Hurd, Heidi. 1989. Sovereignty in silence. *Yale Law Journal* 99:945–1028.
Keil, Geert. 2013. Was lehrt uns das Gettier-Problem über das Verhältnis zwischen Intuitionen und Begriffsanalysen? In *Das Gettierproblem. Eine Bilanz nach 50 Jahren,* ed. Gerhard Ernst and Lisa Marani, 107–144. Münster: Mentis.
Knapp, Steven, and Walter Benn Michaels. 1982. Against theory. *Critical Inquiry* 8:723–742.
Kripke, Saul. 1982. *Wittgenstein on rules and private language: An elementary exposition*. Oxford: Blackwell.
Marmor, Andrei. 2005. *Interpretation and legal theory*. Oxford: Hart.
Moore, Michael S. 1995. Interpreting interpretation. In *Law and anterpretation. Essays in legal philosophy,* ed. Andrei Marmor, 1–30. Oxford: Clarendon.
Patterson, Dennis. 1996. *Law and truth*. New York: Oxford University Press.
Salmon, Nathan. 2005. Two conceptions of semantics. In *Semantics versus pragmatics,* ed. Zoltán Szabó, 317–328. Oxford: Oxford University Press.
Schauer, Frederick. 1993. *Playing by the rules. A philosophical examination of rule-based decision-making in law and in life*. Oxford: Oxford University Press.
Waldron, Jeremy. 2001. Legislators' intentions and unintentional legislation. In *Law and disagreement,* ed. Jeremy Waldron, 119–146. Oxford: Oxford University Press.
Wittgenstein, Ludwig. 1953. *Philosophical investigations*. (Trans. Gertrude Anscombe). Oxford: Blackwell.
Zelazo, Philip. 2014. The development of higher-order rule use: Reflection, rule hierarchies, and cognitive control. In *This volume*,

Chapter 22
The Ordinary Meaning of Rules

Brian G. Slocum

Abstract Judges typically claim that rules contained in legal texts are interpreted in accordance with their ordinary meaning. It follows that the constituent question of what makes some meaning the ordinary one and the evidential question of how the determinants of ordinary meaning are identified and conceptualized are of crucial importance to the interpretation of legal texts. While a comprehensive analysis of these questions is beyond the scope of this chapter, it is possible as well as important to outline how such questions must necessarily be approached. Certainly, there are a variety of ways in which courts habitually go beyond or reject the linguistic meaning of the relevant text. Normatively based desires to, for example, ensure fair notice or avoid constitutional questions may cause a court to give a text a legal meaning that does not correspond with its linguistic meaning. The ordinary meaning principle, though, is necessarily concerned with the linguistic meaning of the text and not normative matters. As such, certain views about meaning and interpretation can be rejected as being incorrect. In particular, certain claims made by actual intentionalists are fundamentally inconsistent with how the ordinary meaning doctrine must be conceptualized. In short, the intentionalist position that a text means what its author intended it to mean, as well as the associated claims about the nature of natural language that often accompany this assertion, must be rejected. Instead, the ordinary meaning doctrine must be explicated on the basis of systematicities and conventions of language.

Keywords Textualism · Intentionalism · Ordinary meaning · Statutory interpretation · Legal interpretation · Linguistics

---

B. G. Slocum (✉)
University of the Pacific, McGeorge School of Law, Sacramento, USA
e-mail: bslocum@mcgeorge.edu

M. Araszkiewicz et al. (eds.), *Problems of Normativity, Rules and Rule-Following*,
Law and Philosophy Library 111, DOI 10.1007/978-3-319-09375-8_22

22.1 The Ordinary Meaning Doctrine and the Problem of Actual Intentionalism

22.1.1 *Judicial Reliance on Ordinary Meaning*

By what standard should rules contained in legal texts be interpreted? The Supreme Court of the United States believes, as do numerous courts around the world, that rules should be identified on the basis of general principles of language usage that apply equally outside of the law. For instance, the Supreme Court recently reasoned, in rejecting what it viewed as an unordinary meaning, that just because a "dictionary definition is broad enough to encompass one sense of a word does not establish that the word is *ordinarily* understood in that sense" (emphasis in original).[1] The judicial reliance on the ordinary meaning of language should not be surprising. A characteristic feature of legal texts is that they employ natural language in order to accomplish their purposes (Mattila 2002). Further, legal texts are widely viewed as a form of communication (McCubbins and Rodriguez 2011; Van Schooten 2007). Ideally, assuming that successful communication is the goal in most cases, these texts should be understood by different people in the same way. One aspect of this broad requirement is that legal texts should be understandable to the general public, as well as to judges and sophisticated practitioners. As Cappelen (2007, p. 19) explains, "[w]hen we articulate rules, directives, laws and other action-guiding instructions, we assume that people, variously situated, can grasp that content in the same way". Such a goal would seem to require that absent some reason for deviation, such as words with technical or special legal meanings, the language used in legal texts should be viewed as corresponding with that used in non-legal communications (Mellinkoff 1963).

22.1.2 *Framing Actual Intentionalism*

Due to the centrality of the ordinary meaning doctrine to legal interpretation, the constituent question of what makes some meaning the ordinary one and the evidential question of how the determinants of the ordinary meaning of legal texts are identified are of crucial importance to the interpretation of legal texts. Both questions are greatly undertheorized in legal scholarship. That is, there are no systematic accounts of the constitutive and evidential questions. This chapter does not attempt to offer a systematic account of the ordinary meaning doctrine but rather addresses a few issues that are integral to it. Specifically, the chapter develops the claim that the interpretation of legal texts, and consequently the elaboration of legal rules, must necessarily be a hypothetical exercise that relies on conventions of language, which largely constitute the ordinary meaning doctrine. In establishing

[1] Taniguchi v. Kan Pacific Saipan Ltd., 132 S.Ct. 1997, 2003 (2012).

this position, particular attention is given to the claims of intentionalists regarding language and meaning. Intentionalist arguments deserve special attention because, if valid, they pose a challenge to any theory that gives the ordinary meaning concept a central role in determining the meaning of legal texts.

The ordinary meaning concept is necessarily based on an 'objective' view of meaning because its communicative content is not constituted by the content of the author's communicative intentions. In contrast, intentionalism is based on a Gricean conception of communication where the communicative content of an utterance is the content that the speaker intends the hearer to understand by recognizing that very intention (Greenberg 2011b). The so-called 'strong' version of intentionalism posits both a constitutive claim that (1) the meaning of a conversational utterance or a text is identical to the speaker or author's intended meaning (*meaning thesis*), and an epistemic claim that (2) interpretation consists of determining the speaker or author's intended meaning (*interpretation thesis*). In the intentionalist model, the determination of authorial intention is thus indistinguishable from interpretation, which simplifies how intentionalists view the meaning of language (Fish 1999).

Consider a typical situation where a sentence may express two (or more) linguistic meanings represented by (A_1) or (A_2), and the author intends to express only one of the meanings. In considering the meaning of (A_1) and (A_2) distinctions can be made, at least according to non-intentionalists, among (i) the linguistic meaning or meanings that a sentence *S* has in a language *L,* (ii) the linguistic meaning or meanings that a sentence *S* conveys in a language *L* in its context of utterance, and (iii) the meaning that an utterance *S* in a language *L* expresses on a given occasion of use. The first category, (i), can be referred to as the word-sequence meaning or 'sentence meaning', which is the meaning of a sequence of words taken in the abstract following the relevant language's syntactic and semantic rules. It excludes all information about the context in which the sentence was uttered or written and is treated as a token of a sentence type in a given language. The second category, (ii), can be referred to as the 'utterance meaning' (or 'what is said'), which is the meaning a sequence of words conveys in its context of utterance. The third category, (iii), can refer to 'utterer's meaning', which is the meaning the speaker or author had in mind to convey by use of the sequence of words. The 'utterer's meaning' holds regardless of whether the meaning was recognized via lexical items and syntactic structures or other publicly available indicators of meaning, or, for some, regardless of whether the meaning was recognized at all by the relevant listeners or hearers.

For an intentionalist, 'utterer's meaning' is all that matters (or, more strongly, all that can be said to exist), and in determining utterer's meaning, one must ascertain the communicative intent of the author. A text can therefore never fail to mean what the author intends it to mean. Further, intentionalists argue that without resort to the author's communicative intent, every text would mean everything its words could potentially mean in the language in which it was written. Thus, any sentence *S* would always mean both (A_1) and (A_2), and perhaps multiple other meanings. In light of these arguments, one would think that an intentionalist should be committed to the view that actual authorial intentions can be determined with "some epistemically respectable degree of warrant" (Iseminger 1996). For these reasons, the intentionalist meaning thesis rejects the traditional distinction between 'sentence meaning' (or 'what is said') and 'utterer's meaning'. Further, intentionalists argue that in legal contexts deviations from intentionalism by judges may sometimes be wise for reasons specific to law, such as 'fair notice', but such deviations nevertheless represent a rejection of a statute's true meaning in favor of some artificial meaning.

Both the meaning thesis and the interpretation thesis pose a challenge to the ordinary meaning concept. If, as intentionalists argue, the meaning of an utterance or text is identical to the speaker or author's intended meaning and the goal of interpretation is to uncover this meaning, it is not immediately clear why the ordinary meaning concept should have a prominent role in the determination of meaning. Any evidence, such as independent word meaning found in dictionaries or corpora, not connected to the author's actual intent would be irrelevant (Azar 2007). Even worse, if words do not have established or conventional meanings in a language, the ordinary meaning concept would be incoherent since, by its very nature, it assumes that words have conventional meanings. Consider, for example, Fish's (2005, p. 633) view that the definition of 'interpretation' is limited to the search for authorial intent because "words do not carry fixed or even relatively fixed meanings". At the least, it is not clear why evidence of ordinary meaning should act as more than a pragmatic constraint on the 'true meaning' of the text, or perhaps serve as a concession that the true meaning of the text cannot be determined due to insufficient indications of authorial intent.

Due to the intentionalist view of language, the importance of the ordinary meaning concept to interpretation can only be realized through an examination of the determinants of meaning and the limits of textual interpretation, and a consequent rejection of the meaning and interpretation theses. As well, the constraints of textual interpretation, and the rejection of the meaning and interpretation theses, underscore the legitimacy and necessity of the ordinary meaning doctrine. As developed in this chapter, the ordinary meaning of a phrase or sentence must, constitutively, be a properly contextualized, public meaning, rather than an idiosyncratic meaning that can only be discerned, if at all, based on non-textual inferences from intent. Ordinary meaning must therefore be based on theories of linguistic phenomena (including conventions of meaning) external to the author and is thereby inherently theoretical. It relies on, to use Hogan's (1996) term, a notion of "semantic objectivism" that posits that there are facts about what words mean and these facts are independent of what individual people mean by the words they use.

Intentionalists claim that it is "embarrassingly obvious" that textual meaning and authorial intention are the same thing (Campos 1996). Their position, however, cannot be sustained. The meaning and interpretation theses must be rejected because the interpretive process is not, as intentionalists would ideally conceive it, telementational where a thought is transferred from the author's mind to the interpreter's mind (Harris 2001). Levinson (2002) observes that our interests in literature are communicative ones but are not more narrowly conversational ones. The same is true with respect to legal texts. Texts are dissimilar from oral utterances in various important ways, and these differences are crucial to how texts can be interpreted.

Most importantly, it changes how we conceptualize authorial intention. An author's so-called semantic intentions—the intent to use a word or phrase and mean something by it rather something else it may mean—are relevant to what the author means, and indeed may be said to constitute it, but they are not determinative of what the *text* means. Contrary to intentionalist arguments, the interpretive process should not be viewed as involving merely an archaeological excavation-like search for authorial intent. Rather, it should be conceptualized as a theoretical and structured enterprise where, among other things, courts apply linguistic and cognitive science insights to determine the meaning of the text, taken from an interpreter's standpoint.

This chapter seeks to explicate the principle that the ordinary meaning of legal rules found in texts is necessarily based on a hypothetical intentionalism that focuses on utterance meaning rather than utterer's meaning. As a consequence, the arguments made by actual intentionalists about textual interpretation must be rejected. Specifically, the chapter highlights the important distinctions between oral conversations and texts, rejects various intentionalist arguments about the nature of natural language, and, finally, argues that a hypothetical view of interpretation is consistent with the current approaches to interpretation. In doing so, this chapter considers arguments about intentionalism and language made by literary theorists, as well as legal theorists (and linguists and philosophers). Of course, intentionalism is not monolithic. Different theories of intentionalism exist depending on the views and needs of a particular community and the kinds of communications that must be interpreted. For instance, legal theorists who advocate for an intentionalist view of legal interpretation undoubtedly have some justifications for intentionalism that differ from those offered by those who are concerned with literary interpretation. These concerns and motivations may have no direct correspondence to non-legal interpretation of texts. Nevertheless, the basic intentionalist position on the nature of language and interpretation is the same, regardless of the type of text at issue.

22.2 Actual Intentionalism and the Distinction Between Oral Conversations and Texts

Perhaps the biggest flaw in the intentionalist view of interpretation is that it does not adequately consider the fundamental differences between the interpretation of verbal utterances and texts. Yet, one of the most important, and constraining, realities of interpretation concerns the differences between oral and written communications. Grice's intentionalism was built on a model of spoken language, but other intentionalists have dismissed the differences between spoken and written language. In fact, as Davies (2006) notes, intentionalists make the comparison central to their claims. Carroll (1992, pp. 117–118), for example, states that "[w]hen we read a literary text … we enter a relationship with its creator that is roughly analogous to a conversation."

The different system of signs utilized in writing is driven by the separation, in typical texts, of the context of utterance from the context of interpretation. In typical written discourse, in contrast to typical spoken discourse, the context that concerns the physical setting in which an utterance is produced does not correspond to the physical setting in which the utterance is interpreted. This physical context (which Ivanic (1994) terms "Context A") is not shared in typical written discourse because the interlocutors are separated in time and space.[2] The text is thus a closed, unilateral speech act with no opportunity for linguistic replies that can help precisify indeterminate messages. Unlike the case with much oral communication, the reader of a text cannot immediately, or often ever, seek clarification from the writer of the text. This limitation on communicating via text caused Socrates to compare writing with paintings because like writing, "the creations of the painter have the attitude of life, and yet if you ask them a question they preserve a solemn silence" (Plato 360 B.C.E., 274–277).

In addition to the unilateral nature of a written communication, vital cues that allow for the ascertainment of a speaker's intent in an ordinary conversation are not available to the interpreter of a text. With a text, the entire message must be expressed in words. Such a message cannot convey the paralinguistic cues that typically assist the listener in a conversation in discerning the speaker's meaning. Thus, important cues such as winking, facial expressions, posture, stance, laughing and gestures are unavailable to help discern the meaning of the utterance. In addition, with a text the words must obviously be written, making unavailable cues from prosody (rhythm, rate, stress, pitch, pitch contour and intonation of speech), which serve an important role in determining meaning in ordinary conversation. Along with offering semantic clues, these prosodic cues contribute to the emotive or attitudinal quality of an utterance, and consequently its meaning.

Routine and important aspects of conversational interpretation are thus unavailable to the interpreter of a typical text. The lexico-grammatic choices may be the same in a given oral conversation and in a text, but the message sent by the speaker in an oral conversation can be modified by adjusting the paralinguistic and prosodic cues that are unavailable in textual utterances. Further, the lack of a shared physical context means that in typical written discourse there is no possibility for each interlocutor to monitor the other's comprehension and degree of agreement and to adjust utterances accordingly. The lack of a shared physical context should not be underestimated because language comprehension hinges on voice-based and stereotype-dependent inferences about the speaker (Van Berkum et al. 2008). Language comprehension is immediately context-dependent and is processed by the same early interpretation mechanism in the brain that constructs sentence meaning based on just the words. Language comprehension thus takes very rapid account of the social context, particularly information regarding the speaker, which indicates the centrality of these contextual cues in the final interpretation given an

[2] Of course, not all written language involves a context of interpretation that is far removed from the context of utterance. For example, a note passed in class would involve a context of interpretation that is very similar to the context of utterance.

utterance. Little is known about how the brain actually constructs an interpretation (Van Berkum 2008). Nevertheless, research indicates that the linguistic brain uses heuristics, particularly regarding the speaker, to arrive at the earliest possible interpretation. Instead of the standard two-step model of language processing where listeners first compute a local, context-independent meaning for the sentence and then determine what it really means given the wider communicative context and the particular speaker, Van Berkum et al. (2008), maintain that research supports a one-step model in which knowledge about the speaker is brought to bear immediately by the same fact-acting brain system that combines the meaning of individual words into a larger whole.

The differences described above between the interpretive cues available in a prototypical conversation and those available for a text are relevant to the interpretation of most texts and are particularly relevant to the interpretation of legal texts. For various reasons, legal texts are paradigmatic examples of autonomous texts which differ greatly from the prototypical personal communication context. Consider the interpretation of statutes. Unlike the typical oral conversation, the legislative context is impersonal. Legislators and interpreters do not, generally, know each other personally, making clarification impossible (absent further legislation, of course, which nevertheless cannot be seen as the continuation of a conversation). Contextual information regarding the legislators' intent is often either not available or is of questionable value. For statutes, the typical source of contextual information termed 'legislative history' has been widely attacked as being unreliable and subject to manipulation. Part of the reason is that the legislative process is a far less cooperative one than is the typical communicative context. The common strategic behavior is such that some have questioned the applicability of Grice's maxims of cooperation to legislation (Marmor 2012; Poggi 2011). Due to strategic behavior, and other legislative practices, the words of the legislative text may reflect, in a general sense, the intent of the legislature to modify the content of the law but may not have been chosen to implement the legislators' communicative intentions. Further, the relevant interpreters, including judges, may have to interpret the text decades or centuries after it was created.

The unsponsored nature of statutes should have various consequences, including underscoring the necessity of the ordinary meaning doctrine. Interpreters must place sustained, if not exclusive, attention on textual rather than extra-textual authorial evidence. More precisely, the unsponsored nature of statutes would seem to require that textual meaning, as opposed to authorial meaning, be the primary determinant of the communicative meaning of a legal text. Designating legal texts as unsponsored also illustrates the unpersuasiveness of the common intentionalist arguments that use examples from ordinary conversations (see Fish 2005 for one such example). An intentionalist account of interpretation that fails to address the fundamental differences between ordinary conversations and legal texts undermines any argument that the meaning of a text is identical to the author's intended meaning and that interpretation consists of discovering that meaning.

22.3 The Nature of Language and Intentionalist Arguments About Meaning

22.3.1 'Fixed' Meanings

Viewing legal texts as unsponsored and not analogous to ordinary conversations supports a theory of interpretation that would give a prominent role to the ordinary meaning concept and its reliance on conventions of meaning, but intentionalists make other arguments about meaning not yet considered that, if persuasive, would undermine reliance on conventions. Stanley Fish (2005, p. 633), for example, argues that the definition of 'interpretation' is limited to the search for authorial intent because "words do not carry fixed or even relatively fixed meanings". Thus, for Fish (635), "lexical items and grammatical structures by themselves will yield no meaning—will not even be seen as lexical items and grammatical structures—until they are seen as having been produced by some intentional agent". Fish's position that words do not have even relatively fixed meanings would, if true, seriously undermine any reliance on conventions of meaning. If fact, if taken seriously, it would counsel that authors are the only parties qualified to interpret their own works.

Notwithstanding the ideality of language, assertions about the absence of inherent lexical meaning or the reality of diachronic fluctuations in word meanings do not further an intentionalist agenda. In a narrow sense, any linguist or philosopher of language should agree with certain intentionalist assertions about language. With respect to natural language, it is the users of language that determine whether signs will convey meaning and what meaning the signs will convey (Cruse 1983). That is, the marks on a page that any given community of speakers agrees to interpret as words do not contain any *inherent* meaning. As Jackson (1995, pp. 18–19) observes, neither the sound d-o-g nor the written characters 'dog' inherently refer to a member of the subspecies *canis lupus familiaris* (which is itself a conventional term). Rather, the reference is natural, and seemly inherent, to English speakers due to the strength of the convention that 'dog' refers to [dog]. Saussure (2011, p. 67) referred to this phenomenon as the "arbitrary nature of the sign". That is, there is an arbitrary connection between a 'sound-image', or signifier, and a 'concept', or signified. Saussure explained that "if words stood for pre-existing concepts, they would all have exact equivalents in meaning from one language to the next; but this is not true" (2011, p. 116)For the most part, the connection between signifier and signified is not rational or natural but is instead conventional. Thus, it would be just as rational for d-o-g to refer to a member of the group of organisms that consist of all gill-bearing aquatic craniate animals that lack limbs with digits (i.e., 'fish') as it would for it to refer to a member of the subspecies *canis lupus familiaris*.

While words have the meanings that are assigned to them by the users of language, these meanings are independent of any particular authorial intention. Indeed, as has been observed by various scholars, various combinations of words can create meaningful sentences that have never been uttered at all. The nature of language easily allows for such possibilities. Verbs select the events and nouns select the entities that allow us to individuate happenings and events in the world. Identifying the meanings of verbs and nouns requires distinguishing their meanings from the happenings and entities in the world that they describe in a particular use. The lexicalized, or context-invariant, meaning, determined on the basis of grammatical behavioral patterns in the data, consists of those properties that are shared across all uses or a verb or noun, regardless of context. When a noun is chosen to describe an entity in the world, a claim is being made that the entity has the attributes lexicalized by the noun, though it may also have other attributes. Two nouns may refer to the same entity, but in lexicalizing different attributes, they may construe it as an entity in different ways. Similarly, a single verb can be applied to quite different happenings, and two verbs may lexicalize distinct but partially overlapping sets of attributes yet be able to refer to the same happening out in the world. Nevertheless when a verb is chosen to describe an event, a comment is made regarding certain attributes present in the chain of happenings in the world being referred to by that verb. For example, Botne (2001) has produced a crosslinguistic study which shows that verbs of dying fall into four major types that can be differentiated according to which stages of the dying process they lexicalize. The Acute type lexicalize the point of death alone, while the Transitional type lexicalize the onset, the point of death, and the result.

Speakers are thus constrained by the lexicalized meaning of verbs (and nouns). Consider a situation where the speaker wishes to convey that a table has been dried. In choosing an appropriate verb, the speaker must consider that there are verb pairs where each member lexicalizes distinct sets of attributes in the same stream of happenings (Levin and Hovav 1995). The speaker could describe the scenario using the verb 'wipe' or the verb 'dry'.

(1) a. Kelly wiped the table with a tea towel.
    b. Kelly dried the table with a tea towel.

'Wipe' is a manner (as opposed to result) verb that involves nonscalar changes, which means that it is not characterizable in terms of a scale, that is, an ordered set of degrees along a dimension representing a single attribute. The lack of an ordering relation and complexity are the two properties that contribute to making a change nonscalar (Hovav and Levin 2010). The vast majority of nonscalar change verbs, such as 'wipe', involve a complex combination of many changes at once, so that there is no single, privileged scale of change. If the speaker uses 'wiped', as in (1a), the speaker will have said nothing about whether the table has actually been dried, though perhaps most hearers would assume that it has been.[3] Unlike 'dry', 'wipe', like 'scrub', involves a specific pattern of movement of the hand and arm that is repeated an indefinite number of times against a surface but, collectively, does not represent a change in the values of one attribute, nor is any one element in the sequence of movements a necessary starting point of the activity. Thus, absent additional, revealing facts in the context that would add information about the lexicalized meaning of the verb, the speaker cannot use 'wipe' and insist that the hearer should understand that the table has been dried.

[3] If the speaker uses 'dried', as in (1b), the speaker will have said nothing about how the trying came about, though the use of a tea towel, and 'wiping' is one possibility.

22.3.2 *The Creativity of Language*

Fish and other intentionalists argue that existing linguistic conventions do not impose any constraints on the ability of individuals to give words new meanings. From a diachronic perspective, it is, of course, correct that the meanings of words can change. Knapp and Michaels (1987) correctly point out that in everyday life people frequently give new meanings to words and phrases and that this is a natural way in which language develops. The existence of linguistic conventions does not preclude these items from obtaining new meanings, as conventions can change. Thus, the philosopher Wittgenstein (1953, p. 18) is correct that one can say 'bububu' and mean 'If it doesn't rain I shall go for a walk'. Under certain conditions (unusual if a text is involved), a successful communicative effort may even result from these instances of linguistic creativity.

Conceding the uncontroversial fact of linguistic creativity does not, however, entail that individual speakers have autonomy over the meanings of their utterances, nor does it undermine the reality that word meanings are independent of authorial communicative intention. As Wilson (1992) argues, there are an unbounded number of 'available' meaningful sentences in any natural language that have never been uttered, and may never be uttered. They are meaningful due to conventions of meaning, and any speaker is part of a linguistic community in which conventions thrive. Meaning may originate in individuals, but conventional meaning derives from individuals as restricted by their group's conventions (von Savigny 1985). While conventional meanings undoubtedly change over time, it does not follow that the rate of linguistic change exceeds efforts to determine a word's conventional meaning at any particular time. If this were true, successful communication via texts, as well as a great deal of oral communication, would be impossible.

Much literary and linguistic analysis is based on the understanding that words have meanings outside of any specific author's intent, and language could not get started if they did not. If signs did not contain meanings outside of authorial intent, literary concepts like symbolism, simile, metaphor, irony, synecdoche, metonymy, exaggeration and sarcasm which depend on a gap between sign and signified, would be incoherent. Due to autglottic space (i.e., the distance between author and text), these concepts are more difficult to discern in texts than in oral conversations. Nevertheless, their effectiveness depends on conventions of meaning. Similarly, if the effort to capture specific authorial intent represented the only permissible definition of interpretation, there could only be "empirical" failures (as Fish puts it) to discover meaning, but there could be no such concept as ambiguity.[4] At the least, there would be no such thing as *unintentional* ambiguity. Natural languages (and

[4] Vagueness could still exist, however, because it is tied more to the nature of language and less to authorial intent. For example, a term is vague if it presents borderline difficulties (Sorensen 1989). Wasow et al. (2005, p. 2) note that "[m]ost expressions in natural languages are vague—that is, the denotations of most expressions are fuzzy around the edges". When, for example, is something green instead of brown or blue? The answer to the question, whatever it may be, is orthogonal to any concept of ambiguity.

especially legal language), though, are considered to be pervasively indeterminate by linguists (Tabossie and Zardon 1993).

Further, if words had no meaning outside of an author's specific intent, there would be no need to distinguish between semantics and pragmatics. At a basic level, though, such a distinction is important and necessary, although the dividing line between two has been subject to much debate. One common conception of semantics is that it involves computing truth conditions of utterances compositionally according to the types of expressions used in the utterances and the ways they are combined.[5] Of course, sentences are not always compositional, and violations of compositionality are said to create a syntagmatic conflict between form and meaning (Moravcsik 2006, p. 111). In addition to being an issue within semantics, violations of compositionality are studied within the field of pragmatics, which concerns information "generated by, or at least made relevant by, the act of uttering the sentence" (Bach 2002, p. 284). In a general sense, the field attempts to explain how "extra meaning (in a broad sense) is 'read into' utterances without actually being encoded in them" (Levinson 1983, p. 11). Thus, a fundamental, and well-established, principle of a central area of study in linguistics (namely semantics) is that words have meanings outside of any specific context, even if context is often highly relevant to such things as precisification, disambiguationj and reference determination.

22.3.3 Necessary Authors and Communicative Intentions

Notwithstanding the existence of author independent word meanings, intentionalists make various related arguments that insist that interpretation of a text is impossible without reference to an author. If, so the arguments go, reference to an author or authors is a necessary aspect of interpretation then all interpretation is intentionalist in nature (Robertson 2009). Some of these intentionalist arguments are true, sometimes trivially so, but none establish the intentionalist meaning or interpretation theses. Contrary to intentionalist arguments, one can agree that generalized assumptions about authorial intent are unavoidable in any interpretive effort but disagree that ascertaining specific communicative authorial intent is necessary to determining meaning.

One intentionalist argument about the necessity of an interpreter's reference to authorial intent is that the interpreter must either actually know or assume various things about texts. Thus, for example, intentionalists assert that no text by itself declares the language in which it is written (Alexander and Prakash 2003; Knapp and Michael 2005). An interpreter must therefore assume that the Constitution and statutes, and other legal documents, are written in English, thereby giving the interpretation an intentionalist focus. This observation, though, does not add support to any intentionalist arguments and, if anything, undermines them. Simply put, why

[5] "The principle of compositionality states that the meaning of a complex linguistic expression is built up from the meanings of its composite parts in a rule-governed fashion" (Murphy and Koskela 2010, p. 36).

would a document (at least one that is more than a word or two) *need* to proclaim the language in which it is written?

Deciding that a text is written in English does not depend on assumptions about authorial intent. One does not need to know *anything* about an author, or any broader non-textual context, to discern the language in which a document is written. Sufficient clues about the language of the text can be found in the text itself. Determining the language of a text depends on the interpreter's ability to identify the English language based on syntactic, semantic, morphological and other linguistic evidence. Under normal circumstances, it is not clear why an author's intent would even be relevant in such a situation, or why an author would bother to make such an intent known. Further, if the author proclaims that a given text is written in language *X* (say, French) but the syntax, morphology and lexicon is clearly that of language *Y* (say, English), in what sense could the author's proclamation sensibly be said to govern? Even if one accepts Knapp and Michael's (2005) hypothetical where two languages (which they term English and "Schmenglish") look exactly alike except for their semantics, there is no doubt that an interpreter could identify a text (again, unless it is very short), with no reference to the author, on the basis of its semantics.[6]

A related argument regarding the inevitability of intentionalism is that an interpreter must acknowledge or assume an author with an intention whenever the interpreter is interpreting a meaningful text (Knapp and Michaels 1982). Thus, Alexander and Prekash (2004, p. 976) argue that "one cannot look at the marks on a page and understand those marks to be a text (that is, a meaningful writing) without assuming that an author made those marks intending to convey a meaning by them." Similarly, Fish (635) argues that "lexical items and grammatical structures by themselves will yield no meaning—will not even be seen as lexical items and grammatical structures—until they are seen as having been produced by some intentional agent." At the outset, it seems as though the argument regarding the necessity of intentions should be summarily rejected. One problem is that the intentionalist arguments beg the meaning of 'meaningful'. For instance, language is perfectly capable of being analyzed for various purposes without referencing an author, or even assuming that one exists. That is, marks are analyzable as lexical items and grammatical structures without referencing an author in any concrete way. More importantly, though, even if this point is conceded, referencing the existence of an author's general intent to communicate via a text is using the concept of intent at a very high level of generality, rather than in a narrow way to signify the communicative intent of some specific meaning. By itself, the high level of abstraction at which intent is framed makes the fact of intent a triviality. Who would deny that an author of a text had an intention of conveying *some* meaning through the text? For what other purpose are texts created?

Despite the triviality of the intentional author argument, intentionalists intend for a strong inference to be drawn from the indisputable fact that an author has a communicative intention when creating a text. More specifically, for the same reasons

[6] For a somewhat similar response to this claim and others by Alexander and Prakash see Sinnott-Armstrong (2005).

that it is impossible to have a text without an author, the intentionalist position is to deny the possibility of a distinction between textual meaning and author's meaning. Thus, Knapp and Michaels (1982, p. 724) assert that: "The clearest example of the tendency to generate theoretical problems by splitting apart terms that are in fact inseparable is the persistent debate over the relation between authorial intention and the meaning of texts." This strong intentionalist inference is not, however, persuasive. A concession that a text has been created by an author with some general intent to communicate does not entail that authorial intention and the meaning of texts are coterminous. Rather, it is possible to concede the relevance of broad authorial intent yet deny the relevance (or at least the decisiveness) of authorial intent to communicate some specific meaning.

As the above arguments illustrate, a fundamental problem for intentionalists is their tendency to conflate distinct aspects of intent with different degrees of generality. Instead, a distinction must be made between intentionally creating something in a simple agentive sense and creating it with a specific intention (Kiefer 2005). Artworks may be intentionally created, but Kiefer questions whether many of them are created with a specific intention. He mentions in this connection examples such as Pollack's action painting, minimalist sculpture, and a hypothetical painter who claims he is just painting, period. He argues that if artworks are not created with specific intentions, understanding that they are the product of intentional activity will give us little or no information that could contribute to an appreciative understanding of them. Similarly, with literary works consider a division based on the type, and generality, of intention. With respect to these works, Levinson (2002) distinguishes between *semantic intentions* and *categorical intentions*. Categorical intentions, which are actual intentions, relate to the status of works as literature and to their categorical or genre location within literature. Thus, a categorical intention is a desire that a text be classified, taken, or approached in some specific or general way, such as literature or art (232). They amount to metasemantic intentions regarding what sorts of meaning are to be sought in given works. They therefore involve intentions regarding the approximate nature of the work, but not the precise import (314).

The distinction drawn by Levinson between categorical and semantic intentions, and his assertion that categorical intentions rest on actual authorial intent, may have flaws, but the arguments underscore the conflation of different types of intent in the intentionalists' arguments.[7] As discussed above when establishing that legal interpretation is theoretical in nature, there are multiple levels of generality associated with the concept of 'intent'. When interpreting a statute, one can, for example, consider intent narrowly as what was said or, more broadly, as how the legislature intended to modify the content of the law (Greenberg 2011a). Of course, intent can be framed even more broadly as the intent to author a text with a meaningful content. These different levels of intent are not, however, freely substitutable. An assertion, posed at a very high level of generality, that an author must have had a communicative intention when creating a text does not suggest, let alone entail, that the identity of much more specific intentions can be determined or are relevant to meaning or

[7] A distinction between categorical and semantic intentions is irrelevant to most legal texts because there is no doubt as to their proper categorization as legal texts.

interpretation. One can concede intent on a meta-semantic level yet deny it at more specific levels without any inconsistency. Thus, one can acknowledge, for example, that Congress (almost certainly) had an actual intent to write in English or to enact a binding statute yet deny that any actual authorial intent is relevant to the resolution of any particular interpretive dispute.

Further issues complicate intentionalist claims that the meaning of a text is coterminous with authorial intent. Somewhat related to intentionalists' conflation of different levels of intent is their failure to recognize that the supposed 'actual' intentions to which they refer are frequently assumed rather than discerned. Often, if an appeal to authorial intent is made, the basis must be a generalized assumption, such as one that authors intend to write in the language that is expected by the audience for which the document is written, not one based on any specific communicative intent. Such generalized, and often fictional, assumptions, however, cannot be seen as intentionalist, within the definition of intentionalism that actual intentionalists defend, but instead are similar to the conventions that intentionalists criticize. A generalized assumption may be framed by the interpreter as something that captures authorial intention, but it is one that is imputed to the author and is thus not an actual intention. Fish (1989, p. 329) argues that interpretation is not a two-stage process in which the interpreter first finds the context-independent meaning and then consults the relevant context. Instead, the 'semantic meaning' cannot be selected independently of a context of assumptions, concerns, priorities and expectations. But, even if Fish is correct, these constraints must apply to all interpreters and methodologies. Similar to other methodologies, an intentionalist therefore cannot determine actual authorial intent independent of assumptions, concerns, priorities and expectations, which are not tied to any actual intent but which will invariably shape and distort that task.

22.3.4 The Necessity of Reference to Authorial Intent

Apart from the intentionalist claim that an interpreter must, in a general sense, always acknowledge or assume an author with an intention, intentionalists make other arguments regarding the necessity of reference to authorial intent. One of these arguments is that language, being polymorphic, is indeterminate without reference to authorial intent, even if one concedes the well-established principle that words have conventional meanings independent of any individual author's specific intention. Consider intentionalist examples used to make the point that authorial intent is necessary for disambiguation. Knapp and Michaels (2005), taking an example from Scalia (1997), argue that the sentence

(2) I took the boat out on the bay

can be interpreted as meaning 'I went sailing' (A_1) as opposed to *both* 'I went sailing' (A_1) and 'I used the horse to carry the dingy' (A_2) only by reference to an author's specific communicative intent. If the point is merely that the meaning of a term or sentence *in abstracto* can be indeterminate, the point is obvious but trivial.

Clearly, at least some content is context-dependent. Consider indexicals (such as 'I', 'now', 'here', and 'today'), which necessarily have content that is relative to the context of utterance. Words such as 'now', 'here', and 'today' similarly depend on consideration of context in order to determine their references. The reference of 'I' obviously shifts depending on the identity of the speaker. Another common example of context dependence involves quantifiers. Thus, using an example from Wilson (1992), if a speaker asserts, 'Every napkin is frayed', it is likely that the seemingly universal quantifier 'every' was meant to be restricted to some smaller domain such as 'in the house' or 'on the table'. The linguistic meaning that a sentence *S* expresses is not, therefore, as a rule sufficient to determine what Wilson terms the 'context-loaded linguistic meaning' that *S* expresses on an occasion of utterance.

Intentionalists, though, make claims about clarity and indeterminacy that are broader than the principle that expressions are context dependent. Knapp and Michaels (2005, p. 655), for instance, argue that if one believes that the meaning of a text is the sort of thing that authors can try to express clearly, and of clarity as something they can either achieve or fail to achieve, then a commitment has been made to the idea that the text means what the author meant by it. They argue that in (2) if one is not interested in what the author meant by the text, the interpreter might look up 'bay' in the dictionary but not have any idea which of the multiple meanings is the appropriate one. Knapp and Michaels claim that the problem would be an ontological one, rather than an epistemic one, because the meanings would be correct. To them, the conclusion is that every text would mean everything its words could mean in the language in which it was written. Thus, the only way a sentence like 'I took the boat out on the bay' can be interpreted to mean 'I went sailing' instead of 'I used the horse to carry the dingy' is by reference to what its speaker means.

The broader intentionalist claims about the necessity of ascertaining specific communicative intent are unpersuasive. While authorial intent, if available and discernible, may, of course, serve to disambiguate language, other evidence can also disambiguate. Under any circumstances, the mental intention of the utterer or author is not directly observable or assessable. If a text is involved, especially a legal text, prosodic and other author specific evidence is also unavailable, as is asking the author for clarification. For purposes of resolving the communicative indeterminacy of a text, a competent interpreter's rational belief regarding the author's intentions is more effective than ascertaining those intentions themselves. In such cases, meaning is discerned through determinants that may surpass the author's intentions, such as conventions of language and context (including earlier expressions). Thus, Wimsatt and Beardsley (1946) correctly reject the idea that an author's intent is a valid ground for arguing the presence of a meaning but indicate that this rejection does not cover situations where the intention is found in, or inferred from, the work itself.

Authorial intent found in the work itself may include sentential evidence, which can disambiguate words, and broader textual evidence, which can disambiguate words as well as sentences and paragraphs. Thus, in (2), even without any evidence of specific authorial communicative intent, the sentence 'I took the boat out on the bay' means 'I used the horse to carry the dingy' if, for example, surrounding sentences describe the horse and the hitching of the dingy to the horse. Similarly, it is not difficult to imagine surrounding sentences that would disambiguate the syntactic ambiguity in (2). Thus, contrary to intentionalist assertions about meaning, it can be argued that non-textual evidence of specific authorial intent may be *sufficient* to disambiguate words and sentences, but it is incorrect to assert that it is always *necessary* evidence. Rather, sentential and broader context is often sufficient to disambiguate. While an intentionalist would respond that sentential and other context is relevant because it is evidence of what the author actually meant, such a response would be inaccurate. Context is not evidence of what the author actually meant, it is evidence that an intended interpreter could use to gauge what the author was trying to convey in employing a given verbal vehicle in the given communicative-context.

22.3.5 Anomalous Meanings

As the above discussion illustrates, discerning actual authorial intentions is not necessary to determine meaning, and these intentions are typically unavailable in any case. Interpreters must rely instead on conventions of meaning, and other objective determinants of meaning. Intentionalists attempt to integrate conventions of meaning into an intentionalist framework by arguing that if an interpreter views a text as having a clear conventional meaning it is because the interpreter either assumes or knows that the author intended to employ those conventions (Robertson 2009). As was argued earlier, an interpreter utilizing a generalized assumption that an author intends to employ conventions should not be seen as actual intentionalism. Rather, such an act is itself the creation or application of a convention, not the evaluation of evidence that would reveal actual communicative intent. Intentionalists argue, though, that while conventional meanings and context may be relevant evidence to a choice between two or more meanings, an interpreter can never rely upon conventional meaning alone (or, one would assume, syntax or other text related information) to determine the meaning of a text. The reason is that the speaker may have intended some anomalous meaning. Thus, in any given situation, an interpreter cannot know whether any word or sentence has the conventional meaning or some unconventional meaning unless reference is made to the intention of the author.

Knapp and Michaels (1987) argue that conventions have no intrinsic power to give a text a meaning that it makes sense for an interpreter to select as an alternative to, or in addition to, the author's intended meaning. Such a position suggests that it is always (or at least usually) possible to discern an author's actual intended meaning without regard to conventions and other generalized assumptions about intent. But unless the author and interpreters are members of the same speech community, sharing a lexicon and similar rules of grammar, linguistic communication is impossible. Considering the unsponsored nature of many texts, a position that it is routinely possible to determine authorial communicative intent without the aid of conventions and other generalized assumptions is naive. Conventions exist, at least partly, because they are devices necessary to interpretation, especially the interpretation of legal texts. Often, there is no other relevant evidence on which to rely.

Apart from the practical necessity of reliance on conventions, a determination that the author intended some unconventional meaning is inherently problematic. Of course, if there is accessible public evidence of such an intention, such as a stipulated definition or persuasive contextual information, determining that an unconventional meaning was intended is often uncontroversial. Imagine, though, that an author intends for the text to have an unconventional meaning but gives no explicit indications of this intent. In such a situation, intentionalists still insist that the meaning of the text conforms to the author's intent. In fact, they argue that although it is sensible to use conventional meanings in order to achieve successful communication with others, doing so is a pragmatic decision, rather than a meaning constraint, and is determined by the outcome one wants to achieve. Intentionalists must therefore be committed to the following proposition: a text T means p, even in situations in which the audience is justified in concluding that the text means q, if and only if the author intended it to mean p. Tellingly, the intentionalist position does not recognize that the author's actual semantic intentions may have been unsuccessfully implemented, making the text mean something other than what the author intended it to mean.[8]

The insistence that an utterance or text means what its author intends it to mean, even if the audience is justified in giving it some other meaning, is unconvincing. The problem is that the intentionalist argument about the potential of anomalous meanings ignores essential constraints on meaning, thereby making communicative success mysterious. By privileging the speaker's intent, intentionalism adopts Humpty Dumpty's philosophy:

'When I use a word', Humpty Dumpty said, in rather a scornful tone, 'it means just what I choose it to mean-neither more nor less' (Carroll 1971, pp. 190–191).

With authorial intentions as the basis for meaning, a speaker's uses of expressions refer to anything the speaker chooses. Humpty Dumpty is claiming the right to change the meaning of a word not through ex-ante public stipulation but through a private mental act. Given speaker confusion, carelessness, mistake or a disordered mental state the possibilities for anomalous meaning are vast. As Gorvett (2005) argues, if intentionalism is accepted, there would appear to be nothing preventing bizarre referring expressions, such as using 'I' to refer to one's uncle, boss or the Pope. While intentionalists argue that such bizarre referring expressions are perfectly acceptable as a linguistic matter (in the sense that there are no inherent language based constraints on the dynamic use of language), hearers have little access to what people have in mind apart what they say or write. Hearers, thus, cannot accurately utilize an interpretive method that depends on the hearer's ability to have independent insight into the speaker's intentions. Interpretation would be potentially unsolvable if hearers were required to have knowledge of the speaker's intent in order to ascertain the content of the context. In order for interpretation to proceed via a reliable method, the interpreter must therefore have access to the determinants of meaning, independently of what proposition the speaker attempts to express.

[8] Such a mistake is not limited to verbal communication. Trivedi (2001) points to an example where a sculptor intended a sculpture to be curvaceous but it instead looks angular.

Faced with the damaging Humpty Dumpty problem, some intentionalists nevertheless maintain the meaning thesis even when the author's intention fails. Other intentionalists, referring to themselves as 'moderate intentionalists', concede, however, that an author may intend his text to mean something but fail to give it that, or perhaps any, meaning (Goldsworthy 2005). Where the author's intention is not realized, the work does not mean what was intended and the interpretive efforts focus on constructing a meaning that is different from the one that was unsuccessfully intended (Davies 2006). In such cases, the meaning of the work is its textual meaning (Carroll 2011).

While moderate intentionalism is an improvement on the circularity of actual intentionalism (which holds that a text *T* means *P* if and only if the author intended it to mean *P*), it fails to undermine the necessity of utterance meaning. Inserting a constraint, as moderate intentionalists have done, undermines the intentionalist meaning and interpretation theses, but it does not solve the dilemma created by actual intentionalism. Consider the typical moderate intentionalist constraint where a text *T* means *P* if and only if the author intended it to mean *p and* that intention has been successfully realized in the text. If only successfully realized communicative intentions serve as the criteria of textual meaning a circularity problem still results. The reason is that successful communicative intentions cannot be given a coherent sense that does not presuppose an independent notion of work meaning to which a communicative intention can be compared to determine if it has been successfully realized (Levinson 1996). One way to avoid circularity is to stipulate that a communication is successfully realized when (a) the author intends that an appropriately backgrounded audience discern *P* in *T*, and (b) such an audience discerns *P* in *T*. Such a stipulation, though, renders successful intent superfluous as a criterion of meaning since (a)+(b) offers a sufficient explanation of it (Trivedi 2001).

22.4 Hypothetical Intentionalism and the Interpretation of Legal Texts

A few literary scholars, including Levinson (2010) and Tolhurst (1979), have recognized that an interpreter centered approach, which they term 'hypothetical intentionalism', is the most defensible form of intentionalism. A basic tenet of hypothetical intentionalism is that a text should be viewed as an utterance, produced in a public context by a historically and culturally situated author. The meaning of the text is its utterance meaning as opposed to either a textual meaning or utterer meaning. Levinson (2010, p. 139) describes the utterance meaning as being determined on a "pragmatic model according to which what an utterance means is a matter, roughly, of what an appropriate hearer would most reasonably take a speaker to be trying to convey in employing a given verbal vehicle in the given communicative-context". Thus, while the interpreter makes a hypothesis regarding authorial intent to convey a meaning to an audience, the hypothesis is based on evidence external to the author.

A hypothetical intentionalist conception of interpretation fits well with the realities of how legal texts must be interpreted. Greenawalt (2000, p. 1620), although arguing for the relevance of "mental states", asserts that "no viable approach to legal meaning can wholly exclude reader understanding approaches". The concession is warranted. The meaning of legal texts must be based on optimal hypotheses about authorial intention, rather than on actual authorial intent. Considering the unsponsored nature of legal texts, and the necessity of relying, in least in part, on generalized assumptions about authorial intent, a claim that actual intent is being sought is, in virtually all instances of interpretation, a fiction. With such texts especially, interpreters must assume that authors intend to comply, in general, with conventions of meaning. Otherwise, to be interpretable, each text would need to be accompanied by a dictionary created by the author that could be used to decode the text. Of course such a dictionary would itself inevitably need to be interpreted. An intentionalist might point to a supposed direct source of authorial intent, but specific assistance from such sources is not always available. With statutes, one might point to the legislative history of a particular provision, but any relevant information is usually stated at a high level of generality, making any specific inferences drawn from it hypothetical in nature. Even when the legislative history is relatively specific, the collective intent issue must be addressed, and there is no way of dealing with it without imputing intent—and thus making the interpretation hypothetical—to some of the members of the legislature.

Not surprisingly, a hypothetical view of interpretation is congruent with the dominant theories of legal interpretation. For the reasons indicated above, any intentionalist practice of legal interpretation will be, in essence, comparable to Levinson's hypothetical intentionalism. Despite the asserted goals of textualism, the theory also cannot ignore communicative intentions, especially considering that textualists argue that context and pragmatic factors may properly be considered. Flanagan (2010), as well as others, argues that these considerations indicate that the textualist interest in literal meaning, rather than authorial intent, might be fictional. This conclusion is not necessary, however. A more accurate view of textualism is that it posits a hypothetical author (seen from the viewpoint of a reasonable interpreter) who complies with conventions of meaning. Consider Marmor's (2012, p. 10) description of textualism:

> What the law says is at least partly determined by what a reasonable hearer, knowing all the relevant background, would infer that it says. In other words, textualism can concede the idea that legal interpretation aims to ascertain the communication intentions of the legislature, as long as it is granted that the relevant communication intentions are understood objectively—that is, as they would be grasped by a reasonable hearer.

The description is similar to the textualist John Manning's (2003, pp. 2392–2393) description of meaning as "how a reasonable person, conversant with the relevant social and linguistic conventions, would read the text in context". Others, including Solan (2005) have also described the similarities between textualist and intentionalist approaches to interpretation.

Of course, there are fundamental differences between textualism and intentionalism, such as textualism's focus on literal rather than utterance meaning as the correct meaning of a text. As a linguistic matter, textualists seem more likely than intentionalists to confuse literal meaning and ordinary meaning. Further, textualists are more likely than intentionalists to reject the possibility that some of a text's contents are determined by relations holding between its purely interior elements and matters lying beyond its boundaries. Intentionalists are thus more willing than are textualists to conclude that the textual meaning does not represent the correct communicative meaning of the text. In addition, some have claimed that textualists prefer to interpret statutory provisions as establishing rules, as opposed to more open ended standards, that narrow judicial discretion in their application (Marmor 2012; Nelson 2005). Textualist preferences for determinate texts and legal rules with objective meanings, as well as interpretive rules that are easily and objectively applied by judges, can come at the expense of adhering to sound interpretive principles.

In addition to the above distinctions, textualists and intentionalists differ in their views regarding various evidential aspects of interpretation. Nevertheless, in both intentionalism and textualism, because access to the actual communicative intentions of the author are unavailable, interpretation must rely on generalized assumptions about intent, such as the assumption that authors of legal texts intend for their words to have their ordinary meaning. Thus, in both methodologies, properly conceived, legislative intent must necessarily be determined from the perspective of the interpreter, and reference to authorial intent is of a hypothetical nature.

Similar to intentionalism and textualism, a purposivist approach to interpretation also posits a hypothetical author. The hypothetical nature of purposivism is obvious. A purposivist interpreter does not attempt to determine the actual intentions of the legislators, but rather may ask something along the lines of what a reasonable legislature wanted to achieve, or would have wanted to achieve if it had foreseen the issue, by enacting the legislation at issue (Marmor 2012). A focus on the legal effects intended by the legislature may seem to render conventions of meaning unimportant, as conventions focus narrowly on communicative meaning while purposivism purports to view language at a higher level of generality. Yet, it is difficult to claim that the communicative meaning of the text does not act, at the least, as a constraint on the available interpretations that a purposivist judge is willing to consider. In fact, in some areas of law, such as criminal statutes, it must be acknowledged that the communicative meaning of the text has to be given priority.

Conclusion

This chapter has attempted to establish that the ordinary meaning concept should be viewed as a central aspect of the communicative content meaning of a legal text and not merely a pragmatic constraint on the true meaning of the text. Further, the communicative content of a legal text is relevant to the legal content of the text, if not decisive of it. Such a view is possible only if one accepts an objective approach to interpretation. Under an objective view, the meaning of a text is the meaning that a competent interpreter would give it by means of a method of interpretation that the interpreter could reliably employ on the basis of features of the situation of which the interpreter is aware (Gauker 2008). Intended meaning can therefore constitute work meaning only if it is accessible to the relevant interpreter (Stecker 2006). An author's perceived actual communicative (semantic) intentions cannot therefore directly serve as one of the criterion of utterance meaning.

Basing the communicative content of a text on objective features of the relevant context avoids the Humpty Dumpty problem, where words mean anything an author intends them to mean. Even part from the Humpty Dumpty issue, it is clear that conventions of meaning underlie all theories of interpretation. Such a conclusion is obvious with objective theories of interpretation, but it is also true with actual intentionalism. When interpreting legal texts at least, actual intentionalists must endemically rely on conventions of meaning. Analogous to the intentionalist claim that textualists must make assumptions about a text that are not based solely on the text, actual intentionalists must make assumptions about the author that are not based on actual evidence of the author's communicative intent. Even if one assumes that a text means what its author intended it to mean, the relevant interpreter must be capable of ascertaining this intended meaning. Because utterances are typically made in order to communicate some intended meaning that is accessible, interpreters typically assume that the author intended to follow conventions of meaning. These generalized assumptions about meaning are not tied to the author's actual intent but instead are the basis of the fundamental concept that works in legal texts are to be given their ordinary meaning.

Acknowledgements The author would like to thank the organizers of Rules § 2013 and Jagiellonian University for hosting a terrific conference and the participants for their comments on my paper.

References

Alexander, Larry, and Prakash, Saikrishna. 2003. Mother may I? Imposing mandatory prospective rules of statutory interpretation. *Constitutional Commentary* 20:97–109.

Alexander, Larry, and Prakash, Saikrishna. 2004. Is that English you're speaking? Why intention free interpretation is an impossibility. *San Diego Law Review* 41:967–94.

Azar, Moshe. 2007. Transforming ambiguity into vagueness in legal interpretation. In *Interpretation, law and the construction of meaning,* eds. A. Wagner, W. Werner, and D. Cao, 121–137. New York: Springer.

Bach, Kent. 2002. Semantic pragmatic. In *Meaning and truth,* eds. J. Campbell, M. O'Rourke, and D. Shier, 284–292. New York: Seven Bridges.

Botne, Robert. 2001. To die across languages: towards a typology of achievement verbs. *Linguistic Typology* 7:233–278.

Campos, F. Paul. 1996. A text is just a text. *Harvard Journal of Law & Public Policy* 19:327–333.

Cappelen, Herman. 2007. Semantics and pragmatics: some central issues. In *Context-sensitivity and semantic minimalism,* eds. Preyer Gerhard and Peter Georg. 3–22. Oxford: Clarendon.

Carroll, Lewis. 1971. *Alice's adventures in wonder-land and through the looking-glass and what alice found there,* ed. Green, R. Oxford: Oxford University Press.

Carroll, Noël. 1992. Art, intention and conversation. In *Intention and interpretation,* ed. G. iseminger, 117–118. Philadelphia: Temple University Press.

Carroll, Noël. 2011. Art interpretation: The 2010 richard wollheim memorial lecture. *British Journal of Aesthetics* 51:117–135.
Cruse, D. Alan. 1983. *Lexical semantics*. Cambridge: Cambridge University Press.
Fish, Stanley. 1989. *Doing what comes naturally: change, rhetoric, and the practice of theory in literary and legal studies*. Durham: Duke University Press.
Fish, Stanley. 1999. *Response: Interpretation is not a theoretical issue*. Yale Journal of Law and the Humanities, 11:509–515.
Fish, Stanley. 2005. There is no textualist position. *San Diego Law Review* 42:629–650.
Flanagan, Brian. 2010. Revisiting the contribution of literal meaning to legal Meaning. *Oxford Journal of Legal Studies* 30:255–271.
Gauker, Christopher. 2008. Zero tolerance for pragmatics. *Synthese* 165:359–371.
Goldsworthy, Jeffrey. 2005. Moderate versus strong intentionalism: knapp and michaels revisited. *San Diego Law Review* 42:669–682.
Gorvett, Jonathan. 2005. Back through the looking glass: On the relationship between intentions and indexicals. *Philosophical Studies* 124 (3): 295–312.
Greenawalt, Kent. 2000. Are mental states relevant for statutory and constitutional interpretation? *Cornell Law Review* 85:1609–1672.
Greenberg, Mark. 2011a. Legislation as communication? Legal interpretation and the study of linguistic communication. In *Philosophical foundations of language in the law,* eds. A. Marmor and S. Soames, 217–264. Oxford: Oxford University Press.
Greenberg, Mark. 2011b. The communication theory of legal interpretation and objective notions of communicative intent. Unpublished. http://papers.ssrn.com/sol3/papers.cfm?abstract_id=1726524. Accessed 20 Aug 2014.
Harris, Roy. 2001. *Rethinking writing*. New York: Continuum International Publishing Group.
Hogan, Patrick. 1996. *On interpretation: Meaning and inference in law, psychoanalysis, and literature*. Athens: University of Georgia Press.
Iseminger, Gary. 1996. Actual intentionalism vs. hypothetical intentionalism. *The Journal of Aesthetics and Art Criticism* 54 (4): 319–326.
Ivanic, Roz. 1994. Characterizations of context for describing spoken and written discourse. In *Writing vs. speaking: language, text, discourse communication: Proceedings of the conference held at the czech language institute of the academy of sciences of the czech REPUBLIC, prague, october, 14–16, 1992*, ed. Čmejrková, Světla, Daneš, František and Havlová, Eva, 180–186. Narr Francke Attempto Verlag GmbH & Co. KG.
Jackson, Bernard. 1995. *Making sense in law: Linguistic, psychological and semiotic Perspectives*. Liverpool: Deborah Charles.
Kiefer, Alex. 2005. The Intentional Model of Interpretation. *The Journal of Aesthetics and Art Criticism* 63 (3): 271–281.
Knapp, Steven, and Michaels Benn Walter. 1982. Against theory. *Critical Inquiry* 8 (4): 723–742.
Knapp, Steven, and Michaels Benn Walter. 1987. Against theory 2: Hermeneutics and Deconstruction. *Critical Inquiry* 14:49–68.
Knapp, Steven, and Michaels Benn Walter. 2005. Not a matter of interpretation. *San Diego Law Review* 42:651–668.
Levin, Beth, and Rappaport Malka Hovav. 1995. *Unaccusativity*. Cambridge: MIT Press.
Levinson, Jerrold. 2002. Hypothetical intentionalism: statement, objections, and replies. In *Is there a single right interpretation?* ed. M. Krausz. 309–318. University Park: The Pennsylvania State University Press.
Levinson, Stephen. 1983. *Pragmatics*. Cambridge: Cambridge University Press.
Levinson, Jerrold. 2010. Defending hypothetical intentionalism. *British Journal of Aesthetics* 50 (2): 139–150.
Manning, John. 2003. The absurdity doctrine. *Harvard Law Review* 116:2387–2486.
Marmor, Andrei. 2012. *Textualism in context*. Unpublished manuscript. http://papers.ssrn.com/sol3/papers.cfm?abstract_id=2112384. Accessed 20 Aug 2014.
Mattila, Heikki. 2002. *Comparative Legal Linguistics* (Trans. Goddard, C). Burlington: Asgate.

McCubbins, Mathew, and Rodriguez, Daniel. 2011. Deriving interpretive principles from a theory of communication and lawmaking. *Brooklyn Law Review* 76:979–995.

Mellinkoff, David. 1963. *Language of the law*. Boston, Massachusetts: Little Brown & Co Law & Business.

Moravcsik, Edith. 2006. *An introduction to syntactic theory*. New York: Continuum International Publishing Group.

Murphy, Lynne, and Anu Koskela. 2010. *Key terms in semantics*. New York: Continuum International Publishing Group.

Nelson, Celeb. 2005. What is textualism? *Virginia Law Review* 91:347–418.

Plato. 360 B.C.E. *Phaedrus* (Jowett, B., Trans.). http://classics.mit.edu/Plato/phaedrus.html. Accessed 20 Aug 2014.

Poggi, Francesca. 2011. Law and conversational implicatures. *International Journal for the Semiotics of Law* 24:21–40.

Hovav Rappaport Malka, and Beth Levin. 2010. Reflections on manner/result complementarity. In *Syntax, lexical semantics, and event structure,* eds. Edit Doron, Hovav Malka Rappaport, and Sichel, Ivy, 21–38. Oxford: Oxford University Press.

Robertson, Michael. 2009. The impossibility of textualism and the pervasiveness of rewriting in law. *Canadian Journal of Law and Jurisprudence* 22 (2): 381–406.

Saussure de, Ferdinand. 2011. *Course in general linguistics,* P. Meisel & H. Saussy (Eds.), trld. W. Baskin. New York: Columbia University Press.

Scalia, Antonin. 1997. *A matter of interpretation: Federal courts and the law*. Princeton: Princeton University Press.

Sinnott-Armstrong, Walter. 2005. Word meaning in legal interpretation. *San Diego Law Review* 42:465–492.

Solan, Lawrence. 2005. Private language, public laws: The central role of legislative intent in statutory interpretation. *Georgetown Law Journal* 93:427–486.

Sorensen, Roy. 1989. The ambiguity of vagueness and precision. *Pacific Philosophical Quarterly* 70:174–183.

Stecker, Robert. 2006. Moderate actual intentionalism defended. *The Journal of Aesthetics and Art Criticism* 64 (4): 429–438.

Tabossi, Patrizia, and Zardon, Francesco. 1993. Processing ambiguous words in context. *Journal of Memory and Language* 32:359–379.

Tolhurst, William. 1979. On what a text is and how it means. *British Journal of Aesthetics* 19:3–14.

Trivedi, Saam. 2001. an An epistemic dilemma for actual intentionalism. *British Journal of Aesthetics* 41 (2): 192–206.

Van Berkum, Jos J. A. 2008. Understanding sentences in context: What brain waves can tell us. *Current directions in psychological science* 17:376–380.

Van Berkum, Jos J. A., Danielle, van den Brink, Cathelijne M. J. Y Tesink, Miriam Kos, and Peter Hagoort, 2008. The neural integration of speaker and message. *Journal of Cognitive Neuroscience* 20 (4): 580–591.

Van Schooten, Hanneke. 2007. Law as fact, law as fiction: A tripartite model of legal communication. In *Interpretation, law and the construction of meaning,* eds. Wagner Anne, Werner Wouter, and Cao Deborah, 3–20. New York: Springer.

von Savigny, Eike. 1985. An emergence view of linguistic meaning. *American Philosophical Quarterly* 22 (3): 211–220.

Wasow, Tom, Amy Perfors, and David Beaver. 2005. The puzzle of ambiguity. In *Morphology and the web of grammar: essays in memory of Steven G. Lapointe,* ed. Orgun C. Orhan and Sells Peter, 1–17. Stanford: CSLI.

Wilson, George. 1992. Again, theory: on speaker's meaning, linguistic meaning, and the meaning of a text. *Critical Inquiry* 19 (1): 164–185.

Wimsatt, K. William Jr., and C. Monroe Beardsley. 1946. The intentional fallacy. *The Sewanee Review* 54 (3):468–488.

Wittgenstein, Ludwig. 1953. *Philosophical investigations*. New York: Macmillan.

Chapter 23
Blindly Following the Rules: Revisiting the Claritas Doctrine

Hanna Filipczyk

Abstract Drawing on Wittgenstein's position on automatic ("blind") rule-following and certainty, this paper re-examines the claritas doctrine as a tool used in the interpretation of legal provisions. The paper focuses on the maxim clara non sunt interpretanda expounded by the Polish philosopher of law, Jerzy Wróblewski, and also comments on the acte clair and acte éclairé doctrines of the Court of Justice of the European Union (ECJ).

The aim of this paper is to investigate whether the claritas doctrine can be put forward in a legal dispute as a valid argument. The mere existence of a legal dispute appears to exclude the claim of interpretative clarity. One party in a dispute cannot invoke the claritas doctrine in order to counter or refute the claims of another party; allowing this would allegedly be contrary to the ethics of legal discourse. On the other hand, however, a party acting in bad faith may bring into play artificial doubts as to the normative content of an otherwise clear legal provision and challenge the opponent (or the authority deciding the case) to prove them wrong. In this case, should "legitimate" and "illegitimate" doubts be discerned—and who would be in a proper position to do it?

Drawing on the philosophy of Wittgenstein, one way out of this dilemma is to shape a new incarnation of the argument from clarity. The argument should refer not to what people should think of the meaning of words (that is, in the context of this paper, how they should construe a legal provision), but rather to how people act when following such a provision. This paper's argument is that the routine practice of rule-following serves to substantiate the claim of clarity in a legal case. Such an understanding allows for the restoration of the claritas argument, though in a new form.

Keywords Certainty · Pragmatic clarity · Claritas doctrine · Legal discourse · Rule-following

H. Filipczyk (✉)
Enodo Advisors Sp. z o.o., Warsaw, Poland
e-mail: hanna.filipczyk@enodo.pl

M. Araszkiewicz et al. (eds.), *Problems of Normativity, Rules and Rule-Following*,
Law and Philosophy Library 111, DOI 10.1007/978-3-319-09375-8_23

23.1 Introduction

The influential *claritas* doctrine essentially entails that what is clear in legal cases is not or should not be subject to interpretation (*in claris non fit interpretatio*). I endeavour to show that Wittgenstein's remarks on rule-following can inform the debate on how this doctrine should be understood and applied in legal discourse. This paper intends neither to fully articulate Wittgenstein's position nor to give it thorough analysis. Rather, it intends to show that Wittgenstein's remarks can be fruitfully employed to resolve a problem in legal practice.

23.2 The Claritas Doctrine of Jerzy Wróblewski

The below account of the *claritas* doctrine is based on a late paper titled *Pragmatyczna jasność prawa* (*Pragmatic clarity of law*) by the prominent Polish philosopher of law, Jerzy Wróblewski (Wróblewski 1988). In this paper, Wróblewski presents an embodiment of the doctrine that is deeply rooted in many legal traditions (MacCormick and Summers 1991). This particular account was chosen as a main point of reference for the current discussion not only due to its lucidity, but also because of the major impact it has on the practice of applying law in Poland.

Wróblewski's account (as is suggested by his paper's title) follows that the clarity of a legal provision should be understood in pragmatic terms. This means that the clarity of a given expression, including one used in a legal provision, should be judged both in terms of a given "communication act" (legal text) and in the context of a given "situation of communication" (p. 9). The latter is affected by a multitude of factors, including, among others, the linguistic competence of the users of a text, their epistemic attitudes and knowledge, the factual circumstances within which a text is used, and in the case of the law, the systematic and functional background of the legal system in which a text belongs.

Wróblewski distinguishes between the "direct understanding" of a (legal) expression and its "interpretation"[1] (p. 5). In the everyday use of "natural" (common) language, the meaning of an expression may be thoroughly clear ("transparent") between interlocutors (i.e., not giving rise to any doubt). In such cases, expressions are not subjected to interpretation, but treated as given. This observation, first formulated with regard to natural language, is then applied by Wróblewski to legal language, which he considers to be the register of the former with the same characteristics.

Wróblewski proposes four different maxims that together pertain to the *claritas* doctrine:

[1] To be exact, Wróblewski gives as many as four different meanings of the term "interpretation". It is the strict (in his own words, "pragmatic") meaning of the term that he finds the most operative in the presentation of the *claritas* doctrine.

I. Thesis D1: *clara non sunt interpretanda* in the descriptive version of the doctrine claims that a clear legal text is not subjected to interpretation (i.e., it is "understood directly").
II. Thesis N1a: *clara non sunt interpretanda* in the normative version calls for a ban on interpreting a clear legal text (i.e., you must not interpret what is clear).
III. Thesis D2: *interpretatio cessat in claris* in the descriptive version claims that once a legal text is rendered clear, it is not further interpreted.
IV. Thesis N2a: *interpretatio cessat in claris* in the normative version calls for a ban on further interpreting an already clarified legal text (i.e., you must not interpret further what has already been rendered clear).

Departing from Wróblewski's account of the doctrine, it is important to point out that the normative interpretation of the doctrine may take different shape, i.e., its versions weaker than N1a and N2a are available. Such versions may involve not the prohibition of interpretation, but the permission not to interpret a legal provision. Consequently, one may read "you are allowed not to interpret what is clear" (thesis N1b) and "you are allowed not to interpret further what has already been rendered clear" (thesis N2b).

The *acte clair* and *acte éclairé* doctrines of the ECJ bear a certain degree of similarity to the N1b and N2b theses of the *claritas* doctrine. These permit the national court of the last instance, which is otherwise obliged to do so, not to refer to the ECJ for a preliminary ruling either when "the correct application of community law[2] is so obvious as to leave no scope for any reasonable doubt" (*acte clair*)[3], "when the question raised is materially identical with a question which has already been the subject of a preliminary ruling in a similar case," or when the answer to the question can be derived from the ECJ's 'settled case-law' (*acte éclairé*)[4]. The *acte clair* and *acte éclairé* doctrines contain similarities to the N1b and N2b theses in that they permit the court to refrain from acting, in this case, from making use of the preliminary ruling procedure.

23.3 The Descriptive Face of the Claritas Doctrine, and Wittgenstein's 'Blind Rule-following'

Thesis D1 of the *claritas* doctrine speaks to the fact that in the everyday practice of understanding and "using" the law (be it abiding by it by all its addresses or applying it by administration and courts), the majority of legal rules are immediately comprehensible and automatically followed. That is, they do not give rise to any

[2] Presently—of course—the EU law.

[3] The milestone judgment of the ECJ, foundational for the doctrine, was rendered on 6 October 1982 in 283/81 *CILFIT vs Ministry of Health* case, [1982] ECR 3430.

[4] The initial source of the doctrine is the ECJ judgment of 27 March 1963 in Joined Cases 28 to 30/62 *Da Costa en Schaake* [1963] ECR 38 (*acte éclairé sensu stricto*). It was significantly widened and developed by further case-law.

doubt as to their proper understanding. Their meanings are transparent to their users and devoid of discursive potential, seemingly agreed upon in a silent and inconspicuous consensus[5]. Accordingly, this phenomenon, although predominant in legal practice, often escapes attention—which is naturally focused on cases of interpretative doubt (such cases attract attention as easily observed). Once acknowledged, however, this phenomenon strikes us as easily evident or even commonplace.

In this respect, Wróblewski's account broadly corresponds with Wittgenstein's. Wittgenstein famously stated, "[w]hen I obey a rule, I do not choose. I obey the rule *blindly*" (§ 219, PI[6]). "One follows a rule *blindly* not with the blindness of the sightless but with the blindness of complete certainty, i.e., without further reflection" (Baker and Hacker 2009, p. 31). Such practice of rule-following is characterized by full confidence in the correctness of one's behaviour, and the unreflective and automatic practice of following legal rules is a prominent example of such confidence (Marmor 1992; Brożek and Zyzik 2010)[7]. Thanks to the uncontroversial meanings the entire edifice of law subsists, it does not fall apart due to inexorable universal doubt. Doubt is parasitic on certainty: "If you tried to doubt everything you would not get as far as doubting anything. The game of doubting itself presupposes certainty" (OC 115). Importantly, social practice built upon a legal text is formative for a rule—and not the text as such. To play on the word, one could say that a legal text is but a *pre-text* for a rule[8]. This notion is akin to the pragmatic aspect of Wróblewski's account[9].

23.4 The Normative Face of the Claritas Doctrine—a Problem in Need of a Solution

Within the normative claims of the *claritas* doctrine an issue arises. This issue is of much practical relevance, as the doctrine influences the practice of legal interpretation and the application of the law (as it is often claimed, having an adverse impact on it) in its normative, not descriptive, aspect. By definition, the doctrine's descriptive face, while theoretically interesting, does not dictate such practice, but merely reflects it.

[5] It is inconspicuous to the participants in the language-game; it is perspicuous "from outside" the practice.

[6] "PI" throughout this chapter means Wittgenstein's "Philosophical Investigations" (Wittgenstein 1986), "OC"—"On Certainty", and numbers given refer respectively, to paragraphs or notes of the works cited.

[7] Contrary (Wittgenstein 1969) view was expressed in Hershovitz (2002).

[8] Even if we question the Kripkean position that social practice is *all* that accounts for the normativity of rules, it plays a role in it.

[9] A word of caution: let us not be misled by the formulation of the D1 thesis, making reference to "legal text". Wróblewski does not embrace textual approach to the interpretation of law.

Let us call "decision-makers" all those (be it courts or administrative authorities) who are under the law both entitled and obliged to resolve disputes pertaining to the content of the law in adversarial legal proceedings. The problem with the power of decision-makers to authoritatively assert that a legal provision is clear and in no need of interpretation is as follows. The mere existence of a dispute focusing on the proper reading of a legal provision seems to exclude any claim of interpretative clarity. If one party in a legal proceeding raises doubt as to the meaning of a legal text, it would be unfortunate (i.e., allegedly unjust or contrary to the ethics of the legal discourse) for another party or for a decision-maker to invoke the *claritas* doctrine—to claim that a provision is clear and therefore does not need to be interpreted—in order to counter or refute such a claim for interpretation[10]. Consequently, the doctrine cannot justify a refusal to interpret a disputed legal provision. Thus, it seemingly has no role to play in legal discourse. This is how the *claritas* doctrine fails in its normative version(s) (N1a and N1b), or so it seems.

If so, however, a party acting in bad faith in a dispute may abuse his rights by bringing into play fake, artificial, groundless doubts as to the normative content of a clear legal provision and oblige his opponent or a decision-maker (depending on the structure and legal nature of the proceedings) to prove them wrong. Multiplying such interpretative claims, such a party may engage an opponent or a decision-maker in the endless process of legal interpretation. This should not be accepted as well. In this case, should the difference between a legitimate and illegitimate doubt be discerned? If so, what would be the criterion of distinction between them? How might easy cases, suitable for a quick resolution on the basis of a clarity claim, and hard cases, deserving fully-fledged legal discourse, be discerned?[11]

The problem with clarity of a legal provision may be seen as boiling down to the authoritative judgment of whether a legal provision is one capable of direct understanding. In many (in fact, most) cases, the judgment of all users of a legal text (including disputing parties and decision-makers) is unanimous, and as a consequence, no such issue arises. This is the situation that the D1 thesis depicts. However, if the correct reading of a legal provision is central to a dispute and parties disagree as to whether a provision is clear or not, whose judgment should prevail, and what should be the basis for it? The discussion concerning clarity runs the risk of being futile and inconclusive if it consists in one party declaring a legal provision clear and the other rejecting this claim. In such circumstances, if a conclusion that a legal provision is clear is reached, it is imposed by a decision-maker—and he may impose it in an unwarranted way.

---

[10] Or rather: it *is* unfortunate, for it is exactly what typically happens a lot in the proceedings. Robert Alexy places the following among the "Rationality Rules" (within the "Rules and Forms of General Practical Discourse"): "Every speaker must give reasons for what he or she asserts when asked to do so, unless he or she can cite reasons which justify a refusal to provide a justification" (Alexy 1989, pp. 192–193). I contend that the mere declaring the clarity of the provision whose meaning has been called into doubt is insufficient as a reason.

[11] Nb. the distinction between easy and hard cases may be drawn according to many criteria—this is only one of them.

The germ of this problem is already included in Wróblewski's list of aforementioned factors for determining the clarity of a provision (or its lack of clarity). These factors are potentially divergent in the guidance they provide as to whether a disputed provision is clear. If such divergence occurs, which indication should prevail? What is more, Wróblewski's account does not expressly explain how and by whom (if at all) the existence of these factors should be established. One can assume that this person must be a decision-maker. It seems that the faculty which a decision-maker uses for this purpose is his linguistic intuition. Intuition, however, is liable to err. This is particularly true for intuition of a decision-maker, since as an educated lawyer he is professionally biased and he may not have easy access to the way in which a legal provision is understood by all addressees of law.

Consequently, theses N1a and N1b practically authorize decision-makers to decide on a dispute arbitrarily, in a way dictated by their own subjective judgment. Such entitlement makes the *claritas* argument particularly prone to abuse and mistakes made by decision-makers, which is a reality all too often, and one that should not be accepted.

23.5 Wittgenstein—Practice as Criterion of Clarity

Confronted with the difficulty in ascertaining clarity of a legal provision in a dispute, we can resort to the philosophy of Wittgenstein to shape a new incarnation of the argument from clarity. The argument refers not to what people should think (in this context, how they should construe a legal provision), nor necessarily what they actually think (in this context, how they argue the content of a provision), but rather how they act (that is, how they manifest their understanding in practice).

"How one understands a rule is exhibited *not only* in how one interprets it, but also in what one *does*, in the *behaviour*, that is called 'following the rule' and 'going against it'" (Baker and Hacker 2009, p. 29, cf. also pp. 125–126). According to Wittgenstein, social practice furnishes the lacking criterion of clarity. That is, the regular, uniform, and unproblematic practice of using a legal text (e.g., following its directives, much like following a signpost) is normative. The practice shows what a legal text means and determines how it should be understood.

Whoever claims a legal text to be clear should be ready and able to present justification for the claim. However, what kind of justification can be given in support of such clarity claims, are we in need of a complex legal analysis? Not at all. "Giving grounds, …justifying the evidence, comes to an end … It is our *acting*, which lies at the bottom of the language game" (OC 204). "If I have exhausted the justifications I have reached bedrock, and my spade is turned. Then I am inclined to say: 'This is simply what I do.'" (§ 217, PI). A party or a decision maker who assert the clarity of a provision should be ready to show evidential support for their claims: demonstrate that "this is simply what people do" when they follow a disputed legal provision. One who makes a clarity claim should point to rule-governed regularities in a legal practice in order to substantiate this claim. He should demonstrate that established patterns of behaviour with a given legal text are in conformity with a rule as it stands in his understanding. This in turn may require research into sources such as newspapers, specialized magazines, and internet publications which illustrate the routine practice of rule-following.

"Interpreting" in the standard meaning of the term means resorting to intricate legal reasoning. However, the need to have recourse to practice should not be understood as resulting from the communicative shortcomings of legal texts, nor a shameful avowal of the helplessness of incompetent interpreters. According to Wittgenstein, it is inevitable that every social practice (language game) finally appears to be the only reason for itself and cannot be supported by any justification or explication external to it. "If that [i.e., how do I know how to continue the pattern?] means 'Have I reasons?' the answer is: my reasons will soon give out. And then I shall act, without reasons" (§ 211, PI)[12]. A language game "is not based on grounds. It is not reasonable (or unreasonable). It is there—like our life" (OC 559). A language game called "applying law" is no exception.

There are two advantages offered by referring to social practice in order to support the claim of clarity. First, showing social practice objectifies claims of clarity, making it insufficient to abruptly and arbitrarily state that a disputed provision is clear. If a declaration of doubt is upheld, relevant practice of understanding a provision needs to be shown[13]. Second, it reconciles the need to respond to doubt raised by a party in a dispute with the fact that such doubt may pertain to what reasonably should not have caused it. Neither of these two claims is rejected: doubts are addressed, but by demonstrating that they are misplaced.

Of course, one might inquire here as to whether illustrating the practice of a law is a form of interpreting a law. According to Wittgenstein, interpretation is restricted to the "substitution of one expression of the rule for another" (§ 201, PI). Evidencing the practice is certainly a valid argument in legal discourse, a *ratio* put forward for the resolution of legal disputes. Whether we classify showing the practice as an interpretation of law or not is a secondary, verbal issue. After all, interpretation is not the sole activity of decision-makers when they aim at resolving a dispute.

23.6 Implications

The above argument, linking clarity claims with social practice, addresses theses N1a and N1b of the *claritas* doctrine. It is not applicable to theses N2a and N2b. One should consider theses N2a and N2b as concerning only the brute pragmatic

[12] Interpreting the rule is *part* of the practice establishing its meaning (competent language user should be able to explain the meaning of the term by which he interprets it—it is one of the ways to demonstrate proper understanding). It is however impotent as a *method* of establishing the meaning: it "does not *mediate* between a rule and what accords to it" (Baker and Hacker 2009) or "bridge the gap between rule and action" (Marmor 1992, p. 149).

[13] Cf. the difference between "groundless, logical, nonepistemic certainty" and subjective certainty, resting on individual intuition, not rooted in the social practice in Moyal-Sharrock (2005, p. 78; also OC 194).

necessity of constraining every human activity in terms of time and effort invested in it. These theses are claims of procedural economy. This is not to say that, whenever brought up to put an end to a dispute, theses N2a and N2b do not suffer from the risk of arbitrariness. Yet the argument proposed above does not seek to address this risk. This means also that the theses jointly referred to as the *claritas* doctrine do not have the same denominator—they cannot be explicated together.

In addition, the similarity between the *acte clair* doctrine and thesis N1b is superficial[14]. According to the ECJ, the absence of "reasonable doubt" as a reason to waive the national court's duty to call for a preliminary ruling must be assessed on the basis of "characteristic features" of EU law (including multilingualism, which requires analysing 24 "equally authentic" language versions, the duty to account for systematic context, and objectives sought by EU law[15]). Given far-reaching research demanded by the *acte clair* doctrine, consisting of advanced legal analysis, it is evident it assumes a concept of clarity that differs from the one discussed above. The concept of clarity that it assumes is certainly not mutually exclusive with the interpretation[16].

A possible objection to the proposed argument might be that in many cases no practice can be invoked to support a claim of clarity. Such is the case for newly enacted laws that have little practice built upon them. However, Wittgenstein's philosophy speaks to the fact that practice always has a certain amount of relevance when it comes to resolving disputes concerning the allegedly clear meaning of a legal provision. Otherwise, on what basis can a provision be claimed to be clear?

Granted, parties in a legal dispute sometimes raise purely artificial doubts as well as challenge the obviousness of what admits no reasonable doubt, what Wittgenstein calls the incontestable "scaffolding" of our thoughts (OC 211) or the immovable "hinges" on which our legitimate doubt rotates (OC 341, 655)[17]. How should be explain such a challenge and deal with it in the legal context? In Wittgenstein's *On Certainty*, he speaks of aberrant, inadmissible doubts that are targeted by a sceptic at what "stands fast" (OC 153). According to D. Moyal-Scharrock, doubts that attack what is certain are considered as queer (OC 553), incomprehensible (OC 347), a joke (OC 463), or even signs of a speaker being demented (OC 467; Moyal-Sharrock 2005, p. 90). To this list we could add another item: doubts put forward in bad faith, for such doubts also represent a flagrant deviation from the regular, rule-governed practice. What is important, however, is that there is an

[14] And it does not hold at all for the *acte éclairé* doctrine, which resembles rather the N2b thesis.

[15] CILFIT, para. 16–20.

[16] In the literature it is often claimed that this concept is detached from reality and the criteria proposed by the ECJ in order to establish such certainty—utterly impracticable. Cf. also the opinion of advocate-general Srix-Hackl delivered on 12 April 2005 in the case C-495/03 Intermodal Transports BV, para. 87: "the application of any provision, even one which seems 'unambiguous' or 'clear,' in principle requires prior interpretation," true if assessed against the CILFIT criteria of clarity.

[17] Even if in the sphere of law doubts which "a reasonable man does *not have*" (OC 220) seem rather scarce—do we get here many assertions enjoying the certainty of "I know that here is my hand"? This is not to claim, however, that there are none at all.

adequate answer available even to the doubts of a vicious doubter. The more rock-solid and unquestionable the understanding of a provision is (or an expression it contains), the more it will be embedded in the practice of "law-following", and the more a practical testimony for it (including all the dealings and acts that presuppose a challenged understanding) will be easier to submit within the discourse (by an opponent or a decision-maker, depending on the nature of the legal procedure)[18]. After all, "foundation-walls are carried by the whole house" (OC 248), in the context of law: by the edifice of legal practice. The meaning of an entirely obvious legal provision is manifested in countless acts of addressees of law, therefore it should rather be easy for a party or a decision-maker to point to few of them in order to support a clarity claim.

Whether a doubter will accept such practical evidence as convincing is yet another matter. According to Wittgenstein, one who doubts may refuse to accept explanations in the same vein as he originally doubted in what was certain. He may act with devious consistency, driven by what we might call an incurable "legal scepticism". Still, by referring to social practice, we gave a doubter the argument other than an "empty", declarative claim of clarity—and we can argue that as a result, the burden of proof is shifted to him. If he wishes to uphold his claim for interpretation, he must either prove us wrong by showing that social practice of following a disputed legal provision is different than we argue (or that it is not uniform), or demonstrate that the reading of a provision established in social practice is unacceptable (e.g., it conflicts with fairness).

The requirement to present the evidence of social practice, though possibly not excluding any further doubt, whether genuine or strategic in a litigation, provides a constraint on claims of clarity. In a number of cases, the attempt to base claims of clarity on social practice rather than on the fallible intuition of a decision-maker would prove unsuccessful, as no such practice could be shown or evidenced. And the possible failure to supply proper evidence would make clarity claims groundless.

We should also bear in mind that clarity of a legal provision is subject to change. As Wittgenstein writes, "[a] language-game does change with time" (OC 256). What is clear (or certain) may cease to be given circumstances that reveal new discursive potential of a provision. On the other hand, past doubts may vanish, or rather be eliminated thanks in particular to the intervention of courts and other decision-makers. This can lead to a legal provision being cleared of doubt and its understanding becoming "hardened" or "fossilized" (OC 657) in the perception and use of this provision by the community of law's addressees. As Wittgenstein states, even "the shift of the river-bed", or in other words, the dramatic revision of the most well-founded and undeniable meanings is possible. However it happens rarely, and normally, "the movement of the waters" is not the same as "the shift of the bed

[18] It is less engaging than it seems—it suffices (or even is only appropriate) to show the practice concerning the entire provision or even larger normative whole, crucial for the disputed case, without studying one-by-one the individual expressions it contains, isolated from the context.

itself' (OC 97). That is, what is certain and clear is inertial and provides firm ground for the dispute of what is shaky, not yet fixed, and controversial.

Doubting what (seems to be) clear may also prove in the favour of a community. This is what happens when the meaning of a legal provision previously agreed upon and undisputed makes law unfair and therefore deserves to be subverted. As a consequence, a trouble-making doubter may in reality be a Socrates-like gadfly: he may provoke uneasiness by undermining the fixed understanding of a legal provision, but thanks to that he may finally bring more fairness into the law. This is how challenging clarity, which is part and parcel of the language-game played by lawyers, can be beneficial for the community as a whole.

Conclusion

The *claritas* doctrine can be dissected into theses which do not have the same theoretical status and deserve separate discussion. The fact that the law is not predominantly interpreted but acted upon unreflectively is quite obvious. Nevertheless, as a normative claim (thesis) the doctrine is problematic. It may be (and often is) brought into play in legal discourse to the detriment of a party when clarity is declared in an unwarranted and arbitrary manner.

The main contention of this chapter is that this deficiency can be addressed and alleviated through the recourse to the routine practice of rule-following. The claim of clarity is well-founded and justified in a legal discourse only if a person asserting it is able to support a claim (if asked to do so) in regular and uniform practice. Admittedly, even the argument in its new form does not come without its weaknesses. That is to say, it is not abuse-proof. It may trigger costs of time and effort. Still, it gives hope to the possibility of reducing arbitrariness in the settlement of legal disputes.

Other aspects typically found in the doctrine that refer to the obligation or permission to stop the interpretation of a legal provision that has been sufficiently clarified as well as the doctrines of the ECJ differ substantially from the above in respect to their understandings of clarity, which is regarded as not mutually exclusive with legal analysis. However, investigation into these aspects exceeds the interests of this paper.

Acknowledgements The Author thanks Professor Zygmunt Tobor for suggesting the linkage between Wittgenstein and Wróblewski. The usual disclaimer applies.

References

Alexy, Robert. 1989. *A theory of legal argumentation*. Oxford: Clarendon.

Baker, Gordon P., and Peter M.S. Hacker. 2009. *Wittgenstein. Rules, grammar and necessity*. Oxford: Wiley-Blackwell.

Brożek, Bartosz, and Zyzik, Rarosław. 2010. Reguły prawne z perspektywy dociekań filozoficznych. *Ruch Prawniczy, Ekonomiczny i Socjologiczny* 2:113–132.
Hershovitz, Scott. 2002. Wittgenstein on rules: The phantom menace. *Oxford Journal of Legal Studies* 4:619–640.
MacCormick, Neil, and Robert S. Summers, eds. 1991. *Interpreting statutes: A comparative study*. Dartmouth: Dartmouth.
Marmor, Andrei. 1992. *Interpretation and Legal Theory*. Oxford: Clarendon.
Moyal-Sharrock, Danièle. 2005. Unravelling Certainty. In *Readings of Wittgenstein's On Certainty,* ed. Danièle Moyal-Sharrock and Wiliam H. Brenner, 76–99. New York: Macmillan.
Wittgenstein, Ludwig. 1969. *On certainty*. Oxford: Blackwell.
Wittgenstein, Ludwig. 1986. *Philosophical investigations*. Oxford: Blackwell.
Wróblewski, Jerzy. 1988. Pragmatyczna jasność prawa. *Państwo i Prawo* 4:3–13.

Chapter 24
Why Legal Rules Are Not Speech Acts and What Follows from That?

Marcin Matczak

Abstract The speech-act approach to rules is commonplace in both Anglo-American and continental traditions of legal philosophy. Despite its pervasiveness, I argue in this paper that the approach is misguided and therefore intrinsically flawed. My critique identifies how speech-act theory provides an inadequate theoretical framework for the analysis of written discourse, a case in point being legal text. Two main misconceptions resulting from this misguided approach are the fallacy of synchronicity and the fallacy of a-discursivity. The former consists of treating legal rules as if they were uttered and received in the same context, the latter consists of treating legal rules as relatively short, isolated sentences. Among the consequences of these fallacies are an excessive focus on the lawmakers' semantic intentions and the neglect of the semantic and pragmatic complexity of rules as sets of utterances (discourses). To redress these flaws, I propose analysing legal rules through the prism of complex text-acts. My paper presents the consequences of this revised approach for legal interpretation, supporting Joseph Raz's idea of minimal legislative intent.

Keywords Legislative intent · Legal interpretation · Rules · Speech acts · Writtenness in law

24.1 Aim and Structure of the Paper

The aim of this paper is to show that using speech-act theory to analyse legal rules is based on an incorrect assumption. According to this assumption, legal rules can be analysed in the same way as

(i) single oral utterances,
(ii) utterances addressed by a speaker to a hearer where both are in the same place at the same time.

I will call assumption (i) the fallacy of a-discursivity and assumption (ii) the fallacy of synchronicity. I show below that both these fallacies arise from the nature of speech-act theory, which traditionally focuses on analysing simple oral utterances

M. Matczak (✉)
University of Warsaw, Warsaw, Poland
e-mail: marcinsmatczak@gmail.com

M. Araszkiewicz et al. (eds.), *Problems of Normativity, Rules and Rule-Following*, Law and Philosophy Library 111, DOI 10.1007/978-3-319-09375-8_24

made in a *face-to-face* speech situation.[1] Speech-act theory has never been fully elaborated to analyse complex written discourses, which are used for diachronic communication—communication involving different moments in time and different locations. Nonetheless, a version of speech-act theory which is not adjusted to written communications has gained popularity in legal philosophy. My argument is that, in order to avoid the fallacies of a-discursivity and of synchronicity, speech-act theory has to be revised and legal rules have to be treated not as simple, single speech acts, but as more akin to complex text acts. This approach acknowledges the pragmatic complexity (in linguistic terms) of the lawmaker's intention and thereby prevents excessive focus on its semantic aspect.

In the first part of this paper I briefly discuss the role that speech-act theory plays in the analysis of legal rules. In the second part I demonstrate that speech-act theory is ill-equipped to analyse written communication and I identify areas in which its shortcomings are most apparent. The third section of the paper is dedicated to showing that legal rules can be analysed through the prism of complex text acts[2] (rather than be treated as speech acts) and to identifying the main consequences that this approach has on legal text interpretation, in particular on the understanding of the lawmaker's intention.

24.2 The Significance of Speech-Act Theory for Legal Philosophy

Legal philosophy's interest in speech-act theory began with the co-operation between H.L.A. Hart and J. L. Austin. The most widely-known legal rule in jurisprudence, i.e. *No vehicles in the park* (Hart 1958), is analysed in a manner characteristic of this theory. Although Hart treats this rule as a written—not spoken—one, he treats it as a single statement made by a single author. As I will show in part 3, in reality legal rules are not single statements but are more the effect of several—sometimes many—statements.[3]

[1] This applies to both J. L. Austin and J. Searle, and their commentators: K. Bach, R. Harnish and P. Grice, though the latter touches upon communications directed in writing to an unspecified group (cf. e.g. P. Grice's solution in *Studies in the Way of Words* devoted to signs such as '*Keep off the grass*'). This analysis is of an auxiliary nature and does not affect the nature of their conclusions. Another exception is the work of Hancher (1979) and Edmondson (1981) on co-operative speech acts, and the work of T. van Dijk on complex speech acts and pragmatic macrostructures (van Dijk 1980). None of these, however, take into account the specifics of writing.

[2] It is not the purpose of this paper to determine whether the rules are text acts (or acts in any sense) or if they are the outcomes of such acts.

[3] The criticism presented here refers to so called expressive theories of legal norm, i.e. the theories which equate legal norms with linguistic expressions. The critique does not apply to those theories defined as hyletic i.e. those which distinguish between the normative act and the norm as the outcome of this act (and not necessarily a linguistic one). The work of K. Opałek and J. Woleński, can be taken as an example of the latter. I am grateful to the reviewers of this paper for indicating the need to clarify this matter.

Concurrently with the development of linguistic analyses in legal philosophy, the application of speech-act theory to analyse legal rules has become increasingly popular. This especially concerns the concept of an illocutionary act (e.g. Visconti 2009), and the concept of illocutionary uptake (e.g. Solum 2008). The role played in legal philosophy by speech-act theory has been neatly stated by P. Amselek:

> The theory of speech acts is, in my opinion, a general foundation which provides legal philosophy with an adequate method of approaching the legal utterances with which it is confronted. It also provides a general orientation and framework for analysis and research. (Amselek 1988)

Besides such explicitly expressed belief in its value, most analyses of legal rules in accordance with speech-act theory are carried out using the following implicit assumptions:

(i) Legal rules are uttered or treated as utterances (e.g. Cyrul 2007, p. 45). Even if we agree that the term "*utterance*" may also refer to written communications, calling a rule an "*utterance*" indicates that it is a statement made at a single point in time, being one indivisible whole (as distinct from a collection of utterances (discourse)).
(ii) Legal rules are addressed by a speaker to a hearer (e.g. Cao 2007, p. 73).
(iii) The primary context in which legal rules are subject to linguistic analysis is the mental context of the utterer, the key element of which is his semantic (locutionary) intent (e.g. Solum 2008; Marmor 2013).
(iv) Taking the recipient's context into account when analysing rules is not deemed a linguistic analysis but an attempt to depart from one and to promote values other than fidelity to the legal text, e.g. the flexibility of law or the freedom of the interpreter (e.g. Eskridge and Frickey 1990).

The foregoing assumptions constitute the underlying structure of thinking about legal rules among legal philosophers. Uncritical acceptance of these assumptions leads to a kind of theory-induced blindness, i.e. failure to observe the differences between simple face-to-face communication and communication in which legal rules are used. The vast majority of legal rules are written rules directed at an unspecified group of addressees commonly external to the immediate context in which the legal rules are created. Among them are the legal rules that are most important for legal philosophers, i.e. those set out in statutes, constitutions and contracts.

24.3 Lacunae in Speech-Act Theory

Some authors dealing with speech-act theory show that it is not fully suitable to analyses of written communications, the communicative aim of which falls outside the face-to-face speech situation. W. Ong states that:

> Speech-act theory could be developed not only to attend more to oral communication, but also to attend more reflectively to textual communication precisely as textual. (Ong 2000, p. 166)

Ong's critique is supported by M. Stubbs:

> Much of speech act theory has difficulty in freeing itself from two assumptions (…). One is the assumption that speech act theory should take, as its paradigm cases, the conveying of messages in face-to-face two-party interaction. The other is the assumption that speech act theory can be based on invented, isolated sentences (…) invented sentences are isolated and not connected discourse. (Stubbs 1983, p. 485)

The primary factor in the inadequacy of speech-act theory is the diachronic nature of written communication. This communication is employed to go beyond the face-to-face speech situation in order to communicate with persons who are beyond the reach of the human voice, in a different place and particularly at a different time. This communication covers not one but two contexts—the context of the utterer and that of the recipient.

The second feature of written communication not acknowledged by speech-act theory is its discursiveness, understood as involving a number and/or variety of utterers and a complexity of communications between and among them. This discursiveness allows written communications to be built with simpler elements, each uttered by a different person, while still remaining a single text. It also allows for elements to be added to or removed from the original text; in this sense, discursiveness is not possible in oral communication, as in speech, words cannot be re-analysed at a later date and nothing can be added to or removed from an oral communication that has already been made (if it was not recorded).

Lacunae in speech-act theory are visible if we take a closer look at the structure of the locutionary act performed within the framework of a written communication. A locutionary act covers utterances of certain words with sense and reference and is composed of three sub-acts: a phonetic act, which is the act of uttering certain noises, a phatic act, which is the uttering of words, and a rhetic act, which is the uttering of words with a definite sense and reference (Austin 1962).

In speech these three aspects of a speech act arise at the same time and are therefore synchronous. The case is different with written text. The equivalent of a phonetic act in written communication is the physical creation of a sign, e.g. leaving traces of ink on a page. The equivalent of a phatic act in writing would be leaving a sign that has meaning. At this point doubt arises as to the perspective from which the meaning of the signs should be assessed—from the utterer's perspective or from that of the recipient? Is a phatic act performed effectively if the signs are written, but never reach the recipient? The latter does not seem a reasonable assumption.

The key differences between speech and writing can be seen in the case of a rhetic act. In certain situations, the speaker is clearly referring to his own context, e.g. by using indexicals ("here", "now", and "I"). In many other cases, however, doubt could arise as to the context—that of the utterer or that of the recipient—to which a text refers. This is the case with texts that constitute instructions on how to proceed in a situation that may arise, e.g. instructions on how to proceed in the event of fire. The phrases and the words contained therein definitely do not refer to the context of the author—we do not expect fire-fighting instructions to be written during a fire. Like fire-fighting instructions, legal texts apply to future situations. Hence, a doubt arises as to choice of relevant context which constitutes the framework of reference for the language of such texts.

This doubt may give rise to the theory that a text recipient is necessary for a rhetic act, and therefore a locutionary act, to occur. This theory seems to go too far, particularly in the case of legal texts that have binding effect without having to be received by the addressees, in accordance with the adage ignorantia iuris non excusat. This notwithstanding, the reference of a locutionary act in written communication has to be considered in the context of the recipient to a much greater extent than it does in the case of an oral rhetic act.

The specifics of a locutionary act performed in writing raises the question of whether a written illocutionary act is performed at the moment that the writing of the text is finished or at that when the text is read. The uncertainty increases when consideration is given to a third, frequently omitted possibility, i.e. that an illocutionary act is performed when a text written earlier is used. This option is considered by Bianchi (2014), who analyses illocutionary acts in recorded speech, which she calls "delayed speech." Bianchi notes that in the case of recorded speech doubts arise as to whose intention determines the nature of the act—the intention existing at the time the communiqué is produced (i.e. when the text is written) or the intention at the time the text is used. Bianchi uses the example of the cartoon character Homer Simpson, who in his office writes a note saying "Don't leave" and then goes on to use it several times, putting it in his wife Margie's handbag, leaving it on his butler's desk, and finally giving it to his son Bart. Bianchi separates Homer's intention at the time the note was composed from the intentions each time the note was used. According to Bianchi, the intention that defines the nature of the illocutionary act is not the intention from the moment of writing, but the intention with which the text was subsequently used.

It can be argued that separating the moment a text is written and the moment it is used in order to perform an illocutionary act is in reality separating a locutionary act from an illocutionary act. This separation in turn enables the locutionary intention to be separated from the illocutionary intention (Skinner 1972). The former is the intention of giving words a specific meaning (sense and reference) and the latter—the intention to perform a specific illocutionary act (e.g. giving an order or making a promise). This proves that a written illocutionary act is much more complex than a similar speech act, not least in terms of intentions.

24.4 The Fallacy of Synchronicity and the Fallacy of A-discursivity; Their Impact on Identifying the Lawmaker's Intention

The difference between speech and writing requires a new approach to the analysis of legal rules. A useful theoretical framework has been provided by Horner (1979) and his concept of text-acts, which share the characteristics of complexity, diachronicity and discursivity. I argue specify below what the fallacies committed by legal philosophers involve and what consequences they have for any deliberation on the interpretation of legal rules.

24.4.1 *The Fallacy of Synchronicity*

The fallacy of synchronicity involves a failure to take into account the diachronicity of legal language. This means that a legal rule is treated as if it were a statement uttered by the utterer and received by the recipient at the same moment in time.

Additionally:

a. an illocutionary act—which is what a legal rule is—involves the use of a text written by someone else, usually at a time other than that at which is it used; the person using such text plays the role of reader, not author;
b. to perform an illocutionary act, a locutionary act is required and this in turn requires a rhetic act, which—as I have already shown—requires the participation of the recipient.

Consequently, this gives rise to doubt as to whether it is possible to analyse legal rules without taking into account contexts other than that of the utterer. The text of an act in law, once written and adopted, may subsequently be amended or derogated. This means that despite the process of writing the text having ended, a rhetic act and therefore a locutionary act and an illocutionary act—do not bring about effects for the persons to which the amended or derogated text is to apply. Treating a legal rule in a synchronous manner is therefore mistaken.

24.5 The Fallacy of A-discursivity

The fallacy of a-discursivity involves treating a legal rule as if it were a relatively short, single statement, similar to an oral order and able to be interpreted in isolation from other statements. Treating a legal rule in this way is derived from unquestioning acceptance of the assumptions of speech-act theory, of which the model example of an utterance is an isolated and self-sufficient statement: "No vehicles in the park". However, a legal rule is the outcome of the linkage of several lawmaker statements and therefore the outcome of a discourse.

Legal philosophy generally overlooks the discursiveness of rules, thus there is no broadly recognised theoretical standpoint that would enable the complexity of the matter to be observed. An exception here is the work of M. Zieliński (Zieliński (1972), who states that legal rules are recorded in legal text by using the "breakdown" technique in individual provisions. This means that several provisions may comprise one rule, which Zieliński calls a "legal norm". The reconstruction of a legal rule starts with selecting a so-called base clause. Then "modifying clauses" and "supplementing clauses" are selected from the legal text. An example of the difference between a base clause and supplementing or modifying clauses is the use of legal definitions and clauses containing the defined terms. In this case, the reconstruction of a rule requires the use of both these clauses at the same time. The same applies to clauses on crime (e.g. murder) and clauses providing for lawful excuses (e.g. self defence), and also clauses providing for specified general decisions and clauses providing for exceptions to such decisions. All these examples require a legal rule to be treated as the outcome of several statements being linked and therefore treated as the outcome of a mini-discourse, not as a single stand-alone statement.[4]

24.6 Impact of the Two Fallacies on Identifying the Lawmaker's Intention

Both fallacies bring about an incorrect understanding of the lawmaker's intention, which consists in the latter being equated with the locutionary intention of the person uttering the rule. This is an oversimplification. As already shown in the Homer Simpson example, using a text in order to perform an illocutionary act requires the separation of at least two intentions: that of the text author and that of the person who is using the text. In the Homer Simpson case, the same person is both the author of the text and the one who is then to use it. In the case of the law, the actual author of a legal text (e.g. a ministry official) is not usually a person who may then use the act to perform a valid illocutionary act, as he is not recognised through the appropriate procedure (in the Austinian sense) as the person appropriate to perform the act. Thus in the case of the law, the person or group of persons having the appropriate authorisation to perform an illocutionary act (e.g. issue an order) use a text written by someone else.

The necessity of differentiating pragmatic linguistic roles within the framework of the concept of lawmaker is also emphasised by Maley, who on the production side calls for a distinction between 'draftsman' and 'source' (Maley 1987, pp. 31–32). Goffman, with regard to the entity performing an illocutionary act, distinguishes between the author, who selects and encodes the message, and the principal, who is committed to the propositions and acts expressed. He states that the author and the principal typically coincide in face-to-face conversation, but not in written communication (Goffman 1981). This distinction can also be applied to the lawmaker.

Treating a rule as discursive in nature makes it more difficult to identify the legislative intention. Although it is possible in the case of a typical independent oral statement to analyse the specific semantic intention of the statement utterer, it is not possible where a rule is treated as the outcome of a discourse, as a discourse does not have only one author.

Given that there are at least two types of entity engaged in performing a legal text act, a distinction between the locutionary and the illocutionary intention of the utterer (Skinner 1972) can be applied to the lawmaker. The locutionary intention may be understood to mean the intention given to words of a specified sense and reference. This intention guides the text author who, when writing it, builds up a meaningful discourse. The illocutionary intention is the intention to perform an illocutionary act of a specified force, e.g. an order. This intention is key to

[4] Distinguishing the fallacy of a-discursivity leads to a question as to the ontological status of a legal rule. This is a version of the question about the individuation of laws (Raz 1980, p. 77).

giving an act adopting a law the appropriate normative meaning, which cannot be achieved merely by writing the text. The illocutionary intention is manifest only in people who are appropriately authorised in the procedure to perform a given illocutionary act.

The distinction between locutionary and illocutionary intentions is not acknowledged in the contemporary analyses of legislative intention (Ekins 2012). The closest to it is Raz's idea of the "intention to make law" (Raz 2009a, p. 329) or the minimum intention (Raz 2009b, p. 284), which seems to be illocutionary in its nature. Thus, this paper provides additional support for the Razian concept—support that stems from linguistic analysis of intentions in written communication.

Conclusions

There are three main conclusions of this paper. Firstly, revision of the speech-act theory as applied to legal rules makes it possible to distinguish between locutionary and illocutionary intentions of the lawmaker. Secondly, what gives the rule its normativity is the illocutionary intention, because this intention defines the type of illocutionary act performed. The role of the lawmaker's locutionary (i.e. semantic) intention is then not so crucial for legal rules as may otherwise seem. Thirdly, it is not possible to base the identification of the semantic content of the rule exclusively on the analysis of the lawmaker's context. If the process of identification is to be comprehensive and reliable, there are other contexts to be taken into consideration. Amongst these the recipient's context, on which the completion of the locutionary act that creates the content of the rule partially depends. This last insight may constitute a starting point for a linguistically-based dynamic theory of legal interpretation, the development of which is beyond the scope of the current paper to explore.

References

Amselek, Paul. 1988. Philosophy of law and the theory of speech acts. *Ratio Juris* 1 (3): 187–223.
Austin, John Langshaw. 1962. *How to do things with words*. Oxford: Oxford University Press.
Bianchi, Claudia. 2014. How to do things with (recorded) words. *Philosophical Studies* 167:485–495.
Cao, Deborah. 2007. Legal speech acts as intersubjective communicative actions. In *Interpretation, law and the construction of meaning,* eds. Anne Wagner, Wouter Werner, and Deborah Cao, 65–82. Dordrecht: Springer.
Cyrul, Wojciech. 2007. Lawmaking. Between discourse and legal text. In *Legislation in context. Essays in legisprudence,* ed. Luc J. Witgens, 43–54. Burlington: Ashgate Publishing.
Edmondson, Willis. 1981. *Spoken discourse: A model for analysis*. London: Longman.
Eskridge, Wiliam N. Jr., and Philip J. Frickey. 1990. Statutory interpretation as practical reasoning. *Stanford Law Review* 42:321.
Ekins, Richard. 2012. *The nature of legislative intent*. Oxford: Oxford University Press.
Goffman, Erving. 1981. *Forms of talk*. Oxford: Blackwell.

Hancher, Michael. 1979. The classification of co-operative illocutionary acts. *Language in Society* 8 (l): 1–14.
Hart, Herbert L. A. 1958. Positivism and the separation of law and morals. *Harvard Law Review* 71:593–607.
Horner, Winifred B. 1979. Speech-act and text-act theory: "theme-ing" in freshman composition. *College Composition and Communication* 30 (2): 165–169.
Maley, Yon. 1987. The language of legislation. *Language in Society* 16:25–48.
Marmor, Andrei. 2013. Truth in law. In *Law and language. Current legal issues,* eds. M. Freeman and F. Smith, vol. 15, 46–47. Oxford: Oxford University Press.
Ong, Walter Jackson. 2000. *Orality and literacy: The technologizing of the word.* London: Routledge.
Raz, Joseph. 1980. *The concept of the legal system.* Oxford: Oxford University Press.
Raz, Joseph. 2009a. On the authority and interpretation of constitutions: some preliminaries. In *Between authority and interpretation.* New York: Oxford University Press.
Raz, Joseph. 2009b. *Intention in interpretation. In Between authority and interpretation.* New York: Oxford University Press.
Skinner, Quentin. 1972. Motives, intentions and the interpretation of texts. *New Literary History,* Vol. 3, No. 2, On Interpretation: I (Winter, 1972) 393–408.
Solum, Lawrence. 2008. Semantic originalism. *Illinois Public Law and Legal Theory Research* Papers Series, Nos. 07–24, Nov 22.
Stubbs, Michael. 1983. Can I have that in writing? Some neglected topics in speech act theory. *Journal of Pragmatics* 7:479–494.
van Dijk, Teun A. 1980. *Macrostructures. An interdisciplinary study of global structures in discourse, interaction, and cognition.* Hilsdale: Lawrence Erlbaum Associates.
Visconti, Jacqueline. 2009. Speech acts in legal language: introduction. *Journal of Pragmatics* 41:393–400.
Zieliński, Maciej. 1972. *Interpretacja jako proces dekodowania tekstu prawnego.* Poznań: Wydawnictwo UAM.

Chapter 25
The Validity of Moral Rules and Principles as a Legal Problem

Andrzej Grabowski

Abstract The validity of moral rules and principles becomes legally important in any case involving the application of law in which a judge (or any law-applying authority) is obligated to take into account moral rules, principles or standards. In the paper, this problem is analysed from the legal point of view in reference to such moral rules and principles that cannot be simultaneously classified as legal ones (or as legally valid). First, the concept of an original normative situation is introduced. Next, the three basic questions are clarified: the question of the meaning of validity statements, the question of the recognition (identification) of valid moral rules and principles and the question of the justification of validity. The possible development of a coherent juristic conception of the validity of moral rules and principles is outlined through indicating the possible jurisprudential answers to such questions. Finally, the methodological approach based on the adoption of a morally detached and impartial point of view is recommended for further research.

Keywords Validity · Moral rules and principles · Adjudication

25.1 Introduction

It is commonly believed that moral rules, principles and standards play an important role in the process of law application. Two obvious examples can be pointed out here (Gizbert-Studnicki and Pietrzykowski 2004, pp. 64–70). The first is related to the judicial decision-making process in particular cases in which a judge has to apply legal norms that include moral concepts such as "good faith", "reasonable care", "social justice", "human dignity" etc. The second example refers to the constitutional courts' decisions on the constitutionality of legislative acts (statutes). In such a case, the moral rules, principles or standards can constitute the criteria of legal validity. Generally speaking, the influence of morality in the legal domain is a phenomenon that is under constant investigation by the legal sciences. As Moore convincingly argues, we can distinguish at least seven relations between law and morality that contemporary legal philosophy deals with (Moore 2012, pp. 436–443). What is more,

A. Grabowski (✉)
Jagiellonian University, Krakow, Poland
e-mail: andrzej.grabowski@uj.edu.pl

M. Araszkiewicz et al. (eds.), *Problems of Normativity, Rules and Rule-Following*,
Law and Philosophy Library 111, DOI 10.1007/978-3-319-09375-8_25

many influential legal philosophers claim that morality—moral principles, rules or standards—can (the inclusive legal positivists, e.g., Coleman, Waluchow, Kramer and Moreso) or have to (the non-positivists, e.g., Dworkin, Dreier and Alexy) be incorporated into the law. The so-called Incorporation Thesis is often questioned by the supporters of exclusive legal positivism—for instance, by Raz (1994, 2004, pp. 1, 7–17)—however, it is worth noting that even the representatives of such a hard version of legal positivism provide the reasons against the classic positivistic Separation Thesis (Green 2008) or argue for certain interpretations of the Necessary Connection Thesis (Raz 2009, pp. 167–169, 179–181).

I do not want to enter into a probably pointless discussion here that leads nowhere on whether the positivistic Separation Thesis is true or the non-positivistic Necessary Connection Thesis is more plausible. In my opinion, despite disregarding this fundamental jurisprudential controversy concerning the nature of the relations between law and morality, it is methodologically acceptable that we directly focus on a very important, specific practical problem: the validity of moral rules and principles. This problem is usually treated as a philosophical, psychological or sociological one (Maluschke 2007). In what follows, I will propose a somewhat unorthodox approach by analysing this problem from the legal point of view—more precisely, from the point of view of a law-applying agent, especially a judge.

25.2 Formulating the Problem

Naturally, it can be questioned that the approach adopted herein is "unorthodox" in effect. If we consider the well-known test of institutional support and the co-related concept of the sense of appropriateness (Dworkin 1977, pp. 40–41, 64–68), it can be argued that the legal (or jurisprudential) approach to the problem of the validity of moral rules and principles is not innovative at all. Yet this statement seems to be incorrect. As Putnam (1995, p. 5) rightly reconstructs Dworkin's view on the relation between legal validity and moral validity:

> [W]hile legal validity and moral validity unquestionably differ [...], still, in what Dworkin calls "hard cases" [...] the judge is obligated to decide in such a way that the outcome is the morally best possible, given the constraints imposed by the system. In effect, moral thinking replaces legal thinking, at least in arriving at the decision (and perhaps even in justifying it) in "hard cases".

Thus, the "unorthodoxy" of our analysis consists, in fact, that in what follows, juristic thinking replaces moral thinking: some jurisprudential ideas will be used to explicate the problem of the validity of moral rules and principles.

Before going into detail, a brief description of the normative situation of a law-applying agent is necessary. The problem of the validity of moral rules and principles becomes legally important in any case involving the application of law in which a judge (or any law-applying authority) is obligated to take into account moral rules, principles or standards. At this point, two normative situations have to be contrasted. The first is when a given moral rule, principle or standard has already been incorporated into the law—for instance, when it is frequently used by the judiciary. And the second concerns when such incorporation has not yet taken place. In this context, it has to be stressed that our analysis refers exclusively to the second case, because in the first situation, we should rather speak about the "legal validity" of the moral rules and principles that have already been incorporated into the legal system. In other words, we are only interested in such an "original normative situation" in which a law-applying agent has to take into consideration a certain moral rule or principle for the first time; a rule or principle that cannot be simultaneously classified as a legal one (or as legally valid).

25.3 Basic Questions

It can be assumed that a law-applying authority that is obligated—during the process of legal decision-making—to take into account morality, will direct her/his attention to the set of valid moral rules and principles. Hence, the issue of the validity of moral norms arises as a legally relevant problem. However, it is obvious that the validity of moral rules and norms has to be analysed in a different way than in the case of the validity of legal norms. For instance, the juristic conception of the systemic validity of law, commonly used in legal practice, and based on the concept of a due enactment and some formal criteria of legal validity (Wróblewski 1988, pp. 96–98), is probably completely useless in reference to the extra-legal moral rules and principles. Therefore, the starting point of the analysis has to consist in the careful identification of the most fundamental questions that have to be answered by the law-applying agent who is obligated to take into consideration valid moral rules and principles. However, it should be noted that we will identify these questions *per analogiam* to the questions that are typically articulated concerning the problem of legal validity, thus replacing moral (ethical, philosophical) thinking with juristic (legal) thinking.

25.3.1 The Question of Meaning

The first basic question concerns the appropriate meaning of the concept of validity that is used by lawyers in reference to moral rules and principles. What does it mean that a moral rule or principle is valid? For a jurist, it is primarily a question that is connected to the semantics of juristic language. Simultaneously, it is a practical question, since an answer can directly imply the solution to the question of recognition (*cf.* next subsection) and—indirectly—to the content of the legal decision in a given case.

The juristic conceptions of the legal validity provide us with many concepts that can be used (individually or in combination) to clarify the meaning of the juristic concept of the validity of legal norms (Garzón Valdés 1977; Bulygin 1982, pp. 65–67; Grabowski 2013, pp. 271–354, 413–422, 433–441). There is no doubt that some of these concepts can be used analogously for the elucidation of the juristic concept of the validity of moral rules and principles. In my opinion, when lawyers speak about "validity" in reference to moral norms, two possible meanings come to the fore.

The first explanation of the meaning of the predicate "valid", which is used by jurists in reference to moral rules and principles, originates from the pure theory of law. Kelsen's view of morality as a static normative system (Kelsen 1945, pp. 112, 399–400; Kelsen 1967, pp. 195–198; Opałek 1991) has strongly influenced the comprehension of morality by lawyers and the legal sciences. According to his view, the relations between moral rules and principles are static in the sense that they are related to the content of these norms. Consequently, the meaning of the expression "a valid moral rule or principle" has to somehow be related to the content of a given moral rule or principle. For instance, it can be explicated by a provisional definition: "A moral rule or principle is "valid" if and only if it is just (right, good)", which means that it will be elucidated by referring to the fundamental idea of justice or moral good. As arguably, it is justice or the moral good that fulfils the function of the basic norm of a static normative moral system.

The second proposal is based on the juristic conception of the axiological validity of legal norms. According to Wróblewski (1988, p. 100):

> axiological validity can be treated as the acceptability of legal norms.

For Aarnio, who follows Wróblewski in his analysis, the core of the concept of axiological validity is expressed through the idea of rational acceptability:

> a legal norm is in force if and only if it would be generally accepted on the basis of the (dominant) system of values, if matters were to be considered rationally. (Aarnio 1983, p. 160)

This means that:

> the majority of the members [of a community], after having rationally considered the matter, would bind themselves to accepting N_i as a legal norm to be followed. (Aarnio 1987, p. 44)

We see that without any substantial amendments, the concept of axiological validity can be applied in reference to moral rules and principles. By doing this, we obtain the second provisional-meaning explication: "A moral rule or principle is "valid" if and only if it is rationally accepted by the members of a given society".

25.3.2 The Question of Recognition (Identification)

The question of the recognition (identification) of valid moral rules and principles is very complicated. Firstly, it can be formulated in various ways—for instance, "When is a moral rule or principle valid?", "Which moral rules or principles are valid?" or "Is a moral rule R_m or a moral principle P_m, valid or invalid?". Secondly, the solution to the question of recognition will strongly depend on the answer given to the above-mentioned question of meaning. Thirdly, it will also be influenced by the jurisprudential position that is dominant in the particular national legal culture (e.g., by legal positivism, non-positivism, iusnaturalism etc.) and by the personal views of the law-applying agent. Finally, we can expect that in fact we will need to find two, presumably slightly different answers related to the recognition of valid moral rules and of valid moral principles, respectively.

Before we point out three general jurisprudential ways in which we can tackle the problem of recognition, it has to be noted that our analysis focuses on the "original normative situation." Consequently, the validity of moral rules and principles, which have been incorporated into a certain legal system, is beyond the scope of our investigation. Therefore, the above-mentioned test of institutional support or other methods that are usually applied by practicing lawyers for the identification of non-positivised legal principles can be regarded as an apparent solution to the problem discussed here.

The first possible jurisprudential solution to the problem of identification of valid moral norms and principles consists in determining the criteria of their validity. For the law-applying agents and practicing lawyers, these criteria will probably be viewed as a part of the juristic rule of recognition, since they are accustomed to dealing with the problem of the validity of legal norms by establishing the validity conditions. So, the analogy looks quite natural here. However, it can be questioned whether this way of reasoning is not misleading, because the rule of recognition in a Hartian sense:

> separates law and morality in another, and more important, way: from *within* the system it is the criterion of what is and is not valid law. (Simmonds 1979, p. 365)

And in the case of the recognition of valid moral rules and principles from the legal point of view, the purpose is entirely the opposite: the criteria-based identification of valid moral rules and principles will be the starting point for their anticipated incorporation into the law. Moreover, the seeking criteria for the validity of moral rules and principles have to be of extra-legal provenance, as the positive law has nothing to do with them.

The second solution is connected to non-positivistic legal thinking. In the frame of his procedural theory of practical reason (practical rationality), Alexy defines the practical correctness (*praktische Richtigkeit*) of the normative sentences in such a way that it can be almost directly applied to moral rules and principles (Alexy 1981, p. 178; Aarnio et al. 1981, p. 261):

> A normative sentence N is correct (*richtig*) exactly when it can be the result of procedure P.

This definition shows the possibility of recognising valid moral norms through the procedure of a general practical discourse. Yet, this kind of solution is also very controversial; since Alexy's discursive rehabilitation of practical reason is doubtful (Grabowski 2013, pp. 91–117).

The third solution is non-positivistic as well. It is based on the argumentative approach to juristic reasoning and legal practice (Neumann 1986; Atienza 1993; Feteris 2011). To put it simply: If the arguments supporting a validity statement concerning a moral rule or principle are convincing (i.e. strong and adequate), then a given moral norm could be considered as valid. This possibility reveals that the argumentative solution to the question of recognition is dependent on how we resolve the problem of the justification of validity. Without the proper justification of a validity statement, this solution comes down to trivial tautology: we recognise moral rules and principles as valid if we are certain that they are valid.

In any case, the law-applying agents have to use their own discretion very carefully, because the recognition of a valid moral rule or principle is a prerequisite for its subsequent incorporation into a legal system.

25.3.3 The Question of Justification

How can one justify the statement that a given moral rule or principle is valid? Presumably, the question of the justification of validity is the most complicated one. The answer involves a large number of purely philosophical, ethical, sociological or psychological puzzles, yet it can be taken for granted that the law-applying agents are not competent enough to deal with them. Moreover, it is not a judge's task to solve extra-legal scientific problems. For this reason, we can assume that a law-applying organ will probably adopt a philosophically minimalist approach to these problems. To continue in a similar vein, first of all I will point out two questions, which seem to be indispensable for justifying the validity of moral rules and principles. Then, the juristic, that is, the philosophically minimalist methods of resolving these questions will be outlined.

The first essential question touches on the sources of the arguments supporting validity statements. A law-applying authority has to know where they can be found, especially because the positive law or law textbooks hardly provide any useful information on this specific issue. The second question concerns the methods of justification used by the law-applying agents. It refers to the problems of how the supporting arguments should be constructed and which methods of justificatory reasoning (deductive, inductive, argumentative etc.) are the most adequate.

When answering the first question, a judge (more generally: a law-applying authority) has to decide whether the source of moral arguments has an internal or external character. Without entering into the ethical debate between internalism and externalism (Wong 2006), to justify a validity statement, a law-applying agent has to choose between three theoretically available approaches: it uses either exclusively autonomous or heteronomous reasons, or both. I suppose that the lawyers will deal with this trilemma by adopting—as the adequate remedy—one of the points of view (*cf.* next section) that are typically used in juristic practical reasoning and theoretical reflection (internal, external, committed, detached, deliberative etc.). Considering that in our analysis, a normative system of morality is treated as independent from the legal system, and that we are analysing an "original normative situation," which precedes the incorporation of the valid moral rules and principles into a legal system, it seems that, above all, the point of view adopted by a law-applying agent has to be as critical as possible.

As for the second question, the solution directly depends on the previous answers to the questions of meaning and recognition (identification). Yet, taking into account the *Münchhausen Trilemma* (Albert 1991, pp. 15–24) and the requirements of the economy of thinking, it can be generally observed that the law-applying agents have to content themselves with a contextually sufficient justification. What is more important is that they have to construct the justificatory argumentation in such a way that it will simultaneously satisfy all the potential addressees of the subsequent legal decision: that is, the litigants' audience, interested in the fairness of the decision; the legal audience, interested in the consistency of legal system; and the general audience, interested in the social utility of the decision (Pincoffs 1971). It implies that the choice and construction of a given justification should be based on the evaluation of the argumentative force and adequacy of any supporting arguments.

25.4 Some Methodological Remarks

The above analysis is at best a sketch of how a coherent juristic conception of the validity of moral rules and principles might be developed. Instead of proposing definite solutions to the questions enumerated above, I will conclude with a few remarks concerning the methodology of further research.

The problem of the validity of moral rules and principles in an "original normative situation" is one of the specific subject matters of the jurisprudential theory of adjudication. The juristic reasoning involved in solving the questions of meaning, recognition (identification) and justification can be investigated in accordance with various methodological standpoints. The research work can be based on analytical methodology, wherein a conceptual analysis constitutes the privileged scientific method. On the other hand, the research can be empirical and focused on the actual actions of law-applying authorities. Furthermore, a juristic conception of the validity of moral rules and principles, grounded on analytical and/or empirical research, can be a descriptive, a normative or a mixed theory.

However, I think that the choice of the appropriate point of view for jurisprudential analysis is of crucial importance here. The contemporary analytical legal theory provides many possibilities for adopting diverse points of view in jurisprudence, mainly related to the original distinction made by Hart between the internal and the external point of view (Hart 1961, pp. 55–56, 86–88, 96, 99–107, 197–99). In my opinion, the most appropriate point of view to adopt in jurisprudential reflection is that which is both morally detached and impartial (Grabowski 2013, pp. 226–237). As Raz states (1996, p. 8), detached legal statements express:

> what a speaker believes the law requires, without commitment on his part as to whether there is any reason to act as the law requires.

According to Hart (Páramo 1988, p. 351), the detached statements in the Razian sense involve taking into account a belief in law's moral binding force without the actual necessity (i.e. with the actual possibility) of sharing it (*cf.* Raz 1999, p. 177). And impartiality involves refraining from definite moral decisions but, on the other hand, entails taking into account, in a critical way, both others' as well as our own personal moral views in situations where a moral or axiological reflection seems to be necessary or, at least, useful. Therefore, in my opinion, by adopting a morally detached and impartial point of view, a legal scientist is also free to express a certain moral position; however, in full awareness of the fact that other people's moral views may be better justified. I suppose that such a methodological freedom is essential, in particular where the elaboration of the adequate juristic conception of the validity of moral rules and principles is concerned.

References

Aarnio, Aulis. 1983. On the validity, efficacy and acceptability of legal norms. In idem, *Philosophical perspectives in jurisprudence. Acta Philosophica Fennica* XXXVI:152–162.
Aarnio, Aulis. 1987. *The rational as reasonable. A treatise on legal justification.* Dordrecht: D Reidel.
Aarnio, Aulis, Alexy, Robert, and Aleksander Peczenik. 1981. The foundation of legal reasoning. *Rechtstheorie* 12:133–158, 257–279, 423–448.
Albert, Hans. 1991. *Traktat über kritische Vernunft.* 5th ed. Tübingen: Mohr Siebeck.
Alexy, Robert. 1981. Die Idee einer prozeduralen Theorie der juristischen Argumentation. *Rechtstheorie Bh.* 2:177–188.
Atienza, Manuel. 1993. *Las Razones del Derecho. Teorías de la argumentatión jurídica.* 2nd ed. Madrid: Centro de Estudios Constitucionales.
Bulygin, Eugenio. 1982. Time and validity. In *Deontic logic, computational linguistic and legal information systems*, ed. A. A. Martino, vol. II, 65–81. Amsterdam: North-Holland.
Dworkin, Ronald. 1977. *Taking rights seriously.* Cambridge: Harvard University Press.
Feteris, Eveline T. 2011. *Fundamentals of legal argumentation. A survey of theories on the justification of judicial decisions.* Dordrecht: Kluwer.
Garzón Valdés, Ernesto. 1977. Modelle normativer Geltung. *Rechtstheorie* 8:41–71.
Gizbert-Studnicki, Tomasz, Tomasz Pietrzykowski. 2004. Positivismo blando y la distinción entre Derecho y moral. Trans.: R. Gama Leyva. *DOXA* 27:63–79.
Grabowski, Andrzej. 2013. *Juristic concept of the validity of statutory law. A critique of contemporary legal nonpositivism.* Heidelberg: Springer.
Green, Leslie. 2008. Positivism and the inseparability of law and morals. *New York University Law Review* 83:1035–1058.
Hart, H. L. A. 1961. *The concept of law.* Oxford: Clarendon.
Kelsen, Hans. 1945. *General theory of law and state.* (Trans.:Wedberg, A.). Cambridge: Harvard University Press.
Kelsen, Hans. 1967. *Pure theory of law.* (Trans.:Knight, M.). Berkeley: University of California Press.
Maluschke, Günther. 2007. Validity of moral norms: perspectives of philosophy and psychoanalysis. *Revista Interamericana de Psicología* 41:205–214.
Moore, Michael S. 2012. The various relations between law and morality in contemporary legal philosophy. *Ratio Juris* 25:435–471.
Neumann, Ulfrid. 1986. *Juristische Argumentationslehre.* Darmstadt: Wissenschaftliche Buchgesellschaft.

Opałek, Kazimierz. 1991. Statisches und dynamisches Normensystem. In *Staatsrecht in Theorie und Praxis. Festschrift für Robert Walter zum 60. Geburtstag*, ed. H. Mayer, 507–518. Wien: Manzsche Verlags- und Universitätsbuchhandlung.

Páramo, Juan Ramón de. 1988. Entrevista a H. L. A. Hart. *DOXA* 5:339–361.

Pincoffs, Edmund. 1971. The audiences of the judge. In *Legal reasoning: Proceedings of the World Congress for legal and social philosophy*, ed. H. Hubien, 337–344. Bruxelles: Bruylant.

Putnam, Hilary. 1995. Are moral and legal values made or discovered? *Legal Theory* 1:5–19.

Raz, Joseph. 1994. Authority, law, and morality. In idem, *Ethics in the public domain. Essays in the morality of law and politics*, 194–221. Oxford: Clarendon.

Raz, Joseph. 1996. On the nature of law. *Archiv für Rechts- und Sozialphilosophie* 82:1–25.

Raz, Joseph. 1999. *Practical reason and norms*. 2nd ed. Oxford: Oxford University Press.

Raz, Joseph. 2004. Incorporation by law. *Legal Theory* 10:1–17.

Raz, Joseph. 2009. About morality and the nature of law. In idem, *Between authority and interpretation. On the theory of law and practical reason*, 166–181. Oxford: Oxford University Press.

Simmonds, N. E. 1979. Practice and validity. *The Cambridge Law Journal* 38:361–372.

Wong, David B. 2006. Moral reasons: internal and external. *Philosophy and Phenomenological Research* LXXII:536–558.

Wróblewski, Jerzy. 1988. *Sądowe stosowanie prawa [The judicial application of law]*. 2nd ed. Warszawa: Państwowe Wydawnictwo Naukowe.

Chapter 26
Implicatures Within the Legal Context: A Rule-Based Analysis of the Possible Content of Conversational Maxims in Law

Izabela Skoczeń

Abstract In the present paper, I will provide an account of general-pragmatic theories, such as Grice's theory or 'relevance theory'. Secondly, I will detail the insufficiency of 'relevance theory' in defining the content of maxims within the legal context. The accounts of possible maxims' content in law tend to treat the subject in a strictly Gricean way. They neglect other theories in modern linguistics or philosophy of language. However, it appears that neither of these theories can provide us with a sufficient vision of legal maxims. Although there exist some similarities between the ordinary and legal speech, I will provide for differences which render them two almost incompatible projects. The relevance-theoretic approach appears only fairly narrowly applicable to the realm of law, as its basic assumption of increasing effect while decreasing effort is a flawed statement in the legal domain. Legislative speech is a collective speech act, while the analytical tools developed in Sperber and Wilson's theory are designed to explain individual speech. The fact, that an interpretation is easily accessible does not make it automatically more relevant in law. However, intentions are a central notion in the legal discourse. The communicative intention defined by Sperber and Wilson is an adequate reformulation of the legislator's will to convey a normative content of its propositions. Nevertheless, neither the content of maxims defined by Grice, nor by Sperber and Wilson, provide a fully adequate account of what their content in law could be. There remains a need to search for a more exact theory.

Keywords Grice · Implicature · Maxim of conversation · Pragmatic enrichment · Relevance theory

26.1 Introduction

This paper aims to provide an analysis of the possible content of conversational maxims in law, defined in Gricean terms as rule-like assumptions, in theories advanced by modern pragmatics. While noticing that contents of utterances in human

---

I. Skoczeń (✉)
Department of Legal Theory, Jagiellonian University, Krakow, Poland
e-mail: izabela.skoczen@uj.edu.pl

M. Araszkiewicz et al. (eds.), *Problems of Normativity, Rules and Rule-Following*,
Law and Philosophy Library 111, DOI 10.1007/978-3-319-09375-8_26

languages contain more than just an amalgam of the words used, Grice provided a substantial leap in the methods of analysis of meanings. He noticed that for linguistic communication to be successful, the hearer of a proposition must make certain assumptions; that the speaker is following some rules (or maxims), which are directed at achieving the specific aim of a conversation. Grice considered conversation only in a narrow sense, that is, a conversation is aimed at an exchange of information. I will begin the analysis by providing a brief account of general-pragmatic theories that address the question of the possible content of the maxims of conversation, such as Grice's theory or 'relevance theory', which was developed by Sperber and Wilson. Secondly, I will detail the inadequacy of 'relevance theory' in defining the content of maxims' content within the legal context. I would like to underline the fact that the accounts of possible maxims' content in law (such as those provided by Marmor or Poggi) tend to treat the subject in a strictly Gricean way. They omit or neglect other theories in modern linguistics or philosophy of language. However, it appears that neither of these theories can provide us with a sufficient vision of legal maxims. The issues I considered in this paper were as follows: What is the content of maxims in law? Why cannot relevance theory be straightforwardly applied to describe legal parlance? Which of its notions could provide us with a more adequate representation of communication in legal contexts than does the Gricean theory?

26.2 Gricean Account of the Maxims of Conversation

Paul Grice noticed that, together with the asserted content of the words used, we can distinguish meanings that are closely tied to the contextual embodiment of an utterance. This led him to the conclusion that human beings must make use of some tools that enable them to understand the implicated content. He created a theory that aimed to explain the formation of conversational implicatures by formulating a general cooperative principle (Grice 1975, 1989). The assumption that the parties to a conversation are cooperating in the aim of exchanging information is specified in the form of four maxims of conversation: QUALITY (try to make your contribution one that is true.), QUANTITY (make your contribution as informative as is required for the current purposes of the exchange), RELATION (be relevant), and MANNER (be perspicuous, avoid obscurity of expression, ambiguity, be brief and orderly) (Horn 2006, p. 7). Grice treated "these rules not as arbitrary conventions, but as instances of more general rules governing rational, cooperative behavior" (Davis 2013). F. Poggi proposed that maxims be defined as "formulations of customary hermeneutic, technical rules". According to von Wright's classification, "technical rules (or directives) indicate a means to reach a certain goal, aiming not at directing the will of the receivers, but at indicating to them that their will is conditioned: in other words, that if they want to reach a certain goal, then they must maintain certain behavior" (Poggi 2011, p. 7). It is the purpose of the conversation that shapes the content of the maxims and not *vice versa*. The sole identification of the existence of implicatures, together with rules that enable us to predict their content, is insufficient to explain why and how technically implied meaning is conjured up. Therefore, we require three additional formulations:

> (…) A speaker *S* conversationally implicates *q* by saying *p* in context *C*, if—
> (a) *S* is presumed to observe the relevant conversational maxims in *C*;
> (b) The assumption that *S* meant (or intended that) *q* is required in order to make sense of *S*'s utterance of *p* in context *C*, given the conversational maxims that apply;
> (c) *S* believes/assumes that his/her hearers can recognize condition *b*, and can recognize that *S* knows that. (…). (Marmor 2011, p. 152)

Conversational implicatures must also somehow be calculable by the hearer with the use of maxims (calculability assumption; Davis 2013). In fact, only the cooperative principle and the calculability assumption combined can create a successfully implicated utterance. The hearer must be capable of inferring the implicature in order for the communication to achieve its goal. A generative assumption is also identified: "Implicatures that are conversational exist because of the fact that the cooperative presumption, determinacy, and mutual knowledge conditions hold. Whereas the Calculability Assumption is epistemological, the Generative Assumption is ontological, explaining the constitution of conversational implicatures. (…)" (Davis 2013). The formation of an implicature is due to a range of factors that enable the prediction of its content. Without a speaker intention that is directed at the creation of a definite implicature, the communication could not be successful (Davis 2013). We sometimes fail to communicate (exactly) what we intend. However, it appears that the existence of an intention is not only necessary for production of an utterance, but it can also be one of the reasons why a hearer must infer the implicature from the proposition heard.

Grice noticed that speakers sometimes flout maxims. Such action appears to be even more complex than the description of a lie, because, in cases of maxim-flouting, the hearer is perfectly aware that the speaker is breaking these rules and successfully infers meanings from such utterances. Another interesting phenomenon is the case of irony. Griceans define irony as a deliberate action of conveying just the opposite of what is being said, while Sperber and Wilson provided a slightly different account of irony; they considered it as an echoic utterance that refers to some other occurrence in the past. Another often discussed example of maxim-flouting is poetry. The followers of Grice explain it by formulating an additional principle of style: "be stylish, so be beautiful, distinctive, entertaining and interesting (…)" (Davis 2013). Consequently, formal or polite utterances that involve a large dose of unnecessary statements or conventions of courtesy are explained by a principle of politeness.

In an effort to improve Grice's theory of linguistic communication and, especially, the definitions of the content of maxims that have posed the most problems, many, including Laurence Horn and Stephen Levinson, have formulated new theories. In this paper, I will primarily consider Sperber and Wilson's 'relevance theory.'

26.3 Relevance Theory: An Alternative to the Gricean Account of Communication

Linguists and philosophers of language have created very different visions of the process of utterance formation. This has also triggered substantial disagreement concerning the possible content of the maxims, even within a standard day-to-day or, to put it in Gricean terms, information-oriented communication. One can imagine that the situation is even more complex when a non-standard specific form of communicating is in play. Multiple forms of communication exist within the large social phenomenon called law, for example, the communication that occurs within the legislature, or between the legislature and the judicial powers, which Andrei Marmor called 'strategic speech.' (Marmor 2011, p. 157). It should be emphasised that most of the debate on maxims' content within the legal domain has been strictly dominated by Grice's view of the cognitive processes involved in human communication. Philosophers who considered the issue straightforwardly (Marmor and Poggi) have assessed the processes described using Gricean vocabulary. Their work was mainly based on comparisons of information-oriented communication of the speech in the legal framework. This has led to interesting, but fairly one-dimensional, conclusions. The aim of this section is to combine other visions of human linguistic-cognitive processes and their possible applications within legal speech-contexts.

Let us attempt to debunk the common misconception that the Gricean framework is the best, and only possible, categorisation of notions. As relevance theory has shown, we must search for a theory that is not only adequate in the descriptive sense, but also conforms to the architecture of our minds. The work of Marmor, which considers the content of 'legal maxims', is based on a division of content of speech between semantic content (the literal meaning of the words used, combined with syntactical structures), assertive content (the truth-evaluable content of speech) and implicated content (that which goes beyond what is literally conveyed) (Marmor 2009, p. 3). This distinction is sufficient in a project aimed at providing a normative account of what must be the case to warrant certain inferences and conclusions. Nevertheless, while analysing the maxims issue, it is worth glancing at another project: cognitive psychology, which aims to give an account of the way in which the mind actually works. As B. Shaer noted: "(…) legal interpretation is as much cognitive as it is institutional 'all the way down'—that it is a particular kind of linguistic activity, carried out as part of the culture of law. This indicates that a plausible account of it must ultimately meld institutional and cognitive analyses, showing how the later perspective is compatible with, and can actually elucidate, the former" (Shaer 2013, p. 261). As philosophers and neuropsychologists have noticed, it is often the case that we should differentiate the process of understanding an utterance and give reasons for why we have understood it in that specific way (Sperber and Wilson 2002, p. 263). A similar differentiation is involved while making decisions; the cognitive process of decision-making is rather holistic, despite the fact that we often present *ex post* reasons for making a decision in a more sequential manner. The hermeneutical *hunch* appears to be a similar concept to modern neuropsychological descriptions of decision-making mechanisms. The previously mentioned differentiation perfectly fits analytical, *ex post* queries for the reasons behind understanding the content of a proposition in a specific way. Nevertheless, it does not aim to convey the way in which understanding of a proposition is actually processed within the mind. The reason why the pragmatics of the legal language have primarily been considered in Gricean terms, is that they are useful in discourse, providing reasons for understanding a legal regulation in a specific way and, furthermore, in deciding whether a legal regulation is applicable to a specific case. This somehow traditional way (at least in continental legal systems) of grounding decisions by providing reasons for a specific understanding or interpretation of a given regulation has a Grice-oriented order. It starts with considering the literal meaning, then considers the systemic and functional contents, which are linguistically viewed as pragmatically enriched, rather than expressly stated. Let us make an attempt to consider the communication and understand the problem in the novel notions proposed by more cognitively oriented theories, such as the aforementioned 'relevance theory'.

Relevance theory proposes the replacement of all four Gricean maxims of conversation with a single principle of relevance; that the utterer ought to be as relevant as possible in the circumstances. It is a cognitive theory that purports to solve the conflict between the two neo-Gricean heuristics deriving from Horn's Q and I principles. The Q principle 'say as much as you can' leads to the following heuristic: 'What is not said is not the case'. The I principle 'say no more than you must' creates: 'What is simply/briefly described is the stereotypical or normal (default) instance' (Carston 2013, p. 14). The clash of the aforementioned heuristics is particularly relevant to lawyers. Consider the following example: "There's a vehicle blocking the driveway" (Carston 2013, p. 16). The I heuristic should lead someone who hears this sentence to infer that it is a motor car that is at stake. Quite the contrary, the Q heuristic suggests that the speaker has something other than a simple 'motor car' in mind, otherwise they would not have used the more general term 'vehicle'. This tension is strikingly similar to the Hartian example of 'no vehicles in the park' provision and could be resolved by an underlying, generalised principle of relevance (Carston 2013, p. 16).

The idea of relevance theory is based on two primary factors: effort and effect. Speakers tend to utter propositions that enable the hearer to attain maximum cognitive effect with minimum effort. If we are to choose between two utterances that require similar effort, we will choose the one that provides us with maximum cognitive effect. If the cognitive effect of two utterances is comparable, speakers choose the one that will require less effort from the hearer. Briefly, agents act so as to attain maximum efficiency of their parlance. Relevance theory, just as Grice's theory, is particularly interesting for lawyers, because it concentrates on a feature that is partly verbal and partly non-verbal; the expression and recognition of intentions (Sperber and Wilson 2002, p. 1). This feature is also central to legal theory and the interpretational debate between textualists (proponents of the literal meaning of statutes) and intentionalists (advocates of the intentional meaning of the lawmakers).

Nevertheless, relevance theory provides for a framework that is rather incompatible with this division: its "view of speaker's intent as integral to interpretation is thus very much at odds with the outright rejection of legislative intent by some textualists. Yet, the theory's recognition of the key role of 'ostensive stimuli' in communication appears to place it equally at odds with the view of intentionalists that 'the actual words used by the legislature may be strong evidence of its intent, but they are merely windows on the legislative intent (or purpose) that is the law', 'so that 'a thing may be within the letter of the statute and yet not within the statute, because not within its spirit, nor within the intention of its makers. Such a view of statutory text seems difficult to square with relevance theory, which takes 'sentence meaning' not to be a mere 'window' on 'speaker's meaning', but rather the basic vehicle for communicating it" (Shaer 2013, p. 282). Every utterance is considered as an input. "An input is relevant to an individual when its processing in a context of available assumptions yields a POSITIVE COGNITIVE EFFECT. A positive cognitive effect is a worthwhile difference to the individual's representation of the world—a true conclusion, for example. False conclusions are not worth having. They are cognitive effects, but not positive ones" (Sperber and Wilson 2002, p. 3). If we were to treat the legal texts issued by a legislative body as an input that is supposed to yield a positive, cognitive effect, we would have to consider it as producing true, normative conclusions, rather than descriptive true or false conclusions. These normative conclusions could consist of either providing agents with good reasons to act in accordance with a regulation, or failing at this task. Consequently, the worthwhile difference after processing the input would not be a true or false descriptive conclusion about the world state, but rather a conclusion with a prescriptive content; how and why agents ought to behave. The negative-normative cognitive effect could consist of a failure to provide the agent with good reasons to act in accordance with the law (fail to answer the question: Why?), or a failure to provide the agent with the correct prescription of behaviour (fail to answer the question: How?). Therefore, legal regulations are supposed to generate only positive, cognitive effects in the normative sense. Processing of an input results in a contextual implication. This is a conclusion deducible from two factors: the input and the context. The use of only one factor is strictly insufficient (Sperber and Wilson 2002, p. 3). In the realm of law, when the utterer (legislator) is a collective agent, so the context lacks a number of important factors that a 'face-to-face' communication provides. In fact, a fully-fledged contextual implication is achieved only when the court interprets a legal regulation in an individual case. It is only then that the legislative utterance gains its full power. Relevance theory emphasises that the greater the processing effort required to understand an input, the less (technically) relevant the input will be; a conclusion drawn by the definition of relevance in this theory. The application of this statement to the formulations of legal texts is rather perilous. There exists some, especially postmodern, views that postulate the need to simplify legal texts, so as to enable their full understanding by laymen. This approach has been criticised for obvious reasons: we cannot sacrifice precision or adequacy provided by complexity in the sole aim of issuing a more understandable text. In a hierarchy of objectives of legal regulations, it is rare for understandability to be privileged.

The described theory has created further assumptions: The existence of the cognitive principle of relevance (human cognition tends to be geared to the maximisation of relevance) and the ostensive-inferential communication, which consists of two intentions:

a. The informative intention: The intention to inform an audience of something.
b. The communicative intention: The intention to inform the audience of one's informative intention. (Sperber and Wilson 2002, p. 7)

In the realm of law, the intention of the legislator is not merely informative, but also normative. The legislator is not only informing, but also regulating. Their communicative intention is to inform their audience of their normative intentions—that they have reasons for obeying the enacted laws[1]. From that angle, relevance theory becomes fairly useful in explaining some legal-linguistic issues. Sperber and Wilson also introduced the communicative principle of relevance, which states that every ostensive stimulus conveys a presumption of its own optimal relevance (Sperber and Wilson 2002, p. 8). "An ostensive stimulus is optimally relevant to an audience if:

a. It is relevant enough to be worth the audience's processing effort;
b. It is the most relevant one compatible with communicator's abilities and preferences (Sperber and Wilson 2002, p. 9).

We should note that the legislator's abilities are restricted to an ostensive stimulus that is formed almost solely of input consisting of written words, as the social context of creating a regulation cannot be fully ostended in court. Therefore, the ostensive context comes into play only when we consider a concrete case. Condition (b) guarantees that the ostensive stimulus gives maximum effect with a minimum of effort; so it is the most relevant that the communicator is WILLING and ABLE to produce (Sperber and Wilson 2002, p. 10). In this way, the distinction of ostensive and non-ostensive silence is resolved. "If you are clearly willing to answer, I am entitled to conclude that you are unable, and if you are clearly able to answer, I am entitled to conclude that you are unwilling" (Sperber and Wilson 2002, p. 10). Within the legal domain, the legislator is sometimes unable to say more, due to lack of sufficient context (they must make a more general statement and lower the cognitive effect) or due to the inability to reach an agreement within a legislative body; the necessity of compromise. Sometimes, the legislator is unwilling to say more, for example, when they want to leave some discretion to the court. This account is sufficient to explain problems created by the legal language. The inability to be more informative, or to be informative at all (remaining silent) in the legislature can be due to the unpredictability of the facts of specific cases that are going to be decided by the judges. For example, the legislator wishes to forbid the use of drugs having a certain effect and enacts a statute with a list of their names. The last point on the list is a formulation 'other drugs having similar effects'. It is a general clause or a 'blank cheque'. The legislator is aware that a new drug having similar effects can be developed at any time, and so is unable to say more at the time of the statute's enactment. Another example of the inability of legislatures to be more informative

[1] I am using J. Raz's definition of normativity as reason for action.

is the situation in which there is a major disagreement within the legislative body as to the implications of enacting a statute. Imagine two conflicting parties, one wishing a statute X to be implicating Q and the other wishing the statute X to be implicating not Q (Marmor 2008, p. 436). If an agreement cannot be reached, the effect is a compromise consisting of a deliberate enactment of the statute X without deciding on its implications. As a result, the legislator is unable to say more than X and is unable to state the implications of X. Both described instances of inability of the legislature to be more informative are a major cause of interpretative issues at the judicial level. Nevertheless, it can be the case that, even though the legislator is perfectly capable of being maximally informative and enacting a complex, strict and full regulation of a specific domain, they refrain from doing so. This particularly occurs when a strict regulation could yield controversial effects in some cases, and it seems more reasonable to allow the courts a degree of discretion such that they can decide on a case-by-case basis. Although relevance theory claims to offer a better, or more thorough, explanation of incomplete utterances (or even silence and lack of utterances) by differentiating the inability and unwillingness to give an answer, it actually describes the same ('Gricean') issues in other terms.

Let us consider another key thesis of relevance theory: "Since relevance varies inversely with effort, the very fact that an interpretation is easily accessible gives it an initial degree of plausibility. It is also reasonable for the hearer to stop at the first interpretation that satisfies his expectations of relevance, because there should never be more than one" (Sperber and Wilson 2002, p. 10).

This is not so in law; we often search for further interpretations, while accepting that there can be more than one. The claimant and respondent will often search for interpretations of legal statutes that are not the most relevant in terms of effort and effect, but which satisfy their client's wishes. Therefore, the cognitive goal is different. It is the judge's task to find the most (and not the first) relevant interpretation of the legislator's words. Shaer developed a similar view: " (…) the process of inferring meaning in legal and literary interpretation, while arguably still guided by a general trade-off between effort and effect, just as scientific theorizing is, involves a trade-off that is not between cognitive so much as professional or institutional effort and effect" (Shaer 2013, p. 286). Let us consider an example from statutory interpretation: A legal text stating that deadlines for appeal are being suspended during statutory-defined days or periods of public holidays. Imagine that, in the given system, there is no statute that would define Saturdays as such days. Speaking in terms of effort, the first accessible interpretation is that which states that Saturdays are not to fall within the scope of that regulation. It is a literalist view, taking into consideration the literal meaning of the statute, and a textualist view, allowing here a co-textual implicature, as no legal act defines Saturdays as vacation days. Conversely, speaking in terms of effect, it is common knowledge that a vast majority of society does not work on Saturdays, most offices are closed or have limited working hours, which creates hurdles, delays, etc. This approaches the so called purposivist view; aiming to fulfil the purpose of the act with interpretive actions. The results of the above considerations are two equally cognitively plausible outcomes. The solution, according to relevance theory, should be to choose the more relevant option. As Carston pointed out, "paying attention to the cognitive processes of and the constraints on ordinary utterance comprehension, such as that offered by relevance theory" could be helpful (Carston 2013, p. 33). Nevertheless, in the example presented above, neither cognitive, nor linguistic arguments appear to be sufficient. In such cases, judges often resign from such (presumably more objective in the technical sense) arguments and succumb to some subjective moral or political argumentation (Marmor 2013, p. 2).

One parameter appears to have been neglected in this definition of relevance. While considering the cognitive effort of both speaker and hearer, the effort of time of uttering is often crucial. Implicatures are quite useful to redouble the conveyed content of an utterance. By a single utterance that takes an acceptable time to utter, we convey twice as much to a cooperative hearer. Consider the following example of a yes/no question:

1. Tom: Are you coming to Paul's party?
2. Jane: I have to work (Davis 2013).

An answer: 'No, I have to work' would be easier to process, but would take more time to utter. Therefore, the notion of effort in the definition of relevance should include time. In legal texts, the tendency is rather to avoid utterances that are highly inferential or context-dependent; utterances that are usually the shortest and quickest to utter. The risk of being misunderstood is too elevated and extremely costly.[2] Moreover, it is not the time of uttering that is the focal problem, but rather the time between the utterance being made and it being interpreted by a hearer (the judge). The controversy is blatant in the originalists' (proponents of favouring the intention of the drafters of the American Constitution) versus anti-originalists' (advocates of the modern meaning of interpreters) debate over transtemporal constitutional interpretation in the United States (Shaer 2013, p. 288).

Conclusions: The Possible Content of the Maxims within the Legal Domain

Marmor argued that the Gricean framework, with an information-oriented communication, is not of much use when a description of legal situations is required. This view has been put under scrutiny by Endicott, who emphasised that a myriad of striking similarities exist between ordinary communication and 'strategic speech' (described by Marmor) used, for example, within a legislative body. Ignoring implicatures or using double-talk (conveying different content to different hearers with the same utterance) is commonplace in every day speech, equally as in legislative speech. Moreover, ordinary speech can serve an infinitely broad range of purposes,

[2] "I think this condition is an instance of the sort of phenomenon stated in Zipf's law. I think there is operating in our language, as in most forms of human behaviour, a principle of least effort, in this case *a principle of maximum illocutionary ends with minimum phonetic effort*, and I think [this] condition is an instance of it. (Searle 1965, pp. 234–235, my emphasis)" (Horn 2004).

including strategic purposes. Restricting it to a strictly informative exchange is an idealisation (Endicott 2013, p. 7).

Another proponent of the view that maxim content in the legal and ordinary speech remains similar is R. Carston. She emphasised that the Gricean programme has a single and very broad goal, which is common to all forms of human linguistic communication: " (…) There is a thin notion of cooperative, purposive activity that might cover all these kinds of linguistic communication, including legal language: the producer of the language wants to get a certain meaning across to an audience and the audience wants to grasp that meaning. There is then a joint cooperative activity here—in a perhaps somewhat attenuated sense" (Carston 2013, p. 17). Consequently, legal canons of construction and the problems that they create are compatible with the neo-Gricean heuristics; Q 'what is not said is not the case', and I 'what is simply/briefly described is the stereotypical or normal (default) instance'), while often clashing with one another. For example, the canons '*Espressio unius est exclusio alterius*' (expression of the one is exclusion of the other) and '*Eiusdem generis'* (of the same kind) can lead to mutually inconsistent results, while deploying analogous content to the aforementioned heuristics. Consider the following example of a statutory provision (given by Carston): 'Exceptions to the prohibition (on employment of foreign workers) are professional actors, singers, artists, lecturers [and others].' Following the second canon we get the result that similar professions (ex. dancers) are to be included in the exception, while others (ex. doctors) are subject to the prohibition. This is consistent with the I-heuristic, which "licences the interpreter to enrich in a stereotypical, uncontroversial sort of way". In contrast, the application of the first canon and Q heuristic provides evidence to the contrary, especially when the phrase 'and others' is not within the wording of the provision. Therefore, any employment category not explicitly mentioned in the text would be excluded (Carston 2013, p. 18). Thus, the neo-Gricean maxims may have an almost identical content in both natural and legal speech, while generating contradictory interpretations. The choice of a maxim or heuristic may either depend on some elusive underlying principle of relevance or rely on an "antecedent decision (…) about whether the appropriate conditions for applying any given canon are met" (Carston 2013, p. 19). This decision could be based on extra-linguistic considerations, which are only backed *ex post* with a matching linguistic argumentation; the previously described neo-Gricean Q or I principles.

While some similarities undeniably exist in maxim content within natural and legal speech, it seems to be going a conclusion too far to state that the differences between those forms of communication can be neglected. The time gap between the uttering of the speaker (here the legislature) and the interpreting of the utterance by a hearer (the courts) in particular provides legalese with a unique and descriptively challenging trans-contextual character.

Every context of legal communication is problematic at the descriptive stage: Within a legislative body, the communication is oriented towards making one's intentions to prevail (strategic speech) and it is not clear who are the parties of the conversation (Marmor 2011, p. 154). In the exchange between the legislature and the judicial powers, the maxims' content in such a communication could be "norms about the ways in which courts interpret statutory language" (Marmor 2011,

p. 157) or, in this context, no cooperative principle could be in force at all. (Poggi 2011, p. 20) The latter view is highly controversial. "In legislation, if cooperation breaks down, the rule of law breaks down. And the separation of powers between legislature and court depends on adherence by the courts to legal analogues of the conversational maxims." (Endicott 2013, p. 8) Some jurists, such as Ronald Dworkin, William Eskridge and Justice Antonin Scalia, even claimed that this was not a conversation at all (Shaer 2013, p. 260). It could be that it is something similar to a monologue formed by two independent agents, the legislator (conveying literal meanings) and the judicial authorities (being more than a standard hearer, indicating what a reasonable hearer would have understood in the context of a concrete case, and pragmatically enriching the received meanings). The hearer indirectly becomes the speaker when they suggest to the legislator that if they do not amend the law, then it will not be understood as the legislator intended. Consequently, a strictly information-oriented maxim content is also inadequate when considering the speech of parties in the courtroom. The majority of the time, the claimant and respondent are unwilling to disclose each and every piece of information that they make use of. The relevance-theoretic approach appears only fairly narrowly applicable to the realm of law, as its basic assumption of increasing effect while decreasing effort is a fundamentally flawed statement in the legal domain. Legislative speech is a collective speech act, while the analytical tools developed in Sperber and Wilson's theory are designed to explain individual speech. Precision and adequacy cannot be sacrificed to boost understandability. Furthermore, the fact, that an interpretation is easily accessible does not make it automatically more relevant in law. However, it is true that intentions are a central notion in the legal discourse and the communicative intention defined by Sperber and Wilson, and are an adequate reformulation of the legislator's will to convey a normative content of their propositions. The distinction of ostensive and non-ostensive silence appears to be an interesting reformulation of issues already identified by Griceans.

Nevertheless, neither the content of maxims defined by Grice, nor by Sperber and Wilson, provide a fully adequate account of what their content in law could be. There remains a need to search for a more exact theory.

Acknowledgments I would like to thank Tomasz Gizbert-Studnicki and Andrei Marmor for their helpful comments on this paper. This research has been supported by the Polish Ministry of Science and Higher Education (grant no. DI2012 019042).

References

Carston, Robyn. 2013. Legal texts and canons of construction: A view from current pragmatic theory. In *Law and language current legal issues*, vol. 15, ed. M. Freeman and F. Smith, 8–33. Oxford: Oxford University Press.

Davis, Wayne. 2013. Implicature. http://plato.stanford.edu/archives/spr2013/entries/implicature/. Accessed 25 April 2013.

Endicott, Timothy. 2014. Interpretation and indeterminacy. *Jerusalem Review of Legal Studies*. doi:10.1093/jrls/jlu005.

Grice, Herbert Paul. 1975. Logic and conversation. In *Syntax and semantics: Speech acts*, ed. P. Cole and J. Morgan, vol. 3, 41–58. New York: Academic.
Grice, Herbert Paul. 1989. *Studies in the way of words*. Cambridge: Harvard University Press.
Horn, Lawrence R. 2004. Implicature. In *The handbook of pragmatics*, ed. L. R. Horn and G. Ward, 3–28. Oxford: Blackwell.
Marmor, Andrei. 2008. Pragmatics of the legal language. *Ratio Iuris* 21(4): 423–452.
Marmor, Andrei. 2009. Can the law imply more than it says? *USC Legal Studies Research Paper* 3:1–22.
Mamor, Andrei. 2011. *Philosophy of law*. Princeton: Princeton University Press.
Marmor, Andrei. 2013. Meaning and belief in constitutional interpretation. *USC Legal Studies Research Paper* 134:1–23.
Poggi, Francesca. 2011. Law and conversational implicatures. *International Journal of Semiotics in Law* 24:21–40.
Searle, John. 1965. What is a speech act? In *Philosophy in America*, ed. M. Black, 221–39. Ithaca NY: Cornell University Press.
Shaer, Benjamin. 2013. Toward a cognitive science of legal interpretation. In *Law and language current legal issues*, ed. M. Freeman and F. Smith, vol. 15, 8–33. UK: Oxford University Press.
Sperber, Dan, and Deirdre Wilson. 2002. Relevance theory. In *The handbook of pragmatics*, ed. L. Horn and G. Ward, 607–632. Oxford: Blackwell.

Chapter 27
Why are Words not Enough? Or a Few Remarks on Traffic Signs

Michał Dudek

Abstract In this study two general theses are presented. In the first thesis—about integral character of traffic signs—it is proposed to stop treating traffic signs as only a subsidiary (illustrative) instruments—an alternatives to written linguistic utterances. It is shown that the construction of legal regulations of road traffic justifies the thesis that traffic signs are in fact an integral part of certain provisions and encoded norms, and not just a way of communicating them. This integral character and the fact that traffic signs as a means of visual-nonlinguistic communication have specific features which are extremely difficult to verbalize in an accurate, intelligible, and concise manner (e.g., angles, pictograms, or ideograms) or are even impossible to verbalize (colors) leads to second thesis—about inadequacy of concept of legal norm as a linguistic utterance in context of traffic signs. Concepts of interpretation of law which adopt a vision that legal norm (reconstructed from legal provisions—linguistic utterances of specific properties included in texts of legal acts) is an object of purely linguistic nature are inadequate, when one considers, for example, some of the provisions of Road Traffic Law, which refer to traffic signs. Their example clearly shows that in contemporary legal orders one can find legal norms, which cannot be accurately and intelligibly presented only with words. Thus, if the result of the interpretation of certain legal provisions must be made not only with words but also with broadly understood graphics, the cited concepts of interpretation of law cannot be actually realized in all of the instances. This makes them inadequate from the perspective of whole legal order.

Keywords Interpretation of law · Traffic signs · Visual communication

27.1 Context of the Study

M. Radin (1930, p. 871) in his known essay *Statutory Interpretation* says that "[a] statute which presented a photograph of two automobiles and printed the legend beneath it that drivers who get into the situation pictured above would be prosecuted

M. Dudek (✉)
Department of Sociology of Law, Faculty of Law and Administration,
Jagiellonian University in Krakow, Bracka 12, Kraków 31-005, Poland
e-mail: michal.dudek@uj.edu.pl

M. Araszkiewicz et al. (eds.), *Problems of Normativity, Rules and Rule-Following*,
Law and Philosophy Library 111, DOI 10.1007/978-3-319-09375-8_27

would not be a statute, although intention would be no less easily, and perhaps more easily, discoverable in this way than in set words." As far as the second argument in this statement does not raise any doubts, the first argument causes confusion. Namely, M. Radin seems to completely reject the inclusion of means of visual-nonlinguistic communication (graphics) in texts of legal acts (e.g. statutes, regulations, etc.). Over 30 years after the publication of aforementioned essay and over 10 years after death of M. Radin, C.B. Nutting (1964) explicitly questions outlined standpoint. He shows that in certain instances various kinds of graphics are not only included in broadly understood legal regulations, but their inclusion and actual taking them into account is necessary for the appropriate functioning of particular regulations. His examples are: inclusion of the so-called Ringelmann Chart in regulations concerning air pollution; use of maps in land-use planning regulations and decisions; inspection marks on food products; and, last but not least, traffic signs and signals. The very last example C.B. Nutting gives, clearly refutes the first argument of the quoted statement by M. Radin. There are statutes—fully deserving 'statute' name—which include in their content not only written linguistic utterances, but also graphics, such as traffic signs.

Since the publication of C.B. Nutting's very often overlooked note, scientific reflection on broadly understood visual-nonlinguistic phenomena in law (not only in texts of legal acts) have been significantly developed, mainly but not only by German-language scholars.[1] In contemporary studies on this issue the focus seems to be placed on the theoretical and practical problems with visualizations of various kind of legal contents,[2] like elements of and whole contracts or legal norms—expressing them in a strictly visual-nonlinguistic manner.

The subject of this short study is different. It is not concerned with efforts to express visually written utterances of legal provisions (their meaning). It is concerned with the specific kind of visualizations prepared not by the legal scholars or legal practitioners, but prepared by the legislators themselves and included by them right in the texts of legal acts. Of course, one can venture to say that most people associate law with whole tomes containing more or less complex written linguistic utterances. C.R. Brunschwig's (2011, pp. 573, 650) diagnosis of "verbocentrism" in thinking about the law is definitely correct. However, means of visual-nonlinguistic communication[3] are in fact used in legal regulations, or—as F. Studnicki (1968, p. 177) states—"normgivers of various kinds and ranks are expressing legal norms created by themselves by optical signs, which are not expressions of ethnic written language." Still, there is no room for exaggeration in this field. The use of graphics by legislators themselves and including them in texts of legal acts is rather a small exception, not a rule in the whole of the modern law-making.

This negligence of images can be explained by, for example, highly complex subjects of contemporary legal regulations, which is not irrelevant for the difficulty of the written formulations included in texts of legal acts. Consequently, these contents

[1] See, e.g., Boehme-Neßler (2011) and Brunschwig (2011) and literature quoted by them.

[2] Briefly on functions of visualizations of law, see, Wahlgren (2012, p. 22).

[3] Characteristic features and functions of visual communication are discussed by, e.g., Boehme-Neßler (2011, pp. ix, 52, 55–57, 58–71, 74–75, 77, 80–81, 129, 151, 183).

can be extremely difficult to visualize in a relatively adequate, intelligible and, at the same time, concise manner. Visualization of normative, legal contents is possible when the subject of visualization is relatively simple and concrete (Dudek 2011, pp. 171–172). Otherwise, one has to take into account that efforts to visualize some legal regulations (or parts of them) can be unsuccessful or only partially successful.

27.2 Subject of the Study

Not going into these and other possible explanations of the correct observation of V. Boehme-Neßler (2011, p. 101) that "in the modern law there are almost no images", hereinafter one focuses on one particular kind of regulations in which legislators themselves include, next to 'traditional' legal provisions, graphics (means of visual-nonlinguistic communication). Although the emphasis is placed on traffic signs—"perhaps the most common instances of graphic law or at least the kinds of graphic law most commonly applicable to the general public" (Nutting 1964, p. 781)—or, more generally speaking, legal regulations of road traffic, one has to remember that similar means to traffic signs are used in regulations not concerned with traffic.[4]

27.3 Fundamental Distinction

Modest size of this study makes it impossible to discuss and argue with a number of multi-threaded scientific analyses of traffic signs.[5] However, due to the clarity of the analysis proposed below, it seems necessary to recall here one fundamental distinction made in the semiotics of traffic signs. F. Studnicki (1968, p. 178), inspired by sign-type and sign-token distinction in Peircean semiotics, distinguishes sign-types and sign-realizations. Sign-types are simply graphical models (images) of particular signs which are included in the text of legal act. On the other hand, sign-realizations are specific physical objects which replicate graphical models (sign-types) and are placed in a given location in space. Thus, for example, the image of 'yield' sign included in a particular legal act is a sign-type, while the sign 'yield' on the nearby street is a sign-realization. This distinction seems to be complementary to the position of A. Beck (1988, p. 11) who claims that the exercise by the sign of the assumed effects on humans is dependent on the physical placement at a given point in space. Without it, sign is taken out of context and therefore incomplete (Beck 1988, p. 10).[6]

[4] See, e.g., Polish Regulation of the Minister of Internal Affairs of 29 December 2011 on the determining the designs of mandatory, prohibitory, information and warning signs applied in the mountains and organized ski areas—Journal of Laws 2011, no. 295, item 1751. All legal acts and their provisions mentioned in this study are in force at the date of 30 January 2014.

[5] See, e.g., literature quoted by Nöth (1995, p. 220) or papers in Posner (1995).

[6] The role of the placement of a sign is noticed also by other scholars, e.g., Wagner (2006, pp. 318–319).

27.4 Integral Character of Traffic Signs

After this short reminder, one can begin the analysis which questions the idea that graphics (means of visual-nonlinguistic communication, such as sign-types of traffic signs) appearing in texts of specific legal acts are only the expressions, illustrations of some content. Namely, such an approach seems to be taken not only in the wording of specific regulations,[7] but also in some scientific deliberations.[8]

This position seems to be flawed because it does not recognize that the role of traffic signs is not only the substitution in its meaning suggested above. References to these particular means of visual-nonlinguistic communication are also a very important part of the content of the particular legal provisions encoding specific legal norms. Therefore, one can formulate a thesis that graphics, in the discussed context, traffic signs (both their designs included in texts of legal acts—sign-types—as well as their actual, physical placement at a given site—sign-realizations) can be regarded as an integral, not secondary part of certain legal provisions and legal norms encoded by these provisions. Example of traffic signs clearly shows that, although the statutes and regulations are thought of in terms of specific linguistic expressions, their strictly visual dimension should also be taken into account. Otherwise, one can say that somc of the linguistic expressions in the texts of legal acts would be in a specific way empty. Some legal provisions, having the form of specifically structured written linguistic utterances can realize their assumed functions, only when one takes into consideration the actual, physical realizations (sign-realizations) of a particular graphical models (sign-types), sometimes contained in parts of legal acts to which given legal provision belongs, or in another legal acts to which it refers.

Not to be groundless, consider the following example. Article 24 paragraph 7 of already mentioned Polish Road Traffic Law[9] prohibits "overtaking a moving motor vehicle on the road", amongst others, "on the bend marked with warning signs." Sign-types of warning traffic signs are included in another legal act, a specific regulation (Fig. 27.1). One cannot in an intelligible and relatively concise (non-redundant) manner reconstruct and communicate norm encoded in this provision (and other similar) excluding particular means of visual-nonlinguistic communication, in this case, traffic signs. Moreover, not only the sign-type (included in particular legal act) is needed, but also the actual, physical placement of a sign in a specific location (sign-realization). Without it a given norm would lose its meaning (it could not be followed or broken), and so the provision, in which norm is encoded could never be

[7] See, e.g., Article 7 paragraph 1 of the Polish Law of 20 June 1997—Road Traffic Law—Journal of Laws 1997, no. 98, item 602—reads as follows "Traffic signs and signals express warnings, prohibitions, orders or information"; see also Regulation of Ministers of Infrastructure and Internal Affairs and Administration of 31 July 2002 on the traffic signs and signals—Journal of Laws 2002, no. 170, item 1393—which accompanies Polish Road Traffic Law and includes sign-types of traffic signs and signals.

[8] See, e.g., Wagner (2006, pp. 311–312), who treats traffic signs as a kind of substitute for written linguistic expressions.

[9] See above, footnote 7.

Fig. 27.1 Warning traffic signs in Poland, according to Regulation of Ministers of Infrastructure and Internal Affairs and Administration of 31 July 2002 on the traffic signs and signals. Journal of Laws 2002, no. 170, item 1393. Due to the editorial requirements, signs in Fig. 27.1 are not presented in their original color palette. Polish warning signs have basically three colors: red

applied. Therefore, without a sign-type and actual, physical juxtaposition[10] of a sign (sign-realization), legal provisions, which refer to means of visual-nonlinguistic communication (not just traffic signs, but also, for example, traffic lights) become, in principle, irrelevant as incomplete, unintelligible, one that cannot be subject of conformity, or nonconformity, thus deprived the basis for their application.

Because of this, it must stressed once more, that means of visual-nonlinguistic communication present in some of the texts of legal acts seem to be not only used to illustrate some content. References to these graphics are also a very important part of the content of the particular legal provision that encode specific legal norm. One can venture an assertion, that these means may be treated as an integral part of certain provision and encoded norms. On this ground, it seems appropriate to dispense the more or less directly formulated claims of 'subsidiarity' of traffic signs—treating them only as illustrations, or an alternatives to written linguistic expressions.

Of course, this partial conclusion may be regarded by some as merely a statement of the obvious. One can even say that this proposal is simply a more complex version of too perfunctory, or even metaphorical statement of C.B. Nutting (1964, p. 781), that traffic signs "have their basic authorization in words", but "their impact (…) is not through words but through graphic or similar representations. When one sees an arrow bearing left he bears left. For all practical purposes the arrow is the law." Similar possible criticisms, however, still seem to be oblivious to significant problems for many of the issues discussed in broadly understood legal science, to which the above diagnosis of the role and characteristics of the traffic signs can lead. Therefore, one should present at least one of the more or less troublesome consequences of the occurrence in the texts of legal acts the means of visual-nonlinguistic communication, that are not merely to illustrate the ideas expressed by written utterances.

27.5 Inadequacy of a Concept of a Legal Norm as a Linguistic Utterance in a Context of Traffic Signs

In contemporary legal science there are still present various standpoints, according to which legal norm is a kind of linguistic utterance reconstructed from legal provisions, that is, another kind of linguistic utterances, but of very specific properties.[11] Adoption of such a fundamental assumption in the interpretation of the law is at least problematic when one considers the above-quoted provision from Polish Road

[10] Term used after Beck (1988, p. 11).

[11] E.g., in Polish legal science such an approach is adopted in the so-called derivative concept of interpretation of law, see Zieliński (2010, p. 14).

(border), yellow (background) and black (graphics on background, if there are any; see 'yield' sign—A-7). However, there are two exceptions from this 'three color rule'—graphics on background of signs A-19 and A-29 have, respectively, white and green elements)

Traffic Law, which prohibits "overtaking a moving motor vehicle on the road", amongst others, "on the bend marked with warning signs", or other similar examples. In order to reconstruct the legal norm, understood as a clear, self-evident, almost autonomous linguistic utterance, it would be necessary to literally put into words the whole catalogue of diverse warning traffic signs (Fig. 27.1),[12] to which the cited provision refers. Below, it is argued, that in this particular case (and other similar), it is impossible to realize the vision of legal norms (results of interpretation of law) as the objects of purely linguistic nature. Consequently, concepts of interpretation of law assuming such a vision of legal norms prove to be inadequate from the perspective of the whole legal order. Regulations of road traffic clearly show that in the set of all the texts of legal acts in a given time and place, one can find encoded norms, which cannot be accurately and intelligibly presented only with words. The result of the interpretation of certain provisions must be made not only with words but also with graphics. Of course, it is not to say, that messages conveyed by traffic signs cannot be verbalized, 'put into words'; that one cannot describe (in speech, writing, etc.) particular information or instruction presented by a given sign. Message communicated by a particular traffic sign can be verbalized.

What cannot be fully and unambiguously verbalized is the sign itself, but such a linguistic description seems necessary as well, if one wants to actually realize the cited vision of interpretation of law. One cannot only by means of linguistic utterances accurately and intelligibly describe the mere medium for the message, that is in given context, traffic sign. Such elements of traffic sign like its general shape, specific angles, particular pictograms[13] and ideograms (e.g., arrows, slashes)[14] are describable, but their accurate and intelligible linguistic description would have to be significantly long. Otherwise, not all relevant features and subtleties of a given sign would be included in prepared specification. Because of this, one can venture to say that the use of graphics such as traffic signs can be regarded as a way of avoiding or reducing wordiness in expressions of language of law.[15]

At this point, one may object the above statement that linguistic description of graphics like traffic signs is impossible; that, in given context, words are not

[12] In context of concept of legal norm as a linguistic utterance, the description of each sign individually, and not just general common characteristics of given kind of traffic signs (like their shape or color palette) would be necessary in order to, i.a., avoid a potential problem connected with false signs. Namely, someone can, for example, for a prank, produce and place at a given site a sign which looks like a kind of traffic sign (e.g., has the same shape, size and color palette), but is not included in the catalogue from a particular legal regulation. In such a situation, reconstructed legal norm, in which content relevant traffic signs are only generally specified, and not individually described, can be regarded as incorrect. Hypothetically, such insufficiently specified legal norm could be applied to the infinite number of false signs, which could be similar to traffic signs, but, legally speaking, are not traffic signs. Needless to say is that it could have the potential to cause negative situations for law's addressees and to be detrimental to legal certainty.

[13] E.g., cow in Polish sign A-18a—see, Fig. 27.1—represents not only cows, but also other livestock.

[14] On the pictograms and ideograms in traffic signs, see Kjørup (2004, p. 3506).

[15] Generally—without references to visual-nonlinguistic means of communication—on redundancy in legal provisions, see, Kłodawski (2012a, pp. 128–132; 2012b, pp. 160–162).

enough. Namely, one can say that it is still possible. Indeed, it is possible, but highly nonfunctional. The result of such a linguistic description can be extremely long and complex. Moreover, even the most elaborated description of a particular graphic can be still inaccurate (may not represent all of the features of the subject of specification) and unintelligible for someone who does not already know what sign is being linguistically specified.

However, this way of argumentation seems to be sound, it yet does not show that even if one is not concerned with accuracy and intelligibility, completely autonomous, self-evident linguistic description of a particular mean of visual communication, like traffic sign, is impossible from one particular reason. Color cannot be 'put into words'—it is indescribable in the sense of famous passages from *Principia Ethica*. One cannot accurately give through language (in speech or in writing) the exact specifics of given color and its particular shade she or he experiences to another subject, who did not experience the same visual stimulus. G.E. Moore (2002, p. 59) convinces that one "cannot, by any manner of means, explain to anyone who does not already know it, what [for example] yellow is" and adds (2002, p. 62) that "[w]e may try to define it [color], by describing its physical equivalent; we may state what kind of light-vibrations must stimulate the normal eye, in order that we may perceive it. But a moment's reflection is sufficient to shew that those light-vibrations are not themselves what we mean by yellow [or other color]. *They* are not what we perceive. Indeed we should never have been able to discover their existence, unless we had first been struck by the patent difference of quality between the different colors. The most we can be entitled to say of those vibrations is that they are what corresponds in space to the yellow which we actually perceive." Or, to put it way simpler—color has to be seen with one's own eyes, not be heard or read about. That is why words are not enough. Thus, the nonverbalizability of such a feature of traffic signs like their color (colors)—explicitly regarded as the most important one (Cygan 2007, p. 414)—seems to be the final argument in support of the following thesis. Concepts of interpretation of law, which assume solely linguistic form of results of interpretation (treating legal norms as linguistic utterances) are flawed with a specific form of inadequacy from perspective of whole legal order.

27.6 Final Remark

Of course, the above remarks are far from an extensive study on traffic signs. Even though they are generally concerned only with two particular issues ('integrality' instead of 'subsidiarity' of traffic signs and their nonverbalizable features in context of strictly linguistic accounts of results of interpretation of law—legal norms) they still seem to show that traffic signs have consequences for many issues discussed in broadly understood legal science, which are far from being trivial and insignificant. Considerations in this study can be regarded as a call to try to take a closer look by legal scholars at the means of visual-nonlinguistic communication used in law—not the ones created by legal academics or legal practitioners, but the ones created by the legislators themselves and included by them in texts of legal acts. Their role, relations with other elements of legal order and specific properties still seem to be overlooked and discussed not thoroughly enough by legal scholars. It is rather astonishing, especially when one tries to imagine such an important part of legal order as road traffic without traffic signs (vertical and horizontal), traffic lights or policemen's gestures. These visual means are of crucial importance, but, maybe because of their mundane character, they seem to be not sufficiently and thoroughly reflected upon. Fulfilling this gap seems to be a valuable enterprise, not only for purely theoretical discussions.

References

Beck, Anthony. 1988. Adjudication and the sign. *International Journal for the Semiotics of Law* 1:7–22.

Boehme-Neßler, Volker. 2011. *Pictorial law. Modern law and the power of pictures*. Berlin: Springer.

Brunschwig, Colette R. 2011. Multisensory law and legal informatics—a comparison of how these legal disciplines relate to visual law. In *Strukturierung der Juristischen Semantik—Structuring legal semantics. Mit einem Beitrag zum Multisensorischen Recht. With an essay on multisensory law. Festschrift für Erich Schweighofer. Festschrift for Erich Schweighofer*, eds. Anton Geist, Colette R. Brunschwig, Friedrich Lachmayer, and Günther Schefbeck, 573–667. Bern: Editions Weblaw.

Cygan, Jan. 2007. Rzut oka na semiotykę znaków drogowych [A look at the semiotics of traffic signs]. In Jan Cygan, *Papers in languages and linguistics. Selected writings published in English and Polish*, 409–414. Wrocław: Wydawnictwo Uniwersytetu Wrocławskiego.

Dudek, Michał. 2011. Paternalistic regulations expressed through means of visual communication of law? Contribution to another distinction of paternalistic legal regulations. In *Argumentation 2011. International conference on alternative methods of argumentation in law. Conference proceedings*, eds. Michał Araszkiewicz, Matěj Myška, Terezie Smejkalová, Jaromír Šavelka, and Martin Škop, 167–179. Brno: MUNI Press.

Kjørup, Søren. 2004. Pictograms. In *Semiotik. Semiotics. Ein Handbuch zu den zeichentheoretischen Grundlagen von Natur und Kultur. A handbook on the sign-theoretic foundations of nature and culture. 4. Teilband, Volume 4*, eds. Roland Posner, Klaus Robering, and Thomas A. Sebeok, 3504–3510. Berlin: Walter de Gruyter.

Kłodawski, Maciej. 2012a. Pleonazmy i analityzmy—wyrażenia redundantne pragmatycznie w języku prawnym [Pleonasms and analytisms—pragmatically redundant expressions in language of law]. In *Język współczesnego prawa* [*Language of modern law*], eds. Adam Niewiadomski and Ewa Sztymelska, 121–132. Warszawa: Lingua Iuris, Międzywydziałowe Koło Naukowe Kultury Języka Prawnego i Prawniczego, Uniwersytet Warszawski.

Kłodawski, Maciej. 2012b. Trzy ujęcia nadmiarowości w polskim prawie stanowionym [Three understandings of redundancy in Polish statutory law]. In *Rzeczywistość społeczna w badaniach młodych naukowców* [*Social reality in research of young scholars*], eds. Zbigniew Dziemianko and Wiesław Stach, 151–166. Poznań: Wydawnictwo Naukowe Wyższej Szkoły Handlu i Usług.

Moore, George Edward. 2002. *Principia ethica*. Revised edition. With the Preface to the Second Edition and other papers. Edited and with an introduction by Thomas Baldwin. Cambridge: Cambridge University Press.

Nöth, Winfried. 1995. *Handbook of semiotics*. Bloomington: Indiana University Press.

Nutting, Charles B. 1964. Graphic law. *American Bar Association Journal* 50:780–781.

Posner, Roland, ed. 1995. *Zeitschrift für Semiotik* 17 (Kommunikation im Straßenverkehr).

Radin, Max. 1930. Statutory interpretation. *Harvard Law Review* 43:863–885.

Studnicki, Franciszek. 1968. Znaki drogowe [Traffic signs]. *Studia Cywilistyczne* [*Private law studies*] 11:177–211. English version: Studnicki, Franciszek. 1970. Traffic signs. *Semiotica* 2:151–172.

Wagner, Anne. 2006. The rules of the road, a universal visual semiotics. *International Journal for the Semiotics of Law* 19:311–324.

Wahlgren, Peter. 2012. Visualization of the law. In *Legal stagings: The visualization, medialization and ritualization of law in language, literature, media, art and architecture*, eds. Kjell Å Modéer and Martin Sunnqvist, 19–24. Copenhagen: Museum Tusculanum Press.

Zieliński, Maciej. 2010. *Wykładnia prawa. Zasady, reguły, wskazówki* [*Interpretation of law. Principles, rules, tips*], 5th ed. Warszawa: LexisNexis Polska.

Part IV
Rules in Legal Logic and AI&Law

Chapter 28
In Defense of the Expressive Conception of Norms

Andrej Kristan

Abstract Against a background of the past three decades of critique directed towards the expressive conception of norms, the author argues first that paradigm expressivists can well account for facultative states of affairs without introducing inconsistencies into the normative system. He then shows how to describe the propositional content of a meta-rule without semanticizing the force indicator of object-rules. Finally, the author provides a formal reconstruction of conditional norms and of permissive closure, without admitting the conceptual autonomy of acts of permitting. The first parts of this chapter are of a clarifying nature, whereas the last parts purport to present an advancement in the expressivist theory.

Keywords Expressive conception of norms · Normative system · Inconsistency · Rules of preference · Permissive closure · Conditional norms

28.1 The Issue in Question

The objective of 'The Expressive Conception of Norms' (1981), co-authored by Carlos E. Alchourrón and Eugenio Bulygin, was "to explore [the] possibilities [of the expressive conception] in order to uncover its limitations and show the differences" between the expressive (or pragmatic) conception of norms and the hyletic (or semantic) one. In the end, they came to the conclusion that "the same conceptual distinctions appear in both conceptions, though, of course, expressed in different

Revus. Journal for Constitutional Theory and Philosophy of Law 22 (2014)

A. Kristan (✉)
Tarello Institute for Legal Philosophy, University of Genoa,
Via Balbi 30/18, Genoa 16126, Italy
e-mail: andrej.kristan@istitutotarello.org

Faculty of Law, University of Girona, Spain
e-mail: andrej.kristan@udg.edu

M. Araszkiewicz et al. (eds.), *Problems of Normativity, Rules and Rule-Following*,
Law and Philosophy Library 111, DOI 10.1007/978-3-319-09375-8_28

languages".[1] In the past three decades, strong objections have been raised against this claim.

In particular, it has been argued that the expressive conception in the form presented by Alchourrón and Bulygin cannot give an account of strong permissions or (at least) of facultative states of affairs (§ 28.2) without introducing a contradiction into the normative system (§ 28.3). In the alternative, the argument continues, their Expressivist cannot successfully describe the propositional content of the rules of preference we use to resolve conflicts of ambivalence, for example, without semanticizing the indicator of illocutionary (normative) force (§ 28.4). This, of course, would imply adopting the hyletic conception. Some also hold that the Expressivist of Alchourrón and Bulygin (1981) cannot account for a permissive rule of closure, if she does not grant the existence of a special normative act of permitting. And, what is more, critics say that the Expressivist is unable to give an adequate representation of conditional norms (§ 28.5). I intend to show that the opposite is true.[2] The following two sections of this chapter are of a clarifying nature and they merely formalise the views of Alchourrón and Bulygin. Most definitions introduced in there will not be used in the last two sections, which purport to make an advancement in the expressivist theory. They serve instead to avoid confusion and misunderstanding—which is, in my opinion, the reason for an important part of the critiques mentioned in this paragraph.

28.2 Fundamental Distinctions

The two major conceptions of norms mentioned in the introduction both assume that 'norm sentences' (that is, act-sentences expressing norms) can be analysed into (*a*) a descriptive component—hereinafter also called 'propositional content'—which is a description of an action or state of affairs resulting from an action, and (*b*) the normative operator. Where they differ is in how they view this latter, prescriptive component.[3]

The *hyletic conception* consists in regarding the normative operator

> as a sign in a *semantic capacity*, so that it contributes to the semantic meaning of norm sentences, in which case a norm becomes the semantic meaning of a norm sentence, in much the same way in which a proposition can be said to be the meaning of a descriptive sentence.[4]

[1] Alchourrón and Bulygin (1981, p. 389).

[2] Contra: Weinberger (1985 and 1986). Navarro and Redondo (1990a and 1990b). Calzetta and Sardo (2014). But even Alchourrón and Bulygin (1991, xxvii), who conceded one major point to Weinberger: the Expressivist's inability to give a satisfactoriy reconstruction of conditional norms. See also Caracciolo (1993, p. 507). I pressume that the reader is familiar with the notations of classical logic and axiomatic set theory. The notations in this paper follow the ISO standard 31–11 (with the addition of '$\Leftrightarrow$' for the biconditional connective). We will assume all the usual inventory of classical logic and axiomatic set theory (if not stated otherwise), plus three axioms which will be introduced later on.

[3] See Alchourrón and Bulygin (1981, pp. 384–385; and 1984, p. 454).

[4] Alchourrón and Bulygin (1984, p. 454). *A footnote is omitted.*

Therefore, a descriptive proposition '*p*' and a normative operator 'O' (for obligatory), 'Ph' (for prohibited) or 'P' (for permitted) both belong to the conceptual import of the norm.[5]

The *expressive conception*, on the other hand, takes the normative operator to be

> a sign in a *pragmatic capacity*, that has no semantic meaning whatsoever and so does not form part of the conceptual import of a norm sentence.[6]

Norms, as such, are speech acts and cannot be negated or combined by means of propositional connectives. For the purposes of the logical theory of systems of norms, the force of a norm shall thus be represented by the membership of its descriptive component in a set.

Relying on this set-theoretic approach introduced by Alchourrón and Bulygin (1981), an expressivist can account for conceptual distinctions between what is obligatory, prohibited and (strongly or weakly) permitted. This is what they say:

> 'It is obligatory that *p* in *A*' is true if and only if *p* is a member of the [normative] system Cn(*A*)—that is, if and only if *p* belongs to the consequences of [the axiomatic basis of the system, also called the commanded set] *A*. This means that *p* is obligatory in *A* if and only if *p* has been [explicitly] commanded or *p* is a consequence of the propositions that have been commanded. In this last case we say that [...] *p* is a *derived obligation.*[7]

Since the commanded set *A* is, by definition, a subset of the set Cn(*A*)

Def. 28.1 $A \subseteq \mathrm{Cn}(A)$

their Expressivist (hereinafter: *our* Expressivist) can distinguish derived obligations from explicit ones by the fact that *derived obligations* figure only as members of the set Cn(*A*), whereas the *explicit obligations* figure as members of both sets, the axiomatic basis *A* and the normative system Cn(*A*). Although a norm can thus belong to both these two sets, the concept of derived norms and that of explicit norms are mutually exclusive:

Def. 28.2 *Obligation* (O):

$\forall p(\mathrm{O}_A(p) \Leftrightarrow p \in \mathrm{Cn}(A))w$

For every *p*, 'It is obligatory in *A* that *p*' if and only if *p* belongs to the set Cn(*A*).

Def. 28.3 *Explicit obligation* (**O**):

$\forall p(\mathbf{O}_A(p) \Leftrightarrow p \in A)$

For every *p*, 'It is explicitly obligatory in *A* that *p*' if and only if *p* belongs to the set *A*.

[5] Alchourrón and Bulygin (1981, p. 384).

[6] Alchourrón and Bulygin (1984, p. 454). *A footnote is omitted.*

[7] Alchourrón and Bulygin (1981, p. 391). *Square brackets are mine.* The identification of the axiomatic basis of the system with the set *A*, and the normative system with the set Cn(*A*) is made on the same page.

Def. 28.4 *Derived obligation* ($\underline{\mathrm{O}}$):

$$\forall p(\underline{\mathrm{O}}_A(p) \Leftrightarrow p \in \mathrm{Cn}(A) \wedge p \notin A)$$

For every p, 'It is implicitly obligatory in A that p' if and only if p belongs to the set Cn(A), but not to its subset A.

In the same way, our Expressivist can define the concepts of prohibition and permission for normative propositions (or states of affairs).

A proposition (or state of affairs) p is prohibited in A if and only if the negation of p (or, shortly, not-p) has been explicitly commanded or is a derived prohibition, that is a consequence of the propositions that have been commanded. To put the same in terms of sets again: "p is prohibited in A if and only if the negation of p (not-p) is a member of the [normative] system Cn(A)",[8] or of both the normative system Cn(A) and its axiomatic basis, the commanded set A.

Just as in the case of obligations, our Expressivist can thus distinguish derived prohibitions from explicit ones by the fact that *derived prohibitions* only figure as members of the set Cn(A), whereas *explicit prohibitions* figure as members of both sets, the axiomatic basis A and the normative system Cn(A):

Def. 28.5 *Prohibition* (Ph):

$$\forall p(\mathrm{Ph}_A(p) \Leftrightarrow \neg p \in \mathrm{Cn}(A))$$

For every p, 'It is prohibited in A that p' if and only if not-p belongs to the set Cn(A).

Def. 28.6 *Explicit prohibition* (**Ph**):

$$\forall p(\mathbf{Ph}_A(p) \Leftrightarrow \neg p \in A)$$

For every p, 'It is explicitly prohibited in A that p' if and only if not-p belongs to the set A.

Def. 28.7 *Derived prohibition* ($\underline{\mathrm{Ph}}$):

$$\forall p(\underline{\mathrm{Ph}}_A(p) \Leftrightarrow \neg p \in \mathrm{Cn}(A) \wedge \neg p \notin A)$$

For every p, 'It is implicitly prohibited in A that p' if and only if not-p belongs to the set Cn(A), but not to its subset A.

A proposition (or state of affairs) p is permitted in A if and only if the negation of p (shortly, not-p) has not been explicitly commanded and is not a derived prohibition, that is a consequence of the propositions that have been commanded. In terms of sets: p is permitted in A if and only if "the negation of p (not-p) is not a member of the [normative] system Cn(A)".[9] Here is a formula:

Def. 28.8 *Permission* (P):

$$\forall p(\mathrm{P}_A(p) \Leftrightarrow \neg p \notin \mathrm{Cn}(A))$$

For every p, 'It is permitted in A that p' if and only if not-p does not belong to the set Cn(A).

[8] Alchourrón and Bulygin (1981, p. 392).

[9] Alchourrón and Bulygin (1981, p. 392).

This holds for both weak or negative permissions and strong or positive permissions (inasmuch as the sufficient conditions of the former are necessary conditions of the latter). But it does not let us distinguish between the two. So, how can the Expressivist of Alchourrón and Bulygin (1981) account for the difference between them? As we will now see, the authors faced this question directly.[10]

Say that Rex is to permit *p* by saying: "I hereby allow that *p*!" Our Expressivist can analyse this speech act in (at least) two ways.[11] She can describe this act either (*a*) as the act of rejection of not-*p* or (*b*) as the act of permitting *p*. I will call the former an Ockhamite reduction and the latter a Moritzian analysis.[12] In either case, the rejected or permitted content cannot be put in the commanded set *A*, and this for two obvious reasons:[13] (i) on the one hand, we could not distinguish permitted states of affairs from the obligatory ones and the prohibited ones if we were to put all these contents together; (ii) on the other hand, we would do nothing but introduce contradictory propositions into the normative system.

In order to avoid these problems, Alchourrón and Bulygin (1981) propose to form separate sets: the *derogandum* or the rejected set *D* in the first case, the permitted set *P* in the second.[14]

An expressivist allowing for the normative act of giving or granting permission—that is, a Moritzian expressivist—can distinguish the *strongly permitted* propositions or states of affairs from *weakly permitted* ones by the fact that only the former figure as members of the permitted set *P*:

Def. 28.9 *Strong permission* (**P**):

$$\forall p(\mathbf{P}_A(p) \Leftrightarrow p \in P)$$

For every *p*, 'It is strongly permitted in *A* that *p*' if and only if *p* is an element of the permitted set *P*.

Def. 28.10 *Weak permission* ($\underline{\mathrm{P}}$):

$$\forall p(\underline{\mathrm{P}}_A(p) \Leftrightarrow \neg p \notin \mathrm{Cn}(A) \wedge p \notin P)$$

For every *p*, 'It is weakly permitted in *A* that *p*' if and only if not-*p* does not belong to the set Cn(*A*) and *p* does not belong to the permitted set *P*.

On the alternative (Ockhamite) analysis of "I hereby allow that *p*!", our Expressivist can distinguish the *positively permitted* propositions or states of affairs from *negatively permitted* ones by the fact that only the negations of the former figure as members of the *derogandum* or the set of the explicitly rejected propositions:

[10] Alchourrón and Bulyin (1981, 393 ss and 406 ss).

[11] Alchourrón and Bulygin (1981, p. 406).

[12] Moritz (1963) is the expressivist who explicitly admitted the act of permitting as a particular normative speech act different in nature from that of commanding. Consequently, he also admitted two types of norms: imperative norms (establishing obligations and prohibitions) and permissive norms (conferring power and permissions). Ockham's name, on the other hand, is employed here to allude to the principle of parsimony used in problem-solving (also known as Ockham's razor).

[13] For the act of rejection, see Alchourrón and Bulygin (1981, p. 394). For the act of permitting, see Alchourrón and Bulygin (1981, p. 408).

[14] Alchourrón and Bulygin (1981, pp. 398 and 408).

Def. 28.11 *Positive permission* ($^{+}$P):

$\forall p(^{+}P_A(p) \Leftrightarrow \neg p \in D)$

For every *p*, 'It is positively permitted in *A* that *p*' if and only if not-*p* is an element of the rejected set *D*.

Def. 28.12 *Negative permission* ($^{-}$P):

$\forall p(^{-}P_A(p) \Leftrightarrow \neg p \notin \mathrm{Cn}(A) \wedge \neg p \notin D)$

For every *p*, 'It is negatively permitted in *A* that p' if and only if not-*p* belongs neither to the set Cn(*A*) nor to the rejected set *D*.

That having been said, one can find all of the fundamental distinctions (explicit and derived obligations, explicit and derived prohibitions, strongly and weakly permitted states of affairs) in the expressive conceptions of norms. Q.E.D.[15]

28.3 Facultativity Without Contradiction in the System

The fact of working with separate sets (the commanded set *A* on the one hand and, on the other, the permitted set *P* and/or the *derogandum D*) saves us from having contradictions in the system in case there is some facultative state of affairs. This can be demonstrated by answering the following question: What effects does an act of rejection produce on the normative system Cn(*A*),[16] and, alternatively,[17] what happens with *p* as a result of its being permitted?—Let us play with two examples.

First example Suppose Rex is to say "I hereby allow you to smoke!" and that *p* stands for <you, smoking>. Now, we can describe this act of Rex as the act of rejection of not-*p*. This is an Ockhamite reduction. If not-*p* is not a member of the normative system Cn(*A*) (smoking has not been explicitly prohibited nor is the prohibition of smoking a consequence of other propositions that have been commanded), then the Cn(*A*) stays unchanged. However, if not-*p* were promulgated later, or if it were a consequence of some propositions commanded in the future, this fact would give rise to a 'conflict of ambivalence' between Cn(*A*) and *D*,[18] which is a special case of what I would call a conflict of non-cotenability:

Def. 28.13 $\exists x\,(x \in \mathrm{Cn}(A) \wedge x \in D)$

There is at least one *x* such that *x* belongs to the set Cn(*A*) and *x* belongs to the set *D*.

Def. 28.14 $\mathrm{Cn}(A) \cap D = \{x \mid x \in \mathrm{Cn}(A) \wedge x \in D\} \neq \{\varnothing\}$

The intersection of Cn(*A*) with *D* is not an empty set.

[15] Lat. *Quod erat demonstrandum.* (Eng. That which was to be demonstrated.)

[16] Alchourrón and Bulygin (1981, p. 399).

[17] Alchourrón and Bulygin (1981, p. 407).

[18] See Alchourrón and Bulygin (1981, p. 396 and 399).

Def. 28.15 $\mathrm{Cn}(A) \setminus D = \{x \mid x \in \mathrm{Cn}(A) \wedge x \notin D\} \neq \mathrm{Cn}(A)$

The difference between Cn(*A*) and *D*—that is, the set of elements which belong to Cn(*A*) but not to *D*—is not equal to Cn(*A*).

If we want a normative system capable of guiding behavior effectively, such a conflict needs to be resolved by the application of some rule of preference,[19] just as it needs to be resolved when the explicitly rejected proposition is already a member of the normative system Cn(*A*).

If the explicitly rejected proposition not-*p* is a member of the normative system Cn(*A*)—that is, if smoking has been prohibited either explicitly or as a consequence of other explicitly commanded propositions before Rex uttered "I hereby allow you to smoke!"—then we have a conflict of ambivalence and need some rule of preference to resolve it. If it is resolved in favor of rejection, then the proposition not-*p* must be eliminated by subtraction from the commanded set *A* and from the normative system Cn(*A*). This subtraction henceforth makes the (normative) proposition $O_A(\neg p)$ false. If the conflict is resolved in favor of promulgation, then the proposition not-*p* must be subtracted from the rejected set *D*.

On the alternative (Moritzian) analysis of "I hereby allow you to smoke!", we can describe this act of Rex as an act of permitting. The explicitly permitted proposition *p* is thus added to the permitted set *P* and another conflict of non-cotenability takes place between Cn(*A*) and *P* (it is slightly different from the one between Cn(*A*) and *D*):

Def. 28.16 $\exists x\,(x \in \mathrm{Cn}(A) \wedge \neg x \in P)$

There is a least one *x* such that *x* belongs to Cn(*A*) and not-*x* belongs to *P*.

Def. 28.17 $\mathrm{Cn}(A) \cap \{x \mid \neg x \in P\} = \{x \mid x \in \mathrm{Cn}(A) \wedge \neg x \in P\} \neq \{\varnothing\}$

The intersection of Cn(*A*) with the set of negations of the elements of *P* is not an empty set.

Def. 28.18 $\{x \mid x \in \mathrm{Cn}(A) \wedge \neg x \notin P\} \neq \mathrm{Cn}(A)$

The set of the elements of Cn(*A*) the negations of which do not belong to *P*—is not Cn(*A*).

In order to resolve such a conflict, Alchourrón and Bulygin (1981) invite us to apply the rules of preference and subtract either *p* from the permitted set *P*—if the preference is given to prohibition—or the negation of *p* from *A* and Cn(*A*), if the preference is given to permission.[20] In this respect, the permission of *p* gives rise to the same operation as the rejection of not-*p*.

Second example Suppose that Rex says also "I hereby allow you not to smoke!" To wit, there are two authoritative pronouncements: "I hereby allow you to smoke!" and "I hereby allow you not to smoke!" Following Weinberger (1985), some fear that this would bring about a contradiction in the normative system Cn(*A*).[21] However, if we follow Alchourrón and Bulygin (1981) there is no reason for fear.

[19] Alchourrón and Bulygin (1981, p. 397).

[20] Alchourrón and Bulygin (1981, p. 408).

[21] See Weinberger (1985, 173 s). Most recently, also Calzetta and Sardo (2014, § 2.1.1).

As a result of the second pronouncement of Rex, the Expressivist of Alchourrón and Bulygin (1981) will either add *p* to the *derogandum D* or not-*p* to the permitted set *P*. On the first analysis, you will now find in the *derogandum D* both not-*p* (because of the first normative act of Rex) and *p* (because of the second normative act of Rex); however, neither *p* nor not-*p* will be in the normative system Cn(*A*). On the second analysis, the permitted set *P* is composed of two elements: *p* and not-*p*, but again none of these two elements is part of the normative system Cn(*A*). In either way, the mere fact that both smoking and not smoking is permitted in the Commonwealth of Rex generates no contradiction in the normative system Cn(*A*) as described by our Expressivist.[22] Q.E.D.

Some may, however, be of the opinion that my response does not do the trick, because we still have *p* and not-*p* in the derogated set *D*. Navarro and Redondo (1990a) saw that as a problem some 20 years ago. Their argument (in different words) was this:[23] From *p* and not-*p* anything follows, meaning that the set of all the logical consequences of *D*, say Cn(*D*), is all-inclusive. Consequently, everything must be eliminated by subtraction from the commanded set *A* and the normative system Cn(*A*). That would leave us with empty sets *A* and Cn(*A*), which is counter-intuitive and, at any rate, highly problematic.

Indeed, the conclusion is sound but the reasoning went way too far in my opinion. The Expressivist of Alchourrón and Bulygin (1981) has no need to operate with Cn(*D*) as the set of all the logical consequences of *D*. In order to know what to eliminate from *A* and Cn(*A*), our Expressivist has to identify the "propositions and sets of propositions that imply some of the propositions belonging to [*D*]".[24] In other words: she needs to operate with propositions and sets of which the elements of *D* are a logical consequence, and not *vice versa*.[25] The problem, therefore, does not exist.

I know that, intuitively, some will find it hard to buy the claim that there is *in general* no need for our Expressivist to operate with Cn(*D*) or Cn(*P*). But I am unaware of any interesting challenge, and as long as they do not provide one, only few things can be added.

One should think of two rejections, or of two permissions, that—by ways of logical inference—give rise to a third one. However, the examples of the kind usually provided by the skeptics are inadequate. (I conjecture this is because they are influenced by the Hyleticist worldview.)[26] Suppose the following two rules are promulgated in the Commonwealth of Rex:

(R_1) "If φ-ing is permitted, then ψ-ing is permitted."
(R_2) "φ-ing is permitted."

[22] Following Alchourrón and Bulygin (1981, p. 391), the normative system has been defined as Cn(*A*) *supra* in Sect. 28.2.

[23] See Navarro and Redondo (1990a, pp. 251 and 254).

[24] Alchourrón and Bulygin (1981, p. 399).

[25] See already Alchourrón and Bulygin (1979, pp. 91–92).

[26] See, at least, Alchourrón and Bulygin (1979, Chap. 8), where formal representations of conditional norms in the expressive conception are clearly put in the Hyleticist key: If *p*, then [commanded] *q*. We will face this problem *infra* in Sect. 28.5.

These two rules do give rise to:

(R_3) ψ-ing is permitted.

But—unlike the Hyleticist—our Expressivist would analyze R_1 as a command, and not as a permission. The propositional content of R_1 (which is yet to be precised, but for the present purposes pretend it were: if *p*, then *q*) will, therefore, appear in the axiomatic basis *A*.[27] The propositional content of R_2 (that is, *p*) will appear in the permitted set *P* (or, in the Ockhamite alternative, its negation will appear in the *derogandum D*). The introduction of *q* in *P* (or the introduction of not-*q* in *D*) is thus not a logical consequence of two elements of *P* (or two elements of *D*); it is a logical consequence of an element of *A* and an element of *P* (or *D*). This example therefore cannot show the need to operate with Cn(*P*) or Cn(*D*) in order to explain the introduction of *q* in *P* (or that of not-*q* in *D*).

It is important to stress at this point that the introduction of a propositional content to a set, or its elimination thereof, is just a metaphor. If a content does not belong to a certain set, it never starts belonging to it. And if it belongs to a certain set, it never ceases to belong to it.[28] What really happens is the performance of a normative speech act (commanding, rejecting; permitting if you will), which is an empirical fact. Each time a new fact occurs, we get new descriptions of the world in terms of sets. Thus in the course of time we have not one, but a sequence of sets ($A_1, A_2, \ldots A_n$; Cn(A_1), Cn(A_2), … Cn(A_n); $D_1, D_2, \ldots D_n$; $P_1, P_2, \ldots P_n$). Following this proposal of Alchourrón and Bulygin (1981), a consecutive set *A*, *D* or *P* may always be defined in relation with the previous set of the same sort *and* the propositional content which is the object of the newly occurred speech act. If we use the signs '!', '¡' and '*' to indicate the kind of normative speech act performed (command, rejection or permission), and '*p*' for its propositional content, then we can represent as follows three (additional) axioms of the expressivist theory, which have not been explicitly formulated by the authors:

Axiom 1 $\forall p\big((!p \Rightarrow (A_n = \{p\} \cup A_{n-1}) \wedge (D_n = D_{n-1}) \wedge (P_n = P_{n-1})\big)\big)$

For every *p*, if *p* has just been commanded, then the new set A_n consists of *p* and all the elements of the previous set A_{n-1}, whereas the new sets D_n and P_n equal the previous sets D_{n-1} and P_{n-1}, respectively.

Axiom 2 $\forall p\big(¡p \Rightarrow (D_n = \{p\} \cup D_{n-1}) \wedge (A_n = A_{n-1}) \wedge (P_n = P_{n-1})\big)$

For every *p*, if *p* has just been rejected, then the new set D_n consists of *p* and all the elements of the previous set D_{n-1}, whereas the new sets A_n and P_n equal the previous sets A_{n-1} and P_{n-1}, respectively.

Axiom 3 $\forall p\big((*p \Rightarrow (P_n = \{p\} \cup P_{n-1}) \wedge (A_n = A_{n-1}) \wedge (D_n = D_{n-1})\big)\big)$

For every *p*, if *p* has just been permitted, then the new set P_n consists of *p* and all the elements of the previous set P_{n-1}, whereas the new sets A_n and D_n equal the previous sets A_{n-1} and D_{n-1}, respectively.

[27] For the purpose of the present section, there is no need for a more detailed reconstruction of the propositional content of conditional norms. As announced above, I will return to this point later.

[28] See Alchourrón and Bulygin (1981, p. 395).

The normative system $\mathrm{Cn}(A_n)$, on the other hand, is just the set of all the logical consequences of A_n—exactly as it was explicitly defined by Alchourrón and Bulygin.[29]

28.4 The Propositional Content of Rules About Rules

It is natural to consider rules of preference as meta-rules. The question, then, is how can our Expressivist represent the propositional content of such a meta-rule without semanticizing the indicators of illocutionary (normative) force of the object-rules (*cf.* Weinberger 1985, p. 175; Calzetta and Sardo 2014, § 2.2)?—An elegant solution is to represent the propositional content of a meta-rule as operating not on object-rules, but on sets containing the (explicit or implicit) propositional contents thereof. These sets are the commanded set A_n, the derogated set D_n, the permitted set P_n, and the normative system $\mathrm{Cn}(A_n)$.

The propositional content, say w, of the rule of preference ($!w$) usually known as *lex posterior priori derogat* [30] could thus be represented (see Def. 28.19) as a conjunction of conditionals to the effect that consecutive sets do not include those propositional contents of older norm sentences (or the consequences thereof) which in relation with the newer ones bring about some conflict:[31]

Def. 28.19 The propositional content of *lex posterior* (w).

$$\begin{aligned}
&\forall x\left[(x \notin D_{n-1} \wedge x \in D_n) \vee (\neg x \notin P_{n-1} \wedge \neg x \in P_n) \wedge (x \in \mathrm{Cn}(A_{n-1}) \wedge x \in \mathrm{Cn}(A_n))\right.\\
&\quad\left.\Rightarrow (D_{n+1} = D_n) \vee (P_{n+1} = P_n) \wedge (\mathrm{Cn}(A_{n+1}) = \mathrm{Cn}(A_n) \setminus \{x\}) \wedge (A_{n+1} = A_n \setminus \{x\})\right]\\
&\wedge \left[(x \in D_{n-1} \wedge x \in D_n) \vee (\neg x \in P_{n-1} \wedge \neg x \in P_n) \wedge (x \notin \mathrm{Cn}(A_{n-1}) \wedge x \in \mathrm{Cn}(A_n))\right.\\
&\quad\left.\Rightarrow (D_{n+1} = (D_n \setminus \{x\})) \vee (P_{n+1} = (P_n \setminus \{\neg x\})) \wedge (\mathrm{Cn}(A_{n+1}) = \mathrm{Cn}(A_n)) \wedge (A_{n+1} = A_n)\right]\\
&\wedge \left[(x \notin \mathrm{Cn}(A_{n-1}) \wedge x \in \mathrm{Cn}(A_n)) \wedge (\neg x \in \mathrm{Cn}(A_{n-1}) \wedge \neg x \in \mathrm{Cn}(A_n))\right.\\
&\quad\left.\Rightarrow (\mathrm{Cn}(A_{n+1}) = (\mathrm{Cn}(A_n) \setminus \{\neg x\}) \wedge (A_{n+1} = (A_n \setminus \{\neg x\})))\right]\\
&\wedge \left[((x \in \mathrm{Cn}(A_{n-1}) \wedge x \in \mathrm{Cn}(A_n)) \wedge (\neg x \notin \mathrm{Cn}(A_{n-1}) \wedge (\neg x \in \mathrm{Cn}(A_n))\right.\\
&\quad\left.\Rightarrow (\mathrm{Cn}(A_{n+1}) = (\mathrm{Cn}(A_n) \setminus \{x\}) \wedge (A_{n+1} = (A_n \setminus \{x\}))\right]
\end{aligned}$$

For every x, if x has just been rejected (or not-x has just been permitted), while being a member of the normative system $\mathrm{Cn}(A)$, then the new sets A and $\mathrm{Cn}(A)$ are composed of all the elements of the previous ones, except x, whereas the new set D (or the new set P) equals the previous one;

[29] See *supra* the definition 28.1 in Sect. 28.2. See also Alchourrón and Bulygin (1981, p. 391).

[30] Following the terminology of Alchourrón and Bulygin (1981, p. 397), whose Expressivist distinguishes what they call *lex posterior* from what they call *auctoritas posterior*, this rule would correspond to *lex posterior & auctoritas posterior*. I decided to give a unitary formal presentation for the sake of simplicity, though the two rules might easily be separated.

[31] The representation works both for those expressivists who admit the existence of a special act of permitting and for those who do not. In case of the latter, the set P_n will simply be an empty set.

—and if x has just been commanded, while being a member of the set D (or not-x a member of the set P), then the new set D is composed of all the elements of the previous one, except x (or the new set P is composed of all the elements of the previous one, except not-x), whereas the new sets A and Cn(A) equal the previous ones;
—and if x has just become a member of the normative system, while not-x is also a member of the normative system, then the new sets A and Cn(A) are composed of all the elements of the previous ones, except not-x;
—and if not-x has just become a member of the normative system, while x is also a member of the normative system, then the new sets A and Cn(A) are composed of all the elements of the previous ones, except x.

When Rex issues $!w$, the proposition w becomes a member of the commanded set A. As we will see, this assures the preference of a posterior normative act (irrespective of whether it is a rejection or a promulgation, or even a permission if you accept the Moritzian variety of the expressive conception) over the anterior ones.

Take, for example, that Rex begins his rule with the system of his late King-father still in place in which there is one (and only one) prohibition ($\neg p$):

(t1) "Thou shall not touch the property of the King!"

Rex thinks to himself: This is nice! I like being king and will rule just like my father. But I want to be able to change any rule!—Consulting with the crown lawyer, Rex decides to promulgate a rule of preference called *lex posterior* ($!w$):

(t2) "Lex posterior priori derogat!"

To see if the system really works as he wanted, Rex decides to introduce communism and proclaims ¡($\neg p$) or $*p$:

(t3) "What is mine is yours, dear brothers!"

This last decision does not really help either the economy of the Commonwealth of Rex or the social relations therein and so Rex soon decides to reestablish *dominium plenum*$!(\neg p)$:

(t4) "Thou shall not covet your neighbor's house. You shall not covet your neighbor's wife, or his manservant or maidservant, his ox or donkey, or anything that belongs to your neighbor!"

Of course, these translations of natural language expressions into p and not-p are oversimplified. But if the above-given formal representation of w is correct, we should be able to show what is important: first, that the legislative intervention ¡($\neg p$) at (t3) eliminated not-p from the normative system Cn(A); and, second, that the intervention $!(\neg p)$ at (t4) reintroduced not-p into the system Cn(A).

At (t1) we have the following sets:

$$\text{(Ockhamite analysis) } A_1 = \{\neg p\}, D_1 = \{\varnothing\}$$

$$\text{(Moritzian analysis) } A_1 = \{\neg p\}, D_1 = \{\varnothing\}, P_1 = \{\varnothing\}$$

Our normative system Cn(A_1) contains all the logical consequences of not-*p*.

As a result of the first promulgation of Rex, !*w* at (t2), we get:

$$\text{(Ockhamite analysis) } A_2 = \{\neg p, w\}, D_2 = \{\varnothing\}$$
$$\text{(Moritzian analysis) } A_2 = \{\neg p, w\}, D_2 = \{\varnothing\}, P_2 = \{\varnothing\}$$

and the normative system Cn(A_2) contains all the logical consequences of not-*p* and *w*.

The second lex of Rex at (t3) may be represented as ¡($\neg p$) or, alternatively, as **p*. This legislative intervention brings about:

$$\text{(Ockhamite analysis) } A_3 = \{\neg p, w\}, D_3 = \{\neg p\}$$
$$\text{(Moritzian analysis) } A_3 = \{\neg p, w\}, D_3 = \{\varnothing\}, P_3 = \{p\}$$

and the normative system Cn(A_3) with all the logical consequences of not-*p* and *w*. As you can see, we have a conflict of ambivalence toward *p*,[32] for the intersection of Cn(A_3) and D_3, or the set of elements which belong both to Cn(A_3) and D_3, is $\{\neg p\}$ and not an empty set.

I will make no more representations with the elements of *P* instead of *D* from now on, for if we manage to give a successful description of how rules of preference function, without admitting the existence of a special normative act of permitting, then we could certainly be successful in the other case (that is, of the Moritzian analysis) as well. That having been said, we can move on and demonstrate how the presence of *w* in the commanded set *A* actually resolves the conflict.

On the basis of *w*, the conflict is resolved in favor of permitted *p*, which gives us these sets:

$$\text{(Ockhamite analysis) } A_4 = \{w\}, D_4 = \{\neg p\}$$

and the normative system Cn(A_4) with all the logical consequences of *w* and without not-*p* or its logical consequences.

Here is a formal proof for Cn(A_4):

Proof 1

1. $A_2 = \{\neg p\}$	*description of facts*
2. $A_3 = \{\neg p, w\}$	*description of facts*
3. $A_i \subseteq \mathrm{Cn}(A_i)$	*by* (Def. 28.1) *of* Cn(*A*)
4. $\neg p \in \mathrm{Cn}(A_2) \wedge \neg p \in \mathrm{Cn}(A_3)$	1, 2; *conjunction*; 3
5. $D_2 = \{\varnothing\}$	*description of facts*
6. $D_3 = \{\neg p\}$	*description of facts*
7. $\neg p \notin D_2 \wedge \neg p \in D_3$	5, 6; *conjunction*

[32] There is a conflict of ambivalence (Cn(*A*), *D*), when there is at least one *x* such that *x* belongs to the set Cn(*A*) and *x* belongs to the set *D*. The intersection of Cn(*A*) with *D* is thus not an empty set. See *supra* the definitions 28.13 and 28.14 in Sect. 28.3.1.

$$
\begin{aligned}
8.\ \forall x\Big[&(x \notin D_{n-1} \wedge x \in D_n) \vee (\neg x \notin P_{n-1} \wedge \neg x \in P_n) \wedge (x \in \mathrm{Cn}(A_{n-1}) \wedge x \in \mathrm{Cn}(A_n)) \\
&\Rightarrow (D_{n+1} = D_n) \vee (P_{n+1} = P_n) \wedge (\mathrm{Cn}(A_{n+1}) = \mathrm{Cn}(A_n) \setminus \{x\}) \wedge (A_{n+1} = A_n \setminus \{x\})\Big] \\
&\wedge \Big[(x \in D_{n-1} \wedge x \in D_n) \vee (\neg x \in P_{n-1} \wedge \neg x \in P_n) \wedge (x \notin \mathrm{Cn}(A_{n-1}) \wedge x \in \mathrm{Cn}(A_n)) \\
&\Rightarrow (D_{n+1} = (D_n \setminus \{x\})) \vee (P_{n+1} = (P_n \setminus \{\neg x\})) \wedge (\mathrm{Cn}(A_{n+1}) = \mathrm{Cn}(A_n)) \wedge (A_{n+1} = A_n)\Big] \\
&\wedge \Big[(x \notin \mathrm{Cn}(A_{n-1}) \wedge x \in \mathrm{Cn}(A_n)) \wedge (\neg x \in \mathrm{Cn}(A_{n-1}) \wedge \neg x \in \mathrm{Cn}(A_n)) \\
&\Rightarrow (\mathrm{Cn}(A_{n+1}) = (\mathrm{Cn}(A_n) \setminus \{\neg x\}) \wedge (A_{n+1} = (A_n \setminus \{\neg x\}))))\Big] \\
&\wedge \Big[((x \in \mathrm{Cn}(A_{n-1}) \wedge x \in Cn(A_n)) \wedge (\neg x \notin \mathrm{Cn}(A_{n-1}) \wedge (\neg x \in \mathrm{Cn}(A_n)) \\
&\Rightarrow (\mathrm{Cn}(A_{n+1}) = (\mathrm{Cn}(A_n) \setminus \{x\}) \wedge (A_{n+1} = (A_n \setminus \{x\}))\Big]
\end{aligned}
$$

2; *substitution of w by* (def. 28.19)

$$
\begin{aligned}
9.\ &(\neg p \notin D_2 \wedge \neg p \in D_3) \wedge (\neg p \in \mathrm{Cn}(A_2) \wedge \neg p \in \mathrm{Cn}(A_3)) \\
&\Rightarrow (\mathrm{Cn}(A_4) = (\mathrm{Cn}(A_3) \setminus \{\neg p\}))
\end{aligned}
$$

8; *simplification, determination of the index* $(n = 3)$ *and the variable* $(x = \neg p)$

$.:\ \mathrm{Cn}(A_4) = (\mathrm{Cn}(A_3) \setminus \{\neg p\})$ 9, 7, 4; *modus ponens*

Formal proofs for A_4 and D_4 reiterate the one for Cn(A_4) from steps 1 to 8; at this point, I skip the obvious step 9 to reach the conclusions $(D_4 = D_3 = \{\neg p\},\ and\ A_4 = (A_3 \setminus \{\neg p\}) = \{w\})$ by *modus ponens*. The argument for the Morizian analysis $(A_4 = \{w\}, D_4 = \{\varnothing\}, P_4 = \{p\})$ is very similar and also simple.

As one may see, the presence of w in the commanded set A has the expected result: it assured priority to the second lex of Rex from (t3) as a posterior normative act over the prior lex of his King-father from (t1). We could go on to demonstrate that w assures the desired result also in the case of the subsequent legislative intervention of Rex at (t4), but that seems unnecessary—for now anyone can do it for themselves, by adopting (roughly) the same argument. This would show, first, that the promulgation of not-p at (t4) brings about a conflict of ambivalence; then, you would see that on the basis of *lex posterior* (w) the conflict is resolved in favor (this time) of the prohibition not-p—leaving us with sets:

(Ockhamite analysis) $A_6 = \{w, \neg p\}, D_6 = \{\varnothing\}$

and the normative system Cn(A_6) with all the logical consequences of w and not-p.

At the end we can thus conclude that our Expressivist can well describe the functioning of *lex posterior* without semanticizing the indicators of (normative) force. Q.E.D.

In a comment to the preprint of this text, Žarnić and Bašić (2014, § 2.2) showed that the Def. 28.19 of *lex posterior* works only for a limited number of special cases (such as our example) where the initial norm-set is independent, that is, where no member of the set is entailed by the rest. I happily concede their point and recognize my mistake. (Alchourrón and Bulygin themselves were much more careful than me in explaining the consequences of an act of rejection, as can be observed also from the citation accompanied by footnote 24 above.)—If x has just been rejected (or not-x has just been permitted), while being a member of the normative system Cn(A), then the operation of derogation results in new sets A and Cn(A) which are—differently from what has been stated in the Def. 28.19—maximal subsets of the previous ones that do not entail x. This means that "the operation of derogation is subdetermined since, typically, there will be more than one maximal subset" of both A and Cn(A) not entailing x. In such cases, the norm-applier will be forced to choose between these maximal subsets—and play the norm-giver's role. The representation of the operation therefore "needs an additional choice operator γ" to pick only one of them.[33] But since the exact propositional content of *lex posterior* is not in the scope of this contribution, I will not amend the Def. 28.19 as needed and will leave that for some later occasion (or to the interested reader, here and now).

For the sake of the clarity of demonstration—and brevity—I have assumed that *lex posterior* is the only rule of preference in the Commonwealth of Rex. Nonetheless, I owe you at least a hint to the solution for the rule of preference *lex superior derogat inferiori* (!s):[34] we shall assume that the promulgated and rejected (or permitted) contents go to different subsets of the sets A and D (or P)—for example, to Aa, Ab, Ac, etc.—depending on the hierarchical level (a, b, c, etc.) of the normative authority which performs the normative act in question. Making use of these subsets, one should be able to formulate the propositional content s of *lex superior* (!s) with no trouble.

We can now move on to deal with one final hurdle.

28.5 The Rule of Closure and Other Conditional Norms

Before we conclude with a possible representation of conditional norms, we shall tackle the problem of the rule of closure.

28.5.1 A Permissive Closure Needs No Permissive Rule

It had often been discussed and is now widely acknowledged[35] that the 'permissive rule of closure'—namely, "what is not prohibited is permitted"—is the only closing rule that does not lead to inconsistencies in the normative system.[36] Calzetta

[33] Žarnić and Bašić (2014, § 2.2). See also Alchourrón and Bulygin (1981, p. 400).

[34] The third rule of preference, *lex specialis*, does not raise the concerns expressed by Weinberger (1985) and Calzetta and Sardo (2014). See also Alchourrón and Bulygin (1979, p. 86).

[35] For discussion see at least Alchourrón and Bulygin (1971, Chap. 7 and the references thereof).

[36] With one practically irrelevant exception of a normative system where it can be inferred that p is not facultative ($\neg \mathrm{I}p = \neg(\mathrm{P}p \wedge \mathrm{P}\neg p)$). "As p is not forbidden, we may infer by means of the

and Sardo (2014) raise this claim against the Ockhamite variety of the expressive conception which denies the existence of permissive norms (or acts of permitting).[37] But the claim is false or, at best, inapplicable and misleading.

It is one thing to say (*a*) that in order to preserve consistency, a normative system can be completed with a closing rule only if this rule is to the effect that what is not prohibited is permitted. It is quite another thing to say that (*b*) only a permissive rule of closure will have this permissive effect, character or normative function. Whereas (*a*) is true, but does not bite (the Ockhamite Expressivist also admits the existence of permitted states of affairs),[38] (*b*) is false, for a rejection of prohibition of *p* has that same permissive function as a permission of *p*. Here is a test:

Suppose that Rex decides to close the system of the Commonwealth and issues the following rule of permissive closure (!*c*):[39]

(t5) "What is not prohibited is permitted!"

The propositional content *c*, which thus becomes an element of *A*, could be formalized as follows:

Def. 28.20 *Rule of permissive closure* (c):
$\forall x\,(\neg x \notin \mathrm{Cn}(A_n) \Rightarrow \neg x \in D_{n+1})$
For every *x*, if *x* is not prohibited—that is, if not-*x* does not belong to the normative system $\mathrm{Cn}(A_n)$—then not-*x* belongs to the derogated set D_{n+1}.

Put in this form, !*c* achieves the exactly desired results of a permissive closure: (i) It has no (direct) effect on private addressees of norms; the introduction of such a closing rule does not affect deontic qualifications of individual conduct. (ii) By making *p* positively permitted,!*c* eliminates normative gaps and, therefore, judicial discretion in cases of *p* (relative to the normative system of *A*). (iii) As the addition of not-*p* to the derogated set *D* is conditional, future acts of explicit rejection do not lose their relevance, as we will shortly see, and (iv) may even be made by authorities subordinated to the one that promulgated *c*.

Please bear with the logical exercise for one final simulation, especially if you are skeptical about my claims *sub* (iii) and (iv). Otherwise, just skip the next four paragraphs.

Suppose that the axiomatic basis A_1 is composed of constitutional norms *a*, *c*, *s*, *w* and that $\neg x \notin \mathrm{Cn}(A_1)$. Therefore, $\neg x \notin D_2$ on the basis of the (conditional) rule

---

[permissive] rule of closure that *p* is permitted. But as $\neg p$ is not forbidden either, the permission of $\neg p$ may also be inferred. However, the joint permission of *p* and $\neg p$ is incompatible with $\neg[\mathrm{I}]p$, so that the [permissive] rule of closure has introduced an inconsistency." Alchourrón and Bulygin (1971, 140, n. 4).

[37] See Calzetta and Sardo (2014, § 2.1.2).

[38] Alchourrón and Bulygin (1981, p. 406).

[39] In order to avoid the ambiguity of the expression 'permissive rule of closure'—in which the adjective 'permissive' may be used to specify the function of the rule, the form of the rule, or both—, I choose to use the term in question only in the second sense (fixing the reference to the form), and express the first sense (that of the function) with the 'rule of permissive closure.'

of permissive closure c (saying that if x is not prohibited in $\mathrm{Cn}(A_n)$, then not-x belongs to D_{n+1}).[40] Moreover, $A_1=A_2$ and $\neg x \notin \mathrm{Cn}(A_2)$. This means that x is positively permitted.[41]

Now, imagine two different scenarios. On the first scenario, a town council issues b with the content $(a \Rightarrow \neg x)$. As a consequence of b, we get $A_3=\{a, b, c, s, w\}$ and $\neg x \in \mathrm{Cn}(A_3)$—which brings about a conflict of ambivalence between $\mathrm{Cn}(A_3)$ and D_3 $(=D_2)$. On the basis of *lex posterior* (w),[42] the conflict is resolved so that $D_4=(D_3\backslash\neg x)$, whereas $A_4=A_3$ and $\neg x \in \mathrm{Cn}(A_4)$. In other words: x gets prohibited as a consequence of the town council provision b, even though it had been hitherto positively permitted on the basis of the conditional (constitutional) rule of permissive closure c. Note that *lex superior* (s) played no role in the resolution of our conflict of norms.

Now, think of another scenario in which not-x is rejected (unconditionally) by the legislator before the town council issues b. Consequently, $\neg x \in D_3$, whereas $A_3=A_2=A_1$ and $\neg x \notin \mathrm{Cn}(A_3)$. This, too, means that x is positively permitted. However, the consequences of the provision b issued later by the town council will be quite different in this case. The conflict of ambivalence will now be resolved on the basis of *lex superior* (s) and not on that of *lex posterior* (w). The preference will be given to the rejection of not-x. As a consequence, x will not be prohibited but will remain positively permitted.

The two simulations demonstrate: (iii) that future acts of explicit rejection do not lose their relevance under the rule of permissive closure c with the above given formalisation—just as they actually do not lose it in legal systems with permissive closure; and (iv) that future acts of explicit rejection may well be made by authorities subordinated to the one that promulgated c.

Here is not the place to discuss the four characteristics of a permissive closure just described. The point is elsewhere. We have shown that the permissive function of the closing rule to the effect that what is not prohibited is permitted may well be represented without granting the existence of a special illocutionary (normative) act of permitting. Q.E.D.

28.5.2 Conditional Norms

What is more, our Ockhamite Expressivist has already exposed by now all the necessary tools to reconstruct conditional norms, including this one:[43]

(R_4) "If and only if it is raining, you ought not to leave the house!"

Whereas the Hyleticist would represent R_4 as a conditional imperative, our Expressivist shall make use of one further set—namely, F, the set of relevant facts and

[40] See *supra* the definition 28.20 in this section.

[41] For every p, 'It is positively permitted in A that p' if and only if not-p is an element of the rejected set D. See *supra* the definition 28.11 in Sect. 28.2.

[42] See *supra* the definition 28.19 in Sect. 28.4.

[43] The example is from Alchourrón and Bulygin (1979, Chap. 8).

actions occurring in the context of application of the rule—to represent R_4 as an imperative conditional or, more precisely, a command that the conditional proposition be made true:

(R_4 in the Hyleticist representation) $p \Leftrightarrow O\neg r$

(R_4 in the Expressivist representation) $!((p \in F_n) \Leftrightarrow (\neg r \in A_{n+1}))$

where p stands for raining and r for leaving the house.

One may prefer the first representation or the second one for reasons of intellectual and other tastes. Yet as far as instrumental power is concerned, the Expressivist representation provides every expected result of R_4: If it is raining (p), you have an explicit prohibition to leave the house. If it is not raining (not-p), you are negatively permitted (and thus not obliged) to leave the house.[44] This can easily be verified, if we recall our definitions of explicit prohibition (Def. 28.6) and of negative permission (Def. 28.12).[45]

When R_4 is issued, its propositional content enters the axiomatic basis A_n. For the sake of simplicity, suppose this is the only rule we have in the Commonwealth of Rex and that D_n is an empty set, whereas Cn(A_n) contains all the logical consequences of R_4. Now, if it is not raining, leaving the house (r) is negatively permitted,[46] since D_n remains an empty set and Cn(A_n) does not contain staying in the house ($\neg r$). On the other hand, if it *is* raining, you are explicitly prohibited to leave the house,[47] since $\neg r$ belongs to A_{n+1}.

This is how one could rebut the objection posed by Weinberger (1985 and 1986) and finally conceded even by Alchourrón and Bulygin (1991): namely, that their Expressivist cannot give a satisfactory reconstruction of conditional norms.[48]

If the Expressivist makes use of (i) sequences of (ii) separate sets (including the set F of relative facts and actions occurring in the context of application), and if she renders conditional norms not as conditional imperatives, but as (iii) commands that conditionals be made true, then she can easily translate the Hyleticist representation of conditional norms as follows:

	Hyleticist representation	Expressivist representation
Def. 28.21	If p, then Oq.	$!((p \in F_n) \Rightarrow (q \in A_{n+1}))$
Def. 28.22	If p, then Phq.	$!((p \in F_n) \Rightarrow (\neg q \in A_{n+1}))$
Def. 28.23	If p, then Pq.	$!((p \in F_n) \Rightarrow (\neg q \in D_{n+1}))$

[44] See Alchourrón and Bulygin (1979, Chap. 8), whose tentative representation of conditional norms admittedly fails to meet this challenge.

[45] The definitions have been introduced *supra* in Sect. 28.2 and will also be reported in the following paragraph.

[46] For every x, 'It is negatively permitted in A that x' if and only if not-x belongs neither to the set Cn(A) nor to the rejected set D. See *supra* the definition 28.12 in Sect. 28.2.

[47] For every x, 'It is explicitly prohibited in A that x' if and only if not-x belongs to the set A. See *supra* the definition 28.6 in Sect. 28.2.

[48] See Weinberger (1985, 175 s). See also Alchourrón and Bulygin (1991, xxvii), but especially Caracciolo (1993, p. 507).

Admittedly, however, some will find the price is too high to be paid—for now our axiomatic basis and, therefore, our normative system changes along with the weather conditions and other factual circumstances over and above commands and derogations.[49] But there are at least two ways to avoid the alleged problem (for those who care):

a. From the general norm R_4 ("If, and only if, it is raining, then you ought not to leave the house!") the fact p (it is raining), we want to obtain as a consequence the obligation to stay in the house. But this may be regarded as an individual obligation in a particular case at hand. The said obligation is derived from a general norm (or its propositional content) and a factual premise. Now, if we assume that such individual obligations are not part of the normative system itself, but are rather applications of its contents to factual circumstances, then we can preserve the normative system's independence from the ever-changing facts: Instead of putting $\neg r$ (or, staying in the house) in the axiomatic basis A_{n+1}, we shall simply put it in a separate set of individual obligations in a case at hand: say, I_{n+1}. R_4 shall then be represented as $!((p \in F_n) \Leftrightarrow (\neg r \in I_{n+1}))$. Accordingly, we shall also modify the above given definitions of what is obligatory, prohibited and permitted (Def. 28.2 – Def. 28.12); but that cannot undermine the claim that conditional norms may be adequately represented by Expressivists.
b. Another way to avoid the alleged problem of an ever-changing normative system consists in identifying the normative system with the commanded set A and not with the set Cn(A) which includes all the logical consequences of the explicitly commanded propositions. One could thus stick with the initially proposed representation of conditional norms (Def. 28.21– Def. 28.23) and with the idea that normative systems do not change together with factual circumstances different from the acts of promulgation and derogation. This solution is also in line with the objections Žarnić and Bašić (2014) raise against my adoption of the usual definition of a normative system (with deductive closure) in their comment to the preprint of this text. I find their arguments convincing and although I will not repeat them here—since they do not go against the expressive conception as such—we can conclude by putting their (general) proposal in connection with our (special) issue of conditional norms: A norm-applier performs deduction from the general norm R_4 ("If, and only if, it is raining, then you ought not to leave the house!") and the fact p (it is raining), but there is "no deductively closed set Cn(A) that needs to precede or can result from the thus obtained determination of the deontic status of the state of affairs brought about by a norm-subject act or by forbearance" (Žarnić and Bašić, 2014, § 2.1). The relation between R_4 and the individual obligation (in the case of raining) or individual permission (in all other circumstances) concerns one's reasoning with ought-statements. In other words, the rules of inference that make us derive implicit and/or individual norms from the explicit and general ones define the metanormative context for

[49] Indeed, for some, the very idea of a normative system is appealing only if it does not change together with factual circumstances different from the acts of norm-promulgation and norm-derogation. I shall thank Moreso (private conversation) for bringing up this issue.

the norm-appliers and have no necessary connection with a normative systems itself.[50] In this view, the issue of the ever-changing normative system disappears.

Of course, the expressive conception (and, in particular, its Moritzian variety) may have other flaws and even serious problems.[51] But if the above demonstrations are correct, the Expressivist of Alchourrón and Bulygin (1981) can perfectly account for facultative states of affairs (§ 28.2) without introducing inconsistencies into the normative system Cn(*A*) (§ 28.3). She can successfully describe the propositional content of a meta-rule without semanticizing the indicator of (normative) force of the object-rules (§ 28.4). And she can give an account of a permissive closure—and of other conditional norms—even if she denies the conceptual autonomy of acts of permitting or, in different words, their irreducibility to other normative forms (§ 28.5).

Acknowledgment I wish to thank Alejandro Calzetta and Alessio Sardo for some long and vivid discussions of the topic. I also thank Eugenio Bulygin, Damiano Canale, Diego Dei Vecchi, Alessandro Ferrari, Pablo Rapetti, Giovanni Battista Ratti, Sebastián Figueroa, José Juan Moreso, Pablo Navarro, Cristina Redondo and Jan Woleński for their valuable comments on various parts of the draft of this text. Last, but not least, I have benefited from two negative reviews. Whereas an anonymous referee of *Doxa* found my formalisations erroneous, another one of *Studia Logica* considered them mostly simple and obvious to the extent that makes this contribution trivial. In the end, I sticked to my original formalisations with only some minor corrections. It is my impression that they shall not attract logicians, but they will spark a thought or two among legal theorists—and so I decided to leave it to the broader community to make an informed judgement.

References

Aguiló, Josep. 1995. *Sobre la derogación. Ensayo de dinámica jurídica*. Mexico: Fontamara (Biblioteca de ética, filosofía del Derecho y política; 41).

Alchourrón, Carlos E. and Eugenio Bulygin. 1971. *Normative systems*. Wien: Springer (Library of Exact Philosophy; 5).

Alchourrón, Carlos E. and Eugenio Bulygin. 1979. *Sobre la existencia de las normas jurídicas*. Valencia: Universidad de Carabobo. (Page numbers in my text refer to the reprint in Mexico: Fontamara 1997).

[50] See Žarnić and Bašić (2014, especially § 1.1 and § 2.1). Their references to John Broome, Lou Goble, and Jürgen Habermas are here omitted.

[51] I will not take positions on other issues here and will stop at indicating further readings. Although already mentioned, Weinberger (1985 and 1986) is the best starting point, as it dwells on various issues not touched upon in this chapter. The argument of Opałek and Woleński (1986, 1987, 1991) goes against the Expressivist treatment of permissions. Navarro and Redondo (1990b, 238 s) point out some questions related to the configuration of the rejected set (with its subsets) as lacking a clear answer in the works of Alchourrón and Bulygin. Navarro and Moreso (1992, p. 1089) purport to identify an ambiguity of positive permission. Aguiló (1995, 59 ss and 63 ss) invokes a problem with derogations for reasons of incompatibility. Caracciolo (1996, nn. 15, 25 and 31) raises the issue of identifying the normative system of the expressive conception with the law. Finally, see also Ferrer Beltrán and Rodríguez (2011, Chap. 1), claiming that there are two different conceptions of meaning, and not of norms.

Alchourrón, Carlos E. and Eugenio Bulygin. 1981. The expressive conception of norms. In *New studies in deontic logic*, ed. Risto Hilpinen, 95–124. Dordrecht: Reidel. (Page numbers in my text refer to the reprint in Litschewski-Paulson, Bonnie and Stanley Paulson, eds. 1998. *Normativity and Norms*, Chapter 21, 383–410. Oxford: Oxford University Press).

Alchourrón, Carlos E. and Eugenio Bulygin. 1984. Pragmatic foundations for a logic of norms. *Rechtstheorie* 15: 453–464.

Alchourrón, Carlos E. and Eugenio Bulygin. 1991. *Análisis lógico y derecho*. Madrid: Centro de estudios políticos y constitucionales.

Calzetta, Alejandro and Alessio Sardo. 2014. The expressive conception revisited. (Under review. Quoted with permission.) In Spanish: Una nueva visita a la concepción expresiva. *Doxa* 37.

Caracciolo, Ricardo. 1993. Entrevista a Eugenio Bulygin. *Doxa* 14: 499–513.

Caracciolo, Ricardo. 1996. Esistenza di norme e di sistemi normativi. In *Struttura e Dinamica dei Sistemi Giuridici*, eds. Paolo Comanducci and Riccardo Guastini. Torino: Giappicheli Editore. (In Spanish: Existencia de normas. *Isonomía. Revista de teoría y filosofía del Derecho* 7: 159–178. Reprinted in Ricardo Caracciolo, *El Derecho desde la filosofía*, Madrid: Centro de estudios políticos y constitucionales 2009 (El Derecho y la Justícia)).

Ferrer Beltrán, Jordi and Jorge Luis Rodríguez. 2011. *Jerarquías normativas y dinámica de los sistemas jurídicos*. Madrid: Marcial Pons (Filosofía y Derecho).

Moritz, Manfred. 1963. Permissive Sätze, Erlaubnissätze und deontische Logik. In *Philosophical Essays Dedicated to Gunnar Aspelin on the Occasion of His Sixty-fifth Birthday* eds. Alf Ahlberg, Rolf Ekman et al., Lund: Gleerups. 108–121.

Navarro, Pablo E. and María Cristina Redondo. 1990a. Permisiones y actitudes normativas. *Doxa. Cuadernos de filosofía del Derecho* 7: 249–255.

Navarro, Pablo E. and María Cristina Redondo. 1990b. Derogations, logical indeterminacy and legal expressivism. *Rechtstheorie* 21: 233–239.

Navarro, Pablo E. and José Juan Moreso. 1992. Normas permisivas, sistemas jurídicos y clausura normativa. Un analisis de la evolución de las ideas de Carlos Alchourrón y Eugenio Bulygin. *Theoría. Revista de Theoría, Historia y Fundamentos de la Ciencia*. Segunda época 7 (16–17-18, Tomo B): 1079–1100.

Opałek, Kazimierz and Jan Woleński. 1986. On weak and strong permissions once more. *Rechtstheorie* 17: 83–88.

Opałek, Kazimierz and Jan Woleński. 1987. Is, ought, and logic. *Archiv für Rechts- und Sozialphilosophie* LXXIII: 373–385.

Opałek, Kazimierz and Jan Woleński. 1991. Normative systems, permissions, and deontic logic. *Ratio Juris* 4: 334–348.

Weinberger, Ota. 1985. The expressive conception of norms: An impasse for the logic of norms. *Law and Philosophy* 4:165–198. (Reprinted in Litschewski-Paulson, Bonnie and Stanley Paulson, eds. 1998. *Normativity and Norms*. Chapter 22, 411–432. Oxford: Oxford University Press).

Weinberger, Ota. 1986. Der normenlogische Skeptizismus. *Rechtstheorie* 17: 13–81.

Žarnić, Berislav and Gabriela Bašić. 2014. Metanormative principles and norm governed social interaction. *Revus. Journal for Constitutional Theory and Philosophy of Law* 22: 105–120.

Chapter 29
Rule-Following and Logic

Jan Woleński

Abstract This paper applies some logical devices taken from standard deontic logic and general metalogic to analysis of rule-following and its paradoxes as formulated by Ludwig Wittgenstein in his later works and recently popularized and analyzed by Saul Kripke. In particular, the paper argues that the Kripkenstein problem, related to the arithmetical operation called *quus* is apparent. In the final part, the question of rule-following of logical rules is discussed.

Keywords Normativity · Obligation · Prohibition · Permission indifference · Arithmetic · Rules of inference

29.1 Introduction

If you write the phrase 'rule-following problem' in Google and click, more than 66 millions of results is displayed. Of course, not all are related to the question formulated by Wittgenstein several years ago and widely popularized by Kripke in recent times. I did not calculate the number of items in the Google-list addressing to views of Kripkenstein and their variations. Anyway, few first pages are almost entirely related to Wittgenstein and Kripke. What is fairly surprising is that we do not find too many attempts clarify the concept of rule in the context of rule-following. Most authors take for granted that normativity and correctness are involved into thinking about rules as followed. Although this intuition is certainly right, its insufficiency for a satisfactory account of rule following immediately appears as obvious. The first part of this paper offers an analysis of rule-following based on a more complex basis. In particular, some devices taken from deontic logic are employed in my proposed solution of the issue. The second parts considers the problem of rules of pure logic and their following in making inferences.

J. Woleński (✉)
Jagiellonian University, Krakow, Poland
e-mail: wolenski@if.uj.edu.pl

M. Araszkiewicz et al. (eds.), *Problems of Normativity, Rules and Rule-Following*, Law and Philosophy Library 111, DOI 10.1007/978-3-319-09375-8_29

29.2 The Concept of Rule-Following and Wittgenstein's Paradox

As it is customary I with start with Wittgenstein's formulation of the paradox concerning rule-following. Wittgenstein says (1953, sections 201, 202, 203, pp. 81[e], 82[e]):

> This was our paradox: no course of action could be determined by a rule, because every course of action can be made out to accord with the rule. The answer was: if everything can be made out to accord with the rule, then it can also be made out to the conflict with it. And so there would be neither accord nor conflict here.
> It can be seen that there is a misunderstanding here from the mere fact that in the course of our argument we give one interpretation after another; as if one is contended us at least for a moment, until we thought of yet another standing behind it. What this shews is that there is a way of grasping a rule which is *not an interpretation*, but which is exhibited in what call "obeying the rule" and "going against it" in actual cases.
> [...]
> And hence also 'obeying a rule' is a practice. And to *thing* one is obeying a rule is not obey a rule. Hence it is not possible to obey a rule 'privately': otherwise thinking one was obeying a rule would be the same thing as obeying it.
> [...]
> Following a rule is analogous to obeying an order.

I do not intend to give a new interpretation of Wittgenstein. In fact, I think that it is impossible to give a coherent interpretation of the quoted passages.

Let us take seriously Wittgenstein's declaration that following a rule is analogous to obeying an order. This immediately suggests its reading as 'following a rule is analogous to obeying an imperative'. Now, imperative are expressed by sentences of the form OA (reading: it is obligatory that A, A is obligatory; I will use the latter phrase for verbal expressing of deontic sentences, because it is more coherent with ordinary parlance). Furthermore, according to standard deontic logic, we have $FA \Leftrightarrow O\neg A$ (reading: A is prohibited if and only if not-A is obligatory), $PA \Leftrightarrow \neg FA$ (reading: A is permitted if and only if A is not prohibited), and $IA \Leftrightarrow PA \Leftrightarrow P\neg A$ (reading: A is indifferent (optional) if and only if A permitted and $\neg A$ is permitted). Let **X** be a consistent (this assumption excludes trivial cases of normative regulations) set of initial obligations (that is induced by imperatives captured by a suitable set of O-sentences). A normative system **NS** is defined as the set $Cn\mathbf{X}$, relatively to a given set **X** (in fact, we can work with initial obligations, because their consequences do not increase the content of **NS**). Every non-empty set **X** divides the entire universe of all possible actions into three mutually exclusive spheres: obligatory ($\mathbf{OB}^{\mathbf{X}}$), prohibited ($\mathbf{PR}^{\mathbf{X}}$) and indifferent ($\mathbf{IN}^{\mathbf{X}}$; I will omit the upper index in further considerations). Formally speaking (**a** refers to the action described by the sentences A), $\mathbf{a} \in \mathbf{OB}$ if and only if $OA \in \mathbf{NS}$; $\mathbf{a} \in \mathbf{PR}$ if and only if $O\neg A \in \mathbf{NS}$; $\mathbf{a} \in \mathbf{IN}$ if and only if $OA \notin \mathbf{NS} \wedge O\neg A \notin \mathbf{NS}$ (this last condition is justified by definitions taken from deontic logic).

Take an obligation expressed by OA. What does it mean to follow this obligation? Clearly, to follow OA consists in undertaking the action described by A or a sentence B which is logically equivalent to A. Let A describes and action and C (also a sentence about an action) is its logical consequence. Observe that, due to the so-called Ross paradox ($OA \Rightarrow (O(A \vee B)$, where B is arbitrary) undertaking the action described by C does not mean the action to which A refers is realized, unless A and C are logically equivalent. And, of course, any action described by $\neg A$ (or sentence equivalent with it) does not follow the imperative expressed by OA. Using the well-known construction known as the Lindenbaum algebra, we can form the class $[A]$ containing sentences logically equivalent with A, symbolically $B \in [A]$ if and only if $\vdash A \Leftrightarrow B$. Consequently, a suitable Lindenbaum algebra represents actions that follow a given obligation expressed by OA. On the other hand, every action belonging to **IN** agrees with OA, although we cannot assert that it follows OA. Yet such an action does not disobey the imperative OA. Note that although indifference and permission are related, the former is stronger than the latter ($IA \Rightarrow PA$), but the converse entailment does not hold).

Taking into account hints and suggestions stemming from deontic logic directly leads to the conclusion that Wittgenstein's paradox of rule-following disappears, because it is not true that every course of action can be made out to accord with the rule in question. If OA is a rule (expresses a rule), then every element of $[A]$ follows this order and every element of **IN** (I will omit upper indexes indicating references to **X** or **NS**) is coherent with it. Eventually, one can distinguish between direct following (satisfying) OA and indirect following, that is, acting in such way that OA is not disobeyed and $O\neg A$ is not disobeyed. Otherwise speaking, this distinction qualifies elements of $[A]$ as describing actions directly following OA and elements of **IN** as indirectly following this imperative. Direct rule-following and indirect rule-following (not disobeying-rules) are both normative concepts but they essentially differ. The normative character of the former is primitive and directly induced by **NS**, but normativity of **IN** obtains this status derivatively. Now, no interpretation can justify Wittgenstein's paradox of rule-following. Interpretation, at least in its legal understanding, contributes to borderlines between **OB**, **PR** and **IN**. The logical aspect of the discussed issue is entirely independent of accepting, interpreting or grasping rules.

Wittgenstein correctly says that obeying a rule is a practice. Consider the following example. I see a person x who does not smoke. This observation neither suggests that x obeys the rule 'Do not smoke!' nor support the conclusion that x never used to smoke. Similarly, if I see a person y smoking in a place in which is not allowed, it neither suggests that y disobeys the order 'Do not smoke!' nor support the conclusion that y overlooked information prohibiting smoking in this place. In order to say (by a person x') that x obeys (disobeys) a rule OA, at least following ingredients are required: (a) there is a rule OA; (b) the rule OA is grasped by x; (c) x intentionally follows OA; (d) x' grasp OA; (e) x' observes how x behaves and correctly ascribes to x intentionality to act in the way A.[1] Contrary to Wittgenstein, there is nothing incoherent in a private (in fact, his quoting words by no means are easy to understand them) obeying rules, unless 'privately' is synonymous with 'exclusively by thinking'. However, if we assume this equivalence, the issue becomes

[1] The ascribing of intentionality (see (c)) can be more complex in the case of abstaining from an action.

trivial: performing any action is not the same as thinking that we perform this action. Another problem is much more interesting, namely the question 'Is it possible to follow a rule *OA* without its internalizing?' The first suggestion that we should distinguish direct following and indirect following. Whereas one can argue that the latter can obtain (not: obtains) without internalizing rule, the former seems to require internalization.[2] Anyway, the points (a)–(e) and the issue of internalization of rules are strongly associated with the question of the role of social practice in obeying rules.

29.3 Kripke's Mathematical Example

Saul Kripke interprets Wittgenstein's paradox of rule-following by employing a mathematical construction (see Kripke 1982, pp. 8–9). If we add normally 68 and 57, the sum of these numbers is equal to 125. However, define a new function *quus* (Gary Ebbs calls it *plush*; see Ebbs 1997, p. 140), denoted by the symbol $\oplus$. The meaning of $\oplus$ is established by the conditions (i) $x \oplus y = x + y$, if $x, y > 57$; (ii) $x \oplus y = 5$, otherwise.[3] Now, the question appears whether $\oplus$ is 'the function [...] previously meant by +' (Kripke 1982, p. 9). Kripke says (Kripke 1982, pp. 10–11):

> Ordinarily, I suppose that, in computing '68+57' as I do, I do not simply make an unjustified leap in the dark. I follow directions I previously gave myself that uniquely determine that in this new instance I should say '125' What are these directions? By hypothesis, I never explicitly told myself that I should say '125' in this very instance. Nor can I say that I should simply 'do the same thing I always did,' if this means 'compute according to the rule exhibited by my previous examples.' That rule could just as well have been the rule for quaddition (the quus function) as for addition. The idea that in fact quaddition *is* what I meant, that a sudden frenzy I have changed my previous usage, dramatizes the problem.

Appealing to being frenzy is naturally a rhetorical figure. According to Kripke, the problem is that we can invent several definitions of functions pretending to being interpreted as denoted by the symbol x and still to argue that we obey rules for addition, relatively to proposed conventions governing various usages of the phrase 'following rules of addition'. He says that his mathematical example sharpens the problem of various possible interpretations of rules.

Kripke locates his version of Wittgenstein's paradox as pertaining to skepticism about meaning. I will not enter into this issue, except making one general remark below. I will also ignore externalism, internalism, behaviorism, truth, warranted assertibility or realism (see Ebbs 1997) for a comprehensive picture of various links of Wittgenstein's paradox and its Kripkensteinian treatment with various philosophical problems (see also Brożek 2012), because these connections make the issue darker.

[2] This statement is simplified due to possible exceptions.

[3] The point (i) is formulated by the formula $x \oplus y = x + y$, if $x, y > 57$ in the first edition of Kripke (1982). It is an obvious error, because $57 \oplus 68$ should give 125 as the result. Further editions corrected this mistake.

Like in the case of rule-following in a general logical setting, the problem seems to be much simpler than Kripke suggests. It is true that a person x who performs the old addition operation usually (perhaps not never) asks himself or herself that he or she should answer 125 as the result of adding 68 and 57. The crucial point is that x can always ask himself (herself) or someone else, why $68+57=125$. The final answer belongs to arithmetic and its standard interpretation. Formally speaking, we have the theory **PA** (Peano arithmetic) and its customary interpretation generating the normal model of **PA**. This codification (or formalization if someone prefers) induces definite rules of calculation for + and other arithmetical operations.

We can change, wisely or not, interpretation and propose new rules of calculation, for instance, involving non-traditional models.[4] Consider ⊕ once again. Truly, it give 125 as the output for 68 and 57 taken as the input values. However, the meaning of ⊕ differs from the sense of +. Although both operations are commutative (in particular, $8+7=7+8=5$), but their other properties appear as unclear without further ado. To see this, consider the formula $(8\times 5)\oplus(7\times 5)$, where the symbol × refers to ordinary multiplication. According to (ii), 5 is the result for these values. Since $(8\oplus 7)\times 5=25$, the *quus* operation is not distributive over multiplication, unless we introduce new constraints on × in order to define a new function, let say, *quimes*, denoted by the symbol ⊕. In general, we have no straightforward answer to the question whether ⊕ is distributive over ⊕ or not. Another, and perhaps a more important question, concerns the meaning of + in (i). It seems that Kripke understand this symbol as referring to addition without further qualifications. However, it is problematic. The operation + is defined in **PA** by conditions (a) $0+n=n$; (b) $m^*+n=(m+n)^*$, where the star expresses the successor function. Now, we have $0^*+56+68=(0+56+68)^*=125$ as required, but, on the other hand and according to (i), $0^*\oplus 56\oplus 68=5$. Thus, either Kripke should change (a) and (b), which is equivalent to changing the meaning of + as defined in the official arithmetic, or his definition of *quus* cannot be satisfactory from the mathematical point of view for its vague properties.

Clearly, both (i) and (ii) change the ordinary meaning of addition, independently whether + and ⊕ give the same outputs for some selected input values. Kripke asks (see Kripke 1982, p. 9): 'Who is to say that this is not the function I previously meant by '+'?' Although it is not sure whether Kripke forwards this question in his own name or assumes the position of the skeptic, an answer does not present special difficulties and refers to **PA**. Even if we agree that choosing of the standard interpretation of **PA** as official and recommending it as deserving rule-following invokes social practice of mathematicians does not exclude other alternatives, this assertion does not suffice to support the thesis that we have here various equipollent (that is, having the same calculable force) rules of addition. We have a good arithmetical theory, which exactly defines +, × and univocally generates their properties on the one hand, and *ad hoc* outlined operations ⊕ and ⊕ without determining their features. Eventually, and it is the already announced remark, one could appeal to

[4] I do not speak about standard and non-standard models, because principles governing arithmetic with *quus* are unclear (see above).

typical arguments of skeptics pointing out that if we normalize a theory **T** and its rules in a language **L**, we must refer to the metalanguage **ML** and its meaning-rules. Thus, although rule-following in **L** finds its justification in rules of **ML**, but the latter are not unconditionally settled in the metalanguage. Then we pass to **MML**, **MMML** and further *ad infinitum*. In fact, Kripke alludes to this strategy, but this move adds nothing new to the old-fashioned skepticism, which always maintained that every criterion of correctness (validity, truth, justification, etc.) is plagued by the regress fallacy.

How to locate rules for + and various other possible *quuses* by using respective, that is generated by arithmetic, regions **OB**, **PR** and **IN**? Accepting **PA** as our official arithmetic, we automatically decide that we should follow its axiomatically stated or derived rules as governing correct calculations employing addition (denoted by +) and other arithmetical operations.[5] In particular, we cannot coherently characterize the spheres **OB**, **PR** and **IN** related to rule-following generated by various *quuses*, unless we prove which newly proposed operations of addition constitute admissible (consistent) alternatives to *plus* within an arithmetic. Correspondingly, all computations determined by rules producing different to those required by **PA** belong to **PR**. However, it is still an incomplete answer. Assume that **R** is a rule which is consistent with **PA**, for example, the rule for ⊕, provided that all unclear points are explained (it can be done, for instance, by introducing ⊕ as a partial arithmetical function). Otherwise speaking, we can introduce various *quuses* in order to execute particular cognitive tasks (for instance, calculating in special areas) or for pedagogical aims of teaching children how to compute inside a definite (usually small) subset of natural numbers, for example, how to add numbers smaller than 68. Yet the analogy between Wittgenstein and Kripkenstein appears as considerably limited. On the one hand, adding such rules is fairly optional (we can, but there is no duty to make such additions), but, on the other hand, if we decide to supplement our arithmetical machinery by new admissible operations, we create new obligatory regions, possibly different than the **PA**-arithmetical **OB**. I have no simple answer to the question whether we should say here about optional spheres or conditionally obligatory subdomains, but I am inclined to the latter qualification.

29.4 Logical Rules and Rule-Following

Some psychological research, for example the Wason selection test, suggest that inferential logical rules are not followed by agents performing inferences in this sense that even students of logic are committed to elementary errors in making inferences. On the other hand, other investigations suggest something different. For instance, students usually prefer natural deduction over truth-table method if they are asked

---

[5] I disregard here the problem of non-standard (in the technical sense) arithmetic, for example, arithmetical theories used in non-standard analysis. I only remark that we can either note that we theories belong to the same arithmetical class or to operate by various spheres of arithmetical **OB**.

to check whether a given formula is tautological or not. This seems justify the thesis that our actual cognitive equipment favors genuine inferential strategies over mechanical procedures. Anyway, accessible empirical data do not speak very much to which extent rules of logic determine the logical rule-following. The only lesson to be derived from various data says that inferential agents sometimes correctly follow logical rules and sometimes fail to do that or that sometimes they perform definitely spontaneous inferences. However, as I will argue, logical rules have some peculiar features as far as the issue concerns their following. These properties are generated by metalogic and are entirely independent of how inferential agents behave.

A typical explanation of the main property of logical inferential rules (**LIR**) is that they are sound, that is, cannot lead from truths (true premises) to falsehoods (false conclusions). If $\mathbf{X} \vdash A$ s a rule with **X** as a set of premises and A as a conclusion, we have

$$\text{If } \mathbf{X} \vdash A \in \mathbf{LOG}, \text{ then } \neg\Diamond(X \in \mathbf{TRUTH} \wedge A \in \mathbf{FALSE}). \quad (29.1)$$

If we remain within pure logic, **LIR** produce theorems from other theorems, ultimately from logical axioms. If A is a logical theorem, we write

$$\vdash A, \quad (29.2)$$

where the symbol $\vdash$ refers to the provability operator. Intuitively speaking, Eq. (29.2) says that A is a logical axiom or a theorem deduced from axioms. Consequently, logical theorems (axioms are a kind of theorems) are said to be inferred from the empty set of assumptions. Thus, the operator $\vdash$ magazines, so to speak logical inferential machinery.

What is the relation between $\vdash$ and $\models$ ($\models A$ means 'A is a logical truth')? If a **LOG** is complete (I consider this property as a substantial feature of logic), we have

$$\vdash A \Leftrightarrow \models A. \quad (29.3)$$

Thus, provability from the empty set of premises is equivalent to universal (logical) validity. Interpret logical rule-following as 'obey rules collected by $\vdash$.' Consider the implication

$$\models A \Rightarrow \vdash A. \quad (29.4)$$

The last formula says that if A is universally valid, A generates a rule to be logically followed. A special case of Eq. (29.4) (it is justified by the deduction theorem) is captured by

$$\text{If } \models (A \Rightarrow B), \quad \text{then } A \vdash B. \quad (29.5)$$

Thus, if $A \Rightarrow B$ is universally valid, asserting B belongs to rule-following of asserting A. Observe that $\models(A \Rightarrow B)$ is devoid of any explicit normative content. On the other hand, the concept of logical inference rule has obvious normative connotations. If so, Eqs. (29.3) and (29.5) suggest that either the Hume thesis (ought cannot be inferred from is) is broken in the domain of the logical or the concept of universal validity has a normative content.

How, to characterize **OB, PR** and **IN** as generated by logic? One could eventually propose an analogy between logic and arithmetic: rule of logic determine **OB**, their negations (in turn, logical inconsistencies) created **PR**, but we can add various extralogical rules in order to enrich logical inferential machinery. The issue is more complicated. Since propositional calculus is Post-complete (every formula is either its theorem or added to it produce inconsistency), the spheres **OB** and **PR** exhaust the entire domain related to $\vdash$. Yet we can divide all formulas into universal validities, universal inconsistencies and factual truths (or falsehoods). Thus, logical rule-following in propositional calculus does not preclude dividing our assertions into **OB**, **PR** and **IN**. If we pass to predicate logic, which is complete but not Post-complete, we can form theories consisting of logical theorems and extralogical assertions (for instance, statements of the form 'there are *n* objects'). Logical validity and being provable from the empty set of premises still coincide, the Hume thesis is broken (or the concept of universal validity is broken), we have theories belonging to **OB** and theories belonging to **IN** (first-order logic extended by adding extralogical assertions) and the tripartite division of all formulas into spheres **OB**, **PR** and **IN.** Thus, we have a quite interesting situation. Propositional calculus possesses the strongest force with respect to rule-following, but its expressive power is the smallest one. First-order logic has a greater expressive power, but the force of its rule-following is smaller than propositional calculus. Generally speaking, because pure logic does not distinguish of any extralogical content, the force of their rule-following is strong. On the other hand, extralogical theories are associate with a smaller force of rule-following. If we could measure how strong is rule-following in particular cases, it we would probably have a good device to treat paradoxes offered by Kripkenstein. Unfortunately in general, but fortunately for philosophers, no such method is available.

References

Brożek, Bartosz. 2012. *Rule-following. From imitation to the normative mind.* Kraków: Copernicus Center.

Ebbs, Gary. 1997. *Rule following and realism.* Cambridge: Harvard University Press.

Kripke, Saul. 1982. *Wittgenstein on rules and private language.* Cambridge: Harvard University Press.

Wittgenstein, Ludwig. 1953. *Philosophical investigations.* Oxford: Blackwell.

Chapter 30
Negating Rules

Giovanni Battista Ratti

Abstract The paper is intended as a first, tentative, contribution to the clarification of the place that negation has in prescriptive discourse. In particular, the paper analyzes the ways in which rules may be said to be negated and the meanings they assume when they are so regarded. In so doing, the differences between external and internal negation of conditional rules are examined. The paper also deals with the effects of inconsistency between conditional rules, understood as the conjunction of a conditional rule and its corresponding conditional denial. The main result of the paper is that both rules negation and rules inconsistency are unclear concepts, casting their shadows over the very concept of rule.

Keywords Conditionals · Inconsistency · Negation · Rules

30.1 Foreword

Analytic philosophers generally hold that propositions, to be regarded as meaningful, must be liable to being genuinely negated. Conversely, if a certain proposition cannot be meaningfully negated must be regarded as meaningless, despite possible appearances[1].

It is not clear, however, how this applies to rules and assertion about rules. This paper is intended as a first, tentative, contribution to the clarification of the place that negation has in prescriptive discourse.

In so doing, I shall analyze the (highly problematic) ways in which rules may be said to be negated and the meanings they assume when they are so handled. In Sects. 30.1 and 30.2, I will stress the differences between external and internal negation of conditional rules, that is between a denied conditional rule and a conditional rule-denial. In Sect. 30.3, I shall examine the effects of inconsistency between conditional rules.

[1] For discussion, see Nárvaez (2010).

G. B. Ratti (✉)
Tarello Institute for Legal Philosophy, Department of Law, University of Genoa,
Via Balbi 30/18, 16126, Genoa, Italy
e-mail: gbratti@unige.it

M. Araszkiewicz et al. (eds.), *Problems of Normativity, Rules and Rule-Following*,
Law and Philosophy Library 111, DOI 10.1007/978-3-319-09375-8_30

The analysis will bring about a first result: that of showing that both rules negation and normative inconsistency are unclear concepts, casting their shadows over the very concept of "rule."

30.2 Negation in Prescriptive Discourse

As is known, negation inverts the truth-value of a (descriptive) proposition. The proposition

[1] Snow in white

is negated by asserting

[2] Snow is not white

If [1] is true, [2] is false, and vice versa. The conjoined truth of [1] and [2] is logically avoided by embracing the principle of non-contradiction: "$\sim(p \mathbin{\&} \sim p)$". This principle in turn is propositionally equivalent to the principle of bivalence "$(p \vee \sim p)$": one of two propositions, of which one is the negation of the other, must be true in that they are exhaustive of a certain universe of discourse. As is easy to see, both principles are equivalent to (one of the possible formulations of) the principle of identity: "$p \supset p$".

When a certain proposition and its negation belong to the same set of sentences, such a set is said to be contradictory. It is also trivialized according to the *ex falso quodlibet* (EFQ) principle, in the sense that it contains any proposition whatsoever among its consequences. This may be easily proved:

[1] $p \mathbin{\&} \sim p$	ASS.
[2] p	[1], elimination of conjunction
[3] $p \vee q$	[2], introduction of disjunction
[4] $\sim p$	[1], elimination of conjunction
[5] q	[3], [4], disjunctive syllogism

Rules are neither true nor false. So, it is not clear which is the logical value (if any) that is to be inverted by negation. Deontic logicians and legal theorists have often referred to the value of "validity"[2]. However, validity is a highly contested concept, liable to be reduced to other, more nuanced, notions[3].

Here I will use a quite abstract notion of efficacy as the logical value of rules[4]. I will hold a rule efficacious if its propositional content is always true in so far as

[2] Cf. Soeteman (1989, p. 132 ff.).

[3] Bulygin (1982).

[4] A more nuanced analysis regarding logical values relevant for rules' consistency is found in the analysis of Hage (2000), based on the idea of rules as constraints possible worlds, and Sartor (1992), relying, *inter alia*, on the application of AGM logic of belief change to normative inconsistencies.

commands (Op and O~p) are concerned, and sometimes true when authorizations (~Op and ~O~p) are concerned. In other terms, a command may be said to be efficacious if it is always complied with during its normative existence (i.e. its membership in a normative system), whereas an authorization is efficacious if it is sometimes used during its normative existence.

In so far as categorical rules are concerned, negation is easily applied. If rule Op is efficacious, its contrary O~p and contradictory ~Op cannot be efficacious, and vice versa. More precisely, 'Op' and 'O~p' are dubbed "contrary" in that they may be both inefficacious, but not both efficacious. 'Op' and '~Op' are contradictory in that if one is efficacious, the other one cannot be efficacious, and vice versa. As a matter of course, the same relation holds for 'O~p' and '~O~p'. 'Op' implies '~O~p' because if 'p' is always the case, '~p' cannot sometimes be the case. The same holds for 'O~p' and '~Op'. The members of the relation of implication are usually called "subalterns." Finally, '~Op' and '~O~p' are "subcontraries": they can be both efficacious, but not both inefficacious.

When two contradictory categorical rules belong to the same system, such a system is usually regarded as trivialized, i.e. any rule whatsoever will be a consequence of it. This is easily provable, in analogy to propositional calculus:

[6] Op &~Op	ASS.
[7] Op	[6], elimination of conjunction
[8] Op ∨ Oq	[7], introduction of disjunction
[9] ~ Op	[6], elimination of conjunction
[10] Oq	[8], [9], disjunctive syllogism

30.2.1 Negating Conditional Rules

Things are not so easy when it comes to hypothetical (*viz.* conditional) rules[5], i.e. those rules which connect a certain normative solution to a determinate (non-empty) set of conditional operative facts or properties: e.g. "If it rains, you ought to close the window".

In propositional logic, denied conditionals are very simply reconstructed as "~(p ⊃ q)". There is a contradiction between conditionals whenever the same set allows one to derive, at the same time, "p ⊃ q" and "~(p ⊃ q)"—or equivalent sentences such as "~(p & ~q)" and "p & ~q". Any sentence will follow from a set containing such two conditionals.

[5] It is interesting to observe that Soeteman's (1989) classical treatment of the negation of normative expressions mainly deals with the negation of categorical norms and the principle of prohibition, whereas I am here interested in conditional norms and I will not explore the mentioned principle. Moreover, his discussion of conditional norms—like Ross's and von Wright's—relies on the so called "insular conception" (which places conditions within the scope of deontic operators), whereas I shall resort to the so called "bridge conception" (which place conditions outside the scope of deontic operators).

By contrast, the conjunction of the two conditionals "p ⊃ q" and "p ⊃ ~ q" is consistent and equates to the negation of the common antecedent: i.e., "~ p"[6].

If one "translates" such simple tenets into the terms of prescriptive discourse, surprising results are obtained.

Assuming (the controversial) tenet that a conditional rule can be reconstructed as the connection of a (generic) case with the deontic qualification of a state of affairs (in symbols: p ⊃ Oq), the negation of a conditional rule would be expressed by the formula "~ (p ⊃ Oq)". By contrast, "p ⊃ Oq" and "p ⊃ ~ Oq" would not bring about any inconsistency.

If it were correct, some remarkable consequences would follow:

1. There would be a contradiction between conditional rules, whenever the same set of rules allows one to derive, at the same time, "p ⊃ Oq" and "~(p ⊃ Oq)". From such a set any rule would follow.
2. Analogously to what happens in propositional logic, the conjunction of the conditional rules "p ⊃ Oq" and "p ⊃ ~ Oq" would be equivalent to the negation of the common antecedent: that is "~ p"[7]. A set containing such two rules would not be inconsistent or trivialized.

Both tenets are debatable indeed[8]. Let us examine them in this order.

30.3 Denied Conditional Rules

The (presumptive) contradiction stemming from the simultaneous presence in a normative system of two conditional rules such as "p ⊃ Oq" and "~ (p ⊃ Oq)" is not easy to construe. Understood as a relation between rules, it prima facie asserts that the second rule is incompatible with the first rule: but are we sure that the latter sentence really expresses (or is commonly taken as expressing) a rule? What does it mean to assert that "It is not the case that (if p, then it ought to be that q)"?

There are at least four possible answers to this question.

[6] This is easily seen from the following truth-table:

p ⊃ q	&	p ⊃ ~q	≡	~p
1 1 1	*0*	1 0 0	**1**	*0*
1 0 0	*0*	1 1 1	**1**	*0*
0 1 1	*1*	0 1 0	**1**	*1*
0 1 0	*1*	0 1 1	**1**	*1*

[7] Ross (1968, § 36) for a very interesting critical discussion. See also Hage (2000, p. 371)

[8] A third tenet is that their disjunction, in turn, is equivalent to the formulation of the so-called "conditional excluded middle"—"(p ⊃ q) ∨ (p ⊃ ~q)"—which allows one to derive, by disjunctive syllogism, the truth of a conditional by denying the other.

30.3.1 Equivalence of External and Internal Negations

A first reading understands the expression at hand—"$\sim$(p $\supset$ Oq)"—as a sentence according to which "p $\supset \sim$Oq": this is a typical thesis of LS logics[9], which are intended to reconstruct counterfactual sentences. In LS systems, this reading is predicated on the fact that, in ordinary language, we negate, say, the counterfactual conditional

[11] If Scott Norwood had scored the free kick against the Giants in Super-bowl XXV, then the Bills would have won four Super-bowls in a row

by means of the other conditional.

[12] If Scott Norwood had scored the free kick against the Giants in Super-bowl XXV, then the Bills would have not won four Super-bowls in a row

the latter being tantamount, on this reading, to the sentence "It is not the case that 'If Scott Norwood had scored the free kick against the Giants in Super-bowl XXV, then the Bills would have won four Super-bowls in a row'".

Analogously, it would suffice to take notice of the fact that, in prescriptive language, in order to negate the conditional rule "If it rains, then it is obligatory to close the windows", one enacts the other conditional rule "If it rains, then it is not obligatory to close the windows", to maintain that the negation of a conditional rule is the same rule with the denied consequent (so-called "conditional rule-denial").

It must be observed that, if this thesis is accepted, the contradictoriness of two conditional rules *exclusively* depends on the configuration of an inconsistency between categorical rules, connected to the occurrence of a state of affairs which both the antecedents of the conditional rules bear upon.

Once one has established the criteria to determine in which cases two categorical rules are incompatible[10], it suffices to control whether such rules are connected to the same universe of cases: if this universe is void, then the rules are categorical and an inconsistency between them occurs, as it were, in any possible world; if it is not empty, then the occurrence of the relevant case (say, *p*) triggers the contradiction between the two categorical rules (i.e. the consequents) only regarding the world *p*. We will elaborate on this point in Sect. 30.3, in dealing with the conditional denial.

30.3.2 The Biconditional Reading

Another way of reconstructing "$\sim$(p $\supset$ Oq)" as equivalent to "p $\supset \sim$Oq" consists in reading the negated conditional rule as a biconditional.

Given that, for the biconditional, external negation and internal negation are equivalent[11], it would be possible to maintain that the negation of a conditional

[9] See Stalnaker (1968) and Lewis (1973).

[10] For discussion, see Alchourrón (1991).

[11] The formal representation of the corresponding propositional equivalence is as follows: $\sim$(p $\equiv$ q) $\equiv$ (p $\equiv \sim$q). Cf. Quine (1961, p. 57).

rule is materially equivalent to a sentence having the same operative facts and the denied consequent: respectively, "$\sim(p \equiv Oq)$" and "$(p \equiv \sim Oq)$". The second rule-formulation provides that non-*q* is permitted if, and only if, *p* occurs[12]. And this would be equivalent to negating the rule that provides that if, and only if, *p*, then *q* is obligatory.

This reading presents some shortcomings. If one wants to reconstruct what normally goes on in normative reasoning, it is highly problematic, for the biconditional construal of conditional rules would (conceptually) preclude the emergence of normative gaps and the subsequent application of analogy. It must also be noticed that the rational reconstruction of a prima facie conditional rule is not a genuinely interpretive act, but an act of creation of a new rule, for it introduces a biconditional clause which, *ex hypothesi*, was not present in the original formulation.

30.3.3 Ambivalence

The third interpretation regards the conflict between conditionals not as a relation of contradiction *stricto sensu*, but rather as a relation of "ambivalence"[13]: namely, a "pragmatic contradiction," consisting in enacting and rejecting the same normative content. However, in this case, external negation would have a completely different meaning from the internal one. While the latter would be a quasi-semantic operator, inverting the relevant logical value, the former would be a pragmatic operator, used to represent the attitudes of the normative authority. It follows from that that one needs to introduce different symbols to represent such operators. If we symbolize the act of enactment by "!", and the act of repealing by "¡", we can represent an ambivalence in the following way: "$!(p \supset Oq)$" and "$¡(p \supset Oq)$." This does not exclude the possibility of configuring a (presumed) conditional contradiction through an internal negation, as the enactment of two incompatible norms, which we can represent as follows: "$!(p \supset Oq)$" and "$!(p \supset \sim Oq)$".

This reading has the manifest feature of explaining away—rather than reconstructing—external negation as a quasi-semantic operator.

30.3.4 The Descriptive Reading: Propositions About Rules

The fourth reading construes "$\sim(p \supset Oq)$" not as a rule, but rather as a descriptive statement which negates the membership of the conditional rule "$p \supset Oq$" in a certain set of rules. So construed, however, the expression "$\sim(p \supset Oq)$" is ill-formed, for it lacks references to the "meta-linguistic" character of negation and to the normative system under examination. It follows from it that it is necessary to introduce two different symbolisms for the external negation (having a propositional character)

[12] In standard deontic logic, "Non-obligatory q" ($\sim Oq$), in fact, is equivalent to "Permitted non-q" ($P\sim q$).

[13] Alchourrón and Bulygin (1981).

and the internal negation (having a genuine prescriptive character) of a rule, as well as the necessity of binding the deontic qualification of a certain state of affairs to a certain normative system. Understood as a descriptive proposition bearing upon a rule, the expression at hand has the following logical form: "$\neg((p \supset Oq) \in \alpha)$" or, what is the same, "$(p \supset Oq) \notin \alpha$", where "$\neg$" represents the external negation, "$\in$" is for the predicate "being an element of", "$\notin$" represents the predicate "not being an element of", and "α" represents the normative system to which the statement refers. In this reading, obviously, "$\sim(p \supset Oq)$" does not express the rule-negation of "$p \supset Oq$", but a statement which denies that the latter conditional rule is not an element of the normative system referred to. No need to observe that no contradiction or trivialization stem from this reading of external negation, since it is a meta-operator, changing the level of discourse of the negated formula.

30.4 Conditional Denial and the Concept of a Prescriptive Contradiction

Despite "$\sim(p \supset Oq)$" being the natural candidate for reconstructing the logical form of negation in prescriptive discourse, it is not the concept generally used by normative agents or practical philosophers to account for a contradiction between rules. Many of the interpretive options we have sketched are viable, but—as we have just mentioned—they have the remarkable shortcoming of explaining away, rather than reconstructing, the problems of (external) negation of conditional rules and inconsistency between conditional rules.

It must be noted that normative agents and practical philosophers (and, in particular, jurists and legal theorists) usually call a *normative contradiction* a sentence of the kind "$(p \supset Oq)$ & $(p \supset \sim Oq)$"—or "$(p \supset Oq)$ & $(p \supset O\sim q)$"—which, as we have seen, is not a contradiction at all in propositional logic, but the conjunction of a material conditional and a conditional denial. They also hold that it is not the case that from such a contradiction, $\sim p$ follows. And this for an intuitive reason: if, say, the case of "raining" is connected to inconsistent normative consequences (say, "it is obligatory to close the window" and "it is not obligatory to close the window"), nobody would derive from that that the normative authority has asserted that it is not raining.

Moreover, according to the received view, the EFQ principle would not affect normative systems, since a normative contradiction would at most trivialize only the case referred to by the antecedent to which two incompatible consequences are connected[14].

This view, though, is too optimistic. From a normative contradiction, connected to the occurrence of a certain case, not only does it follow that such a case is connected to any consequence, but also that it is connected to any conditional rule.

[14] See Atienza (1992).

This can be explained by affirming that, if one accepts enrichment (alias, strengthening the antecedent)[15], a normative inconsistency connected to *p* brings about the trivialization of the entire normative qualification of the world *p*, in the sense that, if *p* occurs, then any further property whatsoever would be connected to any consequence. Indeed, if "$p \supset \sim K$"[16] holds, then "$p \ \& \ s \supset \sim K$" also holds (through enrichment). Nonetheless, if *p* occurs (i.e. if we are in a world where *p* is instantiated), we can derive "$s \supset \sim K$". Such a derivation can then be generalized regarding any marginal property whatsoever.

It follows that the current reading of the conditional denial can perhaps be useful to reject an unlimited trivialization of an inconsistent normative system. However, it is not capable of rejecting a highly paradoxical consequence: the trivialization of half of the universe of discourse corresponding to the operative fact(s) connected to the normative inconsistency. Let it be noted that, the wider is the set of relevant operative facts to which inconsistencies are attached, the smaller is the space which remains free from trivialization. For instance, if both *p* and *r* are connected to inconsistent consequences, then both worlds *p* and *r* are wholly trivialized from a normative standpoint. It follows from that that the worlds $p \ \& \ r$ and $p \ \& \sim r$, as well as the world $\sim p \ \& \ r$ would be deontically trivialized. Only the world $\sim p \ \& \sim r$ would remain free from such effects.

It is reasonable to think that such a conceptual web leads, for practical aims, to as trivialized normative systems as those which may be derived from an unrestricted application of the EFQ principle to normative inconsistency: so, a narrower concept of inconsistency is needed.

30.4.1 A Narrower Concept of Inconsistency

We have seen that it is widespread, among practical philosophers and normative agents at large, the intention of limiting the effects of normative inconsistency to the operative facts, the occurrence thereof leads to the applicability of two incompatible normative consequences. This entails that only from two conflicting categorical rules it is possible to derive any rule whatsoever, whereas, as for conditional rules, this consequence holds only for the case involved in the antecedent. We have also seen, though, that the effects of trivialization are much wider than a single case: they extend at least to half the universe of discourse at hand.

Now, we must see whether there is the conceptual space to envisage another concept of (normative) inconsistency, whose effects of trivialization are more limited than the effects of classical inconsistency. Indeed, this space seems to exist, but it is far away from that of propositional logic.

---

[15] Formally, enrichment is usually represented by the following sentence: "$(p \supset q) \supset (p \ \& \ r \supset q)$". In deontic logic, "$(p \supset Oq) \supset (p \ \& \ r \supset Oq)$."

[16] "K" is for "consistency.

The central element of this second concept consists in stressing the *relevance* of the properties contained in the antecedents of the rules in order to identify inconsistent (conditional) rules and determine the effects of inconsistency.

We may say that a certain property *p* is relevant if, and only if, *p* and its complementary property (i.e. $\sim p$) have a different normative status, that is both properties are connected by the same normative system with two different normative solutions, or one of them, unlike the other, is connected by the system with no normative solution[17].

If one stresses this aspect of properties, one can hold that enrichment has a limited scope: it would apply only to *relevant* properties[18]. This would allow one to exclude all those inferences which, by means of an unlimited use of enrichment, would produce the trivialization of great part of the universe of discourse, through the occurrence of the case to which inconsistency is attached. In other words, properties capable of strengthening the antecedent would only be those which expressly appear in the other rules of the normative systems to which the conflicting rules belong.

Being such properties relevant *qua* presupposing a difference of status with their complementary properties, it is rather difficult that a normative contradiction regarding a case brings about the trivialization of the normative system with regard to all the relevant properties and their complementary operative facts.

Though promising, this strategy is not without difficulties. According to a theorem of deontic logic, if a normative system is inconsistent with regard to a certain universe of cases, then it is inconsistent with regard to finer universes of cases (i.e. universes of cases more specific as for relevant properties)[19]. As a consequence, it would be possible to merge different rules, apparently unrelated, in order to derive, from an inconsistent set, any solution for any case, by adding to the inconsistent set a conditional rule whatsoever, which makes the original universe of cases more specific. Subsequently, thanks to enrichment, it would be possible to connect to the antecedent of the rule, added to the normative system, any solution derived from normative inconsistency.

Let's imagine a normative system composed of R1 which provides that "One ought to stop at the red light" and R2 which provides that "One ought not to stop in front of a military premise". By enrichment, such rules collide when one is in front of a military premise, at the red light. One may add to this normative system another rule, which provides that "If one commits murder, then he must be punished." But, what if one commits murder in front of a military premise, at the red light? This case is connected though enrichment to the inconsistency between R1 and R2, and consequently it is connected to any consequence whatsoever: even the consequence that who commits murder must not be punished.[20]

---

[17] Alchourrón-Bulygin (1971, pp. 101–102).

[18] For discussion, see Moreso (1996).

[19] Alchourrón and Bulygin (1971, p. 98 ff.).

[20] See Rodríguez (2002, p. 110).

This conceptual challenge has been attacked on empirical grounds. As Alchourrón and Makinson (1981, p. 134) point out: "Now imagine the situation of a judge or administrative officer who is called upon to apply an inconsistent code and reach a verdict on a specific question. What ways are open to him to mitigate or transcend the contradiction? One idea is to distinguish between those parts of the code that are directly *relevant* to the case in hand, and those which are not". Rules on traffic would be, generally, irrelevant as for murder cases, and vice versa.

Such a thesis is, without a doubt, totally reasonable in terms of rules application. Nonetheless, to be held, it must presuppose a notion of a conditional rule very different from that of a material conditional, typical of propositional logic. As a matter of fact, the EFQ principle is one of the most paradoxical consequences of propositional logic, and, by rejecting it, one must be ready to abandon several parts of such logic. As we have seen, negation, understood as the inversion of logical values, is a major part of it.

30.5 Final Remarks and Future Research

The difficulties we have surveyed, as a first step towards the clarification of the notion of negation in prescriptive discourses, lead to the tentative conclusion that, in so far as the negation of rules has not a clear scope, the concept of rule cannot have a clear scope either. This is not a minor problem, for it adds a good argument to those skeptical views that deny that rules exist, or guide behavior in the way we think they do. A satisfying logical reconstruction of the negation of rules is a powerful challenge to those who hold a rule-based account of prescriptive discourses and human behavior. But the burden of proving that negation, and inconsistency, can be indeed accommodated within such an account is a future inescapable task for the entire community of practical philosophy.

Acknowledgments The author thanks Riccardo Guastini for his comments and observations on a previous version of the present paper.

References

Alchourrón, C. E. 1991. Conflicts of norms and the revision of normative systems. *Law and Philosophy* 10:413–425.

Alchourrón, C. E., and E. Bulygin 1971. *Normative systems*. New York: Springer.

Alchourrón, C. E., and E. Bulygin 1981. The expressive conception of norms. In *New studies in deontic logic*, ed. R. Hilpinen, 95–124. Dordrecht: Reidel.

Alchourrón, C. E., and D. Makinson 1981. Hierarchies of regulations and their logic. In *New studies in deontic logic*, ed. R. Hilpinen, 125–148. Dordrecht: Reidel.

Atienza, M. 1992. Sobre los límites del análisis lógico en el derecho. *Theoria* 7:1007–1018.

Bulygin, E. 1982. *Time and validity*. In *Deontic logic, computational linguistics and legal information systems*, ed. A. A. Martino, 65–81. Amsterdam: North Holland.

Hage, J. 2000. Rule consistency. *Law and Philosophy* 19:369–390.
Lewis, D. 1973. Counterfactuals. The British Journal for the Philosophy of Science 27 (1976): 403–414. (Oxford: Blackwell).
Moreso, J. J. 1996. On relevance and justification of legal decisions. *Erkenntnis* 44:73–100.
Narváez, M. 2010. Detectar concepciones: El test de la negación. *Doxa* 33:553–570.
Quine, W. V. 1961. *Mathematical logic*. Cambridge: Harvard University Press.
Rodríguez, J. L. 2002. *Lógica de los sistemas jurídicos*. Madrid: Centro de studios políticos y constitucionales.
Ross, A. 1968. *Directives and norms*. London: Routledge & Kegan Paul.
Sartor, G. 1992. Normative conflicts in legal reasoning. *Artificial Intelligence and Law* 1:209–235.
Soeteman, A. 1989. *Logic in law*. Dordrecht: Kluwer.
Stalnaker, R. 1968. A theory of conditionals. *Studies in Logical Theory, American Philosophical Quarterly Monograph Series 2,* ed. N. Rescher, 98–112. Oxford: Blackwell.

Chapter 31
Legal Rules: Defeasible or Indefeasible?

Michał Araszkiewicz

Abstract This paper proposes a middle-ground solution in the dispute between legal defeasibilism and indefeasibilism. Several different readings of the concept of the defeasibility of legal rules are considered. The focus is on the concept referred to as the strong defeasibility of legal rules as defined by Frederick Schauer, that is, the alleged feature of rules according to which their conclusions may be contested on the basis of unspecified list of reasons. The paper analyzes the arguments of both proponents and opponents of legal defeasibilism. The opposing views are analyzed from the point of view of argumentation schemes theory. Certain points of disagreement in the ongoing debate between these two approaches are assessed as apparent only. Ultimately, the strong defeasibility thesis is rejected. A conception of contextually complete legal rules is presented and justified. The presented theory offers a third way in the debate between legal defeasibilism and indefeasibilism, preserving important insights that are present in the two competing theories.

Keywords Contextualism · Defeasibility · Exceptions · Logic · Rules

31.1 Introduction

The problem of the defeasibility of legal rules and legal reasoning has become one of the most debated topics in legal theory during the last three decades. The 1990s and early 2000s can be declared as the age of defeasibilism in analytical legal theory, mainly due to the development of alternative logical systems that have proved very useful concerning the representation of many important issues in legal reasoning: modeling exceptions to rules, reasoning with burdens of proof, etc. The notion of defeasibility has also been employed in the discussion of more general topics in legal theory. However, the criticism of defeasibilism was also present in the literature, and it seems that, in recent years, it has attracted attention again. This paper has three interrelated aims. The first aim is to provide an overview of the contemporary state of the art concerning the discussion of defeasibility with a particular emphasis

M. Araszkiewicz (✉)
Faculty of Law, Jagiellonian University, Kraków, Poland
e-mail: michal.araszkiewicz@uj.edu.pl

M. Araszkiewicz et al. (eds.), *Problems of Normativity, Rules and Rule-Following*,
Law and Philosophy Library 111, DOI 10.1007/978-3-319-09375-8_31

on defeasibility in legal theory. The second objective is to provide a typology of arguments that support or attack the thesis concerning defeasibility of legal rules. The third purpose is to provide a middle-ground theoretical account that would preserve valuable intuitions developed in legal defeasibilism and indefeasibilism yet be free of certain fallacies that are present in each of these theories. The order of investigations is as follows. In Sect. 31.2, we outline the general conclusions that follow from the discussion on the concept of defeasibility. In Sect. 31.3, we focus on the defeasibility of legal rules and formulate a thesis, referred to as the strong defeasibility thesis, concerning legal rules. Moreover, the chosen arguments supporting and attacking the central thesis concerning the strong defeasibility of legal rules are discussed. Section 31.4 is devoted to the methodological analysis of the ongoing discussion concerning the defeasibility of legal rules. In Sect. 31.5, an original application of basic ideas of epistemic contextualism to the problem of the defeasibility of legal rules leads to the formulation of a conception of contextually complete rules. The concept is used to overcome the difficulties that stem from the debate between legal defeasibilism and indefeasibilism. Section 31.6 concludes.

31.2 The Concept of Defeasibility: Defeasible Rules

During the last three decades, defeasibility has become one of the most discussed topic in analytic legal philosophy and in Artificial Intelligence (AI) and Law research. The peak of interest in the subject in legal domain was in the 1990s, although recently this topic still attracts attention (cf. Ferrer Beltrán and Ratti (eds.) 2012 for a comprehensive discussion of the contemporary state of the art). The discussion of defeasibility in legal domain has had numerous interconnections with the ideas developed in the field of general epistemology, formal logic and artificial intelligence research concerning argumentation (Pollock 1987; 1992; 1994; 1995; Loui 1987, Simari and Loui 1992; Prakken and Vreeswijk 2002).[1]

The discussion should be assessed as very important because of its theoretical (what is the actual logical form of legal reasoning) and practical (implications for creation of intelligent legal databases and support systems) aspects. From the bird's eye view it is now possible to formulate a few general statements emerging from this discussion.

First, it is very clear nowadays that defeasibility is an ambiguous concept. For instance, Hage distinguishes (at least) three understandings of defeasibility (Hage 2005, pp. 9–14), and Prakken and Sartor also point out three distinct readings of this term in the context of law (Prakken and Sartor 2004).[2] In particular, the concept of

[1] From the point of view of legal theory, it is often indicated that H. L. A. Hart in one of his early papers (Hart 1948/1949) introduced certain ideas that provided the foundation for contemporary research on defeasibility in law.

[2] For a discussion of the concept of defeasibility in the context of deontic logics, see van der Torre and Tan (1997).

defeasibility is not only discussed in the context of legal interpretation and application of law (cf. for instance Guastini 2012), but it has important connections with the notion of legal validity as well (Ferrer Beltrán and Ratti 2010). Consequently, it would be misleading to formulate any single general "authoritative" definition of the concept.

Second, defeasibility may be ascribed to different objects (concepts, theories, rules reasoning, etc.), and in these different cases, the meaning of defeasibility may vary.

Third, defeasibility ought to be distinguished from non-monotonicity. The latter is a property of formal logics. We claim that a given logic L is monotonic if and only if the following condition holds. Let us assume that a conclusion C follows logically from a set of premises P. If this is the case, then for any set of premises P′ such that P′ is a superset of P, C also follows logically. We state that logic is non-monotonic if and only if it is not monotonic. Although non-monotonic logics are natural tools for modeling defeasible reasoning, there is no necessary connection between non-monotonicity and defeasibility.[3] However, non-monotonic logics capture an important intuition that is encompassed in any reading of the concepts of defeasibility such that the introduction of new information may lead to the defeat of previously accepted conclusions.

The ambiguity of the term "defeasibility" leads to a variety of possible definitions of the defeasibility of rules. However, it is possible to indicate exemplary properties of defeasible rules (Hage 2005, p. 14):

- The strengthening of antecedent principle does not apply to defeasible rules;
- Defeasible rules do not warrant the *Modus Ponendo Ponens* rule as valid;
- Defeasible rules do not warrant any valid derivation of q from $p \rightarrow q$ and p in even weaker sense than referred to in *Modus Ponendo Ponens* rule.

Obviously, precise definitions of properties of defeasible rules can be given in the framework of concrete systems of defeasible logics (see Prakken and Vreeswijk (2002) for an overview). However, independently of different logical systems, a general idea behind the defeasibility of rules (understood here as conditional expressions of the form "IF [conditions] THEN [conclusion]") is that (1) the conclusion of a rule does not have to follow even if all conditions of this rule are satisfied, and (2) this does not mean that a rule in question is modified or revised. Conversely, we may state that an "IF [conditions] THEN [conclusion]" rule is indefeasible (or conclusive) if and only if it is always the case that, if its conditions are satisfied, the conclusion holds (we may reject the conclusion stemming from the rule in the case of revision of the rule or by considering it invalid or inapplicable).

Although this general idea is adopted in legal-theoretical discussion on the defeasibility of legal rules, it is necessary to introduce further distinctions to avoid oversimplification of the problem. The peculiarities of the context of legal discourse lead to several different readings of the concept of the defeasibility of rules.

[3] Cf. Hage (2005, p. 8).

31.3 Defeasibility of Legal Rules

The peculiarities of the context of legal discourse lead to several different readings of the concept of the defeasibility of rules in the field of legal theory. To make the argument of this paper clear and to delimit the scope of inquiry, let us first distinguish between the notion of the defeasibility of rules and the problem of interpretation of the rules' conditions.

Defeasibility should not be identified with problems of determining the extension of antecedents of a rule. Due to the many features of linguistic formulation of a given statutory provision, it may be problematic to determine whether a given state of affairs is or is not within its scope of application. The literature on the topics of ambiguity, vagueness, open texture, and the evaluative openness of statutory terms is too vast to be reviewed here. The problems with the determination of the scope of statutory expressions are dealt with by means of canons of legal interpretation and various kinds of legal arguments. It is necessary to stress, however, that problems concerning the determination of the scope of a rule should not be confused with the (alleged) defeasibility of this rule. It is even possible to state that the contrary is the case. Lawyers (both theorists and practicing lawyers) are so concerned about different methods of legal interpretation and about argumentation related to determination of the scope of rules because they implicitly assume indefeasibility of rules: once it is successfully argued that a given object is within the scope of a given rule, the legal consequences as prescribed by this rule should become effective regarding this object. What should be stressed here is that notorious problems in determining of the scope of a rule do not imply defeasibility of rules; these two issues are conceptually independent.

There are several phenomena concerning actual legal argumentation that have led scholars to formulate different arguments for and against the defeasible nature of legal rules.

Let us begin with the preliminary insight that, in the domain of legal argumentation, there are strong intuitions for both the indefeasible (conclusive) and defeasible character of legal rules. As for the former one, it has roots in the famous distinction of legal norms into legal rules and legal principles as introduced by Dworkin (1978) and refined and modified by Alexy, according to whom legal rules are applied by means of a deductive Subsumption Formula (Alexy 2003, pp. 433–434). In general, lawyers are inclined to think that, if in a given case all conditions for the application of a rule are fulfilled (provided that the rule has been properly reconstructed from the relevant sources), the conclusion of the rule should follow. In other words, legal rules are often perceived as formulating the sufficient conditions of their application.

On the other hand, there are numerous phenomena in the application of legal rules that seem to support the thesis of their defeasibility. Rules are subject to (explicit and implicit) exceptions, they may conflict with other rules, they may be excluded from application by means of other rules, etc. (cf. Gordon and Walton 2009; see Schauer 1998 for distinguishing seven different accounts of the defeasibility of legal rules). Below, we present three different readings of the defeasibility thesis concerning legal rules, and we show that only one of them is actually challenging from legal-theoretical point of view.

1. Procedural defeasibility of legal rules. According to this argument, legal rules are defeasible due to the specific character of their operation within the context of procedures before the courts and due to the institution of the burden of proof existing there. In the context of proceedings before a court, an active side (for instance, the plaintiff) is obligated only to prove the facts that provide for the grounds of her claim; it is the task of the defendant to prove that some exceptions or justificatory circumstances hold. This distinction is discussed in the literature under the name of *probanda* and *non-refutanda* by Giovanni Sartor (Sartor 1995; cf. the recent contribution to the subject in Sartor 2012; let us note that Sartor's discussion of defeasibility of rules encompasses broader topics than just procedural defeasibility). The argument, claims that legal rules are defeasible because, even though the antecedent of a rule invoked by a plaintiff is established in proceedings (proven), it still may happen that the conclusion of this rule will not follow because of a successful defense by the defendant. Consequently, following of a conclusion from a certain formulation of a legal rule seems to be contingent on the behavior of other parties to legal disputes, because if they do not question certain *non-refutanda* successfully, these parts of the rule in question will be considered as holding.
   Procedural defeasibility is a well-known and interesting phenomenon, although it is not an actual problem as regards the legal-theoretical discussion of defeasibility of legal rules. It has been convincingly pointed out by Bayón (Bayón 2001, pp. 332–333) that from the point of view of the judge that no phenomenon of defeasibility is present in this context because the rule actually contemplated and applied by the judge encompasses both (not-)proving of grounds for the claim by the plaintiff and (not-)proving of grounds for exceptions by the defendant. In consequence, from the point of view of the judge, the applied rule (with respect to the rules concerning burden of proof) may have an entirely indefeasible character. In consequence, the procedural defeasibility of legal rules is not the full-fledged defeasibility that leads to genuine legal–theoretical disagreement.
2. Epistemic defeasibility. According to this argument, our whole knowledge and system of beliefs is inherently defeasible, which means that legal knowledge is also defeasible, which should lead to the acceptance of a conclusion concerning inherent defeasibility of legal rules (cf. a broad discussion of this argument in Bayón 2001, p. 333 ff.). However, this argument misses the point concerning a legal–theoretical thesis concerning the defeasibility of legal rules. What we are asking now is whether legal rules are *actually* defeasible, not whether the system of beliefs of an agent applying the law is defeasible (there are strong arguments that it is, but this contention is irrelevant in the context of our discussion). As a consequence, an indefeasibilist may claim that the treatment of a given legal rule as defeasible stems from its incompleteness resulting from epistemic failures (lack of memory, lack of knowledge of the legal system of a given agent, errors

concerning the identification of rules colliding with the rule in question, etc.) and not from the features of the legal rules themselves. Although this type of defeasibility is important from a practical point of view and leads to numerous important insights concerning reasoning with rules, it is not relevant with respect to the legal–theoretical question concerning the defeasibility of legal rules.

3. Strong defeasibility. According to this argument, all legal rules are *actually* defeasible; that is, it is always possible that, even though the scope of the rule has been determined correctly and the rule is applicable to a given case to produce a conclusion C, it is possible that a reason R will be formulated that leads to the rejection of conclusion C. This understanding of the defeasibility of rules is captured well by definition referred to as D5, as discussed by Schauer (1998, p. 232):

> [A] rule is defeasible when its application is contingent not only upon the non-occurrence of events specifiable in advance by particular or type, but also by the non-occurrence of conditions specifiable in advance neither by particular nor by type.

We will refer to this type of defeasibility as strong defeasibility and a thesis according to which all legal rules are strongly defeasible as the strong defeasibility thesis (SDT).

Let us paraphrase the SDT thesis in a more thorough manner. We begin with a consideration that any case may be described by means of an infinite number of sentences. Hence, let us assume that we have a rule R and a set of cases $C_i \in C$ ($i = 1, 2, \ldots n$), where each case C_i is a set of facts describable by conditions c_{i-1}, $c_{i-2}, \ldots c_{i-n}$.

Let us assume that each of the cases from the set C is such that they are encompassed by the list of conditions of the rule R (as a consequence, the rule R is *prima facie* applicable to each of these cases).

According to the SDT, for any C_i belonging to the set C, there may be a condition c_{i-j} that makes the rule R inapplicable to this case. Even more explicitly, for each rule R and case C_i such that the rule R is applicable to C_i, there may exist (although it does not necessarily exist) an element in C_i that makes R inapplicable to C_i (or it brings about a legal consequence that differs from the legal consequence prescribed by R). In consequence, it is always possible that rule R will not be applied to a given case even if the case is within the scope of antecedent of the rule. It is worth emphasizing that the defeating element is not chosen from the set of explicit exceptions to the rule, prevailing constitutional norms, etc.

This thesis is an actual challenge to legal theory because it seems to undermine the conclusive character of arguments built on legal rules and delimits the possibility of adequate modelling of law by means of monotonic logics. Let us emphasize that the thesis discussed here is a theoretical one, and it should be distinguished from practical considerations related to the creation and maintenance of legal knowledge databases, where nonmonotonic logics are actually useful tools for knowledge representations due to several features (resemblance to actual structure of legal provisions, modularity, etc.; see Prakken 1997, p. 104 and Brożek 2004,

p. 143). According to the SDT consequences stemming from arguments based on legal rules are not deductive consequences, and for any legal rules constructed from relevant sources, its conditions are not sufficient conditions for its application, but at best, they are necessary conditions of sufficient conditions of the derivation of a conclusion from this rule (Rodriguez 2012, p. 92).

As for the arguments for the SDT, they are often formulated in the context of the discussion of the aforementioned distinction between legal rules and legal principles introduced by Ronald Dworkin. For instance, Sartor questions the possibility of construction of the so-called perfect conditional norms (such norms that prescribe sufficient conditions for their application). Let us quote the following passage illustrating the author's point:

> (….) [T]he rewriting of the legal system in the form of a set of perfect conditional norms could never be completed. In any case the resulting formulations would be extremely complex—there would be an infinite number of prescriptions, each of them with an endless antecedent; (….) [E]very norm possesses the characteristics Dworkin attributes to principles: it is defeasible in a set of circumstances not abstractly predetermined (….) (Sartor 1995, pp. 143–144).[4]

The argument presented here is convincing because the construction of perfect conditional norms seems to be an impossible task.

It follows that the idea of indefeasible legal rules may serve only as a kind of regulative idea in the Kantian sense: if legal scholars are interested in enhancing certainty in the application of rules, they should attempt to determine the content of the rules' antecedents to the greatest extent possible, but they can never succeed in eliminating the inherent feature of legal rules, which is their (strong) defeasibility.

Although arguments supporting the SDT seem to be strong, the thesis also provokes sound criticism. For instance, in one of this recent contributions, Rodriguez argues that the adoption of SDT makes any rule-based argument in the domain of law useless, and he insists on the deductive character of this type of argument, rejecting also defeasibility theses that are weaker than the SDT (Rodriguez 2012, p. 98; for a discussion of a weaker defeasibility thesis, see Schauer 1998, p. 238). He also claims that, at least in the light of the main theses of legal positivism, it is in principle possible to construct exhaustive sets of conditions for rules' application because these conditions should be identifiable from relevant social sources (Rodriguez 2012, p. 107).

Ratti (2013) also adopts a critical stance concerning legal defeasibilism by pointing out that, by rejecting a (deductive) *Modus Ponens* rule and the strengthening of antecedents of implication, defeasibilists are unable to represent genuine normative conflicts and inconsistencies (2013, p. 130 ff.).

The short presentation of arguments for and against the SDT leads to a tentative conclusion that they are similarly compelling. Both legal defeasibilism and indefeasibilism possess certain troubling features. Therefore, it is worthwhile to look at the discussion from a broader methodological perspective.

---

[4] Similar considerations are advanced by Brożek (2004, p. 142; 2007, p. 133 ff.).

31.4 Methodological Perspective

The discussion of the defeasibility of legal rules is endangered by both confusion and triviality. Regarding the former problem, it is often possible to mix the considerations concerning the defeasibility of legal rules with other important topics in legal theory, such as problems of the determination of the meaning of legal terms, collisions between legal rules, etc. The second factor that may lead to confusion regarding the discussion of defeasibility in the law is that the developed theories may have different aims. For instance, a theory of the representation of legal knowledge as defeasible rules designed for a practical purpose (such as development of AI-enhanced legal databases) does not influence theories that aim at an adequate description of the structure of legal reasoning. More accurately, a practical statement that "it is useful to formulate legal rules as defeasible ones for the sake of computational purposes" is entirely independent of a legal–theoretical statement that "legal systems are sets of defeasible rules." Consequently, in any discussion concerning legal defeasibility, the purpose of the developed theories or models should be clarified carefully.

The latter danger (that is, triviality) is a more serious one. The discussion of the defeasibility of legal rules may be easily disregarded by first showing that the acceptance of theses concerning the defeasibility or indefeasibility of legal rules is implied by general legal–philosophical assumptions and then by pointing out that the controversies in legal philosophy are long lasting and presumably inconclusive. For instance, Rodriguez' argument presented in the preceding section might be attacked on the basis that this statement is sound only if one adopts legal–positivistic assumptions. In consequence, the discussion of the SDT would be transformed into a general discussion concerning legal positivism and non-positivistic theories of law. Fortunately, there are no strict dependencies between an adopted theory of law and the discussion of the defeasible character of legal rules. Neither the SDT nor its negation follows logically from the assumptions of positivism or non-positivistic conceptions of law (although it is a fact that rejection of the SDT is coherent with the social sources thesis adopted by legal positivism). Therefore, the question of the defeasibility of legal rules may be discussed, as such, separately from the most fundamental questions of legal philosophy.

Let us now ask a methodological question concerning the nature of the discussion on the SDT and on the problem of the defeasibility of legal rules in general. Let us emphasize again that we are not interested here in a discussion of the concept of the defeasibility of rules in the context of the realization of a practical aim but from a legal–theoretical perspective. However, in this context, the SDT may be understood in at least three different ways:

1. The SDT as an empirical thesis. In this reading, the SDT is a thesis that aims at an adequate description of the actual argumentative behavior of the judges and other agents taking part in legal discourse. The defeasibility (or lack thereof) of legal rules is not viewed here as an essential property of them but rather as a

contingent feature, the presence of which may differ in different jurisdictions, and it may also vary in degree.[5]

2. The SDT as a conceptual thesis. This reading seems to be present in the majority of legal—theoretical papers dealing with this subject (including the aforementioned papers by Sartor (1995), Rodriguez (2012), and Ratti (2013). In this reading, defeasibility is seen either as an essential property of legal rules or a feature that leads to serious incoherencies in a developed theory of law; these incoherencies are viewed as falsifying the defeasibility theses. Although empirical research may contribute to the conceptual discussion, it cannot be decisive in this perspective. The theorists who are interested in this type of discussion focus on the deep rather than on the superficial (actually represented in the wording of judicial opinions) structure of legal reasoning.
3. The SDT as a normative thesis. According to this reading, the SDT should be adopted for the sake of realizing certain values. The normative thesis may be formulated by different types of actors and directed toward different types of addressees (for instance, defeasibility may be advanced as a conceptual tool for judges to enhance the elasticity of the legal system or its economic efficiency, or it may be advocated among legal scholars as a useful tool for knowledge representation).

The normative reading of the SDT is not relevant for the purposes of this paper (with one exception: the SDT should be accepted by scholars if it is an adequate conceptual thesis; however, in this interpretation, the normative SDT is strictly dependent on the soundness of the conceptual SDT, which is the main topic of our discussion). The relations between the empirical and conceptual reading of the thesis are more complicated. Because the conceptual SDT deals with essential properties of law, empirical research is of limited significance for it. Although it may provide important inspiration for the conceptual analysis, the results of the empirical research can falsify neither the conceptual SDT nor its negation. Consequently, an adherent of the SDT may always question empirical data suggesting the indefeasible (conclusive) character of legal rules either by assessing the judicial decision from which the data is taken as a pathology of legal practice or by stating that, on a superficial level, the wording of the court may suggest the indefeasible character of legal rules but the actual, deep structure of legal reasoning (as reconstructed by the defeasibilist) supports the claim to the contrary. An advocate of legal indefeasibilism may behave accordingly,[6] so if the dispute between them can be solved at all, it must be solved on conceptual grounds by showing that the criticized theory leads to undesirable incoherencies or even that it is internally inconsistent or otherwise incompatible with certain accepted statements. As shown previously, this is the direction chosen by

---

[5] In one of this recent contributions, Frederick Schauer (2012, (87)) adopts a similar (albeit more nuanced) position according to which "defeasibility is not a property of rules at all, but rather a characteristic of how some decision-making system will choose to *treat* its rules".

[6] See Rodriguez (2012, p. 96), discussing Schauer's views.

scholars quoted in the preceding section. However, this strategy is also problematic, for the parties to this legal–theoretical dispute may indicate that the assumptions adopted by them are incompatible, which either moves the discussion to a higher level concerning basic legal–theoretical assumptions or leads to the contention that the dispute is inconclusive (or trivial and should be disregarded as meaningless). To avoid this consequence, both views should be reconstructed in a broad conceptual scheme that is neutral with regard to assumptions of both advocates and critics of the SDT. Such scheme is outlined and applied in the next section.

31.5 A Proposal of a Solution

The structure of the argument in this section is as follows. First, we reconstruct the SDT and its negation in the broad frame of argumentation schemes theory. Second, a proposal for a "third way" between defeasibilism and indefeasibilism is outlined. The proposal is referred to as the thesis of the contextual defeasibility of legal rules.

Various theories of legal argumentation have been developed in the field of legal philosophy and theory during the last several decades.[7] This approach revolutionized legal philosophy and established a paradigm according to which argumentation is essential to legal reasoning. In addition, in the field of AI argumentation and in particular legal argumentation has received much attention and contemporarily is one of the most frequently discussed topics up to now (for an overview, cf. Rahwan and Simari, eds. (2009)).

In particular, the argument schemes approach has become very influential both in the philosophy of argumentation and in AI and law (also due to very important contributions to this field by Gordon and Walton (2006)). In short, 'argument schemes are argument forms that represent inferential structures of arguments used in everyday discourse, and in special contexts like legal argumentation, scientific argumentation, and especially in AI' (Walton and Reed 2002, p. 45). Argument schemes may be constructed around deductive inferences, but a majority of the arguments used in everyday reasoning have a non-deductive character, so they are types of patterns of defeasible reasoning. For instance, in Walton (2006), nine basic forms of defeasible arguments are presented and discussed. The main idea behind the presumptive character of argument schemes is that their premises support the conclusion only if their premises are not successfully contested by means of the so-called critical questions. The existence of critical questions strongly indicates the non-monotonic character of inferences encompassed in argument schemes. This is because a conclusion supported by an argument may cease to hold when additional elements of reasoning are introduced by means of critical questions.

The argument schemes approach offers a fruitful perspective concerning the theoretical structure of legal reasoning. In particular, this approach is neutral with regard to the deductive and non-deductive character of different legal arguments. The

[7] Cf., for instance, Alexy (1989).

discussion of the SDT may therefore be transformed into the question of whether an argument scheme based on legal rules is deductive (which would lead to the rejection of the SDT) or non-deductive (which would support the SDT).

Below, we present a proposal for a rule-based argument scheme.

Rule-Based Argument Scheme

Premise 1. There exists a legal rule LR that is an ordered tuple (ANT, CON), where ANT: (C_1, … C_n) is the set of conditions of LR, and CON: (N_1, … N_n) is the set of consequences of LR.

Premise 2. Let us assume that a case F is a set of facts f_1, … f_n such that these facts are describable by means of a set of predicates PRED: (P_1, … P_n) and that there exists a relation PRED $\subset$ ANT. In plain language, the facts of the case may be qualified as instances of the antecedent of the LR.

Conclusion: CON holds.

Note that this scheme is actually neutral with regard to the dispute between legal defeasibilism and indefeasibilism. The legal rule RL may be interpreted as either defeasible of indefeasible. If the rule RL is interpreted as an indefeasible one, the relation between the premises, and the conclusion of the arguments scheme will have a deductive character[8]; otherwise, the relation will be interpreted as only a presumptive one.

The use of the scheme presented above enables us to state explicitly what is actually at stake in the dispute between defeasibilists and indefeasibilists. A proponent of the SDT may claim that:

1. The rule LR is essentially incomplete in the sense that there may be a reason specified by neither token nor type that will lead to rejection of the conclusion of the LR (CON), or, in other words,
2. That there may be a reason (unspecified by neither token nor type) that will lead to construction of a competing argument that will override the original argument generated from the rule-based argument scheme.

An indefeasibilist may reject the SDT in the following ways:

1. Either by stating that until the reason mentioned by the defeasibilist is specified by either token or at least type, he or she is entitled to hold that the rule LR is complete (and therefore that the conclusion CON follows) or
2. By admitting that the reason provided by the defeasibilist is actually compelling and by revising the rule LR by adding a new condition to the set ANT; the indefeasibilist would insist at this point that the original formulation of the LR was actually incomplete, though the incompleteness stemmed not from conceptual but from epistemic defeasibility.

---

[8] In this reading, the rule-based argument scheme may be considered as an informal description of application of the *Modus Ponens* inference pattern.

The analysis presented above suggests that both stances (defeasibilism adopting the SDT and indefeasibilism rejecting it) are mutually translatable. Any statement of a defeasibilist concerning the defeasible character of any rule-based argument in the law may be translated into a relevant statement of an indefeasibilist asserting epistemic failure in the original formulation of the rule and complementing its ANT set with a new condition.

The rules of translation from the language of defeasibilism to the language of indefeasibilism are useful tools that may be used for revealing apparent problems concerning the dispute in question. However, they are not sufficient for the formulation of a proposal of a solution to the dispute that would be satisfactory for indefeasibilists. Let us note that the discussion built around the rule-based scheme leads to conclusions that are very similar to those in the account referred to as a "weak version of defeasibility" by Rodriguez (2012, p. 98) and formulated by Schauer (1998, p. 238) in the following manner:

> (….) [A] rule is defeasible when its application is contingent upon the non-occurrence of an unspecifiable list of very good reasons for not applying the rule, such reasons having strength greater than would have been sufficient for those reasons to determine the outcome in absence of the rule.

The only difference that follows from the discussion concerning the rules of translation between the language of defeasibilism and indefeasibilism is that, in this latter language, the rule in question would be assessed as incomplete due to epistemic limitations of the proponent of the rule-based argument.

The core issue is whether it is a theoretically sound statement that it is "always possible" to attack legal rules on the basis of their "essential incompleteness." Our discussion around the rule-based argument scheme together with Schauer's definition of weak defeasibility quoted above suggest that the person attacking the rule should state concretely the "very good reason" for non-application of the rule in question and that she or he should justify that these reasons are actually strong enough to result in non-application of this rule. An indefeasibilist would claim that this thesis is still too strong with regard to the scope of accepted defeasibility of rules, and he would claim that, in a majority of situations concerning legal discourse, it is not possible to even initiate such attack and simultaneously remain in the field of legal discourse. Empirical data also support the thesis concerning rejection of the SDT in this context (although it should be noted that these data cannot be conclusive in the context of purely conceptual analysis): legal rules that are actually applied in civil, criminal, and administrative proceedings are not continuously attacked on the basis of novel and surprising reasons that were not specified before (by either token or type).

The question is whether the conclusion stemming from arguments of an indefeasibilist can be justified without adopting a doubtful concept of perfect conditional norms as discussed by Sartor. The answer to this question is affirmative, and it will be formulated by means of the application of certain ideas of epistemic contextualism.

Epistemic contextualism is a view in epistemology according to which

> (….) [T]he proposition expressed by a given knowledge sentence ('S knows that p', 'S doesn't know that p') depends upon the context in which it is uttered (….) (Rysiew 2011).

Changes in the context may thus lead to a change in the ascription of logical values to knowledge ascription statements. Several variants of epistemic contextualism have been developed by, for instance, DeRose (2009), Cohen (1986), and Lewis (1996), and although they employ different conceptual schemes, they are in accordance with respect to the main idea that certain elements of the context of the utterance of a statement concerning the ascription of knowledge may affect the logical value of this statement.

The application of this idea to the discussion of the SDT may be presented as follows. Let us begin with a formulation of a legal rule as it was presented earlier in the rule-based argument scheme:

There exists a legal rule LR that is an ordered tuple (ANT, CON), where ANT: (C_1, … C_n) is the set of conditions of LR, and CON: (N_1, … N_n) is the set of consequences of LR.

The discussion in this section leads to the conclusion that the core difference between the SDT and its negation lies (in the language of defeasibilism) in the problem of the possibility of non-application of the rule due to overriding reasons or (in the language of indefeasibilism) on the possibility of attacking the thesis concerning the completeness of this rule. Let us now consider the following proposition:

[*Contextual completeness statement*]. *The legal rule LR is complete in the context of case F.*

The aforementioned proposition is an ascription of the feature of completeness to the rule LR in the context of a given case. The intuition that is behind the concept of the contextual completeness of legal rules is that, in a majority of cases, they are actually viewed as complete in the sense that there is no applicable legal argument that would lead to the conclusion that they are incomplete (in the language of indefeasibilism). If a legal rule is contextually complete in a given context, then there is no possibility of formulating a sound legal argument that would lead to their non-application.

A question arises: when can legal rules be considered contextually complete? The answer to this question is simple and complex at the same time: it depends on the context in which the rule is (re)constructed and applied. The factors that are important for establishing this context are, *inter alia*, the procedural norms governing a particular type of proceedings (rules of burden of proof, etc.), the active or passive attitude of the parties to the dispute concerning suggestions for answering the questions of law, the constraints stemming from the authority of higher courts, etc. In particular, the presence of controversial moral issues in a given case may raise the contextual standards of the ascription of truth to the contextual completeness statements.

Although it is not possible here to investigate in depth the concept of context that is relevant for establishing the contextual completeness of legal rules, a few comments are in order. The very criteria of identification of factors that are relevant of establishing the elements of this context may be very debatable not only in concrete cases, but also in general. There exist no fixed and uncontroversial theory that would determine the scope of types (and in consequence, of tokens) of these elements. In this connection, it might be claimed that the introduction of the notion of contextual completeness of legal rules simply moves the discussion of defeasibility of legal rules to a meta-level argumentation. This claim would be partially right, but with an important qualification. It may be claimed that if a legal theorist does not intend to assess the existing practice of application of law as generally misled, this practice may be a useful source of information as regards the types (and tokens) of factors that are actually employed for determining that a legal rule in question is contextually complete. What is more, the knowledge concerning this, perhaps to some extent vague, set of factors, will presumably constitute an important part of knowledge of any professional lawyer or judge in any jurisdiction. The topic of factors that are actually relevant for establishing contextual completeness of legal rules should be regarded as an important open question in contemporary legal theory. In our opinion, the topic does not belong to the theory of law itself, but to the theory of legal knowledge (see Guastini 2012, p. 192).

What are the consequences of the adoption of the concept of the contextual completeness of legal rules for the debate between the SDT and its negation in particular and between defeasibilism and indefeasibilism in general? In our opinion, the addition of a contextual completeness statement brings about the following results.

First, the rule-based argumentation scheme may be easily accounted for as a deductive one. This embraces important arguments raised by indefeasibilists. If a disputant argues for the non-application of a rule in question (we assume here that the argument is well formed and that its premises are true), he or she must first show that the rule in question is (contextually) incomplete. However, this does not alter the deductive character of the applied reasoning pattern. In addition, genuine normative conflicts are possible between contextually complete rules. These results give answers to questions raised by Rodriguez (2012) and Ratti (2013).

Second, the concept of contextually complete rules shows that it is possible to circumvent the SDT without adopting infinite, perfect conditional norms (cf. Sartor 1995).

Third, the applied concept of contextual completeness leaves open the question concerning the possibility of the use of novel types of reasons in the legal discourse (as advanced by the SDT). However, it moves this topic to another level of dispute, that is, to the level of elements of context that influence the standards concerning the ascription of the feature of completeness to a legal rule in question.

In summing up the above considerations, an answer to the main question concerning the soundness of the SDT should be formulated. Let us recall that, according to the SDT, a rule is defeasible when its application is contingent not only upon the non-occurrence of events specifiable in advance by particular or type but also by the non-occurrence of conditions specifiable in advance by neither particular nor type. The investigations in this paper lead to a negative answer to this question: the SDT is untenable. However, important intuitions that are encompassed in it should be embraced at another level of legal discourse: the level concerning the contextual completeness of legal rules.

Conclusion

This paper argues for a middle ground in the dispute between legal defeasibilism and indefeasibilism. The concept of the contextual completeness of legal rules was introduced to supply a traditional rule-based argument scheme to obtain two results: preservation of the deductive character of legal rule-based reasoning and embracing the openness and contextual sensitivity of legal discourse as advanced by the strong defeasibility thesis. The paper's original import was preceded by a detailed review of the discussion of the concept of the defeasibility of legal rules in the literature of the subject. In particular, rules of translation were formulated concerning the account of certain problems in the application of law from the point of view of defeasibilism and indefeasibilism.

The concept of contextual completeness is obviously a controversial proposal, in part because it is based on the basic ideas of a contestable epistemological theory: epistemic contextualism. As for perspectives of further research on this issue, the elements of legal context that are relevant for the ascription of the feature of relative completeness to legal rules should be scrupulously investigated.

Acknowledgments The author thanks Jaap Hage, Giovanni Battista Ratti, and Andrej Kristan for their valuable comments in connection with the presentation of this paper during the RULES 2013 (September 27–29) conference in Kraków.

References

Alexy, Robert. 1989. *A theory of legal argumentation. The theory of rational discourse as theory of legal justification*. (Trans: R. Adler, N. MacCormick). Oxford: Clarendon. (1st German ed. 1978).

Alexy, Robert. 2003. Balancing and subsumption. A structural comparison. *Ratio Juris* 16:433–449.

Bayón, Juan Carlos. 2001. Why is legal reasoning defeasible? In *Pluralism and law*, ed. Arend Soeteman, 251–278. Dodrecht: Kluwer.

Brożek, Bartosz. 2004. *Defeasibility of legal reasoning*. Kraków: Zakamycze.

Brożek, Bartosz. 2007. *Rationality and discourse. Towards a normative model of applying law*. Warszawa: Oficyna a Wolters Kluwer Business.

Cohen, Stewart. 1986. Knowledge and context. *Journal of Philosophy* 83:574–583.

DeRose, Keith. 2009. *The case for contextualism: Knowledge, skepticism, and context*, Vol. 1. Oxford: Clarendon.

Dworkin, Ronald. 1978. *Taking rights seriously*. Cambridge: Harvard University Press.

Ferrer Beltrán, Jordi, and Giovanni Battista Ratti 2010. Validity and defeasibility in the legal domain. *Law and Philosophy* 29:601–626.

Ferrer Beltrán, Jordi, and Giovanni Battista Ratti, eds. 2012. *The logic of legal requirements. Essays on defeasibilism*. Oxford: Oxford University Press.

Gordon, Thomas F., and Douglas Walton. 2006. The Carneades argumentation framework—using presumptions and exceptions to model critical questions. In *Proceedings of the first International Conference on Computational Models of Argument (COMMA 06),* ed. P. E. Dunne, 195–207.

Gordon, Thomas F., and Douglas, Walton. 2009. Legal reasoning with argumentation schemes. In *ICAIL*, 137–146. New York: Association for Computing Machinery.

Guastini, Riccardo. 2012. Defeasibility, axiological gaps and interpretation. In *The logic of legal requirements. Essays on defeasibilism,* eds. Jordi Ferrer Beltrán and Giovanni Battista Ratti, 182–192. Oxford: Oxford University Press.

Hage, Jaap. 2005. Law and defeasibility. In *Studies in legal logic,* 7–32. Berlin: Springer.

Hart, Herbert L. A. 1948/1949. The ascription of responsibility and rights. *Proceedings of the Aristotelian Society New Series* 49:171–194.

Lewis, David. 1996. Elusive knowledge. *Australasian Journal of Philosophy* 74:549–567.

Loui, Ronald. 1987. Defeat among arguments: A system of defeasible inference. *Computational Intelligence* 3:100–106.

Pollock, John. 1987. Defeasible reasoning. *Cognitive Science* 11:481–518.

Pollock, John. 1992. How to reason defeasibly. *Artificial Intelligence* 57:1–42.

Pollock, John. 1994. Justification and defeat. *Artificial Intelligence* 67:377–408.

Pollock, John. 1995. The structure of defeasible reasoning. In *Cognitive carpentry. A blueprint for how to build a person,* 85–140. Cambridge: MIT Press.

Prakken, Henry. 1997. *Logical tools for modelling legal argument. A study of defeasible reasoning in law*. Dordrecht: Kluwer.

Prakken, Henry, and Gerard Vreeswijk. 2002. Logics for defeasible argumentation. In *Handbook of philosophical logic*. 2nd ed. Vol. 4, eds. Dov Gabbay and Franz Guenthner, 219–318. Dodrecht: Kluwer.

Prakken, Henry, and Giovanni Sartor. 2004. The three faces of defeasibility in the law. *Ratio Juris* 17:118–139.

Rahwan, Iyad, and Guillermo Simari, eds. 2009. Argumentation in artificial intelligence. Berlin: Springer.

Ratti, Giovanni Battista. 2013. Normative inconsistency and logical theories: A first critique of defeasibilism. In *Coherence: Insights from philosophy, jurisprudence and artificial intelligence,* eds. Michał Araszkiewicz and Jaromír Šavelka, 123–135. Dordrecht: Springer.

Rodriguez, Jorge. 2012. Against defeasibility of legal rules. In *The logic of legal requirements. Essays on defeasibilism,* eds. Jordi Ferrer Beltrán and Giovanni Battista Ratti, 89–107. Oxford: Oxford University Press.

Rysiew, Patrick. 2011. *Epistemic Contextualism*. The Stanford encyclopedia of philosophy (Winter 2011 Edition), ed. Edward N. Zalta. http://plato.stanford.edu/archives/win2011/entries/contextualism-epistemology/. Accessed 30 Jan 2014.

Sartor, Giovanni. 1995. Defeasibility in legal reasoning. In *Informatics and the foundations of legal reasoning,* eds. Zenon Bankowski, Ian White, and Ulrike Hahn, 119–137. Dordrecht: Kluwer.

Sartor, Giovanni. 2012. Defeasibility in legal reasoning. In *The logic of legal requirements. Essays on defeasibilism,* eds. Jordi Ferrer Beltrán and Giovanni Battista Ratti, 108–136. Oxford: Oxford University Press.

Schauer, Frederick. 1998. On the supposed defeasibility of legal rules. In *Legal theory at the end of the millennium, current legal problems,* vol. 51, ed. M. D. A. Freeman, 223–240. Oxford: Oxford University Press.

Schauer, Frederick. 2012. Is defeasibility an essential property of law? In *The logic of legal requirements. Essays on defeasibilism,* eds. Jordi Ferrer Beltrán and Giovanni Battista Ratti, 77–88. Oxford: Oxford University Press.

Simari, Guillermo, and Ronald Loui. 1992. A mathematical treatment of defeasible reasoning and its implementation. *Artificial Intelligence* 53:125–157.

Van der Torre, Leendert, and Yao-Hua Tan. 1997. The many faces of defeasibility in defeasible deontic logic. In *Defeasible deontic logic,* ed. Donald Nute, 79–122. Dordrecht: Kluwer.

Walton, Douglas. 2006. *Fundamentals of critical argumentation.* Cambridge: Cambridge University Press.

Walton, Douglas, and Chris Reed. 2002. Argumentation schemes and defeasible inferences. Workshop on computational models of natural argument. In *ECAI 2002. 15th European Conference on Artificial Intelligence,* ed. Giuseppe Carenini, Floriana Grasso and Chris Reed, 45–55.

Chapter 32
The Role of Argumentation Theory in the Logics of Judgements

Marcello Ceci

Abstract The present paper represents an effort towards the acquisition of an acknowledged standard for the rule and logics layer of the semantic web stack of technologies. It is part of a broader research trying to improve the state-of-the-art of legal knowledge representation by facing its main issues: the gap between document representation and rule modeling, and the need for a shared standard in the logic layer to represent legal reasoning. The paper focuses on the upper part of the semantic web stack, namely the rules and logics layers: here, the Carneades Argumentation System supports the reproduction of judicial argumentation through a ruleset and a knowledge base imported from an OWL/RDF ontology. Being based upon the theories of argumentation developed by Gordon and Walton, Carneades supports argumentation schemes and uses them as templates while instantiating rules, ontology and cases into argument graphs. We argue that using argument schemes is the only viable choice to represent legal reasoning properly, and for this purpose, the concept of argument scheme should include templates that represent procedural aspects of legal processes, such as the acts available to the parties during a court trial. Even if emerging standards in rule representation (such as LegalRuleML) overcome many of the limitations of precedent languages, they lack a complete model of the argumentation process. This, as the paper tries to demonstrate, prevents the representation of legal arguments in their procedural aspects and in those aspects related to patterns and tasks of argumentation, hindering its capability to perform a correct evaluation of the acceptability of legal arguments. In order to support that claim, two examples are provided. The concluding remarks broaden the perspective to include the general need for a standard in legal reasoning engines.

Keywords Legal rules · Case-law · Argumentation schemes · Defeasible logics · Clojure

---

M. Ceci (✉)
AFIS GRCTC—University College Cork, College Road, Cork, Ireland
e-mail: marcello.ceci@ucc.ie

M. Araszkiewicz et al. (eds.), *Problems of Normativity, Rules and Rule-Following*,
Law and Philosophy Library 111, DOI 10.1007/978-3-319-09375-8_32

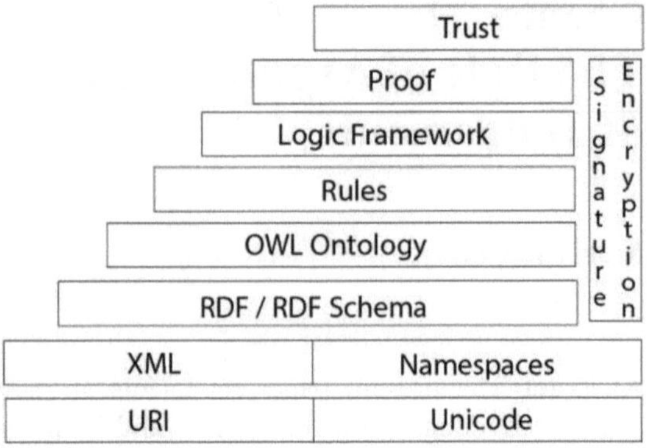

Fig. 32.1 The Semantic Web stack of technologies

32.1 Introduction: A Framework for Representing Judicial Decisions

The considerations presented in this paper stem from the author's research on a framework for case-law semantics (see Ceci 2012; Ceci and Gordon 2012) whose goal is to exploit Semantic Web technologies in order to achieve isomorphism between the text fragment (the only legally binding expression of the norm) and the legal rule, thus *filling the gap* between document representation and rules modelling (Palmirani et al. 2009). More precisely, the framework models the content of judicial documents, such as decisions of courts. The consideration guiding the research is that the features of the new OWL2 standard for computational ontologies[1] could greatly improve legal concepts modelling and reasoning, if properly combined with defeasible rule modelling. The aim of the framework is therefore to formalize the legal concepts and the argumentation patterns contained in the judgement in order to check, validate and reuse the legal concepts as expressed by the judicial decision's text. To achieve this, four layers along the Semantic Web stack of technologies (Fig. 32.1) are necessary:

- a *document metadata structure*, capturing the main parts of the judgement to create a bridge between text and semantic annotation of legal concepts;
- a *legal core ontology*, describing the legal domain's main elements in terms of general concepts through an LKIF-Core extension;
- a *legal domain ontology*, an extension of the legal core ontology representing the legal concepts of a specific legal domain concerned by the case-law, including a set of sample precedents;
- *argumentation modelling and reasoning*, representing the structure and dynamics of argumentation.

The research is based on a middle-out methodology: top-down for modeling the core ontology, bottom-up for modeling the domain ontology and the argumentation

[1] An ontology is a shared vocabulary, a taxonomy and axioms representing a domain of knowledge by defining objects and concepts with their properties, relations and semantics.

rules. Its sample consists in 27 decisions of Italian case-law, from different courts (Tribunal, Court of Appeal, and Cassation Court) but all concerning the same legal subject: *consumer law*.[2] The research relies on the previous efforts of the community in the field of legal knowledge representation (Hoekstra et al. 2009) and rule interchange for applications in the legal domain (Gordon et al. 2009). The issue of implementing logics to represent judicial interpretation has already been faced, albeit only for the purposes of a sample case. The aim of the present research is to apply these theories to a set of real legal documents, stressing the definitions of OWL axioms as much as possible in order to provide a semantically powerful representation of the legal document for an argumentation system that relies on a defeasible subset of predicate logics.

The Legal Ontology (Palmirani and Ceci 2012) creates an environment where the knowledge extracted from the decision's text can be processed and managed in order to perform deeper reasoning on the interpretation instances grounding the decision itself. This reasoning is based on the argumentation model of the Carneades Argumentation System.[3] The framework is capable of creating argumentation graphs in favour (*pro*) or against (*con*) a given legal statement, not only when all the premises for the argument are accepted in the knowledge base: Carneades is in fact capable of *suggesting* incomplete arguments (Ceci and Gordon 2012), thus highlighting critical aspects of the case which were not been taken into consideration by the judge (in the precedent case) or by the user (in the query). This means that, given a set of judicial decision encoded in the OWL ontology, the program is capable not only to represent the argumentation path followed by the judge, but also possible alternative paths that lead to different outcomes.

32.2 Representing Argumentation Patterns

32.2.1 Introduction

Any standard devoted to the representation of legal rules should include a unification of the logic layer into a single language. Some argue that the various aspects of argumentation can be properly represented through logics: in particular,

[2] The matter is specifically disciplined in Italy through the "Codice del Consumo" (Consumer Law) and articles 1341–1342 of the Civil Code. This discipline is also present in all foreign legal systems, which will allow an extension of the research to foreign decisions and laws. It also concerns conflicting norms of various sources, with different addressees (those of the legal system versus those contained in the contract).

[3] Carneades (Gordon and Walton 2006b) implements Walton's argumentation schemes (see paragraph 2.2) to reconstruct and evaluate past arguments in natural language texts, but also as templates for manual generation of arguments graphs representing ongoing dialogues. It can therefore be used for studying argumentation from a computational perspective, but also to develop tools supporting practical argumentation processes. It is capable of importing knowledge from the ontology set and of applying rules on them (Gordon 2008). The new version of Carneades (2.x, under development) uses s-expressions encoded in a proprietarty rule language based on Clojure, while the latest complete version (1.0.2) relies on the LKIF-Rule language (Gordon 2010).

Governatori (2011) shows how proof standards proposed in the Carneades framework correspond to some variants of defeasible logics, which could imply that an implementation of defeasible logics is able to compute acceptability of arguments. However this doesn't seem to be the case, in the light of the following considerations:

- Logics provide abstract formulas to represent relationships between concepts. With fine tools such as defeasible logics it is possible to successfully represent the complex relations between legal rules, but can they manage the *application* of these rules, a fundamental step towards the computation of the acceptability of an argument? In theory it could be the case, since the act of *substitution* of abstract symbols in formulas with the values of the situation we want to compute should be an automatic process where it doesn't matter which material concept is added as the interpretation of that abstract symbol. For example, if we have a+b=c, we can interpret this simple rule as meaning many different things (for example a=1, b=2, c=3, +=addition, or a=blue, b=yellow, c=green and +=mix) and this would not affect the *truth function* of the equation. On the contrary, in the concrete legal field the single elements bring with them particular conditions (minor rules or meta-rules), assumptions, exceptions, values, which can significantly alter the outcome of the abstract formula representing the rules.
- Most of the application scenarios of legal language are centered on *dialogues* with two or more parties in which claims are made and competing arguments are put forward to support or attack these claims (this includes judgements, which are the focus of this paper, but also parliamentary debates and other legal acts). Following Walton, we recognize there are several kinds of dialogues, with different purposes and different protocols (Fig. 32.2). This view of arguments as dialogues (or processes) contrasts with the mainstream, relational conception of argument in the field of computational models of arguments, typified by Dung (1995), where argumentation is viewed not as a dialogical process for making justified decisions which resolve disputed claims, but as a method for inferring consequences from an inconsistent set of propositions. To see the difference between these conceptions of arguments, notice that a proposition that has not been attacked is acceptable in this relational model of argument, whereas in most dialogues a proposition that has not been supported by some argument is typically not acceptable, since most protocols place the burden of proof on the party that made the claim.

Before exploring those two themes, a preliminary presentation of argument schemes is necessary.

32.2.2 Argumentation Schemes and Critical Questions

An argumentation scheme is a pattern of reasoning used in everyday conversation and other contexts, such as legal and scientific argumentation. Argumentation schemes serve the same purpose as their ancestors, the τόποι (*topics*) of Aristo-

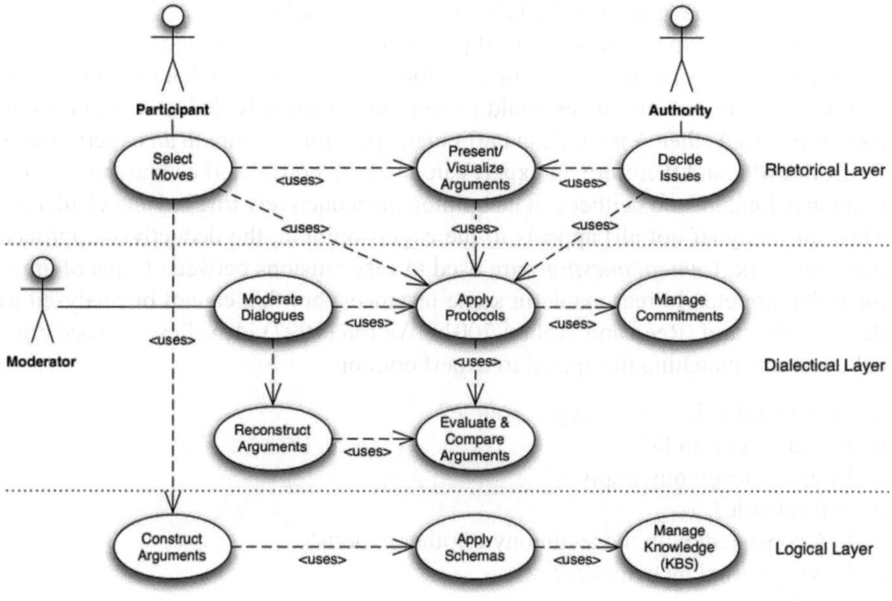

Fig. 32.2 Argumentation use cases in Gordon and Walton (2009)

tle: they are useful to create, evaluate and classify arguments. In recent times, the Artificial Intelligence field has become increasingly interested in argumentation schemes, due to their potential for making improvements in the reasoning capabilities of agents (Verheij 2003; Garssen 2001; Dung and Sartor 2011). Two functions of argumentation schemes can be distinguished in the legal field: as argument patterns useful for reconstructing arguments from natural language texts, and as methods for generating arguments from argument sources, such as legislation or precedent cases.

In argumentation theory, argumentation schemes are evaluated through a set of critical questions[4] (CQs), specific for each scheme. Each question reveals possible weak points in the argumentation, and if not answered adequately may render that specific argument useless in supporting the speaker's position in the dialogue. Evidently, critical points in arguments should be formalized in a dialogical structure, in order to maintain the notion of defeasibility of every argument in the scheme, including those introduced to answer one or more critical questions. The example from Walton's analysis of expert opinion (Walton 1997) perfectly explains this dialogical structure. Following is the model of *argument from expert opinion*:

Source E is an expert in domain D
E asserts that proposition A is known to be true (or false)
A is within D

[4] Critical questions were first introduced by Arthur Hastings (1963) as part of his analysis on presumptive argumentation schemes.

Therefore, A may plausibly be taken to be true (or false).

As shown by experiments in social psychology, however, there is a tendency to defer to experts, sometimes without questioning, resulting in fallacious appeals to authority. Many circumstances could prevent the apparently deductive conclusion that "if E says A, then A is true": in particular, epistemic closure in an expert field is far from truth, and therefore an expert can never be considered as knowing everything in a domain, and neither can its opinion be deductively true beyond challenge. Thus for many (if not all) appeals to the expert opinion, the deductivist approach does not work. *Critical questions* are used to ease tensions between forms of argument that are clearly reasonable in some instances, but that cannot be analysed as deductively valid (Reed and Walton 2001). Walton (1997) identifies six basic critical questions matching the appeal to expert opinion:

a. How credible is E as an expert source?
b. Is E an expert in D?
c. Does E's testimony imply A?
d. Is E reliable?
e. Is A consistent with the testimony of other experts?
f. Is A supported by evidence?

Please notice that, in many cases, asking one of the basic critical questions above will lead to critical sub-questions at a deeper level of examination. This is one way to create argumentation graphs (Gordon 2010).

32.2.3 The Procedural Aspects of Argumentation

Robert Alexy's discourse theory of legal argumentation explains how judicial discretion can be restricted without resorting to mechanical jurisprudence or conceptualism. In the early works of AI & Law on the subject, argumentation was modelled as deduction in a non-monotonic logic, i.e. as a defeasible consequence relation. The Pleadings Game—introduced in (Gordon 1994)—still uses non-monotonic logics and in particular defeasible logics to represent legal reasoning, but these logics are have a procedural layer on top of them which treats the whole argumentation as a process, with a sequence of *moves* by the players which are affected by the precedent ones.[5]

Following the mathematical model of Doug Walton's philosophy of argumentation and Aristotle's classification, Gordon in (Gordon and Walton 2009) describes argumentation as being divided into three layers: logic, dialectic, and rhetoric. While logics deal with the so-called relational aspects of argumentation, dialectic directly addresses the *procedural* aspects of it. In the light of this first distinction, the claim that Defeasible Logics can manage the acceptability of arguments appears

[5] Moreover, the task of that game is not that of winning a claim, but that of identifying the main issue of what Toulmin (1958) defines as *substantial arguments*.

to be an effort to flatten the representation of the first two layers into mere logics, which does not seem to take into consideration the difference of tasks evoked by different argumentation patterns (or, as they will be called from now on, argumentation schemes—see, nor the dialectical (or *procedural*) aspects of argumentation.

Walton's argumentation theory identifies a sequence of stages in a dialogue-like argument, where in each stage some *moves* are allowed to the player (as in The Pleadings Game) and those moves influence the possibilities for further stages. In particular, the concept of stages of the argumentation process is fundamental for the allocation of the burden of proof, which brings us back to the consideration in Sect. 32.2.1 about the relationship between Dungean Semantics and the dialogical conception of argumentation contained in (Walton 1998). Proposable exceptions, tacit acceptance, second grade preclusions, irrelevance: logics alone, no matter how powerful, cannot properly evaluate the acceptability of those argument if they cannot identify the stage of the process at which those arguments are introduced and consequently correctly allocate the burden of proof on one of the competing parties, and this in turn is not possible without a dialogical (or *procedural*) conception of argumentation. Defeasible logics can effectively manage complex interaction of rules such as the concept of proof standards. But an argument is much more than just rules, and representing the tasks and patterns presented above by relying only on a set of rules would require a huge effort, and yet produce an undesirably complicated and ungovernable result. This is, because these rules would have to simulate dialogical characteristics of argumentation, which are very different from relational ones.

In the Pleadings Game argumentation was viewed procedurally—as dialogues regulated by protocols—but this was accomplished by building a procedural layer on top of a non-monotonic logic. In LKIF, the relational interpretation of rules is abandoned entirely, in favor of a purely procedural view, and is thus more in line with modern argumentation theory in logics (Prakken 1995), philosophy (Walton 2006) and legal theory (Alexy 1989). Argumentation, as Gordon (2008) puts it, "cannot be reduced to logic."

In the Carneades Application, therefore, argumentation schemes are managed in an upper layer than rules. In this perspective, rules are just one of many sources for argument construction along with ontologies (OWL) and cases (Cato), whose different logics and formats are translated and mixed into an argument graph. The architecture used to instantiate these sources into argument schemes is presented in (Gordon 2011).

32.3 Two Examples

The AI & Law community uses famous US courts precedents, such as Pierson versus Post in (Gordon and Walton 2006a) and Popov versus Hayashi in (Gordon and Walton 2012; Prakken 2012) as a test field for its theories. These demonstrations are aimed at showing how to model arguments starting from the legal concepts, and how the reliance on argument schemes and competency questions is necessary in order to achieve a reconstruction of the original arguments and to correctly evaluate them. However, those tests do not pay attention to the connection of those concepts with the metadata contained in the source legal document. This is also the approach of Ashley's seminal contributions to the subject: the systems presented in (Ashley 1991, p. 34) and (Aleven 2003) are in fact oriented to the teaching of argumentation in law classes, rather than to the performing of automatic reasoning on the metadata contained in the legal documents.

The approach of the present research is more practical, as described in Sect. 32.1, and this approach will be kept also in finding evidence of the need for a modeling of the procedural aspects of argumentation into the emerging rule standards. The modeling of argument schemes seems the only viable choice to properly perform legal reasoning, and for this purpose the concept of argument scheme should include templates which represent procedural aspects of legal processes (such as the acts available to the parties during a trial). The two examples that follow are in fact taken from the sample of 27 decisions concerning consumer contracts which constitute the knowledge base of the research described in Sect. 32.1.

32.3.1 First Example

The first example is the decision issued on October 31, 2006 by the First Section of the Tribunal of Salerno, concerning the acceptability of an arbitration clause contained in a public statute (the statute of the Italian Football Federation). The argument put forward by the defender is that the judge is incompetent, since the litigation had to be settled by means of an arbitration following article 24 of the statute. The argument, however, was presented to the court only at a late stage of the trial. The judge, therefore, specifies that if the claim was formally qualified as a request for *competence regulation* (as the defender himself defined it), it would be inacceptable since those kind of claims can be presented only in the early stages of the trial. The judge, however, decides that the claim concerns the object of the trial, not a competence regulation. Therefore, the claim is acceptable and the judge declares his incompetence in favour of the arbitration court indicated in the statute.

Without recurring to argumentation schemes, representing this situation would require abstract structures for rules, which would astray from the original structure of the multi-logical process. To provide an example of this, Figs. 32.3 and 32.4 show how this information can be captured in LKIF and Clojure: the LKIF syntax doesn't allow to be dynamic and the sentences are manually applied to the rules during the argumentation modelling, while with Clojure the expressiveness can be enhanced including dynamicity with the rules, Boolean operators and also a meta-scheme of the argument to be applied. This is a typical example of how procedural aspects of the legal argumentation can influence the outcome of a claim, and therefore the application of rules (and more generally the logic layer) has to take into account these aspects, in order to achieve a correct evaluation of the acceptability of arguments.

```
<statements>
  <s id="s122"> applies TribSalerno_I Judge_not_competent</s>
  <s id="s222">considers TribSalerno_I StatutoFIGC_clause10</s>
  <s id="s322">contained_in StatutoFIGC_clause10 StatutoFIGC</s>
  <s id="s422">contains StatutoFIGC StatutoFIGC_clause24</s>
  <s id="s522">applies StatutoFIGC_clause24 Arbitration</s>
  </statements>
<arguments>
   <argument id="arg1">
     <conclusion statement="s122"/>
     <premises>
          <premise statement="s222"/>
          <premise statement="s322"/>
          <premise statement="s422"/>
          <premise statement="s522"/>
     </premises>
</argument>
```

Fig. 32.3 LKIF representation of the first example

32.3.2 Second Example

A second example shows how arguments, even arguments from legal rules, can be introduced in the judgement for tasks different from that of applying the rule contained in the legal norm. In the decision given by the Tribunal of Rovereto on July 13, 2006, an article of the Civil Code concerning oppressive clauses, which lists these by subject and considers as oppressive all clauses introducing "a limitation in concluding certain contracts with third parties" is used as an argument to prove that "there is a general disfavor in the system towards all pacts introducing limitations to competition." The argument of the oppressive clause is used together with the argument coming from article 81 of the EC Treaty, which explicitly forbids such pacts.

```
(def a1 (make-argument
    :header (make-metadata
    :description {:en "the judge of Salerno is incompetent, because art.
24 of the FIGC statute introduces a mandatory arbitration for all claims
concerning the statute" })
    :scheme "competency regulation"
    :conclusion (not (applies TribSalerno_I Judge_not_competent)
    :premises [((considers TribSalerno_I StatutoFIGC_clause10))(pm
'(contained_in StatutoFIGC_clause10 StatutoFIGC))(pm '(contains
StatutoFIGC StatutoFIGC_clause24))(pm '(applies StatutoFIGC_clause24
Arbitration))]
```

Fig. 32.4 Representation of the first example in the Clojure language

We can see how, in this case, the article of the Civil Code is evoked in the decision's text, and must therefore be marked up and linked to the text of the law. But how do we tell the reasoner that this rule doesn't have to be used for its general purpose (which is defining an oppressive clause) but rather for the purpose of supporting the statement that "there is a general disfavor in the system towards pacts introducing limitations to competition"? This can be done only by defining a framework for argumentation and by modeling argumentation schemes. In the example, the argument involving the article of the Civil Code would not be an argument from legal rules, but rather an argument from authority, and therefore the article of the Civil Code would not be transformed into an argument by translating the logic form of the rule it expresses, but rather by referring to the authority of the Civil Code and of the institution that issued it (which in this case is the Italian Parliament).

Conclusions: The Need for a Standard in Legal Reasoning

The present paper focuses on the logic layer of the semantic web stack, arguing that in order to properly process legal knowledge it is necessary to give account not only for deontic and defeasible extensions of logics, but also for argumentation schemes. Among the existing standards, LegalRuleML (Palmirani et al. 2011) includes most of the features required to represent legal rules and thus represents an improved standard language in comparison to LKIF-Rules. It can be taken as a cornerstone for the requirements that a reasoner must met in order to manage legal reasoning. However the LegalRuleML TC has not yet introduced in its language the support for the concepts of argumentation theory such as argumentation schemes and competency questions. An extension of the rule language in that direction would allow providing a standard set of metadata and logical operators for the reasoning layer to apply the state-of-the-art of legal argumentation theory. This engine could in turn consist of a standard set of libraries to be implemented into existing engines in order to introduce a complete management of defeasibility, deontics, temporal dimensions and argumentation schemes. The intention, in the upcoming research on this behalf, is to rely on a Drools-based application under construction by CIRSFID (Palmirani et al. 2012) and on NICTA's SPINdle (Lam and Governatori 2009), both based on LegalRuleML.

Acknowledgements The Author thanks prof. T. F. Gordon for the fruitful discussions from which the considerations contained in this paper arose, and prof. M. Palmirani (as well as those in CIRSFID involved in the "Fill the Gap" project) for providing meaningful references to the general framework.

References

Aleven, Vincent. 2003. Using background knowledge in case-based legal reasoning: A computational model and an intelligent learning environment. *Artificial Intelligence* 1:183–237.

Alexy, Robert. 1989. *A theory of legal argumentation*. New York: Oxford University Press.

Ashley, Kevin. 1991. Reasoning with cases and hypotheticals in HYPO. *International Journal of Man-Machine Studies* 34:753–796.

Ceci, Marcello. 2012. Combining ontologies and rules to model judicial interpretation. In *Proceedings of the RuleML@ECAI 6th international doctoral consortium*, vol. 874, ISSN:1613-0073. Center for European Union Research.

Ceci, Marcello, and Thomas F. Gordon. 2012. Browsing case-law: An application of the Carneades argumentation system. In *Proceedings of the RuleML2012@ECAI challenge*, eds. H. Aït-Kaci, Y. Jin Hu, G. J. Nalepa, M. Palmirani and D. Roman, 874:79-95. Center for European Union Research.

Dung, Phan Minh. 1995. On the acceptability of arguments and its fundamental role in nonmonotonic reasoning, logic programming and n-person games. *Artificial Intelligence* 77 (2): 321–357.

Dung, Phan Minh, and Giovanni Sartor. 2011. The modular logic of private international law. *Artificial Intelligence and Law* 19 (2-3): 233–261.

Garssen, Bart. 2001. Argument schemes. In *Critical concepts in argumentation theory*, ed. F. H. Van Eemeren, 81–100. Amsterdam: Amsterdam University Press.

Gordon, Thomas F. 1994. The pleadings game-an exercise in computational dialectics. *Artificial Intelligence and Law* 2 (4): 239–292.

Gordon, Thomas F. 2008. Construting legal arguments with rules in the legal knowledge interchange format. In *Computable models of the law: Languages, dialogues, games, ontologies*, ed. 4884:162–184 Pompeu Casanovas. Heidelberg: Springer.

Gordon, Thomas F. 2010. An overview of the Carneades argumentation support system. In *Dialectics, dialogue and argumentation. An examination of Douglas Walton's theories of reasoning*, ed. C. W. Tindale and C. Reed, 145–156.

Gordon, Thomas F. 2011. Hybrid reasoning with argumentation schemes. In *Proceedings of the 5th international RuleML2011@BRF challenge* 103–110. Center for European Union Research Workshop Proceedings.

Gordon, Thomas F., and Douglas Walton. 2006a. Pierson versus Post revisited-a reconstruction using the Carneades argumentation framework. In *Proceedings of the first international conference on computational models of argument (COMMA 06)*, ed. P. E. Dunne and T. Bench-Capon. Liverpool: IOS.

Gordon, Thomas F., and Douglas Walton. 2006b. The Carneades argumentation framework: Using presumptions and exceptions to model critical questions. In *Proceedings of the first international conference on computational models of argument (COMMA 06)*, ed. P. E. Dunne and T. Bench-Capon. Liverpool: IOS.

Gordon, Thomas F., and Douglas Walton. 2009. Legal reasoning with argumentation schemes. In *Proceedings of the twelfth international conference on artificial intelligence and law* 137–146. New York: Association for Computing Machinery.

Gordon, Thomas F., and Douglas Walton. 2012. A Carneades reconstruction of Popov versus Hayashi. *Artificial Intelligence and Law* 20:1.

Gordon, Thomas F., Guido Governatori, and Antonino Rotolo. 2009. Rules and norms: Requirements for rule interchange languages in the legal domain. In *Rule interchange and applications. International symposium*, RuleML 2009 282-296. Berlin: Springer.

Governatori, Guido. 2011. *On the relationship between Carneades and defeasible logic. In ICAIL 2011 proceedings of the 13th international conference on artificial intelligence and law*. New York: Association for Computing Machinery.

Hastings, Carl Arthur. 1963. *A reformualtion of the modes of reasoning in argumentation*. PhD Thesis, Illinois: Northwestern University.

Hoekstra, Rinke, Joost Breuker, Marcello Di Bello, and Alexander Boer. 2009. LKIF core: Principled ontology development for the legal domain. *Law, Ontology and the Semantic Web* 1:21–52.

Lam, Ho-Pun, and Guido Governatori. 2009. The making of SPINdle. In *RuleML 2009*, ed. G. Governatori and A. Pashke, 5858:315-322. Berlin: Springer.

Palmirani, Monica, and Marcello Ceci. 2012. Ontology framework for judgement modelling. In AI approaches to the complexity of legal systems-models and ethical challenges for legal systems, legal language and legal ontologies, argumentation and software agents 7639:116-130. Berlin: Springer.

Palmirani, Monica, Giuseppe Contissa, and Raffaella Rubino. 2009. Fill the gap in the legal knowledge modelling. In *Proceedings of RuleML 2009*, ed. G. Governatori, J. Hall and A. Pashke, 5858:305-314. Berlin: Springer.

Palmirani, Monica, Guido Governatori, Antonino Rotolo, Said Tabet, Harold Boley, and Adrian Paschke. 2011. LegalRuleML: XML-based rules and norms. In: rule-based modeling and computing on the Semantic Web, Berlin: Springer, 298–312.

Palmirani, Monica, Tommaso Ognibene, and Luca Cervone. 2012. Legal rules, text, and ontologies over time. In *Proceedings of the RuleML@ ECAI 6th international rule challenge,* Montpellier France.

Prakken, Henry. 1995. From logic to dialectic in legal argument. In *Proceedings of the fifth international conference on artificial intelligence and law,* ICAIL '95, May 21–24 College Park, Maryland, USA. ACM, 165–174.

Prakken, Henry. 2012. Reconstructing Popov versus Hayashi in a framework for argumentation with structured arguments and Dungean semantics. *Artificial Intelligence and Law* 20 (1): 57–82.

Reed, Chris, and Douglas Walton. 2001. Applications of argumentation schemes. In *Proceedings of the fourth OSSA Conference, Ontario.*

Toulmin, Stephen. 1958. *The uses of argument*. Cambridge: Cambridge University Press.

Verheij, Bart. 2003. Deflog: On the logical interpretation of prima facie justified assumptions. *Journal of Logic and Computation* 13 (3): 1–28.

Walton, Douglas. 1997. *Appeal to expert opinion*. University Park: Penn State.

Walton, Douglas. 1998. *The new dialectics: Conversational contexts of argument.* Toronto: University of Toronto Press.

Walton, Douglas. 2006. *Fundamentals of critical argumentation.* Cambridge: Cambridge University Press.

Chapter 33
Towards Multidimensional Rule Visualizations

Vytautas Čyras and Friedrich Lachmayer

Abstract This paper reviews visualizations in legal informatics. We focus on the transition from traditional rule-based linear textual representation such as "if *A* then *B*" to two- and three-dimensional ones and films. A methodology of visualization with the thought pattern of *tertium comparationis* can be attributed to Arthur Kaufmann. A *tertium* visualization aims at a mental bridge between different languages. We explore how visualizations are constructed and what types can be found here. Review criteria comprise comprehension, relations, vertical-horizontal arrangement, time-space structure, the focus of attention, education, etc. Pictures for review are selected from JURIX 2012 proceedings. We conclude that making visualizations as avant-garde as JURIX projects themselves is a tough task that requires knowledge of law, computing, media and semiotics.

Keywords Diagrammatic models · Legal education · Legal informatics · Legal visualization · Soft visualization

33.1 Introduction

This paper reviews visualizations in legal informatics by asking the question "How is multidimensionality exploited?" There are multiple criteria to review and in turn different means to achieve multidimensionality in visualizations: colours (including black-white-grey), mixed types of graphical elements, 1D-2D-2½D-3D, quantity-quality, statistics, etc.

The mainstream of the visualization in law, legal science and legal informatics can be determined with reference to JURIX, the Dutch Foundation for Legal

This author was supported by the project "Theoretical and engineering aspects of e-service technology development and application in high-performance computing platforms" (No. VP1–3.1-ŠMM-08-K-01–010) funded by the European Social Fund.

V. Čyras (✉)
Faculty of Mathematics and Informatics, Vilnius University,
Naugarduko 24, Vilnius 03225, Lithuania
e-mail: vytautas.cyras@mif.vu.lt

F. Lachmayer
Faculty of Law, University of Innsbruck,
Innrain 52, Innsbruck 6020, Austria

M. Araszkiewicz et al. (eds.), *Problems of Normativity, Rules and Rule-Following*, Law and Philosophy Library 111, DOI 10.1007/978-3-319-09375-8_33

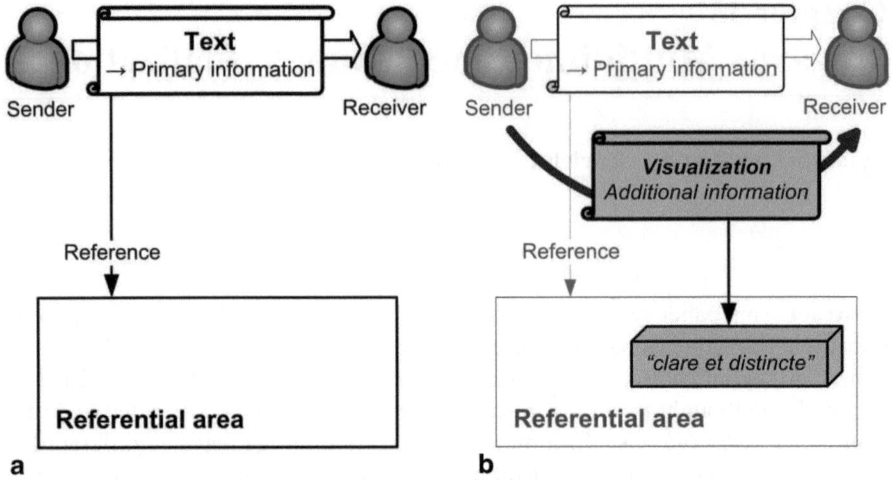

Fig. 33.1 **a** A text is communicated from a sender to a receiver. **b** A visualization refers to clear and distinct knowledge and hence contributes to understanding

Knowledge-Based Systems and its annual conference proceedings.[1] On the one hand there are formal notations, which go beyond the textual ones; on the other hand, there are visual representations that also occur in competition with the text. In the visualizations in turn two different types can be distinguished: first, the visualizations formed according to strict formal rules; second, the more intuitive pictures which can detect situations better. A very good overview of legal visualization can be found in the book of Klaus Röhl and Stefan Ulbrich (2007).

There are also quite different approaches to visualization, for instance, through semiotics (Fig. 33.1). The classical philosophy of law, however, as approximately represented by Arthur Kaufmann (see Lachmayer 2005), has provided a methodological introduction to visualization with the thought pattern of *tertium comparationis*. Especially in the European Union with its many official languages, a visualization, which appears as a *tertium*, can form a mental bridge between different languages.

The annual JURIX conferences are among the most important in legal informatics regarding both the content and the form of scientific presentations. The leading projects in the world are presented here. In many cases visualizations make the text easier to understand, at least in terms of key points. On a meta-reflection level, however, the empirical question is how these visualizations are constructed and what types can be found therein. Such an analysis may also affect the future design of visualizations in legal informatics, especially as corresponding design principles are not yet in the canon.

[1] http://www.jurix.nl/?page_id=8.

33.2 Types of Multidimensionality in Legal Visualizations

First we explain what we mean by multidimensionality in rule representations.

33.2.1 One-dimensional (1D) Visualization

Traditional norms (rules) are represented linearly: in text, both in natural languages and in artificial languages including mathematical notations, formal logic (propositional logic, predicate logic) and programming languages such as Prolog. A traditional notation is "If *A* then *B*", $A \rightarrow B$ or $N(A/B)$, read "when a state of affairs *A* is given, then the legal consequence *B* applies". There are other notations such as Polish prefix notation that comprises a deontic modality and was used by Ilmar Tammelo (1978). An example of a Prolog-like notation is the logical legal sentence in Hajime Yoshino's Logical Jurisprudence (2011).

33.2.2 Two-dimensional (2D) Visualization

Metaphors and symbols can also be employed to represent norms and hence pictorial two-dimensional representations emerge (Röhl and Ulbrich 2007, pp. 42–62). An ancient example is the frontispiece of the book *Leviathan* by Thomas Hobbes,[2] where the state allegory is encapsulated in the sovereign Leviathan that is represented by a giant crowned figure. Besides pictorial visualizations, logical diagrammatical visualizations including info-graphics are widely used to represent legal content such as argumentation graphs, storytelling, legal workflow, etc. (Kahlig 2008).

33.2.3 Two and Half-dimensional (2½D) Visualization

2D diagrams can include pictures of three-dimensional real world bodies such as cubes, cylinders, people, computers, houses, etc. and their icons, producing so-called 2½ representations. The icons of three-dimensional real bodies are used to contrast 2D diagramming elements and abstract concepts.

33.2.4 Three-dimensional Visualization and Films

An example of three-dimensional visualization is the "Menzi Muck timber case—the Film!",[3] which presents situational visualization. The case concerns the liability

[2] http://en.wikipedia.org/wiki/Leviathan_(book).

[3] http://www.youtube.com/watch?v=KI7zeuayum4. See also the lawyer Arnold Rusch's comment, http://www.arnoldrusch.ch/pdf/130311_menzimuck.pdf.

for damages suffered by a volunteer. This 4-min film takes a familiar case from 2002 (BGE 129 III 181 ff.). The Swiss Federal Court defined demarcation criteria between favour (*Gefälligkeit*), gratuitous contract (*unentgeltlicher Auftrag*), agency without specific authorisation (*negotiorum gestio, Geschäftsführung ohne Auftrag*) and the compensation claim of a volunteer (*Schadenersatzanspruch der unentgeltlich helfenden Person*).

33.3 Visualization Criteria

We further examine selected pictures from JURIX 2012[4] papers. This examination is done on the reflexive level of legal informatics. First we discuss systematically different criteria:

- *Citation*. The names of laws and article numbers can be included in diagrams (Winkels and Hoekstra 2012, p. 160).
- *Colours*. In black–white press, dark and light grey tones aid comprehension (Winkels and Hoekstra 2012, pp. 158–166).
- *Dimensions*. Multiple dimensions on the paper can be achieved with 2½D. For instance, a wire-cube representation in Pace and Schapachnik (2012, p. 111) is supplemented with transitions and represents strength diagrams.
- *Domains*. Different problem domains can be referred to (Winkels and Hoekstra 2012, p. 158).
- *Elements with text*. Abbreviations may be difficult for non-experts (Szöke et al. 2012, p. 150). Similar may be with suspension points; see e.g. (Robaldo et al. 2012, p. 137) and (Szöke et al. 2012, pp. 150, 152).
- *Focus*. This is represented by bold face and a dark background. Important elements are coloured in dark grey and less important in light grey or white (Szöke et al. 2012, p. 154). There are also different shapes (angled, rounded).
- *Mindmapping*. Visualizations in the form of mindmapping are creative. An ontology design (Poudyal and Quaresma 2012, p. 118) is shown with no cross-links.
- *Mixed types*. Different types of elements are combined (Szöke et al. 2012, p. 150). This is good for legal education, but may be not very useful for formal semantics.
- *Quantity*. Too many elements confuse the issue. Therefore layers, levels and subelements are used (Winkels and Hoekstra 2012, p. 158).
- *Relationships*. Various relationships are depicted with different connectors. Different types of arrows are normally used: arced, curved, down, etc. Relationships can have a predefined or a newly defined meaning and are represented with edges in graph-like diagrams. Examples of relationships can be found in argument diagrams and defeat graphs in argumentation-based inference (Prakken 2012,

[4] The 25th International Conference on Legal Knowledge and Information Systems, http://justinian.leibnizcenter.org/jurix/.

pp. 127–128), dependency relations (Robaldo et al. 2012, pp. 137–139), document generation and versioning (Szöke et al. 2012, pp. 150–154), relationships between concepts in the tax domain (Winkels and Hoekstra 2012, pp. 158–160).
- *Tables*. They contain much textual information but are not always creative (Pace and Schapachnik 2012, p. 113). Transitions can be added (Ramakrishna et al. 2012, p. 132).
- *Traditional formal diagrams*. Examples are argument diagrams (Lynch et al. 2012, p. 84) and statistical data visualization (Poudyal and Quaresma 2012, p. 118; Winkels and Hoekstra 2012, p. 166). They are clear, look good, but are nothing special.
- *Vertical and horizontal axes*. Placing elements top-down can mean different orders: hierarchy, time axis, etc. Horizontal arrangement from left to right can denote ordering in time. Other meanings can also be defined (Robaldo et al. 2012, pp. 137–139), where both the left arrows and right arrows show the rule-triggering sequence.

33.4 Visualizations in JURIX 2012 Proceedings

Selected JURIX 2012 articles are reviewed below in the order of their appearance in the proceedings, where they are ordered alphabetically.

33.4.1 Refined Coherence as Constraint Satisfaction Framework for Representing Judicial Reasoning

A constraint satisfaction framework as a potent tool for representing judicial reasoning is reported by Araszkiewicz and Šavelka (2012). Figure 1 on p. 8 shows a constraint network for conversion claim in the Popov v. Hayashi case. The picture is interesting, primarily from the point of view of relations, and open. A drawback of the picture is the absence of a legend for nontrivial abbreviations (FA—factual assertion, LA—legal assertion, FLR—FA to LA rules, LLR—LA to LA rules, LA_1—'Hayashi *is* liable…,' LA_2— 'Hayashi *is not* liable…,' etc.) and three types of relationships (positive constraints, negative constraints, and the positively constrained chain). The reader has to guess whether the vertical arrangement means hierarchy and the horizontal one means flow.

33.4.2 Computational Data Protection Law: Trusting Each Other Offline and Online

A collaborative project to develop a communication in infrastructure that allows information sharing while observing data protection law "by design" is reported in

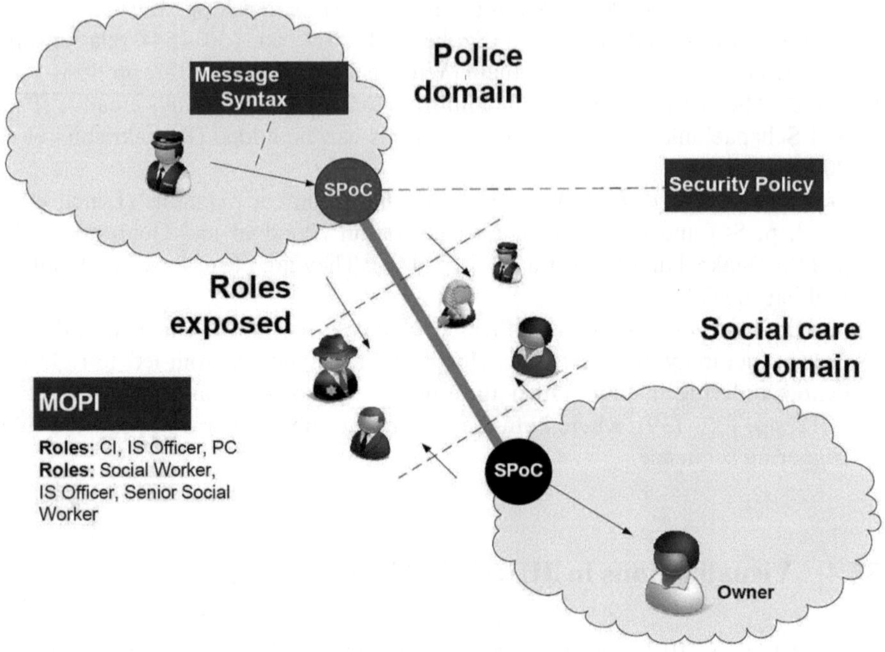

Fig. 33.2 Overview of the architecture (Buchanan et al. 2012, p. 36)

Buchanan et al. (2012). Figure 1 on p. 36 shows an overview of the architecture; see Fig. 33.2. This 2½D space-structured picture is composed of different subsystems. Two cloud-shaped "islands" that are connected with the "bridge" look better than white rectangles. Black and white textual elements interplay. Different icons of humans depict distinguished roles. The picture is comprised of different elements but is successful didactically. The same applies to Fig. 2 on p. 38.

33.4.3 Supporting Transnational Judicial Procedures Between European Member States: The e-Codex Project

The e-Codex project is meant to implement building blocks for a system to support transnational procedures between EU member states so as to increase cross-border relations in a pan-European e-justice area (Francesconi 2012). Figure 1 on p. 43 is composed of mixed elements that suggest clouds or islands and look like a territory map in 2½D. This is interesting; however, much of the text and graphics is too small and barely legible. Figure 2 on p. 47 is composed of mixed elements and a vertical static dichotomy between two models. It is interesting that dynamic flow is shown above with the interchange of grey and white ellipses. Figure 3 on p. 48 is composed of screenshots and arrow flows, but the dynamics is not elaborated.

33.4.4 Argument Analysis System with Factor Annotation Tool

An argumentation support tool which is based on a Toulmin diagram is reported in Kubosawa et al. (2012). Figure 1 on p. 62 shows the architecture of the system. The flow is represented by arrows and rounded white and angled grey rectangles. The reader might be familiar with this type of flow diagram which dates from the 1970s. Figure 2 on p. 63 shows a screenshot that is composed of mixed elements (a table of textual factors and an argument graph) and contains two flows. Figure 3 on p. 65 does not define the meaning of the vertical placing: a hierarchy or a process in time? The meaning of computer symbols can only be guessed ("documents" or something else?). Do the dashed elements exist or not exist? Figure 4 on p. 66 is too abstract because contrasting white and grey circles is not intuitive, although the labels α, β, Λ, z, w, K, etc. are explained in the text of the paper. Figure 5 on p. 68 is also not intuitive. Figure 6 on p. 69 is a bad design pattern: the primary screenshots in the background are too small and illegible and the callout recalls comics.

33.4.5 An Argumentation Model of Evidential Reasoning with Variable Degrees of Justification

A gradual argumentation model of evidential reasoning is reported in Liang and Wei (2012). The research work is interesting and mature. At first glance, however, Fig. 1 on p. 74 seems too abstract. Time and space structure, different arrows and abbreviations are not clear. Likewise, Fig. 2 on p. 79 is elegant but also lacks a legend. This may be justifiable if the reader is familiar with argument graph formalisations, John Pollock's critical link semantics and the *ASPIC*⁺ framework.

33.4.6 Comparing Argument Diagrams

Lynch et al. (2012) report the results of an empirical study into the diagnostic utility of argument diagrams in a legal writing context, namely, how law students employed the LASAD program. Figure 1 on p. 84 is a type diagram. It is drawn to read from right to left although one might expect time axis from left to right. Some texts are in an excessively small font, which may be the fault of a student.

33.4.7 Types of Rights in Two-Party Systems: A Formal Analysis

A formalisation of Kanger's types of rights in the context of interacting two-party systems, such as contracts, is reported in Pace and Schapachnik (2012). Figure 1 on p. 111 looks elegant although very formal and the reader has to judge if semantics complies with it. This picture recalls the logical square and cube which are known in modal logic (Philipps 2012, pp. 69–81). The table on p. 113 is not detailed although this may be reasonable for summarising just yes/no in each cell.

33.4.8 An Hybrid Approach for Legal Information Extraction

An approach and prototype software for legal information extraction is reported in Poudyal and Quaresma (2012). They aimed to populate an ontology automatically. The approach combined a statistically-based method (machine learning) and a rule-based method. Figure 1 on p. 116 represents the ontology design. A reader could view it as a mind map and also ask whether the square of four concepts is a logical deontic square. All elements are in grey and therefore barely distinguishable. Figure 2 on p. 118 is not very creative.

33.4.9 Formalising a Legal Opinion on a Legislative Proposal in the ASPIC⁺ Framework

Prakken (2012) presents a case study in which the opinion of a legal scholar on a legislative proposal is formally reconstructed in the *ASPIC*⁺ framework. Figure 1 on p. 127 demonstrates well-defined relations. This is achieved with texts in the boxes, dashed lines, labels and white vs. grey. Figures 2 and 3 on p. 128 look elegant thanks to the abbreviations, white/grey tones and arrows. Abbreviations make it hard to comprehend, however. A question arises about the patterns within the figures. The meaning of the horizontal-vertical arrangement—hierarchy or time—can be understood only after a thorough reading.

33.4.10 The FSTP Test: A Novel Approach for an Invention's Non-obviousness Analysis

A mathematical approach called the FSTP Test for determining a non-obviousness indication in patent application during the examination stage is proposed in Ramakrishna et al. (2012). A table in Fig. 2 on p. 132 is a hybrid with process curves. This would benefit from elaboration, probably in a longer paper.

33.4.11 Compiling Regular Expressions to Extract Legal Modifications

Prototype software for automatically identifying and classifying types of modifications in Italian legal texts is reported in Robaldo et al. (2012). The work employs the

Italian standard NormeInRete (NIR), which was the outcome of a previous project. Figures 2–5 on pp. 137–139 attract attention with arced arrows (and a loop in Fig. 5) and two reading directions (from left to right and vice versa).

33.4.12 A Unified Change Management of Regulations and their Formal Representations Based on the FRBR Framework and the Direct Method

A unified change management of legislative documents and their representations is introduced in Szöke et al. (2012). This is based on the Functional Requirements for Bibliographic Records (FRBR) framework and the direct method of legislative change management. Although Figs. 1 and 2 on p. 150 appear side by side, they have opposing reading directions. With regard to contents, Fig. 1 is very interesting because of the intermediate forms and four steps (Item-Manifestation-Expression-Work). Abbreviations (and formulas) make Figs. 2–6 on pp. 150–154 hard to comprehend for non-experts although bold face is used. Figure 6 has an opposing reading direction, ellipsis and rectangle-shaped elements with grey background and one with "dramatic" black. Relations are well-defined but formulas make the framework hard to comprehend.

33.4.13 Automatic Extraction of Legal Concepts and Definitions

Winkels and Hoekstra (2012) present the results of an experiment in automatic concept and definition extraction from the sources of law which are expressed in a simple natural language and standard semantic web technology. The software was tested on six laws from the tax domain. Relations in Fig. 1 on p. 158 are well identified and good for learning purposes. Although composed of four layers, the figure seems too quantitative. White and grey elements are used and a dark grey in the focus, but the whole is confusing and not heuristic. Figures 2 and 3 on p. 160 are good for citations, but three schemes in two figures to save space is undesirable. The processes in Fig. 4 on p. 165 are bottom-up and right-left, and not usual. Therefore the picture is schematic and not intuitive. A line-approaching curve is shown in Fig. 6 on p. 166.

Conclusions

Producing elaborated visualizations is a work that requires the mastery of several problem domains: law, informatics, visual media and semiotics. This is a tough task.

References

Araszkiewicz, Michał and Jaromir Šavelka. 2012. Refined coherence as constraint satisfaction framework for representing judicial reasoning. In *Legal knowledge and information systems, JURIX 2012. The twenty-fifth annual conference,* ed. Burkhard Schäfer, 1–10. Amsterdam: IOS.

Buchanan, William, Lu Fan, Alistair Lawson, Burkhard Schafer, Russell Scott, Christoph Thuemmler, and Omair Uthmani. 2012. Computational data protection law: Trusting each other offline and online. In *Legal knowledge and information systems, JURIX 2012. The twenty-fifth annual conference,* ed. Burkhard Schäfer, 31–40. Amsterdam: IOS.

Francesconi, Enrico. 2012. Supporting transnational judicial procedures between European member states: The e-Codex project. In *Legal knowledge and information systems, JURIX 2012. The twenty-fifth annual conference,* ed. Burkhard Schäfer, 41–50. Amsterdam: IOS.

Kahlig, Wolfgang. 2008. *Rechtsmodellierung im e-Government: Fallbeispiele zur Legistik.* [*in German.*] (*Modeling Law in e-Government: Case Examples for Legistic*). Saarbrücken: VDM Verlag Dr. Müller.

Kubosawa, Shumpei, Youwei Lu, Shogo Okada, and Katsumi Nitta. 2012. Argument analysis with factor annotation tool. In *Legal knowledge and information systems, JURIX 2012. The twenty-fifth annual conference,* ed. Burkhard Schäfer, 61–70. Amsterdam: IOS.

Lachmayer, Friedrich. 2005. Das tertium comparationis im Recht. Variationen zu einem Thema von Arthur Kaufmann. [in German.] (Tertium comparationis in law. Variations on a theme of Arthur Kaufmann). In *Verantwortetes Recht—die Rechtsphilosophie Arthur Kaufmanns (Responsible Law—the Philosophy of Law of Arthur Kaufmann), Archiv für Rechts- und Sozialphilosophie,* eds. Ulfrid Neumann, Winfried Hassemer, and Ulrich Schroth, 67–77. Wiesbaden: Franz Steiner. (ARSP, Beiheft Nr. 100)

Liang, QingYin, and Bin Wei. 2012. An argumentation model of evidential reasoning with variable degrees of justification. In *Legal knowledge and information systems, JURIX 2012. The twenty-fifth annual conference,* ed. Burkhard Schäfer, 71–80. Amsterdam: IOS.

Lynch, Collin, Kevin Ashley, and Mohammad H. Falakmasir. 2012. Comparing argument diagrams. In *Legal knowledge and information systems, JURIX 2012. The twenty-fifth annual conference,* ed. Burkhard Schäfer, 81–90. Amsterdam: IOS.

Philipps, Lothar. 2012. Von deontischen Quadraten—Kuben—Hyperkuben. [in German.] (On deontic squares—cubes—hypercubes). In *Endliche Rechtsbegriffe mit unendlichen Grenzen: Rechtlogische Aufsätze.* (*Finite Legal Concepts with Infinite Limits: Essays on Legal Logic) Anthologia*, ed. Lothar Philipps, 69–81. Bern: Editions Weblaw.

Pace, Gordon J. and Fernando Schapachnik. 2012. Types in two-party systems: A formal analysis. In *Legal knowledge and information systems, JURIX 2012. The twenty-fifth annual conference,* ed. Burkhard Schäfer, 105–114. Amsterdam: IOS.

Poudyal, Prakash and Paulo Quaresma. 2012. An hybrid approach for legal information extraction. In *Legal knowledge and information systems, JURIX 2012. The twenty-fifth annual conference,* ed. Burkhard Schäfer, 115–118. Amsterdam: IOS.

Prakken, Henry. 2012. Formalising a legal opinion on a legislative proposal in the *ASPIC*⁺ framework. In *Legal knowledge and information systems, JURIX 2012. The twenty-fifth annual conference,* ed. Burkhard Schäfer, 119–128. Amsterdam: IOS.

Ramakrishna, Shashishekar, Naouel Karam, and Adrian Paschke. 2012. The FSTP test: A novel approach for an invention's non-obviousness analysis. In *Legal knowledge and information systems, JURIX 2012. The twenty-fifth annual conference,* ed. Burkhard Schäfer, 129–132. Amsterdam: IOS.

Robaldo, Livio, Leonardo Lesmo, and Daniele P. Radicioni. 2012. Compiling regular expressions to extract legal modifications. In *Legal knowledge and information systems, JURIX 2012. The twenty-fifth annual conference,* ed. Burkhard Schäfer, 133–141. Amsterdam: IOS.

Röhl, Klaus F and Stefan Ulbrich. 2007. *Recht anschaulich. Visualisierung in der Juristenausbildung* [*in German*] (*Law Graphically. Visualization in the Education of Jurists*), *edition medienpraxis, 3*. Köln: Halem.

Szőke, Ákos, András Förhécz, and Strausz György. 2012. A unified change management of regulations and their formal representations based on the FRBR framework and the direct method. In *Legal knowledge and information systems, JURIX 2012. The twenty-fifth annual conference,* ed. Burkhard Schäfer, 147–156. Amsterdam: IOS.

Tammelo, Ilmar. 1978. *Modern Logic in the Service of Law*. Wien: Springer.

Winkels, Radboud and Rinke Hoekstra. 2012. Automatic extraction of legal concepts and definitions. In *Legal knowledge and information systems, JURIX 2012. The twenty-fifth annual conference,* ed. Burkhard Schäfer, 157–166. Amsterdam: IOS.

Yoshino, Hajime. 2011. The systematization of law in terms of the validity. In *Proceedings of the 13th international conference on artificial intelligence and law* (*ICAIL'11*) ed. Tom van Engers, 121–125. New York: ACM.

MIX
Papier aus verantwortungsvollen Quellen
Paper from responsible sources
FSC® C105338

If you have any concerns about our products,
you can contact us on
ProductSafety@springernature.com

In case Publisher is established outside the EU,
the EU authorized representative is:
Springer Nature Customer Service Center GmbH
Europaplatz 3, 69115 Heidelberg, Germany

Printed by Libri Plureos GmbH
in Hamburg, Germany